The Grail Cypher

The secrets of Arthurian history revealed

Cover swords:
D&D Toledo SL
Rio Jarama, Poligono Sta Maria,
45007, Toledo, Spain.
dydtoledo.com (no www)

Toledo Swords
Marlton, NJ 08053, USA.
www.toledosword.com

The
Grail Cypher

The secrets of Arthurian legends revealed

by
Ralph Ellis

Edfu Books

Adventures Unlimited

The Grail Cypher

First published in 2015 by Edfu Books

Published in the U.K. by:
Edfu Books
PO Box 165, Cheshire
CW8 4WF, UK
www.edfu-books.com
info@edfu-books.com

Published in the U.S.A. by:
Adventures Unlimited
303 Main Street Box 74
Kempton, IL 60946 USA
www.adventuresUnlimitedPress.com
info@adventuresunlimitedpress.com

First edition Sept 2015

v1.5

Paperback edition
ISBN 978-1939149558

And in the blast there smote along the hall,
A beam of light seven times more clear than day:
And down the long beam stole the Holy Grail,
All over covered with a luminous cloud.
And none might see who bare it, and it past.
But every knight beheld his fellow's face,
As in a glory, and all the knights arose,
And staring each at other like dumb men,
Stood, till I found a voice and swore a vow.

Alfred, Lord Tennyson (1809-1892)

Acknowledgments

My sincere thanks go to John Hart of the National CV project for all his support and advice. The National CV has an interesting section on the history of Britain, extracted from the many obscure chronicles written during the Medieval and Tudor periods. http://www.thenationalcv.org.uk

Thanks are also due to Michael Tsarion, Chris Russak and David Whitehead for their support during the daunting days of research. Voices in the wilderness crying out for the contortions of Arthurian history to be made straight. And it would be remiss of me not to give due credit to the many educational establishments who have translated and preserved the many manuscripts that comprise Arthurian history, over the many years and centuries. Their contribution to Arthurian research is indispensable, but often overlooked. These include:

Robbins Library, The Camelot Project, University of Rochester.
Project Gutenberg.
Fordham University, Internet Medieval Sourcebooks.
Internet Archive.
Christian Classics Ethereal Library.
The Online Library of Liberty.
Wikisource.
Early Manuscripts at Oxford University.
Come and Hear Talmud.
Perseus Digital Library, Tufts University.
D. S. Brewer publishing, Cambridge.

And my sincerest of **no** thanks goes to the The Leverhulme Trust, one of many charitable trusts established back in the 19th century by well-meaning philanthropists, that still give grants out even to this day. And while the Leverhulme Trust has previously given funding to several authors involved in Arthurian research, they treated the grant application for this book as if it had been delivered by a carrier of the plague. One gets the impression that many of these venerable trusts are going down the same perfidious path as the The Rowntree Trust, which delights in funding politically correct fantasies and dangerous fanatics who wish to destroy Western civilisation.[1]

Ralph Ellis
September 2015
Spain

www.edfu-books.com
info@edfu-books.com

Contents

Intro

Historical Chasms

Walter Kayo sat at his desk in the scriptorium, the cold chill of winter half broken by a flickering fire in the hearth. The velum page before him was still not finished, yet already his eyes felt heavy and refused to focus. As he dipped his quill to begin the final paragraph there was a commotion outside, accompanied by the tramp of heavy boots. Three burly men strode in bearing armour and arms, their white mantles emblazoned with large splayed red crosses. They introduced themselves as being ambassadors of King Baldwin of Jerusalem, and deposited a large manuscript on his desk.

Kayo wafted away the large cloud of dust they had disturbed, and looked balefully at the enormous volume before him. He had no idea what it was about, but it obviously meant a lot more work for his small understaffed scriptorium. The officer in charge pointed to some marked pages, so Kayo hefted the manuscript open and started to slowly read. But the text was old, tattered, often illegible, and in Aramaic, which was not his favourite language. Half way down the page his eyes started to widen and his jaw took it upon itself to drop down. He looked up bearing an expression that clearly stated: "what the hell is this!"

The officer understood Kayo's perplexion and returned a wry smile, which was reinforced by muffled laughter from the two soldiers behind. The officer approached more closely, disturbing some sheaves on the desk and creating another cloud of dust. He lowered his voice to a whisper and said: "King Baldwin wants you to turn this into an interesting story." Kayo's jaw was now beyond control, but he managed a small nod in acknowledgement.

Historical crossword

The story of King Arthur and his gallant knights that this semi-mythical Walter Kayo eventually crafted is complex, frustrating and fraught with contradictions and impossibilities. In the hands of subsequent Arthurian authors it became a compilation of two histories blended together in such a clumsy manner that it betrays confusion in both its broad outline and finer detail.

Very few of the names and events recorded in these chronicles exist in the historical record, and so the text represents a huge historical crossword puzzle that is almost impossible to crack. But how can we derive an answer for two-down in this puzzle, if we have not discovered the solution for five-across? That is the central problem that has faced all previous researchers of Arthurian history, because starting this decypherment is next to impossible. Happily, Tyche-Fortuna has smiled upon these endeavors, because the previous historical analysis in the *King Jesus Trilogy* has already answered the question for five-across, and so we can now confidently begin to fill in the rest of the crossword. And the result will be a latticework of answers and conclusions that will be both controversial and challenging.

Arthurian history is traditionally set in the 5th or 6th centuries, the era of the Dark Ages. This is a period in British history that is not simply 'dark' because of an economic and social collapse following the decline and fall of the Western Roman Empire, it is also 'dark' because it lacks any historical records. This makes it difficult to decypher what was happening in this era, and it is this lacuna or chasm in British history that has enabled the life of King Arthur to remain enigmatic and semi-legendary for so long. Had Arthur been a king of the 4th or 9th centuries, we could easily have determined if these legends were fact or fiction, but Arthur has managed to slip into a historical crevasse where there are many known unknowns and several unknown unknowns.

But this simple observation is interesting, and begs two obvious questions. Did a real King Arthur become semi-legendary simply because he lived in a Dark Age era of historical phantoms? Or did a mythical King Arthur get deliberately placed into this historical lacuna, because Walter Kayo and the other 12th and 13th century scribes and chroniclers knew that they could hide a semi-fictional legend in the poorly documented confusion of the Dark Ages?

We have seen similar techniques before in this series of books, where the chronology has been amended to cover up the truth. The books *King Jesus* and *Jesus, King of Edessa* have positively identified Jesus as a minor Syrio-Judaean monarch from the AD 60s, who fomented and led the Jewish Revolt. But because this real history of a warrior monarch did not equate with the semi-mythical history that the gospel authors were crafting, the history of King Jesus was deliberately moved back into the relative calm of the AD 30s - to completely divorce their new 'pauper prince of peace' story from the wealthy martial and monarchal persona upon which it was actually based. And so a semi-mythical story was deliberately crafted upon a deliberate chronological dislocation, to put future researchers and historians off the scent. The gospel authors did not want a real Jesus, all they required was an idealistic semi-mythical icon to hold aloft.

So could something similar have happened to King Arthur? Could Arthur have been a real monarch from a different era, who has been shoe-horned into the depths of the Dark Age chasm to hide him from the prying eyes of future historians? Or even to hide him from the prying eyes and barbarous torture techniques of the Catholic Inquisition? Surprisingly, the second possibility is the more likely of the two, for the true story of King Arthur and his twelve knightly disciples of the Round Table trod upon some very sensitive priestly toes, as we shall see later.

1st century Judaea

This book will often stray into regions and eras that no Arthurian research has ever previously dared to venture into, because the complete corpus of Arthurian history is much more diverse and complex than readers might imagine. And this is not simply a matter of wild reinterpretations of the texts, because the many manuscripts that comprise the standard corpus of Arthurian history do overtly go off onto some wild tangents, both geographically and chronologically. Classical Arthurian historians will simply ignore these baffling interludes because they do not understand them. But how can we determine the literary and political goals of the many Arthurian authors, if we do not understand the full spectrum of the story they crafted?

In fact, many Arthurian researchers only tackle Gildas, Bede, Nennius, and Monmouth, and then profess to have understood Arthurian history. But how can we understand anything, when we have only browsed ten percent of the available literature? What about *High History, Perceval, Parzival, Merlin Grail*, or the many impenetrable and soporific volumes of the *Vulgate Cycle*? And there are many other minor texts, besides these. Unless we also understand these texts, we can never understand the true meaning and import of Arthurian history.

For instance, several of the traditional Arthurian manuscripts detail the life of Joseph of Arimathaea and his friendship with Emperor Vespasian and his son Titus. One gives an account of St Peter as the Guardian of the

Holy Grail. Another gives us a hidden history of Pompey Magnus, the Roman commander of the 1st century BC, and his links to Mithras and his cosmic bull. Another appears to give us a history of Minoan Crete. Wolfram von Eschenbach even recounts the bringing of the Holy Grail to Earth by aliens. While yet another strange diversion recounts the life of Hippocrates, the Greek physician from the 4th century BC. But we will never understand the intricacies of Arthurian legend if we simply ignore these inexplicable diversions, because they are actually central to the story. In which case, an understanding of the fundamental aspects of the previous books in the *King Jesus Trilogy* is essential to understanding this book and to understanding Arthurian history.

It would be worthwhile readers starting with *Cleopatra to Christ,* the first book of the *King Jesus Trilogy,* and working up from there. But if time is of the essence, then the following three points represent the main conclusions from the previous books that will impact upon this research:

a. Josephus Flavius the historian is one and the same as Saul (St Paul). This conclusion was determined way back in 1998 with the publication of *Jesus, Last of the Pharaohs,* and it has withstood the test of both time and criticism. The reasons for this connection were further researched and expanded in *King Jesus,* and the resulting conflated character is often called Saul-Josephus.

b. Due to the conflation of Saul and Josephus just mentioned, the era for the gospel events has to move from the AD 30s to the AD 60s. And there are numerous other events within the gospel stories that also point towards an AD 60s date. But Arthurian history does exactly the same, because each time it mentions Joseph of Arimathaea it sets the story in the early AD 70s, just after the Jewish Revolt. And if Joseph of Arimathaea was an AD 60s and 70s character, then the biblical crucifixion story most probably was too.

c. The gospel stories are closely linked to the history of the Babylonian Jews, who were exiled from Parthia to Syria at the turn of the 1st century. This group of exiles established the Kingdom of Edessa (and Palmyra) in northern and eastern Syria, and Saul-Josephus Flavius confirms that it was a king from this small principality who started the Jewish Revolt in Judaea in the late AD 60s. This will become a central topic in later chapters, because according to Arthurian history Joseph of Arimathaea was a contemporary and colleague of Emperor Vespasian and his son Titus, and a leader of the Simple Judaic Christians in the early AD 70s. In other words, both Joseph of Arimathaea and Saul-Josephus were allies of Vespasian, and both were opposed to King Izas Manu of Edessa - the biblical Jesus.

Britons, Welsh and English

The history of Dark Age of Britain can sometimes be perplexing. There were great migrations at this time, and so our modern terminology for the people and languages of this region can fail us and lead to confusion. So let us quickly review the major events of this era.

Up until the beginning of the 5th century, Britain was populated by Britons but ruled by a Roman administration, just as Pontius Pilate was the Roman governor of the Jews of Judaea. To all intents and purposes, Britain was a province of Rome. But this small province was never as wealthy as Syria or southern Gaul, which were resplendent with many great temples and amphitheaters, and nor was it as integrated into the Roman system as these other provinces.

The primary language of the common people in Roman Britain was Celtic, the antecedent to the many modern Celtic languages like Gaelic, Welsh, Cornish and Breton. And it is often claimed that Welsh is the closest modern equivalent to the original language of the Britons. But the aristocracy, administration and army of Britain spoke Latin, and so the Celto-Welsh language of the common people became infused with many Latin interpolations. Exactly the same has happened in the modern era, and so the Welsh for a computer is a *compiwtorau* while a telephone is a *ffonau*.

So while Welsh may sound quite peculiar to the English ear, it is far from being a unique language. Like all languages, Celto-Welsh is actually a colloid of many influences over many centuries, with terms and expressions being borrowed from Latin, Greek and Aramaic. The highly influential biblical texts were written in Latin (and Greek and Aramaic) and the Roman governmental system of Britain was also Latin, and so Latin became the primary language of the Welsh aristocracy and priesthood. Norris Lacy, the translator of the *Vulgate Cycle*, goes as far as saying that Welsh in this early era was primarily a spoken language, while the educated Welsh elite composed their written records, chronicles and epistles in Latin. For example, Gildas, who was a 5th or 6th century Breto-Welsh cleric and chronicler, wrote his *De Excidio et Conquestu Britanniae (On the Ruin and Conquest of Britain)* in Latin, and goes on to say that Latin was 'our language'. [1]

But if the Dark Age chroniclers of Britain, Wales and Brittany were using Latin in most of their works, then why do modern Arthurian researchers look to Welsh for their translations? In fact, the situation is even more complex than this, because the ultimate foundation for many Welsh proper nouns is not Welsh or Latin, but Aramaic. Take, for instance, the most popular Welsh male name: David Jones. There could be nothing quite so Welsh as a 'Davey Johnes'. However, David was derived from the Aramaic Dawvid דויד, the name for King David; while Jones was derived from the

Aramaic Yochanan יוחנן and the Greek Johannes Ιωαννης, the name for John the Baptist. So the very foundation for many popular Welsh personal names is not Welsh, and nor is it Latin, it is actually Aramaic.

There is an interesting book called *How the Irish Saved Civilization*, which details the many literary triumphs of Ireland during the darkest days of the 6th and 7th century, when expensive manuscripts were not a high priority within the ravaged and decimated lands of northern Europe. And the many obscure texts these Celto-Irish monks and scribes were copying included Greek philosophy and science and, of course, the Latin Vulgate Bible. And the majority of the proper names in the Latin Vulgate Bible are direct transliterations from the original Aramaic. This is just one of many routes through which Aramaic, Greek and Latin influenced the formation of the many branches of the Celtic language.

Back in the history of Britain, we then come to the era of the infamous Dark Ages. In the early 5th century Roman command and control of Britain officially ended, by imperial decree no less, and the local Britons reluctantly took control of the region. And this reluctance was genuine, because lowland Britain was being invaded and ravaged by Picts, Scots and Saxons, and so the Britons made three appeals to Rome for military assistance at the turn of the 5th century. But with Roman organisation and protection of the province at an end, significant numbers of Anglo-Saxons came from modern Holland and northern Germany to rape, pillage and then to settle and farm. These new immigrants spoke the language of the Angles, a Germanic language. And it is this Anglish language that became what we know today as English.

But modern English is not simply the Anglish of the Angles (ie: something akin to modern Dutch). When these new immigrants began to take control of regions in Britain, they came up against the language of the British administration, aristocracy, army and priesthood, which was primarily Latin rather than Celto-Welsh. As we have seen, Gildas wrote his *De Excidio et Conquestu Britanniae* in Latin, not Welsh. Thus the Angelish language of the Angles became infused with a large number of Latin words and phrases. And this Latin component was greatly expanded in later centuries via the influence of the Latin Roman Catholic Church and the Latino-French of the Normans. And so the resulting modern English language is approximately one-third Angelish, one-third Latin, and one-third Latino-Norman French.

Most of the later manuscripts we shall be investigating in this book were originally written in Norman French, and were then translated into Latin and Welsh. Even Monmouth claims that much of his *History of Kings* was derived from a manuscript discovered in Brittany, which he translated into Latin. But Norman French and Latin may not have been the original language of Arthurian history, because some of these chronicles claim that one of the original authors came from 1st century Judaea and was called Josephus. Which Josephus this refers to will become one of the first problems to be solved in this investigation. Other manuscripts say that Walter Kayo derived much of his information from a manuscript written by a gnostic-scientist called Flegetanis 'in a heathen tongue'.

However, since Josephus came from Judaea and Flegetanis was said to be from the line of Solomon, we might surmise that some of these original manuscripts were written in Aramaic rather than Norman French. So if we take these seemingly wild claims at face value - and there will be a great deal of evidence uncovered later that supports these claims - then why do Arthurian researchers invariably look to Welsh for their translations and explanations? How can we make sense of the Peshitta Bible from Syria, which was originally written in Edessan Aramaic, if we attempt a clarification using the Welsh language?

Because of this fundamental misunderstanding the majority of classical Arthurian explanations make no sense whatsoever, and it is no wonder that previous researchers and authors have failed to discover the true origins of Arthurian history. So from the very outset of this new evaluation, we need to adjust our perspective and expectations. From the very first chapters of *High History* and *History of the Grail*, which detail the life of Joseph of Arimathaea, it is perfectly clear that there is a vast amount of material in these stories that has come directly from 1st century Judaea. And these are not simply rehashed gospel stories, but highly independent renderings of familiar stories that add to our understanding of this era. But if these Arthurian manuscripts begin with new and often heretical accounts from 1st century Syrio-Judaea, then what about the rest of the story? From which era and region did they emanate from? That is one of the key questions that this book will attempt to resolve, because answering that question will unravel the many mysteries of Arthurian history.

Languages and People

The movement of cultures and peoples during the Dark Ages has caused some conflict with modern terminology, resulting in much confusion. In clarification, this book will attempt to use the following terms:

Britain and British people:
The native Celto-British people living alongside the Roman aristocracy all over the British Isles, prior to the Anglo-Saxon invasions of the mid 5th century.

England and English people:
The Anglo-Saxons living in Angle-land from the mid 5th century onwards, a region which equates well with the borders of modern England.

Wales and Welsh people:
The Celto-British people who were displaced to western Britain, following the Anglo-Saxon invasions of the mid 5th century

Brittany and Breto-British people:
A great deal of Arthurian history involves Armorica, which is now known as Brittany on the northwest tip of France. Brittany became predominantly inhabited by exiled Britons in the late 4th century, and a Breton prince became the 5th century king of Britain. Thus the British Bretons from Brittany are sometimes referred to here as the Breto-British.

Celts and Celtic people:
Although some people frown on the term 'Celtic', it is a useful generic term for all the Celtic-speaking peoples. The Celts were not all of the same ethnicity but were united by language and culture, just like many other cultural groupings are. Americans are not monoethnic by any means, but they are still Americans.

Celtic language:
According to the standard linguistic classification the Celtic language springs directly from the main Indo-European linguistic stem, and is then subdivided into Gaelic and Brito-Welsh. This book is more concerned with the British, Welsh and Breton branches of the Celtic language, rather than the Gaelic branch.

Decoding the Arthurian Cypher

Within this book, some conflated characters will emerge. Since these names can get a little confusing, there follows a short explanation.

Saul-Josephus:
It was conclusively proved in the *King Jesus Trilogy* that Saul (St Paul) and Josephus Flavius the historian were the same person, so he is named within this book as **Saul-Josephus**.

Joseph of Arimathaea:
Joseph of Arimathaea is confused on many occasions within Arthurian history with Josephus Flavius the historian, and so he is often named within this book as either **Joseph(us)** or **Joseph(us) of Arimathaea**.

Josephus:
Josephus is the son of Joseph of Arimathaea, and he was often confused with his father, Joseph of Arimathaea, and also with Josephus Flavius. And this confusion is often deliberate. He is named within this book as **Josephus**.

There are many reasons for the multiple pseudonyms within these biblical and Arthurian texts. The primary reason for them is to cover up the true identity of these people. The Church could not admit that Saul (St Paul) was Josephus Flavius, because that would imply that the majority of the New Testament was written by a Jewish traitor who was working for the Romans. Similarly, the Church could not admit that Josephus Flavius was Josephus of Arimathaea, because that would imply that Jesus was crucified in AD 70, after the Jewish Revolt. And that was a heresy worthy of a slow-roasting.

The result was a plethora of names for the same individual, a confusion that was only enhanced by other historians and traditions choosing their own pseudonyms for these characters. The result is that Arthurian history can be quite a muddle. However, when looking for order within the chaos, all we need is character combinations and conflations that make sense of the available records. Like a cryptographer looking for order within the chaos of an encrypted text, we too shall be on the lookout for recognisable patterns and meaningful paragraphs. And when we find a solution that makes sense of the entire corpus of Arthurian history, then we shall know that we have solved the Arthurian Cypher.

Manuscript Translations used:

Manuscript	Author	Translator	Date
Chronicle Kings of England	Malmesbury	J A Giles	1847
History of the English	Huntingdon	T Forester	1879
Chronicle of the Kings	Oxford	Acton Griscome	1929
Chronicle of the Kings	Oxford	William Cooper	2002
History of Kings of Britain	Monmouth	Sebastian Evans	1903
Antiquities of Glastonbury	Malmesbury	Frank Lomax	1908
Roman de Brut	Wace	Eugene Mason	1912
History of English Affairs	Newburgh	Joseph Stevenson	1861
Tristan et Iseut	Beroul	Ernest Muret	1861
Perceval, Story of the Grail	Troyes	Burton Raffel	1999
Perlesvaus (High History)	Anon	Sebastian Evans	1898
Perlesvaus (High History)	Anon	Nigel Bryant	1978
Parzival	Eschenbach	A T Hatto	1980
Willehalm	Eschenbach	M Gibbs, S Johnson	1972
History of Holy Grail	Vulgate	Carol Chase	1992
History of Merlin	Vulgate	Rupert Pickens	1992
Lancelot Grail	Vulgate	Norris Lacy	1992
Lancelot Grail	Vulgate	W Kibler, C Carroll	1992
Quest for the Holy Grail	Vulgate	Jane Burns	1992
The Death of Arthur	Vulgate	Norris Lacy	1992
Merlin and the Grail	Boron	Nigel Bryant	1988
The Post Vulgate Quest	Vulgate	Martha Asher	1992
The Post Vulgate Death	Vulgate	Martha Asher	1992
The Post Vulgate Merlin	Vulgate	Martha Asher	1992

Approximate Manuscript dates:

Date	Manuscript	Author
530s	Ruin and Conquest of Britain	Gildas,
500s	Y Gododdin	Aneirin
730s	Ecclesiastical History of English	Bede
800s	History of the Britons	Nennius
800s	Anglo Saxon Chronicles	Anon
900s	Armes Prydein	Anon
1120	Annales Cambiae	Anon
1125	Chronicle of Kings of England	William Malmesbury
1130	History of the English	Henry Huntingdon
1135	Chronicle of the Kings	Walter Oxford (Tysilio)
1135	History of the Kings of Britain	Geoffrey Monmouth
1135	Antiquities of Glastonbury	William Malmesbury
1155	Roman de Brut	Robert Wace
1160	History of English Affairs	William Newburgh
1160	Tristan et Iseut	Beroul
1180	Lancelot, the Knight of the Cart	Chretien de Troyes
1180	Perceval, Story of the Grail	Chretien de Troyes
1190	Chronicle of Britain	Layamon
1210?	High History (Perlesvaus)	Anon
1210	Parzival	Wolfram Eschenbach
	The Vulgate Cycle ('V' - six works)	
1220s	History of the Holy Grail	(V) Walter Kayo
1220s	History of Merlin	(V) Anon
1220s	Lancelot Grail	(V) Anon
1220s	Quest for the Holy Grail	(V) Walter Map
1220s	Death of Arthur	(V) Walter Map
1230?	Merlin and the Grail	Robert de Boron
1230s	Post Vulgate Cycle	(V) Anon
1400s	The Death of Arthur	Thomas Malory

Abbreviations within this book:

Abbreviation		Book	Author or translator
English Kings	-	Chronicle Kings of England	Malmesbury
English History	-	History of the English	Huntingdon
Brut Oxford	-	Chronicle of the Kings	Walter Oxford (Tysilio)
History of Kings	-	History of Kings of Britain	Geoffrey Monmouth
Glastonbury History	-	Antiquities of Glastonbury	Malmesbury
History of English	-	History of English Affairs	William Newburgh
Roman	-	Roman de Brut	Robert Wace
High History	-	Perlesvaus (High History)	Unknown
Perceval	-	Perceval, Story of the Grail	Chretien de Troyes
History	-	History of the Holy Grail	(V) Walter Kayo
Merlin	-	Merlin	(V) Anon
Lancelot	-	Lancelot	(V) Anon
Quest	-	Quest for the Holy Grail	(V) Walter Map
Mort	-	The Death of Arthur	(V) Walter Map
Boron Merlin	-	Merlin and the Grail	Robert de Boron
Post Quest	-	The Post Vulgate Quest	(V) Anon
Post Mort	-	The Post Vulgate Death	(V) Anon
Post Merlin	-	The Post Vulgate Merlin	(V) Anon

Repetitions and duplications:

A certain amount of repetition has been retained in this book, in order to assist the reader and reduce the amount of cross-referencing between chapters that is required. The term 'as mentioned previously' can also refer to previous books in this series.

The occult:

This book sometimes refers to items being 'occult'. The intended meaning here is that they are 'hidden' or 'concealed', which is the original meaning of this term.

Robert de Boron - Merlin and the Grail:

This short work by Robert de Boron is a concise summary of all of the manuscripts that comprise the *Vulgate Cycle,* and so instead of having a separate chapter for *Merlin Grail,* extracts from this work are interspersed throughout this book. Boron, who also worked on the *Vulgate Cycle,* has managed to force the entire *Vulgate Cycle* and much more besides into just 160 highly readable pages. And since this manuscript reads as a later summary of the *Vulgate Cycle,* it has been placed in the chronology as a later work. So if readers want to discover all of the elements that comprise Norman Arthurian history, this short summary by Robert de Boron is invaluable.

Caution

All who proceed beyond this point must be prepared to have their view of Arthurian and Biblical history challenged

You have been warned

I

Early Accounts

The history of King Arthur and his wealthy and influential royal court has a credibility problem among modern historians, and it is not difficult to see why. Here is a very famous monarch who is said to have valiantly fought to save Britain from successive invasions by the Picts, Saxons and Romans, and yet he is not visible in the archaeological record and barely mentioned by the early British chroniclers. And he is certainly not mentioned in the manner that we might expect, with descriptions of his vast and wealthy court based at Castle Camelot populated by heroic knights like Sir Lancelot and Sir Galahad. These detailed accounts of a famous and influential monarch of Britain only arose in the 12th and 13th centuries, and mostly from Norman France. So the history of King Arthur and his knights has a credibility gap - a six hundred year chasm that requires an explanation. As Professor James Bruce said in the opening chapter of his comprehensive 1922 study of Arthurian literature:

> Did any such person (as Arthur) actually exist? The candid historian must admit that the evidence on the subject is meagre, relatively late, and almost wholly fantastic; and that consequently an affirmative answer to this question is by no means inevitable. [1] (Author's brackets.)

Professor Bruce is trying to let his expectant readers down gently here, for he finds no credible evidence for a famous monarch called Arthur whatsoever. Although it has to be said that Bruce was looking more at the literature than the history, and there may be a possible candidate for a historical Arthur lurking within British history. As to the fantastic (unbelievable) nature of Arthurian history, well that again depends upon the interpretations we apply to these fantastic stories and as we shall see, some of them make a great deal of sense when viewed from an alternate perspective. Another problem is the distinct possibility that the cloak of a very famous 'Arthur' may have been placed over a relatively unknown British monarch, forming a composite character who is by necessity full of geographical and chronological contradictions. And attempting to decypher the identity of a composite character is going to be fraught with impossibilities and complications.

But readers of the *King Jesus Trilogy* will have noted a trend here, for we have faced the problem of missing or displaced characters several times before. From Adam and Eve, to Jacob and Joseph, to kings David and Solomon, and onto Saul and Jesus, many of the great biblical heroes of the past seem to be missing from the historical record. In the case of these particular individuals we have a great deal of information about them from the comprehensive but semi-legendary accounts of the Torah, Talmud and gospels, but there is nothing tangible within the historical record to substantiate the claims being made there. Not, that is, until we take a lateral and rational look at the evidence and open our eyes to the complete corpus of evidence before us. Suddenly, these mythological apparitions from the Torah and New Testament stop shimmering, draw into focus, and become documented components of real history.

Adam and Eve were rediscovered to be living in Amarna in Egypt; the great Israelite Exodus out of Egypt became the Hyksos Exodus out of Egypt; the capital city of kings David and Solomon was based at Zoan (Tanis) rather than Zion (Jerusalem); while the revolutionary 1st century leader called King Jesus Em-Manuel was actually the revolutionary 1st century leader called King Izas Manu of Edessa. The evidence is there, if we dare open our eyes to the possibilities, and suddenly the presumed mythology coalesces into a real history that is much more logical and believable than the fantasy stories we are usually presented with.

So does King Arthur and his wealthy court reside within the same category as these biblical characters? Is he yet another well-known historical character who has been incorrectly identified and categorised, and so placed into the wrong era or the wrong location? This is entirely possible, and the first clue that points us in this direction is the great centuries-long lacuna or chasm in the accounts that mention King Arthur. There are several British chronicles that document the 5th and 6th century eras in which King Arthur was supposed to have lived, and yet the surprising fact and problem about these ancient chronicles, is that they do not mention a famous King Arthur. In fact, most of them don't mention any Arthur at all, whether famous or not. In chronological order we have the following manuscripts that chronicle this era, followed by some bullet-points of the content of these accounts:

Gildas *Ruin and Conquest of Britain*	5th or 6th century
Emperor Magnus Maximus invades Gaul, Spain, Rome.	(c. 383) *
Upon the failure of Maximus, Britain is without an army.	(c. 388)
Scots and Picts begin to invade Britain.	(c. 392)
Britons plead for Roman help. Receive a legion.	(c. 397 ?)
Turf wall built to keep out invaders	(c. ??)
Britons again plead for Roman help. Receive a legion.	(c. 402 ?)
Another wall built of a 'different nature'.	(c. 405 ?)
Britons plead with Agitius for help, but are refused.	(c. 406)
Foreign invasions and civil wars wrack the nation.	(c. 412 ?)
Unpaid Saxon mercenaries rebel against Britons.	(c. 414 ?)
Retreat and exile of the Britons to hills and forests.	(c. 418 ?)
Britons crown Aurelius Ambrosius, an emperor's son.	(c. 420 ?)
(Probably a son of Constantine III.)	(d. 411)
Wars culminate in the battle of Badon or Bath.	(c. 465).

No mention of King Arthur.

Aneirin *Y Gododdin* 6th century?

Describes a hero warrior, and says: 'he was no Arthur'.

No mention of King Arthur.

Bede *Ecclesiastical History of the English*	8th century *	
Magnus Maximus, usurper emperor of Western Rome.	(c. 377,	383)
Arcadius made emperor.	(c. 394,	395)
Gratian and Constantine usurper emperors of the West.	(c. 407,	392-407)
Roman rule ends 470 years after Caesar's invasion.	(c. 415,	406)
Britons appeal to Roman assistance. Receive a legion.	(c. 420,	397 ?)
Turf wall built to keep out invaders	(c. ??)	
Britons appeal to Roman assistance. Receive a legion.	(c. 425,	402 ?)
Stone wall built to keep out invaders	(c. ??)	
Theodosius made emperor	(c. 423,	423)
Britons appeal to Agitius-Aetius for help, but refused.	(c. 446,	406)
Invasions of Picts. Britons driven to hills and forests.	(c. 447,	418)
Vurtigernus (Vortigern) king, invites Horsa & Hengist.	(c. 448,	411)
Marcian and Valentinian made emperor.	(c. 449,	450)
Saxons ravage the land and terrorise the people.	(c. 452,	418)

*
The dates for Gildas are from the author, because *Ruin and Conquest* is undated.
The dates for Bede are from Bede's chronology, plus the Author's alternate date.
The dates for Nennius are from the author, because *History of Britons* is undated.

Aurelius Ambrosius, a prince of Rome, became king. (c. 454, 420?)
Battle of Badon fought 44 years after Saxon invasion. (c. 492, 462)
No mention of King Arthur.

Nennius ***History of the Britons*** 9th century
Britain settled by Brutus of Troy.
Maximus the 7th emperor of Britain, usurps Rome (c. 383)
Invasions of Picts and Scots. (c. 392 ?)
Britons appeal to Rome for assistance. Receive help. (c. 397 ?)
Another usurper emperor of Rome (Constantine III?) (c. 407 ?)
Britons appeal to Rome for assistance. Receive help. (c. 402 ?)
Vortigern becomes king. (c. 411 ?)
Arrival of Horsa and Hengist. (c. 413 ?)
The Saxon invasion is dated by Nennius to AD 477.
No mention of King Arthur. (Just a warrior called Arthur.)

Anon ***Anglo Saxon Chronicles*** 9th century
Maximus, the usurper emperor of Rome. (c. 381, 383)
Theodosius made emperor (c. 423, 423)
Britons appeal to Rome for assistance: refused. (c. 443, 392 ?)
Vortigern invites Horsa and Hengist. (c. 449, 413 ?)
Horsa and Hengist battle with Vortigern. (c. 455, 417 ?)
Saxon invasions dated to AD 449.
No mention of King Arthur whatsoever.

Anon ***Armes Prydein*** 10th century
An account of Saxon invasions of Britain, and how they will be expelled.
No mention of King Arthur.

Anon ***Annales Cambiae*** 10th or 12th century
Arthur won the battle of Badon in AD 516.
Arthur and Medraus perished at the battle of Camlann in AD 537.
Arthur is not called a king. (But others are.)

Malmesbury ***Chronicle of English Kings*** 12th century
One page describing King Arthur as an army commander for Aurelius Ambrosius.
No mention of King Arthur.

Huntingdon ***History of the English*** 12th century
One paragraph mentioning Arthur as an early 6th century warrior and 'chief of the kings'. This paragraph is mostly taken from Gildas.
A 'chieftain' Arthur is mentioned in one paragraph.

Monmouth ***History of Kings of Britain*** 12th century
Almost the complete story of a famous, wealthy and powerful King Arthur. All that is missing from this account, is a few famous characters like Lancelot, Perceval and Galahad.
Almost the complete King Arthur story.

Newburgh ***History of English Affairs*** 12th century
Newburgh ridicules the claims made by Monmouth, about a wealthy and powerful king called Arthur.
The possibility of a powerful King Arthur is ridiculed.

And this is the sum total of all the evidence for King Arthur and his famous royal court, for the first six or seven centuries after the presumed era for his life. Apart from Monmouth's late account of Arthur, there is no wealthy royal court, no knights in shining armor, no Sirs Lancelot, Perceval or Galahad, and not a trace of a Queen Gwenevere. In fact, even King Arthur is not mentioned in these early texts, bar a passing reference to a 'Duke of War' bearing that name. Readers can perhaps see why Professor James Bruce and others have said from the very outset that the existence of a historical King Arthur was 'by no means inevitable', for at this stage it looks like the story of a wealthy and powerful King Arthur was invented by Geoffrey of Monmouth.

And we appear to be losing historical information, when progressing from Gildas to Bede and then to the sparse references in Nennius, and onto the threadbare references in the *Anglo Saxon Chronicles*. But this is what we might expect - information is more often lost to the sands of time, than long-forgotten scrolls are unexpectedly discovered. So why, after losing so much information about the Arthurian era between the 5th and 10th centuries, do the 12th century authors from Normandy and Germany suddenly know a thousand times more about these events than these early British chroniclers? The data, as it is being presented to us, does not make a great deal of sense. So let us look more closely at what these Dark Age authors knew about the centuries surrounding Arthurian history, and the influential characters and events within that era.

Gildas **6th century**

The really peculiar aspect of *Ruin and Conquest of Britain*, is the fact that Gildas does not mention King Arthur at all. Gildas is surnamed Sapiens, meaning the Wise, so why does the wise Gildas know nothing about a famous king called Arthur? And this is despite Gildas' obvious chronological proximity to this story and his accounts of invading Saxons, which is a primary topic of later Arthurian history. So why did the only historian contemporary to these events fail to mention Britain's most wealthy and powerful monarch of this era? It is stretching credulity to its limits to say that Gildas somehow missed the life of this famous king, or perhaps omitted him out of political opposition. Gildas was desperately looking for a British champion to rid the nation of the hated Saxons, and he could easily have found just such a hero in the life of King Arthur. So why didn't he?

The plot in Gildas' chronicle is tailor-made for King Arthur and his gallant knights to come riding out of the swirling mists in the very last paragraphs of the chapter, with their pennants flying and their lances lowered ready for action with the despised Saxons. The plot has been laid, the reader is expectant and turns the next page with trepidation and .... and there is no King Arthur and no liberation. And Gildas not only misses out King Arthur, he also completely forgets about Uther Pendragon, Queen Gwenevere, Sir Lancelot, Sir Perceval, Sir Galahad and the wise wizard, Merlin. And nor is there any mention of Camelot, Excalibur or the Holy Grail. So how did this happen? Why does our knowledge about King Arthur and his court only blossom when we get to the 12th century? It does not make sense.

The only solace for classical Arthurian history here, is to assume that Aurelius Ambrosius must be a pseudonym for King Arthur. Geoffrey of Monmouth says that Aurelius Ambrosius was the brother of Uther Pendragon and therefore an uncle of King Arthur, and so it is possible that Gildas has placed the emphasis on the wrong royal and elevated Ambrosius to hero status instead of Arthur. But if Arthur was Aurelius Ambrosius, or perhaps his nephew, the political and economic environment of northwest Europe just could not have sustained a wealthy court of Camelot in that era, as we shall see later.

And so we come to the dating of Gildas and the chronology of his work. Caradoc of Llancarfan in his 12th century *Life of Gildas* has Gildas as a contemporary of Arthur, whose 23 other brothers rose up in a revolt against Arthur. This strange tale not only sounds apocryphal, it also has obvious similarities with Arthur's twelve battles and with the design of the zodiac, as we shall see again shortly. Gildas himself seems to say that he was born the same year as the Battle of Badon, and that this battle was fought 44 years after the victories of Aurelius Ambrosius over the Saxons.

I *Early Accounts*

The date for the Saxon invasions, the Battle of Badon and the life of Gildas are all unclear or unknown; and so our starting point for this chronology will be the date for the reign of Emperor Magnus Maximus, the 'British' usurper emperor of Rome, which is known to be AD 383. Maximus was executed in 388, and Britain was left without an army at that time according to Gildas. Because of this lack of defence two appeals were made to Rome for assistance, while the third appeal was actually made to Emperor Arcadius in 406, as we shall see in the following pages. But the third plea for help was refused and Britain was cut adrift from Rome at that time.

This early date for the withdrawal of Roman forces from Britain is confirmed when Walter of Oxford and Geoffrey of Monmouth both appear to assert that Constantine III only became king of Britain and then usurper emperor of Rome, because the Romans had already abandoned the country. Yet the historical record suggests that Constantine III was crowned in 407, and so the Roman administration of Britain must have already ended by that time. This seemingly trivial point will become more significant when we come onto the similar accounts of Bede and others, because it is a key element in determining a date for the reign of this British manifestation of King Arthur.

This Arthurian evidence for an early Roman withdrawal from Britain is confirmed by the numismatic (coin) evidence, which suggests that there were no Roman legionnaires in Britain after AD 406. The Roman army would have brought coinage to pay its troops, which would have been traded with the locals and a proportion lost into the detritus of life; and yet no significant coinage post 406 has been discovered in the resulting archaeological record. So we can safely say that the two successful appeals to Rome for military assistance must have been made prior to 407 - before Constantine III usurped the throne of Britain and then of Rome. Some invading Saxons may have arrived while Constantine was campaigning in Gaul, but the main waves of immigration are more likely to have arrived after his death in 411. The Battle of Badon is said to have been waged about 44 years after Aurelius Ambrosius' victories over the Saxons, and so from all of this evidence we can derive the following rough chronology:

End of Roman presence	406
Constantine III crowned	407
Constantine III executed	411
Saxon invasions	415
Aurelius Ambrosius king	420
Battle of Badon	465
Gildas writes 'On the ruin...'	490

These dates are on the early side for the dating of the Battle of Badon and the chronology of Gildas' chronicle, with the former typically being dated to about

530. But this preliminary chronology does make sense of all the information available in Gildas' fragmentary record, and it will be demonstrated shortly that many of the chronologies that give later dates are following some obvious errors in Bede's account. The key component to remember here is the all-important date for the withdrawal of the Roman presence in Britain, which has been placed here at before AD 407. And remember that although Bede may have had other records to work from, his main guide was obviously Gildas. And the same goes for Geoffrey of Monmouth and Walter of Oxford, who were also relying on Gildas and Bede for their history of this early era.

Although this rough chronology will become more important in the next chapter, perhaps the most important aspect of Gildas' chronicle is what he omits. Gildas was almost contemporary to these events, and yet he does not mention King Arthur. In fact, he does not mention anyone called Arthur. So why did Gildas, who was contemporary to these events, not know of a famous king called Arthur? So from the very outset of this investigation, we can safely say that there is something fundamentally amiss with classical Arthurian history.

Gildas never mentions any Arthur whatsoever

Bede **8th century**

The Venerable Bede was writing at the beginning of the 8th century, some two centuries after Gildas, and he was plainly using Gildas' manuscript as a guide as the two accounts are almost identical. But Bede had a major problem, which was that Gildas did not give a chronology for his history. Conversely, Bede was trying to write a comprehensive and accurate chronicle, annotated with all the correct dates, and these dates were obviously derived through reference to the reigns and consulships of the emperors of Rome. But Gildas did not mention Constantine III in his chronicle, who happens to be a key chronological peg in this history, and this may have caused some confusion.

The result of this was that Bede made an error in his chronology, and identified the third appeal for assistance to Rome as being sent to consul Flavius Aetius in 446. Why Bede focused upon Aetius, who was merely a commander and consul of Rome, is not known. Surely the Britons would be appealing to the emperor himself, rather than to an army commander. But the error is fairly clear to see, for Bede says that:

> The Romans ceased to rule in Britain, almost 470 years after Caius Julius Caesar came to the island. (Ecclesiastical History, 1:11.)

470 years after Julius Caesar's invasion would equate to AD 415, which is a reasonable date for the end of Roman rule in Britain; and it agrees reasonably well with the 406 date obtained from the numismatic evidence and the 407 date for the usurping reign of Constantine III, as we have already seen. Following Bede's 415 date for the end of Roman rule, Bede then says that the Britons made two appeals for assistance from Rome and received legions to protect the islands and build protective ramparts or walls. These are the same pleas for assistance mentioned by Gildas, but the date that Bede gives makes no sense whatsoever. If the Romans had withdrawn from Britain in AD 406 and absolved themselves of all responsibility for the islands, and if Constantine III had initiated a rebellion against Rome in 407, then why were the Romans sending legions across to help Britain in the AD 420s? There is an obvious error here.

The answer is that Bede has misidentified the chronological position for Constantine III, and also misidentified the recipient of the third appeal for Roman assistance. Bede was looking for a thrice elected consul who was called Agitius in Latin or Gittiws in the Welsh translation. Bede has presumed that this must be a reference to commander Aetius, who was thrice consul in 446, but he was wrong. In reality, Gittiws, Gittius or Agitius was a poor transliteration of the name for Emperor Arcadius, who reigned in Constantinople from AD 395. The nominative progression (in reverse) is as follows:

Welsh	**Latin**
Gittiws	A--gitius
Gatius	A--gatius
Gadius	A--gadius
Ar-Cadius	Ar-cadius
Arcadius	Arcadius

Just as important as the nominative progression given here, is the fact that the identification of Emperor Arcadius makes much more sense than commander Aetius. Choosing similar names at random is of no use in making a historical identification, because the surrounding narrative and chronology also have to make sense. And in this case, they do.

One reason that Bede may have dismissed this alternate identification, is that it seems odd for the Britons to be writing to an Eastern emperor in Constantinople for assistance, rather than to a Western emperor (or commander) in Rome. But as we shall see in the next chapter, the Western emperor had already refused help and so the Britons were merely appealing over the heads of the administration in Rome, to the emperor in Constantinople instead. And so if we choose Arcadius as the recipient of the third plea for assistance, rather than Aetius, both the reasoning and the chronology fit like a glove:

Emperor Magnus Maximus	....	383
Death of Maximus	....	388
Britain no army	....	388
Gratian usurps the throne	....	390 or 406
Two appeals for Roman assistance		397 & 402
Romans refuse further assistance		404
Picts and Scots invade	....	404
End of Roman presence in Britain		406
Unsuccessful third appeal to Arcadius		406
Constantine III made usurper emperor		407
Constans the Monk made emperor		409
Death of Constantine and Constans		411
Vortigern takes the throne	....	411
Saxons invade	....	415
Aurelius Ambrosius (the son) king		420
Battle of Badon	....	465
Gildas writes 'On the ruin...'	....	490

As gloves go this one is made from the finest peccary leather with a cashmere lining, with not a wrinkle or blemish in sight. And that is what makes for an accurate chronology and therefore a trustworthy history. And so the real problem here is not that Bede made a very obvious error in his chronology, by identifying Aetius in 446 instead of Arcadius in 406, but the disappointing fact that so many modern translators and academics have missed this error completely. And despite the fact that the resulting chronology resembled a baggy mitten made from horse-hair, they still championed it as being the ultimate in received wisdom.

The other major problem with Bede's account, which is perhaps more pertinent to this investigation, is that Bede again never mentions King Arthur and his wealthy and influential court. Bede's chronicle dates from the 8th century, just a couple of centuries after the presumed era for King Arthur, and yet just like Gildas, Bede knows nothing about this famous royal family and their cadre of valiant knights. Yet two centuries of displacement is just a drop in the historic ocean; it is the equivalent of a modern historian writing about the Industrial Revolution. Evidence for this vibrant and influential royal court that conquered much of northwestern Europe should still have existed at this time, and yet Bede knows nothing about it.

Bede never mentions any Arthur whatsoever

Nennius and Saxon Chronicles **9th century**

As we proceed onto the 9th century accounts of Nennius, matters get worse not better, for the story begins to fragment and thin. The entire history from Maximus to Vortigern now occupies four short paragraphs. And the warrior called Arthur that this chronicle briefly mentions, is not attached to this genealogy at all. And the situation in the *Anglo Saxon Chronicles* is even more dire, with the data reducing to just four sentences. As evidence for a Celto-British king called Arthur, this is of no use whatsoever.

Nennius never mentions King Arthur

Welsh prophesies and annals **10th century**

And that is not the end of the many Arthurian woes, for the *Armes Prydein (Prophesy of Britain)* and *Annales Cambiae (Welsh Annals)* do not mention a king called Arthur either. While Gildas ended up living in Brittany in northern France, and might be excused for not knowing too much about a King Arthur of the Britons, the *Armes Prydein* is a poem from Wales. Furthermore, this is fictional tale about the great Celto-Welsh dream - the expulsion of the Saxons from all of Britain. Once again, this is the very expulsion of a hated enemy that an Arthurian warrior-hero should have been actively involved in, and yet the author does not use King Arthur as the hero of this fantasy. Why?

Similarly, the *Annales Cambiae* is a Welsh chronicle created at St David in Dyfed, and yet it merely has two short entries for an otherwise unknown Arthur, and fails to call him a king. Why? If the 10th century Welsh bards and chroniclers had not heard of a King Arthur of the Celto-Britons, and did not celebrate his great achievements, then who had and did?

The prophesies never mention King Arthur

Malmesbury **12th century**

The surprising thing about William of Malmesbury's *English Kings* is that we have already arrived in the all-important early 12th century. This is just a decade before Geoffrey of Monmouth started to write his great epic about the famous and wealthy royal court of King Arthur in his *History of Kings*, and yet Malmesbury knows nothing about the history of King Arthur whatsoever. All Malmesbury says is:

> When (Vortigern) died, the British strength decayed ... and they would soon have perished altogether had not Ambrosius, the sole survivor of the Romans ... quelled the presumptuous barbarians by the powerful aid of warlike

> Arthur. It is of this Arthur that the Britons fondly tell so many fables, even to the present day; a man worthy to be celebrated, not by idle fictions, but by authentic history. He long upheld the sinking state, and roused the broken spirit of his countrymen to war. (English Kings, 1:1:10.)

Malmesbury's Arthur is merely a heroic Herculean army commander figure of the early 6th century; a *Dux Bellorum* or a Duke of War as Nennius calls him. And there is no sign whatsoever of this warrior Arthur being a famous, wealthy and powerful British monarch with a vast royal court. But this observation is pivotal. Malmesbury was writing a chronicle of Britain (England) in the early 12th century and it is obvious that the only sources he had access to were the standard chronicles of Gildas, Bede and Nennius. Yet Malmesbury obviously had no access to the Breto-Norman manuscript(s) that Monmouth was going to use just a decade later to craft his epic Arthurian history, and therefore no idea whatsoever that there could have been a heroic king called Arthur who had a wealthy and influential court. Monmouth himself acknowledges this problem when he says:

> William of Malmesbury and Henry of Huntingdon, who I bid to be silent as to the kings of the Britons, seeing that they have not that book in the British (Breton) language which Walter of Oxford did bring here out of Brittany. (History of Kings, 12:20.) (Author's brackets.)

This is a reference to the Armorican or Breton manuscript that formed the foundation for Oxford's *Chronicle of the Kings* and Monmouth's *History of the Kings*, which are the subject of the next chapter. Monmouth was obviously in contact with Malmesbury and Huntingdon, or had read their manuscripts, and is pleading with them to be silent (and not to mock him), because they have not read the secret Breton manuscript that detailed the life of a wealthy and powerful King Arthur.

Quite obviously the Celto-British bards had not been singing tales of a heroic King Arthur over the preceding centuries, for if they had then surely Malmesbury, Huntingdon, Newburgh and the Welsh chroniclers would have devoted many chapters to this old legend. In which case, we can quite confidently state that Monmouth's assertion in the previous quote must be correct - the history of a wealthy and powerful King Arthur came from Normandy and Brittany, and not from Anglo-Britain or Celto-Britain. And it did so via an obscure manuscript that will be discussed in the next chapter.

And if classical Arthurian history was a Breto-Norman story about events that were not even known in Britain at that time, then this story may not be all it is claimed to be. The three main choices that would explain this paradox seem to be:

a. The Breto-Normans found an ancient manuscript about Dark Age Britain and published it. But why would the Normans be interested in a relatively obscure British history?

b. Since this was just after the Norman invasions of Angle-land or England, the Normans had created a fake history of Britain to keep the natives happy. But this seems highly unlikely. The Angelish or English aristocracy had been Anglo-Saxon at the time of the Norman invasions in 1066, not Celto-Welsh. For the Normans to have created a fake history about a Celto-British king slaughtering the Anglo-Saxons would have been undiplomatic and unproductive to say the least.

c. The Breto-Normans had an occult (concealed) but heretical story to tell. And in order to cover up its origins they attached it to a convenient historical event - the campaigns of the Breton-British usurper king and emperor called Constantine III.

While option c. may seem like a fantasy at this stage, it may well be closer to the truth than readers might imagine. The Normans must have either discovered or created this story about 'Arthur the wealthy monarch', because this was obviously not a Celto-British or Saxo-English tradition. And so one of the central tasks for the rest of this book is to discover the motive and meaning for this great literary and historical venture, that was organised and funded by the Norman aristocracy. The Arthurian enterprise was far too expensive and far too expansive to be a hoax or a whimsical jest, so there had to be a very serious motive and rationale for the creation and promotion of these many manuscripts. But what was it?

Malmesbury never mentions King Arthur

Malmesbury II **12th century**

A decade after writing *English Kings* Malmesbury was invited to Glastonbury to promote the heritage and history of the famous abbey there. The resulting *Antiquities of Glastonbury* is a compendium of hearsay and rumour that does manage to mention a King Arthur in passing. And yet by only mentioning one Arthurian knight, the relatively unknown Yder, Malmesbury does not appear to have taken his new information from Monmouth. We shall come across the shadowy Yder again in later chapters. Instead, Malmesbury credits the otherwise unknown *Acts of the Illustrious King Arthur* as his source. And despite Malmesbury's bold claim that King Arthur was buried at Glastonbury, he gives us just two paragraphs of text about this supposedly illustrious king.

Malmesbury never mentions the story of King Arthur

Huntingdon **12th century**

Like Malmesbury, Henry of Huntingdon knows nothing of a wealthy and influential King Arthur. Huntingdon has produced a very interesting and readable history of the English, but during this early era it basically follows the chronicles of Gildas, Bede and Nennius. And while Huntingdon does introduce some new material, which makes his chronicle worth reading, the Arthurian King Arthur is not one of those additions. The only mention we have of Arthur, is a single page about a 6th century warrior and 'chief of the kings', who was victorious against the Saxons. But the title 'chief of the kings' makes this Arthur sound more like a tribal chieftain than an influential monarch, and the 6th century date for his life precludes any interaction with the Romans, for there were no Romans in Western Europe this era.

Huntingdon mentions a chieftain King Arthur

Monmouth & Oxford **12th century**

The similar histories narrated by Monmouth and Oxford are discussed in the next chapter.

Monmouth and Oxford give the full history of King Arthur

Newburgh **12th century**

William of Newburgh was writing after the publication of Monmouth's *History of Kings*, which is the first of the classical Arthurian sagas that detail the full life of a powerful and wealthy King Arthur. But Newburgh knows nothing whatsoever about this wealthy and powerful monarch called King Arthur, from his many historical sources, and so he savages Monmouth for producing a litany of fictions and falsehoods.

Newburgh says Monmouth's King Arthur is fictional

I Early Accounts

The missing king

However we work the many excuses, it is a given fact that the most famous king of the British Isles following the decline of Roman Britain, goes missing for some six hundred years. Yes, the most famous British monarch of the Dark Ages era is not mentioned for more than half a millennium. Is that not strange? The similarity here with the missing archaeology in Israel for kings David and Solomon is obvious, but in Britain this famous Arthurian royal family goes missing not only from the archaeological record, but also from the contemporary chronicles. But if kings David and Solomon can both be rediscovered in the historical record by moving the location of their capital city from Zion to Zoan, can King Arthur be rediscovered by similarly altering our perceptions - by either moving his capital city or perhaps by readjusting the chronology a little?

The first hint of a solution to the many problems with Arthurian history, can be glimpsed in the sudden 12th century blossoming of Norman and Breton accounts that mention a heroic king and his magnificent royal court - an Arthur who can be recognised as the classical Arthurian Arthur. And yet we don't reach this point until the publication of *History of Kings of Britain* by Geoffrey of Monmouth in about 1135, and *Chronicle of the Kings* by Walter of Oxford around the same date. This is some 300 years after the short account of a warrior Arthur attributed to Nennius, and more than 600 years after King Arthur is supposed to have lived. And just as importantly, this is only ten years after Malmesbury wrote his *English Kings,* and about five years after Huntingdon wrote *English History,* and yet both Malmesbury and Huntingdon knew absolutely nothing about this famous royal Arthur.

Then a veritable torrent of Arthurian manuscripts began to stream out of Northern France and even Germany, Holland, Italy and Spain, in the early 12th and early 13th centuries. But why this late era and these odd locations? Why did a Celto-British King Arthur only surface, as a fully fledged monarch with a grand royal court and expansionist political strategies, within the 12th and 13th century literature of Normandy and Europe? The answer probably lies in the history of the Knights Templar.

The Templars were founded by Hugues de Payens in 1119, but they were not officially recognised by the Church until 1129 and only became rich, powerful and influential from that time onwards. If the Knights Templar in Syria and Judaea had shipped some manuscripts back to Europe, they would not have arrived until about 1130. This is five years after Malmesbury wrote his chronicle of England and likewise too late for Huntingdon to have seen them. But this date would be just five years before Monmouth and Oxford published their very different chronicles of Dark Age Britain, which detailed almost the complete history of the classical King Arthur. So if classical Arthurian history was linked in some manner to Templar manuscripts, as will be strongly argued in later chapters, then Gildas, Bede, Nennius, Malmesbury and Huntingdon would not have had access to them. But Monmouth and Oxford, writing just a few years after Malmesbury and Huntingdon, may well have access to some novel, challenging and heretical ideas that were emerging from the newly liberated Christian Near East.

However, Geoffrey Monmouth and Walter Oxford were obviously keeping their dangerously heretical information within a tight cabal of trusted colleagues, because just 30 years later William of Newburgh savaged Monmouth's *History of Kings* as being a complete fiction, saying:

> No one, but a person ignorant of ancient history ... can for a moment doubt how impertinently and impudently (Monmouth) falsifies in every respect ... Whatever Geoffrey has written ... is a fiction, invented either by himself or by others, and promulgated either through an unchecked propensity to falsehood, or a desire to please the Britons, of whom vast numbers are said to be so stupid as to assert that Arthur is yet to come, and who cannot bear to hear of his death.
>
> First, he makes (Arthur) triumph, at pleasure, over Angles, Picts, and Scots ... Next, he makes him attack, and speedily triumph over, Gaul ... Next this fabler makes (Arthur) declare war against the Romans ... Then, with a wider license of fabrication, he brings all the kings of the world in league with the Romans against him; that is to say, the kings of Greece, Africa, Spain, Parthia, Media, Iturea, Libya, Egypt, Babylon, Bithynia, Phrygia, Syria, Boeotia, and Crete.
>
> And he relates that all of them were conquered by him (Arthur) in a single battle; whereas, even Alexander the Great, renowned throughout all ages, was engaged for twelve years in vanquishing only a few of the potentates of these mighty kingdoms. Indeed, (Monmouth) makes the little finger of his Arthur more powerful than the loins (penis) of Alexander the Great. (History of English Affairs, Newburgh, Preface.) (Author's brackets.)

Clearly, Newburgh was not a member of Monmouth's Normo-Breton Arthurian cabal, and regarded everything he recorded as being a complete and worthless fiction. Note also in this quote that we have the common euphemism of loins meaning 'penis', which will become important in later chapters. This penile comparison between Arthur and Alexander was actually derived from a biblical verse in 1Kings 12:10, where King Rehoboam declares that he will be mightier than his father, King Solomon.

And having outlined the unlikely events and impossible exaggerations within Monmouth's *History of Kings*, Newburgh then comes to the central problem with Monmouth's sensational new history of King Arthur:

> For how would the elder historians, who were ever anxious to omit nothing remarkable, and even recorded trivial circumstances, pass by unnoticed so incomparable a man, and such surpassing deeds? How could they, I repeat, by their silence, suppress Arthur, a British monarch who was superior to Alexander the Great? (History of English Affairs, Newburgh, Preface.)

This is indeed a tricky problem for classical Arthurian history, for how could such a powerful, influential and famous king go unnoticed by so many chroniclers for so many hundreds of years? We have many records that detail the life and times of the mighty Alexander, and yet nothing was written about Arthur for some six hundred years. One possible solution to this inconvenient omission is that Arthur has had a change of name; and so he might be rediscovered in the historical record if we look for a monarch who had similar family connections and performed similar deeds. However, while this may appear to be a viable solution, as soon as we try to make use of it we hit another complication that brings yet more creases to the researcher's already furrowed brow.

These new 12th century accounts, by both Geoffrey Monmouth and Walter Oxford, say that King Arthur was so powerful he refused to pay tribute to Rome, and led an expedition down through Gaul to conquer the Western Roman Empire. And while this is a magnificent story of nationalistic revival and chivalric deeds, almost on a par with Alexander the Great's celebrated campaigns in the East, it rather restricts the possible time-frame for these events. In fact, there is only a very small window of opportunity - between the decline of Roman control in Britain and the end of the entire Western Roman Empire - within which such an invasion by a wealthy and powerful Celto-British monarch could have taken place. The various options on the table are as follows:

A 4th century Arthur.

There were not many opportunities for a local British monarch to usurp the authority of Rome in this era, let alone embark on an expedition down through Gaul to conquer Rome. The nation was still administered by the Romans, and while the Empire was faltering on occasions there was little opportunity for a local monarch to usurp the authority of Rome. Likewise, the history of 4th century Britain is fairly well documented, and so there is little scope for an Arthurian rebellion going unnoticed and unreported.

The only possibility in the 4th century would be for King Arthur to be Emperor Magnus Maximus, a British leader of uncertain heritage who usurped the Western Roman Empire from Gratian and Theodosius I in 383. Maximus is thought to have been Spanish but he was also said to have married Helen, a daughter of a British king called Octavius. His rebellion was eventually quashed by Theodosius and Valentinian in 388, and the remnants of this semi-British royal-imperial family and their army retreated back to Armorica (Brittany). Many Britons had likewise emigrated to Armorica over the preceding decades, and so the growing Briton population there enabled the region to get involved in another yet another rebellion just over two decades later. So there ***was*** a 4th century rebellion against Rome under a 'British' king, but very little of this particular revolt matches with known Arthurian history.

Having said that, there is a slim possibility that the Maximus rebellion was directly related to the story of a British King Arthur, especially since Gildas does not mention the second rebellion by Constantine III at all. However, the adjustments that have to be made to the established Arthurian storyline to achieve this are so great, that this explanation has been relegated to the appendix. But this alternative chronology is worth a read at a later time, because the resulting narrative makes a great deal of sense and explains many of the claims being made for the early Celto-British segment of Arthurian history. But even if this proposed equivalence with Maximus and Constantine is accepted, it cannot alter the fact that the Arthurian story narrated in *High History*, *Parzifal* and the *Vulgate Cycle* is something completely different, and mostly concerned with 1st century events.

An early 5th century Arthur.

It is almost a certainty that a large section of the chronicles narrated by Bede and Monmouth were based upon the life of Emperor Constantine III, the second British usurper emperor of Rome. Gildas has the chronology of this era correct, but fails to mention Constantine. Bede relied upon Gildas for his information, and although he got the chronology wrong he did place Constantine III and Constans II in roughly the right location. But the mistake in Bede's chronology is fairly easy to spot and correct, which results in a good agreement with Gildas. And yet the royal-imperial succession of Constantine and Constans is also the basis for the Arthurian succession narrated by Geoffrey of Monmouth, as the following table demonstrates:

Historical lineage	Date	Monmouth lineage	Date *1	Ref
Honorius		not mentioned		
Gratian the usurper	(406?)	Gratian the usurper	(390?)	(6:1)
Constantine III	(407)	Constantine (III?)	(411?)	(6:4)
sons		sons		
Constans the Monk	(411)*2	Constans the Monk	(423?)	(6:6)*3
not mentioned		Aurelius Ambrosius		(6:5)
not mentioned		Uther Pendragon		(6:5)
grandson		grandson		
not mentioned		King Arthur		(8:20)

*1 Arthurian dates vary. These are from thenationalcv.org.uk and are typical.

*2 Constans is called a 'monk who became a caesar' by Orosius and Zosimus.

*3 Constans is called 'the monk' by Bede in 1:11, and by Monmouth in 6:6.

We can see that there is a close agreement here, between the established history of Roman Britain and the Arthurian history of Monmouth and Oxford. However, what we do not have in the historical record, in order to complete this comparison, is the names of the other sons of Emperor Constantine III. But what we do have is the same region; the same royal title; the same dates; the same names; the same ecclesiastic title; and the same family relationships. Thus we do end up with a broad agreement between the uncertain story by Monmouth and Oxford, and the presumably historical accounts narrated by Gildas, Bede, Orosius and Zosimus. For instance, both of these early British chroniclers say that Aurelius Ambrosius was the son of an emperor:

> They took arms under the conduct of Aurelius Ambrosius, a modest man, who of all the Roman nation was then alone in the confusion of this troubled period by chance left alive. His parents, who for their merit were adorned with the purple, had been slain in these same broils. (Ruin and Conquest, Gildas 25.)

> They had at that time for their leader, Aurelius Ambrosius, a man of worth, who alone, by chance, of the Roman nation had survived the storm, in which his parents who were of the royal race had perished. (Ecclesiatical History, Bede 1:16)

Nearly all Arthurian researchers and historians will agree that the Aurelius Ambrosius mentioned here by Gildas and Bede is the brother of Uther Pendragon, and therefore the uncle of King Arthur. And so this Aurelius Ambrosius joins directly onto the genealogy given by both Monmouth and Oxford and the rest of Arthurian history, as can be seen in fig 1.2. But what many modern researchers fail to mention, is that this Aurelius Ambrosius was a son of a Roman emperor. Not simply the son of a British monarch, but the son of an aristocrat who was of the 'Roman nation' and of the 'royal race' who had been 'adorned with the purple'. And the only aristocrats in the Roman Empire who were allowed to wear the imperial purple cloak, were the emperors themselves.

But how can Arthurian researchers possibly divine the ancestry and provenance of this otherwise unknown King Ambrosius, if they do not use all the information available? This is similar to the many histories of Christianity that refuse to acknowledge that 'christ' and 'messiah' both refer to the anointed king of the Israelites and Jews, and then complain that they cannot find a heroic carpenter in the historical record. Well, if they spend all their time looking for an artisan instead of a king, that is not really surprising. And the really sad thing, is that these Christian historians will deliberately look into this incorrect location because they don't want to find their hero figure - because they are too afraid of what they might find.

Surprisingly, the same attitude is also prevalent within Arthurian historical research, where otherwise competent and dedicated historians will avert their gaze from the reality they have discovered because they do not like what they see. And this conspiracy of silence emanates from both sides of the Arthurian divide. To those who believe that King Arthur was a real historical figure, the imagery of the glorious knights seated around the Round Table in the British royal court is highly seductive, and it would seem that nobody wants to terminate that dream. Conversely, Guy Halsall and others pour scorn on the whole concept of an Arthurian monarchy, and yet fail to mention that Aurelius Ambrosius was said to be the son of a murdered emperor. But how can they possibly divine who Ambrosius was, if they do not acknowledge his imperial heritage?

So what we are looking for here is a murdered Roman emperor whose son became a British prince, and that leaves us with very few options. This has to be a record of the late 4th or early 5th centuries and so the only options in the historical record are the 'British' usurper emperor Magnus Maximus, or perhaps the Breto-British usurper emperor Constantine III. The Maximus option is an outside chance, and so it will be discussed in Appendix I.

Regards the Constantine option, both Monmouth and Oxford claim that this Aurelius Ambrosius was the son of a Constantine and the brother of a Constans the Monk. And of course Constantine III, the British usurper emperor who took the throne of the Western Empire between 407 and 411, did have a son called Constans the Monk. It would appear to be undeniable that Monmouth and Oxford were both pointing towards

Constantine III as being the father of Aurelius Ambrosius. This is why Ambrosius was said to have had a murdered emperor as a father, because Constantine III was executed by Emperor Honorius in Arles, Gaul. But if Aurelius Ambrosius was the son of an emperor, then so too was his brother, Uther Pendragon. And so the grandfather of King Arthur must have been Emperor Constantine III.

From the available evidence, it would appear to be reasonably certain that Monmouth's and Oxford's King Constantine, the grandfather of King Arthur, was actually Emperor Constantine III, the British usurper emperor who briefly ruled Britain, Gaul and Hiberia in the early 5th century. See the short genealogy in fig 1.2 for details. But are Monmouth's and Oxford's additions to Constantine's genealogy real, or have these authors deceitfully fabricated a new fictional story and added it onto the history of Constantine III, just as Newburgh claimed? Or, more interestingly, have Monmouth and Oxford spliced a real history from a different era onto the line of Constantine III?

All these authors needed to do was give Emperor Constantine two additional sons that nobody else knew about, and then they could have hung an entirely new genealogy from the line of Constantine. And who would be able to spot such a cunning deceit, in the fragmentary records of a Roman Britain that was rapidly disintegrating? And while this

Fig 1.1
A gold solidus of Emperor Constantine III, the father of Emperor Constans II the Monk. Both of these emperors were of British extract and usurped control over the Western Roman Empire.

-- Constantine III may be the grandfather of King Arthur --

The legend reads: Constantinus PF AVG ~ Victoria AAAVGGGG ~ L-D. The multiple 'G's indicate that there were four emperors at this time. The L-D is the mint at Lugdunum or Lyon.

suggestion may sound unnecessarily conspiratorial, there is a real problem with King Arthur being a grandson of Emperor Constantine III - the fact that this chronology forces him to be a mid to late 5th century monarch.

A late 5th century Arthur.

There is a problem for Arthurian history with this later era, and it is a big problem. The 12th and 13th century Arthurian manuscripts all relate that King Arthur undertook a military campaign down through Gaul to conquer Rome. Funnily enough, this is a campaign that sounds very similar to the one organised by Constantine III in AD 407, which is a subject taken up in Appendix I. However, by the mid 5th century Britain was in no fit shape to finance any such expedition, and the Western Roman Empire collapsed completely in about 480. By the end of the 5th century, there was no Rome left to conquer, and certainly no Rome left to have had a tax dispute with.

The many classical Arthurian histories that spontaneously erupted in the 12th century onwards all say that King Arthur refused to pay tribute to Rome, and yet both Monmouth and Oxford say that the Romans had already refused to accept any tribute from Britain way back in 404. To

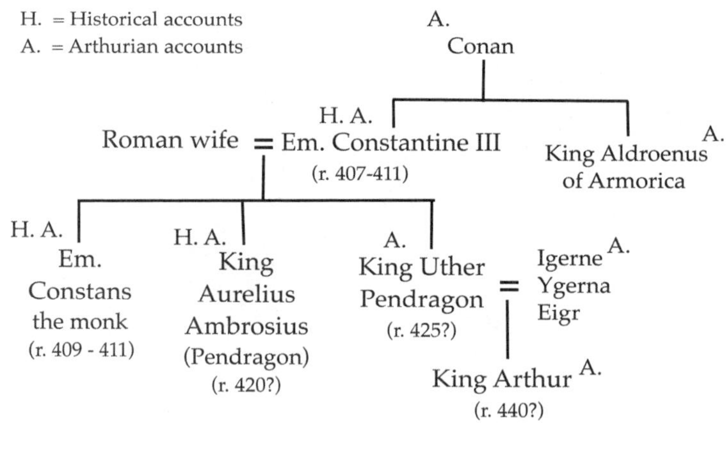

Fig 1.2
The first beginnings of an Arthurian genealogy, with the British usurper emperor, Constantine III, as the father of Uther Pendragon and the grandfather of King Arthur. The Arthurian accounts have added extra details and characters to this genealogy, but were these addition historically correct or later interpolations - a new story hung upon an old history?

accept tribute gave Rome an obligation to protect Britain from invaders, which Rome was no longer prepared or capable of doing, and so Britain had been cut adrift from the Empire at the turn of the 5th century. So if King Arthur lived the mid to late 5th century **he could not have had a tax-dispute with Rome**, let alone have had a British economy vibrant enough to muster an invasion force.

It is sometimes contended that King Riotimus could have been the historical role model for King Arthur, even though this king is not mentioned by any British chronicler. It is recorded by Jordanes of Constantinople that in the late 5th century Emperor Anthemius asked Riotimus of Britton *(sic)* for assistance against the invading Visigoths:

> Their King Riotimus came with twelve thousand men into the state of the Bituriges by the way of Ocean, and was received as he disembarked from his ships. Eurich, king of the Visigoths, came against them with an innumerable army, and after a long fight he routed Riotimus, king of the Brittones, before the Romans could join him. (Origins and Deeds of the Goths, 45.)

It is argued that because King Riotimus came across the sea he must have been British, and therefore possibly a prototype for King Arthur. But it would seem obvious that these were Bretons, not Britons. The Bituriges were based in modern Bordeaux, and the quickest route from Brittany to Bordeaux is down the coast by ship - sailing through the ocean just as the quote says. And so this small army did not have to cross the English channel and were unlikely to be British. But if this uncertain one-line afterthought comment about a Breton king's military manoeuvres is historically correct, then could Riotimus have been the foundation for Arthurian history?

This would seem unlikely: because Riotimus was an ally of the Romans rather than the sworn enemy; this battle was a matter of survival rather than a tax-dispute; and the troublesome invaders were Visigoths not Saxons. In fact, there appear to be few if any points of contact between this short, unsupported account and standard Arthurian history. But it is interesting to see that Rome was still trying to organise a military defence of the Empire right to the very end - as indeed they did with the botched and unsuccessful attempt to destroy the Vandals in North Africa in 468. The problem that Rome faced in this era, was that it now had too many fifth columnists in positions of power. The Roman commander and *de facto* King of Gaul at this time who was tasked with defending Rome against the Visigoths, was Ricimer, whose mother was a Visigoth. The problem Rome faced here is not too difficult to discern.

Rome had the same problem at the beginning of the 5th century, when the most senior Roman commander was Flavius Stilicho, the son of a Vandal. And when Stilicho was sent to counter Alaric's Visigoth invasion force he agreed the infamous 'pact of servitude', where Rome effectively bowed before Alaric and paid him protection money. Ricimer was cast from exactly the same mould as Stilicho, and so instead of defending Rome against the Visigoths, he marched on Rome and deposed Emperor Anthemius. And following that unhelpful stab in the back, Western Rome had less than eight tumultuous years to endure before it ceased to exist completely.

In conclusion, the proposed mid to late 5th century version of King Arthur could only have been an impoverished local chieftain in Britain, battling with foreign invasions and muttering unspeakable profanities about Picts and Saxons, much as Nennius suggests. But if this is so, then all these fine Norman, Italian, Dutch, Scandinavian and German stories about a vibrant Arthurian royal court and a valiant Arthurian conquest of Rome, must have all been fabricated. In other words, the vast bulk of Arthurian history, including most of the *Vulgate Cycle*, must therefore be fictional.

The Edessa trove

However, there is another possible explanation for these later stories of a wealthy and powerful Arthurian court and this comes from the location and era in which these stories blossomed, and also from the information gleaned thus far in the *King Jesus Trilogy*. The early 12th century is a generation after the First Crusade in 1096, and the first Christian city in the East to be liberated from Muslim subjugation was Edessa, the city that has already been named as the capital city of King Izas Manu of Edessa. And it will be a continuing refrain in this book that much of Arthurian history was rediscovered by Count Baldwin of Boulogne, after he liberated this very city and reestablished the Christian County of Edessa. But if this is so, then we can begin to make some predictions about the chronology, nature and presentation of Arthurian literature as we know it. And surprisingly, Arthurian manuscripts conform very well with these simple predictions.

The first prediction we might propose, is that any names mentioned in Arthurian texts written prior to the 12th century, are unlikely to have been derived from the Aramaic language. In contrast, the later *Vulgate Cycle* overtly claims that many of the names it uses are Chaldean (Aramaic). So Vortigern, Horsa and Hengist are less likely to be Aramaic names and are more likely to be derived from the local languages of northwestern Europe. Horsa and Hengist are a good case in point, because these brothers were said to be Saxon princes and their names are Saxo-Germanic meaning 'horse' and 'gelding' respectively. Conversely, the name for Vortigern appears to come from the

Celto-Welsh *wor tigern* meaning 'great ruler', and so Vortigern is the direct equivalent of Gildas' Latinised *tyrannus superbus* meaning 'arrogant tyrant'. So yes, these are not Chaldean-Aramaic names at all, and so these early proto-Arthurian histories by Gildas, Bede and Nennius are most certainly of Celto-British inspiration.

And then we come to the name of King Arthur himself. As most people already know, the name for King Arthur was derived from the Celto-Welsh *arth* meaning 'bear', or even *arth-fawr* meaning 'great bear'. But, as with so many words in the Celto-Welsh, *arth* was derived from another source entirely. In this case the word came from the Latin name for Ursa Major, the constellation of the Great Bear, which was either called Arctus or Ursa. And we know that Monmouth was using 'bear' as a reference to the northern constellations and to Ursa Major, because he says of the dawn of a new day:

> But when the Bear began to turn her chariot, as it drew towards dawn, Uther called the earls and princes to meet with him in council. (History of Kings, 8:18.)

The Bear here is capitalised as a proper noun and so this Bear and chariot are clearly a reference to the constellation of Ursa Major, which turns in the northern skies and can be used to determine the time of the dawn. And the seven major stars of Ursa Major look like and are often referred to as a chariot or cart - King Arthur's cosmic cart. And Monmouth's cosmic chariot-bear is even said to be female, giving Ursa instead of Ursus in the Latin. But the constellation of the Great Bear was also the Arctos Maxima in the Latin, which was derived from the Greek *arktos* αρκτος meaning 'bear'; and it is from the Greco-Latin Arctos that we derive Arctic, referring to the north, because the Great Bear was the northern constellation.

However, if we are drifting away from a Celto-Welsh origin for Arthur's name, then we must also question its origins. Did it really spring from Celto-Welsh traditions, or was it from the quills of an eastern chronicler or scribe? As we have already seen, Gildas and Bede never mention an Arthur and the first reference we get is a half-hearted mention of a 'Duke of War' called Arthur in Nennius' *History of the Britons*. And not only is there is no further mention of an Arthur until we get to the 12th century, but the sons of the Celto-Welsh nobles were not being called Arthur either.

One would have thought that the great Celto-British hero called King Arthur would have inspired many a parent to call their son by this name, just as the names royal names Harry, Henry and William have produced many a subsequent son of that name. But what we actually find is that Adomnan mentions a Prince Arturiur in his 7th century *Life of St Columba* (ref 1:8), while an Arthur Petr is mentioned as a 7th century prince of Dyfed in Wales. And yet these sparse references are hardly what we might expect if King Arthur had really been a famous 5th or 6th century Celto-British hero. And so if there was a real Arthurian-style prince in this early era, we might surmise that he was more commonly known by another name.

In fact, there were no notable Celtic aristocrats called Arthur for more than 600 years, until we arrive in the 12th century. And even then the majority of these newly minted 'Arthurs' came from Normandy, Brittany and even Italy, rather than Wales.[2] But if Arthur's name (or new name) had been derived from the tales recounted by returning Templar Crusaders in Normandy, the evolving theory suggests that 'Arthur' should not be a Latin or Greek name, but instead derived from an Aramaic original. And surprisingly, the Latin Arctus and Greek *Arktos* were most probably derived from the Aramaic *uwsh* עוש or *uwth* עות, which are the roots for the Torah's name for Ursa Major.

These two variants utilise either a 'sh' or a 'th' consonant. And yet we see exactly the same consonant shift between the Latin *ursus* meaning 'bear' and the Celtic *arth* meaning 'bear', and so it is likely that the true origin of this name is indeed Aramaic. A later chapter will discuss the references to Ursa Major within the Torah, and discover that the Jewish rabbis and scribes also knew and documented the precessional movement of the constellations with the passing millennia. So the name for Ursa Major in the various languages we have looked at are as follows. The Aramaic versions shown here include the 'u' ו to 'r' ר transliteration error, that crops up quite often in these texts:

name	diction	meaning
עוש	Uwsh	Ursa Major
עות	Uwth	Ursa Major
ערש	Arsh	Ursa Major
ערת	Arth	Ursa Major
Welsh	arth	bear
Latin	ursa	bear
Greek	arktos	bear
Latin	arctos	bear
Latin	arctos	north
Greek	Arktouron	Ursa Major
Latin	Arcturum	Ursa Major

The reasoning for the change in pronunciation between Uwsh (Arsh) and Uwth (Arth) is not mentioned, but both derivations are given in the Aramaic Lexicon. The original of the two appears to be Uwth meaning 'bent' or 'crooked' and so Ursa Major was the crooked constellation, which is a reasonable description of the outline of these stars. The Latin *arcus* also refers to things that are 'bent' and became the English 'arc' or 'arch'. Incidentally, the Greek Septuagint Bible translation for Ursa Major is *Arktouron* Αρκτουρον, while the Latin Vulgate Bible gives Arcturum. We shall come across these verses in Chapter IX.

The result of this long introduction, is that the Celto-British name for King Arthur is not very Celto-British at all. The Celtic bards have borrowed this name from the Romans, who occupied Britain and influenced the Celto-British culture and language for nearly 400 years; while in their turn the Romans have borrowed it from the Greeks and the Jews. Or perhaps the Celtic scribes had a copy of an Aramaic Tanakh (the Old Testament), and were translating and copying directly from the Aramaic.

The reason why this royal Arthurian bear-king was named after a constellation, rather than a fierce animal from the forest, has already been explained in *Mary Magdalene, Princess of Orange*. The original tenets and symbolism of Fourth Sect Nazarene Judaism revolved around the precessional zodiac, rather than big game hunting. And the central character in the middle of a zodiac can either be the Sun, in the guise of Helios, Ra, Aton or Malakbel; or it can be the Pole Star and the constellations of the northern skies. And the greatest of the constellations in the northern heavens is Ursa Major, the Great Bear. And so the central character or king on a zodiac can

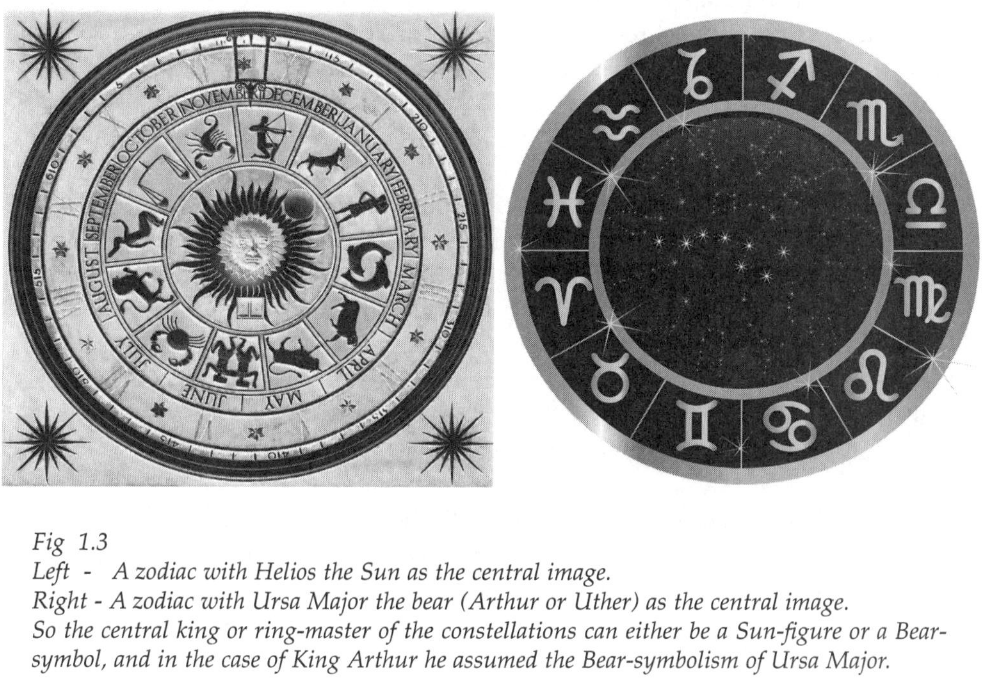

Fig 1.3
Left - A zodiac with Helios the Sun as the central image.
Right - A zodiac with Ursa Major the bear (Arthur or Uther) as the central image.
So the central king or ring-master of the constellations can either be a Sun-figure or a Bear-symbol, and in the case of King Arthur he assumed the Bear-symbolism of Ursa Major.

be represented either as an image of the Sun-god or it can be symbolic of the Great Bear - the image of King Arthur, the bear-king of the northern heavens.

And if Arthur was originally an Aramaic name, then the emerging theory says that it will not be found in the early Arthurian manuscripts of Gildas and Bede. And that is exactly what we find, for there is no mention of Arthur in these early chronicles. And there is no mention of a Pendragon either, and for the very same reason as we shall see in a later chapter.

Ring Master

However, the constellation of Ursa Major was not the only king or arbiter of the cosmos in these ancient astrological creeds, and perhaps the most important monarch in the heavens above was actually the constellation of Orion. It was Orion who was often portrayed as the ring-master of the heavens, who ensured that the precession of the zodiac ran smoothly through the constellations, as will be explained in later chapters. And Orion was often portrayed as Hercules, because he held the shield of the Nemean Lion in his left hand and a great club in his right. Thus Helios (the Sun) and Arthur (Ursa Major) were the primary referees or ring-masters of the heavens above, but they could sometimes be confused with or replaced by Orion, in the image of Hercules.

It was because of this alternate cosmic symbolism that Nennius, in his *History of the Britons,* recounts that Arthur was a *Dux Bellorum* or Duke of War who was involved in twelve great battles, including the famous battle of Badon. But these were not real battles at all. Instead, Nennius is claiming that the Britons were being led into battle against the Saxons by the semi-divine hero, Hercules. But being a Christian, Nennius could hardly invoke the assistance of Hercules directly and so he has called him Arthur instead - the alternate arbiter or ring-master of the heavens. So this account by Nennius is not historical at all, and nor does it refer to a historical prince, king or knight of Britain. This story is actually a Celtic version of the Twelve Labours of Hercules, a legendary Greek story that is again closely related to the precession of the zodiac through the twelve monthly constellations. Guy Halsall's highly critical and partisan account of Arthurian history, said of King Arthur's battle-list in *History of the Britons*:

> One other point must be stressed. With the exception of Caledonian Forest, which ought to be north of Hadrian's Wall, and Linnuis, which might be Lindsey in Lincolnshire, the locations of all of these battles are unknown and unknowable. This is of supreme importance if reading these modern pseud-histories (about King Arthur), so I'll say it again: the locations of all of these

> battles are unknown and unknowable. (Worlds of Arthur, p66) (Author's brackets.)

Halsall does not investigate Arthurian history so much as pour scorn upon it from an academic bed-pan, located high up in an impregnable academic tower. And this from an author who wrote a complete critique of Arthurian history without mentioning the *Vulgate Cycle* once. To put this into its proper perspective, it is a bit like writing a critique of Christian history without ever mentioning the gospels. Which is one reason why the erudite scholars of the 19th and early 20th century are much to be preferred than their vapid and vacuous modern counterparts. When James Bruce comes across an uninspiring manuscript he merely observes:

> It will be observed that this manuscript, whose main merit is its brevity, consists of two parts... (Evolution of Arthurian Romance II:218.)

What more needs to be said? In great contrast, while Halsall was busy applying derision with a trowel, he failed to notice the obvious connections between a warrior called Arthur (Ursa Major, the Great Bear) and his twelve battles in Britain, and a remarkably similar warrior called Hercules-Orion who also had twelve Labours or battles.

Since the Twelve Labours of Hercules are most probably related to the precession of the twelve constellations of the zodiac, it is likely that each of these twelve Arthurian battles will be similarly related to a particular sign of the zodiac. And this is why Halsall could not satisfactorily equate any of these battle-names to locations in the British Isles, because they are not place names at all they are constellations. However, since Nennius was probably utilizing the astrological signs and names that were in use in 9th century Wales, solving that particular cosmic conundrum would represent a whole new book in itself.

This close connection between Arthur and Hercules would also explain Arthur's peculiar conception story. Starting with Geoffrey of Monmouth's *History of Kings*, we have a semi-mythological story of this conception which was subsequently copied into most of the later Arthurian manuscripts. In this story, King Uther is enamoured with Igerne, the wife of Gorlois the Duke of Cornwall, and desires to sleep with her. So Uther asks Merlin to give him the exact likeness of Gorlois, Igerne's husband, so he can sneak in to Tintagel castle and sleep with her while Gorlois was away fighting a battle.

This devious scheme goes according to plan, and it is from this illicit union that King Arthur was born. But then Monmouth realises that Arthur cannot be king if he is a common bastard, and so a cover-story is further arranged to say that Gorlois was killed in this battle on the very evening of Arthur's conception, and so Igerne was a widow (just) when this union took place. But Arthur was still half a bastard because his parents were not married, so it is not clear how this amendment helps justify Arthur's claim to the throne. And so some of the later manuscripts have Merlin covering up this deceitful episode by arranging for the infant Arthur to be fostered by Ector or Hector, which is why Arthur is only later identified as being the true king through being able to pull the sword Excalibur from a stone.

So why do we have this convoluted and deeply unsatisfactory story for the birth of the future King Arthur? Surely it would be much better to have the exemplary Arthur as the son of two famous and devoted royal parents, rather than as a by-product of lust, disloyalty, adultery and abandonment? The answer to this perennial problem is that Arthur can often be equated with Hercules, as we have already seen, and so this entire dismal story is actually an account of the conception of Hercules.

In Greek mythology a beautiful maiden called Alcmene catches the eye of Zeus, who always had an eye out for a pretty earthly maiden. So Zeus devises a plan to impregnate Alcmene, as he had done many times before. Zeus had already turned himself into a swan to seduce the beautiful Leda of Sparta, and from this mythological union Helen of Sparta was born. And similar tricks were devised so that Zeus could seduce Europa and Danae. But with Alcmene, Zeus decides that the best strategy is to assume the likeness of Amphytrion, her husband, and to trick her into sleeping with him while her husband is away in a battle or war. And the result of this deceitful union was the demigod Hercules, who also became a ring-master of the constellations just as King Arthur did. But because of the wrath of Hera, the wife of Zeus, the infant Hercules ends up being fostered by Athena, and then (unknowingly) by his own parents. So the similarities between these two conceptions are:

A king who wants to sleep with a beautiful woman.
Her husband is away at war.
The king takes on the likeness of her husband.
From this union a strong champion is born.
The infant is taken away to be fostered.
He is recognised as being semi-divine through feats of strength.
He goes on to perform twelve labours or battles.
He becomes the ring-master of the zodiac.

Quite plainly, Monmouth is dressing King Arthur up as being the new Hercules. And this would comprehensively explain the deeply unsatisfactory nature of Arthur's conception and childhood, and also explain the twelve battles that he fought. So there is no point whatsoever looking for the site of the Battle of Badon in southwestern England. If it is going to be found at all, we need to raise our perspective towards the heavens above and seek the Battle of Badon there. And this link between Arthur and Hercules was not simply arranged because Monmouth wanted Arthur to be a strong hero, but also because the name 'Arthur' is intimately linked to the great ring-master of the heavens above. We have already seen how the name 'Arthur' is linked to Ursa Major, but the other great arbiter of the heavens was Orion-Hercules. So later chapters will go on to explain the many connections between Ursa Major and Orion-Hercules, and the cosmic characteristics of this astrological dimension to King Arthur.

However, perhaps it should be stressed here that this mythological and astrological dimension to King Arthur does not mean that he did not exist as a real character in the historical record, just that he was styled on occasions as being the great arbiter and ring-master of the heavens. In a very similar fashion Gilgamesh may well have been a real king of Sumer, but he was also portrayed in the image of Orion killing the Bull of Heaven or Taurus. Alexander the Great was a real king, but he was often portrayed wearing the two ram's horns of the Great Month of Aries. And Jesus was also a real historical character, as was proven in *Jesus, King of Edessa*, but he was likewise portrayed as a fisherman to represent the constellation and Great Month of Pisces. And there are many other similar examples besides these. No monarch from antiquity was truly great, until he had been linked to the appropriate constellation in the heavens above.

Mortal king

The second prediction we can make from this assumption, about a Near Eastern Crusader-Templar source for these later Arthurian manuscripts, is that the early Welsh and British histories of King Arthur are likely to contain very little detail. If the primary source manuscripts for Arthurian history came from Crusaders returning from the Near East in general, and from Count Baldwin's liberation of Christian Edessa in particular, then it is highly unlikely that previous chroniclers would have known anything about a wise and wealthy king called Arthur. There may have been the odd reference to a heroic warrior assuming the guise of Orion-Hercules, but this is not the classical King Arthur by any stretch of the imagination. Again this is what Arthurian history provides us with - a complete dearth of information about a wealthy and influential king called Arthur, until a few Templar Crusaders began to return from Syria.

And since the great flowering of Arthurian history not only started in the early 12th century, but also primarily sprang from Norman France, perhaps we can again implicate Count Baldwin in all of this. Baldwin not only became the Count of Edessa and the King of Jerusalem in the early 12th century, he was also the Count of Boulogne in northern France. And so if Baldwin had sent some of his knights or courtiers back home from Syria, they would have ended up in Norman France in the early 12th century - the very location and era in which the majority of classical Arthurian history flourished.

But if this is so, then we might also surmise that the characters that these later manuscripts were describing would have had less to do with local events in Britain, and a much greater affinity with events on a European scale. Why would an influential Christian city in eastern Syria have housed historical accounts taken from 5th century Britain? And even if it did, why would Count Baldwin have been interested in them? The answer, of course, is that the real King Arthur was of much greater international stature than he is portrayed within traditional Arthurian history, which is why his fame and story spread all over Gaul, Germany, Italy, Spain, Portugal, Greece, Scandinavia and Holland. Surprising as it may seem, Arthurian stories were devised and produced in all of these diverse regions, which demonstrates the pan-European appeal of Arthurian history.

And so the primary task of this book will be to identify the influential character that lies behind this enduring historical legend, and explain what this great corpus of material meant to its composers and their wealthy patrons. These were very expensive hand-written texts, with the *Vulgate Cycle* alone representing nine volumes and about 3,500 pages, even in the compact modern typed format. That is an enormous amount of time, effort and hard cash to spend, if these Arthurian stories were merely romantic legends for the entertainment of maids and matrons. And so from the very outset we can confidently predict, from the era, location and great expense of these manuscripts, that there was something reasonably important that prompted their composition and production.

One last result of these assumptions about a Near Eastern manuscript source, is that we can safely assume that the *Welsh Annals* cannot have been composed in their current form prior to the 12th century. The *Annals* contain a reference to the death of Arthur and Medraus, who must therefore be Mordred, the son of King Arthur who died during a battle with his father. And yet it will be conclusively demonstrated in a later chapter that 'Mordred' is a very obscure Aramaic royal title that originated in Babylonia. It is highly unlikely that the name Mordred - or rather the correct usage of this ancient Sumerian name - would have been known about until Templar Crusaders began to return to Normandy in the early 12th century. And so the *Welsh Annals* cannot date from the 10th century, as is commonly claimed. And when we look at the reasoning for this modern 10th century attribution, we find that the extant copies of this manuscript actually date from the 12th century, but the entries in this chronicle end in the mid 10th century. And so it has been assumed that this is a late 10th century document when that may not be the case at all.

The result of this short introduction, that covers the first six or seven hundred years of Arthurian literature, is that these early manuscripts conform very closely with what we might expect if the first classical accounts of Arthurian history had been brought back from the Near East by the knights and courtiers of Count Baldwin of Boulogne. And later chapters will not only confirm this budding supposition, but build upon it. Especially when we reach the many turgid and soporific accounts that comprise the *Vulgate Cycle*, whose material is demonstrably Near Eastern in nature. More surprisingly, perhaps, these later accounts will also demonstrate a close affinity with the 1st century, rather than the 5th or 6th centuries, with a heavy concentration on the lives of Joseph of Arimathaea and Emperor Vespasian. And so the result of these readjustments to our perceptions, will be that much of Arthurian history will be transposed both geographically and chronologically.

But this relocation will not be without merit or evidence, because in these new lands and new eras the hazy historical apparition that presently represents Arthurian history will at last come into sharp focus. There ***was*** a real King Arthur in the historical record, and he did have a court of twelve knights seated around a Round Table, but his true identity may come as a bit of a surprise to many people.

II

Monmouth & Oxford

History of the Kings of Britain - Geoffrey of Monmouth
Chronicle of the Kings - Walter of Oxford (Tysilio)

Monmouth

The first classical history of King Arthur, as we know the story today, was narrated by both Walter of Oxford and Geoffrey of Monmouth in the early 12th century. But it was Monmouth who popularised the story, with his rather more poetic Latin version called *Historia Regum Britanniae* or the *History of the Kings of Britain.* Monmouth was a minor cleric from Monmouth in south Wales who became the bishop of St Asaph in North Wales, and his patron in this enterprise is said to have been Robert Duke of Gloucester. Interestingly, Professor James Bruce indicates that Geoffrey Monmouth was probably the son of an officer at the Norman garrison at Monmouth, and was therefore most probably of Breto-Norman extract rather than Welsh descent.

The manuscript in the form we know it today comes from about 1135, which is nearly a full century before the many accounts of the *Vulgate Cycle* that will dominate the second half of this book. And it is worth noting that this early 12th century date is still a generation or more after the First Crusade in 1096. It will be the contention in this and later chapters that much of the new information that embellished the meagre history of King Arthur that we have seen thus far, came from Crusaders returning from the Near East.

Monmouth's *History of Kings* sets out to record the history of Britain from its very foundations in the early 1st millennium BC through to the 10th century AD, and it makes King Arthur one of the central characters in the story. So this new improved and reconstituted (king) Arthur is not a heroic army commander of little consequence occupying two lines of text, as he was in the pre-crusading accounts of these events, he is now one of the cornerstones of the entire story. At the end of *History of Kings* Monmouth says that the original source manuscript for his chronicle came from Brittany, as we saw in the previous chapter, and at the very beginning of his account he again credits Walter of Oxford for obtaining it:

> While I was thinking on such matters (the kings of Britain), Walter Archdeacon of Oxford, a man learned ... in the histories of foreign lands, offered me a certain most ancient book in the British (Breton) language that did set forth the doings of all of them in due succession ... I have been at pains to translate this volume into the Latin tongue. (History of Kings, 1:1) (Author's brackets.)

By 'British language' Monmouth means Celto-Breton, the language of Armorica or Brittany, the region where this manuscript originated. So large sections of *History of Kings* were derived from an unknown ancient manuscript, written by an unknown author possibly from Brittany in northern France, that had been brought to Britain by Walter of Oxford. But Oxford's most notable expertise was said to be 'the histories of foreign lands', not the history of Britain.

Monmouth has translated and obviously considerably reworked this story into its current Latin format, because it is quite different to Oxford's more prosaic version of the same story. And while this claim to an unknown source manuscript is often presumed to be a literary device to confer age and authenticity onto a work, the majority of Arthurian manuscripts did indeed come from Normandy and Brittany, and perhaps originally from far beyond those shores. Besides, how else can an author write a historical chronicle, without copying from older sources? Any chronicler who is not using older sources for his work has to be writing fiction, not history. In addition, Malmesbury, Huntingdon and Newburgh knew nothing about this new Breton history, which again suggests a relatively unknown source document, and so perhaps we should take Monmouth at his word here.

As might be expected, modern literary criticism is not so sure about this claim to a mysterious source manuscript from Brittany, and suggests instead that Monmouth assembled the story himself from a variety of sources including Gildas, Bede and Nennius. And they should have added Saul-Josephus' *Jewish War* and the French chanson *Gormond and Isembart* to this list, as we shall see later. But just because the original source manuscript has not been identified, does not mean that it did not exist. Monmouth was probably of Breton descent himself, so the delivery of a manuscript from his ancestral homeland is not unreasonable. Besides, there were many poets and scribes who reused and reworked Monmouth's manuscript in later years, like Robert

Wace's *Roman de Brut* and Walter Kayo's *History of Merlin*, and so it is entirely possible that Monmouth used a source manuscript in a similar fashion, just as he claims.

Oxford - Tysilio

The second of these two very similar manuscripts is the *Brut y Bryttanait* or *Chronicle of the Kings*, which is sometimes known as *Brut Tysilio* but will be called here the *Brut Oxford*. The translation used in this book is the *Jesus College MS LXI*, which is a 15th century copy of a 12th century original, and written in Medieval Welsh. Modern scholarship suggests that *Brut Oxford* is a prosaic copy of Monmouth's *History of Kings*, but Flinders Petrie, the famous Egyptologist and historian, claimed that *Brut Oxford* was the original text. The third option is that both versions sprang from a common source from Brittany, just as Monmouth says, and so the production of *Brut Oxford* and *History of Kings* would have been virtually coincident. The colophon at end of the *MS LXI* manuscript supports this suggestion when it says:

> I, Walter of Oxford translated this book from Welsh (Breton) into Latin and in my old age I have translated it again from Latin into Welsh. [1] (Author's brackets.)

This Walter of Oxford is the very same Walter who gave the secret Breton manuscript to Geoffrey of Monmouth, which eventually became his Latin *History of Kings*. And Walter has translated the same source manuscript into Latin and eventually into Welsh, to become the *Brut Oxford*, which is why *MS LXI* is written in Welsh rather than Latin or Breton. It is because of these confident accreditations of the original manuscript to Walter of Oxford, from two different sources, that *Chronicle of the Kings* is here called *Brut Oxford* rather than *Brut Tysilio*. But perhaps the most important result of this close connection between Monmouth and Oxford, is that both of their manuscripts appear to be linked to an original source from Brittany. Thus the wellspring region and era for almost all of the later, more complex Arthurian histories, appears to have been 12th century northern France.

And the reason for Geoffrey of Monmouth becoming involved in this heretical literary enterprise is that he was a much better story-teller than Walter of Oxford, and composed a much more entertaining tale. It would appear that Oxford has merely translated and duplicated details from this ancient source manuscript, which has resulted in a very prosaic chronicle, whereas Monmouth crafted an entertaining story that captured the public's imagination and became substantially more popular.

Fiction or fact?

There are many elements of *History of Kings* and *Brut Oxford* that appear fantastical on the surface, and so modern scholarship derides the accounts in these manuscripts as being pure legend. And the venerable historians were no less critical. As a reminder, the 12th century historian and chronicler William of Newburgh said of Monmouth's work that:

> Whatever Geoffrey has written ... is a fiction, invented either by himself or by others, and promulgated either through an unchecked propensity to falsehood, or a desire to please the Britons. (History of English Affairs, Newburgh, Preface.)

As we shall see shortly, it is very easy to regard Monmouth's history as being pure mythology because much of it does not make historical sense - unless you know what he is talking about. And so a classical historian's view of Monmouth would be similar to a cleric's view of the Book of Revelations - a blinkered Christian cleric who did not understand that 'Babylon, the Mother of Harlots' was actually a covert reference to Rome and the Roman Empire. How can anyone understand a historical account, if they do not know who the characters and locations in that history really are? So let us not throw the baby out with the bathwater here, for if we look at the Oxford-Monmouth manuscripts in a more objective fashion we may well find a whole host of historical detail.

This chapter also includes some elements from *Roman de Brut*, which is a reworking of Monmouth's story by Robert Wace, a Norman poet from Jersey in the Channel Islands. This manuscript was written in Norman French in about 1156, some twenty years after *History of Kings*, but it is rather disappointing. Wace clearly did not understand the underlying message in the Oxford-Monmouth chronicle, and so his sloppy treatment of the text detracts rather than adds to the story. For instance, the names of characters are forgotten or changed, with the revisions making no sense whatsoever. Clearly Wace thought that this was a story about valiant knights in shining armour in Britain and France, when it was nothing of the kind as we shall see shortly. The only interesting addition that Wace made to the plot is the first mention of the Arthurian Round Table, and no doubt he purloined that from a source manuscript that would eventually become a foundation for the *Vulgate Cycle*.

Scotichronicon

Both Oxford and Monmouth start their history with a familiar but improbable-sounding story about refugees from the Trojan wars founding Rome, a story that has its roots in Virgil's *Aeneid* and Nennius' *History of the Britons*. If it ever happened this event would have to be dated to the 12th century BC, although modern 'scholarship' tends to place the Trojan war some 60 years earlier than Victorian academics. The quotes that follow are mainly taken from *History of Kings*, but the equivalent quotes in *Brut Oxford* are virtually identical.

Monmouth's version of this story says that Prince Silvius of Rome was the grandson of Aeneas, the hero of Virgil's *Aeneid*, a story which recounts the founding of Rome. In Virgil's tale Aeneas is a Trojan exile who sails initially to Carthage and marries Queen Dido Ellissa of Carthage, before moving to Italy where his descendents would founded the city of Rome. In the Arthurian version Silvius secretly weds a niece of the king of Lavinia in Italy, and they have a child called Prince Brutus. Many years later Brutus accidentally kills his father while out hunting, and is exiled to Greece. In Greece, Brutus becomes the leader of the Trojan slaves, who are still labouring for the Greeks after all this time, and starts a slave revolt. Brutus demands of Pandrasus, the king of the Greeks, that the Trojans are given their freedom. Pandrasus refuses and a war ensues in which Brutus and the Trojan slaves

Fig 2.1
Aeneas fleeing from Troy, by Frederico Barocci. But in 'History of Kings' there was a second flight from Greece or Troy, following the Brutus-Trojan slave revolt against the Greeks.

are victorious. However, despite this victory one of the Trojan leaders, Mempricius, councils caution and says:

> For so long as they remember the slaying of their kinsfolk they will always hold you in eternal hatred ... My option is that we ask (Pandrasus) for his eldest daughter, who they call Ignoge, as a wife for our Duke (Brutus), and along with her gold and silver, ships and corn ... and then we will go on our way. (History Kings 1:10.)

This they do, and they set sail with 324 ships laden with provisions and sail towards the sunset. The scene is poetically described, with Princess Ignoge swooning and weeping in the arms of Prince Brutus at the thought of leaving her homeland and family, and the perils that lay ahead as they head out into the open sea. A familiar story? It should be to anyone who has read Ralph's *Egyptian Testament Series* of books. This is, of course, the story of *Scotichronicon*, the chronicle of the Scots. John of Fordun and Walter Bower, the primary authors of this very similar chronicle, say of the exile of their princely heroes:

> So Gaythelos gathered together all his followers and left Egypt with his wife Scota. Because he was afraid to return to the regions from which he had come (Greece), because of old feuds, he directed his course westwards. (Scotichronicon bk1 c12.)

Yes, in almost exactly the same era and the same region, we have another pair of royal lovebirds who have been exiled from Greece and or Egypt, and are likewise setting off across uncharted waters to find a new homeland in the west. And so *Scotichronicon* is very much the same story, not only of *History of Kings* but also of Virgil's *Aeneid*. *Scotichronicon* and *History of Kings* merely take the story one stage further than the *Aeneid*, by narrating what happened to some of these exiles after they arrived in the western Mediterranean. And so these many similar stories may all be based upon one historical event - the exile of a famous king and queen from Egypt and or Greece. And this duplication of the story may not be a simple case of some authors copying and embellishing a fictional story, for it is entirely possible that some of the descendents of these refugees did end up in Italy and Spain and thence Britain and Ireland.

In *Scotichronicon* Fordun and Bower say that Prince Gaythelos went from Greece to Egypt before being exiled from Egypt with his princess wife. The Egyptian historian Manetho places a slightly different spin on this story by saying that Gaythelos (Dannus) was an Egyptian prince who went to Greece, and then came back to Egypt before being exiled. But the basic story in *Scotichronicon* and *History of Kings* remains the same. We have a prince of Greco-Egyptian extract who is firstly exiled to Greece (from either Rome or Egypt); who ends up marrying a local princess (in Greece or Egypt); and becoming the local king (of Greece or Egypt); before being forcibly exiled and sailing for the western Mediterranean and thence to Greater Britain. And we shall see many more such similarities as this analysis proceeds.

In Monmouth's account, King Brutus and Queen Ignoge and their small flotilla of ships first make landfall in on a small island, where an oracle of Diana tells them to seek an island in the ocean as their refuge (ie: Ireland or Britain). They next go ashore in North Africa to reprovision, much as Aeneas did in Carthage:

> From thence they arrived in Mauritania, where a lack of food and water compelled them to disembark ... when they had revictualed their ships they made for the Pillars of Hercules. (History of Kings 1:12)

It is at this point that *Brut Oxford* adds a little aside, which indicates that Walter of Oxford's original Breton manuscript contained a few interesting details that Monmouth failed to understand and use. Oxford adds at this point that these exiles have to sail around the Rock of Gibraltar, but:

> They came to the Altars of the Philistines and there they fell into great danger doing battle with cruel pirates ... And from there they arrived at the Caves of the Mighty Hercules, where they were surrounded by sea monsters who nearly sank their ships. (Oxford p6)

As the modern translator of *Brut Oxford* says, this is supposed to be the Pillars of Hercules, just as Monmouth describes them, rather than the Caves of Hercules. And so the translator suggests that Oxford has mistaken a *colofn* 'pillar' for an *ogof* 'cave'. Or has he? Interestingly, the *Vulgate Cycle* includes a long description about the pirate caves on the Rock of Gibraltar, and so it is quite possible that Oxford was alluding to those pirate caves. But since the *Vulgate Cycle's* description is very obscure and cryptic, and is recalling a Roman history and religion from the 1st century BC, this would mean that Oxford understood this history quite well - and rather better than Monmouth appears to have done.

These refugees eventually escape the pirates and sail through the Pillars of Hercules and onto the Loire Valley in Aquitaine, in western France. (In antiquity Aquitaine was a larger region than it is today, encompassing much of western France.)

> They then came to Aquitaine, and entering the mouth of the Loire, cast anchor

> there ... and explored the lie of the land. Geoffrey Pictus, the king of the country ... sent envoys to enquire if they demanded peace or war.
>
> Brutus, along with the whole flower of his army, marched forth to meet the enemy ... The Trojans win the day, and drive King Geoffarius in flight before them.
>
> Brutus then lead his army inland with the intention of sacking the whole country and loading his ships with countless treasure. (History of Kings 1:12)

In a very similar refrain *Scotichronicon* says that King Gaythelos and Queen Scota also landed in North Africa to reprovision. They then set sail to the Pillars of Hercules but turned instead to the east and landed on the river Ebro in Spain:

> In this way they wandered for a long time over unknown seas ... until forced at last by lack of food they landed safely on the shores of Spain beyond all their expectation.
>
> The local inhabitants rushed together on all sides ... to oppose them in armed warfare; soon a fiercely contested battle was joined and the inhabitants were defeated and turned to flight. Then, after he had won the victory, Gaythelos pursued the inhabitants and plundered a considerable part of their territory. He returned to the shore and pitched his tents on a small mound on higher ground. (Scotichronicon bk1 ch13 bk1 ch15.)

In both cases the refugees end up fighting pitched battles with the local tribes, which they win with ease (due to their superior weaponry, according to *Scotichronicon*). The only real difference thus far, is that Scota and Gaythelos landed on the Ebro River in Spain, before moving onwards to Ireland; while Brutus and Ignoge first go to the Loire and then to Britain. And the reason for moving on was that both France and Spain were inhabited, and the locals were intent on reclaiming their lands from these invaders from the east. And while the local tribes were always beaten back by these Egypto-Greco-Trojan exiles, through their superior armour and tactics, they were always losing men:

> Brutus was glad at heart to have achieved such a significant triumph, but was very grieved by anxiety on one account, for he saw that, whilst his own numbers were diminished daily, those of the Gauls were daily multiplied. (History of Kings 1:15)

And since Monmouth is simply retelling the same ancient story contained in *Scotichronicon*, it is not surprising that Gaythelos and Scota should encounter exactly the same problem:

> Gaythelos suffered many kinds of calamity in that place ... Although he had been successful in inflicting heavy losses on the enemy on many occasions, he never gained a single victory without some loss to his tiny nation, which he saw would grow smaller as a result of the daily and unending decrease instead of increase in numbers. (Scotichronicon bk1 ch16)

And so these exiles from Greece and Egypt are forced to move on northwards, towards Greater Britain. Brutus and Ignoge land in Totnes in southwest England, while the (descendents of) Scota and Gaythelos land along the Dingle peninsular in Ireland. And having settled the land and built some towns, Brutus needed a name for his new kingdom:

> Then at last, Brutus called the island Britain and his companions Britons, after his own name, for he was minded that his memory should be perpetuated from his name. Whence afterwards the country's speech, which was before called Trojan or crooked Greek, was called British. (History Kings 1:16)

And since this is the same story, Scota and Gaythelos did likewise:

> Since the Hibernians are descended from Gaythelos and Scota they are named Gaitheli (Gaels) and Scoti (Scots). Gaythelos, so they say, invented the Hibernian language which is also called Gaelic. (Scotichronicon bk1 ch20) (Author's brackets.)

So the Britons were named after King Brutus, while the Scottish and Gaelic people were named after Queen Scota and King Gaethelos. And the term 'Scottish' here refers to the Irish, as that is said to have been the original name of that island before many of these Scoto-Irish emigrated to Scotland. Thus the opening chapters in Geoffrey of Monmouth's *History of Kings* and Oxford's *Chronicle of Kings*, are a simple retelling of the accounts in the *Lebor Gabala* and *Scotichronicon*. And Walter Bower claims in Book II of *Scotichronicon*, that his version of the story is more correct than Monmouth's. The many similarities between these texts include:

a. A prince gets into a great deal of trouble with his family.
b. He is forced to go into exile in Greece or Egypt.
c. The renegade prince rises to become king of Greece or Egypt.
d. The prince was of the tribe of Danaoi (the Greeks) or the Dardanaoi (the Trojans).
e. The prince is forced into yet another exile.
f. This new exile is achieved via a large fleet of ships.
g. The exiles land in eastern Spain or western France.
h. The locals engage them in battle, but the exiled prince wins.
i. The prince is concerned that his forces always get smaller.

j. The prince decides to take his people to an uninhabited location.
k. The prince and his people journey to Ireland or England.
l. The prince names the new land and the new language after himself.

So the opening chapters in Monmouth's *History of the Kings* are simply a retelling of the Irish *Labor Gabala* and the Scottish *Scotichronicon,* with each of these traditions amending the story to make it fit into the history and culture of their particular region. But does this mean that this story is a complete fiction, a deliberately crafted fantasy to explain the unknowable and inexplicable past? Is it in any way likely that a Greco-Egyptian king came to Britain and founded the British nation, or is this merely a fantastic mythology?

At first reading this story does indeed appear to be pure fantasy, but readers of *Scota, Egyptian Queen of the Scots* will have already seen that there is a great deal of synergy between the Scottish version of this story, which is much more detailed than Monmouth's version, and real history. There are similar traditions and artifacts that lie all along the suggested route of this ancient exile from the eastern Mediterranean, including very similar boat tombs, truncated round towers, gold torques, gold shoulder-capes, Egyptian necklaces, red gloves, similar ship designs and names. All of these archaeological and literary equivalences reflect and support the itinerary of the Scota and Gaythelos exile, as given by the various versions of this story.

Plus we have the interesting coincidence that *Scotichronicon* focuses on the only era in Egyptian history when an exile of a Greco-Egyptian king and queen could well have taken place. It is highly unlikely that John Fordun and Walter Bower could have known about all these ancient events and coincidences, while sitting in their draughty monastery in Scotland. Especially since the true history of this particular Greco-Egyptian king and queen was not discovered (or rediscovered) until the 19th century. How would Fordun and Bower have known about the unstable and crumbling Amarna dynasty in Egypt, when it had been completely erased from Egyptian history in later generations? And yet of all the royal dynasties in Egyptian history, the Armarna dynasty is one of the very few that may well have been forced into exile.

Yet, Fordun and Bower were not the originators of this story, because it appears to have come from Ireland, and the 6th century *Lebor Gabala Erenn* or the *Book of Invasions*. The compilation of the *Lebor Gabala* as we know it today was achieved in the 12th century, but this text draws upon accounts by Eusebius, Orosius and St Augustine, which date from the 4th and 5th centuries, and also upon the great corpus of so-called pseudo British history that so influenced Welsh chroniclers like Nennius in the 9th century. So in the 6th century, when the native Britons had been pushed out of what became Angleland (England) by the Anglo-Saxons, there may have been scattered

Fig 2.2
The Tudons Naveta, near Ciutadella, Minorca. (top)
The Gallarus Ossuary near Dingle, Co Kerry, Ireland. (bottom)
These upturned boat designs are identical in almost all respects, including the measurements of the front elevation. The Scottish chronicles say that the descendants of Gaythelos and Scota travelled to Spain and Ireland, and so the mythology and the archaeology dovetail precisely.

British or Welsh texts that attempted to explore and explain the ancient heritage of these Celtic peoples. These were eventually gathered together into what became the Irish *Lebor Gabala,* the Scottish *Scotichronicon,* and the English *History of Kings* and *Brut Oxford.*

And the reason for this preoccupation with an exotic heritage is not difficult to discern. By the mid 6th century, the Celto-Britons had been pushed out of what became Angleland or England by the Angles and Saxons, and had retreated all the way back into Scotland, Wales, Cornwall and Armorica or Brittany. The Celto-Britons had become the Celto-Welsh and Celto-Bretons. In the circumstances, it is not so surprising that these conquered and exiled Britons would want to search for and champion their illustrious heritage. But does this mean that Oxford and Monmouth copied and redrafted a fabricated fantasy, to suit the needs of these exiled Celts?

The answer to this has already been given in *Scota, Egyptian Queen of the Scots.* There is too much inside information in *Scotichronicon* for this to have been a completely fictional story, and there are too many common artifacts that give credence to the claims that have been made. And so it is likely that an Egypto-Greek royal family did indeed travel to Ireland and Scotland in a very early era. And this evidence suggests that these royals were actually Pharaoh Aye and Queen Ankhesenamun, who reigned at the very end of the Amarna dynasty.

The initial exodus of this family and their many followers was made in about 1320 BC, but their sojourn in Spain or France may have lasted a few generations and so it is likely that the final exodus to Ireland was not made until a few centuries later. Oxford says that a date

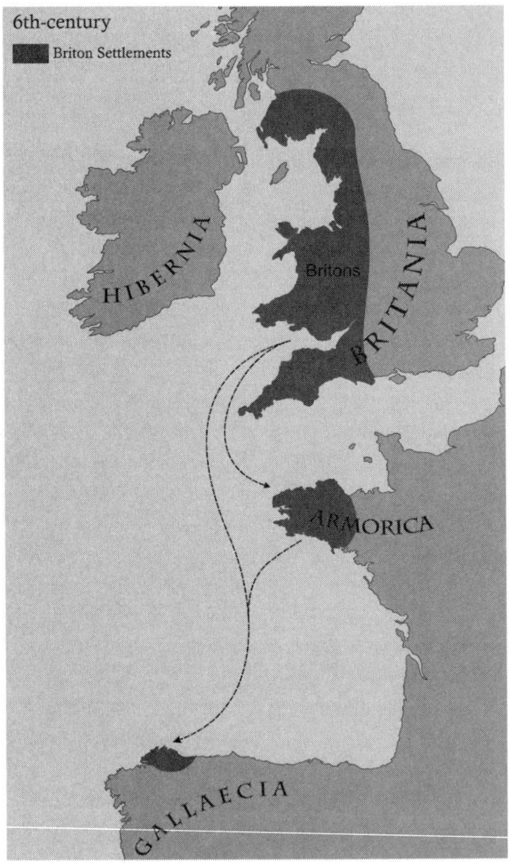

Fig 2.3
The exodus of the Celto-British people from old Britain (new Angleland) to the extremities of Wales, Cornwall, Brittany and even Gallaecia. (Image courtesy of Wiki.)

equating to about 130 years after their arrival in Britain coincides with the reign of King David in Jerusalem (Tanis). The reign of David would equate to about 990 BC and so the Oxford chronology would place the arrival of these Egyptian exiles in Britain in about 1120 BC. This date equates reasonably well with both the Egyptian exodus in about 1320 BC and the modern date for the Trojan War in about 1250 BC.

Roman Britain

Moving on by a millennium or more, Monmouth's sources certainly knew the full name of Caius Julius Caesar and his twice coming to invade Britain in the 50s BC, although he says the landings were two years apart rather than one. Monmouth then relates that due to internal divisions in Britain there was a third landing which is not mentioned by the Roman chroniclers, that landed at Richborough (Rutupi Portus) in Kent. This third invasion was made at the invitation of Androgeus, the duke of Trinovantum* (London), who wanted Roman assistance to gain the throne from King Casswallon. While Rome did not record this third invasion, for whatever reason, it is entirely possible that it did occur. The Oxford and Monmouth chronicles represent the British account of these events, and the British would have had different imperatives and a very different political spin to this story.

Monmouth then says that the Romans withdrew from Britain, on the understanding that the Britons continued to pay an annual tribute to Rome, and sent their sons to Rome as hostages. This was a standard Roman tactic for subduing unruly barbarian tribes at the extremities of the Empire. One can imagine these Britons, who had never seen architecture much beyond a timber-framed hut, arriving in Rome to see the great splendors of that vast, teeming city; where there were temples that looked as if they had been made by giants, and stone columns that could have supported the entire Earth. These British hostages must have whirled around and around wondering if they were perhaps in heaven, or in a city made by the Titans.

And then, far from being clapped in irons and thrown into a dark dungeon, these 'prisoners' were given a fine mansion, a bevy of busty servants and mistresses, and as many exotic luxuries as Rome could muster. And all the while there would be a tutor or diplomat whispering into the ear of this royal barbarian hostage: 'this can all be yours, if you join the Pax Romana'.

So Monmouth assures us that although Britain was nominally

* The name Trinovantum is said to have been derived from Troy.

independent after Julius Caesar sailed back to Gaul (for the third time), the nation was now officially a client state that traded with Rome, paid tribute to Rome, paid export and import duties to Rome, and was subservient to Rome in many respects. And presumably this client status was quietly maintained because of the covert threat that if Britain went against Roman demands there would be yet another invasion. Strabo concurs with Monmouth's claims when he says:

> Some of the chieftains (in Britain), after procuring the friendship of Caesar Augustus by sending embassies and by paying court to him, have ... managed to make the whole of the island virtually Roman property. Further, they submit so easily to heavy duties, both on the exports from there to Celtica and on the imports from Celtica, that there is no need of garrisoning the island. For ... the expense of the army would offset the tribute-money. (Strabo Geography 4:5)

We then pass on through the era of Jesus' crucifixion, which would be the early AD 30s under the classical chronology, and hear that King Guiderius of Britain had refused to pay Roman tributes (taxes), and so Emperor Claudius had invaded Britain once more. This would have been in AD 43. There are a few more detail differences here, with classical history saying that the Romans again landed in Richborough in Kent while Monmouth says that they landed in Porchester in Hampshire. But the classical account of these landings is uncertain and highly confused, with Cassius Dio saying that the Romans sailed from east to west, suggesting a landing closer to the Solent, much as Monmouth and Oxford claim. The case for a Roman landing further to the west was furthered recently by archaeologist John Manley in his book *AD 43, A Reassessment*, and it has become known as the 'Sussex Case'.

Monmouth's account is also a little confused, because he was primarily writing an entertaining story and was not so concerned about military detail. And so the most authoritative and believable account of these Roman invasions is to be found in *Brut Oxford*. This more prosaic version says that the first Roman landing was at Porchester near Portsmouth, where the Romans were besieged by King Guiderius. But a Roman who could speak Celtic slipped into the British ranks and killed Guiderius, and so his brother Arviragus became king to continue the battle. But the native Britons were chased to Winchester, where a peace accord was made, which included Arviragus marrying a daughter of Emperor Claudius.

It was only after King Arviragus again refused to pay tribute to Rome, that Legatus Vespasian was sent to Britain with reinforcements. According to Oxford it was Vespasian who landed at Richborough, but the opposition was so great that Vespasian took to his boats and went down the coast to Totnes near Exeter and made a second landing there. Vespasian then moved up towards London, where another peace treaty was made with Arvirargus. So perhaps the 'Sussex Case', the modern claim to a Roman landing further to the west, should be renamed as the 'Oxford Case'.

Remember that the Roman accounts of these invasions are not the gospel truth. Not only were the Roman historians not actually there, but these accounts were propaganda dispatches as much as they were records for history books. They detailed the marvelous and unbelievable exploits of the indomitable Roman army, with the numbers of enemy forces being doubled or quadrupled to enhance the invincibility and glory of Rome. Had Legatus Vespasian been fought to a standstill at Richborough by the rag-tag British army of Arvirargus, and forced to make an alternative landing down near Exeter, the Romans are not necessarily going to tell everyone about it. So this alternate account of the Roman invasions by Oxford bears all the hallmarks of being based upon the alternate accounts recorded by the British forces. As William Cooper, the translator of Oxford says:

Fig 2.4
The extensive Roman fortifications at Richborough, Kent, where the Romans first landed in AD 43. Were the Romans besieged by the British army here, and forced to send Vespasian down the coast to find another landing site?

> The following account gives the Roman invasion of 55 BC as it was seen through the eyes of the Britons.
>
> Julius Caesar does not name this fort (Odina). Flinders Petrie rightly suggests that this name reveals the genuine though garbled nature of British intelligence reports, for Caesar does state that he sent troops to Lisieux on his return to Gaul. (Oxford p 26, p28)

In other words, these British chronicles are not necessarily wrong simply because they happen to disagree with the Roman accounts of these campaigns - they are simply the opposite political view and an alternate record of these events.

Constantines I, II & III

We then come to Monmouth's genealogy of King Arthur, a subject that was touched upon in the previous chapter. The king of Britain at this time was King Coel of Colchester, the king from the children's nursery rhyme. Then King Constantius arrives in Britain and he is such a powerful monarch that King Coel seeks an alliance with him. This is 'king' is actually Emperor Constantius I, the father of Emperor Constantine the Great. Monmouth says that after the death of King Coel, Constantius took the throne of Britain and a British princess, Helena, as his queen. This is not entirely correct because Constantius became co-emperor of Rome alongside Emperor Maximian,* rather than the king of Britain, while his wife, Helena, is thought to have been from Anatolia. But it is true that Constantius was in Britain in AD 305, fighting the Picts, and so he would have been considered by the Britons as being their local king. This is not unlike the Armenian king-list that was explored in *Jesus, King of Edessa,* where the Armenians had a habit of claiming Parthian kings to be their own domestic Armenian monarchs.

According to Monmouth, Constantius eventually died and his son Constantine became the king of Britain. Again this is very nearly a true account, because Constantius died in Britain in AD 306, and so Constantine I (the Great) was crowned in York. The only minor difference in these details being that Constantine was being hailed as the new emperor of Rome, rather than the king of Britain. Nevertheless, it is not stretching factual history too far to say that Constantine I was now the king of Britain, because he was -

* The Roman Emperor Maximian, not the British Emperor Maximus who will be discussed later.

plus the king of Hiberia and Gaul. However, he was not the sole emperor of Rome at this time because Rome was divided, so perhaps the title 'King of Britain' is more accurate that it at first seems.

And then we enter the first of many chronological confusions. According to *History of Kings* Constantine had three sons, who are named as Constans, Aurelius Ambrosius and Uther Pendragon, with Uther being the father of King Arthur. But the latter two sons are not attested in the historical record, and may be later additions by Monmouth. There are numerous modern books that assume that this Constantine is Constantine the Great, but that is not exactly what Oxford and Monmouth say. The reason for historians confusing this Constantine with Constantine the Great, is because when King Arthur gives a speech about Britons invading Rome he says:

> Comrades ... forasmuch as my ancestors did of days gone by obtain possession of Rome. For Belinus did of old, with the assistance of his brother Brennius ... take the city ... Constantine also, the son of Helena, no less than Maximian (Magnus Maximus) ... did also obtain the throne of the Roman empire. (History of Kings 9:16.) (Authur's brackets.)

This Constantine is obviously Constantine I (the Great), the son of Queen Helena. And since this speech only mentions one Constantine, it is easy to confuse this account with the earlier chronology and assume that the

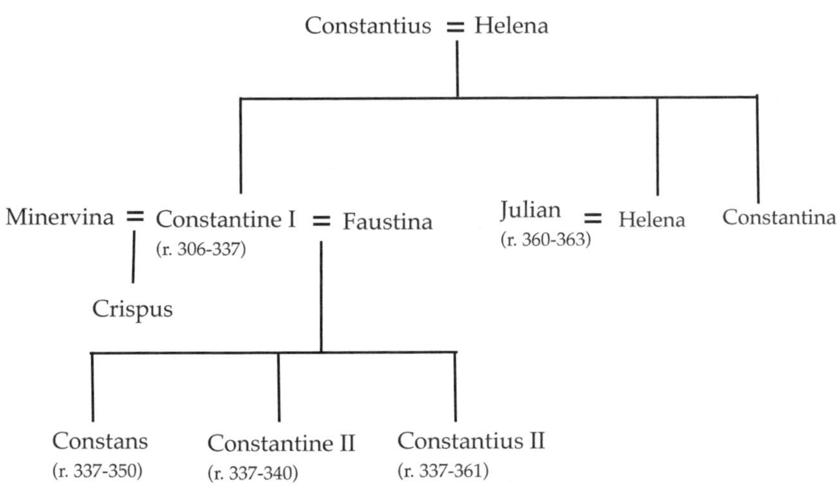

Fig 2.5 The historical genealogy of Emperor Constantine, as given in the Roman record.

Constantine with three famous sons was also Constantine the Great, when it is more likely to have been a reference to Constantine III. The probable reason for Monmouth confusing these two Constantines is that the mother of Constantine the Great was Queen Helena, who became St Helena in Christian tradition following her pious 4th century tour of Judaea searching for the surviving relics of King Jesus. Not surprisingly, the dutiful and avaricious clerics of Judaea managed to find everything that this 4th century Queen Helena (St Helena) wanted to discover, including enough wood from the true cross to build a trireme warship.

However, in a very similar fashion, the mother of King Izas-Jesus of Edessa was also called Queen Helena. This was not the 4th century Queen Helena, the mother of Constantine, but the very famous 1st century Queen Helena of Edessa-Adiabene, who is mentioned on so many occasions by Saul-Josephus and by the Armenian historians. This earlier Queen Helena made a similar trip to Judaea to see her son, King Izas-Jesus. And while she was in Judaea she: saved the nation from famine; furnished the Temple of Jerusalem; built the largest palace in Jerusalem; built the largest tomb in Jerusalem; and became the *de-facto* Queen of Judaea.

In which case, there is a great potential for confusion between Queen Helena and Queen Helena. So if an astute chronicler like Monmouth wanted to conceal a history about the family of the 1st century Queen Helena of Edessa, he could easily place it into the 4th century and say that this was actually a story about Queen Helena the mother of Constantine - honest. In fact, it was speculated in the previous books that St Helena, the mother of Constantine, never went to Judaea at all and this story was deliberately fabricated by the deceitful Church historian, Eusebius. The problem the Catholic Church faced, was the history of a very famous Jewish Queen Helena of Edessa who had become the *de facto* Queen of Judaea in the mid 1st century.

The main difficulty that this presented, was that the life and family of this earlier Queen Helena dovetailed far too closely with the gospel accounts for comfort. But this earlier Queen Helena was far too famous for the Church to simply delete her from history, so what could the ever-deceitful clerics do? The answer was the exact reverse of what Monmouth may have done here. They took the life and times of the 1st century Queen Helena, and said this was all done by the 4th century mother of Constantine the Great. In one simple but very effective stroke, the Catholic Church had deleted the 1st century Queen Helena of Edessa from history and created a great 4th century heroine for Catholic Christianity. In fact, this was not a simple stroke, it was a master-stroke.

However, Monmouth may well have cleverly turned this master-stroke around, and used it to his own advantage. And if so, this would demonstrate that Monmouth and his rich patrons were covert heretics who

List of Roman Emperors

Emperor	Reign	Relation	Notes
Constantius I	293-306		died Britain
Constantine I	306-337	son of Constanius	crowned Britain
Constantine II	337-340	son of Constantine	
Constantius II	337-361	son of Constantine	
Constans I	337-350	son of Constantine	
Valentinian I	364-375		
Valens	364-378	brother Valentinian	
Gratian	367-383	son Valentinian	killed by Maximus
Valentinian II	375-392	son Valentinian	
Magnus Maximus	383-388		British usurper
Theodosius	379-395	in-law Valentinian	
Honorius (W)	393-423	son Theodosius	letter 'no assistance'
Arcadius (E)	395-408	son Theodosius	petition for help sent to
Constantine III	407-411	a Breton?	British usurper
Constans II	408-411	son Constantine	British usurper
Constantius III	421-421	fought Constantine as army commander	
... many others ...			
Anthemius	467-472		killed by Ricimer
Olybrius	472-472		
Glycerius	473-474		
Julius Nepos	474-475		
Romulus	475-476		

--- End of Western Roman Empire ---

Fig 2.6
List of Roman emperors and their reignal dates.
This is not an exhaustive list, as it misses out many Eastern and duplicate co-regency emperors not pertinent to this research. The reignal dates can be confusing too, with many emperors having two or three different dates, depending on which part of the Empire they were ruling and in what capacity.

were discretely challenging the central tenets of the Catholic Church. We shall see much more evidence for this in a later chapter, but what Monmouth may have done here done, is to take the life of the 1st century Queen Helena of Edessa, and hang this true history onto the 4th century St Helena that the Catholic Church had manufactured. And the Catholic Church could hardly complain that someone was wrongly using Queen Helena (St Helena) in their manuscript, because they had created her in the first place.

The chronology

While this link to Constantine the Great and St Helena is interesting, and provides us with the first tentative links to 1st century Judaea, it is not exactly what Monmouth's complete chronology says. There are too many Constantines and Maximuses in this period of Roman history for absolute certainty, but it seems to be clear that the tortuous chronology that Monmouth provides jumps 60 or 70 years, without actually saying so. And that leap takes us from the era of Emperor Constantine I to the reign of Emperor Magnus Maximus, the British usurper emperor of the late 4th century. And so it is highly likely that the Constantine who was the grandfather of the British King Arthur was not Constantine I (the Great) but Constantine III, who was another British usurper emperor of Rome.

The list of events that follows is taken from both Oxford and Monmouth, which are more or less the same with a few minor variations; and from the details and chronology they relate it is quite certain that these authors have utilised Gildas and Bede as their guide in this section of their chronicles. However, there are sensible and seemingly accurate amendments and additions which give the impression that Oxford and Monmouth had additional manuscripts to work from. Each entry in this list is followed by a short explanation from the historical record, plus dates where applicable:

This list is primarily from Oxford.
The square brackets are Monmouth's alternate spellings and history.
References are Oxford's followed by Monmouth's.

- Konstans [Constantius] marries Elen the Fair [Helena] - daughter of King Koel [King Coel]. (p34, 5:6)
- This is Emperor Constantius (r. 293-306).

- Konstans [Constantius] has a son, Kystennin [Constantine]. Monmouth adds that Constantius died in York and gave the throne of Britain to Constantine. (p34, 5:6)
- This is Emperor Constantine the Great. (r. 306-337) He was said to be the 'King of Britain' because he was crowned in York and only controlled Britain, Gaul and Spain at that time.

- Constantine takes Rome from Maxen the Cruel [Maxentius the Tyrant]. (p34, 5:8)
- This is Emperor Constantine the Great defeating the usurper emperors

Maximian and his son Maxentius in either AD 306 or 310.

- Kradowc [Caradoc] and his son Mayric [Maurice] invite king Maxen [Maximian] of Rome, son of Ioelinus [Leoline], to Britain as king. (p34, 5:9)
- It turns out that this Maxen or Maximian of Rome is Emperor Magnus Maximus (r. 384-388). Even taking into account the long reign of Constantine I, this still represents a large chronological jump. It is later explained by Monmouth that there are four generations between the two sections of this story (between Conan and Aldroenus).

- Maxen [Maximian] makes war on [quarrels with] Emperors Grassian and Afalawnt [Gratian and Valentinian]. (Oxford says that Grassian-Gratian was killed at this time.) (p35, 5:9)
- These are Emperors Gratian and Valentinian from the AD 380s. This is confirmation that the Arthurian (king) Maximian must be Emperor Magnus Maximus (r. 384-388), who did have a battle with Gratian and Valentinian, and did kill Gratian. So the story has indeed jumped about 70 years, from the exploits of Constantine the Great just mentioned. Gratian was killed at Lyon in AD 383 but Valentinian II stopped the advance of Maximus, just as Oxford says.

- Maxen [Maximian] defeated Duke Inbalt of Armorica and gave Conan Mairiadawc [Conan Meriadoc] the lands of Armorica or Brittany. (p35, 5:12)
- Again this has to be Emperor Maximus, who was strongly linked with Armorica by Nennius. This must be the AD 380s.

- Oxford says Grassian [Gratian] is now emperor of Rome. (p36)
- This is Emperor Gratian again, so Oxford appears to have gone back in time. But see the later confusion with a Commander Gratian, who became the king of Britain.

- Monmouth says Maximian kills Emperor Gratian and makes Emperor Valentinian flee. (5:14)
- Emperor Maximus killed Emperor Gratian at Lyon in AD 383, but Valentinian II stopped his advance - so the story is correct. And there is less of a chronological error in Monmouth's version, because Gratian is killed at a later point in his version of the story.

- Maxen [Maximian] dies in Rome. (p36, 5:16)
- Emperor Magnus Maximus died in Aquileia in AD 388.

- Maxen [Maximian] had sent commander Grassian [Gratian] to Britain to deal with invasions. But upon the death of Maxen [Maximian], Grassian [Gratian] claimed the throne of Britain, but was killed shortly afterwards. (p36, 6:1)
- Before Constantine III came to the throne, Britain raised two very short-lived kings to the throne, and these were called Gratian and Marcus. So the Gratian mentioned here is the British usurper 'king' Gratian, who only reigned for about four months before he was killed in a local uprising. So this was sometime between AD 388 and 407 - say AD 392.

- There are many invasions of Britain by Scots and Picts, and so the Britons send for help from Rome. They received one legion under (Severus) and built a great stone [turf] wall. (p36, 6:1)
- Monmouth does not mention Severus. Oxford may have been thinking of Emperor Septimius Severus here, who did build a turf wall back in the 2nd century. This turf wall will be discussed later in Chapter IX. Note that there is only one request for assistance here, unlike the account by Nennius which says that there were two. This request for assistance must have been sometime between 388 when Maximus died, and 406 when Roman rule in Britain came to an end. Say AD 400.

- The Romans declare that they can no longer protect Britain, and they must organise their own defences. (p36, 6:2)
- This is an account of the letter from Emperor Honorius, which was delivered to all the major cities of Britain and declared exactly this - that Rome absolved itself from all responsibility for the province. (c. 404)

- The Britons again ask for help, this time from Emperor Gittiws-Agitius, thrice consul of Rome. (p36, 6:3)
- This must be Emperor Arcadius (r. 395 - 408). But all further assistance is refused, and Rome cedes control of Britain completely. Arcadius became consul for the third time in AD 406 and so we can quite precisely date this final plea for Roman assistance to 406.

- In desperation, Bishop Guithelinus is sent to get help from King Aldroen of Armorica or Brittany. Aldroen refuses the throne of Britain, but sends his brother Constantine to Britain with 2,000 men. Constantine is crowned at Silchester. (p37, 6:4)
- This Constantine is sometimes said to be Constantine the Great (r. 306-337). However, if this coronation occurred just after AD 406, as this chronology has clearly demonstrated, then this must be

Constantine III. (r. 407-411) According to Zosimus and Orosius, Britain raised four usurper Kings to the position of Western Emperor between AD 383 and 408, and these were Maximus, Gratian, Marcus and then Constantine III. And this is more or less what Oxford and Monmouth say, although Monmouth places the short reign of Gratian *before* the pleas for help, rather than after. In the historical record Constantine III is said to have been a low-ranking Roman soldier, and it is entirely possible that Prince Constantine, the brother of King Aldroen of Armorica, had been an officer in the slowly disintegrating Western Roman army. Constantine III quickly established himself as king (emperor) of Britain and Gaul, and eventually Spain too.

- Constantine has three sons: Konstant, Emrys, and Ythyr ben Dragown [Constans, Ambrosius, and Uther Pendragon]. (p37, 6:5)
- In the historical record Emperor Constantine III also had a son called Constans, who co-ruled alongside his father.

- When Constantine died, his son Konstant Mynarch [Constans the Monk] of St Amphibalus monastery in Winchester, was raised to the throne. (p37, 6:6)
- Emperor Constans co-ruled with his father from AD 409, and his father died in AD 411. Interestingly, both Zosimus and Orosius remark that Constans, the son of Constantine III, was a monk who became a Caesar. And this is exactly what Oxford and Monmouth say - Constans was a monk at St Amphibalus monastery who became the Emperor of Rome.

- When Constantine went on his campaign he entrusted the rule of Britain to Gwrtheyrn [Vortigern]. (p37, 6:7)
- When Emperor Constans went on his campaign, Zosimus says that he entrusted the rule of Britain to Justinian and his brother Nevigastes; while Orosius says he entrusted the realm to Verinianus and his twin brother. It would seem likely that Verinianus and Ne-Vigastes are alternate spellings for the Arthurian Vortigern.

Verinianus
Ne Vigastes
Vortigern(us)

In which case, we may have just found Vortigern in the historical record. This is the famous Arthurian Vortigern, the traitorous seneschal or governor of the king who usurped the throne from Constantine and had his son

Constans murdered. In the historical record Vigaste(nus)-Vortigern was one of two brothers who had been sent back to rule Britain while Emperor Constantine III was campaigning in southern Gaul, and just like Vortigern, these two brothers (Didymus and Vigastenus-Vortigern) were plotting to take the throne from Constantine:

> Thereupon two brothers named Didymus and Verinianus, who were young, noble, and wealthy, undertook not only to seize the power of the usurper (Constantine), but to protect themselves and their country for the lawful emperor against both the usurper and the barbarians. (Orosius 7:40) (Author's brackets.)

In the Arthurian version of this story it was not Constantine III who led the British army down through Gaul to conquer Rome, but his grandson, King Arthur, and we shall take a look at Arthur's similar exploits later in this chapter. But it is highly unlikely that a grandson of Constantine III could have mustered any army of any significance in this late era. Even before Constantine III's failed invasion, Britain had been cut off from the collapsing Western Roman Empire and was being invaded, raped, and pillaged; so by the mid 5th century Britain was in no position to protect itself, let alone muster another invasion army. In fact, Monmouth says that Britain had no indigenous weapons manufacturing way back in the 400s, let alone in the 450s, and had to be shown what to do by the rapidly retreating Romans. And those instructions were obviously not fully grasped and implemented, because the Britons again appealed for Roman assistance just a few years later.

In real history, the reign of Constantine III represented the last hope and the last gasp of a rapidly fading outpost on the fringes of the Empire, that felt highly aggrieved at being cut adrift from Roman trade and Roman protection. But as Constantine led his Brito-Gaulic-Roman army down through Gaul and into Spain, with the intent of securing rule over the entire Western Empire, there were many setbacks along the way. There were several battles against Roman troops who remained loyal to Emperor Honorius, and a wave of 'barbarian' (ie: Saxon) attacks on Britain which divided Constantine's forces. Finally, only three or so years later, Constantine and his son Constans were defeated by the forces of Honorius and executed. So why did this happen? Why did an impoverished and disintegrating Britain suddenly decide to march on Rome, just as the lights were going out all over the Western Roman Empire?

Roman assistance

The decline and fall of Roman Britain did not begin in the 400s, it actually began two decades before this with the revolt against Rome by (emperor) Magnus Maximus. It is not entirely clear why Maximus fomented this unsuccessful revolt, but its failure drained the nation of many of its finest troops and left the region defenceless, and simultaneously made the Romans disinclined to assist this rebellious province. Just after Maximus was executed in AD 388, one of his commanders called Gratian had claimed the throne of Britain, but he was deposed. According to Zosimus there was another short-lived claimant called Marcus. Following a Pictish and Scottish invasion, the Britons appealed to Rome for assistance and received a legion to defeat them, as has been narrated in the previous list. But the lessons were obviously not learned, because as soon as the Roman legion withdrew back to Gaul the foreign invasions intensified. Emperor Honorius was obviously unimpressed with all the time, effort and expenditure being spent on this rebellious northwestern outpost of the Empire, for so little in return, and so he wrote to all the major cities of Britain saying:

> (Emperor) Honorius, having sent letters to the cities of Britain, counselling them to be watchful of their own security... (Zosimus bk 6.) (Author's brackets.)

The Romans were absolving themselves from all responsibility for the islands, and so the locals would have to organise their own defences. Guy Halsall says that these letters were sent in 410, but it is highly unlikely that they were sent while the Constantine III rebellion was in progress as Britain was not under Honorius' control at this time, and so they must have been sent either before or after this usurpation. Monmouth says that these letters were sent after the usurpation by Gratian and the first pleas for Roman assistance, but before the final plea to Agitius-Arcadius. In other words, these letters were sent out between AD 398 and 406, according to the chronology being established in these chapters. Monmouth's account of this very same letter being written says:

> The Romans then gave a public notice to the country that thenceforth they could in no way be troubled again to undertake any more laborious expeditions of this kind ... for the Romans held it a disgrace to endure fatigues and work for the sake of a pack of cowardly, pilfering vagabonds. (History of Kings 6:2)

Which means that Monmouth knew of Zosimus' chronicle or some similar account of this event. And if Monmouth's version is a fair summary of what the letter from Honorius said, then it was clear that the Romans would never return to Britain or lend assistance to the former province. Monmouth goes on to say that the Romans had not only refused to give military assistance, they had also refused to take any further tribute payments. As has been mentioned previously, to accept tribute from a Roman province was a binding two-way contract which obliged Rome to offer protection. But Rome could no longer protect itself, let alone Britain:

> The (Romans) have now chosen rather to lose the whole of the tribute we pay, rather than any longer endure these fatigues by land and sea. (History of Kings 6:2)

But the British were desperate for military protection, whatever the price and whatever the humiliation. So ambassadors were sent 'with their garments rent and their heads covered with ashes', as Gildas says, to implore Rome for assistance. And because Emperor Honorius had already refused any help, this plea was sent all the way to Emperor Arcadius in Constantinople. And this is interesting, because it did seem odd that the Britons were writing to the Eastern Roman emperor about a problem in the far northwest, which may be why Bede dismissed this as a possibility. But now we know the reason why the Britons did this: Honorius in Rome had already refused to give any assistance and so the Britons were appealing to Arcadius in Constantinople instead:

> Again, therefore, the wretched remnant, sending to Gittiws-Agitius ... address him as follow: 'To Agitius, consul for the third time. The groans of the Britons ... The barbarians drive us to the sea; the sea throws us back on the barbarians. Thus two modes of death await us, we are either slain or drowned.' The Romans, however, could not assist them. (Gildas, On the Ruin of Britain 2:20.)

> 'To Aetius (Agitius), thrice Consul, the groans of the Britons.' And in the sequel of the letter they thus unfolded their woes: 'The barbarians drive us to the sea; the sea drives us back to the barbarians: between them we are exposed to two sorts of death; we are either slaughtered or drowned.' (Bede, Ecclesiastical History, 1:13.)

As we have already seen, Gittiws-Agitius is a Welsh transliteration of the Latin Arcadius. And it has been claimed here that the third consulship of Arcadius was in 406. But that late date may appear to be in disagreement with the classical history of Emperor Arcadius, and so some explanation is required.

The first consulships of Arcadius are said to have been in 385, 392 and 394. But Arcadius was only 8, 15 and 17 years old at the time. What happened here is that his father, Theodosius, had raised his son to co-Augustus in 383, when he was only six years old. It is highly unlikely that anyone counted these honorary consulships of Arcadius, when he was still in his minority, as real appointments. Arcadius did not become the Eastern Roman emperor until 395, and so his real imperial consulships were in 396, 402 and 406.

Consulship dates	Classical ranking	Arthurian ranking
385	1	-
392	2	-
394	**3**	-
396	4	1
402	5	2
406	6	**3**

And just to confirm that the Arthurian consulship numbers and dates for Emperor Arcadius are the more correct of the two, Bede says:

> In the twenty-third year of his reign, Aetius (Agitius), a man of note and a patrician, discharged his third consulship with Symmachus for his colleague. (Bede, Ecclesiastical History, 1:13.)

This quote is a historical muddle of epic proportions. Commander Aetius could hardly have been said to 'reign' as he was not the emperor, and his third consulship was not in the 23rd year of his 'reign' (his third consulship was 14 years after the first). Although it is correct to say that Aetius was consul alongside Symmachus. However, a much more satisfactory result can be obtained if we again assume that Gittws-Agitius was actually a reference to Emperor Arcadius, rather than Legatus Aetius. Arcadius was raised to Augustus by his father in 383, when he was only six years old. And if we add 23 years to 383 the answer is 406 - which was the date of the Arthurian 3rd consulship of Arcadius as emperor.

And this is quite a significant discovery, because the classical date for the end of Roman rule in Britain depends in part upon the date for the letter from Honorius (said to be 410), and the final plea for Roman assistance that went to Gittiws-Agitius (said to be 446). But now we can see that the letter from Honorius refusing any further assistance was written in about 404, while the subsequent plea to Arcadius-Agitius was sent in a much more satisfactory 406. Note that Bede's peculiar 40-year interlude before the Briton's asked for further assistance has just evaporated, as has the peculiar assertion that the Britons went to see an army commander and politician, rather than the emperor himself. In which case, the entire dissolution of the Roman presence in Britain occurred between 390 and 406, some 40 years earlier than previously assumed by modern historians.

And so the final desperate plea from the British aristocracy had gone over the head of Honorius, who had already written a letter refusing any military assistance in 404, and landed upon the desk of Arcadius in Constantinople in 406. But Arcadius was unable to help these remote and beleaguered islands, and so the British ambassadors returned empty handed. Finally, perhaps in desperation, the Britons requested a local prince from Armorica or Brittany. According to Arthurian history the Armoricans were descended from the former British royal line of Octavius and Conan, and were distantly related to Emperor Magnus Maximus who had been married to Octavius' daughter. And it is also claimed that the defeated Brito-Roman army of Magnus Maximus had retreated back to Brittany, rather than going home to Britain (a problem with transport, perhaps?). Thus the requested king or prince from Brittany may have been of both local and imperial heritage, and therefore satisfied the demands of all the aristocratic factions in Britain at the time - both the pro-independence and the pro-Roman.

Although King Aldroenus of Armorica refused the throne of Britain he sent his brother, Constantine, who was crowned as the king of Britain in Silchester. And as we have seen previously, this Arthurian Constantine just has to be the historical Emperor Constantine III. Although Monmouth and Oxford do not mention the campaigns of Constantine (they reserve them for King Arthur himself), Zosimus and Orosius record that Constantine III immediately set out to conquer Gaul, Spain and Rome - leaving the British nation defenceless once more. This strategy does not make a great deal of sense, and so these bold claims of a campaign through Gaul to Rome were assumed to be exaggerations. However, there appears to be more than sufficient historical and numismatic evidence to demonstrate that Constantine III was a real usurper emperor of Celto-British extract who did indeed take over Gaul and Spain between 407 and 411. In fact, the Imperial mints at Lugdunum (Lyon) and Arelatum (Arles) are known to have been striking gold and silver coins for both Constantine and his son, Constans.

And we know that Constantine III was one and the same as the Arthurian Constantine, because both had an elder son who was a monk who became an emperor. Monmouth says of Constans, the son of Constantine:

> Constans, the eldest born, he made over to the church of Amphibalus in Winchester, that he might there be admitted into the order of the monks. The other two, Aurelius and Uther, he gave in charge to Guethelin to be brought up ... On the death of Constantine ... Vortigern took him and led him to London clad in royal garments and made him king. (History of Kings 6:6)

But this is exactly what Zosimus and Orosius say of Constans, the son of Constantine III. The only difference is that the historical record says that Constans was in a co-regency with his father, while Arthurian history says that they reigned consecutively:

> To oppose them, Constantine sent into Spain his son Constans, who, shameful to

> say, had been transformed from a monk into a Caesar. (Orosius 7:40.)

> Having thus arranged affairs throughout all Gaul, he decorated his eldest son, Constans, with the habit of a caesar, and sent him into Spain. (Zosimus bk 6 n174.)

The mention of a 'habit of a caesar' is a reference to the habit or cloak worn by a monk. Presumably this was a humorous play on words in the original Latin, between a *habit* meaning 'garment' and a *habitus* meaning 'appearance'. And so Constans either had the 'priestly cloak of an emperor' or the 'appearance of an emperor'. Very witty indeed.

Oxford and Monmouth say that Constans was a weak leader and so his seneschal or minister, Vortigern (Gwrtheyrn), became the *de-facto* king of the land. Eventually, Vortigern usurped the throne and asked one of his subordinates to behead Constans. This he does, and so the other two young children of Constantine (Aurelius and Uther) were whisked into safety in Armorica (Brittany) by their supporters. The historical record tells a similar story. The chronology just outlined suggests that Vortigern was Vigastes-Verinianus, and the historical record says it was one of his officers, Gerontius, who killed Constans:

> The usurpation of Constantine, who received the purple from the legions of Britain, had been successful, and seemed to be secure ... But this transient prosperity was soon interrupted and destroyed by the revolt of Count Gerontius, the bravest of his generals ... (who) surprised the two emperors, Constantine and Constans, before they could prepare for their defence. The son was made prisoner at Vienna, and immediately put to death.

> The Roman general, indeed, refused to sully his laurels with the blood of Constantine. But the abdicated emperor (Constantine III), and his son Julian, were sent under a strong guard into Italy; and before they reached the palace of Ravenna, they met the ministers of death. (Decline and Fall, Gibbon vol3 ch31.) (Author's brackets.)

The Count Gerontius mentioned here may well be the short-lived usurper king of Britain who is called Gratian by Monmouth and Oxford. The murder or execution of Constantine and his (two) sons is why both Gildas and Bede say that the father of Aurelius Ambrosius was an emperor who had been murdered during the many uprisings and invasions that followed the withdrawal of the Romans from Britain:

> They took arms under the conduct of Aurelius Ambrosius, a modest man, who of all the Roman nation was then alone in the confusion of this troubled period by

> chance left alive. His parents, who for their merit were adorned with the purple, had been slain in these same broils. (Ruin and Conquest, Gildas 25.)

> They had at that time for their leader, Aurelius Ambrosius, a man of worth, who alone, by chance, of the Roman nation had survived the storm, in which his parents, who were of the royal race, had perished. (Ecclesiatical History, Bede 1:16)

And who was the imperial son who managed to escape the murder of the last Brito-Roman Emperor of the Western Roman Empire? The answer is surely one of the two young sons of Constantine III, who had been whisked to safety in Armorica when Vortigern-Vigastes seized the throne of Britain. Once again we see that Arthurian history and real history dovetail time and time again, right up until this point. This is the story that Arthurian history was narrating. And so Emperor Constans II (the monk) must have been the brother of Aurelius Ambrosius and Uther Pendragon, and therefore the uncle of the British King Arthur.

However, it is at this point in time that Arthurian history parts company with real history, and not simply because we lack any historical information about the other sons of Constantine III. They may well have

Fig 2.7
A silver siliqua of Emperor Constans II the Monk, the son of Emperor Constantine III. Both of these emperors were of British extract and usurped control over the Western Roman Empire.

-- Constans II may be the uncle of King Arthur --

The legend is DN Constans NS P F AVG - Victoria AAVGG. The multiple 'G's indicate that there were two emperors at this time. This is not entirely correct, and so this may refer to the father and son in a co-regency. The KONT is the mint at Arelatum or Arles. The two eyes are because the coin has been inadvertently double-struck. [2]

existed, and they may have even had the common names that are ascribed to them, including a grandson called Arthur, but Zosimus and Orosius make no mention of them. And while Orosius could not have mentioned much about the life of the sons and grandsons of Constantine III, because he died in AD 418, Zosimus most certainly could. Zosimus was writing in the late 5th century when these events were still historically fresh, so why did Zosimus not say anything about the famous Aurelius Ambrosius, Uther Pendragon or King Arthur? If Zosimus can mention Constans, then why not his other two brothers and his famous nephew? Was this simply because this history had now become a domestic British issue, and beyond the concerns of a chronicler in Constantinople? Or was it because Uther Pendragon and Arthur were not actually the son and grandson of Constantine III, but belonged to another region and another era entirely?

The reason for questioning the veracity of Arthurian history at this point in time is not simply due to the missing sons of this royal line, but more because the exploits that are related in the continuation of this story are simply not possible. By the mid 5th century Britain no longer had the resources to protect itself, as the many pleas to Rome for military assistance demonstrate, let alone organise an expedition to conquer Rome. And by the time we get to the end of the 5th century there was nothing left of Rome to invade. So the suggestion that Arthur was a wealthy and dynamic monarch in this late era does not ring true at all.

Fig 2.8
The classical image of King Arthur, pulling the sword from the stone, as narrated by Monmouth. Is this imagery merely a fictional fantasy? Window in the Arthur Hall, Tintagel. In the Vulgate Cycle, it is Sir Galahad that pulls the sword from the stone.

But if the accounts of King Arthur's invasion of Rome by Oxford and Monmouth are unlikely to be historically possible, then what was this story about? Remember that we have dropped off the edge of recorded history here, and into the Dark Age abyss, so an author could place any story of his desire into this great historical void and we would have no idea if it was attached to reality or not. And while that cautionary suggestion may seem unwarranted and slightly conspiratorial, it may well be what actually happened. We shall pick up on this story again in a few pages time, but first we need to introduce and demonstrate the many chronological dislocations that occur in Monmouth's accounts, and the first of these involves an earlier British invasion of Gaul and Rome.

Brennius and Belinus

It is *Merlin Grail* that gives us the best and the most succinct introduction to this previous invasion of Rome. As a justification for King Arthur embarking upon his invasion of Gaul and Rome, which will be covered shortly, Merlin says to King Arthur:

> And I will tell you something else. There were two brothers in Britain, one named Brenes and the other Belin, and such was their power that they crossed the sea and conquered Gaul and advanced as far as Rome. (Merlin Grail p163)

The modern translator of *Merlin Grail* not unreasonably suggests that kings Brenes and Belin are alternate spellings for Monmouth's kings Brennius and Belinus. Monmouth's names are simply Latinised variants of these names, and both of these brother-pairs undertook an invasion of Gaul and Rome at some point in the past.

Monmouth says that Brennius and Belinus were two kings of Britain from the BC era, but they are usually assumed to be completely legendary by modern academia. But that is only because modern academia does not understand the history and meaning of this story, as we shall see. Anyway, Brennius sails to Norway to marry a princess and while he is away Belinus takes over his lands. This results in long and bitter struggle between these two brothers that covers several pages. Brennius is the eventual victor in this struggle, while Belinus sails into exile in Gaul. While basking in the glory of his victory, Brennius then decides to embark on some great infrastructure projects:

> He called together all the workmen of the whole island, and commanded a highway to be built of stone and mortar that should cut through the entire length of the island from the Cornish sea (in southwestern Britain) to the coast of Caithness (in northeastern Scotland). And it should run in a straight line from one city to another the whole way along. (History of Kings 3:5.) (Author's brackets.)

This is obviously a description of the Fosse Way, which runs from Exeter (which lies on the Cornish sea) to Lincoln (which not quite Scotland, but certainly in the far deepest north that the Romans had been at the time this road was built). And just as Monmouth describes, this Roman road runs in a dead straight line for 290 km, while never deviating for more than a few kilometers off track. And the Fosse Way is still a major highway, even today.

The only minor (deliberate) error that Monmouth has made here, is to claim that this major infrastructure project was of British inspiration, when it was actually Roman. But this is normal in these texts, where the great achievements and kings of one nation are often claimed as being belonging to another. Monmouth knew of this great arrow-straight road in Britain, so it had to be built by a British king, surely. And he was nearly right about the date of this great construction too, as we shall see.

Then we have the great reconciliation between these semi-legendary brothers. Brennius invades Britain from Gaul, and as the two armies of Brennius and Belinus stand facing each other the mother of these royal brothers bares her breasts and implores them to stop fighting:

Fig 2.9
The Fosse Way strides out across the British countryside. In reality the Fosse is a Roman road that originally marked the frontier of Roman Britain. Fosse means 'ditch' and so one presumes that there was a frontier fortification that ran alongside this road. Or perhaps the road was the fortification, and was later turned into a road. Photo, Thomas Nugent.

> Then, baring her breasts she spoke to (Brennius) ... 'Remember my son these breasts that you have sucked and the womb that bore you ... remember all the anxieties I have suffered for you and grant my petition. Pardon your brother and constrain the wrath you have made against him'. (History of Kings 3:7.)

And while this may seem like a Pagan oath, to swear upon the breasts of your mother, it was also a Judaeo-Israelite custom. In a similar fashion Menelek, the son of King Solomon and the Queen of Sheba, was reputed to have said to his father:

> O my Lord, it is impossible for me to leave my country (Sheba) and my mother, for my mother made me to swear by her breasts that I would not remain here (in Jerusalem) but would return to her quickly. (Kebra Nagast 37 or 14:4.) (Author's brackets.)

And this mammary oath or blessing was still current in the 1st century, and it was Jesus who sought to belittle and end it when he said:

> And it came to pass, as (Jesus) said these things a certain woman ... said unto him, Blessed is the womb that bare thee, and the breasts which you have sucked. But Jesus said: Yes, but rather the blessed are they that hear the word of God and keep it. (Luke 11:27-28)

Not surprisingly, the shock of seeing their mother's breasts being exposed to the world prevented Brennius and Belinus from going to war, and so the brothers make amends and decide to join forces to invade Rome instead. And it is this part of this semi-legendary story that allows us to accurately date these events and decypher who these supposedly mythical monarchs really were. Monmouth says:

> At that time there were two Consuls of Rome, Gabius and Porsena, unto whose government the country had been committed. And when they saw that no people were strong enough to withstand the mighty Brennius and Belinus, came unto them with the consent of the Senate ... to offer presents of gold and silver and tribute every year to hold the peace. (History of Kings 3:9.)

When did Rome ever surrender to the kings of Britain and offer to pay them tribute in gold and silver? Surely this is all mythology, just as modern academia claims. However, the simplistic dismissal of this story is academic indolence and the truth is far more complex.

The first thing we need to know is that a Gaulic king did indeed conquer Rome, and his name was King Brennius. And so the Brennius mentioned by Monmouth was actually a 4th century BC king of Gaul who sacked Rome following the Battle of Allia. But the chronology for this king and his adventures in Rome do not agree with the subsequent chronology in *History of Kings*. And so what Monmouth has done, yet again, is to appropriate another monarch from another land and another era, and claim him as being a heroic king of the Britons. And this is not simply bravado, there is also a degree of nationalistic redress here. In a few pages time the Romans are going to invade Britain, and so it is only right and proper that the Britons did this to Rome first. As ever, these histories are as much propaganda as they are a chronicle of past events.

Fig 2.10 King Brennius, the 4th century BC king of the Senones in Gaul who sacked Rome after the Battle of Allia.

The second thing we need to understand is that, presumably because the Gaulic King Brennius was so famous, the Celto-Welsh name for a king became *brenin*, while a Latinised form of this might well be *breninus*. In which case, the two brothers called Brennius and Belinus may actually be one monarch who was called Brennius Belinus or King Belinus.

The final element in this particular crossword puzzle is the era when all of this actually happened. And the answer to this question is given by the consuls of Rome at this time, who are mentioned in the previous quote. Monmouth says that they were Gabius and Porsena, and this just has to be a reference to Gabinius Secundus and Porcius Cato, who were successive consuls of Rome in AD 35 and 36. So although Monmouth has appropriated a heroic monarch from the 4th century BC, so that the valiant Britons could sack Rome, this is actually a story about the 1st century AD and the subsequent Roman invasion of Britain led by Emperor Claudius and Legatus Vespasian. So we see here how Monmouth can easily readjust his chronology by a few centuries, to suit his political goals. And we shall see another couple of very similar chronological dislocations in Monmouth's account in the following pages.

So who was this British king called Brennius Belinus or King Belinus who ruled in the AD 30s, and had a dispute with Rome? The answer is that he was King Cunobelinus (Cuno-Belinus) or King Cymbeline, of the early 1st century AD:

Brennius	Belinus
King	Cuno Belinus
King	Cunobelinus
King	Cymbeline

And since the Saxo-Norse *kunig,* the Old English *cynn,* and the modern English 'king', are all related and interconnected words, it would appear that Cuno Belinus was actually called King Belinus. Thus Brennius Belinus and Cuno Belinus are the same title and name:

Brennius	Belinus
King	Belinus
Cuno	Belinus
Cynn	Belinus
Cym	Belinus
King	Belinus

Again it would seem highly likely that Monmouth's Brennius Belinus was actually the historically attested 1st century British king, Cuno-Belinus (King Belinus), who has been displaced into the past in Monmouth's account to equate him with King Brennius of Gaul. According to Monmouth, the 1st century Cunobelinus-Cymbeline had been raised in the court of Emperor Octavian Augustus and had been on good terms with the Romans, and regularly paid tribute to Rome. But King Cymbeline had died some time in the late AD 30s or early 40s and his sons, Guiderius and Arvirargus, had refused to pay tribute to Rome. And it was this tax rebellion, so it is said, that prompted Emperor Claudius to invade Britain in AD 43.

Stonehenge

Before we get to Monmouth's description of King Arthur's invasion of Gaul and Rome, readers of *History of Kings* have to trawl through many pages of fanciful accounts of Merlin's prophesies, some of which sound as if they have been dredged out of the New Testament's Book of Revelations. These are actually extracts from Monmouth's own *Prophesies of Merlin,* and presumably they were shoved into *History of Kings* to bulk up the manuscript. The same happens today in authorship, where readers will often see large chunks of standard history cut-and-pasted into a historical investigation. These interpolations are often not there to inform the reader, but merely to bulk up a small pamphlet into a full-size book.

Then we arrive at the story of Merlin bringing Stonehenge from Ireland to Britain, which Monmouth calls the Giants' Dance. The stone circle was originally located at Mount Killaraus or Killara, and surprisingly for such an Irish sounding name this was probably derived from the Aramaic *khil* חיל meaning 'dance'. This fanciful-sounding tale will actually become a major feature of Chapter XIV, because the three authors who mention this great feat of engineering, Monmouth, Oxford and Boron, all say that Stonehenge was erected on Salisbury Plain as a mausoleum for Aurelius Ambrosius and then Uther Pendragon.[3]

Following the great battle of Salisbury Plain, Uther had asked his engineers for a fitting mausoleum for Aurelius Ambrosius, that would last for eternity. The king had, after all, been the son of an emperor of Rome. But the king's architects all said that such a construction was impossible, and so Merlin brought Stonehenge from Ireland, because these giant stones would indeed last for eternity. And as a strange aside, the Bluestone circle within Stonehenge

Fig 2.11
A giant helps Merlin construct Stonehenge. A 14th century illustration from Roman de Brut by Robert Wace. British Library MS, Egerton 3028.

is comprised of stones that came from the Preseli Hills in Pembrokeshire, Wales, and so the story that (some of) Stonehenge was brought from a land far to the west is not quite so absurd as it may at first seem.

But the primary feature of interest about Stonehenge is not its fanciful reconstruction by Merlin, but its design. As we shall see in Chapter XIV, the layout of Stonehenge is based upon the precession of the equinox, and therefore closely linked to the precessional zodiac. And yet the name and court of King Arthur will also become closely linked to the precessional zodiac in later chapters. And so there is a definite link here between Stonehenge and Arthurian history, that requires further exploration.

Roman invasion

Following this mythical interlude, we arrive back into something approaching real history. But this is not real history as we know it, this is a deliberately concealed history. This is a history that could not be told in the Middle Ages, because it was a heresy and therefore worthy of a slow roasting over hot coals. And so this account requires a certain amount of translation and interpretation, to uncover the deliberately hidden historical details. We shall see this same obfuscation again and again in the following chapters, where the events being related are similarly obscured.

Upon the death of Uther Pendragon, King Arthur is crowned as king of Britain. And like King Magnus Maximus before him, King Arthur immediately stops paying tribute to Rome and moves to take over all of Gaul and Rome. Oxford and Monmouth record that the Romans were not impressed by this expansion of King Arthur's realm into Gaul, and his impudence in not paying tribute, and so a letter was sent from Lucius Hiberius, Procurator of the Republic, to King Arthur which said:

> With much amazement do I marvel at the insolence of your tyranny. I do marvel, I say, because of the injury you have done to Rome ... When I recall it to remembrance I am moved to anger ... and in no hurry to perceive what it is to have offended the Senate by your wrongful deeds ... For the tribute of Britain that the Senate has commanded you to pay - and that has been paid since the time of Caius Julius (Caesar) and to his successors in the dignity of Rome - you have presumed to hold back in contempt of an empire of so lofty a rank. You have, moreover seized Gaul ... the kings of which have paid tribute from the time Roman power prevailed in those parts. (History Kings 9:15.)

Rome was obviously outraged with this impudent vassal monarch, King Arthur, who was refusing to pay tribute to Rome. The Arvirargus tax-revolt back in the AD 40s had ended in the Roman invasion of Britain, and it looked as if history was about to repeat itself. So Lucius Hiberius demands that Arthur attends Rome in the middle of August the next year in order to be judged and sentenced, and he further assures Arthur that he will proceed to Gaul and Britain in order to 'restore these lands to the Republic'.

And so we can immediately see that there is something greatly amiss with this story, because this simply could not have happened in this late era. Monmouth's chronology suggests that Constantine, the claimed grandfather of King Arthur, was actually the British usurper emperor Constantine III. This means that Monmouth's Constantine must have died in AD 411. And

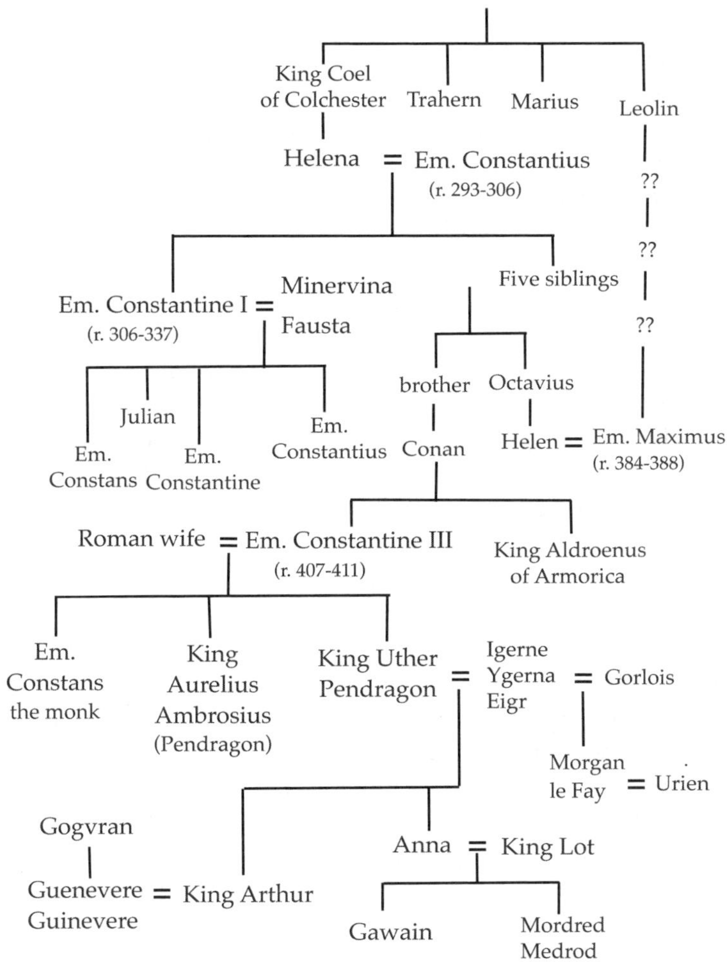

Fig 2.12
The Arthurian genealogy of Emperor Constantine III and his sons, as narrated by Geoffrey of Monmouth. Names in brackets come from Robert de Boron.

since Arthurian history says that Constantine's younger sons, Aurelius and Uther, were both quite young at this time, we might assume they were born in the late 390s and the early 400s respectively.

These dates are perhaps confirmed by the name given to Prince Aurelius Ambrosius, which may have been derived from St Ambrose, the very famous 4th century bishop of Milan. St Ambrose died in 397 and so any royal son born in that year might well have been named after such a famous and influential bishop. And the full name of St Ambrose was Aurelius Ambrosius. And this would have been an especially auspicious name to choose if Constantine III was opposed to Arianism, which St Ambrose had staunchly opposed. The Venerable Bede says that Arianism had 'infected' Britain after the Council of Nicaea in AD 325, and if this teaching was still prevalent in the era of Constantine III, then the king (or perhaps a later chronicler) may have wanted to invoke the authority of St Ambrose to crush it. And so it is entirely possible that Aurelius Ambrosius was named after this very famous Milanese bishop because he was born in 397, and so he would have been 14 years old when Constantine III died.

And if his brother Uther was born in 405, and King Arthur was born to him when Uther was 25 years old, then Arthur would have been born in 430. And if King Arthur was ready to invade Rome when he was 40 years old, then this invasion would have taken place in about 470. And although these assumptions are quite reasonable, this 470s date is actually quite early for the life and times of the classical King Arthur. Because of Bede's chronological error, many Arthurian manuscripts and researchers place the life of Arthur much later than this, and sometimes well into the 6th century. Geoffrey Monmouth, William Malmesbury and Henry Huntingdon, for instance, all confidently place the life of King Arthur in the early 6th century, between 520 and 542.

In which case, having decided not to pay any tribute to Rome in the late 5th or early 6th century, the very last thing King Arthur would have been faced with is an incandescent emperor of the Western Empire threatening to send fire and brimstone and an invasion force upon Britain. As we have seen, Rome had already disowned the entire province way back in 404, and had not taken any tribute since that time. So how could King Arthur be refusing to pay tribute to a Rome that had not requested any tribute for more than 60 years? In fact, in 406 British ambassadors had travelled all the way to Constantinople and demanded that Emperor Arcadius took the nation's tribute, in return for military protection, but he had point-blank refused to do so. So the basic premise of Monmouth's story is false.

But that is not the only problem. While these reports about a tax dispute may be incorrect, the major difficulty with this account is that by the time we get to the end of the 5th century there was almost nothing left of the Western Roman Empire to negotiate with. Rome finally succumbed to the twin evils of uncontrolled immigration and the inevitable internal social divisions this causes, in about 480, and that was the end of the Western Empire. So a rebellious King Arthur who lived in the late 5th or early 6th century would not have even received an unconcerned shrug from Rome, because there was no Rome left to even give a shrug.

The import of this historical reality, is that there must something fundamentally wrong with the latter half of Monmouth's story. The slightly disjointed histories of King Cymbeline and Emperor Constantine III can be reworked reasonably well into the historical record, but a wealthy and powerful late 5th or early 6th century King Arthur champing at the bit to invade Rome cannot. There is no way that this could have happened as it is recorded. And there are not many adjustments to this story that can make any sense of it either. As we saw in the last chapter, the primary options here are:

> King Arthur was a minor 5th century chieftain of Britain, living in a mud hut and muttering unspeakable profanities about Picts and Saxons. But this means that all the embellished stories about a wealthy Arthurian court are a 12th century fantasy.
>
> King Arthur was actually Emperor Constantine III, and so Arthur's invasion of Rome was the historically attested invasion by Constantine. However, this scenario fundamentally alters the Arthurian chronology and so it is unlikely. Nevertheless, elements of this readjustment do make sense and so this possibility will be explored further in Appendix I.
>
> The embellished stories about a wealthy Arthurian court are actually talking about another royal court entirely, and this story has been grafted onto the end of the history and genealogy of Constantine III for religio-political reasons.

Surprisingly, the correct answer is the third one. And so here we begin to enter the new esoteric and occult (hidden) world of Arthurian history. This is the new history that was brought back to Normandy by the Knights Templar, after the First Crusade in 1096, and it found a convenient resting place within the fragmentary Dark Age history of Britain. Which is why all of the classical Arthurian manuscripts originate from 12th and 13th century Normandy, Brittany, and Europe, rather than from 6th or 7th century Britain or Wales.

The first fragments of evidence for this outlandish claim to a secret esoteric history, can be seen in the long reply to King Arthur written by Lucius Hiberius, Procurator of the Republic, that was quoted earlier. The evidence lies in the name and title of Lucius Hiberius, for he may not be who we think he is. As we have seen, a letter from Rome to Britain about a tax-revolt does not fit into the late 5th century era of the Western Empire whatsoever. And it most certainly does not match with the 6th century date for the death of Arthur that Monmouth mentions at the end of his manuscript. But readers of the *King Jesus Trilogy* may see that we are back on familiar ground here. Most of the events researched and explained in the previous books in this series revolved around a bitter tax dispute with Rome. And here we see the same problem, but who is seeking restitution, and from whom?

Monmouth says that the Lucius Hiberius who wrote this letter to King Arthur was only a procurator, while Oxford says he may have been an emperor. But there was no emperor of Rome by that name at this time. Some researchers have declared that Lucius Hiberius was actually Emperor Tiberius Constantine of the late 6th century, because we see here the names Tiberius (Hiberius) and Constantine together. But this suggestion is quite bizarre. The entire Western Roman Empire collapsed in the late 5th century, while Emperor Tiberius Constantine was a Byzantine emperor in Constantinople. It is beyond belief that anyone could claim that a 6th century Byzantine emperor would be expecting tribute from the remotest part of an empire that no longer existed.

So what is the answer to this chronological muddle? The answer lies in the rank being given to Lucius Hiberius, because Monmouth claims that Lucius Hiberius was merely a procurator of the Republic, and a procurator is an officer of equestrian rank who governed the provinces of Rome. Pontius Pilate, for instance, was the procurator of Judaea. So instead of looking for an emperor called Lucius Hiberius, we should be looking for a Roman governor. And surprisingly, we should not be looking for a procurator of Britain or Gaul but a procurator of Judaea, because all of the later components of Arthurian history were derived from manuscripts brought back to Normandy by the Crusaders and Templars. And rather than looking into the 5th century we should be looking at the 1st century, as the accounts in *High History* and the *Vulgate Cycle* will clearly demonstrate.

So for the third time of asking - who is Procurator Lucius Hiberius? Well, he is actually Luceius Albinus (Lucius Alberius), the procurator of Judaea from AD 62 - 64 during the run-up to the Jewish Revolt. And now we can see exactly why a letter from Procurator Lucius Hiberius (Lucius Alberius) would be angry about a local monarch taking over Roman lands and refusing to pay Roman taxes, because this is exactly what happened. In 1st century Judaeo-Syria there was indeed a revolt against Roman taxation, and a local usurper king who was taking over Roman provinces in the east. In fact, the *King Jesus Trilogy* has explained this history in great detail, and the king who was opposing Rome at this time was called King Izas-Jesus of Edessa.

Arthur of Judaea

While this attribution may seem like a leap of faith at this stage, please bear with this suggestion a little longer, because each and every Arthurian manuscript we shall be looking at from this point onwards, will similarly point towards 1st century Judaea in general and the events of the Jewish Revolt in particular. So this is not a rash proposal without merit. And if readers are still sceptical that Monmouth could be saying one thing and meaning something completely different, then please fast-forward to the section in this chapter entitled 'William of Orange' where Monmouth covertly narrates the history of the 8th century Muslim invasion of France, while pretending that this was actually an invasion of Britain.

Anyway, this Syrio-Judaean manifestation of King Arthur talks to his advisers and generals about the Roman reply, and points out that their forces should be strong enough to withstand any attack by Lucius Hiberius and the Roman legions. Besides, the Roman levy of taxes was unlawful, and so anyone with integrity and honour should stand up against this naked extortion by Rome. So King Arthur says to his council of ministers:

> He (Lucius Hiberius) says that it is right and lawful to give (tribute) to him, for it was paid to Julius Caesar and his successors ... who did invade Britain by force of arms and thus by violence subdue everyone under their power ... But nothing that is taken by force and violence can be justly possessed by him that did the violence ... So in like manner I now decree that Rome aught to pay tribute to me, for as much as my ancestors did obtain possession of Rome ... Do you think, therefore, I should ask for tribute from Rome? (History Kings 9:15)

On the surface it seems clear that this claim, that Rome had invaded and subdued these lands by violence, must refer to Britain. And yet such a claim could equally refer to Syrio-Judaea, which had also been taken by force. In fact, since King Jesus-Izas of Edessa owned many of the lands in Syrio-Judaea, then surely the Romans should pay him tribute instead - just as Arthur says in this quote. In fact, we have seen these exact same arguments and phraseology before, with the refusal of the biblical Jesus-Izas to pay taxes to Rome. The gospels say of this seemingly parallel dispute:

> And the whole multitude arose, and led (Jesus) to (the governor). And they began to accuse him, saying: We found this man perverting (subverting) the nation, by forbidding the people to give tribute (taxes) to Caesar and saying that he himself is the anointed king (of the Jews). (Luke 23:1-2) (Author's brackets)

> (Jesus said) 'What do you think, Simon? Of whom do the kings of the earth take taxes or tribute? Of their own children, or of strangers?' (Simon) Peter said unto him, 'Of strangers'. Jesus said unto him, 'Then are the children free'. (Mat 17:24-26.) (Author's brackets.)

Just like King Arthur, King Jesus-Izas was also claiming that he was the rightful annointed king* of Judaea, and telling his followers and people not to pay taxes to Rome. And in the second verse Jesus is saying that Rome should not be taxing its own 'children' - its own princes and the 'Children of Israel'. But this is exactly what King Arthur is also claiming: that Rome is living on his land and therefore it is Rome who should be paying tribute to him. Yet if the claims being made by King Arthur and King Jesus-Izas sound very similar, then so too are the equivalent complaints made by Judas of Gaulanitis and Gamala, who was the father of King Jesus-Izas of Gamala and Edessa. In *Antiquities,* Josephus Flavius says of Judas:

> Yet was there one Judas, a Gaulonite of a city whose name was Gamala, who, taking with him Sadduc a Pharisee, became zealous to draw them to a revolt, who both said that this (Roman) taxation was no better than an introduction to slavery. (Ant 18:1:1) (Author's brackets.)

As has been demonstrated and proven in the previous books in this series, King Izas-Jesus of Gamala-Edessa and the biblical King Jesus were one and the same person, and so it not so surprising that the quotes attributed to them should be very similar. But now we see that the complaints made by King Arthur in Monmouth's account are virtually the same. And in a similar fashion to King Arthur taking over Gaul, King Jesus-Izas of Gamala had taken over Gaulanitis. This did not refer to France of course, but to the lands around Galilee in Judaea. But the similarity and confusion between these 'two' provinces is fortunate to say the least. So if an author wished to divert attention from the true story, he could quite honestly say that King Arthur invaded and captured Gaul, and none bar a select few initiates would realise that the province in question was actually Gaulanitis near Galilee.

Surprising as it may seem at this stage, the tax dispute that King Arthur was having with Rome, is identical to the tax dispute that King Izas-Jesus was having with Rome. The era for this Syrio-Judaean tax dispute with Rome is the AD 60s, as has been amply demonstrated in the previous books in this series, and the Roman procurator who was governing Judaea at the time

* The title 'christ' simply refers to the anointed king of the Jews.

of the Judaean tax revolt was Luceius Albinus (Lucius Hiberius). In reality, it was Luceius Albinus (Lucius Hiberius) who sent this letter to King Arthur, and so the true era of these events was the early AD 60s. Rome was getting fed up with non-payment of its taxes and the expansionist goals of King Izas-Jesus of Edessa, and so both Luceius Albinus (the governor of Judaea) and Cestius Gallus (the governor of Syria) were about to set out to put down this rebellion before it had even started. But these Roman governors were about to get a bloody nose, as Arthurian history explains in some detail.

Varus and Cestius

Knowing and understanding these chronological and geographical dislocations, we can now follow and make sense of Monmouth's story, which is settling down very nicely into 1st century Judaea. This is why, when King Arthur threatened Lucius Hiberius with war, the Roman governor asked the Roman Senate to assemble the kings of the Orient to crush Arthur's army (History Kings 10:1). This novel Roman confederation included the kings of Parthia, Media, Libya, Phrygia, Egypt, Babylon, Bithynia, Syria, and Crete. But why would Rome assemble the kings of the East, to oppose a rogue monarch in Britain, on the far western fringes of the Empire? Within classical Arthurian history this strategy makes absolutely no sense whatsoever. And it makes even less sense for Monmouth to try and pass this off as a real history of Britain, for why would anyone write such nonsense?

However, it does make sense if we understand that these events did not take place in Britain. This alternate manifestation of King Arthur was actually a 1st century monarch of Syrio-Judaea, not Britain, and so these events actually took place in Judaea. So yes, when the Jewish Revolt broke out in Judaea, Rome did indeed gather support and armies from all the loyal vassal kings of the Orient, just as Monmouth relates.

So let us back up a little and see what we have discovered thus far. The question that was asked some pages back was: "who is Procurator Lucius Hiberius?" And the surprising answer was that he was actually Luceius Albinus, the procurator of Judaea from AD 62 - 64 during the run-up to the Jewish Revolt. But a couple of pages later in Monmouth's account we come across a colleague of Procurator Lucius Hiberius who is called Caius Quintilanus. So the next question has to be: "who is Caius Quintilanus, and how does he fit into this 1st century explanation?" Before we answer that question, perhaps we had better look at what actions Caius Quintilanus takes in these events.

An embassy of knights is gathered by King Arthur and sent to the Roman camp to parley, and tell them to withdraw from Gaul or face military action. (As mentioned previously, Gaul may refer to Gaulanitis near Galilee.) Lucius Hiberius replied that he had not come to Gaul just to retreat, while Caius Quintilanus observed that the Britons were better at bragging than deeds and prowess. But perhaps Oxford tells this story better than Monmouth:

> Monmouth:
> Caius Quintilanus observed that the Britons were better men at bragging and threatening than in deeds of hardihood and prowess. (History of Kings 10:4)

> Oxford:
> Caius, who was nephew to the emperor, said: "I have heard it told that the tongues of you Britons are longer than your swords!" (Oxford p55)

This comment angers Sir Gawain, who charges at Caius Quintilanus and cuts him down. This provokes a melee, with limbs being cut and heads being cleaved. The Arthurian knights flee for a while, and then turn back and charge upon the Romans again, before fleeing once more. As diplomatic missions go, this one was a complete failure; although Oxford suggests that this fight was deliberately contrived, to provoke a wider conflict with the Romans.

Reinforcements then arrive on both sides, and so the melee turns into a pitched battle. The Arthurian army flees for a while, but again turns and fights. And when Gawain turns and kills a Roman called Marcellus Mutius, his retort is again much more poetic in the Oxford version. The previous comment by Quintilanus that: 'the tongues of you Britons are longer than your swords,' is reversed to become: 'tell your fellows in hell that the swords of the Britons are longer than their tongues!'

It is clear from this account that Procurator Caius Quintilanus and Lucius Hiberius were both Roman governors who get involved in a major pitched battle with local opposition forces. And if these events do indeed relate to 1st century Judaeo-Syria, rather than the totally impossible 6th century Britain, then this second governor should also be visible in the historical record. And he is, because he is actually Caius Cestius Gallus (Gaius Cestius Gallus), the Roman Procurator of Syria from AD 63 who suffered a major defeat at the hands of the Judaeo-Edessan army in September of AD 66. Thus these two important Roman officials were in the same location at the same time: Lucius Hiberius is Luceius Albinus, while Caius Quintilanus is Caius Cestius Gallus. And so Monmouth's story does indeed make a great deal of sense.

And while Caius Quintilanus and Caius Cestius Gallus may not sound like the same person, the explanation that follows will conclusively prove that they were. And do bear in mind that the obscure connection between these two names was only noticed because these very same events are related in the *Vulgate Cycle* and in Josephus' *Life*. But it is only when these three accounts are brought together does it become obvious who this character really is. The following explanation will run through this deliberate charade fairly quickly as it is explained in more detail in Chapter XI.

The event being described here is King Arthur (ie: King Izas-Jesus) sending an embassy of knights in AD 65 or 66, to Caius Cestius Gallus the Roman governor of Syria, to ask if the Romans will withdraw from Judaea. However, this diplomatic mission turns into a fight in both the historical and Arthurian versions of this event, and many people are killed on both sides. There are many different accounts of this diplomatic brawl, and in Josephus' *Life* the commander is confusingly called Varus, who is said to be a prince of Sohaemus, while in the *Vulgate Cycle* he is called Varlan. However the fact that Varus-Varlan was Roman, rather than a local official, is given in the following quote from Josephus:

> (Philip) wrote to King Agrippa and Berenice, and gave them to one of his freedmen to carry them to Varus, who at this time was procurator of the kingdom. (Josephus Life 11.)

Thus Varus was actually the Roman Procurator of Syria during the pivotal melee and battle that started the Jewish Revolt, and this would have been in AD 65 or 66. But in the historical record there was no such governor called Varus, for the governor of Syria at the time was Caius Cestius Gallus. (Monmouth's Caius Quintilanus.)

What has happened here, is that there has either been an accidental or a deliberate misidentification, and Chapter XI will demonstrate that this error is probably deliberate. The AD 60s Varus has been confused with Publius Quintilius Varus, the governor of Syria from 6 to 3 BC who put down a very similar Jewish uprising after the death of Herod the Great. Note the similar names here - Varus and Varlan, plus Quintilanus and Quintilius. Because of this confusion, the governor of Syria in AD 66 has been called Varus by Josephus, Varlan by the *Vulgate*, and Caius Quintilanus by Monmouth. But his real name was Caius Cestius Gallus.

Source	**Name**	**Rank**
Josephus BC	Publius Quintilius Varus	Governor of Syria 4 BC
Josephus AD	Caius Cestius Gallus	Governor of Syria AD 66
Monmouth	Caius Quintilanus	Governor of (Syria)
Josephus	Varus	Governor of Syria AD 66
Vulgate	Varlan	Governor of (Syria)

The confusion and resulting misattribution of these Roman governors may have been derived from the following quote in Josephus' *Jewish War* which says:

> How our people made a sedition upon Herod's death, while Augustus was the Roman emperor, and Quintilius Varus was in that country; and how the war broke out in the twelfth year of Nero, with what happened to Cestius (Gallus). (Josephus introduction 7.) (Author's brackets.)

Note here the close juxtaposition of Quintilius Varus and Cestius Gallus in the same sentence, alongside the mention of Nero in the AD 60s. Of course Josephus was talking about two different wars and two different governors of Syria here, but it may not seem like that upon a first reading.

While this may be a possible reason for confusing these two Roman governors, it is likely that the main reason for both Saul-Josephus and Geoffrey of Monmouth choosing a Roman governor from the past is that Jesus was supposed to have been crucified in AD 30. As we shall see again and again in later chapters, the events being related in Arthurian history are closely related to the life and times of the biblical Jesus (ie: King Jesus-Izas). Having these pivotal events occurring in the AD 60s during the Jewish Revolt was a trifle embarrassing for the Catholic Church and so the Church has deliberately relocated all of these events, including the crucifixion, into the relatively peaceful AD 30s. And this chronological dislocation has compromised much of 1st century history, including Arthurian history, and dragged many of the events from the AD 60s back into the past. This has led to some absurd cover stories, to account for this 30- or 40-year dislocation in the chronology, and we shall see more of these absurdities in following chapters.

In this particular case the mention of Cestius Gallus, a Roman governor of Syria from the AD 60s, may lead people to link these events to the AD 60s and the Jewish Revolt, which was not desirable. The events that Saul-Josephus was describing when he used the pseudonym 'Varus' had a direct equivalent in the gospel stories, and he did not want a troublesome researcher realising that King Jesus-Izas was involved in the Jewish Revolt in the AD 60s. So a suitable Roman governor of Syria from the past, who had also put down a major Jewish uprising, was found as a replacement. And in this manner Caius Cestius Gallus became Quintilius Varus, or just Varus for short. Josephus has used Varus, the *Vulgate Cycle* chose Varlan, Oxford just calls him Caius, while Monmouth was more bold and decided upon Caius Quintilanus.

Note that Monmouth was not simply copying events from Saul-Josephus' *Jewish War* and *Life*. Far from it. He has realised that the Caius

Cestius Gallus mentioned in Josephus' *Jewish War* is the same person who was called Varus in Josephus' *Life*. And that is not an easy thing to detect, unless you have critically read and heretically understood the gospel stories. And to prove that he knew of this conflation of characters he has called his Syrian governor Caius Quintilanus - which is a deliberate combination of **Caius** Cestius Gallus and **Quintilius** Varus.

And if *History of Kings* has deliberately concealed the identity of the Roman governor of Syria, then its chronology has been extraordinarily concealed. As we have already seen, Monmouth has deliberately distorted his Arthurian chronology to make it appear that he is talking about 6th century events in Britain, Gaul and Rome. And yet we know that these events could never have taken place in the early 6th century, because Rome no longer existed at that time. And so throughout this 'Roman invasion section' of his history, Monmouth is actually giving us a covert but reasonably accurate account of events in 1st century Gaulanitis, Judaea and Syria (and Rome). This is a literary deceit on an epic scale, but it was deliberately contrived so that the authors and their benefactors could avoid being burned as heretics. And as inducements go, that is a very powerful motivation.

This was not an era in which a duke, baron, chronicler or scribe could challenge the Catholic Church on the central issues of Church doctrine. And the possibility that Jesus had been a king of Judaea involved in the Jewish Revolt in the late AD 60s was decidedly heretical. Even though the Catholic Inquisition was not formally created until the 1180s, to assist in genocide of the Cathars, the threat was still there. Yet this was the era that Monmouth and the various authors of the *Vulgate Cycle* were working in. If the Catholic Church can murder hundreds of thousands of people in the Languedoc in the late 12th century, then writing a decidedly heretical story about Jesus in the 1130s (*History of Kings*) or the 1220s (*Vulgate Cycle*) would be foolhardy in the extreme. Precautionary measures were the order of the day, even if this meant distorting the story to fit into a new location and era.

And there is not too much point in merely keeping secrets. The Cathars were very secretive, and were most probably named after the Aramaic term *cathar* סתר meaning 'conceal' or 'secret'. And yet they were still massacred. And the similarly secretive Knights Templar were likewise rounded up and killed on Friday 13th October 1307, which is why Friday 13th is unlucky for some. Secrets are problematic as they can always leak out, and even if they don't, the mere suggestion that a secret is being concealed will invite suspicion and yet more hot pokers.

But Arthurian history does the complete reverse of Cathar and Templar secrecy, because it hides these secrets in plain sight. The paranoid Catholic Church could roast people over hot coals for many reasons, but writing convoluted mythical stories and sweet children's fairytales was not at the top of their list. Having said this, the later works by Robert de Boron do lay claim to there being hidden secrets within the vast expanse of Arthurian history. In *Merlin Grail* Boron says:

> Then Jesus spoke other words to Joseph which I dare not tell you. Nor could I even if I wanted to, if I did not have the *High Book* in which they are written: and that is the teachings of the great mystery of the Grail. (Merlin Grail p22.)

> The next day ... Joseph (of Arimathaea) related to Bron and Petrus everything he had learned from the Holy Spirit - except for the words given to him by Jesus ... which he entrusted to the Rich Fisher (King) privately, in writing. (Merlin Grail p43.) (Author's brackets.)

> When a knight has attained such heights that he is worthy to come to the court of the rich Fisher King, and has asked what purpose the Grail served ... the Fisher King will be healed. Then he will tell him the secret words (that Jesus gave) before passing from life to death. (Merlin Grail p113.) (Author's brackets.)

The *High Book* mentioned here is most probably a reference to *Perlesvaus*, which is also known as the *High History of the Grail*. We shall look at *High History* in the next chapter and while this manuscript is certainly interesting and decidedly heretical, it is not exactly the compendium of wondrous secrets that is being alluded to here. Although do note that Joseph of Arimathaea is talking to King Bron here, who is the grandfather of Sir Perceval. This places Arthurian history squarely into the 1st century, which has to be an Arthurian heresy at the very least. And in masonic ritual, the secret word(s) of Jesus would have been Machabenach. But since Masonry acknowledges that it has lost its secret word to the sands of time, and that Machabenach is merely a substitute word, its import is not very significant.

Given the clandestine nature of these texts, the likelihood of anyone spotting the true foundations of Arthurian history without suitable initiation is fairly low. Even with the enlightenment in this book, the general response will invariably be: 'that is simply not possible'. Hiding secrets in plain sight is a tried and tested formula. It works, and those secrets can slip unnoticed through the generations and millennia. Sometimes the inner secrets are forgotten, as many have been within Masonry, but as long as the mythology remains they can often be retrieved at a later date. And this is going to be one of those concealed, forgotten and resurrected hidden histories.

William of Orange

Monmouth then moves four generations onwards from the death of King Arthur, perhaps to the late 6th century, and onto what appears to be a last-minute addition to the basic story. But Monmouth is still not giving us a true history of Britain in this section, and the clue to this story not being quite as it seems becomes evident when he says:

> The Saxons went to Gormond, King of the Africans in Ireland and, adventuring there with a vast fleet he conquered the people of that country (Ireland). Then, by the treachery of the Saxons, he sailed across with a hundred and sixty six thousand Africans into Britain ... which the Saxons were laying waste. Entering into an alliance with the Saxons, Gormund made war upon Careticus ... and drove him from city to city until he was forced into Cirencester. (History of Kings 11:8)

Again we can see how Monmouth is not narrating a simple history of Britain, but rather blending different stories from different eras and different regions into a single narrative. This technique does make for a few odd-looking bulges and wrinkles in the story, that don't entirely make sense, but it does serve to enhance the political message that Monmouth was trying to convey.

So how does this huge African army invading Britain from Ireland, fit into this supposedly Dark Ages story? It does, but not quite in the manner that most readers are expecting. This is why we have to think laterally and try to interpret what Monmouth is trying to relate; for this account is not pure history, it is a heretical chronicle mixed with elements of subversive propaganda that undermined Church teaching. This does not mean that the story is fictional, just that we need to try harder to understand its meaning. In this particular case the give-away to its true meaning is the sentence that follows the one just quoted, and this says:

> **Gormond** made war on Careticus ... and forced him to Cirencester. Here, **Isembart**, the nephew of Lewis, king of the Franks, came to him (Gormond) and entered into a league of friendship with him and forsook his Christianity upon the condition that he would grant him assistance in seizing the kingdom of Gaul. (History of Kings 11:8)

Interesting. As historical accounts go this is quite cryptic and devious, but it is interesting nonetheless. As it happens we have already touched on this topic and so readers who have fully digested *Mary Magdalene Princess of Orange* will probably see what is going on here. In Norman France during the 12th century, the troubadours were busy manufacturing dozens if not hundreds of *chanson de geste* or songs of heroic deeds. The main topics of these songs were:

Chanson	**Subject**
Geste du Roi	Charlemagne
Geste de Garin de Monglane	Guillaume de Gellone-Orange
Geste de Doon de Mayence	Gormond and Isembart.

Quite! So Monmouth's supposedly late 6th century characters called Gormond and Isembart actually belong to the Norman *chanson de geste* literature, and to the song called ***Gormond et Isembart***. But the story contained in this chanson actually refers to events in the early 8th century, not the late 6th. So within a few short paragraphs Monmouth has jumped from late 6th century Britain (which was actually late 1st century Judaea) into early 8th century southern France and the Muslim-Saracen invasion of the Languedoc. But he has done so without telling his readers what he was really talking about, and thereby consigned his work to the mythological and fictional departments because nobody could understand it.

We can all imagine the standard response to this claim: "Africans invading Britain from Ireland? Pure mythology, don't bother with it." But this is not mythology at all because these were real events that have already been covered in some detail in *Mary Magdalene Princess of Orange.* Unfortunately, most of *Gormond and Isembart* is missing, but we can fill in a few of the gaps by employing the parallel epic stories of *Chanson de Guillaume* and *Willehalm* as a guide. In *Guillaume,* Gormond is renamed as Suleiman Rahman or Terramer, the Saracen Muslim king. Gormond-Rahman's great Muslim army had already conquered Spain, and was moving up into the Languedoc in southern France.

Thus Gormond's peculiar-sounding African army, that was said to have invaded Ireland and Britain, is actually the great Muslim army that conquered Spain and was now invading southern Gaul. All Monmouth has done, is changed Spain into Ireland, and Gaul into Britain. Oh, and he has changed the era too. Wolfram von Eschenbach says of this great Saracen Muslim invasion.

> King Terramer brought (his army) all at the same time across the water, in sailing ships and galleys, in transports and boats. Any man who wants to boast that he has seen a larger army cannot have done so, since that occasion. (Willehalm bk1)

This is a description of a seaborne invasion of the Languedoc in the 8th century. Monmouth has changed this into an invasion of 'Britain', but in the real world this army was actually sailing from North Africa and conquering all of Spain and much of southern Gaul. These were the great Muslim invasions of Europe in the early 8th century, and we shall see why Monmouth has decided to appropriate and incorporate this story into British Arthurian history shortly.

Within real history, the first Muslim invasion of Gaul was in 711, and it was eventually halted by Duke Odo at the Battle of Toulouse in 721. But this vast conquering Muslim army pushed north again in 731, and was stopped again at the decisive battle of Tours in 732. This was the more famous of these two battles, where the Frankish commander Charles Martel won a decisive and crushing victory over the Muslim forces, killing a reputed (and exaggerated) 350,000 Saracen invaders and forcing them to retreat all the way back to Spain. This really was a pivotal moment in European history, because without the intervention of Charles Martel and his 'valiant race', Western Europe would be another Muslim backwater of social oppression, cultural lethargy and economic decay. Edward Gibbon says of these events in his epic *Decline and Fall of the Roman Empire*:

> In this inquiry I shall unfold the events that rescued our ancestors of Britain, and our neighbours of Gaul, from the civil and religious yoke of the Koran; that protected the majesty of Rome, and delayed the servitude of Constantinople; that invigorated the defence of the Christians, and scattered among their enemies the seeds of division and decay. (Decline and Fall, ch52, Limits of Conquest)

> The victory of the Franks was complete and final; Aquitaine was recovered by the arms of Eudes. The Arabs never resumed the conquest of Gaul, and they were soon driven beyond the Pyrenees by Charles Martel and his valiant race. (Decline and Fall, ch52, Defeat of the Saracens).

Note that even Gibbon says that this pivotal battle saved Britain, as well

Fig 2.13
A statue of Charles Martel at the Palace of Versailles. But where is the statue of Guillaume de Gellone (William of Orange)? Is it missing because King Louis XIV exiled the Princes of Orange and all their people from France to Holland?

as Europe, from Muslim servitude. And this is more or less what Monmouth is saying too, albeit more obliquely and covertly.

And while Charles Martel's great victory at Tours was indeed a pivotal moment in history, it was not the only battle that saved Europe from Muslim subjugation. There was another Muslim invasion of Aquitaine and the Languedoc which tends to get left out of modern literature and is not mentioned by Edward Gibbon at all, and it came just two generations later in the 790s. And this was the invasion that is described in some detail in *Chanson de Guillaume,* in *Willehalm,* and also in *Gormond and Isembart.*

Strangely, the epic Norman chansons do not praise the courageous feats of Charles Martel at the Battle of Tours, instead they pay tribute to the heroism, bravery and leadership of Guillaume of Gellone (William of Orange). And Guillaume is said to have been the great grandson of Charles Martel through his daughter, Aldana or Auda. So why have the celebrated triumphs of Guillaume of Orange been lost to the modern history of France and Europe? The answer is that they are considered to be the French equivalent of Arthurian history - a mere legend that has been turned into a historical romance:

> The authors of the *chanson de geste* learned from the monks of Gellone - and could only have learned from them - the few authentic facts they record of their Guillaume and which form the sole historical basis of their voluminous tale. (Joseph Bedier, Legendes Epiques Vol1 p404.)

As Bedier suggests, the Frankish bards and troubadours gathered a few facts about Guillaume of Gellone (William of Orange) and spun an epic story out of almost nothing. But if that is the case, then why did they not sing about the heroic triumphs of Charles Martel instead? And while it is possible that the story of Guillaume-William was fabricated, the events of that era and the subsequent history of the city of Orange would tend to support the history narrated by the troubadours. Anyway, *Willehalm* says that Suleiman Rahman marched into southern France in the late 8th century with a Muslim-Saracen army claimed to be 100,000 strong, easily taking Narbonne. As Monmouth says of this late 8th century Muslim invasion of France (not Britain):

> All the towns were battered to the ground by rams, and all who dwelt therein along with the priests of the churches were delivered up (killed) by the flashing of their swords or the crackling of the flames. The residue of them that were slaughtered in these dreadful visitations had no choice but to flee into whatever shelter might seem to promise safety. (History of Kings 11:8) (Author's brackets.)

And this is exactly the kind of destruction that the Languedoc suffered during the Muslim invasion of the region. In fact, it happened wherever and whenever Islam has invaded a country, from the 8th century destruction of Syria and Jordan, to the 15th century destruction of Anatolia, to the modern campaigns of ISIS who are slaughtering the unbelievers wherever they find them - just as the Koran commands.

In the chanson of *Gormond and Isembart,* which initiated this long discussion about the Languedoc, Prince Isembart is said to have been a nephew of King Lewis I (King Louis the Pious), who was the prince of Aquitaine from AD 780 and king of the Franks from AD 814. (In antiquity, the principalities of Aquitaine and Septimania encompassed much of southern and western France.) Isembart was punished and exiled from Gaul for some reason, and so he goes to King Gormond seeking an alliance with the Saracen Muslims, to take revenge on King Louis. In effect, Isembart is a Frankish analog for Saul-Josephus - the disgraced and disgruntled prince who defects to the enemy, changes his religion, and encourages them to invade and occupy his own lands. Saul-Josephus defected to Rome and used their might to invade Judaea, while Isembart defected to the Muslims and used the might

Fig 2.14
The atmospheric monastery at Guillaume le Desert near Montpellier. Guillaume de Gelone-Orange commissioned this monastery, and then retired there in AD 806.

of Gormond's army to invade Septimania and Aquitaine in southern France.

Although we do not know who Isembart really was, Guillaume de Gellone-Orange, the hero of *Chanson de Guillaume*, was a real historical character. As we have seen previously, he was the Jewish Prince of Orange who used every political, kindred and threatening trick in the book to gather a combined Franko-Orange army together to oppose this late 8th century Muslim invasion of France. (Louis I was Guillaume's brother-in-law, and many of the dukes were his brothers.) And even then the Frankish army rebelled, and had to be taken under the leadership of Guillaume. But at last this fractious army fought the Muslims, and managed to evict them from France. And then, at the turn of the century, they chased the Muslims all the way down to Barcelona. After these successful campaigns Guillaume retired to the charming monastery at Guillaume le Desert, in AD 806. And this is definitely a location worth visiting, for the village and monastery are uniquely atmospheric.

This, then, is what Monmouth was talking about within his supposedly Arthurian history of Britain - he was actually narrating the (true) story of the great Muslim invasions of Spain and France. Note how fluid Monmouth's account is. Monmouth is recording real history here, because an 'African' Muslim king did invade Septimania-Languedoc and quite possibly at the head of an army almost 166,000 strong. But of course these Muslim soldiers would have been predominantly Arab Muslims, not Africans. And yes, the Muslim king was eventually defeated and thrown out of France, by Guillaume the Prince of Orange.

Fig 2.15
A youthful Guillaume de Gellone (William of Orange), by Simon Vouet. Guillaume is wearing his obligatory orange cloak, just as the modern Princes of Orange in Holland do to this day.

But Monmouth is saying that all of this happened in Britain, not Septimania in southern France. So 'Britain' for Monmouth is merely a convenient literary peg, upon which he can hang a multitude of different stories. A moment ago 'Britain' was Syrio-Judaea, but now it is southern France; while 'Ireland' has become a convenient pseudonym for Spain, which had indeed been conquered by the Muslim 'Africans'. No doubt a part of the reason for relocating these pan-European events into Britain, was simply self-preservation from Catholic wrath, but it also made the story more relevant to Monmouth's educated and clerical English audience (he was translating this story from Celto-Breton into Latin).

But why was Monmouth bothering to dovetail this French *chanson de geste* into Arthurian legend at all? What purpose did this serve? The answer is two-fold, and both reasons are strongly related to the Crusades in the Holy Land which had started just a generation before. The previous accounts we have been exploring were actually about King Jesus-Izas in 1st century Syrio-Judaea, but the Crusaders were fighting in this same Near Eastern region in the name of this same Near Eastern king. The Crusades were a bitter fight against the Dark Lord and his Great Protection Racket, in the name of King Jesus-Izas, and the people of Europe needed encouragement to go and prosecute that fight - to continue the 'struggle for freedom' that King Jesus-Izas (King Arthur) had started many centuries ago.

The people needed reminding that this battle against the Muslim invasion of Europe in the 8th century was almost the same struggle for freedom that the Crusaders were waging in Syrio-Judaea in the 12th century. Syrio-Judaea was a majority Christian land, and had been for a thousand years, and it needed liberating from Muslim oppression just as the Languedoc and Spain had required saving from Muslim oppression. And this is why Charles was nicknamed 'Martel', the Hammer. This title was not simply coined because Charles was hammering the Muslims, but also because the equivalent hero in Judaea was Judas Maccabeus, the son of Matthias, who led the revolt against the Greek Seleucid forces. And Judas was called the Maccabeus because this title was similarly derived from *maqqbeth* מקבת meaning 'hammer'.

It would seem that Monmouth was using his history to deliberately link these two or three struggles against invading forces in the minds of his readers. This was a Christian era, and Jesus had been a revolutionary Nazarene (Christian) hero who had tried to free his people from the perceived serfdom of Roman domination. And in that guise Jesus was merely another Judas Maccabeus from Judaea, a Jewish freedom-fighter. And so Charles Martel and Guillaume of Gellone-Orange were simply following in the same footsteps as Jesus and Judas, by protecting the New Jerusalem in Europe from Muslim domination. As Monmouth himself says of these perilous times:

> Oh you neglectful nation, bourne down by the weight of your iniquities and ever thirsting for civil wars, have you enfeebled yourself by these discords in your

> own household. You that did once subdue kingdoms that lie far away; you that was planted (by a) noble vine ... how are you now turned into the degenerate plant of a bitter vine. You can no longer protect your own country, your own wives and children from your enemies. (History of Kings 11:9)

And on and on goes the tale of woe. Monmouth is supposed to be talking about Arthurian history here, but in reality this is not simply a lament about the Saxon invasions of Britain in the 5th century, this is also a covert lament about the Muslim invasions of France and Europe in the 8th century, and by extension also a protest about the contemporary Muslim occupation of the Christian Near East in the 12th century. And the reason for relating this precautionary lament is obvious. Monmouth is saying to his educated Latin-speaking readers in Britain and Norman France: 'if you do not go on this Crusade to the Holy Land, the Muslim barbarians will be back in Europe within a decade, plundering your cities and murdering your women and children.' This is not straightforward history, this is also national and religious propaganda.

Remember that in Monmouth's day, Spain was still ruled by Muslim Caliphs who used the Spanish Christians and Jews as a *dhimmi* serf workforce to maintain their own dominance and lifestyles, just as Islam has always done since its inception. The Koran commands Muslims to form a slave economy ruled by Muslims lashing the whip at subjugated unbelievers who do the work and pay the *jizya* protection-money tax. And so that is exactly what Islam always delivers - an Islamic aristocracy and army who control a subjugated *dhimmi* unbeliever serf workforce via the Covenant of Dhimmitude and *jizya* taxation. And if you don't like the situation the Koran gives you three options: convert to Islam, become a *dhimmi* serf to your Muslim overlords, or die. Your choice.

In Monmouth's view the occupation of the Christian Near East was intolerable, while another Muslim invasion of Europe was obviously a very real threat, and so this rather out-of-place chapter in *History of Kings* was a call to arms. The nations of Europe were too busy fighting amongst themselves to protect Europe from another Muslim invasion into southern France or Austria, and the degenerate nobility of Europe had better wake up and fight for their freedom, before their cities are destroyed and their women and children taken into Muslim *dhimmi* servitude. If only we had a modern equivalent of Monmouth, to fire a warning shot across the bows of our equally degenerate and self-absorbed politicians.

The second answer to this question, of why Monmouth was shoehorning a French *chanson de geste* into Arthurian legend, is that Arthurian legend was itself becoming another of the famous French chansons. Because a significant number of aristocrats now understood the covert and subversive nature of Arthurian history, King Arthur was becoming - or had always been - less of a British king and more of a pan-European hero. Which is why the vast majority of Arthur's biographers were based in Europe, rather than Britain. And so in addition to the myriad of Breton and Norman authors of Arthurian history and romance we also have the following examples:

Manuscript		Author or editor
German		
Lanzelet	....	Ulrich von Zatzikhoven
Tristan	....	Eilhart von Oberge
Erec and Iwein	....	Hartmann von Aue
Tristan	....	Gottfried von Strassburg
Daniel von Blumenthal		Der Stricker
Parzival	....	Wolfram von Eschenbach
Dutch		
Historie van den Grale		Jacob Maerlant
Roman van Walewein		Pieter Vostaert
Torec	....	Jonckbloet
Walewein ende Keye		Jonckbloet
Italian		
Tristano	....	Parodi
La Tavola Ritonda		Filippo Luigi
Il Febusso e Breusso		
La Vita di Merlino		Ireneo Sanesi
Li Chantari di Lancelloto		

And so the list goes on and on. Professor James Bruce records eleven Italian, eleven Dutch, and thirty two German versions of Arthurian romances, plus a few other manuscripts from Scandinavia, Greece, Spain and Portugal. In fact, until we get to Thomas Malory's late and hugely disappointing *Le Morte d'Arthur*, the only region in the whole of Western Europe that did not produce much in the way of influential Arthurian literature was England. Even Monmouth's seminal work, which is often accepted as being Anglo-Welsh - it being funded by a the Duke of Gloucester and written for a predominantly English readership - was derived from a manuscript discovered in Brittany and was written in Wales. Is that not a little odd? The Caxton edition of Malory's *Le Morte d'Arthur* clearly acknowledges this strange lacuna in its preface, when it says:

> For in all places, Christian and heathen, (Arthur) is reputed ... (he is) more spoken of beyond the sea; more bookes made of his noble actes, than there be in

> England, as well in Duche, Ytalyen, Spaynyshe, and Grekysshe, as in Frensshe. (Morte d'Arthur, Preface.)

And this diverse array of foreign editions are not simple translations of Norman texts, but a reworking of the story and history according to local tastes and traditions. Some Italian versions, for instance, have King Arthur becoming the king of Sicily and being buried in Mount Etna. And so by the 13th century, King Arthur had already become an international hero who crossed national and cultural divides, because his true history did not reside solely within Britain.

And if we now go back to the influence of French *chansons* on Arthurian history, perhaps we could actually say that there were four primary Norman *chanson de geste* from the 12th century, rather than three, with Arthurian history being the fourth. And we know that Arthurian history had entered this Norman historical-romance genre because one of the most famous authors of Arthurian history in the Medieval era was Wolfram von Eschenbach, the Bavarian knight and poet. And yet after Eschenbach had written *Parzival*, his great epic about King Arthur and the knights of the Round Table, he went on to compose the not so well known *Willehalm*, his great epic about Guillaume de Gellone (William of Orange) - the very same prince from Languedoc-Septimania who Monmouth has awkwardly forced into his *History of Kings*.

So in the eyes of both Eschenbach and Monmouth, King Arthur and Prince Guillaume could be seen as direct equivalents of each other, with both saving their people by expelling the invading hoards (of Saxons, Romans or Saracen Muslims). And while the line of King Arthur fades from history at the end of the Dark Ages, the descendents of Prince Guillaume governed Orange as an independent principality in France until the city was destroyed by Louis XIV, during the great and tragic Wars of Religion in the 17th century. But by this time the Princes of Orange had relocated to Holland, and it was a much later William of Orange - William III of England - who defeated the Catholic forces of Louis XIV at the Battle of the Boyne in Ireland in 1690. And the result of this pivotal European battle was the Protestant religion, the Church of England, the Enlightenment movement, and the resulting Age of Reason. Thus the Princes of Orange had saved Europe from Muslim domination and subjugation in the 8th century, and saved Europe from Catholic domination and subjugation in the 17th century. We owe a debt of gratitude to the Princes of Orange, and sincerely hope they will continue to honour and protect the ideals of the Enlightenment in the 21st century.

III

High History

High History of the Grail (Perlesvaus) - Anon

We now enter a very different realm within the great corpus of Arthurian history. In *History of Kings* we were grappling with a story that quite obviously contained poorly recalled elements of real British history. But all that has gone now. There is no longer any need to worry if Constantine was Constantine I or Constantine III, or whether the Britons appealed for help in 406 rather than 446, because there is no Constantine and there are no appeals to Rome from this time onwards. In fact, there is almost no mention of anything to do with known British history throughout the entire *Vulgate Cycle. Merlin* gives a short one-chapter summary of a few events copied directly from Monmouth, and that is it. Other than that, it is as if the British half of this story never existed. So we have now entered the realm of 12th century Norman Arthurian literature and as was promised in previous chapters, this is a very different realm indeed.

It is quite obvious that there are two distinct traditions within Arthurian history. One was British and never mentioned a wealthy and powerful King Arthur at all - the 'Arthurian' history of Gildas, Bede and Nennius. The other was derived from Crusader Templars returning to Normandy in the 12th century - and surprisingly they knew a great deal about King Arthur and his royal court, even if they had never been to Britain. And so again we see this same Arthurian peculiarity, where the manuscripts derived from Normandy and beyond knew much more about King Arthur than the local British and Welsh chronicles ever did.

The only Arthurian authors who bothered to include any of the earlier British history in their manuscripts were Monmouth and Oxford, and they did so by adding Aurelius Ambrosius and Uther Pendragon* as extra sons of Constantine III, and thereby joining the presumed Crusader material onto the established (if sketchy) history of Britain. But there is precious little within the bulk of Arthurian history to link Aurelius, Pendragon and Arthur to the line of Constantine III, because Constantine and his son Constans are never mentioned in the later Arthurian histories. And so this tenuous link to British history may have been manufactured for religio-political reasons, as we shall see.

And so we have entered the realm of Arthurian self-deceit here, an overt pretence that has endured for many centuries. In popular literature King Arthur will often be portrayed as being an English monarch from Middle Ages, when that is simply not possible by any stretch of the imagination. However we interpret this history, King Arthur cannot have been a mythical equivalent of King Richard I astride a mighty charger with his pennants flying and his lance lowered, as he is portrayed in the *Vulgate Cycle*. Christians will do much the same, with their popular children's portrayals of a pauper-carpenter Jesus, despite Jesus being called a king on numerous occasions in the gospels. And people will believe these fairytale versions of history because they are nice stories and good morality tales. Besides, as individuals we simply don't have the time to research every subject and so we believe what we are told; while those who control the legend either tell us what we want to hear or tell us what they want to sell. It is a vicious cycle of gullibility and deceit, and it is a cycle that needs challenging and breaking.

Within Arthurian literature, Monmouth and Oxford held out the slim possibility that King Arthur was a British hero; who may have been a wealthy monarch of the early 5th century, but is much more likely to have been a powerless local chieftain of the early 6th century. But subsequent Arthurian literature paints a very different picture, of Arthurian knights campaigning in the Near East and heading out from Jerusalem into Syria and beyond. And so from this chapter onwards, our perception of the Arthurian world is about to change forever. And so we have the three possible histories of King Arthur once more, and the task set for the rest of this book is to decide which of these is the real Arthur:

a. King Arthur may have been the early 5th century's Emperor Constantine III, a

* Uther and Pendragon are often named as separate sons, with Uther adopting the Pendragon title when his brother died.

Breto-British usurper emperor who did have the wealth, power and opportunity to invade Rome. See Appendix I for a discussion about this possibility.

b. Chieftain Arthur would have been a late 5th or early 6th century tribal leader, living in a mud hut and muttering unspeakable profanities about Saxons.

c. King Izas-Arthur actually lived in the Near East, and that is why the returning Templars knew so much about his life and deeds.

And what does this opening polemic about Arthurian history have to do with *High History of the Grail*? The answer is that *High History* is one of those troublesome and problematic Arthurian histories that nobody wants to talk about, because it paints the wrong kind of picture. *High History* is the Arthurian equivalent of the biblical King Jesus sitting on an ornate throne, wearing a gold crown, and ordering the death of his sworn enemies who would not bow down before him, much as it says in Luke 19:27.

High History was written by an unknown author in the early part of the 13th century, some seventy years after Monmouth. The colophons say that the manuscript was commissioned by Lord Cambrein for Lord Johan de Neele, who may have fought at the battle of Bouvines in 1214. So we have a reasonably good idea when this manuscript was copied, but not when it was originally written. In fact, despite the later dates that are often assigned to this manuscript, it was probably written before *Perceval* and *Parzival*, as these Arthurian histories appear to depend upon *High History* rather than the other way around. This is why *High History* will be discussed first.

The dedication in *High History* says that the lettering on the original manuscript that this story was copied from, was so faint that it could hardly be read. And if we take this comment at face value, rather than being a literary device to suggest age and authority, then the original manuscript for this book may have been very old indeed. As we know from manuscripts that have survived the centuries, the lettering does not normally fade until several hundred years have passed. We shall see later that this comment about faded lettering may be more fact than fiction, because the original manuscript upon which *High History* was based may have been very old indeed. The scribe who copied this manuscript in the early 13th century then goes on to say:

> Let Messire Johan de Neele understand that he should treasure this story. Nor should he tell any of it to ignorant folk, for a good thing that is squandered upon bad people is never remembered by them for good. (High History dedication)

The reason for Lord Cambrein telling Lord Johan de Neele to keep this manuscript secret will become obvious later, for this text contained some heretical assertions - not simply about King Arthur and his court, but also about New Testament events. Prof Neale Carmen in his 1946 *Symbolism of Perlesvaus* said that *High History* was:

> A sort of symbolical New Testament ... employing a system of knightly substitutions for Biblical characters ... (the author) has amply provided the hints necessary for a public skilled in exegesis and acquainted with the minutest legends of the life of Christ and his disciples. [1]

Prof Carmen was right, of course, but the character substitutions he provides are incorrect. We shall come to some of the correct substitutions later. And just to add to this heady blend of intrigue Sebastian Evans, a 19th century scholar, said of *High History*:

> Yet we feel as we read, that the words employed are intended to convey some deeper meaning than the fiction bears on the face of it. The romance is more than a romance, it is also a secret written in cypher ... Throughout, there is a continual suggestion of hidden meanings... [2]

High History clearly gives the suggestion to many historians that it is something other than as advertised. There is a hidden meaning here, if we could but decypher it. Sebasian Evans thought that the hidden message involved the Albigensian Crusade against the Cathars in the early 13th century. But the original manuscript upon which this story is based was probably too early to be talking obliquely about the Cathars. Besides, there was a much more explosive secret that needed hiding, rather than the Catholic genocide of the followers of a peaceful religion.

Alternate perspectives

One of the interesting aspects of *High History* is that it represents a complete reversal of standard Arthurian history. As we all know, King Arthur was the righteous and gallant warrior-hero who justly defended his kingdom from the invasions of the evil Saxons and Romans. And this is a given truth of Arthurian history that we all know and accept, whether we think Arthur was rich and powerful or simply a minor chieftain. But in *High History* Arthur has descended from being a righteous king into being the fount of all evil. Yes, Arthur the evil king - interesting, isn't it? This great contrast between *High History* and classical Arthurian literature prompted historian Roger Loomis to call the unknown author of *High History* 'deranged'.[3] But this anonymous author was not deranged at all, as we shall see shortly, he just had a different viewpoint.

In addition to the atypical portrayal of King Arthur, *High History* also exhibits a complete disregard for the chronological conventions of orthodox Arthurian history. In the classical image of these romances, it is a given fact that the author should place the unfolding story in 5th or 6th century Britain, with a few excursions to Brittany and Gaul thrown in for good measure. And then the text should relate sad stories about Saxons and Picts invading the kingdom, and the plucky Celto-Britons defending their lands. That is what Arthurian history is all about. But what ever you do with your Arthurian story, you must never link these brave and righteous Dark Age knights in shining armour with events in 1st century Syrio-Judaea.

But from the very outset, *High History* ignores all of these conventions completely. In fact, there is nothing to positively identify the region as being Britain at all, bar the odd mention of Briton or Wales to keep the Church censors happy. Instead, from the very outset the story links the main Arthurian characters with Joseph of Arimathaea and therefore with the 1st century AD, and most probably with Syrio-Judaea. And in great contrast to the *Vulgate Cycle,* which takes several pages to make a vague allusion to this story possibly being written by Saul-Josephus Flavius, the famous 1st century Judaean historian, *High History* just wades in and says:

> Josephus the good clerk tells us the Good Knight (Perceval) had come, of whom you shall hear the name presently. (High History chI:intro, ch1:1) (Author's brackets.)

> Hear you the history of the most holy vessel that is called the Graal (Grail), wherein the precious blood of the Savior was received on the day he was put on the Rood (the cross) and crucified in order that he may redeem his people ... Josephus has set this in remembrance by annunciation of the voice of an angel, for that the truth might be known by his writing. (High History chI:intro) (Author's brackets.)

> Good Knight (Perceval) was he of right, for he was of the lineage of Joseph of Abarimacie (Arimathea). And this Joseph was his (Perceval's) mother's uncle (nephew), that had been a soldier of Pilate for seven years ... Of this lineage was the Good Knight for whose sake is this High History treated. Yglais was his mother's name, and King Fisherman was his uncle, and the king of the lower folk was named Pelles ... The head of the lineage on his father's side was named Nichodemus. *(sic)* (High History chI:I) (Author's brackets.)

Well that has certainly put the cat in amongst the pigeons. So in its first few paragraphs, *High History* has managed to produce a massive chronological tangle that betrays the true era of these events and the true nature of the characters involved.

Firstly, we see that this history was written by someone called Josephus. Which Josephus the text does not exactly say, but the first two quotes here do give a direct connection between this unknown Josephus and the 1st century crucifixion of Jesus. And the third quote says that Joseph of Arimathaea, who was also closely connected with the crucifixion, had been a soldier working for the Roman administration for a number of years. Now this is a strange thing to say. Joseph of Arimathaea was said to be a member of the Sanhedrin (the priestly parliament) and a secret disciple of Jesus, but nowhere outside Arthurian history does it say that Joseph was a Roman soldier. In fact, that role is likely to have been completely incompatible with his position as a member of the Jewish Sanhedrin. So why does *High History* claim that Joseph of Arimathaea was a Roman soldier?

The answer most probably lies in a conflation that has already been made in the *King Jesus Trilogy,* which demonstrated numerous close connections between Saul-Josephus and Joseph(us) of Arimathaea. And this quote from *High History* is simply confirming this conflation by adding that Joseph was a Roman soldier. And the only Joseph(us) we know of who was both a Roman soldier and became a member of the Sanhedrin was Saul-Josephus, and the only reason he was allowed to enter the Sanhedrin was because he became the *defacto* high priest and king of Judaea after the Jewish Revolt. So we appear to have multiple links here, between the Joseph(us) (of Arimathaea) mentioned in *High History* and Saul-Josephus the historian. Saul-Josephus the historian was:

A Jewish aristocrat and priest.
A Judaic soldier in the Jewish Revolt.
A soldier who worked for the Romans.
A member of the Sanhedrin after the Jewish Revolt.
A scribe or clerk who wrote the secular history of Judaea.
A scribe or clerk who wrote the religious history of the Jews.
A scribe or clerk who wrote much of the New Testament.
A Roman soldier who took King Izas-Jesus down from the cross.
(For a discussion of the latter two claims, please see *King Jesus.*)

In which case, the good clerk and soldier called Joseph(us) (of Arimathaea) can only be Saul-Josephus Flavius, as was demonstrated several years ago in *King Jesus.* As a deceptive deflection, the 13th century author of *High History* then says that Josephus was told this story by 'angels', perhaps to give the illusion of a passage in time. Thus we might be led to think that this is a different Joseph(us) to Josephus Flavius; a later author perhaps from the 5th century. But nobody is really going to believe that, after these opening paragraphs. William Nitze, one of the fathers of Arthurian research, also concluded that this Josephus the Clerk was actually Joseph of Arimathaea, with both being strongly linked to Saul-Josephus Flavius. In his 1903 dissertation Nitze says of this confusion between these similar Joseph(us)es:

> The role of Josephus is of greater importance in our work than that of Joseph. It is Josephus to whom we owe the tale ... he vouches for the truth of the adventures related; he knows of others which are not told here; he was the first person to celebrate the holy sacrament; he explains to Gawain the allegory of his adventures; and he is known as the Good Clerk and the Good Hermit. Twice the text calls him simply Joseph, and twice he is called Josephus, but these variants may be scribal blunders. Nevertheless, it is now generally supposed that the confusion of these two Josephs - Joseph of Arimathea and Josephus Flavius the Jewish historian - gave rise to the legend of Joseph and his son Josephus mentioned above. [4]

Note however that Nitze cannot bring himself to say that Joseph of Arimathaea ***is*** Saul-Josephus Flavius, and so he merely asserts that these two Joseph(us)es were 'confused'. Sorry, but this was not a 'confusion' of names, it was a conflation of characters. But if this is the case, then the many pseudonyms that Saul-Josephus has acquired within these many contrasting accounts of 1st century Judaea have just expanded to include:

Name	**Text**	**Occupation**
Josephus Flavius	Jewish War	soldier and author
Josephus Flavius	Jewish War	colleague of Vespasian
Saul	Gospels	author and apostle
Saul	Gospels	soldier and priest
Joseph(us) of Arimathaea	Gospels	politician and priest
Joseph(us) of Arimathaea	High History	soldier of Pilate
Joseph(us) of Arimathaea	Vulgate	colleague of Vespasian
Joseph(us) of Arimathaea	Robert Boron	colleague of Vespasian
Josephus the Scribe	Vulgate	author, son of Joseph
Josephus the Good Clerk	High History	author
Josephus the Good Hermit	High History	author

For many, many reasons, Joseph of Arimathaea just has to be one and the same as the historian or clerk called Saul-Josephus Flavius. And if we are prepared to accept this conflation, the only real alteration required to the entire gospel story is that the crucifixion must have taken place in AD 70 - just as Saul-Josephus relates in his *Vita* or *Life*.

This new date for the crucifixion story may well bring with it a host of chronological complications that no Christian can entertain, but that is a failing of classical Christianity rather than an error of history. This is the first instance and example of what will become known in this book as the 'chronological dislocation' or the 'chronological chasm' - the 40-year gap that exists between gospel history and real secular history. And we shall see this chasm or dislocation many times in this research, and witness the many absurd and hilarious methods the Arthurian authors have used to bridge it.

However, whether the author of *High History* was Joseph of Arimathaea, Saul-Josephus Flavius, or even the conflated Saul-Joseph(us) of Arimathaea, this attribution gives us yet another chronological problem. These separate or conflated Joseph(us)es were all 1st century characters, and so the events they were recording must have been from the 1st century or before. After all, none of these 1st century Joseph(us)es could have been writing about the kings of Dark Age Britain. Many researchers, like the translator Nigel Bryant, have deflected this problem by saying that these Joseph(us)es have been named as the original author as a literary device, to add age and authenticity to the manuscript - and so the original manuscript could have been written much later than the 1st century, by someone else entirely.

But since most of these manuscripts contain multiple examples of 1st century events, characters and material, as we shall see later, it is more than likely that Saul-Josephus Flavius did have a hand in writing the original manuscript. Besides, the third quote from *High History* just given, says that the Good Knight (Perceval) was of the family line of Joseph of Arimathaea, and that Joseph of Arimathaea was Perceval's mother's uncle. And it is doubly confirmed that this Joseph was Joseph of Arimathaea because it is said that this Joseph worked for Pontius Pilate for seven years.

But if Perceval is a nephew or a great nephew of Joseph of Arimathaea, then Perceval is only one or two generations displaced from the era of the crucifixion, at the very most. So these famous Arthurian knights must be firmly located within the 1st century, and the Arthurian history being narrated must be a 1st century chronicle. Not only that, but Joseph of Arimathaea was a Judaean aristocrat, and so if Sir Perceval was directly related to Joseph of Arimathaea, then surely Perceval must have been a Judaean knight. And if Perceval was a 1st century Judaean knight, then surely Arthurian history must be a chronicle of events in 1st century Judaea.

And so within its first few paragraphs, *High History* has managed to trample all over most of the primary conventions of Arthurian history. The great guardians of Arthurian lore demand that this must be a history of brave Celto-British knights in Dark Age Britain. But we have hardly even started this analysis and *High History* is already indicating that this was actually a story about brave Jewish knights in 1st century Syrio-Judaea. So where does 5th or 6th century Britain fit into this story? Answer: it does not. There is barely a glimmer of recognition within *High History* that Britain even exists. And the only difference between *High History* and the other Arthurian stories we shall look at in later chapters, is that this account is just a bit more open about this troubling aspect of Arthurian history.

But then a strange thing happens, because none of the modern translators mention this heresy. William Nitze, for example discusses the role of Joseph of Arimathaea in this story at great length, but never once points out that this means that Perceval and King Arthur must be 1st century characters who were most probably living in Judaea. [5] But why the silence? The author of *High History* has just trampled all over the classical chronology of Arthurian history, so is this not even worth a footnote or perhaps a lame attempt at a refutation? To simply turn a blind eye to this chronological and geographical heresy and pretend it does not exist, is academic cowardice, and so the reader is being badly let down by these academics.

Venerable mule

This new 1st century chronology and Judaean location for the majority of Arthurian history is confirmed later in this manuscript, in the description of a white mule that belonged to King Hermit (King Pelles):

> King Hermit came from the forest and could not find his nephew (Perceval) in the hermitage, and he is right sorrowful, and he mounted a white mule that he had there. She had a star on her forehead in the shape of a red cross. Josephus the good clerk tells us that this same mule belonged to Joseph of Arimathaea at the time he was Pilate's soldier, and that he had bequeathed her to King Pelles. (High History 8:3)

So this white mule once belonged to Joseph of Arimathaea, and it was given to one of the central characters in Arthurian history: King Pelles, who was the uncle of Sir Perceval and the uncle or father of King Arthur. So either this is an incredibly long-lived mule that should be the first item mentioned in the Guinness Book of Records, or we are still in the 1st century. In which case, King Arthur must have been a 1st century king living in and ruling over Syrio-Judaean lands. But the text continues, and again we have the claim that the mother of Perceval was directly related to Joseph of Arimathaea. Dindrane, the sister of Perceval, is praying to Jesus and speaking of her mother, who is called Yglais, the Widow Queen:

> Lord ... remember that the Good Knight Joseph of Abarimacie *(sic)*, who took

> down your body when it hung upon the rood (cross), was her (Yglaise's) own uncle (nephew). Better loved he to take down the body (of Jesus), than all the gold and all the fee that Pilate might give to him. (High History 15:18) (Author's brackets.)

Again we see that Perceval is directly related to Joseph(us) of Arimathaea, with both being called the Good Knight on occasions, and so *High History* is a 1st century history rather than a 5th century fiction. And when we look at the *Vulgate Cycle* in a later chapter, the Good Knight is called Sir Galahad rather than Perceval. However, since Sir Galahad is never mentioned in *High History*, *History of Kings* or *Perceval*, and his role is completely taken over by Sir Perceval, it would seem likely that Galahad is simply another name for Perceval. In fact, evidence will be shown later demonstrating that 'Galahad' is merely a priestly title, and so this famous Arthurian knight was actually called Sir Perceval the Galahad.

Also, the mention of Joseph(us) of Arimathaea being Yglais' uncle, both here and in the previous quote, is incorrect. If Joseph(us) were Perceval's mother's uncle, then they were hardly of the same lineage, for they would only have been related via a great-grandparent. So the genealogy as given here and in all the other quotes is wrong. What we have here is a deliberate generational leap over the chronological chasm, caused by the standard biblical chronological dislocation that we have seen previously.

The author of *High History* knew that Joseph of Arimathaea had to be of the generation before the Jewish Revolt, because the gospels say so. Joseph of Arimathaea took Jesus down from the cross in the AD 30s, and yet the *Vulgate Cycle* will later confirm that Joseph of Arimathaea was actually a key player after the Jewish Revolt in the AD 70s. And this dual role was not simply a matter of Joseph being very old in the 70s, for the text overtly says that he was not a day older in the 70s than he had been in the 30s.

This leap from the 30s to the 70s made the chronology of any story involving Joseph of Arimathaea highly contradictory, and yet that awkward 40-year chasm was now cast in gospel stone and unavoidable to any author who did not want to become the next Catholic Sunday roast. And so the author of *High History* has deliberately turned Joseph of Arimathaea into the uncle of Yglais, even though this makes little or no sense in the unfolding story. But the author did not want to go to the bother of redrafting the entire genealogy of this royal family, as that was simply far too much trouble, so all he has done is change 'nephew' into 'uncle'.

It is likely that in the original genealogy, Joseph(us) of Arimathaea was actually the nephew of Yglaise, rather than her uncle, and this agrees more closely with the genealogies given in the *Vulgate Cycle*. In reality, Joseph(us) of Arimathaea was the next generation down from King Pelles, but where he sits within this family tree is uncertain. One possibility is that he was a son of King Pelles, because King Pelles was the Hermit King while his son Joseus was the Young Hermit, which is a title that would suit the role of Joseph(us) very well. However, other Arthurian manuscripts sometimes say that King Arthur was the son of King Pelles, rather than Joseph(us), and it is highly unlikely that Arthur and Joseph(us) were brothers. Another possible position is that he was a son of Yglais, rather than the nephew. Later chapters will demonstrate many permutations on this theme, because the Good Clerk was not so good as to positively and irrefutably place himself within this genealogy.

This separation of Joseph(us) of Arimathaea and Saul-Josephus Flavius the historian into two characters, due to the chronological chasm, has caused as great a confusion within these texts. Especially in the *Vulgate*. But as William Nietz observed in the previous quote, even *High History* manages to get itself in a tangle between these 'two' characters when it says:

> Messire Gawain ... came, as you have heard, from the most holy lineage of Josephus and the good King Fisherman. (High History 8:10)

The only Joseph(us) with a 'holy lineage' was Joseph(us) of Arimathaea, and so even *High History* is now calling Joseph of Arimathaea 'Josephus' instead of 'Joseph'. And is doing so because Joseph(us) of Arimathaea was actually Josephus Flavius (of Arimathaea), and this is a reference that has slipped through the censor's net due to sloppy editing.

And here is another missed reference. The young Perceval and his parents are discussing their family lineage, which was of the family of Joseph(us) of Arimathaea as we have just seen. Perceval asks his parents who was laid in a certain sepulchre and he was told that nobody knew, and that only the Best Knight in the world would ever find out because the coffin would open itself to him (High History 1:9). The Best Knight turned out to be Perceval himself, who carried the shield of Joseph of Arimathaea. Many years later Perceval finds this very same sepulchre and:

> He looked at the sepulchre and straight away all the joinings fell apart and the stone lifted up in such a way that a man might see within ... They found a letter which testified that this knight was named Josephus. As soon as the hermits saw the sepulchre open they said to Perceval: 'Sir, now at least we know that you are the Good Knight, the chaste and holy.' (High History 18:25)

Although it is not explicitly stated, it is clear that this was the tomb of Joseph(us) of Arimathaea, who was the previous Good Knight in this story. According to the amended chronology in *High History,* Joseph(us) was already dead and so he had a secret sepulchre that only Perceval could see into. But in this quote we again see that Joseph of Arimathaea was actually called Josephus. And the next example from *High History* says much the same thing:

> The bald damsel signifies Joseu Josephus, who was bald before the crucifixion of our Lord, nor ever had his hair again until such time as he (Jesus) had redeemed his people by his blood and his death. (High History 6:11)

In an earlier passage the bald damsel held the shield of Joseph of Arimathaea (High History 2:1), which was intended for Perceval, and in a later section it is said that she will only regain her hair when the Good Knight (Perceval) has 'achieved the Grail'. So who does the Joseu Josephus in the quote above refer to? It just has to be to Joseph of Arimathaea, who is being called both Joseus and Josephus in *High History*. But we also get the same confusion in reverse, because Josephus is sometimes called Joseph:

> This is the Castle of the Inquest, for nothing you ask it will not be told its meaning, by the witness of Joseph the Good Clerk and Good Hermit, through

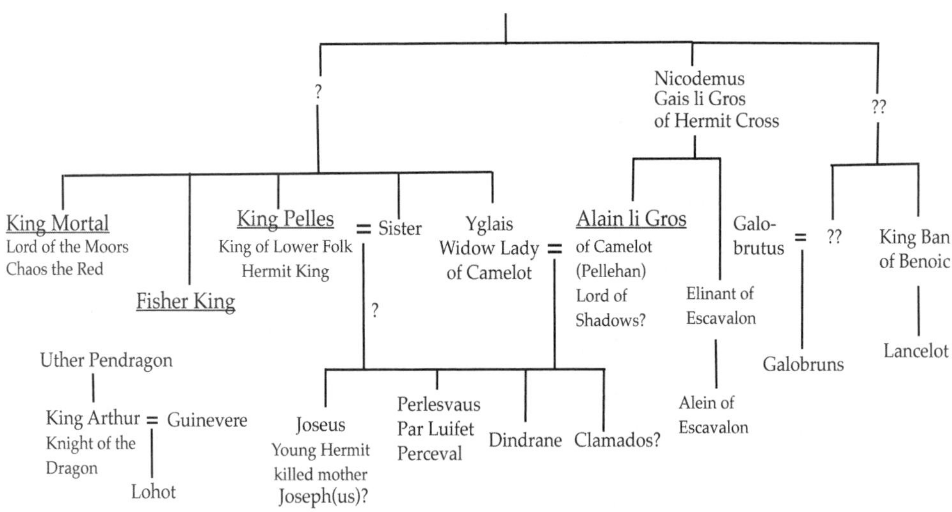

Fig 3.1
The Arthurian genealogy from High History. Joseph of Arimathaea has been moved from being the uncle of Yglais to the nephew or son, to make sense of the family relationships. Note that High History does not attach King Arthur onto this family tree at all. His position within this family will eventually be deduced from comments within the story.

whom we have it (the story). (High History 6:11).

Here we see Josephus the Good Clerk (Josephus Flavius) being called Joseph, which again links him with Joseph of Arimathaea.

The troubling truth that the author of *High History* was desperately trying to conceal here (or trying to surreptitiously reveal here), is that Joseph(us) of Arimathaea was actually Josephus Flavius, the Jewish traitor and historian who became the favourite sycophant and poodle of Legatus Vespasian during the Jewish Revolt. As we have seen, this association is completely unthinkable for classical Christianity, because Josephus Flavius was born in AD 37. This late birth date for the conflated Saul-Joseph(us) of Arimathaea would mean that Jesus could not have been crucified before about AD 67, when Josephus was of sufficient maturity to be an important aristocrat able to ask for Jesus to be taken down from the cross. So by all means this very troubling conflation of characters had to be side-stepped or concealed. However, if we disregard the fears and deceit promulgated by the Catholic Church, we now see that according to *High History,* Joseph(us) of Arimathaea was the author of *Jewish War, Antiquities* and one of the original manuscripts upon which *High History* and the *Vulgate Cycle* were based.

So the author of *High History* has overcome some of these chronological problems by changing Joseph(us) of Arimathaea from a 'nephew' of Yglais into an 'uncle'. And then he has introduced a new scribe and clerk called Josephus (ie: Josephus Flavius) who sounded a great deal like Joseph(us) of Arimathaea but wasn't - honest. And this was a simple and effective method of jumping the 40-year chasm caused by the erroneous classical chronology in the gospels. But this is not the only way in which this chronological leap can be achieved, and in the *Vulgate Cycle* we shall see yet another novel method of achieving the same goal. Bizarrely, the *Vulgate* just makes Joseph(us) of Arimathaea fall asleep for 40 years, and think that only three days have passed.

Such are the chronological absurdities that these authors have had to overcome, in order to stay within the fixed boundaries of classical Christianity. But no matter whether Joseph(us) of Arimathaea was a nephew or an uncle of Yglais, we again see that Perceval was displaced at the very most by just two generations from the life of Joseph of Arimathaea. This version Arthurian history is therefore set squarely in the late 1st century. And there do not appear to be any other events or characters within this particular manuscript that would contradict that early date and era, for there don't appear to be any references to the 5th or 6th centuries at all.

One might be tempted to say that this is the trouble with altering a real history to suit a new chronology, for you have to be very careful that you don't leave one or two references unchanged that give away your deceit. However, *High History's* account of Arthurian history is so sloppy in its concealment of the true era of these events, it is almost as if the author did not care if we knew the true era or not.

Merlin

Just to add to these esoteric and slightly heretical origins of Arthurian history, Robert de Boron's *Merlin Grail* gives us the possibility of there being two original manuscripts rather than one. *Merlin Grail* is one of the most succinct and readable of these Arthurian histories and it will be used from time to time to confirm the events in each manuscript. *Merlin Grail* simply states that Merlin narrated much of this story to a scribe called Blaise, who transcribed it into a manuscript. But Merlin says to Blaise:

> For evermore men will tell of your work and your writings, though your book will have no authority for you are not and cannot be an apostle, and only the apostles wrote about our lord ... Just as I am a figure of secrecy ... so shall your whole book remain a mystery and few will recognise its wonders ... And Joseph and his book will be combined with yours ... for your book will be attached to his and the truth of our work will be revealed. (Merlin Grail p 62.)

Robert de Boron appears to be claiming that one of the original manuscripts for Arthurian history was almost of the same ranking as the gospels, which is not only highly heretical it also implies once more that this manuscript must have originated in the 1st century. And not only was this a 1st century pseudo-gospel, it was also a secret gospel that the Church quite obviously would not acknowledge let alone approve of. And this secret gospel will be combined with the history written by 'Joseph', who must be *High History's* Good Clerk, Joseph(us) of Arimathaea, so once again we see a confusion between Joseph(us) of Arimathaea and Joseph(us) Flavius. And so there were two original ancient manuscripts which when combined would form the basis of the newly emerging 12th century Arthurian history, and that is probably correct as we shall see later.

Merlin is a shadowy figure who is difficult to discern in the historical record, just as Boron readily admits here. Merlin is obviously a magician and therefore the equivalent of a *magus* priest and astronomer from the east, the same as the eastern Magi who visited the birth of Jesus. But in his *Life of Merlin* Geoffrey of Monmouth has lazily borrowed some of Merlin's adventures and perhaps even his name, from the 6th century Celtic story of Lailoken, the wild man of the forest. Lailoken is probably a direct equivalent of the Welsh wild man called Myrddin, and it was from Myrddin that the name 'Merlin' was probably derived. But since the fully fledged Merlin character of Arthurian history was actually a Breton-Norman construct, the respectable authors of northern France could hardly call their wise wizard 'Merdin', for obvious reasons, and so they called him Merlin instead. Names get changed for many reasons within Arthurian history, but the motivation for this alteration is fairly unique.

But the 12th century Arthurian Merlin was closely connected to the 1st century stories of Joseph of Arimathaea and Nicodemus, rather than the 6th century forests of Caledonia and Wales. And if we were to look into 1st century Judaea for an equivalent character to Merlin the magician, then we would just have to point the finger at Simon Magus, the 1st century's most famous magician and wizard. Simon Magus was the foremost pupil of John the Baptist, and so just like Merlin he was of the previous generation to the main players in the gospel saga - a wise old sage who could produce much greater magical tricks or miracles than could Jesus, according to the *Clementine Recognitions*. And if this were the case, then the real Merlin was a more of a Nazarene Magus than a Celtic Druid. James Bruce is in agreement with this when he says of Merlin, in his 1928 analysis of Arthurian romances:

> On first reading ... concerning the great enchanter of Celtic legend ... one is naturally inclined to take for granted that the materials on which it is based are Celtic. But a closer analysis of its elements reveals the fact that the sources are only to a limited degree Celtic, in any proper sense, and that the Orient has supplied a far larger proportion of the motifs. (Evolution of Arthurian Romance, bk1 p140.)

Evil Arthur

High History then gives us the background to the coming events in this story. King Arthur possessed the Round Table, and the knights that sat at this table were the best and most honourable in the world. For ten years Arthur led the 'highest life and was the most gracious king ever'. Arthur had 366 knights in his household, a number that is based upon the astrological layout of the Round Table itself, as we shall see later. If it were possible to build such a vast contraption, the ideal Round Table would be divided into 366 astrological days or degrees, rather than twelve astrological months. And so this famous and successful King Arthur would have had 366 knights around this vast (but hypothetical) Round Table.*

Following these ten heady years of fame and fortune, the court of Arthur had gone into a decline. There were only 25 knights left in the court, and they never went out on knightly adventures. A later comment indicates that Arthur reigned well and righteously for ten years, before going into a decline for a further three. And this may be correct, because in the historical record Arthur's 1st century equivalent may well have been considered a worthy monarch for the ten years between AD 57 and 67, and an evil one for the three years between AD 67 and 70. And *High History* does not spare the punches, regarding the levels that King Arthur had sunk to. A lady is talking about King Arthur but does not realise that she is talking to the king himself, and so she says:

> I was thinking of going to Arthur's court, but I have met twenty knights ... and each told me that the court of King Arthur is the vilest in the world, and all the knights of the Round Table have renounced it because of its badness ... who cares for (Arthur's) good beginning when the end is bad? And it is distasteful that a decent knight such as yourself should have the name of so evil a king. (High History 1:11) (Author's quotes.)

To anyone brought up on a diet of Hollywood depictions of the righteous and virtuous King Arthur, this may seem desperately shocking. So why was King Arthur said to be evil? The answer is simple: if there are two combatants in a conflict, then there will always be two sides to the resulting history. If King Arthur was winning battles against an 'evil enemy', then that enemy would regard King Arthur as being the evil one. And that is the very scenario we see here in this particular version of Arthurian history.

This entire *King Jesus Trilogy* has been about the ongoing dispute and battles between King Izas-Jesus Manu au Kama of Edessa, and Saul-Josephus Flavius, who was not only the spiritual leader of Simple Judaism but also the Jewish army commander in control of Galilee during the outbreak of the Jewish Revolt. (And then the Roman propaganda minister at the end of the Jewish Revolt.) And Saul-Josephus' mortal enemy in Galilee during the late AD 60s was Jesus - Jesus of Gamala (ie: King Izas-Jesus au Kama of Edessa). So in the eyes of Saul-Josephus, Jesus-Izas was the evil one, rather than himself. And Saul-Josephus makes his views pretty clear within his *Jewish War* and *Life*.

* Interestingly, the text says that the Round Table belonged to Queen Gwenevere rather than King Arthur, and when the queen died her brother (?) King Madeglant of Oriande demanded that it be given to him. And he threatened to invade King Arthur's lands if it was not given to him (and if Arthur did not renounce Simple Judaism and marry his sister, Queen Jandree) (High History 26:2). The identity of Madeglant is unknown, but it is worth noting that his name is very similar to 'Magdalene'.

However, *High History* is a history of 1st century Judaea that was quite patently penned by Saul-Josephus himself - the Good Clerk Josephus (of Arimathaea) - just as the text overtly says. There was no other Good Clerk called Josephus who was a chronicler in 1st century Judaea, and so the original author of *High History* just has to be Saul-Josephus. But the mortal enemy of Saul-Josephus within the historical record was King Jesus-Izas, who in these accounts is being called King Arthur. And so in the eyes of the author of *High History,* King Arthur-Jesus was the evil king.

In which case, *High History* represents an original account of Judaeo-Arthurian history in the raw, before anyone else got to it and amended it. King Arthur had to be evil in this original account, because Jesus-Izas of Gamala is described as being evil in *Jewish War* and *Life*. And if this is a copy the original manuscript, before this story was all covered up in the other Arthurian manuscripts, then this account may provide us with some interesting details and a revealing genealogy. Having said this, it was almost impossible to have the King Arthur character being quite as evil as he is depicted in this account, and so someone has provided Arthur with a pseudonym or two, even within this text.

Other evil kings

The next of the evil kings we come across after King Arthur, is the Lord of the Moors. His position and heritage are unexplained, however it is said that it was because of this evil king that Perceval lost his inheritance. So the lands of Perceval's mother and father, Yglais and Alain li Gros of Camelot, became a wasteland and Perceval became disinherited.

In the *Vulgate Cycle* we have the same emphasis on previously good lands that become a wasteland, because of a dispute of some nature. But in the *Vulgate* the blame for this sad state of affairs is placed upon outside influences, which appear to be mostly Roman. But here in *High History* the fault appears to lie within this region, if not within this family. This appears to be more of a bitter family feud than an invasion. And so Perceval's mother becomes known as the Queen of the Wasteland, just as she is in the *Vulgate Cycle*. *High History* then says of this evil Lord of the Moors:

> (Perceval) was the son of Alain li Gros of the Valleys of Camelot and is named Perlesvax (Perceval) ... The Lord of the Moors had plundered him (Alain) of the greater part of the Valleys of Camelot, and therefore he desired that his son should be reminded of this by this name (Perceval). (High History 1:9) (Author's brackets.)

Some explanation of the names of these characters is probably necessary here. The father of Perceval is called Alain li Gros here, but in the *Vulgate Cycle* he is called Pellehan. It is highly likely that Alain was the original name, because there are a series of similar names in *High History* that range from Alain, to Alein, to Elinant. And we only need add a prefixed 'P' to these names to get a reasonable nominative progression.

Alain,
Alein,
Elinant,
(Ellehan),
Pellehan.

The name of the evil knight, the Lord of the Moors, is also interesting and revealing. In Monmouth and the *Vulgate Cycle* Perceval is disinherited by Varus-Varlan, rather than the Lord of the Moors, and Varus-Varlan turned out to be the Roman governor of Syria in the AD 60s. This identification will be explained in more detail later. But the *Vulgate's* account of this conflict is from the opposite viewpoint to *High History,* because the latter was written by Saul-Josephus and he saw things from a very different perspective. So who would Saul-Josephus have blamed, for the lands of Alain li Gros (Pellehan) becoming a wasteland and Perceval being disinherited? Well the opposing forces in the battle with Varus-Varlan were the rebel Nazarene Ebionite Jews led by King Izas-Jesus, the king of Edessa. And so the 'evil' Lord of the Moors, from the viewpoint of Saul-Josephus, has to be closely connected to King Izas-Jesus.

So who was this otherwise unknown Lord of the Moors? While it is possible that the Moors title was a reference to the Moors as they were understood in the 12th century - the Muslims of North Africa - the majority of these names and locations are Aramaic, not Norman French. And so it is more likely that 'Moor' was derived from *morad* מרד, *moriy* מרי, or *moriyah* מריה meaning 'rebellion'. Thus the Lord of the Moors was the Lord of the Rebellion - the leader of the Jewish Revolt. And according to the historical record, the leader of the Jewish Revolt was King Izas-Jesus Manu of Edessa - the biblical Jesus.

Patricide

Incidentally, although *High History* rather sidesteps the issue it is likely that Perceval killed his own father, and there are several references to this event in the many manuscripts we shall look at. There were two knights fighting in a forest, one being the Red Knight and the other the White Knight. The young Perceval (before he was a knight) was out hunting deer and saw the knights fighting and killed the Red Knight with his javelin (High History 1:11). And it was this killing, so it is claimed, that started the bitter family feud that resulted in the persecution of the Widow Lady, the dispossession of Perceval, and the lands of Camelot becoming a wasteland.

But who was the unnamed Red Knight with the Red Shield that Perceval killed? He had to be one of the primary kings in this story, to start such a bitter feud, and that leaves us with very few options. It could not have been:

King Mortal	because he started the war against Perceval.
King Fisherman	because the war was against him too.
King Pelles	because he had retired to a hermitage.

That leaves us with Alain li Gros, Perceval's father, who was the brother-in-law of these three kings. That it was Perceval's father who was killed is possibly confirmed in the next paragraph, where Perceval is told that his father is dead and then inherits a red shield:

> Should you meet him (Perceval) ... he bears a red shield with a white hart. And so tell him that his father is dead and that his mother will lose all her lands ... and the brother of the knight of the Red Shield that he killed in the forest with his javelin makes war upon her (his mother) with the Lord of the Moors. (High History 1:11) (Author's brackets.)

> 'Knight', said he, 'who gave you this shield?' ... 'I bear it on behalf of my father' said (Perceval). 'Did your father bear a red shield with a white hart?' 'Yes', said Perceval, 'Many a day.' (High History 11:4) (Author's brackets.)

It would appear that Perceval had inherited his father's Red Shield bearing a white hart, just after he killed the knight of the Red Shield. So the logical sequence and explanation here is that the knight of the Red Shield and the knight of the White Shield were brothers (or brothers-in-law), and Perceval killed the wrong brother - he killed Alain li Gros, his father, the knight of the Red Shield with the white hart. Perceval then inherited his father's shield.

But the Red Knight's brother (or brother-in-law) - the knight of the White Shield - continued the dispute against the Red Knight (Alain) by attacking his widow, Perceval's mother, thus turning the lands of Camelot into a wasteland. And since this feud was led by the King of Castle Mortal, it is likely that the knight with the White Shield was a knight who served King Mortal.

This short account of Perceval killing his father may be based in part upon the legends of Artemis. Artemis was the goddess of the hunt, who tricked the Aloadae twins into killing each other by posing as a stag, and getting them to shoot arrows at each other. This is also the same story that was given in the founding myth of King Brutus, by Geoffrey of Monmouth. In this earlier mythology Brutus killed his father while out hunting, and so he was exiled from Italy to Greece where he freed the Trojan slaves. So the young Perceval is being cast here as a latter-day King Brutus, the wayward prince with a chequered history who would nevertheless rise to do great things.

The allusion to Artemis in this story is continued in *High History* with the story of the three princesses who arrive at King Arthur's court in a procession that is reminiscent of the Holy Grail procession. One of these princesses arrives in a golden cart pulled by three white harts, and in a similar fashion Artemis had a golden cart that was pulled by four harts. This Artemis-style princess brought the shield of Joseph of Arimathaea to the court of King Arthur. The shield was intended for Perceval, who would eventually exchange it with his red shield bearing a white hart.

But it is not simply Artemis who is being invoked here, for so too is the Roman Fortuna or Greek Tyche, the goddess of fortune. The princess with the golden cart had long golden hair, but then she became bald:

> My head was richly garnished with hair plaited in rich tresses of gold, when the knight came to the hostel of the rich King Fisherman, but I became bald because he (Perceval) did not ask the question... (High History 2:1) (Author's brackets.)

This is likely to be a Medieval interpolation into this story, perhaps from another manuscript, because although the story is told correctly it would appear that the author of *High History* did not fully understand why the princess became bald. The bald princess was obviously Fortuna-Tyche and her baldness was not simply caused by Perceval not asking the right questions (about who the Holy Grail served), instead it was the result of the pivotal moment that Fortuna-Tyche had offered to Perceval being lost. This baldness is a typical Medieval allusion to Fortuna-Tyche, and next chapter will explain this legend in much more detail.

Persian rebels

But now we must return to the story of the Lord of the Moors or Rebels. The fact that this dispute with Perceval's mother was not an all-out war and more of a brotherly quarrel, is confirmed by these two knightly antagonists then attending a jousting tournament. So this was not a war by any means, but a dispute. And when Perceval's cousin, Gawain, the guardian of Camelot, unhorses and defeats the Lord of the Moors, he pretends to take him as a prisoner and to ransom him. Clearly this had been a brotherly contention between two opposing views, strategies, politics or wealth, with one brother (in-law) gaining a political and territorial advantage over the other. But then we have a further complication to contend with, for Dindrane the sister of Perceval says:

> And now the King of Castle Mortal seized the castle (of the Fisher King) in such a manner that ever since the Holy Graal has not appeared ... King Fisherman my uncle is dead and another of my uncles, the King of Castle Mortal, has seized his castle, although my lady mother should have it, or my brother (Perceval) ... Sir, all of this land the Lord of the Moors has taken from my mother and he also wants our castle. (High History 15:19-22)

> Josephus records that this evil king that was so traitorous and false and yet was of the lineage of the Good Soldier Joseph of Abarimacie. This Joseph, as the scriptures witness, was his (Perceval's) uncle (nephew), and this evil king was the brother of King Fisherman, and the brother of the good King Pelles. (High History 18:33) (Author's brackets.)

Fig 3.2
Artemis with her white hart or stag, takes an arrow from her quiver.

Here is yet another king who is trying to dispossess the Widow Lady and Perceval - the king of Castle Mortal. Sebastian Evans, the translator of *High History,* suggested that the name Mortal came from the Old French *mortel* and the Latin *mortalis* which means much the same as it does in the modern English - 'a living being that is subject to death'. In other words the Lord of Castle Mortal would have to be a mortal or secular king, rather than a spiritual king. And so Lord Mortal must refer to the mortal realm, and therefore to the Emperor of Rome.[6]

The only problem with this suggestion is that the King of Castle Mortal is said to be the uncle of Perceval, and the Romans were not related to this Arthurian-Edessan royal family:

> 'Then you are my nephew,' said the King of Castle Mortal (to Perceval) ... 'That I do not like,' said Perceval, 'For you are the most disloyal of my kindred ... Henceforth she (his mother) will have no need to guard against such an evil man as you are' ... Then Perceval called after him: 'Evil King, tell me that I am not of your kindred.' (High History 11:4) (Author's brackets.)

But if the King of Castle Mortal cannot be an emperor of Rome, then who are both he and his alter ego, the Lord of the Moors? The real clue lies in the other evil king who is mentioned in *High History* - King Arthur himself. Remember that *High History* never links King Arthur onto the family tree of Perceval, so where exactly does he fit in to this genealogy? The *Vulgate Cycle* says that King Arthur was the son of King Pelles, but *High History* indicates that Joseph(us) may well have been the son of King Pelles. So if *High History* is not going to hang King Arthur from the line of King Pelles, then where does he belong within this famous lineage? And why cannot *High History* be bothered to give us a more precise genealogy for the most famous king within all of Arthurian history?

There are only a few places that King Arthur can be attached onto this family tree, and that is as a son of either King Mortal or King Fisher, or perhaps of the same generation as these kings themselves. Remember that although the *Vulgate Cycle* places Arthur in the next generation to these kings, in reality this Arthur-Jesus character should be one generation older than Saul-Josephus; and so in this genealogy he should really be of the same generation as King Pelles, King Fisher and King Mortal. In which case, perhaps we should conflate the various evil kings in this narrative and say that kings Mortal and Moors were of the same generation as King Arthur himself.

In which case, we may have simply acquired a new pseudonym for the same evil king. Previously he was being called the Moor מרד meaning 'rebellion', but now he is being called *mortalis* meaning 'death'. But the Latin *mortalis* was derived from the Aramaic *muth* מות meaning 'death', and so we are still working with Aramaic names here. So can all of these evil brother-kings really refer to the immediate family of King Arthur-Jesus? Absolutely, and the evidence for this comes from the apocryphal Acts of Matthew, where the last words of the apostle Matthew were designed to mimic the last words of Jesus from the gospels. But what Matthew is said to have cried out is:

Adonai Eloi Saboath marmari marmuth. (Acts of Matthew)

And in translation these names become:

Aramaic	**Translation**	**Evil king**
Adonai	Lord of the Dawn	
Eloi	Lord of the Sun	
Saboath	Lord of the Stars	
Mar Mari	Lord of the Rebellion	Lord of the Moors
Mar Muth	Lord of the Dead	King of Castle Mortal

In which case, this version of Jesus' dying words on the cross included the 'evil' Lord of the Moors and the 'evil' King of Castle Mortal, who were attacking the lands of the Widow Lady and dispossessing her son, Perceval. So it would seem likely that these two 'evil' kings must be related in some way to King Jesus-Izas himself, perhaps as pseudonyms that were used by his supporters or detractors.

Remember that Arthur is only said to be 'evil' in this manuscript because it is Saul-Josephus who is narrating this history, as the story plainly states in its opening paragraphs. And Saul-Josephus was a traitor to the Nazarene-Ebionite cause who had joined the Romans, and was now fighting alongside Legatus Vespasian against the Nazarene rebels. So of course Josephus would view all the leaders of the Jewish Revolt as being 'evil'. We shall see in later chapters that this great Judaean Revolt against Rome is also covered in some detail in the *Vulgate Cycle*, where it becomes one of the central topics of Arthurian history.

Besides, Saul-Joseph(us) of Arimathaea should not have been one to crow about the contrasting merits of virtue and evil. Saul-Joseph(us) of Arimathaea has already been linked with Joseus the Hermit, but then we find that Joseus-Josephus was linked to a particularly nasty piece of evil himself:

> Perceval ... came to a castle that was burning fiercely with a great flame. He sees a priest at the door and asks him why the castle has caught fire like this. 'Sir,' I will tell you. 'Joseus, the son of King Pelles, killed his mother there. Never since has the castle ceased to burn. And I tell you that of this castle and one other will be kindled a fire that will burn up the whole world and put it to the end.' Perceval looked in wonder, for he knew it was the castle of King Hermit (King Pelles). (High History 35:15) (Author's brackets.)

Did Saul-Joseph(us) of Arimathaea kill his own mother? Is this a reason for his being kicked out of the Nazarene Church of Jesus and James? It is difficult to tell from this short sentence, because much of this is allegory.

The castle that is on fire, that will kindle a fire to burn the whole world, is obviously a reference to the Jewish Revolt that burned Jerusalem and Judaea to the ground. And the spark for that Revolt is said here to be the murder of Joseus' (Josephus of Arimathaea's) mother. So was this a real matricide, or is this symbolic of Saul-Josephus selling out his family by turning to the Romans and becoming a Jewish quisling and a Roman commander? The next quote would suggest the former:

> I have wrought the greatest sin that any man can do, for I have slain my mother who was a queen, because she told me I would not be king after my father's death. Instead she would make me a monk or clerk, and that my other brother who is younger-born than I should have the kingdom. When my father knew that I had killed my mother, he withdrew to a hermitage and renounced his kingdom. (High History 5:3)

This is Joseus being told by his mother that he should become a clerk or a monk, which is exactly what Saul-Josephus became - the Good Clerk and author, and the Good Monk of the Church of Simple Judaism. But what Saul-Josephus did not become, is a king. And because of this royal rejection Joseus-Josephus killed his mother, the queen. Of the many things that might start a family feud and get you dispossessed from your lands, killing your mother and queen is fairly high on the list.

And when it comes to matters of evil, Perceval the Good Knight

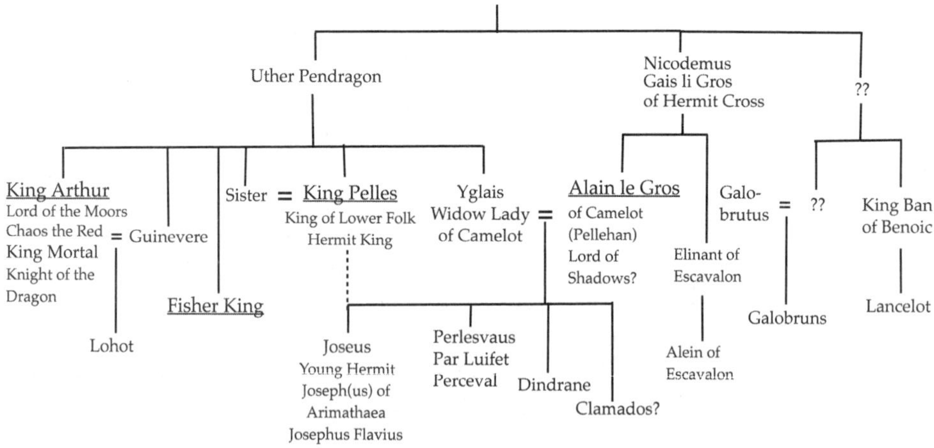

Fig 3.3 A revised genealogy of the Arthurian family, with King Arthur as King Mortal. This makes Uther Pendragon the patriarch of the entire family.

is not much better than Joseus-Josephus. The Lord of the Moors finds an old knight of the Widow Lady (the mother of Perceval) out hunting in 'his' forest, so he kills him. In return Perceval finds five of the Lord of the Moors' knights, and kills one and imprisons the other four. Perceval then finds himself in single combat with the Lord of the Moors and chops his arm off 'together with his sword'.

> But Perceval defended himself as any good knight should, and gave him such a blow as to chop off his arm together with his sword. (High History 15:30)

There then follows a grizzly scene where Perceval empties the blood of eleven of the Lord of the Moor's knights into a large vat, and then drowns the Lord of the Moors in the blood of his own knights. This unlikely scene seems to be some kind of barbarous parody on the Christian eucharist ceremony. At the Last Supper, eleven of Jesus' disciples (twelve minus Judas) were invited to drink his blood. But here, in a complete reversal of the eucharist, the Lord of the Moors (Arthur-Jesus?) is being forced to drink the blood of his own disciple-knights. It is clear from this that Saul-Joseph(us), the original author of *High History,* had a pathological hatred of King Jesus-Izas and of the eucharist ceremony. We shall see yet more demonisation of the eucharist blood-ritual later.

More evil knights

There are three other 'evil' protagonist knights in this battle against Perceval and his Widow Lady mother, and they are Aristot of Moraine, Chaos the Red, and the dreaded Knight of the Dragon who bore a flame-throwing shield. Aristot of Moraine was supposedly a cousin of the Lord of the Moors. It was he who killed King Pelles, and he was killed in turn by Perceval. Note that he bears a similar title to many of the other 'evil' knights who were 'persecuting' Perceval's mother; so we now have evil knights named: Moors Mortal and Moraine. And in later chapters we shall see that King Arthur's evil son was similarly called Mordred and Mordrain.

Chaos the Red is said to be the brother (or brother-in-law) of Perceval's father, Alain li Gros, and a colleague of the Lord of the Moors. Chaos is angry because Perceval had killed his brother, the Lord of the Red Shield. (High History 3:12, 9:9). The Knight of the Red Shield has already been identified as Perceval's father, Alain li Gros, who Perceval killed by accident while out hunting deer. This murder is why Chaos the Red views Perceval as his mortal enemy and wishes to kill him and dispossess his mother. So they engage in mortal combat and Perceval slays this knight in a familiar manner:

> Perceval thought to strike him in the middle of the head, but Chaos swerved aside and so Perceval caught his right arm and cut is sheer from his side, sword and all. (High History 9:10)

The last in this long list of protagonists who wish to dispossess Perceval is the Knight of the Dragon. It is said that the Knight of the Dragon can be found in the Island of Elephants, and it is likely that this refers to the city of Pella in Perea. In Aramaic an Elephant is a *pel* פל, while the city of Pella became a well-known during the Jewish Revolt as a refuge for the Nazarene Ebionites of Jesus and James, as will be related in a later chapter. It is likely that Joseph(us) of Arimathaea had been in Pella too, because the *Vulgate Cycle* says that Joseph(us) of Arimathaea came from Perea, while *High History* continuously refers to him as Abarimacie instead of Arimathaea. But the proper spelling and pronunciation of this name should have been well known to the author from the gospel accounts, and so this misspelling was probably devised because *abarim* עברים refers to the lands to the east of the Jordan - to Perea and the city of Pella.

And the reason for linking the Knight of the Dragon with King Arthur is that his shield was embossed with a fire-breathing head of a dragon. And the Head of a Dragon is a Pendragon, the name of Arthur's father. And then Perceval dispatches the Knight of the Dragon in exactly the same manner as he did to the Lord of the Moors and Chaos the Red.

> Perceval hit (the Knight of the Dragon) with a blow so heavy that he cleaved the habergeon and his right shoulder so that he cut the flesh to the bone. And as he drew back his blow, Perceval caught him and struck with such strength that he cut off his hand, sword and all. (High History 18:6) (Author's brackets.)

What are we to make of this? Either the whole world was out to persecute and dispossess the Widow Lady, Perceval's mother, or there has been a deliberate concealment of the true antagonist in this ongoing family dispute. The 'evil' knights who fought against the Widow Lady include:

King Arthur	Not killed
Lord of the Moors	Arm severed (then drowned)
Chaos the Red	Arm severed
Knight of Dragon	Arm severed
Aristot of Moraine	Lance in chest and beheaded
King Mortal	Suicide with sword

Are we really to believe that so many of the adversaries in this dispute get wounded or killed in the same manner? Or are most of these adversaries different manifestations of the same person? Remember that it was King Arthur who was castigated as the evil king at the beginning of *High History*, and so it would seem likely that many of these 'evil' knights refer to Arthur and his close compatriots. But this close association would have given the author of *High History* two major problems.

Firstly, in the early 13th century King Arthur was becoming a well-known hero figure of popular legend and romance, and so it was difficult to produce a manuscript that repeatedly said he was the fount of all evil. Such a contrarian story was certainly not going to be the top of the Medieval sales charts, and so it is possible that King Arthur was renamed as the Lord of the Moors, King Mortal, Chaos the Red, Aristot of Moraine and even the Knight of the Dragon, in order to spread and soften the claimed wickedness. But if this is so, then we can confidently reattach King Arthur onto the genealogy of this family, as a brother of King Pelles.

However, this gives the author of *High History* a second problem, because this genealogical position would identify Arthur as a 1st century

Fig 3.4 "Tis but a scratch....!" Sir Perceval in combat with the Knight of the Dragon. (Scene from Monty Python and the Holy Grail.)

king, because King Pelles has already been said to be a 1st century king. And yet placing Arthur into that position does make sense of much of the unfolding narrative, and so that is where he will go for the time being. In contrast, the *Vulgate* claims that King Arthur was in the next generation down, which complicates matters slightly, and an attempt to resolve this perennial generational issue will be made in Chapter XIII.

High History

Having looked in great detail at the characters in this text, what is the rest of the story about? Most of the other Arthurian manuscripts detail the struggles that King Arthur has with invading Saxons, Picts and Romans, but *High History* ignores all of that completely and concentrates on this bitter internal feud within the ruling elite. As we have seen, the main topic seems to be the dispossession of the Widow Lady and her son, Perceval. So what is the meaning of all this?

The clue, perhaps, is that Perceval is not simply Perceval. Once in *High History* and many times in *Perceval*, Perceval is called the Welshman, and yet 'Welshman' means 'Galahad', as will be fully explained in later chapters. And in Robert de Boron's *Merlin Grail*, we see that Perceval sits in the Perilous Seat at the Round Table, which was the seat reserved for Galahad

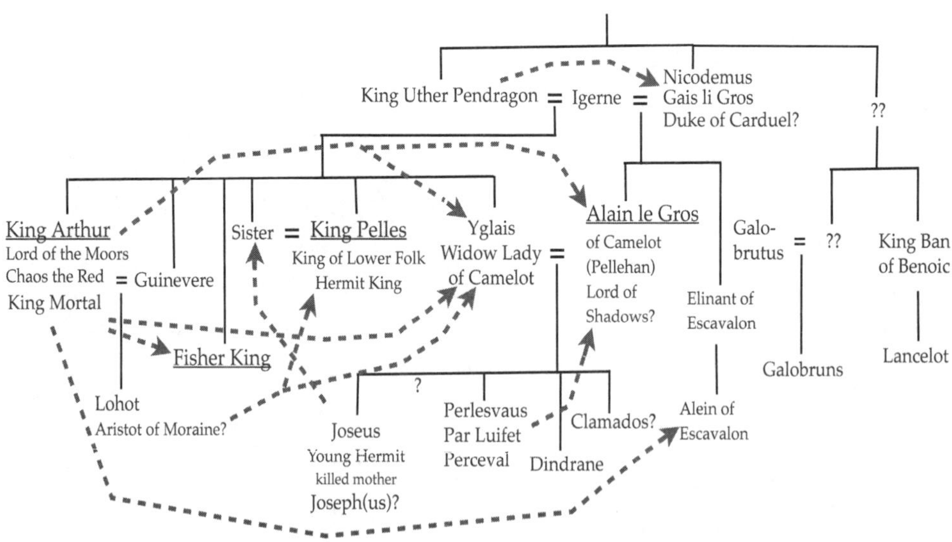

Fig 3.5 A genealogy of this fractious Arthurian family, showing the various lines of murders and persecutions.

in the *Vulgate Cycle* (Merlin Grail p119). And Perceval also takes on some of Lancelot's roles. In fact, *High History, History of Kings* and *Perceval* never mention a Sir Galahad, while the role of Perceval is almost fully replaced by Sir Galahad in the *Vulgate*, which again indicates that these were two names for the same knight.

And yet this new Galahad character is overtly said to be a son of Joseph(us) of Arimathaea, while his other son is called Josephus. Readers can probably see the muddle that we are getting into. Perhaps a tabulated version of these related characters will make more sense of this:

High History

Name	**Title**	**Role**
Joseph(us)	of Arimathaea	the Good Soldier
Joseus	cousin(?) of Perceval	the Good Hermit
Perceval	cousin(?) of Arimathaea	the Good Knight
Josephus	(Flavius-Arimathaea?)	the Good Clerk (but not related)

Vulgate Cycle

Name	**Title**	**Role**
Joseph(us)	of Arimathaea	the Noble Knight
Josephus	son of Arimathaea	the Good Priest and Scribe
Galahad	son of Arimathaea	the Good Knight
Josephus	(Flavius?)	the Scribe (but not related)

Most of these similar-sounding characters appear to be related in some manner to Saul-Joseph(us) of Arimathaea, who has been identified as being one of the original authors of *High History*. But Saul-Joseph(us) was not simply a clerk or scribe, he was also the Judaean army commander who fought a running battle with Jesus-Izas (of Gamala), and then changed sides to become a Roman commander. And so even after his 'flash of inspiration' on the road to Jotapata, Saul-Josephus was still fighting against the Judaean-Nazarene rebels of King Jesus-Izas. So Saul-Josephus Flavius was not simply the Good Clerk and Good Scribe who became the Good Priest of Simple Judaism, he was also the Good Soldier and the Good Knight.

Thus it is entirely possible that this great conspiracy of persecution against Perceval and the Widow Lady in *High History,* is merely a sad lament about the life and fate of Saul-Joseph(us) of Arimathaea and his own family. Saul-Josephus considered himself dispossessed because he had been rejected by the leaders of the Nazarene Church of Jesus and James. And it was because of this rejection and possible dispossession that he joined the Romans, in order to use the might of Rome to regain his position and lands. But Saul-Josephus could hardly say that it was himself who was being dispossessed, because having a story about a dispossessed Saul-Josephus being overtly written by Saul-Josephus was a bit too obvious. The sincerity of the lament gets a bit diluted, if it is merely Josephus complaining about the fate of himself and his family. And so it is possible that Saul-Josephus has invented an alter-ego or two as his heroes.

Evil of Simple Judaism

One of the other main topics within *High History* concerns yet more divisions within this family, this time regarding those who believe in the Old Law and those who believe in the New Law. The Old Law is a reference to the Judaic Law of Moses, which is a reference in this case to the religion of the Nazarene Ebionites of Jesus and James. Conversely, the New Law is Saul-Josephus' new Simple Judaism for Gentiles. And so we see the same old division and contention between these two sects that has already been covered in some detail in the *King Jesus Trilogy*.

But *High History's* obsession with this topic is odd, because this religious dispute had nothing to do with 5th century Britain. There were no Nazarene Ebionite Jews in Britain during the 5th and 6th centuries, or any other kind of Jews come to that. And so this great religious conflict makes absolutely no sense in terms of orthodox Arthurian history. It only makes sense if we extract this history from 5th century Britain, and thrust it back into 1st century Syrio-Judaea where it really belongs.

And if we follow this 1st century Judaean train of thought, this gives us another possible reason for the bitter dispute within the Arthurian royal family, one that accords very well with the history of 1st century Judaea - religion. So another possible reason for Perceval and his Widow Lady mother being dispossessed from their lands, is that Saul-Josephus came from this side of the family, much as the later *Vulgate Cycle* suggests. But Saul-Josephus had created Simple Judaism for Gentiles, which eventually created an irrevocable rift within the Nazarene Church.

To begin with, even James the brother of Jesus had initially consented to Saul-Josephus' new Simple Judaic creed, and it was James who crafted the original Simple Judaic rules himself, as has been discussed in *King Jesus*. But Saul-Josephus had taken the leadership of this new creed much too far, and had started mocking the laws and leaders of Nazarene Judaism and actively opposing their Church. Saul-Josephus had an especial hatred for circumcision, and this loathing would have been greatly reinforced by Jesus' requests for castration in Math 19:12. So this is an equally likely reason for the severe opposition that we have seen towards Saul-Josephus' side of the family.

Many of the knightly adventures that Perceval has, are interpreted by various lay priests and hermits as representing the destruction of the Old Law (of Nazarene Judaism) and the establishment of the New Law (of Simple Judaism). So yes, the entire story in *High History* is being firmly written from the Simple Judaic viewpoint - the viewpoint of Saul-Josephus himself. And so Perceval is being portrayed here as a follower of Saul-Josephus' Simple Judaism (Christianity). Although it has to be said the morality of some of these allegorical stories leaves a lot to be desired.

For instance, a knight was angry with Gawain because he suspected his wife of adultery with him, so he made her stand in a pool and whipped and beat her cruelly, until the water ran red with her blood. Gawain jousts with the knight, in order to prevent this cruel beating, but instead of attacking Gawain the knight thrusts his lance right through his own wife's chest and leaves her for dead. The learned priest says of this brutal murder:

> Much significance was there in her death, for Josephus witnessed that the Old Law was destroyed by a stroke of a sword without recover, and to destroy the Old Law our Lord did suffer to be smitten in the side by a spear. By this stroke the Old Law was destroyed. The lady signifies the old law. (High History 4:3, 6:12)

The allusion to the scourging (whipping) of Jesus, and the spear in his side when he was on the cross is clear enough to see. But what a fine morality tale, upon which a new religion can be established - spearing your wife through the chest with a lance. So was this strange morality tale designed to praise Christianity, or to mock and condemn it? These peculiar parables continue, on and on, and here is another interesting one:

> Sir, said Gawain, I want to ask you about the king (King Gurgalain). When I brought his son back dead, he had him cooked and gave pieces (little slices) of him away to be eaten by all the people of his land.
>
> Sir, said the priest, The king had lent his heart upon Jesus Christ and wanted to make a sacrifice of his flesh and blood to our Lord, and for this reason did he make all those people eat his son ... and therefore was all evil beliefs uprooted from his land. (High History 6:13) (Author's brackets.)

Again the allusion here to the Catholic eucharist ceremony, where slices of the body of Jesus are cut up and eaten by the congregation, is more than obvious. But was this strange morality tale devised to praise Christianity, or to mock and condemn it? The priest says that the king's actions, in cooking and eating his son, were performed in order to end all evil. But is not the act of cooking and eating your son the fount of all evil in itself? Does the king propose that his people should become cannibals?

It is quite clear that these events and their lame explanations represent a devastating criticism and mockery of two of the central tenets of Catholic Christianity. This is most definitely a condemnation, rather than a commendation. But if so, then we have to ask who would have written these peculiar 'morality tales'. It seems highly likely that the original text upon which *High History* was based was written by Saul-Josephus (of Arimathaea) himself, as we have seen. But Saul-Josephus was himself the primary architect and author of Simple Judaic Christianity, so why would Saul-Josephus have set out to mock and condemn his own religion? Or were these strange stories later interpolations by a 13th century translator and scribe?

While the suggestion that Saul-Josephus might condemn his own religion may seem bizarre, this may well be the most likely option. Remember that when Saul-Josephus was selling his Simple Judaism for Gentiles across Anatolia and Greece in the AD 50s, he did not mention any of this scourging, crucifixion, spear-thrusting or man-god eating. Saul-Josephus was peddling faith in Jesus rather than the sacrifice of Jesus. In fact, if one trawls through Saul's epistles he never seems to mention the eucharist at all. Where the 'body of Christ' is mentioned in Saul's (Josephus') epistles it refers to the 'body of the Church', while the 'blood of Christ' is not mentioned at all. There are a few references to the body and blood in the epistles of course, but these are all in Peter, John, and Hebrews, which are not regarded as being epistles of Saul. And there are a couple of references in Ephesians, which is widely considered to be a later pseudographic epistle.

The only references to the eucharist in one of Saul's epistles are in 1Cor 10:16 and 1Cor 11:23-25, but these give the impression of being later interpolations. The first of these verses lies within a section that is condemning the Orthodox Jewish ritual of animal sacrifice. So why condemn Jewish animal sacrifice and then hold up Jesus as a human sacrifice, as if that is a more moral and humane alternative? And the second reference is similarly odd, for the verses just before it say:

> When ye come together therefore into one place, this is not to eat the Lord's supper. For in eating every one eats before his own supper before others: and one is hungry, and another is drunken. Have you no houses for eating and drinking? Or do ye despise the assembly of God, and put to shame them who have not? What shall I say to you? Shall I praise you? In this point I do not praise. (1Cor 11:19-22)

So Saul (Josephus) has just said that the congregation should <u>not</u> partake in a Last Supper eucharist celebration - before then launching into a description of the eucharist. But that makes no sense. Why specifically ban something, before describing and praising it? And the answer to Saul's question 'have you no houses for eating' is not answered until we get all the way down to the very last verse in this chapter, which says:

> If any one be hungry, let him eat at home, that ye may not come together for judgment. But the other things, whenever I come, I will set in order. (1Cor 11:34)

In which case, if we subtract verses 23 to 33 about the eucharist, the entire section would make a great deal more sense than it presently does. So the intervening verses are likely to have been a later interpolation, because this mention of the eucharist is out of place and highly unusual for Saul's letters. But this is very odd. Think about it. Here is Saul (Josephus) writing to his new Simple Judaic congregations, supposedly some twenty or so years after the Last Supper and crucifixion of Jesus, and he never mentions the full crucifixion story once; while the eucharist is only mentioned once within this deceitful interpolation. Is this not strange?

Surely an evangelising Saul should have been banging his drum in the AD 50s about the unjust trial and crucifixion of his man-god. And so the main topics in his many epistles should have included graphic accounts of the unjust trial, the scourging; the cross; the sponge; the spear; the women milling around; the death; Joseph of Arimathaea; the burial; Mary Magdalene; the empty tomb and the resurrection. But Saul (Josephus) does not mention any of this when he writes to his new Simple Judaic congregations in the AD 50s. Why? The answer to this perennial conundrum is that the crucifixion had not yet taken place, because it came at the end of the Jewish Revolt in AD 70. While the concept of a cannibalistic blood sacrifice ritual, the eucharist, was most definitely not Saul-Josephus's idea.

Saul-Josephus may have been a Romophile who despised Jewish circumcision, Jewish separatism and Nazarene castration, but he was still of Jewish heritage. And one of the primary stipulations within Jewish kosher regulations is the prohibition on eating or drinking blood, which is why kosher meats are drained of blood during slaughter. So would Saul have ignored this central kosher regulation, along with his other amendments to Judaic customs and laws?

The answer to this is given to us in Acts of the Apostles. When Saul (Josephus) went to James, the brother of Jesus, and devised the rules for his new Simple Judaism for Gentiles, the four simple rules they decided upon still forbade the eating and therefore drinking of blood. So the message went out from James, to Saul and his mainly Gentile Simple Judaists, that:

> We have sent therefore Judas and Silas, who shall also tell you the same things by mouth. For it seemed good to the Holy Ghost, and to us, to lay upon you no

> greater burden than these necessary things - That you abstain from meats offered to idols, and from blood, and from things strangled, and from fornication. From which if you keep yourselves, you shall do well. Fare ye well. (Acts A15:27-29)

Note that James also sent Judas and Silas with this message, because nobody would ever believe the lying and deceitful Saul (Josephus). And the message from James the Just, who was the leader of the Nazarene Church at this time, was that these new Gentile Simple Judaists that Saul was preaching to in Corinth, Galacia, Philippi and Thessalonica, had to abstain from: sacrificed meat, blood, meat containing blood, and from fornication. Note that circumcision and segregation from other sects were not mentioned in this list, because Saul (Josephus) despised those Jewish customs. But the consumption of sacrificial meats and blood were still banned. In fact, blood was banned twice in this list because the strangled animals were only banned because they still contained their blood.

In this case, how could anyone imagine that Saul (Josephus) would have been travelling around the Mediterranean as a young evangelist, preaching that the Jews and Gentiles of Philippi and Thessalonica should eat sacrificial human flesh and drink sacrificial human blood? Not just any old blood of a pigeon or lamb, but the human blood of a christ, an anointed king of Judaea? It is simply not possible. It did not happen. And so the two suspect references to the eucharist in Corinthians must be later interpolations.

And so we now come back to the savage mockery of the crucifixion and eucharist that we saw in *High History*, with the king's son being cut up and eaten. Surprising as it may seem, this condemnation does not need to have been a later interpolation by a 13th century scribe who detested the Catholic Church, because it may have already been in the text. As we shall see later in the *Vulgate Cycle*, when Saul-Josephus was ordered to go and negotiate with the defeated Nazarene rebels in the east, after the Jewish Revolt, he was told what to say and teach by Emperor Vespasian himself. So it may well have been Vespasian and Titus who added this blood-sacrifice ritual to Saul-Josephus' new creed of Simple Judaism, and they drew these ideas out of the Roman cult of Mithras. So what is Mithrasism, and why it is linked to this investigation?

Mithras

As we shall see in the following chapters, Mithras was one of the foundation-stones upon which Simple Judaic Christianity was built. And it also features in a covert fashion within the *Vulgate Cycle*, so it is worth our while making a short diversion into the origins and rituals of Mithras. And like so many aspects of this story, what is commonly taught about Mithras is decidedly incorrect. And surprisingly, it is the *Vulgate Cycle* that will expose and correct these long-standing academic errors.

It is still often said that Roman Mithrasism was derived from Mithra, a Zoroastrian angelic figure from Persia. This incorrect assumption was derived in the 19th century and although it was challenged in the 1870s by a German scholar, K B Stark, this view has prevailed right up until the 1970s. But there seem to be few if any points of contact between Roman Mithras and the Persian Mithra, for there is no bull-slaying by a Phrygian cap-wearing Mithras within the Persian cult of Mithra. And neither did the Zoroastrian Mithra hold secret initiatory ceremonies in underground chambers. Perhaps, then, we should rightfully conclude that Roman Mithras did not come from the Persia Mithra - it may well have originally been an eastern religion, but it had nothing to do with Mithra.

The true origins of Roman Mithras will have to wait until the next chapter, as it is the Arthurian *Vulgate Cycle* that will point us in the right direction and it would be a shame to spoil that interesting and surprising story. However, we can still look at what the symbolism of Mithras referred to. K B Stark, the German scholar just mentioned, suggested that it was a cosmic religion and that all the characters in this drama were stars or constellations. The bull was obviously Taurus; Mithras was Perseus; the dog drinking the bull's blood was Canis Minor; the scorpion nipping the bull's balls was Scorpio; while the snake was Hydra.

While Stark was correct in the broad outlines of his theory, it is obvious that he lacked a knowledge of the precessional cycle of the zodiac, otherwise he would have quickly understood the symbolism of this bull-slaying scene, or the tauroctony as it is sometimes called. In reality, this standard scene and symbolism, which is replicated in nearly all the lodge-chambers of Mithras, is simply a retelling of the great Babylonian epic of Gilgamesh. There is no point going through an explanation of Gilgamesh once again, as it was fully described in *King Jesus*. Suffice it to say that Gilgamesh - armed with his bow and club or axe, and his sword hanging from his belt - was actually an image of the constellation of Orion. And the task of Gilgamesh-Orion was to kill the Bull of Heaven, which was obviously a manifestation of Taurus the bull.

So why was Gilgamesh-Orion slaying the constellation of Taurus? Because of the precession of the equinox. As has been explained many times previously, the constellations change with the passing millennia, with each of the Great Months for each constellation of the zodiac lasting on average 2,140 years. Some of the constellations and their corresponding Great Months are longer than others, but the eras for these changes in the constellations are written in the heavens above and so we can be quite confident that the

Gilgamesh epic was written in about 1750 BC, when the Great Month of Taurus ended and the Great Month of Aries began. And it was the job of Gilgamesh-Orion, as the ring-master and director of the heavens, to ensure that Taurus (the bull) was killed so that Aries (the ram) could be the victor and the new sovereign of the heavens. So here we see this same connection between the Ursa-Major-Arthur figure and the Hercules-Orion figure, who were both regarded as being the ring-masters of the precessional cycle, depending on how the circle of the zodiac was being depicted. And in the case of Mithras, it was most definitely Orion-Hercules-Mithras who was being portrayed as the king of the cosmos and director of the precessional cycle.

So now we are in a position to fully decypher the tauroctony, the bull-slaying scene of Mithras. The bull is Taurus; Mithras is Orion-

Fig 3.6
Mithras wearing a Phrygian cap and slaying a bull. Note the Sun and Moon in the corners of the image, while Mithras cuts the jugular vein of the bull. Mithras is Orion-Hercules, the ring-master and director of the heavens, while the bull is the constellation of Taurus.

Gilgamesh-Hercules; the dog is Orion's dog or Sirius; the snake is Draco; while the raven is the Phoenix, the sacred avian of the precessionary cycle. And of course there are the Sun and Moon in the upper corners, surveying this scene. So just like Gilgamesh-Orion in the Babylonian epic of Gilgamesh, Mithras is also slaying the constellation and Great Month of Taurus the bull, in order that we might move onto the Great Month of Aries the ram. And so Mithras is symbolic of the constellation of Orion-Hercules. But we know from the predictable precession of the constellations that this event actually happened in about 1750 BC, and so the cult of Mithras was supremely out of date by the time it arrived in Rome in the 1st century BC. In fact, to be more precise it was some 1,700 years out of date. Why this happened and where this cult came from, will be explained in Chapter VI.

And while it may seem strange that an Empire-wide cult of such magnitude and influence could be so supremely wrong about the era of its fundamental beliefs and doctrines, exactly the same has happened with modern astrology. Western astrology obviously saw the chronological errors within Mithras and were able to update their beliefs and predictions in the 1st century AD. And we know this because the modern astrological calendar still points at the first point of Pisces, the cusp between the constellations of Aries and Pisces. But this astrological star-chart has never been updated since that time, and so all of modern astrology is 28 precessional days out of date. And since each day or degree in the precessional cycle equates to about 71.3 solar years, the 'modern' star-chart used by astrologers has not been updated since the birth of King Jesus-Izas and is 2,000 years out of date.

However, it is surprising that Mithras was quite so much out of date,

Fig 3.7
The bull-slaying scene from Mithras is often overtly linked to the circle of the zodiac, as depicted here, demonstrating that this scene is a component in the precessionary cycle of the zodiac. Mithras is Orion-Hercules, the governor and director of the heavens.

because the little we do know about Mithras suggests that its practitioners did know about the precessionary cycle. Origen says of Mithras that:

> Celsus also describes some Persian mysteries, where he says: These truths are obscurely represented by the teaching of the Persians and by the mystery of Mithras which is of Persian origin. For in the latter there is a symbol of the two orbits of heaven, the one being that of the fixed stars and the other that assigned to the planets, and of the soul's passage through these. The symbol is this. There is a ladder with seven gates and at its top an eighth gate. (Contra Celsum, 6:22)

Origen, quoting Celsus, says that these were Persian mysteries. Note that they are not described as being the mysteries of the Persian Mithra, but just Persian mysteries. And they did indeed originally come from Persia, via the Babylonian Jews who came to Syria and Judaea, although their true origin prior to that was from Egypt.

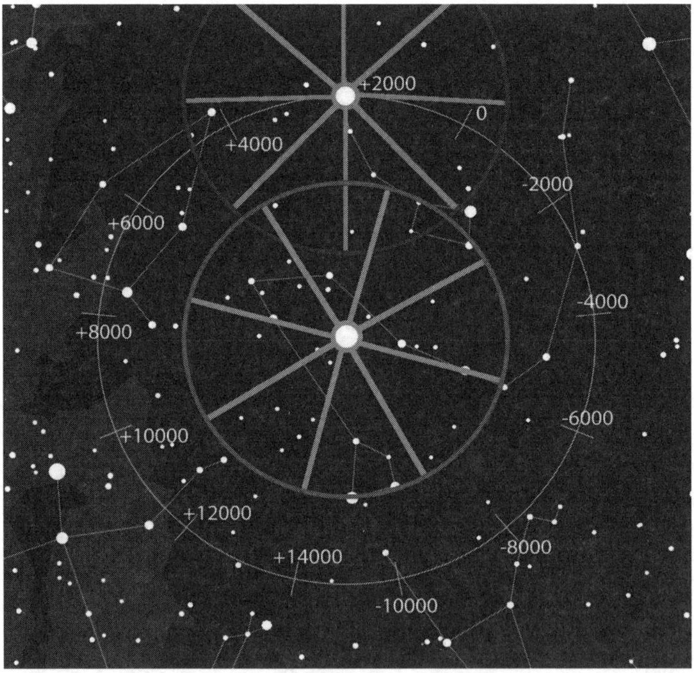

Fig 3.8
The 'two orbits of heaven' as Celsus describes them, or the two wheels of 'King Arthur's cosmic wagon' as Arthurian history sometimes calls them. These two great wheels in the heavens are the wheels of the ecliptic circle (lower red) and the celestial circle (upper blue). It is the slow movement of the celestial wheel around the ecliptic wheel that causes the precession of the equinox and the changes in the Great Months. The numbers around the ecliptic circle are years AD and BC.

Then there is the peculiar description of the two orbits (or wheels) of heaven. This is a description of King Arthur's cosmic cart, and therefore a description of the mechanics of precession. In the diagram shown in fig 3.8, the heavens above rotate daily around the axle of the upper (blue) celestial wheel. But every 71.3 years the entire upper (blue) wheel will move one degree anti-clockwise around the perimeter of the lower (red) ecliptic wheel. This is precessional motion, and this is what drives the change in the Great Months, from Taurus to Aries and onto Pisces. (In reality, these wheels should be slightly larger and intersect more. Their circumferences should touch the center of the other circle.)

But if the Mithraic priesthood understood the layout of celestial precession, then why did their symbolism become 1,750 years out of date? It is difficult to tell. It may be that they did not understand the mechanics of these two precessional cosmic wheels. It may be that the Roman soldiery liked the imagery of killing bulls, rather than slaying sheep. It may be that the symbolism of Mithras killing a ram was held in reserve for only the highest of initiates, but if that was so we have no evidence for this alternate symbolism.

We shall see evidence in later chapters that the knowledge of the precessional zodiac came from the Nazarene Ebionites of Syrio-Judaea, the sect of Jesus and James. Crucially, however, Chapter VI will also demonstrate that it is unlikely that Roman Mithras was derived from that primary source, and so Rome may well have picked up an out-of-date version of this Sabaean astrological-astronomical creed and not realised their error. And so James the Just must have been chuckling into his cassock, about the ignorance of the barbarian Romans venerating an out-of-date Taurus.

No matter how the Romans acquired the cult of Mithras, some elements of it obviously survived. The image in fig 3.9 is from William Blake's *Jerusalem*. The composition is based upon the masonic 1st degree tracing-board, and yet it displays many similarities with the Mithraic bull-slaying scene. There is the Sun and Moon in the upper left and right corners, the association with stars, and the prominent Mithras (Los) character in the center. Then there are blacksmiths tongs that could be seen as a pair of dividers. Blake placed a very similar pair of dividers in the hands of god in another painting, for sub-dividing the regions of the heavens - and so the possessor of these dividers or tongs is the architect of the heavens, just as Orion-Hercules-Mithras is the ring-master and director of the precessional heavens. And then there is the large hammer, and although this appears to be another tool of a common artisan it is also the hammer or axe that was prominently wielded by Orion, Hercules and Gilgamesh.

So the central figure in Blake's composition is again symbolic of Orion-Hercules, the ring-leader and arbiter of the heavens, which is why Los-

Fig 3.9 Los from William Blake's 'Jerusalem' – a symbolic copy of an already symbolic First Degree masonic tracing board. The central character is Los, who is linked here with Stonehenge, and is flanked on the left and the right by the Sun and the Moon. Note the distinct similarity with the Mithra bull-slaying imagery. Undoubtedly Blake must have seen and copied some of these elements from Mithraic symbolism, especially those 'legs' of Stonehenge which are splayed out in the same fashion as the legs of the Mithraic bull.

Orion has an image of the Stonehenge Sun-temple behind him. And if Orion can be directly equated with Hercules, and we shall see further evidence for this in later chapters, then the central figure in this composition is also an image of King Arthur. As we saw in a previous chapter, King Arthur's strange conception story, his adoption, and his twelve battles were all based upon the equivalent events in the life of Hercules. And so it is likely that Blake has placed an image of Stonehenge behind this Orion-Hercules-Arthur figure not simply because it is a Sun-temple, but also because Stonehenge was said to be the mausoleum for King Aurelius Ambrosius and King Uther Pendragon.

IV

Perceval

Perceval, Story of the Grail - Chretien de Troyes

Perceval is the last of the Arthurian manuscripts written by Chretien de Troyes, a late 12th century poet from Troyes in northeastern France, and it remained unfinished at the author's death. So once again we have the peculiar situation where a Norman French poet is more concerned with the history of Britain than the history of France. Although it has to be acknowledged that the Plantagenet kings of England at this time were Norman French, being descended from the Counts of Anjou. Which is why Henry II of England was the Duke of Normandy and Aquitaine until 1189, as was Richard I who reigned after him. And just to add to these links and connections, the Duke of Anjou and Brittany at the turn of the 13th century was a grandson of King Henry II who was called Arthur.

However, despite the monarchs of England being nominally Norman French, it is still odd that Norman French poets would be more concerned with English matters than French. When England produced its own playwright of international renown, William Shakespeare, his historical plays were all about English rather than French monarchs. So why were the Norman French so interested in King Arthur of Britain? The answer, surely, is that Arthur was not a British king, he was an pan-European king whose life and history had been brought back to Normandy following the First Crusade.

In classical Arthurian research it is often claimed that *Perceval* was written before *High History*, partly because it was dedicated to Philip I of Flanders who died in 1190, while *High History* was dedicated to Lord Jehan of Nesle and so is thought to have been a later work than this. But these dates only apply to the extant manuscripts, and there may well have been earlier copies that have been lost or destroyed. Yet Nigel Bryant, the modern translator of *High History* goes even further than the usual arguments by saying:

> It is clear from the very first page of *High History* that the author has assumed a knowledge of Chretien de Troyes' *Perceval*. (High History introduction.)

This 'clear assumption' is not explained by Bryant, and so it remains far from clear why *Perceval* should precede *High History*. The truth of the matter is that Chretien's *Perceval* represents a softer, more humourous, better composed, and much more entertaining version of *High History* - a revised version that leaves out all the blood, gore, dubious morality and Bible-bashing that *High History* revels in. So it is much more likely that *Perceval* was derived from *High History* and sought to improve upon it, which would not be difficult as *High History* is hardly bedtime reading material. But it is most unlikely that the reverse has happened.

Having said this, another option is that Chretien de Troyes has based *Perceval* upon a common source. There are three very similar accounts of Arthurian history: *High History*, *Perceval* and *Parzival*. Yet there are significant differences between these manuscripts too, and not simply added fantasies that an author could create without inside knowledge or an additional source. So the most likely option is that there was another common source manuscript that has been lost to history, and each of these authors has emphasised different events from within that story and interpreted its theology, history, and meaning in a slightly different fashion.

The makeover

The story that Chretien has crafted in *Perceval* follows *High History* very closely, but is much nicer in nearly all respects. But these amendments to the story do mean that much of the original occult (hidden) information has been lost. But it is likely that Chretien did understand who the characters in the story really were, because he has deliberately crafted his work from a very different perspective. For instance, Chretien casts Perceval as a rustic fool, instead of a grievously and unfairly persecuted hero. Clearly, Chretien is approaching this entire story from the opposite viewpoint to *High History's* author.

Nevertheless, it is clear that *High History* followed the original source manuscript much more closely than has *Perceval*. Chretien may have understood who Perceval was in the historical record, but it would appear that he did not understand all of the underlying history that underpins Arthurian literature. And the net result is that he has lost a great deal of the story and therefore much of the covert information. For example, the young Perceval is out in the forest hunting deer when he sees some knights, just as he does in *High History*, but he is so naive and rustic he thinks the shining knights are angels. Perceval then starts asking questions about their equipment, what it was made of and what its purpose was. The sort of questions a simpleton would ask, like 'what is a shield?' Perceval then asks what the knight's hauberk is, his chain-mail vest. The knight replies:

> 'It is my hauberk, young man, and it is as heavy as iron, for it is made of iron as you can see.' ... 'What is it for?' (asked Perceval) 'Young man that is easy, if you tried to throw a javelin or shoot an arrow at me you couldn't do me any injury'. 'Sir knight,' (said Perceval) 'I hope god will never let the hinds and harts have such hauberks, for I would not be able to kill any and could never hunt them again'. (Perceval 270-275) *

The story is now sitting on a literary precipice. It is just waiting for Perceval to test out this new theory of the invincible hauberk on the next knight he sees, which is exactly what he did in *High History*. But in *High History* the hauberk was not as impenetrable as Perceval thought, and his javelin went straight through the armour of the Red Knight and killed him:

> Perceval left tracking the stag ... and he saw the Red Knight was conquering the White Knight. He launched one of his javelins at the Red Knight so hard it pierced his habergeon and made it pass through his heart ... 'I thought,' said Perlesvaus (Perceval), 'that nothing would ever pierce or damage a knight's armour, otherwise I would not have run him through with my javelin.' (High History 1:11) (Author's brackets.)

This is clearly the same story. Perceval had been told that a hauberk is impregnable, but on testing out the theory he discovered it was not quite so invincible as he thought. And in the previous chapter we then launched into a great enquiry as to who this Red Knight (the knight of the Red Shield) really was, because his full identity is not given. He was certainly one of the three or four leading brother-monarchs in the story and quite possibly

* The reference numbers are from the Burton Raffal translation, and refer to the lines-numbers in the original poem.

Perceval's own father.

But Chretien's *Perceval* ignores all of this intrigue completely. There is no accidental murder of a knight and so there is no possibility of fratricide, and so the story is much more suitable for bed-time reading without encouraging nightmares. And yet a great deal of valuable information has been lost in the process. There are no royal knights to name, so there is no genealogy, and we also lose much of the rationale behind Perceval's later concerns and actions. In *High History* it was the killing of this Red Knight that caused the bitter family feud that led to the persecution of the Widow Lady (Perceval's mother), her land becoming a wasteland, and Perceval being disinherited. But if there is no murder of the Red Knight, then the story is lost from the very beginning.

Perceval does eventually kill the Red Knight in *Perceval,* later in the story, but this is a 'legitimate' execution because the Red Knight had stolen King Arthur's gold cup, insulted the queen, and was plotting against Camelot. And Perceval does so by throwing his spear through the eye-piece of the Red Knight's helmet, which will become important in the next chapter. Perceval then takes the Red Knight's armour to become the new and much feared Red Knight, just as Sir Galahad was known as the Red Knight. So again the reasoning for Perceval's dispossession and his desire for revenge are completely lost in this revised version of the story.

Later manuscripts again allude to this fratricide, but even more obliquely than does Chretien. In both *Erec and Enide* and *Roman de Fergus,* the story starts with King Arthur out on a hunt and killing a white hart or stag. The allusion here to the killing of the knight who bore the symbol of a white hart (Perceval's father) is obvious, but only if we already know the original story. So it is possible that these later authors did not understand the underlying history and were only writing pleasant stories. The hero of *Roman de Fergus* is called Fergus, a Celtic name meaning 'Strong Man'. Fergus goes from being a royal rustic to becoming a knight of King Arthur and being challenged to vanquish the Black Knight (instead of the Red Knight); which is exactly the same story that is narrated in *High History* and *Perceval.* So Fergus is quite obviously another name for Perceval, but why his name has been changed in this fashion is unknown. Why change the name of a famous hero into something so obscure that readers no longer know what this story is about?

Another transformation in Chretien's *Perceval,* is evident in the tale of the lady with the jealous husband. Chretien has managed to conflate the 'Tale of the Tent of the Evil Custom' and the 'Tale of the Jealous Husband' into one story. But this is a minor alteration, and the story is still arranged so that the naive Perceval is once more alone with a certain lady, and so her husband suspects adultery. And so the husband exclaims:

> 'He kissed you?' 'Yes,' (said the lady), 'but I assure you it was against my will.' 'No, you liked it and were pleased by it! ... Do you think I don't know you? Indeed, I know you only too well ... You have embarked on a wicked path ... you will follow me naked on foot, until I have cut off his (Perceval's) head, for nothing else will satisfy me.' (Perceval 810-830) (Author's brackets.)

And then the story goes on to tell of Perceval on the road to 'Carlisle', as if nothing had happened.

Once more we are missing the climax to the story. The husband is enraged, he wants vengeance, and in *High History* he takes his wife to a pool, whips her until she is almost flayed and thrusts a lance through her chest. One can see why Chretien would want to leave out the murder of the wife, as it is hardly bedtime-reading material, but again he loses the whole point of the story. These strange events were all supposed to be morality tales about the destruction of the Old Law (Nazarene Judaism) and the introduction of the New Law (Simple Judaism). And although the story in *High History* is rather macabre, the whipped and speared wife is supposed to represent Jesus being whipped and stabbed with a lance, so that the Old Law might be terminated and the New Law established.

Perceval does meet up again with the jealous knight much later in the story, and he is still abusing his wife because of his jealousy. But Perceval defeats him in combat and send him to King Arthur to apologize to the court. So again Chretien has lost the original import of these events, in order to create a nice, readable story. This was originally a Christian morality tale about the persecution of Jesus, and it has been turned into a morality tale about not being a jealous husband. Although the original 'parable' in *High History* conveniently forgets the fact that Jesus held to the Old Law (the Nazarene Church), rather than the New Law (the Simple Judaic Church of Saul-Josephus).

Interesting additions

Having said this, it is also possible that Chretien has added some extra material to his manuscript that is useful to this research. For a start he has turned Perceval into a naive and stupid country bumpkin, who knows nothing about courtly manners or knightly combat. In fact, the Perceval in *Perceval* is a complete idiot, and so one has to wonder why this change to the narrative has been made.

The most obvious answer is that Chretien knew who Perceval was. As was alluded to in the last chapter, in the *Vulgate Cycle* the hero-figure known as Perceval is called Sir Galahad instead. This is why Chretien calls Perceval the Welshman, because 'Welshman' means 'Galahad' as we shall see later. And this is also why Robert de Boron in *Merlin Grail* has Perceval sitting in the Perilous Seat, which was the seat reserved for Sir Galahad. But in the *Vulgate Cycle*, Galahad is the son of Joseph(us) of Arimathaea (ie: the son of Saul-Josephus). So if Chretien was not a Simple Judaic Catholic (the Church of Saul-Josephus), and was leaning instead towards a Templar-style Nazarene Gnosticism (the Church of Jesus and James), it would suit him to portray Perceval-Galahad as an ignorant oaf with no manners, style, education or intelligence. And that is exactly what Chretien has done. And so as we proceed through *Perceval* it is probably worth remembering that this story may be representing a diametrically opposed viewpoint to the one presented in *High History* - instead of pitying the persecuted Perceval, this new story laughs at him.

Another interesting snippet of information that Chretien provides, is that Perceval's father was wounded in the thighs. We shall see exactly what

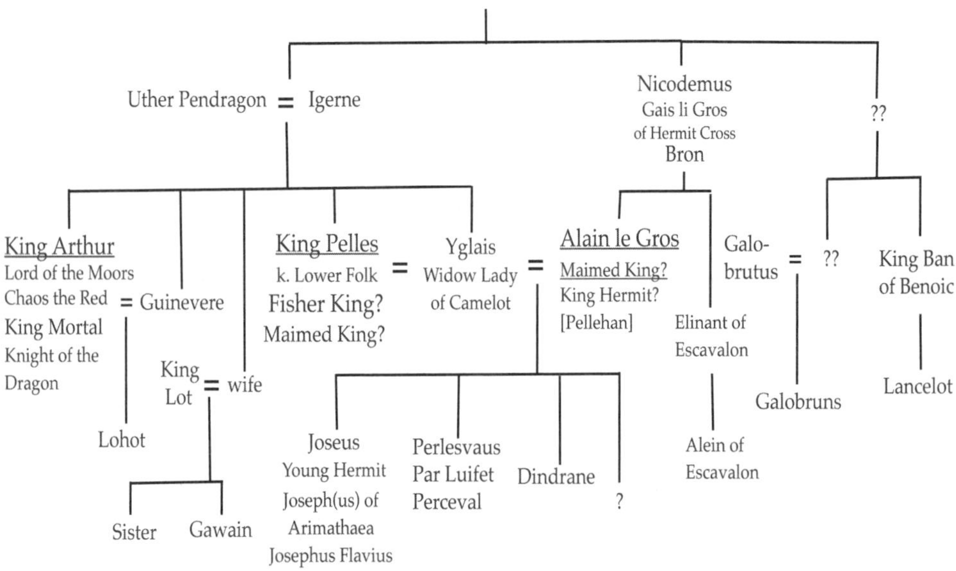

Fig 4.1
The genealogy of Perceval according to Chretien de Troyes. Joseus-Josephus has now moved across to being the son of Alain and the brother of Perceval. But this is also what the Vulgate says, with Josephus being the brother of Sir Galahad. Note that Chretien's manuscript does not mention many of these characters, and so much of this genealogy is taken from High History, with a few amendments mentioned by Chretien.

this means in later chapters, but it does indicate that Alain li Gros, Perceval's father, was seen to be the Wounded King. And the *Vulgate* says exactly the same thing, that the father of Perceval was the Wounded King and therefore also the Hermit King. This means that the Hermit King title should be taken from King Pelles and given to Alain (Pellehan), Perceval's father. And if we do this, then we should also take King Hermit's son, Joseus, and make him a son of Alain too, much as we did in the *High History* genealogy. Joseus was the Young Hermit, and so he must surely follow the line of the wounded Hermit King.

Clamadeu

Perceval then finds the Lady of the Wasteland in her crumbling castle, much as is narrated in *High History*. But here the castle is called Biaurepaire and the lady is named Blancheflor, and in this account she is no longer Perceval's much-persecuted mother but a beautiful princess who falls in love with this oaf-like knight. One can see how Chretien has subtly altered the text here, to introduce a love-scene and a nicer story.

The king who has besieged the lady's castle is no longer her brother (or brother-in-law), but an otherwise unknown King Clamadeu and his seneschal, Anguingueron. But Anguingueron was present at the death of the Wasteland Lady's father, and so he sounds a bit like the many persecutors of the Widow Lady of the Wasteland in the account in *High History*. However, the story has changed quite radically here, because King Clamadeu has come from abroad with a huge army to besiege the Lady of the Wasteland in her castle. But Perceval challenges both Anguingueron and Clamadeu to single combat and defeats them both, and so Clamadeu is forced to sue for peace, although he refuses to be a prisoner of Blancheflor:

> Clamadeu was compelled to beg for mercy and to grant the youth (Perceval) everything he asked ... but nothing could compel him to accept imprisonment in Biaurepaire ... nor would he go to the gentleman's castle magnificent castle for all the empire of Rome. But he was quite ready to swear to offer himself as a prisoner to King Arthur ... He is called Clamadeu of the Isles, and a knight without peer in all the Roman Empire. (Perceval 2685, 2780)

The mention of the Roman Empire here suggests that King Clamadeu is an earlier version of the *Vulgate's* King Claudas, who was also from Rome and prosecuted a war against Kings Bors and Ban and then against King Arthur's forces. But as we shall see later, King Claudas turns out to be a pseudonym for Legatus Vespasian (Emperor Vespasian), who prosecuted the Jewish

Revolt against the Edessan Nazarenes of King Izas-Jesus in Judaea. The nominative progression is as follows:

King Clau...das
King Clam..des
King Clamadeu

However, if King Clamadeu and King Claudas really are equivalent characters in this tale, then we can see here the extent to which Chretien has amended the story not only to make it softer and nicer, but also to divorce it from the real history it was based upon. And this may not be simply due to Chretien not knowing or perhaps disagreeing with the underlying history, it may simply be a case of Chretien not wanting to get any closer to the hot pokers of the Inquisition. The more sensitive data that the author includes in his story, the greater the likelihood that an inquisitive Church censor might discover what this story is really about. And with discretion proving to be the better part of valor, Chretien has obviously decided to reduce the role of Claudas-Vespasian into a minor character involved in an unsuccessful siege.

Fisher King

Later on in the text, Perceval meets with the Fisher King in his castle, but the Fisher King is being described here as the Maimed King (the Wounded King). But Chretien has already said that Perceval's father was the Wounded King, and so Alain li Gros was both the Fisher and Wounded king. This conflicts somewhat with a later comment in *Perceval*; and it also conflicts with *Vulgate Cycle*, which has King Pelles as the Fisher King and King Pellehan (Perceval's father) as the Wounded King.

The *Vulgate's* genealogy would make more sense, as it was Jesus who was the first Fisher King (or the son of the first Fisher King), which is why Jesus led a fishing expedition on the Sea of Galilee and why his disciples were known as fishers of men. Although it should be pointed out that these titles were hereditary and so there were entire dynasties of Fisher Kings and Wounded Kings. The Fisher title referred to the constellation of Pisces, while the Wounded King was a reference to the Galli priesthood as we shall see in the following chapters. But in *Perceval* and *Merlin Grail* the Fisher King and the Wounded King are the same person, and he was also the Guardian of the Holy Grail. And so it is in the castle of the conflated Wounded Fisher King that Perceval finally witnesses the grand procession of the Holy Grail:

> A squire came forth from a chamber carrying a white lance ... Everyone in the hall

> saw the white lance with its white point from whose tip issues a drop of blood ... The youth (Perceval) observed this marvel but refrained from asking how it came about, for he recalled the admonishment given by the gentleman who had knighted him, who taught and instructed him not to talk too much...
>
> Two other squires entered holding in their hands a candelabra of pure gold ... A maiden accompanying the two squires was carrying the Grail with her two hands; she was beautiful, noble and richly attired. After she entered the hall carrying the Grail, the room was so brightly illuminated that the candles lost their brilliance, like the stars and the Moon when the Sun rises. The Grail was of fine pure gold. Set in the Grail were precious stones of many kinds, the best and costliest to be found in earth or sea...
>
> Meanwhile, the Grail passed again in front of them and the youth again did not ask who was served by the Grail ... With each course that was served he saw the Grail pass by completely uncovered before him. But he did not learn who was served from it, even though he wanted to know. (Perceval 3210-3310)

This is the traditional perception of the Holy Grail, that it is a golden chalice that served the knights of the Round Table with the choicest of foods. This golden Grail had been used by Joseph of Arimathaea to collect some drops of blood from the body of Jesus, after he had been wounded with a spear on the cross. And this is supposedly why this chalice became sacred and why we have the story of the bleeding spear; although the symbology of the bleeding lance may be more symbolic of Nazarene circumcision and castration, than of the lance that pierced Jesus on the cross. So the Holy Grail had always been closely connected with the Holy Blood of Jesus and therefore with the Holy Bloodline of Jesus, and we shall see in a later chapter how this Grail cup morphs into a Grail bloodline.

Perceval was highly honoured to have seen and been served by this semi-magical golden Grail-cup, as were Sir Galahad and Sir Lancelot in the later Arthurian manuscripts. But the old and infirm Wounded Fisher King needed to find a successor before he died, to pass on the Grail and its secret traditions. And this was why Perceval was invited to the ceremony, for he was a possible candidate to inherit this esteemed position. But the account in *Perceval* is confused about who the Wounded Fisher King is, and therefore which side of this family should inherit the Grail. It is clearly stated in *Perceval* that the Wounded Fisher King was the maternal uncle of Perceval, and thus from the King Pelles side of this family, while simultaneously forgetting that Perceval's father was wounded in the thighs, and thus the equivalent of the Wounded King.

In great contrast, Robert de Boron in *Merlin Grail* says that the Wounded Fisher King was Perceval's grandfather, who is called Bron or

Hebron in this account. But upon his death, the Wounded Fisher King title jumped a generation down to Perceval, who was therefore forced to 'wound himself in the thighs' to become the next Wounded Fisher King. So it would appear that there was a competition within this history, for who should claim the Wounded Fisher King title and therefore become the Guardian of the Grail. Sometimes it is the family of King Pelles and Arthur who hold this title, and sometimes it is usurped by Alain and Perceval-Galahad. In this extract from *Merlin Grail*, Perceval is speaking to his grandfather, Bron-Hebron:

> 'Sire, you should know that Alain li Gros, your son, was my father.' When the Fisher King heard this his elation redoubled, and he said: 'dear grandson (Perceval) I am very glad you have come' ... Then the aged Bron (the Fisher King) placed the Holy Grail in Perceval's hands ... and taught Perceval the sacred words that Joseph (of Arimathaea) had taught him, which I cannot and must not tell you (the reader) ... And with that he (Bron) passed away ... And with that Merlin took Blaise and led him to the house of the (new) Fisher King, whose name was Perceval. (Merlin Grail p155, 156.) (Author's brackets.)

Fig 4.2
A typical image of the Holy Grail as a golden chalice studded with precious stones. This image is from the front cover of 'Jesus, Last of the Pharaohs', which is why it has an image of Tutankhamen on the front.

In this account the Fisher title is firmly held within Perceval's side of the family, and passes from Bron-Hebron (Gais li Gros) to Perceval-Galahad. But this claim may be a distortion of the truth. Reading between the lines, the real Wounded Fisher King and Grail Guardian was probably King Pelles, on the Arthurian side of this family. But following the events of the

Jewish Revolt, the title and the Grail ended up in the hands of Joseph of Arimathaea and his son Josephus, and was then bequeathed to Perceval-Galahad, as we shall see later in the *Vulgate Cycle's* account of these events.

Another reoccurring theme in all of these stories is the great misfortune that befell the Fisher King and his lands. Because Perceval-Galahad had not asked who the Holy Grail served or honoured, the king's wounds would never heal and his realm became a wasteland, just as the lands of Perceval's mother had become a wasteland in *High History*. But in great contrast with *High History*, this misfortune was no longer the fault of largely unknown evil monarchs, it was the fault of Perceval himself, because he had not asked the pertinent question about the Grail. Perhaps the best description of this sad but puzzling lament is to be found here, in *Perceval*:

> Ah, Perceval, Fortune is bald behind and hairy in front. Cursed be anyone who would greet you, because you did not catch hold of Fortune when you met her.
>
> You entered the castle of the Fisher King and saw the bleeding lance, but it was so much effort for you to open your mouth and speak that you couldn't ask why that drop of blood flowed from the shaft! And you didn't ask what rich man was served by the grail you saw. Wretched is the man who sees that the propitious hour has come, but waits for an even better one.
>
> Cursed be the hour you kept your silence since. If you had asked, the rich Fisher King who is suffering would already be healed of his wounds and would be ruling over the land, that he shall now never again command. And do you know the consequence of the king not ruling and not being healed? Ladies will lose their husbands, lands will be laid waste, and maidens will remain as orphans, and many a knight will die. All these troubles will occur because of you. (Perceval 4645-4680)

The description of the lady with hair in front and bald behind is another description of the Roman Fortuna or Greek Tyche, the goddess of fate or fortune. In a Medieval twist to her story, Fortuna sits on her Wheel of Fortune, which is described as a large Ferris Wheel. And the significance of Fortuna's baldness is that you can grasp Fortuna by the hair as she is approaching you, but there is no hair on the back of her head to grasp as she goes away from you. If you wait until Fortuna has passed by, hoping that something better will come along, you can never grasp and pull Fortuna back again. And that is the allusion being made in this quote. Perceval had three chances to ask what the Grail was and whom it served, but he kept silent and waited for another opportunity at a later time. But once Fortuna has gone, she has gone.

This is also why the Grail princess in *High History,* who had long plaited golden hair, suddenly became bald. The author said it was because Perceval did not ask the question about who the Holy Grail served and honoured, which was correct but not very explanatory. In reality, the princess lost her golden hair because she was Fortuna-Tyche herself, and although she had presented Perceval with a 'golden opportunity' (her golden hair), he had not grasped it.

Again, this subtle difference between these two author's interpretations of this same story would suggest a common source for these manuscripts, rather than straight copying. If Chretien had simply been copying *High History* it would have been very difficult for him to understand from the description there, why the golden-haired Grail princess was bald. But the description in the common source manuscript may well have been more obvious, and each author has used that information in a different fashion. And the similarity of the Medieval Wheel of Fortune to a modern Ferris Wheel is elegantly described in *Mort de Arthur*:

> When (King Arthur) fell asleep it seemed like the most beautiful lady in the world appeared and took him onto the highest mountain he had ever seen; and there she sat him on a wheel. The wheel had seats, some of which rose as others sank. The king saw that his was in the highest position ... "This is the Wheel of Fortune," she said, "and what do you see." "Lady it seems like I see the whole world." "Indeed," she said, "but such are the effects of earthly pride that no one is so highly placed that he can avoid falling from worldly power." And then she took him and dashed him to the ground... (*Mort* 23:227) (Author's quotes.)

The Wheel of Fortune is a popular theme in Medvieval literature. However, the Wheel being described in *Mort* is much more sophisticated than the one illustrated in Siena Cathedral in fig 4.3. There is no need for someone hang onto the Wheel of Fortune in Arthurian history, for this is clearly some kind of Ferris Wheel with seats. And so King Arthur can sit in some comfort and see the entire world and his fortune pass before him. But Arthur's good fortune had passed its peak, and he was about to be dashed to the ground.

But why was the land laid waste and Arthur (or the Widow Lady) dispossessed from their lands, simply because Perceval did not ask who the Grail honoured or served? *Quest for the Holy Grail* from the *Vulgate Cycle* indicates that the reason for King Arthur's court becoming deserted was because the nature of the Grail was not clear, and so the knights all depart on a quest to find out what the Grail is or means. But as Arthur observes: 'once these knights have left they will never gather here again.' And so it was the quest itself that caused the decline of Camelot into a wasteland. In contrast, *High History* intimates that the reason was more pragmatic than esoteric: the dispossession and wasteland had simply been caused by a bitter family feud. The Knight of the Red Shield (Perceval's father?) had been killed, the family was now at war, and the Widow Lady had been dispossessed from her lands.

Another reason for King Arthur's realm becoming a wasteland is given to us in *Lancelot*. Here we have another pragmatic explanation, for the wasteland is blamed upon a Roman invasion of Arthur's lands, which will be explored in later chapters. This was the great invasion by King Claudas (ie: Legatus Vespasian), as was mentioned previously. Yet the New Testament gospels give a very similar description of a king being dispossessed from his lands:

> (Jesus said) Think not that I am come to send peace on earth: I came not to send peace, but a sword. For I am come to set a man at variance against his father, and the daughter against her mother, and the daughter in law against her mother in law. And a man's foes shall be they of his own household. He that loves father or mother more than me is not worthy of me: and he that loves son or daughter more than me is not worthy of me. (Matthew 10:43-37)

> (Jesus said) And you shall hear of wars and rumours of wars ... For nation shall

Fig 4.3
The Wheel of Fortune on the floor of Siena Cathedral, which was originally designed in 1372. There are four main spokes to the Wheel of Fortune. Starting from the left we have: regnabo; regno; regnavi; sum sine regno. (I shall reign; I reign; I have reigned; I have lost my kingdom.)

King Arthur's Wheel of Fortune was much more sophisticated than this, in having seats just like a large Ferris Wheel. The earliest Ferris Wheels are said to date from the early 17th century, but the description in 'Morte d'Arthur' indicates that children's Ferris Wheels were a feature of fairs and fetes even in the 13th century.

> rise against nation, and kingdom against kingdom: and there shall be famines, and pestilences, and earthquakes, in divers places. All these are the beginning of sorrows. (Matthew 24:6-9)

It would appear that the family feud or the war that dispossessed the Fisher King and King Arthur from their lands is very closely related to the gospel's account of the Jewish Revolt, which ended up with the dispossession and exile King Jesus-Izas. And because of this great feud or war, King Arthur-Jesus was now descending to the bottom of the Ferris Wheel of Fortune, instead of ascending to its apex. Fortuna had passed on by, the golden opportunity had been lost, and there was no golden hair on the back of her head to grasp and bring her back.

V

Parzival

Parzival - Wolfram von Eschenbach

Not content with having Norman French writers composing epic poems about King Arthur of Britain, we now have German poets doing the same. Hartman von Aue was the first of the many Germanic Arthurian authors, but it was Wolfram von Eschenbach who became the most famous and celebrated. Eschenbach was a knight from Bavaria who composed a number of epic stories including: *Willehalm,* the story of Guillaume of Gellone (William of Orange), and *Parzival,* the Arthurian story of Parzival (Sir Perceval). Eschenbach's Arthurian history appears to be based upon Chretien de Troyes' *Perceval,* or perhaps upon the common source manuscript that all three of these authors used, but with some interesting additions from another source entirely. But why would a German knightly laureate be interested in the history of British kings, rather than the German monarchy? Again we are faced by the prospect of King Arthur being more international than British.

Eschenbach's patron was Herman of Thuringia, and from this and other clues in the text, historians have derived a date of somewhere between 1200 and 1210 for the composition of *Parzival.* In the middle of this manuscript Kyot the Provencal is credited as being the translator of this story from a heathen tongue to Norman French, while Eschenbach further translated it from French to German. As we shall see later, the original text was probably in Aramaic. Within modern academia Kyot is regarded as being a fictional creation by Eschenbach. However, since the *Vulgate Cycle* credits Walter Kayo as being the source for *History of the Grail,* perhaps there is some substance in this attribution. Who Walter Kayo was is again unknown, but it is quite likely that Kayo and Kyot were the same person, with the Norman version acquiring the traditional French silent 't'.

Since *Parzival* is retelling the history of the famous King Arthur of Britain, Eschenbach starts his tale exactly where you would expect it to start - in Baghdad and Nineveh in modern Iraq! Precisely! As we have seen, time and time again, most of Arthurian history is not very British and not very 5th century either.

For some unexplained reason Gahmuret, the father of Parzival (Perceval), became an errant knight working for King Barus of Babylon, who conquered Pompeius and Ipomedon of Babylon. (Thus Gahmuret is a new name for Alain li Gros or Pellehan.) And if this opening sequence sounds highly unlikely then it is time to readjust our perception of what Arthurian history is all about, because the *Vulgate Cycle* narrates these inexplicable deviations to the storyline all the time, as we shall see in the following chapters. But these unlikely detours into Syria and Iraq are richly embroidered with real and sometimes secret historical facts, so let us indulge Eschenbach for a while, and see where he takes us.

What we have in these opening chapters of *Parzival* is a prequel to the story we have just seen in *Perceval*. This prequel is the story of Parzival-Perceval's father, who became a knight in eastern Syrio-Mesopotamia and then the king of a land somewhere in eastern Syria or Mesopotamia. Yes, this is still supposed to be a 5th century Normo-British story, even though *Parzival* gives us no solid chronological pegs to hold onto and sets the story somewhere in Mesopotamia:

> There were once two brothers of Babylon, Pompeius and Ipomedon, from who the (king) Barus seized Nineveh, which had always belonged to their forebears. (Parzival 236 of 7000)

Nineveh used to lie on the east-bank of the Tigris river and was the capital of Assyria. It was once the largest city in the world, until it was sacked by the Babylonians and Persians in 612 BC and left to the desert sands. And so completely destroyed and deserted was the city, that Nineveh was merely the faded memory of a ghost city, even to the ancient Greeks.

In which case, who were the Arthurian Pompeius and Ipomedon of Nineveh? For a part of the answer to this we have to look into a surprising location, to Gilbert Fitzbaderon, Lord of Monmouth. Gilbert was from the next generation after Geoffrey of Monmouth, but it is axiomatic that Gilbert, as a Lord of Monmouth, would have known and read Geoffrey's earlier *History of Kings*. And because of his love of literature Gilbert Fitzbaderon became a patron of the arts, and more importantly the patron of an errant bard called Hue de Rotelande of Credenhill.

And what does all this have to do with Nineveh and Babylon, readers may ask? Surprisingly, Rotelande wrote a bawdy romance called *Ipomedon*. And the hero of this tale is a prince of Apulia in southern Italy called Ipomedon. Interesting, isn't it. We have to travel from Mesopotamia all the way to Monmouth on the borders of England and Wales, to find out who Ipomedon is. And even then we only find a pseudonym for a prince of southern Italy. And the reason for Rotelande involving southern Italy in these Norman sagas, is that a Norman count called Roger of Hauteville conquered southern Italy and Sicily in the mid to late 11th century. This was not a Norman conquest of Italian Italy, of course, but instead the largely forgotten reconquest of Muslim controlled Italy. So an entire generation before the First Crusade set off to the Near East, Christian knights were already retaking the lands of southern Europe from their Muslim oppressors, who had invaded the region in the 9th century. Calabria was liberated in 1062, Toledo was liberated in 1085 during the Spanish Reconquista, while Roger of Hauteville liberated Sicily and Malta in 1091 and became King Roger I of Sicily.

Strangely enough all of these 11th century events became a part and parcel of Arthurian history, because King Arthur was an adaptable hero who could be recast into many roles. And so in *Floriant and Florete,* an early 13th century Norman manuscript, King Arthur sets off to conquer Sicily, which was being held by the Emperor of Constantinople. The author would have to invoke (Roman) Constantinople as the enemy of King Arthur, as this was the only empire he could possibly have opposed in this supposedly 5th or 6th century era. But in reality, the author of this manuscript is recasting King Arthur as King Roger I of Sicily, while Floriant is a Sicilian equivalent of Sir Lancelot. And the story even relocates King Arthur's eventual burial to Mount Etna. Being educated in Italy, Gervase of Tilbury said much the same in his *Otia Imperialia*. He recorded the improbable claim that there was a deep cave in the side of Mount Etna, that widened into the broad plain of Avalon where King Arthur's tomb resided.

However, the evil empire that this composite King Arthur-Roger was actually opposing in Sicily, was the 11th century Muslim Caliphate, which had invaded and occupied the region a century or so previously. And so in the mid 11th century the Muslims did indeed control most of the Greek islands, Crete, Cyprus, much of coastal Anatolia, most of southern Italy, and almost all of Spain and Portugal. So *Floriant and Florete,* was simply a recasting of the Arthurian story to suit the contemporary events in southern Italy; a region that was badly in need of a conquering Christian hero like King Arthur. Modern playwrights will often do the same, by recasting Shakespearian works into a contemporary setting, thus spreading the fame of well-known Shakespearian characters well beyond their original settings and eras.

Anyway, in Rotelande's pseudo-Arthurian story, *Ipomedon,* the young

Normo-Italian Prince Ipomedon was fostered out to a worthy man called Ptolemy. And it is the wise old Ptolemy who teaches the young Ipomedon the arts of courtesy, horsemanship, martial arts and hunting.

> When this boy (Ipomedon) was old enough to learn he was fostered out to a man named Ptolemy, a very worthy man. There was no man in the entire world, emperor or king, whose court he (Ipomedon) would not have been an asset to. He (Ptolemy) taught the child courtesy, horsemanship, how to wield arms in battle and how to hunt. (Ipomedon I)

This is quite obviously the same story that is narrated in *Perceval*, where the young Perceval was tutored by Gornemant of Gohort (Perceval 1548). And the same as Eschenbach's story, where Parzival was tutored by Gurnmanz of Graharz. This is obviously the same tutor, with two pronunciations, and so this Ipomedon character just has to be a pseudonym for Perceval-Parzival. And we know that *Ipomedon* is closely associated with these interconnected

Fig 5.1
The Muslim conquest of Spain is often said by apologists to have been benign and beneficial, but the Reconquista is still celebrated all over Spain. And nowhere more so than Valencia province, where the Christians still defeat the Moorish Muslims some 700 years after the liberation of the region. The costumes get more flamboyant and less authentic with each passing decade. Moros y Cristianos fiesta, Alcoy.

Arthurian stories because the text goes on to say:

> *Sul ne sai pas de mentir l'art: Walter Map reset ben sa part.*
>
> I am not the only one who knows the art of lying: Walter Map is equally good at it. (Ipomedon 7185). [1]

Water Map is credited along with Walter Kayo as being the author of many of the *Vulgate Cycle* manuscripts, including *Quest for the Holy Grail* which will be studied in detail in a later chapter. What Rotelande is saying here, is that both he and Walter Map are using the same obfuscation techniques to cover up the real import of the story they are telling. And therefore it is highly likely that Rotelande is narrating the same events that are to be found in more standard Arthurian histories.

More importantly, perhaps, this also strongly suggests that these Normo-English writers all knew each other and were all singing from the same hymn-sheet. We have already seen how Geoffrey of Monmouth cleverly used a French *chanson* or song called *Gormond et Isembart,* to weave a story about the invasion of the Languedoc by the Muslims into Arthurian history. And now we see Eschenbach similarly weaving *Ipomedon,* another *chanson* type text that is also connected with Monmouth, into his story about Arthurian history. This is reminiscent of an international literary club, where members are covertly utilising each other's material

Fig 5.2
An image of Wolfram von Eschenbach, taken from the Manesse Codex. It is interesting to see that Eschenbach flies his colours from his helmet, in the same manner that a president will fly the nation's flags on the presidential limousine. Not much has changed over the centuries.

in a self congratulatory fashion - resulting in a series of in-joke's that only a select audience of initiates would recognise and understand.

So the creation of these Arthurian manuscripts was not a disjointed enterprise, with isolated authors spread all across Europe who just happened to have an interest in King Arthur. On the contrary, this sharing of common material gives every impression of being a deliberate and coordinated endeavour. And the ultimate goal of this semi-secret cabal of authors, was obviously to bind this information into the national psyche of Europe, so it would not be forgotten.

And it is a tactic that has obviously worked, for who today in Britain does not know of King Arthur and his brave knights of the Round Table? Conversely, who today knows of kings: Burgred, Beorhtwulf, Sigered, Ecgberht, Ceolwulf, Beorhtric, Cynewulf, or Anarawd ap Rhodri, Idwal Foel ap Anarawd, Hywel Dda, Maredudd ab Owain, or even Æthelstan, Edmund, Eadred, Eadwig, Edgar, and Edward the Martyr. This list starts with a few local Saxon monarchs, moves onto some Celto-Welsh kings, and then lists a few of the descendants of King Alfred the Great. These are real monarchs and minor monarchs of the British Isles, and yet they have all drifted into complete obscurity. But King Arthur - the semi-legendary king who cannot be placed with any certainty into the history or chronology of Britain - well everyone knows about King Arthur. Perhaps readers can see how effective this Arthurian enterprise really was.

Pompey

So the young Ipomedon appears to be another incarnation of Perceval-Parzival, who is now based in Italy rather than in Gaul or Britain. However, in Eschenbach's version of this story, Parzival-Ipomedon's father was a king of Parthia or Persia. Why? The answer is that in real history Perceval was related to King Jesus-Izas-Arthur and the rest of the influential Edessan royal family, and this family did indeed come from Parthia-Persia. And although Eschenbach makes a fine play on words with Perceval's name, saying it means Perce-a-val, the French for 'pierce the heart', it may have been derived instead from Perce-val פרסי-ולד meaning 'Persian Child'.

But if Ipomedon was a convenient and covert stand-in for the semi-Persian Perceval-Parzival, then who is his 'brother' in this story: Pompeius of Babylon? The most obvious answer, for those who have read the *Vulgate Cycle*, is Gnaeus Pompeius Magnus or Pompey the Great, the Roman general and Consul of the Roman Republic. And if that may seem like an unlikely solution to this problem, it should be explained that the *Vulgate Cycle* contains several chapters detailing the history of the Third Mithridatic War against

Mithridates VI of Pontus and Tigranes II of Armenia, which lasted from 73 to 63 BC. And the Roman general who successfully prosecuted that war was Pompey the Great.

And so Pompey did indeed become the lord of Nineveh and much of northern Mesopotamia, and could well have become lauded in later generations as being a 'king' of Babylon. We will explore the highly occult (hidden) reason for Pompey the Great becoming a central character in Arthurian history in the next chapter. However, Eschenbach has seen this obvious connection with Pompey the Great coming, and to render it invalid he says:

> Gahmuret received a reliable message that his lord the Barus (King Barus) has been overrun by Babylonians, the first of whom was Ipomedon and the second Pompeius. The latter was a proud nobleman - not the Pompey who fled from Rome in ancient times in fear of Julius Caesar. His uncle on his mothers side was

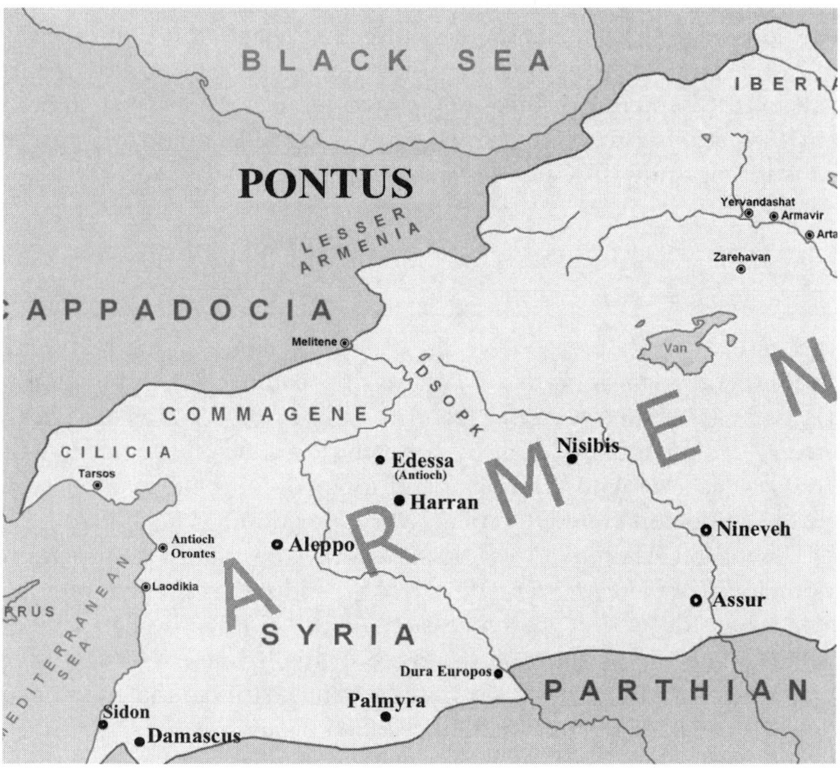

Fig 5.3
Map of the kingdoms of Pontus and Armenia, that were conquered by Pompey the Great in the 60s BC. Note that the region around ancient Nineveh was firmly within the Armenian sphere of influence, before Rome took control of this region.

King Nebuchadnessar, who read in deceitful books that he was himself a god! (Parzival 857 of 7000)

Now that 'clarification' is a chronological pigsty, to say the least. So this Pompeius of Nineveh was not Pompey the Great, because Pompey lived in ancient times. Instead, Pompeius was the nephew of King Nebuchadnessar of Babylon, because he lived in - err - even more ancient times. Actually, this does all make sense, if you know the secrets of the Arthurian cypher. But the answer to this chronological conundrum lies in the *Vulgate Cycle,* which once again implies that these many authors and their heretical patrons were all in contact with one another, and were using the same codes and cyphers in their manuscripts. And in this case, Eschenbach not only knew of the *Vulgate's* secret cypher, he has adopted it and used it in a slightly different fashion.

The first level of this code is simplicity itself. We are not really talking about the 6th century BC Nebuchadnessar here, and so one reason for using this name is simply that it demonstrates that this Pompeius was a Babylonian, rather than a Roman. The second level of this code is both clever and devious in the extreme and points directly towards this Pompeius being a son of the biblical Jesus, but the full explanation of this name will have to wait until Chapter VIII. But perhaps we can clearly see once more that Arthurian history is more concerned with Syrio-Judaea and the East, than with the rolling shires of Celtic or Saxon England.

Patricide

There was a secondary reason for disguising the name of Parzival-Perceval in these opening paragraphs of *Parzival,* by calling him Ipomedon, and that is because when Gahmuret returns to Babylon some years later, this Ipomedon of Babylon kills him by thrusting his lance through his helmet. (Parzival 886 of 7000.) And if Parzival and Ipomedon are the same person, as has just been demonstrated, then Parzival-Ipomedon has just killed his own father, Gahmuret-Alain. And yet this is exactly the same scenario we have seen previously in *High History* and *Perceval,* and will see again later in this chapter, where on two of these occasions Perceval kills the Red Knight by thrusting his spear through the eye-piece of his helmet. And yet this Red Knight turns out to be Perceval's own father, and so this conflated Ipomedon-Perceval-Parzival again appears to have killed his own father. And so we see once again how these Arthurian authors can recount points of history, but distort them sufficiently so that the underlying reality is all but imperceptible to the majority of readers.

In the previous quote we also see that Ipomedon (ie: Parzival) was dispossessed from his lands in Nineveh (ie: his lands in the east), just as Perceval and his Widow Lady mother were both dispossessed from their lands. And in the previous manuscripts we have looked at, this dispossession was caused by the death of the Red Knight (Perceval's father), which resulted in a family feud and the dispossession of Perceval and his Widow Lady mother. *High History* claimed that Perceval had been dispossessed by a combination of kings, who were alternately known as the Lord of the Moors, Knight of the Dragon and King Mortal, and these conflated or related monarch(s) have already been closely identified with King Arthur and his court.

However, in the opening paragraphs of *Parzival* we see that Ipomedon-Parzival was being dispossessed from his eastern lands by King Barus of Babylon. But we have already seen a similar scenario in *Jesus, King of Edessa,* where the Edessan monarchy were involved in a similar civil war or family dispute. And so if this Arthurian dispossession had been caused by a member of the Edessan monarchy, then we might confidently equate this King Barus of Babylon with King Abgarus of Edessa (and Babylon), who was the father of King Izas-Jesus.

It was King Abgarus who took over all these eastern lands in the 1st century AD, forming a kingdom that stretched from Nisibis in the east as far as Edessa and Harran in the west, and down as far as Palmyra in the south (and possibly as far south as Pella). This was the new Kingdom of Osrhoene or the Kingdom of Aurania, or even, when translated into English, the Kingdom of Heaven. And since King A**bg**arus of Edessa was also known in many ancient texts as King A**gb**arus, including the short mention of him in Acts of the Apostles, we can derive a very simple nominative progression that ends in Eschenbach's King Barus of Mesopotamia.

King Abgarus of Edessa and Babylon
King AgBarus of Edessa and Babylon
King Barus of Nineveh and Babylon

So here we appear to have a direct link between Arthurian history and the history of the Kingdom of Edessa: the influential kingdom that led a revolt against Rome in the late 1st century AD. And since Sir Gahmuret was the father of Parzival-Perceval, we can again see that this was really a 1st century story. And in a similar fashion to the previous manuscripts we have looked at, Sir Gahmuret was previously in the employ of the king who eventually opposed him: in this case King Barus of Babylon (King Abgarus of Edessa). And yet although King Barus ruled in the 'heathen' lands of the East, in Mesopotamia, his kingdom still appears to be closely linked to the Christian Church:

> (Gahmuret) had heard that there was a man in Baghdad so powerful that two thirds of the Earth or more were subject to him, and whose name was so revered that, in the Heathen tongue, he was called The Barus ... The Barusate stands today. See how they dispense the Christian rite in Rome ... they get their papal law from Baghdad, and so far as it is free of crooks and crannies, they deem it straight. The Barus gives them bulls of indulgence for their sins. (Parzival 230 of 7000)

There was only one Babylonian royal family who was closely connected with Nazarene Judaism and thence with the Simple Judaic Church that became Christianity, and that was the family of King Abgarus V of Edessa and Babylon. So it does seem likely that this mention of a King Barus of

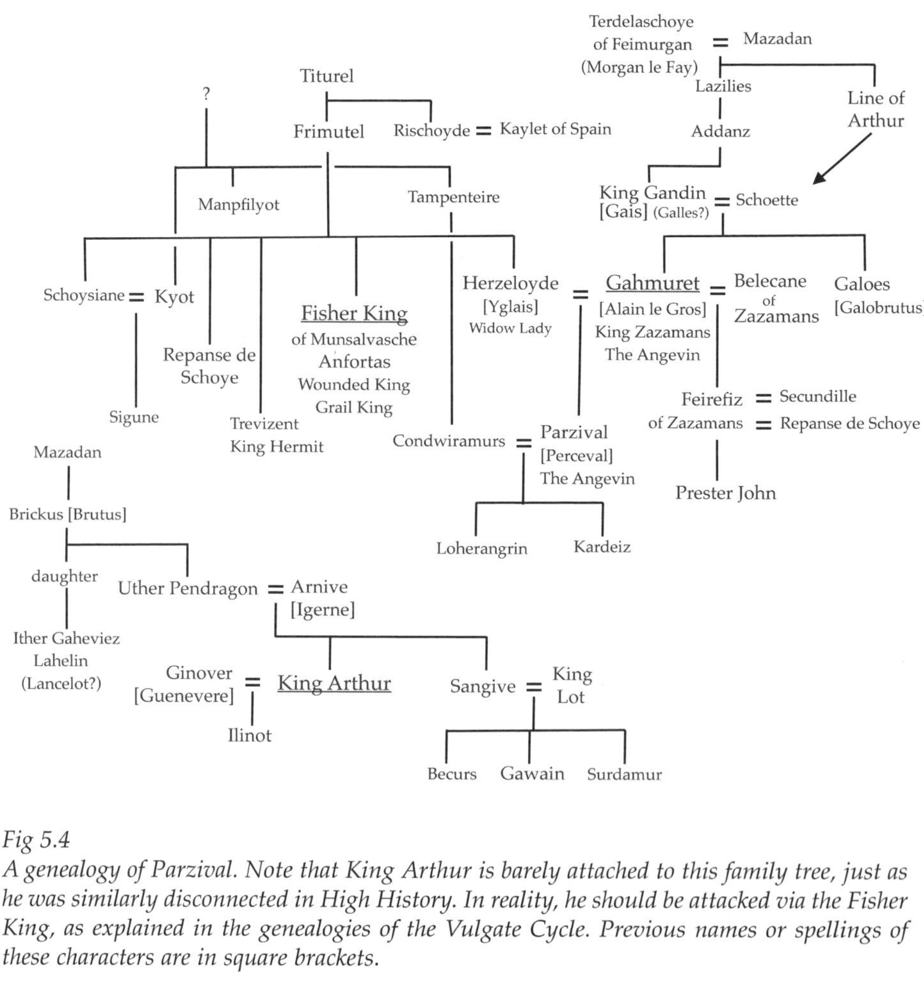

Fig 5.4
A genealogy of Parzival. Note that King Arthur is barely attached to this family tree, just as he was similarly disconnected in High History. In reality, he should be attacked via the Fisher King, as explained in the genealogies of the Vulgate Cycle. Previous names or spellings of these characters are in square brackets.

Nineveh and Babylon was actually a reference to King Abgarus of Edessa and Babylon.

Being a vassal of an eastern monarch, the newly knighted Sir Gahmuret (the future father of Parzival) then seeks knightly fame and fortune in foreign lands, and these include Damascus and Aleppo. Note again that the key players in this Arthurian drama are linked more closely with Syria and Edessa than they are with Britain and Wales. However, since both Damascus and Aleppo lay just south of Edessa, it looks like Sir Gahmuret did not go as far afield in his adventures as the text is intimating. From Aleppo, Sir Gahmuret then traveled to the city of Patelamunt in the Kingdom of Zazamans, where the people were lamenting the death of (Prince) Isenhart.

In which case, Eschenbach is playing games with us, once more, and trawling through the French *chanson de geste* or 'songs of heroic deeds', for yet more pseudonyms. It is quite clear that Gahmuret and this Isenhart are actually the Gormond and Isembart from *Gormond et Isembart*, the very same chanson that was used by Geoffrey of Monmouth. It is difficult to see why Eschenbach has used this chanson to create Gahmuret-Gormond, his new name for Alain li Gros, the father of Parzival-Perceval, apart from the fact that Gormond was said to be a Moor - a Persian. This may be a convoluted way of saying that Gahmuret was of Persian extract, just as Parzival-Ipomedon was also of Persian extract, but this brief mention Gormond and Isembart appears to have little other use.

It is not entirely clear where the Kingdom of Zazamans or the city of Patelamunt are, with many researchers and academics placing it down in Africa for some reason. But since Gahmuret's previous exploits were in Syria we can guess that Zazamans is somewhere fairly close by. One of the problems with Eschenbach's manuscript was that he was fairly ruthless with the names, modifying them considerably. The text is in Middle High German, and this bias towards German shows through in the new proper names he created, and in many of the names he modified. Worst of all, Eschenbach does not use Aramaic proper names very often at all, as appears to be the case in most of the other Arthurian manuscripts, so we don't know if he knew the hidden (biblical) meanings that lay behind many of these Aramaic names.

Anyway, while these two place-names don't make much sense in High German, they may contain an element of Latin, because Latin was the lingua franca of the Catholic Church and therefore the language of the Latin Vulgate Bible. And an educated knight like Eschenbach would surely have understood some Latin. So if we look at the city of Patela Munt in the Latin, we could possibly derive Patella which refers to a grail dish like the Grail itself (or to the top of the head), and Muns meaning 'mountain'. So it is possible that Patelamunt may refer to the Mount of the Holy Grail, but which city that might refer to is unknown.

The etymology of Zazamans may be easier to trace because this eastern-sounding name may well be biblical, and derived from the Latin Vulgate Bible's Zuzim. This was in turn derived from the Aramaic Zuzym זוזים or Zamzummim זמזמים, a fabled biblical people and a land of giants. However, even if this is the correct interpretation, the location of this semi-legendary place is still unknown. The most logical suggestion is that Zazamans refers to the wealthy, independent and influential city of Palmyra, which was located in the Syrian desert to the east of Damascus. We shall see evidence in later chapters that the *Vulgate Cycle* calls Palmyra 'Sarras', and this city becomes the focus for the majority of events in *History of the Grail*.

Being an errant knight, Gahmuret hires himself out to Belacane, the queen of Zazamans. Belacane is described as being a dusky maiden and so we are obviously still in the East: somewhere like Palmyra. The queen accepts his offer, and Gahmuret's small detachment marches into her capital city, which is being besieged:

> The big-hearted Gahmuret rode into town in style. Ten sumpter (mules) ... marched through the streets followed by twenty squires on horseback. His baggage train could be seen ahead: unmounted pages, cooks and scullions has gone on in advance. After the squires rode twelve noble pages, some of who were Saracens. After these, horses with trappers of cendale were led, eight in a group, while the ninth carried Gahmuret's saddle. Next rode the trumpeters. (Parzival 276 of 7000) (Author's brackets.)

Wolfram von Eschenbach was a knight himself, and this shows in the realism of his descriptions. The other authors have these errant knights travelling with no possessions whatsoever, and stumbling across free lodgings each night. In great contrast, *Parzival* describes the knights bearing weighty saddlebags, and packhorses carrying lances packed in bundles of six. And here Gahmuret has acquired a veritable army of attendants and assistants, which may well be how these errant knights toured the country. If the primary role of these knights was to maintain the peace and defend the realm on behalf of the king, there would be no point having a single knight on a charger. The king's 'police force' would have to consist of at least a dozen soldiers plus their attendants, to maintain any sort of control over the region they patrolled.

Anyway Gahmuret established himself as a champion of Belacane, and wins some crucial skirmishes with the besiegers of Patelamunt. And following these minor victories Gahmuret hoists pennants of defiance from the castle walls, with a design that seems quite appropriate.

> Our pennants show a woman with two fingers of one hand raised... (Parzival 343 of 7000)

Appreciative of his assistance in raising the siege, Belacane of Zazamans marries Gahmuret, who then becomes the King of Zazamans; a story that has a degree of resonance with Eschenbach's later epic tale, *Willehalm*. The royal couple have a child called Feirefiz, and because Belacane is a dusky maiden the young Feirefiz is said to be piebald (black and white patches). The name for Feirefiz reflects those skin tones, because it was derived from the Norman *feir* meaning 'piebald' and the common nominative prefix of *fiz* or *fitz* meaning 'son', which is still used today in many English surnames. So Feirefiz means 'Piebald Son', and Wolfram confirms this translation by comparing him to a magpie.

But this long prequel introduction to *Parzival* gives Wolfram von Eschenbach a problem, because this is supposed to be a story about King Arthur of Britain, rather than King Arthur of Syria. And so Gahmuret, the father of the future Parzival-Perceval, walks away from his home and family in Syria and crosses the Mediterranean to France and Britain. There he meets Queen Herzeloyde, the queen of Anjou, Walies and Norgals (Nor-galles). These place-names are said to refer to Wales and Normandy, but we shall see in later chapters that Walles and Galles have a different meaning entirely. In reality, this reference to Walles or Galles is the reason for Parzival's father being known as the Maimed or Wounded King, in both *Perceval* and the *Vulgate Cycle*.

Perceval-Parzival

We then come to the story of Parzival himself, which may well have been lifted directly from Chretien de Troyes' *Perceval*, as the opening sections are virtually identical. Although later on we shall see that Eschenbach adds extra material that again suggests that there was some common source to these three versions of the same story. As we shall see later, Eschenbach once again credits Kyot (ie: Walter Kayo) as being that source, and he in turn is said to have derived some of this material from Flegetanis of Toledo.

The main difference between this section in *Parzival* and the similar story we have already explored in *Perceval*, is that it is openly admitted that Parzival is a prince, instead of the son of a poor widow lady in a forest. Parzival's late mother had been the queen of Anjou, Walies and Norgals, while his late father had been King of Zazamans in Syria as we have seen. (Gahmuret eventually went back to the East, and was killed by Ipomedon.) So all the pretence of Parzival being a pauper is put to one side, although he is still dressed in the rags of a country bumpkin for some reason. But Parzival is still a naive prince of royal bearing who is in great need of a knightly mentor to teach him the customs, manners and politics of the royal court.

On his journey to see King Arthur, Parzival meets the same knights in the forest that he met in *High History* and *Perceval*. But Parzival is merely naive in this version, rather than being the village idiot that was portrayed in *Perceval*. And again nobody is killed at this stage in the story. Then there is the beautiful lady with the jealous husband, a story which now has overtones of titillation rather than romance. And again, while the poor lady get's abused by her jealous husband, she is not stabbed through the chest with a lance to show how wonderful and benevolent the Christian Church is, as she was in *High History*.

Parzival then meets with King Arthur and asks to be a knight, and again Parzival rides out to kill the Red Knight, who is King Arthur's enemy. In *Perceval* the Red Knight was called the Red Knight of Quinqueroy, but now he is named as King Arthur's paternal cousin, Ither of Gaheviez, the king of Cucumerlant. And the reason for the dispute between these kings is made more clear, for Ither is no longer an errant knight with delusions of grandeur, but a king and a cousin of King Arthur who is claiming Arthur's throne. (Presumably because he was descended from the female line rather than the male line, and within Judaism the genealogy runs through the female line.)

It was the death of Ither of Gaheviez (the Red Knight) that caused the bitter family feud and the region to become a wasteland, just as we have seen before. And again Parzival-Perceval kills Gaheviez with a lance through the helmet; and so if this story is following true to form then Gaheviez must be Eschenbach's new pseudonym for Gahmuret, Parzival's father. And the names Gaheviez and Gahmuret do indeed sound very similar. The possibility that Parzival killed his own father is not openly admitted, of course, but the Hermit King then says:

> Dear nephew (Perceval) ... you have slain your own flesh and blood. If you take this misdeed unatoned to the judgement of god, it will cost your life, since you and Ither were of one blood. (Parzival 3529 of 7000)

To which the modern translator remarks dryly that Parzival-Perceval is hardly related to Ither Gaheviez, because they are only related by a great-great-great-grandfather. But the real problem here lies not in Perceval's apparent remoteness from Ither Gaheviez, but with the fact that these authors are continuously misleading us. The family line of King Arthur and Ither Gaheviez are not attached to the main line of the Fisher King and Hermit King, as they are in the *Vulgate*. And depending upon how Arthur's line is attached to the main family line, then Ither Gaheviez would indeed become 'of one blood' with Parzival-Perceval, and quite possibly his father.

Parzival then takes Gaheviez-Gahmuret's armour for his own, to become the new Red Knight, and so Parzival becomes the Red Knight just as Sir Galahad will become the Red Knight in the *Vulgate*. And as just mentioned, the death of Gaheviez (the Red Knight) caused a bitter family feud, despite the fact that the fight between Parzival and the Red Knight had been sanctioned by King Arthur himself. And it caused a personal feud too, because Gaheviez was the brother of the jealous husband, who will meet up with Parzival later in the story. However, quite surprisingly it is Queen Ginover (Queen Gwenevere) who leads the lament for the slain Red Knight, saying:

> Alas, this strange and dire event will shatter Arthur's noble fame. That he who by rights should bear the palm before all at the Round Table should lie slain here ... he did but claim his heritage and was accorded death! When all is said and done, he was a member of our household of such (good) behaviour that none had ever heard a misdeed of his. If perfidy is wild then he is tame. Now and all too soon it is my duty to inter the very Clasp on the Roll of Fame ... A new and fertile seed of grief is sown among us women! ... So red were your locks of hair, your blood could not have made the flowers redder! (Parzival 1270 of 7000)

So what are we to make of this? It was King Arthur whose lands were being plundered by his cousin, Ither of Gaheviez (the Red Knight); it was King Arthur whose life was 'made wretched' by Ither of Gaheviez; and it was King Arthur who authorised Parzival to kill Ither of Gaheviez. And now it is Queen Gwenevere who leads the lament for Ither of Gaheviez and predicts dire consequences from his death.

One suspects that Ither of Gaheviez (the Red Knight) is an earlier incarnation of Sir Lancelot, who becomes the passionate and loyal lover of Queen Gwenevere in the later *Vulgate Cycle*. Remember that both Lancelot and Galahad are never mentioned in these earlier manuscripts, and so it is possible that this deceitful and treacherous love affair was well known by these authors, but they decided to conceal it. And so the redheaded Ither of Gaheviez was probably a literary prototype for the redheaded Sir Lancelot. We shall see a similar scenario in Chapter VIII, where a little-known knight called Yder or Ydern (who was mentioned by Monmouth in Chapter I) also becomes the lover of Gwenevere and again appears to be a forerunner of the later Sir Lancelot. And since the names Ither and Yder are remarkably similar, this may well be two pronunciations of the same name.

However, since we have already linked Ither Gaheviez with Alain Gahmuret, the father of Perceval-Parzival, Ither-Yder-Lancelot may well have been the father of Perceval-Parzival. Chapter VIII will revisit this question, and show an original 12th century carving of Ither-Yder. This may be why King Arthur both admired and detested this proto-Lancelot Red Knight, because he was the best and most loyal knight in his court, and yet he was openly sleeping with his wife. And the *Vulgate* says that this illicit love affair produced a child, the future Sir Galahad, which is why Sir Galahad was also known as the redheaded Red Knight.

But if Ither-Yder-Lancelot was Galahad's father, and Perceval-Parzival is Galahad as we shall see later, then Perceval-Parzival-Galahad has just killed his father once more. And this ties in nicely with the previous suggestion that Ither Gaheviez was Gahmuret-Alain, the father of Perceval. This may well give us a small genealogical contradiction to overcome, but a later chapter will demonstrate the possibility of a missing generation here, and it is Ither-Yder-Lancelot who may well fill in the generational gap between Gahmuret-Alain and Perceval-Parzival-Galahad. In which case, the convoluted connections between these kings and knights are as follows:

> Perceval kills the Red Knight
> The Red Knight appears to be Gaheviez-Gahmuret
> Gahmuret-Alain is the father of Perceval
> Perceval has just killed his father
>
> Ither-Yder is actually an early proto-Lancelot
> Lancelot is the father of Perceval-Galahad
> Perceval-Galahad has just killed Ither-Yder-Lancelot
> Perceval-Galahad has again killed his father
>
> The story may have jumped a generation.

This connection to Lancelot would certainly explain why Queen Gwenevere is leading the lament for King Ither-Yder of Gaheviez, the redheaded Red Knight, because in the guise of Lancelot she would have been sorely grieved at his death and angry with King Arthur for having sanctioned it. However, the later *Vulgate Cycle* has decided to openly admit to this passionate affair between Lancelot and Gwenevere, and all of the family and court tensions that it engendered. And it has also decided to expand the role and life of Sir Lancelot, so that he does not die quite so early in the story.

The Widow Lady

Just as in *Perceval*, the young Parzival rides out and finds a kindly old knight called Gurnemanz, who tutors him in courtly manners and knightly jousting. He then rides on to the castle of the dispossessed Widow Lady.

Again she is not Parzival's mother in this version of the story, as she was in *High History*, but a beautiful princess willing for his love, which makes for a more romantic storyline. As we have seen in previous versions of this tale (and in the similar story of Parzival's father) Castle Belrepeir is being besieged by a king and his wicked seneschal. And again Eschenbach provides us with some slightly different names and spellings:

Item	Chretien	Eschenbach
Queen	Blancheflor	Condwiramurs
Prince	Perceval	Parzival
Castle	Biaurepaire	Belrepeir
King	Clamadeu	Clamide
Seneschal	An-guingueron	Kingrun

Once more there are battles outside Castle Belrepeir, which confidently keeps its gates open despite the threats and attacks. And then Parzival challenges and defeats both Kingrun and Clamide in single combat. The siege of Belrepeir is lifted, and Parzival is free to marry Condwiramurs and become the king of Brobarz.

Continuing on his adventures, Parzival then meets the Fisher King in his magnificent castle called Munsalvasche. In this version the Fisher King is again the Wounded King, and he does not appear to be the father of Parzival-Perceval as he is in the *Vulgate*. Parzival then witness the splendours of the Holy Grail procession which is led by Princess Repanse de Shoye, and again he forgets to ask who the Grail honours or serves.

Parzival then meets his cousin on his mother's side, who is eventually named as Sigune, the daughter of Schoysiane. In this section Parzival is called the Waleis, because he was a prince of Waleis; and this again identifies Parzival as being Sir Galahad, who was a Walles or Galles priest. But Sigune does not view the young Parzival as heroic knight in shining armour, far from it. Because he did not ask the all-important question of who the Grail served she says:

> To think that you could not be bothered to ask in the very presence of the Grail! ... O what prompted you to come here. You dishonourable person, man accursed. You showed your venomous wolf-fangs when the canker took root in your integrity and grew apace! ... You live, yet as far as heaven's favour is concerned you are dead! (Parzival 1940 of 7000)

Clearly this business about not asking who the Grail honoured or served was a subject of great import that generated much anger and resentment. But its precise nature remains a bit of a mystery. One suspects that this is a covert appeal for all readers of Arthurian history to ask questions, especially in regard to things of a spiritual or religious nature. The problem with the oppressive dominance of the Catholic Church in the 12th century, was that the petrified and servile population did not dare ask any difficult questions, for fear of Christian retribution. And so European society and science became moribund - sealed in Church aspic and unable to progress.

The core essence of the 17th century Reformation movement was about asking questions. Not only questions about nature and philosophy, but also questions about Church teachings if they made no sense. If the priest was blathering yet more incomprehensible or self-contradictory nonsense, the virtuous and valiant knight should ask the pertinent question that undermines his fairytale and bursts his inflated ego. Ask, ask, and ask again. And once the Reformation was won, a whole century later, this became the founding and guiding principle of the Royal Society, Britain's premier scientific institution. 17th century science was founded upon the two simple but fundamental questions that the Catholic Church despised and feared the most - 'how' and 'why' - the two words in the English lexicon that were guaranteed to turn a powerful pope into a quivering wreck.

So the seeds of the Reformation were not simply sowed by Martin Luther and his Ninety Five Theses in the 16th century, they were actually being sown within these 12th and 13th century Arthurian romances. Chretien de Troyes and Robert de Boron were the first authors to mention the Holy Grail and the importance of asking questions, and so they were not only challenging the Church by recording a heretical history, the advice they were giving guaranteed that the Church would be harassed by awkward questions for centuries to come. And 95 of those awkward questions were pinned to the doors of Wittenberg church by Martin Luther, at the start of the Reformation. And if a modern equivalent of Martin Luther does not pin 95 equivalent questions to the door of every European mosque, the hard-won Reformation and the resulting Age of Reason may well be lost forever.

Toledo - Edessa

Having recounted the entire story that was told in Chretien's *Perceval,* Eschenbach now gets to what seems to be the primary subject that interested him, which is the story of the Holy Grail. To get this information, Eschenbach has Parzival meet with Trevrizent, who is more commonly known as the Hermit King in the other manuscripts. But here, the Hermit King is definitely a separate character, and not merged with any of the other major monarchs in this story. Eschenbach says of this meeting between Trevrizent and Parzival:

> From Trevrizent Parzival is about to learn matters concerning the Graal that have been hidden. Those who questioned me earlier and argued with me for not telling them earned nothing but shame, because Kyot asked me to conceal it because his source forbade him to mention it until the story itself reached that point where it has to be spoken of. The famous Master Kyot found the original version of this story in the heathen script lying all neglected in a corner of Toledo. He had to learn (the alphabet) beforehand. (Parzival 3380 of 7000) (Author's brackets.)

What Eschenbach means by this, of course, is that the nature of the Holy Grail should be hidden in the middle of his great manuscript, instead of being openly discussed at the very beginning. And this was not simply a literary technique, to persuade his readers to read the whole book, it was also a method of burying sensitive information where Church censors might not find it. The material gets more sensitive as we go through this manuscript, with Parzival declaring himself to be an Agnostic on at lest three occasions, and being an Agnostic in the early 13th century was a dangerous road to travel.

Then we have the location of this newly discovered manuscript, which is said to be Toledo. And so A T Hatto, the modern translator of *Parzival*, has presumed that the 'heathen language' must have been Arabic. This scenario is entirely possible, as Toledo was wrested from Muslim oppression and servitude in 1085, and so European scholars may well have been poking around the forgotten libraries of Toledo at this time. And since the majority of citizens in Spain were still Latino-Spanish speaking Christians, there would have been any number of scholars there who were able to translate an Arabic manuscript into Latin.

However, one cannot help feeling that this entire story by Eschenbach is a diversionary tactic. Within Muslim culture and education, history does not exist prior to the birth of Muhummad, which is why we see Muslim controlled states in the modern Middle East destroying anything and everything that pre-dates Islam. And this is not simply a matter of religious iconoclasm, this is the destruction of anything and everything that is non-Islamic. For instance, the National Museum in Kabul was damaged by rockets in 1993, but the real damage was done when some 4,000 ancient artifacts were looted and destroyed, and every single coin was stolen including those from the great Kabul and Kunduz hoards.

So we have entered a completely new era of warfare. The prerogative of invading armies since the dawn of history was to rape, pillage and loot. In fact, the division of spoils was a primary method of paying soldiers in the army. If you won, you were given a share of the spoils, and if you lost you were probably dead anyway. Which is why Sura 8 in the Koran is entitled 'The Spoils of War', while Sura 48 'The Victory' says:

> Allah has promised you many spoils that you will take ... and other spoils which you have not yet been able to take, god has reserved them for you. (Koran 48:20-21)

Muhummad was a petty warlord from Mecca, and so the entire Islamic religion was founded, advocated and advanced upon the promise that its followers would get rich on the loot stolen from Jews, Christians and Sabeans. But in recent Middle Eastern conflicts the victorious Western armies did not loot a single thing, while the defeated local population set about desecrating, looting and destroying their own heritage, including the Mosul, Baghdad, Palmyra and Kabul archaeological museums. The World Archaeological Congress at the Getty Conservation Institute recorded a statement from Philippe Flandrin, who said of the Muslim destruction of historical artifacts in Afghanistan:

> Three quarters of the (Afghan) collections that have been found were removed without any iconoclastic intent ... On 4 February a line of cars stopped in front the museum. Carrying hammers and axes, the minister of finance and the minister of culture with his adjunct, and the notorious Mollah Rahamn ... ordered that the storerooms be opened. According to a staff member who witnessed the scene: "As they entered the storeroom, they snarled in excitement and started to smash everything while chanting 'Allahu Akbar'." Throughout history, the destruction of a nation's cultural treasures has been the consequence of religious fanaticism, political ideology, or mere ignorance, yet never before had the madness reached such magnitude. [2] (Author's brackets.)

As the Western conservators in Afghanistan said, this looting and destruction had nothing to do with religious iconoclasm, it was all about a complete disregard and loathing for the pre-Islamic world and its history. And the situation is not getting better as the centuries and decades roll on, it is getting worse: mankind is regressing, not progressing. And do note that this was not the actions of a few mindless indoctrinated thugs, who would normally be found roaming the backstreets of Kabul in a hash-fumed stupor, this was the work of the minister of finance and the minister of culture. Yes, the very man who had been tasked with saving the nation's archaeological heritage, had been waiting all this time for the opportunity to destroy it all. This is what fundamentalist Islam does even to educated people: it destroys all reasonable and rational thought.

In which case, it is highly unlikely that a Muslim scholar in the 11th century Near East would have preserved the history of some *kuffer* unbelievers and their heretical Holy Grail, and taken it all the way to Toledo in Spain. And so this was not an Arabic document at all. The most likely option, is that this manuscript was discovered in the capital city of the royal family who appear to be at the epicenter of this story - in Edessa in northern Syria.

When the First Crusade arrived in eastern Anatolia and northern Syria, the very first city that the Crusaders liberated from Muslim oppression was Edessa. But why? There were many closer and perhaps more strategically important Christian cities that could have been wrested from Muslim control, but Count Baldwin chose to leave the main Crusader forces and travel across the Euphrates to save Nazarene Christian Edessa from Muslim occupation and subjugation. Was this because he knew of the connection between Nazarene Christian Edessa and the biblical royal family?

The unlikely nature of this diversionary expedition implies that Count Baldwin already knew that if there was anywhere in the Near East that might house interesting and possibly heretical manuscripts, it was Nazarene Christian Edessa. And these would not have been Arabic documents, of course, they would have been written in Syriac-Aramaic by the many great Syriac Christian academics who populated that region. Islam does not do education, which is why there have only ever been three Muslim Nobel laureates for science:

Jewish Nobel laureates	172	
Jewish population	13	million
Muslim Nobel laureates	3	
Muslim population	1,700	million
Total of all Nobel laureates	723	
Percentage Jewish laureates	23.8%	
Percentage Muslim laureates	0.4%	
Laureates per million Jews	13.2	
Laureates per million Muslims	0.002	

Similarly, we also have the amazing statistic that Spain translates more books in one year, than the entire Arab world has translated in the last thousand years.[3] And since this is such an unbelievable and deeply disturbing statistic, it was checked and double-checked.

This was first reported by the United Nations Development Report on Arabia in 2002, and so the oft-quoted statistic from this report is perfectly correct. However, it is highly likely that the Muslim 'scholars' who compiled this report have made a risible error of magnitude, an error that simultaneously lessens and supports the assertions being made about the Muslim education system. In reality, the Spanish are probably translating more books per year than the entire Arab world has translated in the last century, rather than in the last millennium. The figures for France are similar to Spain. However, this still leaves an alarming literary gulf between Arabia and Europe. Even in the modern era, with the ease of modern publication technology, it was reported by the UN that Arabia is only translating 350 books a year into Arabic. And so Muslim Arabia has always been and remains today, an educational and intellectual backwater far removed from the fast flowing stream of Western intellect, culture and science.

The anti-intellectual foundations of Islam stem from the common assertion that the Koran, a small book no bigger or better than a bodice-ripping novel, contains all the knowledge of the universe. This claim is based upon verses 5:64 and 21:23, which say that nobody, especially the Jews, can question god, and god is omnipotent. But the idea that such a small book contains all the knowledge, science and history of the universe, demonstrates and proves the ignorance of Islam in one short assertion. Especially since the Koran contains numerous basic scientific misunderstandings, including a geocentric solar system; stars being missiles; the Moon emitting light; several verses that imply the Earth is flat; and the Sun setting in a muddy pool. And yet because these errors have been set in koranic stone, modern Muslim 'scientists' are compelled to believe them and try to work around them. But an institutionally schizophrenic mind is not a logical, rational, or scientific mind.

This anti-intellectual bias within Islam was noted even in the very first decades of its existence. When the Parthian capital city of Ctesiphon fell to the Muslim army in 637, it was said that Caliph Omar declared of the library there:

> If the books in it agree with the Koran, they are superfluous. If they disagree with the Koran, they are heretical. [4]

An alternative rendering of the same quote and sentiment says:

> Throw them into the water. If they contain good guidance, god has already given us better guidance. If they are in error, god will have protected us against it. [5]

Gregory bar Hebraeus recorded a similar account during the second burning of the library at Alexandria by the Muslims in 642, under the same Caliph Omar. But Gregory's account contains exactly the same quote that was recorded for the destruction of Ctesiphon. In reality, it is unlikely that there was much left of the Alexandria library after the Christians burned it down in 391, and so Gregory's much disputed account may have been a confusion with the destruction of the Ctesiphon library.

It has been claimed by modern apologists that the many accounts of Islamic destruction of knowledge and history in the Judaeo-Christian Middle

East are apocryphal, for Islam is still held by some as being the saviour of Western wisdom during the Dark Ages. However, the revised history of the so-called Islamic Golden Age narrated in *Mary Magdalene, Princess of Orange,* completely undermines that claim. And likewise the history of the Syriac Christians explored in *Jesus, King of Edessa* tells the story of the great million-book library of Amida near Edessa, which also disappeared after the Muslim invasion in 639. And an interesting book by Robert Reilly has similarly argued that irrationality triumphed over reason within Islam more than a millennium ago, and so the possibility of doing serious science under an Islamic administration was quashed from that time onwards.[6] Reilly rightly calls this abject capitulation to the forces of fundamentalist darkness: 'intellectual suicide'. Even very recently, one of the grand muftis of Malaysia said in a warning to local politicians:

> Islam is based on faith ... Don't make any remarks based on intellect or logic ... intellect is governed by desires and it is influenced by Satan. Don't be ruled by desires and rudderless comments.[7]

How, even within the supposedly enlightened modern world, can intellect and science progress if politics and society are hamstrung by the Neanderthal* notion that intellect, reason and logic are constructs of the Devil? And since intellect is being branded as the work of the Devil, it must therefore be a sure sign of apostasy, and yet apostasy is still punishable by death in many Muslim countries, including Saudi Arabia, Iran, Sudan and Pakistan. How can science progress, when the voyage of intellectual discovery is punishable by death? And this anti-intellectual ethos is widespread throughout the Islamic education system, because the brain-washing Saudi-inspired Madrassas of Islam are run by devout Muslim clerics, and often only teach Arabic and the Koran until the age of eleven.

In great contrast, the higher educational establishments within Islamia always were, and still are, mostly run by non-Muslims. In the 12th century the universities were run by Syriac and Armenian Christians, which is why the oft-claimed Golden Age of Islam was actually a Golden Age of Syriac Christianity and Babylonian Judaism. Similarly, in the modern era many or most Middle Eastern universities are run by Americans and Europeans. For instance, of the 43 universities listed in Dubai, 27 are Western and 2 are Indian.[8]

* This comparison is probably grossly unfair to Neanderthals, who were in all likelihood far more advanced than this.

In which case, if Walter Kayo had been given an Arthurian-type manuscript that had been discovered in Edessa, the likelihood is that it was written in the lingua-franca of that region which was Syriac-Aramaic rather than Arabic. And this is why most of the names within Arthurian history appear to be Aramaic, especially in the *Vulgate*. This is also why Eschenbach says of Flegetanis, the reputed original source for much of the more esoteric material in *Parzival*, that:

> There was a heathen named Flegetanis who was highly renown for his knowledge. This same physicus was descended from Solomon, begotten of Israelitish kin all the way down from ancient times until the Baptism became our shield against hellfire. He wrote the marvels of the Graal. Flegetanis, who worshipped a calf as though it were his god, was a heathen by his father. (Parzival 3390 of 7000)

Flegetanis was an Israelite. So why does the modern translator of *Parzival* assume that Flegetanis was a Muslim, and thus the language of this manuscript must have been Arabic? And while Muslims also profess a descent from the Israelites, through Abraham's son, Ishmael, the chances of a Muslim worshipping a bull are nil to non-existent. Any deviation from the Koran results in one being thrown off a high building or being burned alive in a cage. [9] And this extreme brutality is not a new phenomena within Islam, born within the madness of ISIS or the Taliban, it forms the very foundations of the Muslim Protection Racket. The Koran says that *kuffer* unbelievers should be: subjugated, raped, taxed, crucified, beheaded, amputated, have boiling water poured over them, or merely sent to the fires of hell. And so this obscene brutality towards *kuffer* unbelievers is not a new phenomena devised by a few deranged tyrants within ISIS, it is what unbelievers and heretics have had to suffer and endure in Muslim controlled lands throughout the centuries.

This is the tried and trusted technique for running any protection racket, whether it originates in 20th century Chicago and Palermo, or in 7th century Mecca and Baghdad. The basic *modus operandi* of any protection racket is to brutalise and frighten the population into abject submission, so that they can be controlled by an elite minority, just as ISIS are doing in Syria today. And that is exactly what Muhummad did to the Jewish and Christian populations of the Middle East, when he lined up the 900 men of the Jewish Banu Quraiza tribe in Medina and beheaded them all. This genocide was simply a warning to all the other tribes and cities in the region not to oppose his army and to submit to his protection racket, and to pay the *jizya* protection money that funded Muhummad's band of thugs. Any 12th century bull-worshipping Muslim in Toledo would have suffered the same fate as the Jews of Banu Quraiza, and so the likelihood of the bull-worshipping Flegetanis being a Muslim is nil to non-existent.

However, this account also says that Flegetanis was a child of Israel descended from King Solomon, and so he is much more likely to have been either an Orthodox Jew or a Nazarene Ebionite Jew, the sect of Jesus and James. And surprisingly, both of these branches of Judaism may well have venerated the bull in some fashion or other. Orthodox Judaism was still sacrificing sacred bulls, even in the 1st century, as the Talmud makes perfectly clear. In fact, according to the Talmud it was Kamza (ie: Jesus) deliberately arranging for the gift of (an imperfect) bull from Emperor Nero, that was one of the primary causes of the Jewish revolt. Rather predictably, the scrupulous but short-sighted Jerusalem rabbis refused to sacrifice an imperfect heathen Roman bull, which greatly offended Rome. And so Kamza (Jesus) had sown one of the many seeds that would eventually lead to a conflict with Rome.

Similarly, the Nazarene Ebionite sect of Jesus and James would also have venerated Taurus the bull, to a degree, as the precessionary zodiac was one of the central components of their creed as we shall in see later chapters. However, there was one other religious sect that will become central to Arthurian history and which likewise venerated the bull as if it were a god, and that is Mithras. And if Mithras may seem like an unlikely religious source for Arthurian history, the next chapter will conclusively prove that this Roman cult was a central component within this hugely complex Arthurian story.

So if Wolfram von Eschenbach was using an old manuscript in the fashion that he describes, the likelihood is that Count Baldwin discovered this ancient manuscript in

Fig 5.5
Count Baldwin of Boulogne is hailed as a liberating hero by the priesthood at the gates of Edessa, after delivering this Christian city from Muslim oppression in 1098.

Christian Edessa after its liberation from Muslim occupation. This precious document may well have detailed the life and times of the biblical family, because Christian Edessa had been their capital city during the 1st century AD. And this text would have been hidden from Western Roman Catholic view for all this time not simply because of the 7th century Muslim invasions, but also because of the divisions caused by the Council of Chalcedon in 451, which had separated Eastern and Western Christianity.

Count Baldwin's liberation of Edessa cut through all of these divisions, that had sealed off Edessa from Catholic Christianity for more than 600 years. And so Baldwin was at last able to be initiated into the many secrets of the Syriac Church by the bishops of Edessa. However, Baldwin had not only just become the Count of Edessa and the King of Jerusalem, he was also the Count of Boulogne in Norman France. And it is via this trail of historical events that a manuscript could well have made its way back to Norman France in the early 12th century. And so this esoteric and heretical manuscript, that had been written by Flegetanis many centuries previously, arrived in the right location in the right era to become the foundation for much of Arthurian history - in Norman France in the early 12th century. And in a later chapter we shall not only see who Flegetanis was, but discover that 'he' was most probably a princess.

However, Flegetanis' manuscript did not give the full story that Eschenbach wanted to tell and so one of the original Arthurian authors, who is said to have been Master Kyot (ie: Walter Kayo), made a search of other lands including Ireland and Britain in order to discover the rest of the story. He finally found the story he was looking for in Anjou, which lies on the borders of Brittany and Normandy:

> (Kyot) read the chronicles of various lands ... and it was in Anjou he found the tale. He read the tale of Mazadan ... (and) the account of the latter's whole lineage was faithfully recorded there. And on the maternal side how Titurel and his son Frimutel bequeathed the Graal to Anfortas (the Fisher King) whose sister was Herzeloyde (the mother of Parzival). (Parzival 3390 of 7000) (Author's brackets.)

What Eschenbach means is that all he had was a fragmentary manuscript giving details of a royal family who were responsible for guarding the Holy Grail. And while this was an interesting story in itself, he needed more information about this family. And not simply more information about Edessa. The story that he was about to compose was decidedly heretical, and so what Eschenbach also required was a cover-story to attach this Eastern, Edessan story onto.

Master Kyot (ie: Walter Kayo) found that extra information and cover-story over in Anjou, where yet another Walter - Walter of Oxford - had discovered an old manuscript in Armorica-Brittany, the neighbouring province to Anjou. This was the original source manuscript that Monmouth and Oxford had used, and it gave the impression of being the history of a British rebel king who had waged a similar tax revolt against the Roman Empire and had made similar preparations to invade Rome - Constantine III of Britain. And Monmouth and Oxford had cleverly blurred and blended this British history into Eastern history by calling this rebel king Arthur, which seemed like a reasonable pseudonym and cover-story for this Eastern monarch.

On his travels, Master Kyot (ie: Walter Kayo) must also have found a copy of Chretien's *Perceval,* because the middle portion of Eschenbach's work closely follows Chretien's version of this story. And this is why *Parzival* presents us with a strange sandwich of subjects, topics and families: it starts in Mesopotamia; then we have the story taken from *High History* and *Perceval,* supposedly about Gaul and Britain; and then we have elements from the East once more. Since elements of this story came from Anjou in France we might call the resulting story a *melange* - a mixture of components from a variety of sources designed to conceal the true origins of this story.

This is also why we have two genealogies within *Parzival,* with King Arthur being almost completely separated from the Fisher King's genealogy, and largely incidental to the story. This was a consequence of the main characters of this story being from the 1st century, as *High History* in particular has confirmed, while King Arthur was supposed to be from the 6th century, despite the overwhelming evidence to the contrary. And nobody was ever going to successfully join these two genealogies together without some obvious contortions and discontinuities, and so most of these histories don't even attempt to do so. *High History, Perceval* and *Parzival* all fail to attach King Arthur onto the rest of the Arthurian family, because it is simply too difficult to do so while maintaining the pretence that Arthur is from the 6th century. Only the *Vulgate Cycle* attempts, but largely fails, to make the necessary connection. And so it was obviously better to be accused of delivering a confusing storyline, than receiving a hot poker from the Inquisition.

In *Parzival* these two families are only conjoined via Mazadan, who is the great grandfather of King Arthur (which would still make Arthur a 1st or 2nd century character). But in the *Vulgate* Arthur is said to be the son of King Pelles, the Fisher King, and so he becomes a central component of this family. And the clue to *Pazival's* separation of these families being incorrect, is that the wife of Mazadan is a fairy called Terdelaschoye of Feymurgen. But a fairy within Arthurian history is often a reference to a witch or sorceress, and so we are looking for a magician called Feymurgen. And the obvious answer to this minor conundrum is that Terdelaschoye Feymurgen is a reverse transposition of Morgan le Fay of Terre de la Joye, the sister or half-sister of King Arthur.

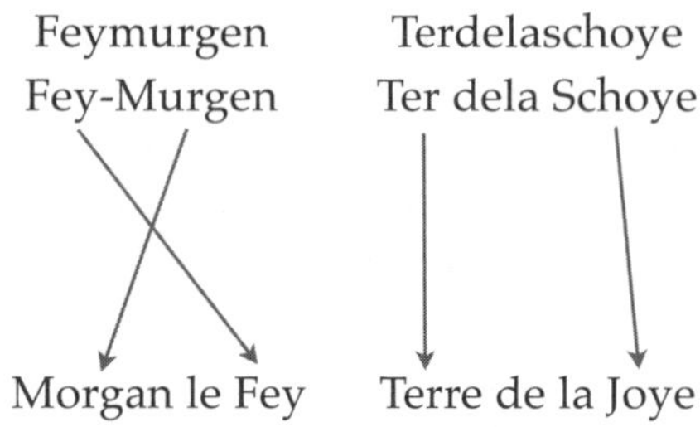

The Terre de la Joye title that Morgan or Morgane has acquired here means 'Land of Joy' and is probably a reference to her palace in Avalon, which was called the 'Fortunate Isle' by Monmouth. But if Feymurgen (Morgan le Fay) was married to Mazadan, then Mazadan was the brother-in-law of King Arthur. And if Feymurgen (Morgan le Fay) was a sorceress who was married to a wizard called Mazadan, then Mazadan was surely an alternate name for Merlin the Wizard. According to Geoffrey of Monmouth and the later *Vulgate,* Morgan le Fay was an apprentice of Merlin who had a palace on the Isle of Avalon, and she was the chief queen of nine sorceress princesses. So the original sorcerer and his apprentice were Merlin and Morgan le Fay, who appear to be named in *Parzival* as Mazadan and Fey Murgen of Ter dela Schoye.

And like Flegetanis, Merlin was well versed in the precessional movements of the heavens, which was the central focus of veneration by the majority of these ancient astrological religions. In *Life of Merlin* Monmouth says that Merlin asked for:

> Before the other buildings build me a remote one with seventy doors and as many windows, through which I may watch fire-breathing Phoebus and Venus and the stars gliding from the heavens by night, all of whom shall show me what is going to happen to the people of the kingdom. (Life of Merlin)

Of what use is a tower with seventy windows to an astronomer or astrologer? What does the number seventy tie into, within the myriad of divisions and periods within astronomy? The answer is probably none.

What has happened here is the standard confusion between the numbers 70 and 72, with some scribes not understanding the significance of the peculiar-sounding number 72. So when Jesus sends out more disciples in Luke 10:1, most Bibles say that there were 70 extra disciples but a significant number of Bibles say that there were 72. For Bibles indicating 72 disciples, please see the 1902 Rotherham or the 1899 Douay Rheims. And the reason for having 72 disciples rather than 70, is because this is six times as many disciples as the original 12. But the concentration on this number 72 within so many diverse manuscripts indicates that there was a more important reason for mentioning it than this. And there was, because this number is intimately associated with the precession of the equinox.

The Great Year of precession is 25,680 years long, which is normally divided into 12 Great Months of approximately 2,140 years. However, if we divide the 25,680 Great Year by the 360 *(sic)* days in a year (or 360 degrees in a circle), the answer is 71.3. In other words, one degree of precession lasts for about 72 years, and so the number 72 is quite symbolic in precessional terms. However, an astronomer can utilise this same calculation in reverse. If Merlin builds a tower with 72 windows, then each window will show about 360 years of precession (25,680 divided by 72). So as the Earth waltzes in its slow precessionary circle, a star in one window will appear in the next window almost 360 years later. And so what Merlin has devised here is a millennial calendar. Each terrestrial year is approximately 360 days long, while each window in this tower represents approximately 360 years in the precessional cycle.

And such a tower could well be used to prophesise the future, just as Monmouth claimed, because the symbology of the reigning monarch depended upon the dominant sign of the zodiac, which changed with each passing Great Month. Which is why Jesus was born as a Lamb of God (Aries) but became a Fisher of Men (Pisces). And momentous events were supposed to happen as these signs and symbols changed from one to another, just as they most certainly did during the 1st century change between the Great Month of Aries and the Great Month of Pisces. But Merlin's many-windowed tower could track this event quite precisely, because if the Great Months were of equal length then six windows will equal one Great Month (72 windows divided by 12 months).

Combined genealogy

If Terdelaschoye of Feymurgen was linked to Morgan le Fay and Merlin, then perhaps we can start to meld these two genealogies together. And so the perennial question becomes: 'which generation'? Was King Arthur of the generation of the Fisher King or was he the son of the Fisher King, as the *Vulgate Cycle* suggests? Unfortunately, Wolfram is of little help here, because he merely calls the Fisher King Anfortas, which was derived from the Latin *infirmitas* meaning 'infirm', because Anfortas was also known as the Wounded King. Again we can see that the names that Eschenbach devised himself were mostly taken from the Latin, rather than the Chaldean Aramaic.

In the previous chapter, King Arthur became the brother of the Fisher King, but where should we add King Arthur within *Parzival's* genealogy? In later chapters we shall see more indications that Arthur was of the previous generation to Parzival-Perceval and Joseus-Josephus, and so he should be of the same generation as the Fisher King. And perhaps King Arthur should even be identified as the Fisher King himself, because King Jesus-Arthur was the leader of fishermen who went fishing on the Sea of Galilee, just as the Fisher King was identified as the Fisher King by his peculiar fishing expeditions where he failed to catch any fish:

> Do not imagine that (the Fisher King) is served pike or lamprey or salmon. A single (eucharist wafer) that is brought to him in that Grail brings comfort to that holy man. (Perceval 8850)

Quite obviously, the Fisher King title had nothing to do with fish or fishing and everything to do with the Great Month of Pisces, which began in the very early 1st century AD. So the era of the Fisher King and the birth of King Izas-Jesus are closely linked; as was the birth of King Arthur, as we saw in Chapter II. Bearing all of this in mind, the following amended genealogy has equated the Fisher King with King Arthur, while Parzival-Perceval becomes Arthur's nephew. This would equate well with the many meetings between Arthur and Parzival-Perceval, where Arthur is portrayed as the troubled and possibly ageing king, while Parzival-Perceval is the eager young knight.

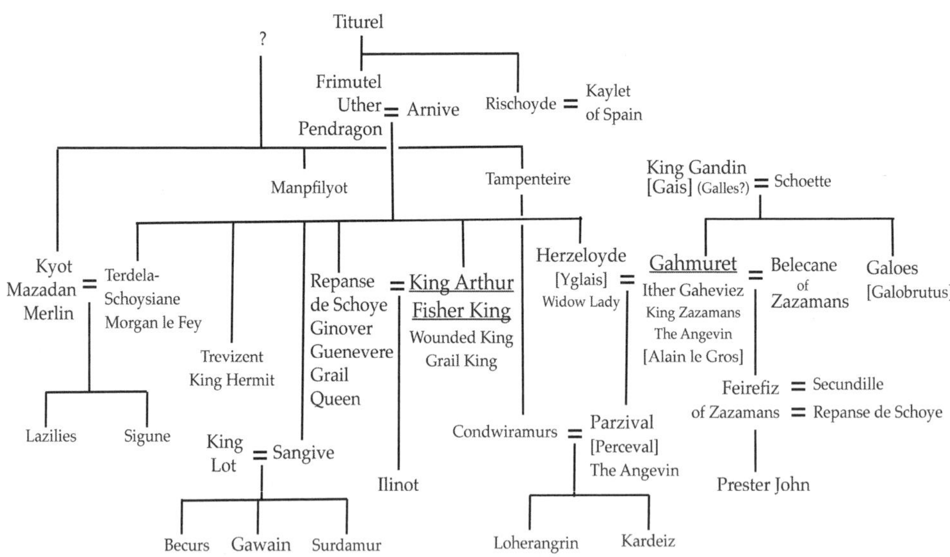

Fig 5.6
A revised genealogy of Parzival, to join King Arthur onto this family line. Previous names or spellings of these characters are in square brackets.

Remember that when Eschenbach talks about the Fisher King he never includes King Arthur in the same paragraphs, and so these could be two accounts of the same individual, perhaps from two different sources. And remember also the evidence in *King Jesus* which demonstrated that King Jesus was wounded but still alive following his crucifixion, although the wounds in the Fisher King's thighs would suggest a religious compliance rather than crucifixion wounds. However, the Fisher King's wounds forced the king to recline, rather than sit or stand, and so this gives us yet another connection with the gospel accounts:

> The King is unable either to ride or walk or even to lie down ... He reclines, he does not sit ... There is a lake called Brumbane onto which he is taken so that the stench of his gaping wound shall be quelled ... From this a rumour went around that he was a fisherman. He had to endure this story ... even though he had no salmon for sale ... The cushions on which he reclined were of brocade of *nourient*, quilted, not just sewn, and his mattress was of *palmat* silk. (Parzival 3650 and 5730 of 7000)

Again we have a description of the Fisher King going fishing, but never having any fish to sell. And again the reason for this lack of success is that this was actually an astrological fishing expedition, and the fish that the Fisher King was interested in was the Great Month of Pisces. Just as King Jesus-Izas went fishing in John 21:6, and caught a net-full of converts to the new Piscean creed of the Nazarene. We also see here a reclining monarch, which is very similar to the Palmyran Last Supper imagery shown in fig 12.1 where the aristocrats or royalty recline while holding a wide-brimmed Grail-type chalice. And it is also similar to the gospel account of the Last Supper, where one of the disciples - probably the 'loved disciple' who may well be Judas - reclines on the breast of Jesus.

> He leaning back, as he was, on Jesus' breast said unto him, lord, who is it? (Who is the betrayer.) Jesus answered, he is the one for whom I shall dip this morsel, and give it him. So when he had dipped the morsel, he took it and gave it to Judas Iscariot, the son of Simon. (Joh 13:25-26). (Author's brackets.)

This description of the disciples lounging would suit the Palmyran and Arthurian description of this Holy Grail Last Supper scene, rather than the formal table arrangement depicted in most cathedrals and churches. And this was, of course, how the Roman aristocracy ate. They did not have formal dining tables, they reclined on a couch and ate with one hand; a position that looks neither comfortable nor good for the digestion. The Roman dining room was called a *triclinium*, from the Greek *triklinion* τρικλινιον meaning 'three beds', and a delightful old book on Roman history and custom by Arthur Gilman says of these dining rooms:

> The dining-room, called the *triclinium* (Greek *kline* or bed) from its three couches, was a very important apartment. In it were three lounges surrounding a table ... Each man lay almost flat on his breast, resting on his left elbow, and having his right hand free to use, thus putting <u>the head of one near the breast of the man behind him</u>, and making natural the expression that 'he lay in the bosom of the other'. As the guests were thus arranged by threes, it was natural that the rule should have been made that a party at dinner should not be less in number than the Graces nor more than the Muses. [10]

So the Gospel of John was correct and Leonardo da Vinci was wrong, the disciples would have lounged on couches or cushions with the head of one man lying almost upon the breast of another. And while the illustration here is laid out for just three guests, Gilman says that the dining arrangements can be expanded from the Graces (three guests) to the Muses (nine guests). And no doubt one could stretch that custom if necessary to the Disciples

Fig 5.7
A Roman triclinium or dining room, with three couches arranged around a table. This basic model could be expanded to nine, or perhaps even twelve couches.

(twelve guests). But this small aside in the Gospel of John does imply that the banqueting hall that King Izas-Jesus was using was inordinately large, and the dining arrangements hugely expensive.

Brumbane

The lake where Anfortas, the wounded Fisher King, bathed his wounds was called Lake Brumbane, and since we know that Eschenbach preferred Germanic or Latin names to Aramaic, the suffix to this name seems to be reasonably certain. The term *bane* was widely used in High German and Old English to mean 'wound' and since Anfortas was the Wounded King who bathed his wounds in this lake this is surely what was intended by this pseudonym. The prefixed *brun* or *brum* is more problematic but may mean 'burn', from which we derive 'brimstone', the Germanic and English biblical translation of *theion* θειον meaning 'sulphur'.

Eschenbach goes on to say that Lake Brumbane was very close to Castle Munsalvasche, which is sometimes called Corbenic in the *Vulgate*. Since this castle was also called Salvasche al Muntane it is readily apparent that the *muns* must refer to a 'mountain', from the Latin *mons* and the Old French *mont* or *munt*. And that leaves us with the Salvasche, which some authors translate as meaning 'wild' from the Latin *silva* and Old French *sylvain* meaning 'woods'. However, since Munsalvasche-Corbenic contained the Holy Grail, which could magically feed the grail knights and prevent Anfortas from dying, the a more logical translation would be from *salvatio* meaning 'salvation'. The Catholic Encyclopaedia gives both options.

Corbenic, the alternative name for Munsalvasche would tend to confirm this translation. But since the name for Corbenic comes from the *Vulgate* it is much more likely to be derived from the Aramaic, as most of the Vulgate's names are. *History of the Grail* confirms the Aramaic origin of this name when it says:

> They found on one of the gates a miraculous inscription in the Chaldean (language) saying, 'This Castle should be called Corbenic'. And in that language Corbenic means 'Holy Vessel'. (History 40:289) (Author's brackets.)

The Chaldean language is Aramaic, but unfortunately Corbenic does not mean 'Holy Vessel' in Aramaic. However, there is only one likely translation of Corbenic in the Aramaic and that is *corben* קרבן meaning 'offering' or 'sacrifice'. It is likely that the Mount of Salvation (Munsalvasche) and the Mount of Sacrifice (Corbenic) were two sides of the same nominative coin.

In which case, we now have the Wounded Fisher King 'fishing' upon the Lake of the Burning Wound, which resides next to the Mount of Salvation, and perhaps where a great Sacrifice had been made. And if this story is related in some manner to the Jewish Revolt, then we might tentatively link these many descriptions to the Dead Sea, which might well be considered to be a *brim* or *brum,* a 'sulphurous' lake. And if one had a festering wound that would not heal, as the Fisher King had, the Dead Sea would be an ideal location to heal that wound. And the wound would 'burn' in this lake, that is for sure. And this is a second reason why the Fisher King was pointedly said to have not caught any fish on Lake Brumbane, because the Dead Sea has no fish. King Jesus-Izas was more successful, as it says in John 21:6, but these were not real fish that Jesus was catching, they were converts to the veneration of the Great Month of Pisces.

But if Lake Brumbane referred to the Dead Sea, then surely Munsalvasche must refer to the only castle that stands on the shores of this great salt-lake, which is the mighty fortress of Masada. And Masada did become a mountain of Salvation for the Nazarene Sicarii rebels, who fled there after the fall of Jerusalem in AD 70. And it was also a mountain of great sacrifice, when the defenders committed mass suicide in AD 73 rather than

Fig 5.8
A fantasy image of Castle Munsalvasche, also known as Corbenic, the castle of the Holy Grail. Image courtesy of Wallpaperswa.

surrender to the Romans. Was Masada Munsalvasche-Corbenic, the original Castle of the Holy Grail? *

Feifefiz

At the conclusion of this epic story Eschenbach then begins to tie up the loose ends by having Feirefiz, the piebald son of Gahmuret by Belacane, travel to France. Parzival and Feirefiz meet in combat for no particular reason, as they often do in these tales, but they finally recognise each other and embrace. And so now the Eastern and Western ends of this story can meet and merge. And King Feirefiz of Zazamans (and many other Eastern kingdoms), promises to give the kingdoms of Zazamans and Azagouc to Parzival. And so the King of the East and the King of the West are as one once more, as if they had never been parted.

Interestingly, because Feirefiz arrives in the West we also get an 'invading army' arriving somewhere in southern France from the Saracen-Moorish East, just as Geoffrey of Monmouth described in *History of Kings*.

Fig 5.9
The fortress of Masada on the shores of the Dead Sea. Is this Castle Munsalvasche-Corbenic, the castle of the Holy Grail?

But here the army is not invading France - or rather the intention was to invade, until Feirefiz realised that Parzival was his half-brother. So we can see that each of these authors has interpreted the original source information in a different fashion. Monmouth describes a mighty battle with the Saracen Moors, perhaps for Crusader-type political reasons, while Eschenbach has the opposing sides embracing each other.

Feirefiz was then invited to Castle Munsalvasche, to see the procession of the Holy Grail. But, as we shall explore more fully in a later chapter, Feirefiz cannot see the Grail because he does not know what he is looking for. Feirefiz is like a child desperately looking for Father Christmas, while his parents are standing in front of him; and perhaps asking his parents to stand to one side, so he can get a better view. It is not that Father Christmas or the Holy Grail are particularly difficult to see, but you have to be initiated before you can understand who or what they are. 'There are none so blind as those who will not see,' as the old saying goes.

Feirefiz then falls in love with Repanse de Schoye, the sister of Anfortas the Fisher King, and asks for her hand in marriage. But he agrees to convert to Christianity before doing so. The intention of both Monmouth and Eschenbach is obvious here. The early 13th century was the era of the Fourth and Fifth Crusades to the Near East, which had the commendable objective of ending the occupation and subjugation of the Christian Near East by the Muslim caliphs. All of Syria, Jordan, Anatolia, North Africa and much of Mesopotamia had been Christian for hundreds of years, before Islam steamrollered through the region and enslaved the Christian and Jewish people of the East, and the Crusades intended to set these people free once more.

Thus Monmouth has readjusted his chronology to include Muslims invading France from Spain in the late 8th century, who are defeated in a great battle. And the propagandist meaning of this story is obvious - the mighty Christian army will always defeat the heathen Muslims. However, Eschenbach takes a different course entirely, but with the same propagandist intent. Eschenbach includes the Knights Templar as the guardians of the Grail, to give the story a contemporary feel, and then he has the heathen (ie: Muslim) Feirefiz converting to Christianity. Eschenbach is saying that when peace breaks out in the Near East, the heathen Muslims will naturally want to convert to Christianity. This is a propaganda double-punch by Monmouth and Eschenbach - Christianity will defeat the Muslims both militarily and spiritually.

* *History* says that a new Corbenic castle was built in a far western land, by the brother of Alain li Gros, who was called Joshua. (History 40:289) This Joshua sounds very similar to Alain's son, Perceval, who also travelled to the west according to *Merlin Grail*. This western land is probably Britain, but this story may be a retelling of the second journey to Sarras, as narrated in Chapter XII.

Prester John

Feirefiz and Repanse then have a child, who is the famous Prester John (Presbyter Johannes) of the East. It is said that the legend of Prester John, who is supposed to have evangelised throughout Ethiopia and perhaps even India, has been derived from the apocryphal Gospel of Thomas. And so Prester John could be equated with Mar Addai, the hero of *The Doctrine of Addai* who converted King Abgarus of Edessa to Nazarene Judaism. The story of Mar Addai has been discussed at length in *Jesus, King of Edessa,* so there is no point reviewing all that material here.

Despite many claims to the contrary, it is fairly well established that Mar Addai only went to Edessa and down the Mesopotamian valley as far as Nineveh, and not onto India or Ethiopia. A similar story was told about Prester John in the 12th century. Otto of Freising in his *Chronicon,* related that Prester John was a Nestorian Christian priest-king, who had regained the city of Ecbatana from the monarchs of Medes and Persia. [11] So once again we see an account of a Simple Judaic (Christian) priest in Mesopotamia, rather than India or Ethiopia.

The era for the life of Prester John is likewise uncertain. However, Papias, who was the 2nd century Bishop of Hierapolis in Anatolia, mentions a very similar character called Presbyter John from western Anatolia. The

Fig 5.10
A traditional view of Prester John, enthroned in Christian pomp and ceremony in eastern Africa on the borders of modern Ethiopia and Somalia.

account of Papias meeting Presbyter John is given to us by the Church historian Eusebius, who says:

> It is worth while observing here that the name John is twice enumerated by him (Papias). The first one he mentions in connection with Peter and James and Matthew ... clearly meaning the evangelist. But the other John he ... places among others outside of the number of the apostles, putting Aristion before him, and he distinctly calls him a presbyter. This shows that the statement of those is true, who say that there were two persons in Asia that bore the same name ... Papias gives ... the traditions handed down by Presbyter John. (History of the Church 3:39) (Author's brackets.)

Again we see the many problems that Arthurian chronology provides. Much of Arthurian history pretends to be based in the 6th century, but if the Arthurian Prester John is the same as the Prester John mentioned by Eusebius, then he must predate the 3rd and 4th century life of Eusebius. And he must also predate the 2nd century life of Bishop Papias, who originally wrote this story. Thus Parzival and Feirefiz must have been 1st or 2nd century characters, and not the 6th century heroes that traditional Arthurian history tries to imply. However, this is in complete agreement with *High History* and the first volumes of the *Vulgate Cycle*, which overtly place their narrative back into the 1st century.

The earliest of these dates is likely to be more correct, and so Prester John was probably an evangelist of the late 1st century who had travelled to western Anatolia and subsequently onto Mesopotamia, evangelising in the name of either Nazarene or Simple Judaism. Bearing this extensive travelogue in mind, perhaps the clue to who Prester John was can be seen in his full Latin title, which is Presbyter Johannes. So Prester John is unlikely to have been Mar Addai, who evangelised in Edessa in the mid 1st century, because Mar Addai has already been strongly linked to the apostle Thaddaeus Thomas Didymus. And so Mar Addai (Thaddaeus) was a disciple, rather than a presbyter, and he was never called Johannes.

But there ***was*** a very famous Johannes who evangelised in western Anatolia and the East in the mid to late 1st century. *Jewish War* and the *Vulgate Cycle* call him Josephus, while the Talmud calls him Johannes, and he was sent to Palmyra and Mesopotamia by Emperor Vespasian, both to evangelise (according to Arthurian history) and to warn the people there about the dire consequences of revolting against Rome (according to orthodox history). Unsurprisingly, his name is Saul-Josephus, the quicksilver-quilled author of much of 1st century history. And the only difference between these many diverse accounts, is that Prester John is being identified here as the son of Perceval-Parzival-Galahad instead of the father.

VI

Gibraltar, Santorini and the Augurs of Rome

History of the Holy Grail - Water Kayo
Book 1 of the *Vulgate Cycle* or *Lancelot Grail*

Before we look at *History of the Grail* in any detail, it may be worthwhile discussing whether the *Vulgate Cycle* contains any real history, or whether it is so fanciful and so mythological that it is not even worth researching. *History of the Grail* is a mixture of storytelling and flights of huge fantasy, especially where the text is introduced by phrases like 'Evalach's vision'. As soon as a character has a vision, we can expect page after page of unintelligible nonsense.

However, many of these flights of fancy are actually quite historical, if you know what the author is talking about. Yet because they appear to be fictional, these fanciful sections have never previously been explained in rational historical terms. So the decypherments that follow represent the first time any of these sections have ever been correctly replaced back into the historical record, from whence they came. And it has to be said that the third in this sequence of novel explanations, represents a deliciously cloaked and hugely comical satire of both biblical and eastern Roman history - which demonstrates that the author of *History* knew a great deal more about these 1st century events than any historian or theologian in the modern era.

As readers may have already gathered, this does mean that the story narrated in *History* is not exactly standard Arthurian material. Almost all of this manuscript is actually concerned with the adventures of Joseph of Arimathaea and his son, Josephus. So this is not the approved 5th or 6th century era of Arthurian legend at all, and most of the characters are not the familiar 'knights in shining armour' that we might expect. And where we do occasionally meet up with a few familiar Arthurian characters, they tend to get completely muddled with the 1st century era of Joseph of Arimathaea once more. So just as with the previous manuscripts we have looked at, the *Vulgate's* Arthurian history appears to be more concerned with 1st century Judaea than 6th century Britain.

And then we have these fanciful interpolations into *History of the Grail,* which appear to have absolutely nothing to do with the primary narrative. Every now and then and for no apparent reason, a character in the story will be whisked off on a semi-mythical journey to some unknown location and unknown era, to experience a strange adventure that defies explanation. It is up to the reader to figure out what is going on in these fanciful sections, but it is quite possible that nobody since the 13th century has understood what they really refer to or mean. So readers are about to be enlightened into some long-forgotten secret histories.

Note:

This translation of *History* is by Carol Chase, and she has taken the paragraph references from Hutcher, books II and III.

VI Gibraltar, Santorini, and Rome

The Rock of the Perilous Port

The first of these strange and obscure additions to the story within *History of the Grail,* is entitled 'The Rock of the Perilous Port'. In summary of the story up to this point, Joseph of Arimathaea had travelled northeast from Jerusalem in about AD 72 and arrived at a city called Sarras, which was ruled by King Evalach-Mordrain and his brother-in-law Prince Seraphe-Nascien. These are real historical characters, as we shall see later.

This decidedly out-of-place insertion into the unfolding story then says that King Evalach-Mordrain travelled seventeen days from his eastern kingdom in a semi-mythical journey, but for what for what purpose we are not told. One suspects that the real reason for this fantastical journey, is simply to introduce this curious and disjointed interpolation into the story. Anyway, at last Evalach-Mordrain arrives at a large rock in the ocean that is said to lie somewhere between Babylon and Scotland, where the Perilous Port was located. This great rock is described as being:

> So high that one could survey the entire Western Sea, as far as those places where land could be seen. And in the other direction ... one could see the land of Cordoba and the entire tip of Spain ... This rock was so unpleasant and uncultivated ... that is consisted entirely of raw stone up to the edge of the sea. (History 16:339)

> Lightning descended from on high and struck the rock so hard that it split straight down the middle, so that half of it remained standing just as it had before, while the other half that broke off from it fell into the depths of the sea and was never seen again. (History 17:385)

Quite plainly King Mordrain of Sarras in Syria was now in Gibraltar for some reason, and the Rock of Gibraltar does indeed look as though one half of the mountain has fallen away into the adjacent sea. And from the remaining half of this cleaved mountain, a good view of the entire Atlantic and much of the tip of Spain can be obtained, just as these quotes say. And bearing in mind that this is either a 1st or a 13th century text, it is interesting to read that the author believes that land can be seen across the other side of the Atlantic.

So what on earth was Mordrain, a late 1st century AD king from northeastern Syria, doing in Gibraltar? Well, although this has absolutely nothing to do with the rest of the story *History* is relating, it is said this rock was inhabited by the meanest of pirates who ever ruled the sea; until Pompey the Great came along and destroyed them all. And here we can immediately see that this interpolated fanciful story is not simply dislocated geographically, but chronologically too. Pompey the Great died in 48 BC, after his eventual defeat by Julius Caesar, so why have we jumped back in time by a century or so?

We shall come back to what the historical Pompey was really doing in Gibraltar a minute, but the text in *History* says of these events:

> Pompey, who was the Roman emperor at the time, crossed the sea of Greece and came to Syria ... he heard about these pirates who killed everyone who passed there. And he said that everything he had done (in the Mithraic wars) would be for nothing, if he did not rid this land of pirates. (History 16:341) (Author's brackets.)

According to *History* it would appear that the Roman Republic's problem with piracy started in the east, somewhere between Greece and Syria, and became an issue of national and international importance. So Pompey gathered a small fleet together to combat these pirates:

Fig 6.1 The Rock of Gibraltar, one of the legendary Pillars of Hercules. History of the Grail says that a lightning bolt split the mountain in two, and one half fell into the sea.

> (Pompey) provided 40 men on his ship with twenty large hooks to hold the galleys (together) when they attacked his ship at sea. Pompey and his men sailed until they saw the high and marvelous rock (of Gibraltar), and they cast anchor to wait for night. After a good part of the night had passed, they sailed close enough to the rock to throw a stone (at it) by hand. And when the pirates heard them, they boarded their ships and prepared to assault them. (History 16:341-342) (author's brackets.)

So *History* is saying that Pompey the Great was an emperor, who became an admiral for a while to rid the seas of pirates. Surprisingly, this potted history of Rome is close to being correct. Pompey had become a consul of the Roman Republic in 70 BC, just three years before these events; and since there was no such position as emperor at this time, a consul was as high as one could climb the political ladder of Rome. So yes, one could easily say that Pompey had become akin to an emperor, but perhaps 'prime minister' might be slightly more accurate. And yes, Pompey did become an admiral, one of the first admirals of the ancient world, which is why the large naval base at Portsmouth in England is called Pompey.

What we have here in *History,* is a large section of the story that appears to have nothing to do with Arthurian history whatsoever; and nor does it appear to have anything to do with 1st century Judaea and the Jewish Revolt. It is tempting to think that an old manuscript was lying upon the desk of the author, who thought to himself: 'hmm, this is interesting, but where can I put this into the story in order to preserve it?' And 'preserve it' may be the correct phrase here, because this information may well have been lost to the rest of modern history. Nevertheless, we shall eventually see at

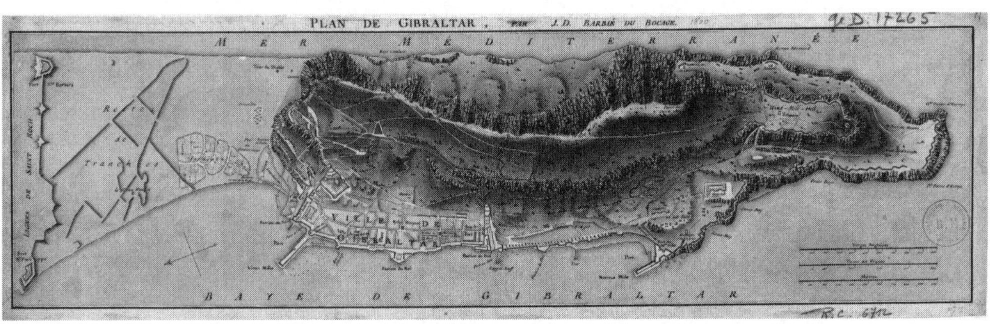

Fig 6.2 A 19th century map of the Rock of Gibraltar, showing how the cliffs used to border the sea.

the end of this section, how this account of Pompey and the pirates is very closely connected to the creation of Simple Judaism, and therefore quite closely connected to this new style of Arthurian history.

So this interpolated story in *History* is actually relating the history of Pompeius Magnus (Pompey the Great) and the Lex Gabinia - a famous law made in Rome and named after Gabinius, the law's proposer. In 67 BC, just two years after Pompey's appointment as consul of Rome, shipping in the eastern Mediterranean was being plagued by pirates and so international trade and therefore the Roman economy was beginning to suffer. So Tribune Gabinius proposed that Pompey be given command of all the Mediterranean, and also control inland from all its coasts to a distance of 50 miles.

Now this was quite some command, perhaps the most powerful position in all of Rome, and so the Lex Gabinia was robustly contested in the Senate. Nevertheless, piracy was such a threat to the state and the all-important grain supplies from Egypt, that Pompey got his command and became the admiral of the entire Mediterranean. And perhaps the senators had been right to question the power that came with this post, because Pompey is said to have ended up with 500 ships and 120,000 men under his command. This sounds like a gross exaggeration, but he obviously ended up with a sizeable navy. Suitably equipped with warships, Pompey then set off

Fig 6.3
A coin of Pompeius Magnus under the authority of Lucius Calpurnius Piso as quaestor, dating from 49 BC. The reverse says 'Magn Procos' (Pompey the Great, Proconsul) and portrays a galley in recognition of Pompey's successful leadership of the Lex Gabinia.

The device above the deck is probably a gangplank hanging from a jib. The Romans were not the best of sailors, so they preferred to lock the ships together, place a bridge between the two, and turn a naval battle into something they were much more familiar with - a standard land-battle with legionnaires bearing shields and swords.

in search of pirates. And perhaps the best description we have of Pompey's escapades on the Mediterranean, comes from Plutarch:

> The power of the pirates had its beginning in Cilicia, and at first its adventure was attended with hazard and sought concealment, but it gained confidence and daring in the Mithridatic war by lending itself to aid the king. Then, the Romans being engaged in the civil wars about the gates of Rome, the sea was left destitute of all protection, and this by degrees drew them on, and encouraged them (the pirates) not to confine their attacks to those who navigated the sea, but to ravage islands and maritime cities. (Plutarch's Lives III, Pompeius, xxiv)

Note the strong correspondence between Plutarch's historical account and this out-of-place story in *History*. In both accounts the threat of piracy is said to have started in the east of the Empire, at Cilicia in southeastern Anatolia according to Plutarch. And this piracy spread quickly because, as Plutarch claims here, King Mithridates of Pontus was encouraging and assisting these seaborne bandits as a part of his Mithridatic war with Rome, which continued from 88 to 63 BC. Pontus was a small principality to the south of the Black Sea, but grew in size and influence to surround the Black Sea and much of Anatolia too. This is why this piracy was primarily based in and around the eastern Mediterranean. Please see the map in fig 5.3.

This is not unlike the episode of the Barbary pirates of North Africa in the 17th and 18th centuries, who raided the coasts of southern and northern Europe and took more than a million white European slaves to their bases in North Africa.[1] And in a very similar fashion to this encouragement by Mithridates of Pontus, the Barbary pirates were likewise selling their booty and their captured slaves into the slave markets of the Ottoman Empire in Anatolia. All that had changed over the many centuries, was the pirate's main base of operation. The Barbary pirates were based along the Barbary coast in North Africa, while the Pontic pirates were based along the coasts of southern Anatolia.

It is clear that the author of *History* knew the events of this era quite well. He knows of the battles with the Pontic pirates, and he also knows of the Third Mithridatic War against Mithridates the Great. The story says of Pompey's campaigns in the East:

> Until it happened that the great Pompey ... crossed the sea of Greece and came to the land of Syria. After he had gone throughout the lands of the East and captured the defended fortresses as far as Babylon, he heard about the pirates... (History 16:340)

While the pirate wars actually came before the major land campaign in the

East rather than after, this is still a reasonable potted history of the events of this era, so we know that *History* is recounting elements of real history, rather than a flight of fictional fancy. And the reason why Arthurian history should be concerned with the Pontic wars in the 1st century BC will be explained shortly because, believe it or not, this largely forgotten dispute with Rome is closely linked with the birth of Christianity.

Coracesium

Anyway, in the 1st century BC the piracy problem grew to unbearable proportions, with Plutarch claiming that the pirates had 1,000 corsair ships at their disposal, which is quite obviously another exaggeration. So the Roman Senate had been forced by Gabinius into accepting a novel solution - to appoint Pompey the Great as the Admiral of the Empire. Plutarch says of these events:

> The power of the pirates extended over the whole of our sea at once in a measure, so that it could not be navigated and was closed against all trade. It was this which mainly induced the Romans, who were hard pressed for provisions and were expecting great scarcity, to send out Pompeius to clear the sea of the pirates. Gabinius, one of the friends of Pompeius, drew up a law which gave Pompeius, not just a naval command, but palpably sole dominion and power over all men. (Plutarch's Lives III, Pompeius xxv)
>
> However, by dividing the waters and the whole space of the internal sea into thirteen parts and appointing a certain number of ships and a commander for each, with his force, which was thus dispersed in all directions, he surrounded the piratical vessels that fell in his way in a body, and forthwith hunted them down and brought them into port. (Plutarch's Lives III, Pompeius xxvi)

So the accounts in *History* and by Plutarch are singing from the same hymn-sheet, because Pompey did indeed become the Roman admiral charged with hunting down these evil pirates, who were disrupting trade throughout the eastern Mediterranean. But note that Pompey divided the seas into thirteen segments, with a commander in each, and so we can already see that this is not a simple tale of admirals and pirates, and may have several pages or chapters firmly located within astrology. But at this point the two accounts diverge slightly.

> Those who ... effected their escape, crowded from all parts and made their way to Cilicia as (bees) to a hive. And against them Pompeius himself went with sixty of the best ships. (Plutarch III, xxvi)

> The greater part and the most powerful of the pirates had deposited their families and wealth ... in garrisons and strong forts among the heights of the Taurus. But the pirates themselves manned their ships and awaited the approach of Pompeius near Coracesium in Cilicia. And a battle was fought in which they were defeated and afterwards blockaded. (Plutarch's Lives III, Pompeius xxvii)

So Plutarch says that the pirate's bases were located along the Taurus mountains in southern Anatolia, which is not surprising considering the kingdom of Pontus encompassed much of central and eastern Anatolia. And the final battle with these pirates was staged at Coracesium near modern Alanya in southern Anatolia. In great contrast, *History* is quite clearly pointing towards Gibraltar for this final last-stand, which is 4,000 km away from Alanya and the Pontic kingdom.

So who is right here, Plutarch and modern historians, or the supposedly fanciful mythology in Water Kayo's *History*? Well, place names are notoriously unreliable in historical texts, because cities often had multiple names in multiple languages, and the same names were often repeated in different locations. Cities called Antioch or Alexandria, for instance, are scattered all over the Near and Middle East, so which of these similar cities is any one particular text referring to? Interestingly, the editor's notes to Plutarch says of Coracesium:

> This place is on the coast of the Rough or Mountainous Cilicia, on a steep rock near the sea. (Plutarch's Lives, Aubrey Stewart notes.)

This editor's note is taken from Strabo's *Geography*, which says:

> The first place is Coracesium, a fortress of the Cilicians, situated upon an abrupt rock. Diodotus Tryphon used it as a rendezvous at the time that he caused Syria to revolt from her kings, and carried on war against them with various success. (Strabo, Geography, xiv:v:2)

So while these two locations for a pirate hideout are situated at opposite ends of the Mediterranean, both of them feature a precipitous rock adjacent to the sea. So the descriptions are consistent, even if the location is not. But who is the more correct here, Walter Kayo or Plutarch?

Well, if accuracy is dependent upon the quantity of detailed information, then the *Vulgate Cycle* wins this historical contest with ease. In his *History,* Walter Kayo goes on to record every detail of the hand-to-hand fighting, as Pompey landed at the foot of the Rock of Gibraltar and engaged the pirates. But since it was too dark to see what was going on, the Roman commander advised Pompey to withdraw until daylight. The pirates had retreated into tunnels deep inside the rock, which they were tenaciously defending. Pompey's commanders did not know what to do, but Pompey suggested smoking them out and so fires were lit at the base of the rock, and:

> Pompey sent forty knights forward to light the fire with pieces of the (pirate) ships that had broken on the rocks. When the fire had caught well, the flames shot up to the entrance of the cave where the pirates were, and much of the smoke went in. Upon seeing this the pirates took fresh water, which they had in abundance, and poured it onto the fire, which became so full of smoke that it was nearly extinguished. However, those at the bottom shot numerous arrows and stones at the pirates, and wounded four of them.
>
> When Pompey saw that the enemy were holding out so long ... he ran up to the fire ... and pursued them so fiercely they did not dare to wait for him. They fled back to the cave with Pompey rushing after them ... When the leader saw that Pompey was alone and a single man had forced his men to flee ... he changed his mind and turned back. Pompey raised his battle-axe to strike Foucaire on the head, but he dodged the blow and the axe struck the rocks so hard that the

Fig 6.4 St Michael's cave inside the Rock of Gibraltar. There are now some 55 km of tunnels and caves inside the Rock.

entire blade shattered, and the handle flew into pieces. (History 16:348).

The text continues, with Foucaire and Pompey continuing the fight and ending up falling off the path and into the fire below. Pompey was dazed but unharmed, and after lighting the fire once more the pirates were all asphyxiated in their caves.

The detail here is incredible, with individual actions described and the leader of the pirates named. But detail within *History* does not always equate to reality, as some of the battle scenes within the *Vulgate Cycle* are equally detailed and yet they seem to be nonsensical fairytales. So was this particular battle fact or fiction? Did the pirates' last stand take place on the southern coast of Anatolia at Alanya, or were they holed up in the Rock of Gibraltar? Well, there are some aspects of this Gibraltarian battle-scene that are historically correct.

Firstly, a sailor could indeed sail right up to the Rock of Gibraltar in the 1st century. Even in the 19th century this was still possible, as the map in fig 6.2 demonstrates. Secondly, there are indeed many tunnels in the Rock that these pirates could have holed up in. There are some vast natural caverns, like the impressive St Michaels Cave, and there are numerous man-made tunnels and caverns too. In fact, these military tunnels now extend for over 55 km, within the Rock of Gibraltar. So yes, there would indeed have been many tunnels and caves that these fugitives could have used to conceal themselves and their booty.

Strabo

But while this is interesting, none of it can be taken as proof that Pompey was fighting the last of the pirates at Gibraltar, rather than at Coracesium in Anatolia. However, there is one final piece of evidence that swings the pendulum of reality firmly in favour of the *Vulgate Cycle*.

The description of Coracesium came from Strabo's *Geography*, as we have seen. And Strabo does link the pirates with this region, because in two sections he says that Pompey made his main base on Rhodes, while conducting his expeditions against the pirates. (See XI:I:6 and XIV:III:3.)

However, Strabo describes many places and cities all across the Roman Empire and beyond, and one of the places he mentions is the southern coast of Spain. The two towns in question are Nebrissa and Onoba, which are identified as being modern Lebrija which is located a short distance to the west of Cadiz, and Gibraleón which lies a bit further to the west. Strabo mentions that these towns are situated on the estuary of the Guadalquiver river, which was tidal in those days for a long way inland, which is why these towns are not on the coast. In fact, merchants could sail right up the Guadalquiver river past Sevilla and onto Cordoba, making this a valuable trade-route. Strabo then says of these two small towns, and others on the Guadalquiver estuary:

> Their trade is wholly carried on with Italy and Rome. The navigation is excellent as far as the Pillars (of Hercules), (excepting perhaps some little difficulties at the Strait), and equally so on the Mediterranean, where the voyages are very calm, especially to those who keep the high seas. This is a great advantage to merchant-vessels. The winds on the high seas blow regularly; and peace reigns there now, the pirates having been put down, so that in every respect the voyage is effortless. (Strabo, Geography III:II:5)

The trade-route from the Guadalquiver estuary to Rome would have taken these merchants through the Straits of Gibraltar, and Strabo, who was writing in about 20 BC or later, says that: 'peace reigns there now, the pirates having been put down'. Strabo is the Roman authority on the geography (the physical features) and chorography (the political and social features) of the Roman Empire. And yet here Strabo is agreeing with the *Vulgate Cycle,* rather than with Plutarch. Although much of the action against the pirates

Fig 6.5 A map showing the Straits of Gibraltar. The small towns of Nebrissa and Onoba reside just to the west of Cadiz. The route that their merchants used to trade with Rome went past the pirate's bases, which were located upon the Rock of Gibraltar.

took place on the south coast of Anatolia, this short extract from Strabo is plainly recording that there was also a very well-known case of piracy near the Straits of Gibraltar, but it had been 'put down' by the time Strabo was writing his *Geography*.

The inescapable conclusion to this short chapter, is that the *Vulgate Cycle* in general, and *History of the Grail* in particular, does contain unexpected elements of real history. And not simply extracts from well-known and broad-brush events in history, but instead giving quite detailed descriptions of specific events. And if *History* can be seen to be correct about the pirates holed-up in the caves of Gibraltar, one can easily imagine that *History* is also correct when it says that their leader was called Foucaire and he and his men were smoked out of their caves by Pompey the Great.

Temple Mount

This same out-of-place story then relates that Pompey the Great went to Jerusalem and desecrated the Temple Mount by stabling his horses there.* Again the general thrust of these paragraphs is correct, because Pompey took control of Syria in 64 BC and of Jerusalem the following year. Josephus Flavius says of these events:

> No small enormities were committed within the temple itself, which, in former ages, had been inaccessible, and seen by none. For Pompey went into it, and not a few of those that were with him also, and saw all that which it was unlawful for any other men to see but only for the high priests. There were in that temple the golden table, the holy candlestick, and the pouring vessels, and a great quantity of spices; and besides these there were among the treasures two thousand talents of sacred money: yet did Pompey touch nothing of all this, on account of his regard to religion. (Josephus Ant 14:4:4)

In contrast *History* says of this very same event:

> There was a very worthy old man called St Simon, who presented Jesus at the Temple on the day of purification (Yom Kippur). When he found out about the great violation Pompey had committed by stabling his horses in the lord's holy

* *History* indicates that Pompey stabled his horses inside the Temple of Jerusalem itself, but this is highly unlikely and disagrees with Josephus' accounts. Besides, the more famous Second Temple was not built until the time of Herod the Great.

> house, he said that he had lived too long ... He went straight to Pompey and began to shout and cry as if he had lost his senses ... (and said): 'We believed that Pompey had killed Foucaire, but Foucaire has killed Pompey.' (History 16:352) (author's brackets)

The latter comment is a highly barbed observation, indicating that Pompey had so debased himself, by stabling his horses on the Temple Mount, that he had become a pirate just like Foucaire (the pirate leader). Of course this could not have happened exactly as it is related here, because Pompey's campaign in Judaea happened long before the era of Jesus, unless the text is implying that St Simon is recalling events from the distant past (some 80 or 90 years before, according to the classical biblical chronology). So why has this account of Pompey the Great conquering Jerusalem been included within *History's* narrative, which up until this interlude had been describing the role of Joseph(us) of Arimathaea during and after the Jewish Revolt?

The initial suspicion is that the author of *History* did not know the difference between the first Jewish Revolt in 66 BC (Pompey started his eastern campaign in 66 BC), and the great Jewish Revolt which started in AD 66. Having never heard of the earlier Roman campaigns in Judaea, perhaps the author thought that these earlier events must all be connected with the later Jewish Revolt.

Fig 6.6 Pompey enters the Holy of Holies in the Temple of Jerusalem, by Jean Fouquet.

That is certainly one possibility, but it is not the only conclusion we can draw. The alternative and more provocative possibility, is that perhaps the author knew rather more than we do. Perhaps he not only knew the difference between these revolts, but also knew that they were historically linked, a possibility that modern history knows nothing about.

Secret rituals

The clue to there being something rather more cryptic or occult (hidden) that underlies this story, can be seen in the peculiar secrecy that it was subjected to. In the final paragraph of this chapter it says:

> And when Pompey left Jerusalem, he forbade his household to ever speak of Foucaire, for he did not want to be reproached for using all his power and forces to attack and capture pirates. Thus this feat was kept silent, for it was not put in writing among his other deeds. The fact that his household kept it secret prevented it from being known, although it was the greatest feat he had ever achieved, and for which he would have been remembered best. (History 16:353)

Thus the story of the pirates on Gibraltar was a secret history that Pompey had not told anyone about. More than that, he had deliberately commanded his household to keep this particular topic secret. But why? The accounts we have from Strabo indicate that the broad outline of the story is true, for there had indeed been an action against a nest of pirates based close to the Straits of Gibraltar. But if this was simply another of the many battles with the Pontus pirates, then why keep it secret? For what reason would any great military leader want to keep a skirmish with the enemy secret?

If the engagement had gone badly wrong and made the commander look foolish, one might expect such a reaction. But this minor conflict did not go wrong for it appears to have been a great victory, both from the viewpoint of Strabo and the author of *History*. So again we must ask: why the explicit requirement for secrecy for such a seemingly trivial event? And if it was so secret, then how did Walter Kayo get to know about it? In addition, readers perhaps need reminding here that this chapter is still an investigation into Arthurian history. So what are we doing in Gibraltar, investigating the heroic deeds and actions of Pompey the Great against a band of cutthroat pirates? Just what, if anything, could link these two disparate and seemingly unconnected slices of history?

Some lateral thinking is required. Savor the moment of mystery for a few minutes. Engage the cerebral cortex and let the synapses spark. We have secrets, caves, Romans, pirates; plus a strong link with Arthurian history, which is closely linked to 1st century Judaean history and thence to Christianity. So what is the common factor in all of this? Where is the silken thread that weaves this disjointed and incoherent history into a perfectly symmetric web?

The answer is Mithras.

As we have already seen, Roman Mithras did not spring from the Zoroastrian veneration of Mithra, instead it was an eastern Sabean astrological cult that venerated the precessional zodiac. And this is why Pompey was said to have divided the seas into thirteen segments. Pompey was indeed the secular admiral of the Mediterranean, but this description of the seas having thirteen segments comes straight from astrology. The seas in question were the celestial seas above, which are divided into twelve segments of the zodiac plus a central circle for the position of either Ursa Major or the Sun, making thirteen. And so Pompey was using his position as admiral to declare himself as the central director or ring-master of precessional astrology. Just as a Mason might declare himself to be a 'pillar of society', in order to announce his affiliation to the Craft, so Pompey Magnus was also declaring his allegiances and his central position within the zodiac of Mithras.

And while the Roman version of Mithras might have been supremely out of date by the time it penetrated the Roman Empire, it was still an astrological creed that venerated the zodiac. And so Mithras had nothing whatsoever to do with the Persian Mithra, and nothing to do with the Nazarene Ebionite creed either, for they knew that the Great Months had moved away from Taurus long ago. That is why King Jesus-Izas was born as a Lamb of God but became a Fisher of Men, because the Nazarene knew that the Great Month of Aries was fading and the Great Month of Pisces was now dominant. If there was any sacrificial killing to be done, Mithras should have been killing a ram, not a bull.

But if Roman Mithras did not come from Mithra, and nor did it come from the Nazarene Ebionites of Syrio-Judaea, then where did it come from? Surprisingly, the answer lies in Walter Kayo's *History of the Grail* and its peculiar account of the Pontic Pirates that Pompey was battling all across the Mediterranean. Plutarch says of these pirates:

> Now the piratical ships had increased to above a thousand, and the cities captured by them were four hundred ... They also performed strange rites at Olympos and celebrated certain mysterious ceremonies, among which were those of Mithras and they are continued to the present time, having been first introduced by them. (Plutarch's Lives III, Pompeius, xxiv)

The Olympos mentioned here is not Mount Olympus, but the ancient city of Olympos to the southwest of Antalya in Anatolia. And since Plutarch mentions 'strange rites' at Olympos, perhaps it is worth mentioning that there was a commune of tree-dwelling European hippies living there until 2014, when the Turkish government evicted them all. But if we go back to the 1st century BC we find that the secret mysteries performed at Olympos involved Mithras. And since the ruler of Pontus at this time was Mithridates VI, it is highly likely that this version of Mithras was born in Pontic Anatolia, rather than in Persia. These were cutthroat pirates who sailed the eastern Mediterranean, so were they going to derive their secret Mithraic rituals from? From across Syria and down into Persia, or from the very coasts that were controlled and governed by their own king, Mithridates? So yes, the cult of Mithras came from Mithraic Anatolia rather than Persia, just as Plutarch says, and it was named after King Mithridates VI.

But the cult of Mithras did not stay with the Pontic pirates in Anatolia. By the turn of the 1st century it had migrated to Rome, with hundreds of *mithraeum* initiation chambers being established in the city of Rome and hundreds more across the Empire. It was a favourite cult and initiation ceremony of the Roman military. And one presumes that one of the pathways by which Mithras migrated to Rome was through the many contacts that Pompey the Great had with the Mithraic pirates he was contending with in Mithridates' kingdom of Pontus. Wars often end in political negotiations, when such secrets might be discussed as a part of a peace agreement. And we shall see further evidence for Pompey's direct involvement in Mithraic ceremonies shortly.

Yet the mysteries of Mithras did not stay enclosed within the secret confines of the *mithraeum* initiation chamber, because they appear to have branched out into the Roman cult of Sol Invictus and into the Romo-Judaic cult of Simple Christianity. And it was these Mithraic blood-drinking aspects of Simple Judaism that Saul-Josephus was mocking in *High History,* as we saw earlier. And if the blood-drinking rituals that Emperor Vespasian had forced into Simple Judaism were derived from the Mithraic initiation ceremonies of the Pontic pirates, rather than from Saul-Josephus' original brand of Simple Judaism, then perhaps these pirates did deserve a mention within these manuscripts. Many of the manuscripts we have looked at have been describing the birth of Simple Judaism after the Jewish Revolt, and the cult of Mithras was one aspect within that complex new creed. Which is why many of the manuscripts that form the foundations of Arthurian history seem to be concerned more with the Jewish Revolt than with the Saxon invasions on Britain.

And the mention of Mithraic rituals within Arthurian history would make even more sense, if those original manuscripts were derived from the quicksilver quilled historian himself - Saul-Josephus. As we saw in *High History* it is likely that Josephus was absolving himself from the cannibalistic flesh-eating and blood-drinking rituals of Simple Judaism by mocking them, but here he may well be absolving himself from those same rituals by explaining where they came from. These decidedly non-Judaic blood rituals were not his idea they came from Foucaire, the leader of the Pontic pirates, and they were brought to Rome and thence to Simple

Judaism by Pompey the Great.

Pompey-Mithras

However, it is possible that this novel conclusion can be taken one dramatic step further. Perhaps we can also propose that Foucaire, the pirate leader, might be a highly cryptic substitute for the Mithraic bull. In other words, when St Simon says in a previous quote: 'We believed that Pompey had killed Foucaire, but Foucaire has killed Pompey,' was he talking about the pirate leader or the Mithraic bull? And while this may seem like unbridled speculation at this point, let us run with this for a while and see where it leads. Luckily *History* gives us good a description of the pirate leader and it is said that:

> This pirate was unusually large and so strong that no man could hold out against the strength of his limbs. This pirate came to this rock, and he made his home out of the rock itself, which he dug out until he had a chamber that could lodge twenty men. In this lodging he and his numerous companions stayed, but they could not all sleep inside the rock for they numbered ... a hundred or more ... during the night when it was very dark they put great brands of burning fire on the rock. (History 16:340)

So Foucaire was big and strong, and he came to Gibraltar and carved out a cavern large enough for twenty people. And this is despite the fact that his band of pirates numbered a hundred or more, and the fact that the Rock of Gibraltar already contained any number of natural caves capable of housing a thousand pirates. So was this 'chamber that could lodge twenty men' a refuge for pirates, or was it a *mithraeum* initiation chamber? It so happens that the standard *mithraeum* is an underground chamber carved out of the rock that held about twenty men, and it would have had burning torches outside to illuminate the entrance during these secret nocturnal rituals.

So was Pompey flushing out dangerous pirates from the caves inside the Rock of Gibraltar, or was he joining them in a secret ritual in a *mithraeum*? The story in *History* continues and says:

> Foucaire and Pompey were engaged in hand-to hand combat, the first to arrive struck Foucaire with his lance so fiercely that he made him stagger and his feet flew out from the path ... the pirate was tall and big and heavy and he made (Pompey) lose his lose his footing ... Once his men had uncovered his (Pompey's) face they saw he was as pale as if he was dead and that he was not moving his legs feet or hands. (History 16:348-349) (Author's brackets.)

Is Pompey's hand-to-hand combat really with Foucaire the pirate, or is this Pompey in the guise of Mithras, in hand-to-hand combat with the Mithraic bull? When Foucaire is struck by a lance, is this the pirate leader receiving a deadly blow or is this the Mithraic bull being stabbed in the neck by Mithras? And when Foucaire loses his footing and his feet fly out from the path, is this the pirate leader stumbling or is it a perfect description of the splayed legs of the Mithraic bull, as is depicted on all the altars of Mithras? See fig 6.8 for an image of this scene. And Mithras is only squatting in that awkward position because he represents the constellation of Orion, and that is generally how Orion is shown in classical depictions, with the left knee bent in exactly that same fashion (where Orion is facing the viewer).

And finally, when Pompey lays down as if he is dead, is this the result of this dramatic fight between two fierce opponents, or is this just a standard component in a secret ritual of death and resurrection, just like the masonic Third Degree? Surprising as it may seem, the answer to all of these questions probably lies in the name of the Pontic pirate leader, Foucaire, for in the Aramaic a bull is called a *buker* בקר or a Boucaire.

Fig 6.7 The subterranean mithraeum below the San Clemente Basilica in Rome. Like all mithraeums, it is a small chamber large enough for about twenty men and one priest, just like the chamber at Gibraltar that Foucaire made.

Pompey's battle	**Mithraic battle**
Pompey vs Foucaire	Mithras vs Boucaire

Interesting, isn't it? The leader of the Pontic pirates in Gibraltar was actually a symbolic representation of the Mithraic bull, Boucaire-Foucaire, and he was being slain by Pompey-Mithras in a secret ceremony in a *mithraeum* initiation chamber inside the Rock of Gibraltar.

But as we saw in Chapter III, Mithras himself is merely symbolic of the constellation of Orion-Hercules, the ring-master and director of the precessional rotation of the heavens and the zodiac. In which case, the

Fig 6.8 Pompey the Great as Mithras in hand-to-hand combat with Boucaire-Foucaire, the Mithraic bull which represents the constellation of Taurus and therefore the end of the Great Month of Taurus. The cult of Mithras was therefore some 1,700 years adrift in its symbolism, for in the 1st century BC Pompey the Great should have been slaying the Mithraic ram of Aries, rather than the Mithraic bull of Taurus. Note the dog, that is drinking the life-giving blood of the bull.

Pontic god Mithras is merely an alternate version of the Sumerian god-king Gilgamesh (Orion). Which is probably why *History* says of Pompey Magnus:

> Thus Pompey killed five of them with his battle-axe, leaving only fourteen ... Ready to reenter the cave after the others, he (Foucaire-Boucaire) changed his mind and turned back. Pompey raised his battle-axe in both hands, thinking to strike him on the head, but Foucaire dodged the blow and the axe struck the slope of the rock so hard the entire blade shattered, and the handle flew into pieces. (History 16:348) (Author's brackets.)

A Roman general wielding a battle-axe? Sorry, but even the Roman soldiery did not use battle axes, let alone their generals. However, Gilgamesh, Hercules and Orion did use a weapon of this nature, which is where this description came from. Orion-Hercules traditionally brandished a huge club whereas Gilgamesh carried an axe, and this is why Pompey is incongruously described as wielding a battle-axe. In this scene Pompey Magnus was the great Orion-Hercules-Gilgamesh, in mortal combat with Boucaire-Foucaire the Mithraic Bull of Heaven - Taurus.

In which case, our previously wild speculations are now resting on much more solid foundations. Yes, the Pontic pirates did exist; and yes, Pompey Magnus did smoke them out of their hideouts all across the Mediterranean, including on Gibraltar. But during that military campaign, perhaps during the surrender negotiations, Pompey was also initiated into a secret ritual that was unknown in Rome at that time: the cosmic ritual of Mithras-Hercules and the precession of the zodiac. So Pompey was initiated into Mithras at the pirate's secret *mithraeum* lodge, possibly inside the Rock of Gibraltar, before persuading these pirates to desist from piracy and engage in more legitimate forms of maritime trade.

But did this pirate lodge really meet in the Rock of Gibraltar, or was this merely the symbolic location of all Mithraic lodges? All masonic lodges are symbolic of the Temple of Jerusalem (or the Great Pyramid), even if they are located in Washington DC or rural Illinois, so did the same kind of symbolism apply to Mithraic lodges too? The reason for thinking this is that the Rock of Gibraltar happens to be one of the Pillars of Hercules, and it was Orion-Hercules (ie: Mithras) who was killing the precessional Taurean Bull of Heaven.

Fig 6.11 shows a 17th or 18th century-looking Orion battling with the Taurean bull, while holding his shield and Herculean club. But in fig 6.12 Orion is not only wielding a Herculean club he is also holding up the Nemean Lion as a shield, which was the primary symbol of Hercules. So Orion is, and always has been, closely linked with Hercules and therefore linked with the twin Herculean pillars at Gibraltar. So now we have Pompey

Magnus as the heroic Mithras (ie: Hercules-Orion) slaying Boucaire-Foucaire the bull (ie: Taurus), in a *mithraeum* lodge inside one of the pillars of Hercules. So were these Pillars of Hercules symbolic of the Twin Pillars of Yachin and Boaz that graced the entrance to the Temple of Jerusalem, and the Master's throne at every Masonic Lodge?

Is all of this a coincidence too far? Was the location of this ceremony at Gibraltar symbolic, or did the Pontus pirates establish a lodge on Gibraltar because of its strategic and symbolic location? Whatever the case, it is highly likely that this symbolic battle between Pompey-Mithras and Foucaire-Boucaire is why Pompey Magnus explicitly told his household never to mention this topic, even after his death. Pompey may have alluded to it during his lifetime, but the household would have only known this event as a real military engagement, and not the symbolic slaying of Taurus in a Mithraic initiation chamber. Only Pompey and a few confidantes knew that,

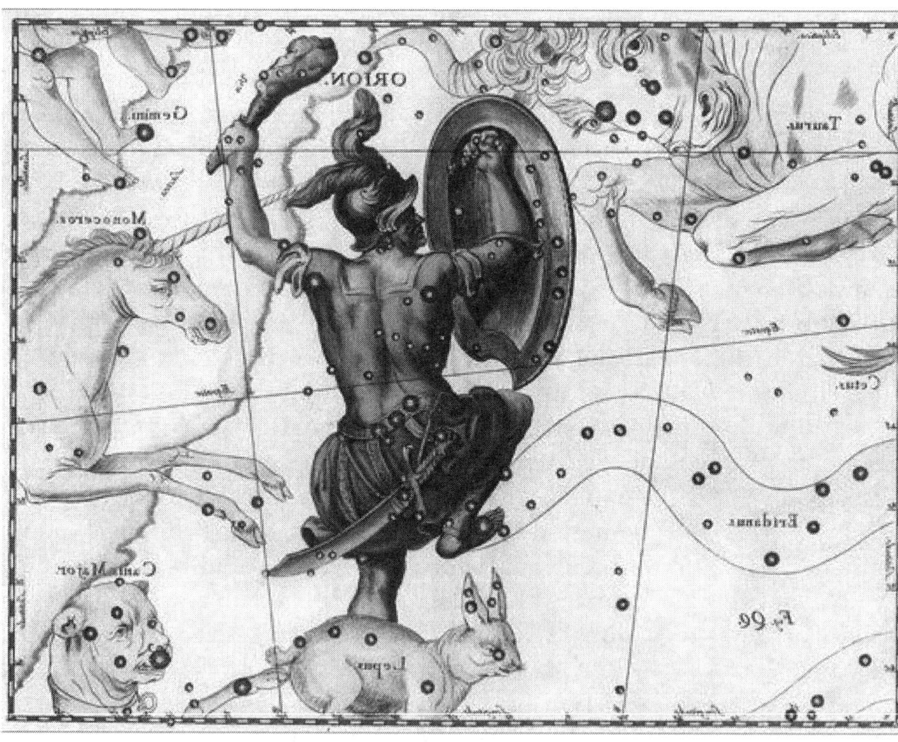

Fig 6.11 Orion-Hercules-Gilgamesh-Pompey, battles with the Mithraic Taurean bull of Boucaire-Foucaire with his great club (or axe); and he has his sword hanging from his prominent belt, ready for the final coup de gras. Normally Orion is facing us, and so it is his left leg that is bent, and the right outstretched, just as we see in the bull-slaying depictions of Mithras-Pompey.

and so he forbade any mention of the subject so as not to cause any confusion or embarrassment.

But perhaps another reason for this secrecy is that Pompey only realised some time later, that he had been sold a phoney religion that was 1,700 years out of date. The center of Sabaean precessional cosmology did not lie within Roman Mithras, for the cult of Mithras was already long out of date by the time it arrived in Rome. According to the cycle of the precessional zodiac, Pompey the Great should have been slaying the Mithraic ram of Aries, rather than the Mithraic bull of Taurus. His sword should have been plunged into the neck of Ayil איל the ram, rather than Foucaire-Boucaire בקר the bull. So Pompey had been a sold a bogus zodiac and a phoney religion that was well past its sell-by date, which is not surprising really. This pirated copy of Sabean astrology had come from a bunch of pirates, so what did he expect? If you trade in an Eastern bazaar, be prepared to be sold a pirated counterfeit.

Fig 6.12
Orion as Hercules, brandishing his club and holding up the Nemean Lion as a shield, during his battle with Taurus. This is definitely Orion in the image of Hercules.

Having said that, the original center for these Mithraic rites was based in the East, for it lay squarely within the Nazarene Ebionite creed of Jesus and James. And in later chapters we shall see many more examples of this Sabaean cult of the precessional zodiac. But like the Roman cult of Mithras, the Nazarene Sabean creed was also occult (hidden) and initiatory. And the Nazarene priesthood had concealed their secrets so well, that nothing had leaked out since the era of Alexander the Great and Ptolemy III of Egypt, as was explained in *Jesus, King of Edessa*. So all Rome was left with, was a pirated copy of the knowledge and science of the last of the Egypto-Persian priesthood.

This is why the few coins that we have bearing an image of Mithras depict a distinctly Eastern scene. The coin below is of Septimius Severus (193-211 AD). Minted in Moesia in Thrace (modern Serbia) and inscribed in Greek, it depicts Mithras on horseback, who can be identified by the raven and the torch. But note the eastern costume worn by Mithras, which is virtually identical to the clothing on the coins of King Abgarus of Edessa that were shown in *Jesus, King of Edessa*. And why would Septimius Severus know the true origins of Mithras better than Pompey? Because he was an eastern emperor from Syria, and his great nephew was Emperor Elagabalus who followed in the same footsteps as King Jesus-Izas. We shall come across Septimius Severus again in a later chapter, when we look at his great wall on the borders of Wales. We will see there that Septimius was well acquainted with the Ophite rites of the Nazarene, and so he presumably also knew a great deal about Mithras.

Fig 6.13
Coin of Septimius Severus showing a mounted Mithra on the reverse. Mithra is dressed in the standard Persian dress of baggy trousers, a tunic with a short skirt, a cape, and a Phrygian cap. This attire was not only typically Persian, it was typically Edessan too.

But it was not just Septimius Severus who knew a thing or two about Mithras, for somehow the authors of the *Vulgate Cycle* also knew a great deal too. They knew of Pompey and the pirates and the fact that Strabo mentioned pirates on Gibraltar. They also knew about Mithras and Pompey's involvement in this cult, and the possibility that he brought it to Rome. And they also knew how to conceal that history within layers of ingenious obfuscation about a fight between an axe-wielding Pompey-Orion-Hercules and an Aramaic pirate-bull called Boucaire-Foucaire.

And there may even be a final layer of Judaic *pesher* surrounding this already convoluted plot. *Pesher* is all about finding events in the past that are similar to those of the present, and utilising our understanding of those past events to conceal the present or divine the future. The original source document that was extensively used in *History* was written in the 1st century AD, as we shall see again in the next chapter. The greatest event in the east of the Empire in the late 1st century was the AD 70 siege of Jerusalem and the destruction of the Temple by Emperor Vespasian. And if the author of this source manuscript looked into the past for an equivalent event, his eye would naturally settle upon Pompey the Great's siege of Jerusalem and his desecration of the same Temple in 65 BC.

Thus within the traditions of Judaic *pesher*, Pompey is the historical equivalent of Vespasian, and so these two characters and their actions can be directly equated to each other in all respects. In which case, their adversaries must be equivalents too. The adversary of Pompey in this story was Boucaire-Foucaire, the bull of Taurus; while the adversary of Vespasian during the Jewish Revolt was King Izas-Jesus of Edessa, the fisherman of Pisces. So Boucaire-Foucaire the pirate must be the *pesher* equivalent of King Izas-Jesus, who was also viewed as being a rebel 'pirate'. And he was. Within Mithras the death of Boucaire-Foucaire represented the Great Month of Taurus turning into Aries, while the death of King Izas-Jesus was symbolic of the Great Month of Aries turning into Pisces. So using our knowledge of *pesher*, perhaps now we can now see a much deeper meaning to the old man's tirade against Pompey-Vespasian. (In this revised quote, Pompey has been renamed as Vespasian, and Foucaire as Jesus.):

> He went straight to Vespasian and began to shout and cry as if he had lost his senses ... (and said): 'We believed that Vespasian had killed Jesus-Izas, but Jesus-Izas has killed Vespasian.' (History 16:352) (with *pesher* characters)

And the old man's *pesher* was absolutely correct. Despite Jesus-Izas losing the Jewish Revolt against Legatus Vespasian and being crucified and taken prisoner, it was eventually Jesus-Izas who became the most revered person of this era. Jesus-Izas had indeed triumphed over Vespasian. And if King

Jesus can be equated with King Arthur, as we shall see again and again in later chapters, then perhaps we can also see why this story was located within a manuscript ostensibly about Arthurian history.

And despite all of this detailed historical knowledge, there are still many historians who think that Arthurian history is mere fantasy and mythology. Yet the occult (hidden) knowledge within the *Vulgate Cycle* goes well beyond the capabilities of any modern historian, who wears the obligatory blinkers of modern academia. So why could modern academia not see any of this? Because they dare not step outside the current orthodoxy, in case a peer might vilify them, thus perhaps reducing their esteem and stipends. Its much easier nowadays to fabricate a new study saying that the Jewish Revolt was caused by Climate Change, and watch the grants flood in.* But the selfless authors, translators and publishers of the *Vulgate Cycle* were operating on a completely different level of probity and commitment. These were truly courageous academics who voluntarily stepped outside the contemporary orthodoxy, despite knowing that one false move might result in their being roasted over hot coals.

* Having already written this passage, one of the greatest acts of academic courage took place in August 2015. The Barbarians of ISIS took over Palmyra and demanded that Khaled Asaad, the former head of antiquities, reveal where he had hidden the artifacts from the Palmyra museum. He refused, and so he was tortured and beheaded. Khaled Asaad joins the esteemed ranks of the scholarly or thespian martyr, alongside Socrates, Hypatia, Giordano Bruno, William Tyndale and perhaps even Theo van Gogh. May he rest in peace.

Santorini-Thera

Within the Cyclades islands north of Crete, there lies the island of Santorini, which was formerly called Thera. The etymology of Thera is unknown, but it is one of the very ancient names for this island. But since Thera has always been known as a volcanic island, that has probably steamed and fumed throughout its long volcanic history, its name was probably derived from *theros* θεροϛ meaning 'summer', which was in turn derived from *theroo* θερω meaning 'hot'. Thera, the Hot Island, is a name that would certainly fit this location very nicely.

Back in the 17th century BC this volcanic island was the site of several thriving Minoan cities, whose people had created a very free, open and wealthy culture. Their cities had no walls, their houses stood three or four stories high, their plumbing was on a par with the best of Roman standards, while their women wore fancy dresses, vibrant make-up, expensive jewellery, and danced while openly exposing their breasts.

But life in this 'Atlantean idyl' was about to take a dramatic turn for the worse, when the island was wracked by earthquakes. The tremors grew in intensity and then the volcano in the center of the island deposited thin layer of ash across the land. The people of Thera consulted their priests and wisely decided to abandon their homes, no doubt in the full expectation that they would return once things had quietened down a bit.

But they never did return, for Mother Nature was not finished with Thera just yet. The volcanic pressure was so great under the island that the magma chamber began to vent, which it did for number of weeks, throwing ash high up into the stratosphere. And then seawater entered the vent, causing violent steam eruptions which grew and grew in intensity, causing earthquakes, tsunamis, ash-clouds and chaos to communities all across the eastern Mediterranean. And then, when the magma chamber under the island had finally exhausted itself, the entire center of the island fell into the void and disappeared beneath the sea, causing one last giant tsunami to ripple out across the Mediterranean (catching pharaoh's army by surprise, just as the biblical scribes noted).

Fig 6.14 A fresco from Knossos, showing the bare-breasted fashions of Minoan Crete, and an artist's impression of Minoan courtly life. However, it should be pointed out that the three ladies displaying their breasts may have been priestesses, who are imitating the fertility symbolism of both the Egyptian Isis and the Minoan snake goddess, and so this bare-breasted fashion may not have extended to the general population.

VI Gibraltar, Santorini, and Rome

Go west

So why is this almost pre-historic eruption of Thera being related here, in a book about Arthurian history? Because one of the characters in *History of the Grail,* known as Prince Seraphe-Nascien (the brother-in-law of King Evalach-Mordrain), was taken upon yet another fantastical journey towards the west. And a later comment says that he was taken to somewhere within the many islands that punctuate the Aegean Sea. Flegetine, Nascien's wife, sent out a search party, and then embarked on her own journey to find him.

Anyway, Nascien arrives at a strange barren island that floats in the sea and turns in synchrony with the heavens. It is explained that this island had floated across the sea for a long time, until it happened upon a large lodestone on the seabed which attracted it magnetically. And so the island became fixed in that spot, but still slowly turned in synchrony with the heavens, which is why it became known as the Turning Isle.

This fantastical adventure is one of the many reasons that *History* is dismissed as being utter nonsense - a mere fable for the entertainment of children and fools. But perhaps this story is not quite as foolish as it may at first appear, because in the first instance the story of the Turning Isle appears to have been derived from the story of the island of Aeolia in Homer's *Odyssey*, which was inhabited by Aeolus, the master of the four winds:

> Thence we went on to the Aeolian island where lives Aeolus son of Hippotas, dear to the immortal gods. It is an island that floats (as it were) upon the sea, iron bound with a wall that girds it. Now, Aeolus ... feasting and enjoying every conceivable kind of luxury. All day long the atmosphere of the house is loaded with the savor of roasting meats, until it groans again, and in the courtyard. (Homer Odyssey 10:1).

This quote from *Odyssey* mentions a similar floating island, but this is a much older mythology than the one to be found in *History*. So was the island that Nascien got stranded upon in *History*, based upon the island that Odysseus discovered in *Odyssey*? Well, apart from both of these islands floating, they both appear to groan in some manner. The translation of 'groaning' in the quote above is omitted from some translations, and so one cannot help feeling that there is something missing here, for the mention of 'groaning' sits uneasily in this sentence. The translators were probably confused by the intent of this wording, but had they known there was another floating island that groaned, as mentioned in *History*, they may have made a better attempt at decyphering the meaning.

However, the discovery of a similar mythology from Greek legend does not help much with our understanding of *History's* floating isle. We still appear to have a fantastical tale about a floating island that has no foundation (*sic*) within real life or real history. Until, that is, we look back to the ancient origins of Homer's *Odyssey* which, like many of these ancient myths, appears to contain not simply fictional fantasies but also snippets of long-forgotten history.

One of the interesting slivers of real history that has survived within Greek mythology, is to be found in *Argonautica* by Apollonius of Rhodes: the famous story of Jason and the Argonauts. Jason's epic journey is set in the era just before the Trojan wars, in a similar fashion to *Odyssey* which is set just after that same war. But while sailing across the Aegean in search of the Golden Fleece Jason meets with the bronze-clad Thalos:

> And from there they were to cross to Crete, which rises in the sea above other islands. And Thalos ... in all of his body and limbs was fashioned out of bronze and invulnerable; but beneath the sinew by his ankle was a blood-red vein; and this, with its issues of life and death, was covered by a thin skin. So the heroes, although worn out with toil, quickly backed their ship from the land in sore dismay.
>
> Medea addressed them (and said): 'Listen to me, for I alone can subdue for you that man (Thalos), even though his frame be (made) of bronze throughout. But keep your ship here beyond the cast of his stones, till he yields the victory to me. And as he was heaving massive rocks to stay them from reaching the haven, he grazed his ankle on a pointed crag; and the *ichor* (the blood of the gods) gushed forth like molten lead. (Argonautica, Bk 4, 1638-58) (Author's brackets.)

Here we have a rock-throwing monster living not far from Crete, whose body looks like bronze, but whose feet have blood-red veins of *ichor* covered by a thin skin. So is this a mythical monster, or is this a very good description of a volcano? It does not take much imagination to see that the blood-red veins covered by thin skins are actually a very good description of the streams of lava pouring out of an open wound at the base of a volcano. These streams do indeed form a thin, dark skin, if they are travelling slowly, and then they will often break that thin skin and burst back into life as a glowing blood-read vein, just like a healing leg-wound might break open and issue fresh blood. And so when Thalos gashes his ankle on a rock the *ichor,* the blood of the gods, runs out like molten lead just as it does in fig 6.15. What better description could we have of an erupting volcano?

In addition, the dreaded Thalos was hurling rocks at the Argonauts, which were no doubt the lethal lava bombs that are an almost obligatory feature of volcanic activity. *Argonautica* is therefore recounting an ancient story about a volcanic eruption in the Aegean, but which one? The Mediterranean is not exactly awash with active volcanos, and the three that spring to mind are Vesuvius, Etna and Thera. So can we decide between these three? Well the story goes on to say that:

> Thalos for a while stood on his tireless feet, swaying to and fro, until at last all his strength left him and he fell with a mighty thud. But straightway as they sped over the wide Cretan sea, a darkness fell upon them, a night which they name the Pall of Darkness. Not even the stars pierced that doom-laden night, nor even the beams of the Moon; but a black chaos descended from heaven, or perhaps rising from the depths of the underworld. And the heroes, did not know whether they drifted on the sea or in Hades ... But Jason raised his hands and cried to Phoebus with mighty voice, calling on him to save them ... Calling on Phoebus the bringer of light, and a glimmer was seen far away and it led to the island they called Anaphe. And they sacrificed all that they could provide for sacrifice, on a desolate beach. (Argonautica, Bk 4, 1694:1730)

Jason is said to have been sailing across the Cretan sea, which would seem to exclude the two volcanos in Italy. And then we have the description of the 'monster falling', a 'pall of darkness', 'blood-red veins', and a 'hail of

Fig 6.15 A long-exposure picture of red hot lava dripping into the sea. These are the blood-red veins of the mighty Thalos. And when he gashed his ankle the ichor, the blood of the gods, flowed into the sea like molten lead.

rocks', which just has to be a description of the mighty eruption of Thera - especially since Anaphe, the island that Jason ended up upon, lies just 20 km east of Thera. The Thera eruption was the biggest volcanic event in the eastern Mediterranean, and it happened between 1600 and 1580 BC, at the very beginnings of recorded history, and it caused the evacuation and the destruction of the small but vibrant seafaring community who were living on Thera.

But this was not the single, unexpected and devastating eruption that is often imagined, for Thera had huffed, puffed and shaken for months prior to the final cataclysm. And then an especially violent eruptive episode had persuaded the people of Thera to abandon their island home, with many fleeing to Minoan Crete. But we can imagine that during periods of relative calm between these many eruptions, the expert sailors of Thera would visit their former island home to see if they could return, or if anything more could be salvaged. There, they would see the veins of the dreaded Thalos pulsating with life, and their blood-red *ichor* pouring into the sea like molten lead. But these intrepid sailors faced an ever-present danger from the ballistic rocks, that Thalos was hurling high into the skies, accompanied by the occasional small explosion. And through the curtains of steam, clouds and falling ash, they had seen the Thalos, the great towering volcano that sat at the very center of the island of Thera.

But one day, while a ship was sailing past Anaphe not far from Thera, the volcano on Thera collapsed into the by now empty magma chamber that lay below it - with an almighty crash and thud that shook the entire eastern Mediterranean. The rebound caused ash and pumice to spew out in a magnificent display of natural pyrotechnics, which covered the entire eastern Mediterranean in a thick ash-laden pall of darkness for three whole days. This was the same three days of darkness that the Israelites suffered and recorded, before embarking on their great exodus. According to Israelite legend, this darkness was caused by Moses throwing ash into the skies:

> The Lord said to Moses and Aaron, 'Take handfuls of ashes from the furnace, and let Moses sprinkle it toward the heaven in the sight of Pharaoh. And it shall become small dust across all the land of Egypt. And there shall be boils breaking forth with blains upon man and beast, throughout all the land of Egypt.' (Ex 9:8-9) (author's brackets)

A better description of the long-range effects of a volcano would be hard to find, especially as this biblical ashfall was coincident with a large tsunami. Clearly there had been a great volcanic eruption and ashfall across the eastern Mediterranean, that had caused a thick darkness to descend upon the land which lasted for a number of days - a highly unusual darkness that was recorded by the Egyptians,* Israelites and Greeks. But this was not simply a darkness caused by a thick layer of cloud above, rather the air was thick and difficult to breathe, and it 'inwardly consumed' the Egyptians:

> A thick darkness, without the least light, spread itself over the Egyptians, whereby their sight being obstructed, and their breathing hindered by the thickness of the air, they died miserably, and under a terror lest they should be swallowed up by the dark cloud ... after three days and as many nights, the darkness dissipated ... their bodies had terrible boils, breaking forth with blains, while they were already inwardly consumed. And a great part of the Egyptians perished in this manner. (Antiquities II:14:4-5)

The darkness, the ashfall, and the thickness of the air that 'inwardly consumed' and killed the Egyptians, just has to be a description of the long-range fallout from a massive volcanic eruption. See the book *Tempest & Exodus* for further commentary on this event. And the only eruption large enough to have effected both Crete and Egypt in this era (in any era during recorded history), was the great eruption of Thera in the early 16th century BC. And this suggestion is confirmed in the account of *Argonautica*, which goes on to say that this is exactly where Jason landed: on the island of Anaphe, just 20 km to the east of Thera. So these Greek and Israelite myths can and do contain elements of real history within their apparently fanciful stories.

The Turning Island

Thus far we have seen three ancient histories that recorded the eruption of Thera in the 16th century BC, and two histories that recorded the strange story of a floating island, that creaked and groaned under your feet. So what, in real recorded history, links these two seemingly incompatible stories and events?

The answer lies in the geology of Thera, which gives us a very good idea of what actually happened when Thera erupted. On Thera the layers of *tephra* created by the fallout of ash and pumice, lie up to 60 m deep. In fig 6.16 the white cliffs that tower above modern Santorini (Thera) are

* See the translation of the Tempest Stele in *Tempest & Exodus*.

composed from layer after layer of ash from the great Thera eruption; with each layer denoting an active phase in the eruption followed by a period of calm. But this thick layer of ash would have covered the entire coastline, as well as the hills, and since *tephra* is light enough to float on water, deposits just as thick as these cliffs would have built up around the coastline of Thera, just like the floating sea ice that extends out from the shores of Antarctica.

But then, either when the volcano reached its dramatic finale, or perhaps in later decades or centuries during some great atmospheric storm, great chunks of this coastal *tephra* could break off and float away - just as huge icebergs regularly float away from Antarctica. And since the ash-layer along the shores of Thera was some 60 m thick, one could easily imagine an island of *tephra* a kilometer or so across, floating off across the Mediterranean. Here, then is the potential source for the enduring mythology of an island that floats across the Mediterranean. So let us now look at what *History* says about this island, to see if it accords in any way with the limited possibilities within geological and physical reality. The first thing that is described is the formation of this island:

> Once god had cleaned and purified heaven of all earthly slag and watery rust and shaken earth and water out of heaven's burning heat, this slag and rust could not naturally rejoin with the earth and water from which they had come ... Because none of them could return whence they came ... and since they had retained some of their lightness and heat from heaven ... all these things had to stay in one mass.
>
> ... this mass fell into the sea, and because it tended in part to be light, in according to what it felt from heaven, which is very light, it floated lightly and could not go to the bottom. In this way it floated for a long time in the sea without being able to stop anywhere... (History 20:430-432)

The formation of *History's* floating island equates quite well with the known mechanics of vulcanism. To the author of *History* the Earthly elements are cold and heavy, while the elements of heaven are hot and light. This floating mass was left over from the formation of the heavens, and so it was hot and light, and it eventually fell into the sea and floated. And in the real world of the Thera eruption, this great mass of hot and light pumice did indeed fall down from the heavens above and float in the sea. So the description being given in *History* is fairly accurate, considering that the author was writing (or copying) this account anything up to 2,800 years after this event occurred. And then we see a description of the floating island itself:

> When Nascien found himself on the Turning Isle ... he was very troubled. All around him he saw the ugly, barren island which was so hot that it was cruel and

Fig 6.16
(top) Pumice is very light, and will float on water. Here we see the wake of a ship, as it ploughs a furrow through a raft of floating pumice.
(bottom) The towering cliffs of pumice deposited on the island of Thera. They are up to 60 m in depth, and sections of these deposits could easily have formed very large floating island.

> grievous to bear. He saw he was alone and lost, and did not know in what part of the sea he could be ... he saw a very great plain, in which there were a great many very beautiful birds. Some flew high, some flew low, and others could not fly and stayed on the ground. (History 20:435, 436)

So the island was barren and hot. Certainly an island of pumice would be very barren, because it would be very new with no soil or water whatsoever, and so nothing could live upon it apart from a few nesting birds. And while birds nesting on open ground may not seem very strange to those of us who have been brought up on a diet of television nature documentaries, it may well seem strange to someone not familiar with a barren coastal island where the birds have no fear of man nor beast. This would be especially so on a brand new island that had no predators.

Then we have the description of the island being hot. Had this island broken away from Thera quite soon after it had formed, it would indeed have been hot, as the volcanic ejecta was still very hot when it landed and formed these great cliffs and rafts of pumice. But this may not have been the true intent of this comment. As we saw earlier, the word for 'hot' in Greek was *theroo* θερω, from which the name for Thera may well have been derived. Thera was a volcanic island, and no doubt it had been blessed with many hot springs and huffing fumaroles throughout its history, and so it would be entirely reasonable that Thera had been named the 'Hot Island'. If so, then the description of Nascien's floating island as being hot, directly links this floating island with the islands of pumice that broke off from Thera.

But this hot and barren island was not static and rooted to the ground, as anyone in this early era would expect, it floated and travelled across the seas. *History* says of this novel feature:

> Nascien (when on the island) heard such a great and marvelous battle and struggle at the bottom of the sea that it seemed to him that the entire island was about to sink and fall into an abyss ... there was not one place on the island that did not tremble violently as a leaf in a strong wind ... thus the contest was so great between the earth and the lodestone that at times the island sank into the sea until the water covered the shoreline ... while sometimes it completely floated on the water. (History 20:438) (author's brackets)

There would indeed have been a great battle between the bottom of the floating island and the bottom of the sea. Pumice will float like an iceberg, with the majority of the island being below the water and only a small portion above the surface. This would especially be so after a number of years, when the island had become thoroughly saturated through sea-ingress and rain. This huge floating island may have drifted for a number of months or even years, but it would inevitably ground itself on a shelving seabed somewhere in the eastern Mediterranean, and come to a halt.

However, since this huge island would have had a great mass but very little weight (because it is mostly floating and only lightly touching the seabed), it will be greatly effected by the winds, currents and tides. And although the Mediterranean tides are very small, averaging just 0.2 meters or so in open water, this difference in water-level will certainly raise and lower this pumice island from the seabed; so it can then be pushed and shoved by the winds and sea currents that swirl around the Greek islands. So yes, there would indeed be a 'great battle and struggle at the bottom of the sea', because the island would tremble violently under your feet as the bottom of the island scraped across the seabed, just as the text describes. In which case, this supposedly fanciful account of a mythical floating island accords very closely with what we might expect, from a vast floating island of pumice perhaps a kilometer or more across.

But there is one final description of this floating island, that may help us decide if this description is fact or fantasy, because the text says:

> Then Nascien stood up, feeling the island tremble beneath him, he looked and saw one of the ends was sinking while the other was rising. And yet the island was not small. Rather the truth attests ... that the island was 1,280 stadia long and 912 stadia wide. (History 20:438-9)

The dimensions are a bit astray here, because if the standard stadia is meant then the islands was over 200 km across. It is more likely that the wrong units have been used here, and if we substitute cubits for stadia we would derive an island that was 700 m across. This is still quite a sizeable chunk of pumice to have broken off from Thera, but quite within the bounds of physical probability.

But the interesting point in this final quote, is that *History* is indicating that this entire island is unstable, and it is possibly in danger of flipping over. But why would an ancient author think that such a huge object, an island perhaps 700 meters or more across, could do something quite as dramatic as start tilting up like a sinking ship? Having watched icebergs do this on television documentaries we are all quite familiar with this process, but why would the author of *History* have known about it?

Descriptions like this are known as Black Swan Events - discoveries or events that are so outside our experience and so unexpected that they are highly unlikely to have been predicted, especially by the original bard or chronicler who lived some 3,500 years ago. So when an ancient author describes an ashfall and a tsunami happening at the same time, as the biblical chroniclers do, we can have good confidence that this was an eye-witness account of a real historical event. An author in the 16th century BC would have no idea that darkness, ashfalls and tsunamis are likely to be caused by the same volcanic eruption, unless they had witnessed that very eruption. Likewise, an ancient author would have no concept of a whole island turning upsidedown, unless they had either been to the Arctic and seen icebergs do this, or had seen a real island of pumice do something very similar in the eastern Mediterranean. In which case, we can have some confidence that the description of Nascien's floating island was originally based upon an eye-witness account of a real event.

Island of fortune

Whether this island was real or not, what we appear to have here is a description of an event from the ancient past that has absolutely nothing to do with the unfolding story in *History* about Joseph of Arimathaea in Syria. So why was this peculiar story forced into a manuscript about Arthurian

Fig 6.17 A large iceberg that has just turned over, exposing its smooth blue undersides. A floating berg of pumice would be almost as unstable as an iceberg, and could easily have tipped up, just as is described in 'History'.

history, and what is its meaning?

For the answer we have to go back to Siena Cathedral once more, the cathedral that has an image of the Wheel of Fortune on its floor. Surprisingly, one of the other mosaics in this rather Pagan cathedral is the Island of Fortune and Wisdom, which was commissioned in 1505 (sometimes called the Hill of Fortune or Mount of Virtue). The scene is quite complex and it starts at the bottom right with a naked Fortuna, who has arrived on this island with a party of men quite by chance, as the boat has no mast. Just like the boats that the Arthurian knights often sail in, that have no crew or guidance, this boat sails wherever Fortuna takes it.

The small throng of men and women make their way to the top of the island, where Socrates and Crates stand. Socrates is the great 5th century BC philosopher who laid the foundations of modern Western philosophy, and so he is holding a book of wisdom. And Crates was a Cynic of the 4th century BC who renounced all his considerable wealth to live in virtuous poverty, in line with the teachings of Cynic philosophy, and so we see Crates emptying his wealth into the sea. Note also how the island is barren, apart from a few weeds and snakes, and how it tips up at each end. Is this island related to Nascien's barren island, that similarly sinks and rises?

The central lady is again Fortuna, enthroned in majesty and holding a palm in one hand and a book in another. She is sometimes said to be an image of wisdom or virtue, seated on the *Sedes Sapientiae,* the Seat of Wisdom. This is probably because the inscription above her head reads:

> *Huc properate viri: salebrosum scandite montem Pulchra laboris erunt premia palma quies.*
>
> Thus, the wise man who has attained virtue will receive serenity as his prize.

This mention of wisdom might suggest that the enthroned lady is the Greek Athena or the Roman Minerva, but she does not resemble either of these. And the central goddess is unlikely be Minerva-Sophia, if this is supposed to be the Island of Fortune, it is much more likely to be Fortuna herself. Which is why the inscription that Seneca holds in the Wheel of Fortune mosaic says something similar:

> *Magna servitus est magna fortuna.*
>
> Great fortune entails great obligation (or burdens).

So the imagery of the lady enthroned on the Isle of Fortune is likely to be based upon eastern traditions, and in the east the goddess who sits on a rock in a lake or river holding a palm frond is Tyche, the Greek name for Fortuna. The coin of Tigranes II illustrated here depicts Tyche (Fortuna), and has a composition that is almost identical to the goddess enthroned on the Isle of Fortune. So this barren island tests one's ability to deal with the vicissitudes of fortune, which is why *History* intimates that Nascien's exile to this island was a test of his faith:

> However, despite the disappearance of joy and despite the misfortune that had befallen him, he did not deviate from his faith. Just as Job, who had so many beautiful treasures in his life, suffered willingly and wisely all his misfortunes ... in the same way Nascien suffered graciously and willingly... (History 20:434)

Fig 6.18 The 'floating' island of Fortune and Wisdom, from Siena cathedral. This is the strange floating island that Nascien sailed to, in order to test his faith. We shall see in a later chapter that Josephus Flavius also came to this hill for his barmitzvah; although Josephus' version of the Hill of Fortune was located in Egypt.

The palm that Fortuna holds is often a symbol of victory, and so perhaps the allusion here is to a victorious or good fortune based upon knowledge and wisdom. As the previous descriptions of the Wheel of Fortune in Arthurian history have suggested, Fortuna is not simply arbitrary and capricious. You can still determine your own fortune by making an informed choice, and grasping Fortuna by the hair as she passes by. But the avaricious or ignorant will probably wait for something better to come along, and find that Fortuna is bald behind and the opportunity has been lost. And the Fortuna mosaic in Siena Cathedral is also clearly stating that attaining good fortune does not simply refer to acquiring high status or great wealth. Both Socrates and Crates were very fortunate - they had grasped Fortuna as she passed by - but one was a simple philosopher while the other was a Cynic who threw all his considerable wealth into the sea. As the inscription says, the truly wise man who is pure of heart will ask Fortuna for serenity, rather than wealth and power.

And the symbolism of Fortuna's palm-frond may go much deeper than a simple token of success or victory, because the palm-frond is a *phoenix* φοινιξ. And this avian palm-frond is not simply symbolic of the fabulous Phoenix bird, but also of the motions of the Sun through the precessional cycle of the zodiac. In which case, the knowledge and wisdom on this inscription may be closely connected to the fortunes of the precessional zodiac. But of course the two are inextricably linked. The Wheel of Fortune, which is also represented on the floor of Siena Cathedral, could be thought

Fig 6.21
A coin of Tigranes II of Armenia, showing Tyche (Fortuna) of Antioch (95-56 BC) sitting on a rock holding a palm-frond. Below Tyche is the river-god Orontes, which demonstrates that this rock is situated within a lake or river.

of as the wheel of the zodiac, the great wheel of the constellations that turns in the heavens above. According to the astrologers of the era, our fortune could be determined by the positions of the stars and planets, and so the wheel of fortune and the wheel of the zodiac were almost one and the same thing. And this is probably why the Turning Island of Arthurian history is said to turn in unison with the heavens above:

> And along with this quality it has yet another one, derived from heaven, which

Fig 6.22
Some of the many fine mosaics on the floor of Siena Cathedral, which date from the 14th to 16th centuries.

> is that every time the firmament turns, the island turns in the same way as the firmament, that is, heaven. In the way you have heard, the island turns. That is why the local people call it the Turning Isle. (History 20:433)

The Turning Island was not simply a geological curiosity, a large island of pumice that could float around the Mediterranean at the commands of Fortuna, it was also an earthly representation of the zodiac. The whole island was turning because of the anticlockwise currents of the Mediterranean, which may well capture such an island in a vortex and slowly turn the island around every day, week or season. And so the floating island appeared to turn in unison with the heavens. And if the rotating heavens above can determine your fortune, then surely the Turning Island can do likewise, and in this manner the floating island became the Island of Fortune.

Hippocrates of Rome

The third of these semi-mythical interludes, that pockmark the main story in *History of the Holy Grail,* is even more devious and humorous than the previous two. It tells the story of Hippocrates, the famous philosopher and physician from Kos in Greece, who travelled to Rome to meet Emperor Octavian Augustus. And anyone with a passing knowledge of Greek history will immediately see that there is something desperately wrong with this story from the very outset, because Hippocrates lived from about 460 to 370 BC, while Octavian Augustus was emperor of Rome from 27 BC to AD 14.

So what is to be done with this wildly inaccurate interpolation? Should we cast it into the fires of 'unreliable mythology', along with all of the other texts from Arthurian history? Or should we persevere a little longer? Perhaps the previous two examples have already demonstrated that there is real history to be found in these strange interpolations, so let us read on and see what else this section says.

The clue to the true era of this story is to be found in the assertion that Hippocrates was shown the tower where King Gatus of Babylon was imprisoned in Rome. It will be demonstrated later that the majority of events within *History* actually occur in the mid 1st century AD, and so perhaps we should look for a King of Parthia (Babylon) called Gatus from this era. Surprisingly, there is such a king, and his name is Gotarzes II. It would appear that *History's* King Gatus or Gotus is simply a shortening of Gotarzes.

So could this Parthian king have ever been in Rome? Quite possibly, because Rome often took princes of Parthia into their care to prevent insurrections back in Parthia. Queen Thea Muse Ourania, for instance, sent all of the king's sons to Rome except for her own son, who then conveniently became the next king of Parthia. And there was a great deal of turbulence in mid 1st century Parthia that may have precipitated the exile of a royal son. Josephus says of these kings:

> Artabanus died, and left his kingdom to his son Bardanes. Now this Bardanes came to King Izates (of Adiabene-Edessa), and would have persuaded him to ... assist him in the war he was preparing to make with the Romans; but he could not persuade him ... But the Parthian king was provoked at (Izates' inaction), and pronounced war immediately against Izates. But he gained no advantage

> by this war, because ... (the people) killed him, and gave his kingdom to his brother Gotarzes. He also, in no long time, perished by a plot made against him, and Vologases, his brother, succeeded him. (Antiquities 20:3:4) (Author's brackets.)

Fig 6.23
An engraving of Hippocrates, the 4th century BC, by Peter Rubens - 1638.

This potted history of Parthia is pretty much how classical history records it. Bardanes (Vardanes) and Gotarzes ruled at about the same time, between 40 and 50 AD, and Vologases I succeeded them in about AD 51. But since Vardanes had been deposed and Gotarzes was invited to take the throne, he could easily have been a guest of Rome in the meantime - to keep him out of the way, as often happened with the Parthian monarchy.

But if this was the case, then we are not looking for a healer called Hippocrates who lived in the 4th century BC, we are looking for a healer called Hippocrates who lived in the 1st century AD. And this was either during the reign of Emperor Augustus in the early 1st century, or perhaps when Prince Gotarzes may have been in Rome, in the AD 40s. Or perhaps during both of these dates, as we shall see later. Now who could this wise healer have been?

Again the answer lies within the Greek and Aramaic languages, rather than Celto-British. But the author of *History*, has been mightily devious here, for he may well have transcribed a Parthio-Aramaic name into Greek, to prevent readers from knowing who this person really was. No doubt this was an in-joke at the time, so that the initiated few could snigger and laugh every time they saw 'Hippocrates' being mentioned in relation to 1st century events. In fact, it may be worth trawling other Greek texts at a later date, to see how many times an oddly positioned character called Hippocrates pops up in the 1st century AD.

So who was this 1st century Hippocrates? Well, first of all we need to decypher the name 'Hippocrates' into the English, to see what it actually means. In fact, this name was derived from ιππο κρατης meaning 'horse power' or 'powerful horse'. So who was this 'Powerful Horse' who came to meet Emperor Augustus in Rome during the early 1st century?

Surprisingly, there was a very famous Powerful Horse in Rome in the 1st century, because if we translate 'horse power' into Aramaic, instead of Greek, we can derive Iz-sus עז-סוס. Now that is interesting, very interesting indeed. It looks like a very cunning and erudite author, who was very familiar with Aramaic, is having a little game with his readers - because if one wants to be exceedingly devious then the name Izas (Jesus) can be very loosely translated into Greek as 'Hippocrates'. And so if someone wished to conceal the presence of this royal prince in Rome, they could wax lyrical about Hippocrates the great healer and avoid the hot pokers of the Catholic Inquisition.

Jesus of Rome

The suggestion here, is that the 1st century Hippocrates mentioned in *History*, is actually a highly occult (concealed) and very humorous pseudonym for the biblical King Jesus-Izas. So does this suggestion make any sense? Does it concur in any fashion with the rest of the story in *History*, and with real and biblical history as we know it?

Unfortunately, although the biblical King Izas-Jesus was certainly honoured and celebrated as a great leader and wise healer, he was never knowingly in Rome. So the history of Izas-Jesus does not suit the role of this 1st century Hippocrates quite as well as we might like. But since we have already seen that the author of *History* possessed some very informative and reliable 'inside information', perhaps we might still find a connection if we look deeper into the story.

History relates that when Hippocrates (Izas-Jesus) arrived in Rome, the nephew of Emperor Augustus was very sick and died. But Hippocrates (Jesus), being a worker of great medical miracles, was able to bring him back to life.

> When he came to the body (Hippocrates) began to inspect that part where he might learn whether the child was dead. Thus it happened that as soon as he put his hands on the body, he knew the soul was still in it. Then he opened the mouth and put inside some liquor made from herbs of great power and strength, so that the child immediately got up. (History 26:31.)

This is the standard method by which (Nazarene) 'Christians' ingratiated themselves into the aristocracy of a nation, by reviving apparently dead people. So one cannot place too much credence on this part of the story being accurate, but it is entirely possible that a strong smelling-salt would produce this kind of immediate reaction on a 'lifeless' body. Anyway, Emperor Augustus was so impressed by this Lazarus-style feat of resurrection, that he commissioned a lifelike bronze statue of Hippocrates (Jesus) healing the young boy.

Then a beautiful princess came to Rome from Gaul, and poured scorn on such a stupid statue, as nobody could bring the truly dead back to life. Hippocrates (Jesus) was most indignant and demanded to see the upstart princess, but when he finally got to see her he fell hopelessly in love. But not she with him. Determined to humiliate Hippocrates (Izas-Jesus), the princess told him to get into a small cage during the night, and her people would pull him up to her window so they could meet in secret. The love-struck but naive Hippocrates (Izas-Jesus) did exactly as she said, but did not realise he had just climbed into the criminal's punishment cage. The petulant princess gleefully hauled Hippocrates up the wall of the tower, and left him hanging there all day, the same as petty criminals would be hung for all to see and mock. And it was not until Emperor Augustus came back to Rome in the evening, that Hippocrates (Jesus) was released from the cage. (History 26:35-51)

Is the general outline of this story, of a wise but impetuous and naive Hippocrates (Izas-Jesus) in Rome, beginning to sound a bit familiar? Readers of *Jesus, King of Edessa* may be able to make the connection here, and see the true origins of this story. If King Jesus was anything like Thomas in the *Song of the Pearl,* he would indeed have been caught out by the petulant princess in just such a manner. In the *Song of the Pearl,* which seems to be a parody on the combined lives of the Old Testament Joseph and the New Testament Jesus, Thomas (the twin) is sent down into Egypt to seek the pearl (of wisdom) but is seduced by the many pleasures and distractions of Egypt. It was not until he received a letter from his family reminding him of his duty, that Thomas (the twin) suddenly remembered why he had been sent to Egypt in the first place. (Song of the Pearl, Acts of Thomas).

This is the interesting thing about almost all of the events narrated in *History* - readers can only understand the (hidden) story if they know that the gospel story was closely related to the Edessan royal family. And also understand that many of the events being described were firmly set within the AD 60s. Without that knowledge, the reader is left floundering in a sea of meaningless narrative that appears to have been assembled into a manuscript by the village cretin. But as soon as the fundamentals of the Edessan association are understood, a wonderful story suddenly emerges from the puzzling prose.

So was this history of Hippocrates really a story about King Izas-Jesus? The answer to this is nearly, but not quite. Instead, this is more likely to be a story about the father of King Izas-Jesus living in Rome in the early 1st century, as has already been discussed in *Jesus, King of Edessa*. So how did the father of Jesus-Izas become confused with his son, and how did he get to Rome? Well, in the previous books we have already seen how these monarchs shared the same titles. The three 1st century Edessan monarchs we are most interested in are:

King Monobazus Izas Abgarus au Kama V	(the father)
King Izas Monobazus Manu V	(James)
King Izas Monobazus Manu VI	(Jesus)

As can be seen, all of these monarchs bore the titles Izas and Monobazus. The meaning of Monobazus is positively known, for it simply means 'Only King', which was a known title of these Adiabene-Edessan monarchs and of Jesus himself. Jesus was not only called the Only Begotten Son (Joh 3:16) he was also called the Only Prince (Only King):

> Which in his times (the time of Jesus) he shall show, who is the blessed and Only Prince, the King of Kings, and Lord of Lords. (1Tim 6:15) (Author's brackets.)

The origin of the Edessan royal title Izas or Izates is less certain. It was suggested in previous works that the name was derived from Asar 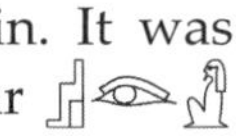 or Osiris, the great god of Egypt. However, in Persian this name is often said to mean 'angel'. As we have seen previously, an angel is simply a messenger from the gods, or god's ambassador on Earth. And to increase their standing and power, the Parthian and Edessan monarchies had claimed that they were god's ambassador or god's angel. Which is why an ambassador or angel in Aramaic is a *malak* מלאך while a king is called a *malek* מלך, because the kings of the East were seen to be ambassadors of the gods. And that is exactly how they were portrayed upon their coinage, as was explained previously.

However, it was later noticed that the Judaic god was sometimes called 'strong and mighty', as in Psalms 24:8. And in the Aramaic this phrase is pronounced as *Izus u Gibbur* עזוז ו גבור. So the name King Izas in Aramaic may well have meant 'strong', referring to a Strong King. And it was this 'strong' title that was then humorously corrupted by the author of *History* into Iz-sus עז-סוס meaning 'Strong Horse'. And if we translate this Izus Strong Horse from Aramaic into Greek the result is 'Hippocrates'.

The result of these similar Edessan royal titles - Izas and Monobazus - is that it would be very easy to confuse the father and the son, the king and the prince, because they bore many of the same titles. And so Izas-Jesus' father could have been humorously called Hippocrates just as easily as Jesus could have been. But how did King Abgarus-Izas of Edessa (Izas-Jesus' father) end up in Rome, as this story in *History* suggests?

The answer is through the standard social manipulation and control that the Roman Empire had employed since its very foundation, with 'captive' barbarian princes from the provinces being taken to Rome and pampered like royalty with every luxury that Rome could offer. And exactly the same thing happened to King Abgarus of Edessa.

When the Edessan monarchy were exiled from Parthia in AD 4, they were warmly greeted by Herod (Archelous) and Emperor Augustus, and given lands on the border between Syria and Parthia in which they could establish a semi-autonomous nation state, which became known as the Kingdom of Osrhoene, the Kingdom of Edessa or the Kingdom of Ourania (the Kingdom of Heaven). And they were allowed to keep these lands free of Roman taxes too, which was quite a concession by the normally tax-hungry Romans. But the deal was that Edessa should use these tax concessions to defend the eastern borders of Rome against Parthian incursions, which they sort of did for a number of centuries.

However, while Augustus may have been feeling generous with his tax concessions, he was not about to trust this upstart rebel king just yet; and so he demanded that the king - King Abgarus Izas au Kama V of Edessa - accompany him to Rome as his guest. In effect, King Abgarus had just become yet another hostage of Rome, to ensure the fidelity and loyalty of the new city state his people were building in eastern Syria. This is why King Abgarus drops out of the history of Edessa for some considerable time, and the main player in these dramas becomes his wife, Queen Helena.

King Abgarus remained in Rome for about seven years, just as 'Hippocrates' (Iz-sus) also spent a great deal of time Rome, and so it is to Rome we must look for further evidence that the story in *History* has any foundations within real history. Unfortunately not much is known about King Abgarus' time in Rome, bar a short account by Procopius of Caesarea, a 6th century historian working for Emperor Justinian. Procopius says of King Abgarus:

> There was a certain Augarus in early times, a prince of Edessa. Now this Augarus was the most clever of all men of his time, and as a result of this was an especial friend of the Emperor Augustus. For, desiring to make a treaty with the Romans, he came to Rome; and when he conversed with Augustus, he so astonished him by the abundance of his wisdom that Augustus wished never more to give up his company; for he was an ardent lover of his conversation, and whenever he met him, he was quite unwilling to depart from him. A long time, therefore, was

> consumed by him in this visit. And one day when he was desirous of returning to his native land and was utterly unable to persuade Augustus to let him go. (Persian Wars 2:11-20)

Note that Procopius calls King Abgarus by the name Augarus. As readers may expect by now, this alteration is not a misspelling nor a mispronunciation, but yet another witty play on words. And with Procopius being a Roman, this will obviously be a Latin play on words. The explanation can be seen in the *augurs* of Rome, who were very important priests who divined the future through observing the flight of birds. And this was not some minor avian cult to be found at the fringes of Roman society, for the *augurs* presided over the inauguration of the magistrates of Rome, which is why this ceremony is known even to this day as an in-augur-ation. These *augurs* looked to the birds in the heavens to find favourable auspices, a word that is derived from the Latin to 'look at birds' and divine the future.

This is what Procopius was alluding to, when he renamed King Abgarus as Prince Augarus. He was plainly saying that King Abgarus had become a *augur* of Rome - a diviner of good omens for Emperor Augustus, much as the biblical Joseph became a diviner of good omens for the pharaoh of Egypt. And since we already know that the divine bird of Edessa was the Phoenix, which was emblazoned upon the Edessan's sacred omphalos-elagabal stone, it is more than likely that the 'birds' that the augurs were observing, were the stars and constellations in the heavens above.

Geoffrey Monmouth claimed that these avian seers were divining the future by looking at the letters that formations of cranes made in the sky:

> While he was speaking thus, the chiefs caught sight of long lines of cranes in the air, circling through space in a curved line in the shape of certain letters ... Marvelling at these they asked Merlin to tell why it was that they were flying in such manner. Merlin presently said to them, 'The Creator gave to the birds as to many other things their proper nature, as I have learned by living in the woods for many days.' (Life of Merlin)

And from the letters that the cranes wrote in the sky, the future could be divined. A similar argument was also put forward for the identification of the Egyptian Thoth, the god of writing, with the ibis or crane. However, the priests of Edessa and Egypt were Sabeans (astronomers), not twitchers (bird watchers). They were interested in the precessional progression of the constellations from Aries to Pisces in the early 1st century, rather than the arrival of the lesser-spotted pink finch in the spring. And so the *augers* of Rome were most probably looking to the skies to divine the future from the positions of the stars and planets in the heavens, rather than the shape of a

Fig 6.24 Emperor Augustus dressed as an augur priest (below), with a bird at his feet and holding the augur's lituus, a curved wand used to mark out the heavens. Christian priests still hold the same lituus wand to this day, but call it a crozier. Above we can see examples of a Roman lituus and a Christian crozier, which are identical in all respects. King Abgarus of Edessa would have held exactly the same augur's lituus, and so he might be considered to be the earliest 'Christian' (ie: Nazarene-Ebionite) bishop of Rome.

flock of birds. But do note that, as with the Turning Isle that has just been described, we are once more back on the subject of Tyche-Fortuna divining the future - the augur's portends - from the arrangement of the constellations on the circle of the precessional zodiac.

Procopius then goes on to claim that Abgarus-Izas (Augarus) was the cleverest of men of his age, just as Izas (Hippocrates) was said to be in *History*. In fact a plaque was attached to the statue of Izas (Hippocrates) in Rome that read:

> This is Hippocrates, the foremost doctor of the philosophers, who through his wisdom brought the nephew of Augustus Caesar back to life. (History 26:33)

So both Izas (Hippocrates) and King Abgarus-Izas were being hailed as being the wisest philosophers in the court of Emperor Augustus. But although King Abgarus relished the fame and attention he had received in Rome, he still wanted to get back to Edessa to see his beloved wife, Queen Helena, and so he devised a clever ruse with some animals in the amphitheater of Rome, to show that all animals missed their homelands. According to Procopius, Abgarus then turned to Augustus and said:

> Then Augarus, suddenly laying hold upon his knees, said: 'But as for me, O Master, what thoughts do you think I have, who possess a wife and children and a kingdom, small indeed, but in the land of my fathers?' And the emperor, overcome and compelled by the truth of his saying, granted not at all willingly that he should go away, and also bade him to ask for whatever he wished. (Persian Wars 2:11-20)

For his final wish, King Abgarus-Izas asked for an amphitheater to be built in Edessa, and Augustus granted him the funds to build it. So at last Abgarus was free and able to travel back to Edessa.

As readers can perhaps see, *History's* account of Izas (Hippocrates) in Rome is pretty much identical in its broader aspects, to the story of King Abgarus-Izas in Rome. Both went to Rome, both were confidants of Emperor Augustus, and both were being hailed as the wisest philosophers and augurs of their age. So it would seem likely that this 'Hippocrates-Izas' who was in Rome in the 1st century AD referred to King Abgarus-Izas au Kama V of Edessa, the father of King Jesus-Izas.

So yes, this incredible 'fictional fantasy' of Hippocrates being in Rome in the early 1st century AD was actually based upon real history - the history of the kings of Edessa. However, whether the finer details of this story are correct, is open to debate. Did King Abgarus-Izas meet with and fall in love with a princess from Gaul? (Remembering that 'Gaul' in Arthurian legend can also refer to Gaulanitis in Judaea.)

It is certainly possible. Rome was awash with princes and princesses from all over the Empire, who were the 'guests of Rome' - including Prince Agrippa II of Judaea, Prince Jubba II of Mauretania, Prince Cymbeline of Britain, and King Caratacus and his daughter Claudia. As mentioned previously, although these 'barbarian' royals were hostages of Rome they were not kept in dark dungeons. Instead, they were pampered with every luxury Rome could provide, in order to demonstrate the huge benefits of agreeing to the Pax Romana - the Roman Peace. After a number of years, these suitably Romanised princes and princesses would then be sent back to their home nations as good Romans and loyal client kings of the Empire - just as King Abgarus was being sent back to Edessa. It was a tried and tested formula that worked.

So did one of these hostage princesses trick a besotted King Abgarus into making a fool of himself? Or was this simply a literary device, to bring a boastful and egotistical Abgarus (Hippocrates) back to Earth? Without further information we cannot be sure, but some of the other details in *History* do dovetail very well with what we know about the life of King Abgarus, as we shall see.

Doctrine of Addai

History goes on to say that a knight who was 'well known to the Romans' arrived in Rome from Galilee in Judaea, bearing information about a wonderful prophet there called Jesus:

> "What news do you bring?" asked (Emperor) Augustus.
> "My Lord, he is a poor man but he has such great power that anyone who did not see it could scarcely relate it. He makes the blind see clearly, the deaf hear and the lame walk straight."
> "I can do this too," said Hippocrates ...
> "but he also brought Lazarus back to life after he had been buried for three days and three nights." (History 26:55) (Author's brackets.)

Here is a knight bringing news of the biblical Jesus, which is another reason why we know that these are really 1st century events. So how does this fit in with the history of King Abgarus? As we have seen, the Edessan king had been released from his seven years under house arrest in Rome, and travelled back to Edessa in about AD 14; so how was news of Jesus in Galilee in the AD 30s (or the AD 50s) reaching him in Rome? The answer comes from the accounts of Procopius once more, who says that this section of the story actually happened at a much later time. He says of King Abgarus:

> At a later time when Augarus was well advanced in years, he was seized with an exceedingly violent attack of gout. And being distressed by the pains and his inability to move in consequence of them, he carried the matter to the physicians ... But later he abandoned these men, for they did not succeed in discovering any cure for the troubles ... But about that time Jesus ... was moving among the men of Palestine ... performing even things impossible.
>
> When these things were reported to Augarus by those who travelled from Palestine to Edessa, he took courage and wrote a letter to Jesus, begging him to depart from Judaea and ... to spend his life with him from that time forward. When Jesus saw this message, he wrote in reply to Augarus, saying distinctly that he would not come, but promising him health in the letter. And they say that he added this also: that never would the city (of Edessa) be liable to capture by the barbarians. This final portion of the letter was entirely unknown to those who wrote the history of that time; for they did not even make mention of it anywhere; but the men of Edessa say that they found it with the letter.
>
> A short time after Augarus received the letter of the Christ, he became free from suffering, and after living on in health for a long time, he came to his end. (Persian Wars 2:20-31)

So the report about Jesus working miracles in Judaea did not go to Emperor Augustus when Abgarus-Hippocrates was in Rome. Instead, this was a much later event and the report actually went to the Edessan king when he was living back in Edessa, and so this could have been at a much later date. So again we can see that *History* is correct in the broad outline of what it relates in this story, even if it got the location and timing wrong in this particular instance. So yes, King Abgarus-Hippocrates-Izas did get to hear of Jesus of Judaea at a later date, but the only thing missing from this report - in all the accounts we have of this event - is that Jesus of Judaea was actually the king's son.

In which case, this account by Procopius (and in *History*) is actually a retelling of the *Doctrine of Addai*, a manuscript that has been discussed and dissected at great length in *Jesus, King of Edessa*. This apocryphal manuscript recounts the story of the king of Edessa suffering from a disease, and sending letters to Jesus in Jerusalem asking for a cure. But Jesus is detained in Jerusalem and sends the king's ambassadors back with letters and a portrait of himself. The ambassador who went to Edessa is given various names, which all point towards him being Mar Addai (ie: Thomas Didymus Thaddaeus, Jesus' twin brother).

But if both the *Doctrine of Addai* and *Persian Wars* are telling the same story as *History*, then this is direct confirmation that this Hippocrates is actually King Abgarus of Edessa. In the *Doctrine* and *Persian Wars* it is King Abgarus who hears of Jesus the healer while he was in Edessa, yet in *History* it was Hippocrates who heard news of Jesus the healer while he was supposedly in Rome. So all three of these stories are speaking about the same person. In which case, the translation of King Abgarus' name at the beginning of this section was correct. Izas or Iz-sus עז-סוס - the name that Saul-Josephus used for King Monobazus Izas Abgarus au Kama of Edessa - can indeed be humorously translated as 'Strong Horse' or 'Hippocrates'.

The *Doctrine of Addai* is a very interesting manuscript that could easily have been claimed by Christians as positive proof that Jesus was a real historical character. But the faithful are prevented from doing so because:

a. This letter-writing episode between King Abgarus and Jesus happened in the AD 40s and 50s, which is inconvenient to say the least.

b. There is a complete ban on mentioning Edessa within Christianity (and within the works of Josephus Flavius). Nobody wants the unthinking

Fig 6.25 St Jude (ie: Thaddaeus-Addai) holding up the Mandylion before a very eastern-looking King Abgarus V of Edessa. Note that the disciple here is being called Jude (Judas) instead of Thomas, Thaddaeus or Addai (Thomas Didymus was also called Judas). Window from Our Lady of Victories Church, Paterson, New Jersey; also known as The Shrine of St. Jude.

> faithful knowing anything about this Egypto-Parthian monarchy, because they might start asking difficult questions and realising that Jesus came from Edessa.

In addition, we also saw conclusive evidence in *Jesus, King of Edessa* that the ambassadors from Edessa, who were taking these letters back and forth between Edessa and Jerusalem, included the apostles Saul and Barnabas from Acts of the Apostles. The gospel accounts say that Saul and Barnabas went to Antioch during these travels, but what they failed to mention is that this city was actually Antioch-Edessa, the full name for this important and pivotal city in northern Syria.

Asclepius and the snake

So what are we to make of this latest flight of fantasy in *History*? Perhaps the most important conclusion we can draw from this, is that the author or translator of *History* knew a great deal more about these events than anyone could have expected.

For example, he knew all about the exile of King Abgarus-Izas to Rome, and his claimed close relationship with Emperor Augustus. But since Procopius knew of these events, one can assume that this was hardly a state secret in the early centuries AD. However, the big difference between the accounts of Procopius and those in *History*, is that the author of the latter also knew that King Abgarus was related to the biblical family and to Jesus himself, because he cryptically called him Hippocrates. Now this is very interesting, because there would have been very few people in the early centuries AD who would have known this, and one might suspect that by the 13th century that circle of high initiates had been reduced to a trusted brotherhood of two or three Templars.

So explosive and dangerous was this secret information, that the author of *History* has had to devise (or possibly resurrect) the most cryptic of pseudonyms for Izas-Jesus that nobody in that era would ever have decyphered, bar those who had been initiated. And so Izas-Jesus has had his name divided into two, to become Iz-sus meaning Strong Horse or Great Horse, which translates as 'Hippocrates' in the Greek. And this clever but devious pseudonym has been chosen because Hippocrates was a great physician and healer, in a similar fashion to the claimed medical miracles performed by Izas-Jesus.

But the similarities and comparisons do not stop there. There may well have been additional reasons for associating King Izas-Jesus with Hippocrates. The first of these is quite interesting, because it directly links this story with known Arthurian history. Surprisingly, the Greco-Egyptian name for Ursa Major may well have been Hippo Crates. And if Ursa Major was known as the Great Horse, as well as the Great Bear, then both King Jesus and King Arthur (King Jesus-Arthur) could have been known as Hippo Crates, the great ring-master of the precessional zodiac. This interesting addition to the Hippocrates story is derived from the Dendera zodiac in Egypt, and will be explored in greater detail in Chapter X.

The second additional connection between Jesus and Hippocrates is that Hippocrates was the primary heir to the traditions of medicine and healing formulated by the Greek god Asclepius. And Hippocrates taught medicine at the Asclepeion, the great temple-hospital on the Greek island of Kos. But the symbol of Asclepius was a snake entwined around a rod. Yet in later chapters we shall see that the symbol of the Nazarene sect of Jesus and James was also the sinusoidal snake; and we shall also see that the snake of Asclepius was a primary symbol of Egypt, the nation that King Izas-Jesus' family came from.

This nominative and symbolic link between King Jesus-Izas and Hippocrates is further confirmed in Naassene Ophite teachings. In later chapters we shall be equating the Naassene with the Nazarene, and demonstrating that their creed is identical in many respects to the Gnostic teachings in the gospels, especially those in the Gospel of John. And yet these Naassene-Nazarene teachings confuse and conflate the sayings of Jesus-Izus and Hippocrates. The following quote is from Hippolytus who is trying to refute Naassene-Ophite teachings:

> And concerning this they hand down a passage, occurring in the Gospel of Thomas, that says: 'He who seeks me, will find me in children from seven years old; for there concealed, I shall be made manifest in the fourteenth age.' This, however, is not (the teaching) of Christ, but of Hippocrates, who uses these words: 'A child of seven years is half of a father.' (Hippolytus, Refutations 5:7:20-21)

Fig 6.26
The entwined snake symbol of Asclepius is also symbolic of a winding river.

It would appear that the Nazarene Sect of Jesus and James was recycling some of the teachings of Hippocrates, the Greek physician and healer. And so it is not so surprising that the great Nazarene healer, Jesus, would be equated with Hippocrates by some of his followers, even if only as a covert pseudonym. But it is interesting that *History of the Grail* should know about these obscure names and associations, and use the same Egypto-Nazarene pseudonym for Jesus in its narrative. So when we get to the explanation of the Naassene-Ophite Sect in Chapter IX, do remember that this belief-system and world-view was also a component within Arthurian history.

St Peter

The last of these semi-mythical interludes is not taken from real history, but from biblical history. But it is being included in this section because it is illuminating and decidedly heretical, and therefore betrays the subversive viewpoint of these Arthurian authors.

As we shall see shortly, this Arthurian story is about the gospels' Simon Peter (St Peter), the disciple who tried to walk on water just like Jesus, but failed. From the gospel accounts we know very little about Simon Peter's family connections and previous life. All we are told is that he was the brother of Andrew and the son of Jonah, from Capernaum on the Sea of Galilee, and he was married. Christians will say that we know very little about Simon Peter because he was just a poor fisherman, but that is merely a story for the kindergarten. The fisher symbolism came from the constellation and Great Month of Pisces, while the Jonah-dove symbolism was a known representation of the Sun-god, Helios-Aton-Ra. And the fact that the authorities came to Simon's house looking for taxes in Math 17:24 would suggest he was a man of some means, as were Saul-Josephus and King Jesus too. And then King Jesus-Izas gave Simon the additional title of Petros Kephas Πετρος Κηφας, which means 'stone' in both Greek and Aramaic respectively. And this was an important title, as we shall see shortly. It is quite obvious from all of this that Simon Peter was actually quite important, despite the mockery and condemnation that we shall see he received.

The gospel story about Simon Peter walking on water starts with the beheading of John the Baptist by Herod Antipas in about AD 33, the very date when the Church says that Jesus died, which is a very convenient confusion in the deaths of two famous Judaean prophets. The gospel accounts say that following this death, Jesus immediately escaped by ship to a 'desert place', which may be a reference to either Qumran or Masada on the Dead Sea (Math 14:13). A multitude of people flock to Jesus, and we then have the feeding of the 5,000 with loves and fishes (Math 14:19). And then the disciples go by ship to the other side of the lake (the Dead Sea?) (Math 14:22), and Jesus decides to follow them on foot (walking on the water). Simon Peter thinks this is a marvelous trick, and so he asks Jesus if he can try it too:

> And Peter answered him and said, 'Lord, if this is you then ask me come to you on the water.' And (Jesus) said, 'Come'. And when Peter was come down out of

> the ship, he walked on the water to go to Jesus. But when he saw the strong wind he was afraid and began to sink. He cried out, saying, 'Lord, save me.' And Jesus stretched out his hand and ... said unto him, 'O ye of little faith...' (Math 14:28-32)

This is a very famous quote from the New Testament that everyone in the 13th century would have known about, and so it is surprising that *History* should try to amend it and improve upon it, as we shall see. And this is especially so since the Church may well have viewed any such amendments to the 'word of god' as being blasphemous, and so in amending this story the Arthurian authors were dicing with death.

But do note how the enlightened 21st century has regressed back into the trepidation and terror of the Medieval period, when blasphemy laws threatened death for every unguarded utterance. Nowadays death comes from the followers of the Great Protection Racket, while Western governments blame the authors, artists, cartoonists and comedians for 'incitement' (ie: blasphemy), and exonerate the terrorists of all blame. The Catholic Inquisition has been resurrected by *dhimmi* politicians in Western Europe, who have surrendered to Islam. And so the very people who extol freedom of thought and speech are helping to bury it.

A new generation of authors in the 21st century will only be able to write obliquely about the genocidal protection racketeer of Persia, just as Arthurian authors of the 13th century could only write obliquely about the warrior-prince known as the Powerful Horse. These courageous Medieval authors were constantly risking their lives to pass on the heretical information they had on their desks, and here the author of *History* parallels those very same biblical verses about Simon Peter by saying:

> Josephus said to the people who were with him: 'follow me, you can be sure you will cross this river without danger' ... then he (went across the river) as confidently as if he was on a rock ... and the people following him went into the water ... and they hardly got wet at all ... Everyone crossed the river except for one person called Canaan ...
>
> Once they were on the other side the twelve brothers (disciples) noticed that their brother Canaan had remained behind ... Josephus said ... if he had gone in the water the burden of his sins would have pulled him down to the bottom and he would have drowned ... Josephus went back to the river and crossed as easily as before. When he reached Canaan he said: 'Canaan, now your lack of faith is apparent... (History 35:219-221) (Author's brackets.)

This is obviously a repetition of the Jesus walking on water story, but with some interesting variations. And the first of these is that the leader of the twelve brothers (or disciples) is no longer Jesus but Josephus the son of

Joseph(us) of Arimathaea, who will again be equated with Saul-Josephus in the following pages. This is a deliberate confusion of names, as readers can probably see. And so Saul-Joseph(us) has achieved his goal of usurping the role of Jesus completely, by leading twelve disciples and walking on water.

Interestingly, the gospel version of this story involves Simon Peter (St Peter), while the Arthurian version is talking about Simon Canaan who is also called Simon Zelotes (Math 10:4, Mk 3:18, Acts 1:13). But in the gospel accounts these are supposed to be two separate disciples. In the gospels, Simon Canaan-Zelotes is always linked with Judas-Theudus (Iscariot) and with James. It was for this and other reasons that he was said to be a brother of Jesus, in *Jesus, Last of the Pharaohs*, while Simon Peter was not linked to this family at all. But here in *History*, the author is explicitly linking Simon Canaan with Simon Peter, which means that Peter (St Peter) may have been a brother (or brother-in-law) of Jesus. And while this assertion is unusual, and not exactly supported by the gospel stories, it does make sense because Peter became a pivotal leader within the Church of Jesus and James. And who better to give the Keys of the Kingdom of Heaven to, than your own brother or brother-in-law.

History says that all of these twelve brothers (or disciples) who crossed the river were of the same father and mother, which is yet another heretical claim. And so these were not simply brothers in a Church, but blood-brothers. Although a later comment in *Merlin Grail* says that some of them were brothers-in-law (p42). To have Jesus as the leader of twelve disciples is one thing, but to have all those disciples as your own brothers or brothers-in-law speaks more of a dynasty than a sect, and more of a familial conspiracy than independent witnesses.

But who was this Arthurian (Simon) Canaan, who is being closely linked here with St Simon Peter by walking on water? As with the works of Saul-Josephus, we have to be very suspicious when a 'certain person' is mentioned, or a character simply leaps into the narrative from nowhere without introduction. And the Arthurian Canaan is one of those suspicious characters: he appears at this very point in the story, is discussed for two short chapters, and then disappears never to be seen again. So who is Canaan? Well the famous Arthurian character with eleven brothers (and brothers-in-law) is Alain li Gros (or Pellehan), the father of Perceval, and as we shall see shortly it is likely that this Canaan is either Alain or his son, Perceval.

However, since Canaan has just been linked to Simon Peter, then we might also tentatively link either Alain or Perceval with St Peter. And while this connection may seem like a leap of faith, another unknown character slips almost unnoticed into *History's* narrative, just before and just after this walking on water episode, and his name is ... Petrus or Peter. This Peter is another of these suspicious characters who appears unannounced, and then disappears from the story after a few short chapters. But the similarity here is so obvious, that even the modern translator places a bracketed (St Peter) in the index section for this Peter.

But according to *History* this Peter (St Peter) was one of the knights of Josephus' Round Table (34:199) and he was related to Josephus (34:206). And so Arthurian history is not only firmly back within the 1st century era of the biblical story once more, but the disciples of Jesus are now being openly equated with the knights of the Round Table. *History* often attempts to separate Joseph(us) (of Arimathaea), Josephus (his son) and Arthur by a number of centuries. But since King Bron was sitting at Joseph(us)' Round Table table alongside Peter (St Peter), and Bron was the father of Alan li Gros (34:207), who was the father of Sir Perceval, it is fairly obvious that this version of Arthurian history is firmly set within the late 1st century. And so the gospel's Simon Canaan Peter (St Peter) may well have been one of the knights of the Round Table.

In the Arthurian walking on water episode, Josephus (the son) is clearly playing the role of Jesus. And in both cases the Jesus-Josephus character places his trust in St Simon Peter (Canaan) but finds that Peter cannot walk on water, and therefore has little faith or little trust. This link to the gospel Simon Peter (Canaan) is further reinforced by the Arthurian Josephus crossing the water 'as if he was on a rock'. But in the gospels this conjoined Simon Canaan was also called Peter and Kephas (Petra Πετρα and Kepha כיפא), meaning 'Rock Rock'. And so this Arthurian mention of a rock is a direct allusion to the gospel Peter, and it confirms that this story is really about a conflated Simon Peter Canaan Kephas, the biblical St Simon Peter.

This radical interpretation is reinforced by another passage in the same chapter, where another biblical episode has crept virtually unnoticed into Arthurian history. This is the peculiar story of the biblical St Simon Peter and the tablecloth, and the two versions of this story are as follows:

> Arthurian version:
> Josephus and his ministers began the service ... They sat down in the middle of a field and began to spread some tablecloths, while others laid folded cloths on the grass, for they wanted to eat at the dinner hour and they had no other tables. Once they were ready to eat Peter, one of Josephus' relatives, carried the Holy Grail before the ranks. It happened that at the coming of the Holy (Grail) Vessel all the tablecloths where the religious worthy men sat were covered in the most beautiful food a mortal heat could conceive. But the sinners ... had nothing to eat. (History 34:206) (Author's brackets.)

> Biblical version:
> Peter ... became very hungry, and would have eaten, but ... fell into a trance. And he saw heaven opened, and a certain vessel descending unto him, as it had been

> a great tablecloth tied at the four corners, and let down to the earth. (And on it) were all manner of four-footed beasts of the earth, and wild beasts, and creeping things, and fowls of the air. And there came a voice to him saying, Rise, Peter; kill, and eat. But Peter said, Not so, Lord; for I have never eaten any thing that is common or unclean. (Acts 10:10-16)

Is this not the very same story, in both Acts of the Apostles and in *History*? Peter and the disciples are hungry, so a tablecloth is spread and the Holy Grail-chalice appears, and so the table becomes full of the choicest of foods. The cornucopian attributes of the Holy Grail are a common theme in the *Vulgate Cycle*, and so it is clear that these miraculous foods were provided to St Peter by the Grail. And so the direct equivalence between these two stories confirms that the Arthurian story ***is*** about St Simon Peter, and it also confirms that the New Testament did know about the Holy Grail, and did covertly record details about it.

So rather than this meal being a pleasant picnic in a park, this 'laying of the tablecloth' is a religious ceremony, just as the Arthurian quote indicates. Due to a lack of purpose-built temples many early masonic lodge meetings were organised in a similar fashion, in the upper rooms of taverns. The masonic 'tablecloth' would be decorated with a black-and-white checkerboard and spread on the floor just like the tablecloth in Acts, while three smaller cloths depicting the symbolism of the 1st, 2nd and 3rd degree tracing-boards would be folded in the middle (waiting to be unfurled). One can imagine that the equivalent biblical 'tablecloth' was decorated with celestial and astrological symbolism in a very similar fashion, and quite possibly laid out as a complete zodiac. Even the venerable theologian Adam Clarke suggests that the gospel 'tablecloth' was an 'emblem of the universe'.

Note the differences between these accounts too. The account in *History* is more prosaic, and downplays the miraculous features of the Grail. And the main point of this version is the separation of worthy knights, who were fed by the Grail, from the unworthy who went hungry; although this 'food' may refer to 'knowledge', as we have seen previously. But in the gospel version the story has become more ethereal and fanciful, just as we might expect. And the point of the story here, is a test of Simon Peter's commitment to Saul-Josephus' new Simple Judaism. Saul-Josephus was the Apostle to the Gentiles and did not keep kosher, while St Peter is trying to remain a pious Jew by not eating unclean foods. But these detail differences merely demonstrate the disparate perspectives of the authors who have crafted these stories.

But perhaps the most interesting aspect of these similar stories are the characters. In the Arthurian version the religious service was led by Josephus (the son), while the Holy Grail was held by an otherwise unnamed Peter, because the Peter was the Grail Guardian. But in Acts of the Apostles it is St Simon Peter who sees the vessel (Grail-chalice) and the tablecloth (masonic floor-cloth), while the voice urging him to eat non-kosher Gentile foods just has to be Saul (St Paul). So here we have Josephus and Peter, and Saul and Peter in exactly the same story. And this is interesting because we can again deduce that Saul (St Paul), and Josephus (the son) must therefore be the same person.

Arthurian	Biblical	Role
Peter	Peter	Grail Guardian
Josephus	Saul	Priest

So the biblical Saul (St Paul) and the Arthurian Josephus (the son) just have to be the same person. But since Saul and Josephus Flavius have already been identified as the same person, on numerous occasions, this means that the Arthurian Josephus (the son) and Saul-Josephus Flavius are also the same person. Once again we see that Arthurian history is not only relating 1st century events, but events extracted directly from the gospels. And it is doing so because these are two alternative accounts of exactly the same story and exactly the same characters. And while we are on the subject of similar or equivalent characters, in this particular section St Simon Peter was staying at the House of Simon (the tanner):

> And now send men to Joppa, and call for one Simon, whose surname is Peter. He is lodging with one Simon the tanner, whose house is by the sea side. (Acts 10:5-6)

But a tanner is a *burseus* βυρσευς, and so this was actually the house of Simon Burseus. However, in Chapter X we shall see that one of the key players in the Jewish Revolt was actually Simon Boethus, who was probably the father of Mary and Martha. And since the disciples often stayed at the House of Simon in Bethany beyond the Jordan, where Mary and Martha lived, it is likely that this well-known gospel house was actually the house of Simon Boethus. Yet it is entirely possible that the Simon Burseus mentioned here was a deliberate mispronunciation of Simon Boethus, and so Simon Peter was staying at another House of Simon. So it would appear that the inordinately rich Simon Boethus also had a holiday cottage by the seaside in Joppa. How pleasant.

The Peter Rock

So the Arthurian Josephus (the son) is definitely Saul-Josephus Flavius, and in the walking on water episode Saul-Josephus is attempting to usurp the role of Jesus by placing his trust in Simon Peter (Canaan Kephas), the Rock. And within the gospel accounts Jesus did just that, when he elevated Simon to the position and title of the Peter, the Guardian of the Stone:

> And (Jesus said to Simon Peter) you are Peter (Petros Πετρος), and upon this rock (*petra* πετρα) I will build my church, and the gates of hell shall not prevail against it. (Mt 16:18) (Author's brackets.)

But the Rock or Stone of the Nazarene Church was not simply a priestly title, it was actually one of the facets of the Holy Grail. As we shall see in a later chapter, in Wolfram von Eschenbach's *Parzival* the Holy Grail is not simply a golden chalice, it was also a sacred omphalos stone - the sacred stone of Jacob, or the Elagabal of Emperor Elagabalus. But St Simon Peter-Kephas was given the prestigious title of The Rock or The Stone by Jesus himself, and so the gospels are clearly saying that Simon Peter-Kephas had become the new Guardian of the Stone - the new keeper of the lithic Holy Grail.

Merlin Grail says that the Holy Grail was given to Bron-Hebron (p41-42),* who became the new Fisher King after Joseph(us) (of Arimathaea). And after Bron, *Merlin Grail* says that the Grail went to Perceval (p155-156), while *Quest* says that the Grail was passed onto Sir Galahad (84:274). And since Perceval and Galahad were probably the same knight, we can be fairly sure that a singular Sir Perceval-Galahad became the new Guardian of the Holy Grail after his grandfather, Bron-Hebron.

But if Bron, and perhaps his son Alain li Gros, and then his son Perceval-Galahad were all Guardians of the Grail, then they must also have become the new Peter-Kephas. The Peter was the Rock or Stone, the Guardian of the Holy Grail-stone, and so all of these three Arthurian characters must have acquired the Peter title. And since we have already seen that Arthurian history is replicating the gospel accounts, then Bron, Alain and Perceval are all potential candidates for the biblical St Simon Peter.

And a possible confirmation for this claim lies in the name that Alain li Gros was given. In many of these manuscripts Alain is called Pellehan, but *History* and *High History* call him Alain li Gros instead. And the clue to this not being an Aramaic name is the 'li Gros' suffix, which strongly suggests a Celto-Breton-Norman origin.

* *Merlin Grail* says that the Grail jumped a generation, from Bron to his grandson Perceval-Galahad. This may be because Alain li Gros forfeited the Grail and its illustrious title. Alain not only detested circumcision and castration, he had an illicit affair which disqualified him from the role. This may be another reason for the 'dispossession' story that we have seen on so many occasions.

The 'li' is from the Norman and is cognate with the Celto-Welsh 'y', with both meaning 'the' or 'of', as in Cor y Cewri meaning Circle of Giants (ie: Stonehenge). The title 'Gros' is incorrectly translated in most Arthurian histories as meaning 'fat', but it much more likely that it refers to the Celto-Welsh and Normo-French word *gros* which refers to a 'dozen dozen' (or the number 144). Since Pellehan-Alain was pointedly said in *History* to be the youngest of twelve brothers, he was quite literally the twelfth of the twelve (History 34:207 **). And so Alain's common nickname became 'li Gros', the twelfth of twelve sons, the dozen dozen.

But this 'Gros' title had a dual function, for Alain li Gros was not simply one of twelve sons, he was also one of the twelve knights of the Round Table. And if Alain can be linked with St Simon Peter, then he was also one of the twelve biblical disciples. In which case, it is likely that 'Gros' was not simply a nickname but more of a formal title, which either referred to Alain being the twelfth of the twelve disciple-knights, as *History* implies, or perhaps the first of the twelve disciple-knights, as *High History* maintains. (In modern Western tradition we tend to think of the first son being the most senior, but in ancient folklore the favoured child was the seventh son of the seventh son: the younger rather than the elder.) And Bron-Hebron, Alain's father, held exactly the same title because *High History* calls him Gais li Gros, and so both Bron and Alain were the twelfth of the twelve - they were both the foremost of the twelve disciple-knights.

And if Alain's title was Celto-Norman, then perhaps his new name was too (the *Vulgate* calls him Pellehan, Parlan or Pellinor). The Celto-Norman *alain* can be linked with Alain li Gros in two ways. Firstly, *alain* means 'deer', which was the symbol on Alain's shield. And secondly, the same Breton and Welsh dictionaries claim that *alain* also means 'small stone'. In which case, the name 'Alain' appears to be the equivalent of the Aramaic Kephas, the Greek Petros, the English Peter, and the English Rock. And so now the gospel's St Simon Peter has four equivalent titles in four different languages:

Aramaic	Shimown	Kephas
Greek	Seemon	Petros
Celto-Norman	Simon	Alain
English	Simon	Peter
English	Simon	Rock

'Peter' is merely a title that is given to the Guardian of the Holy Grail-stone.

** Just to be contrarian, *High History* says that Alain li Gros was the oldest of the twelve brothers.

And so when Perceval-Galahad succeeded his father or grandfather as the Grail Guardian, he would become the new Peter - the new Rock who guarded the Grail-stone. However, it is difficult to decide which of these knights is the gospel's St Simon Peter: was he the grandfather, the father or the son? The initial assessment is that Peter was of a mature age, and must therefore have been either Bron or Alain. However, Chapter XIV will argue that the more famous references to a Peter in the gospels were actually referring to Perceval-Galahad.

Perhaps now we can see why Chretien of Troyes was describing Sir Perceval as being a complete rustic fool in his *Perceval.* The gospel's St Simon Peter was often considered to be the oaf and fool of the Nazarene Church, and yet in this new analysis Simon Peter may well have been Perceval himself. As Jesus said to Simon Peter, only a few verses after making him the Guardian of the Grail-stone:

> But Jesus turned, and said to (Simon) Peter, 'Get yourself behind me, you Devil: you are an obstacle to me: for you do not understand the ways of God, but only those of men.' (Math 16:23)

Jesus appears to have had a change of heart about the promotion of Simon Peter here, because he appears to be bereft of understanding. The Jerusalem rabbis may well have a similar view of Simon because in the Talmud, Simon ben Gamaliel, the son of Gamaliel who will later be identified as the Talmud's Simon Peter, was debating the minutiae of Jewish law. This is the central topic of the Talmud, which manages to debate some of the most bizarre rulings known to man, like the approved methods of inspecting beds and the kosher regulations for snow. Anyway, Simon ben Gamaliel (Peter?) observes yet another Sabbath rule, but it is so obscure and irrelevant that even the other rabbis were obliged to make fun of it:

> R. Simeon b. Gamaliel said: We may also handle fragments of glass (on the Sabbath), because it is food for ostriches. R. Nathan said to him: If that is so, then let bundles of twigs be handled, because they are food for elephants. And R. Simeon b. Gamaliel said: Ostriches are common, whereas elephants are rare. R. Amemar observed: Provided he has some ostriches. (Shabath 128a) (Author's brackets.)

Anyway, Jesus had placed his trust in Simon Peter when he gave him the title of 'Peter' or 'Rock', but Peter did not return that trust by following Josephus-Jesus onto the water as if it were a rock. He either refused to cross or started to sink, depending on the account.

The untrustworthiness of Simon Peter Kephas is further reinforced just after this Arthurian walking on water episode, were we have the confusing and seemingly tragic story of Simon Peter (the gospel's St Peter) murdering all of his brothers. Both Simon and Canaan (Simon Peter Canaan) are jealous of their brothers, because they had received no 'grace' from the Holy Grail. The Grail's 'grace' is said to be 'food' but one presumes that it actually refers to secrets, just as 'bread' often refers to knowledge in the gospels. And so Canaan creeps up upon his sleeping eleven or twelve brothers and cuts off all their heads.

Then we have a real muddle, where Canaan confesses to Simon what he has just done, and so Simon wants to kill his cousin Peter too, but only succeeds in stabbing him in the shoulder. Since this strange detail makes little or no sense, it seems that the only reason for this peculiar murder alliance is to link Simon, Peter and Canaan all together once more, which is what the previous paragraphs in this story have already done. And this confusion of names is not simply an Arthurian artifact, because in the gospels this combined St Peter was actually known as Simon Peter Kephas Canaan Zelotes bar Jonah. Readers can perhaps appreciate how a single Arthurian character can have so many names. With these accounts being recorded by multiple authors in three different languages, and with many secrets to hide, these names and titles can rapidly bifurcate and multiply to absurd levels.

The meaning of this strange story of Simon Peter beheading his eleven or twelve brothers is no doubt allegorical in some manner. And perhaps we can get a better understanding of what this episode means from *High History's* similar account of the murder of eleven knights. In this alternate version, Perceval had captured the Lord of the Moors, who was equated earlier with King Arthur. The Lord of the Moors begs for mercy, but Perceval asks who will repay his mother, the Widow Lady, for the damage and shame done to her. Perceval demands justice and so he:

> Had a great vat made ready in the middle of the court and made the eleven knights be brought. He made their heads be cut off into the vat, and bleed as much blood as might come from them (into the vat). After that ... the Lord of the Moors was brought before the vat ... he hung him by the feet so that his head was in the blood ... until he was drowned and quenched. (High History 15:31.)

This gruesome story is obviously the same as the account of the beheadings here in *History*, but in *High History* it was Perceval who did the head-cutting rather than Simon Peter. And so we see yet another direct link between Perceval and Simon Peter Canaan, because both beheaded the eleven knightly disciples (with Peter or Perceval being the twelfth disciple). It was explained earlier that this story was probably a cruel parody of the Christian eucharist, with the king (Arthur-Jesus) being forced to drink the blood of his disciples, rather than the disciples being made to drink the blood of their god-king. Saul-Josephus did not approve of circumcision, let alone castration and blood-rituals, and so it would appear that Saul-Josephus, as the probable original author, was using this cruel parody to mock these rituals. (We shall see later, that the eucharist blood-drinking aspect of Simple Judaism was probably devised by Emperor Vespasian.)

However, there may be an element of historical truth behind this cruel allegory, as their often is, for it was this very same Simon Peter (Canaan) who used his sword to cut off the ear of the high priest's servant:

> Then Simon Peter having a sword drew it, and smote the high priest's servant, and cut off his right ear. The servant's name was Malchus. Then said Jesus unto Peter: Put away your sword into its sheath. The chalice which my Father has given me, shall I not drink it? (Joh 18:10)

The chalice mentioned here may be the Holy Grail, but it may also be a reference to the proverbial 'poisoned chalice'. Jesus' father (be that mortal or spiritual) had given him the task of changing the religion of the region and becoming its king, and this had placed him on a collision course with both Orthodox Judaism and Rome. (That, plus the little matter of a very secular tax rebellion.) And so Jesus-Izas was styling himself as the new Socrates, who had been convicted of challenging the religious *status quo* of Greece by introducing new gods. And of course the punishment for the wise Socrates was to drink from a poisoned chalice.

In the previous quotes Simon Peter (Perceval) not only used his sword to cut off the heads of his brother disciples, he also used it to cut off the ear of the high priest's servant. So are these two stories linked in some manner? And if so, then how? The verse from John says that Simon Peter cut off the ear of Malchus, but this name is the Greek equivalent of the Aramaic *malchos* מלכוס meaning 'king' or 'kingdom'. So was this a name or a title? And who was this princely Malchus that Simon Peter maimed with his sword?

This gathering of the twelve (armed) disciples on the Mount of Olives was described by Saul-Joseph(us) as being an armed assault on the city of Jerusalem by 30,000 men. And it is highly likely that in this early era the rebel army of Jesus would have performed some kind of blood-ritual sacrifice, to sanctify the impending assault and thus protect the army. The Jews and Pagans might have slaughtered a sheep or bull to ensure success, but since the Nazarene Ebionites did not slaughter animals perhaps they made a sacrifice of another kind.

It is likely that these neo-Israelite Nazarenes would have performed a ceremony similar to the one in Numbers 10:35, where the Ark of the Covenant containing its two sacred stones traveled at the front of the army to ensure success. And since it was demonstrated in *Jesus, King of Edessa* that the Edessan monarchy possessed the Ark of the Covenant in the 2nd century AD, it is likely that they would have used it in a similar fashion. But an Ark and its sacred stones is of little use without a Peter-Kephas, a priestly Guardian of the Grail Stones, and so a pre-battle ceremony may have been held to initiate a new Peter-Kephas, a new Guardian of the Grail-stones. And this is a distinct possibility because immediately after this ear-cutting event and the arrest of Jesus, we appear to have the flight of a new initiate:

> There followed (Jesus) a certain young man, having a linen cloth cast about his naked body; and the young men laid hold on him. And he left the linen cloth, and fled from them naked. And they led Jesus away to the high priest ... And Peter followed him afar off, even into the palace of the high priest. (Mark 14:51-54.)

So what was this semi-naked young man doing, at this famous gathering of

Fig 6.27 The death of Socrates by a poisoned chalice, which is being handed to him by a weeping disciple. Jesus is styling himself as the wise Socrates, while the disciple who hands him the poisoned chalice is presumably St Peter. Note that Socrates often gives the same single-fingered salute as John the Baptist does. Picture by Jaques David, 1787.

the (armed) disciples on the Mount of Olives? Whether this was a gathering for an (armed) prayer-meeting or a gathering of 30,000 men for an armed assault on Jerusalem, the presence of this semi-naked young man needs explanation. As we have seen, a likely answer is that this young man was an initiate, a new princely entered-apprentice into the Nazarene cult of castration that will be discussed at length in Chapter IX. And so perhaps Simon Peter Kephas was cutting an *osfus* οσφυς (the loins) rather than an *ous* ους (an ear). Has a scribe deliberately abbreviated an *osfus*, to prevent a gospel embarrassment?

And since Arthurian history mimics biblical history in so many respects, it is not so surprising that we find a similar story in *Quest*. And rather conveniently, this story involves one of the very same characters we have just been discussing - Perceval the Peter. Perceval and Galahad (Perceval-Galahad) were the pure virginal knights of Arthurian history, but Perceval finds himself tempted by the devil in the guise of a beautiful woman who says:

> Believe me, I had wanted you more than you desired me ... the lady then ordered her servants to prepare her bed ... Perceval happened to catch sight of his sword ... and that made him come to his senses ... Perceval was so disturbed by the adventure that ... he pulled his sword from its sheath and drove it into his thigh, and blood spurted out in all directions ... then he looked down and realised he was entirely naked except for his breeches. (Quest 31:110, 32:110.)

To protect his virtue and chastity Perceval takes his sword and thrusts it into his loins, and then finds himself nearly naked just like the initiate in the gospel story. And since the wounds of the Maimed or Wounded (Fisher) King were exactly the same, and it is widely acknowledged that the Wounded King was castrated, then Perceval must have been castrating himself. And since Perceval became the new Fisher King and Grail Guardian (Merlin Grail p156) he would have to castrate himself, because the title of Fisher King and Wounded King seem to be always linked. The Fisher King had to be a Galli *castrato* eunuch, as we shall see in later chapters.

We appear to have two very similar events here. In the biblical account St Simon Peter (Canaan) takes his sword and cuts an appendage off a prince, and then a semi-naked man runs away. And in the Arthurian story Sir Perceval is a prince who ends up as a semi-naked virgin cutting off an appendage between his loins, in order to become a eunuch - and therefore become the new Peter, the new Guardian of the Grail-stone. So this young princely initiate on the Mount of Olives is likely to have been Perceval Peter, the son of Alain li Gros. And although this young age does not appear to suit the role of the gospel's St Simon Peter very well, Chapter XIV may give us a potential solution to this perennial problem.

Summary

In summary, while it is not possible to positively link the biblical St Simon Peter's sword wielding escapade with the equivalent by the Arthurian Sir Perceval, we can quite confidently link St Simon Peter with Bron, Alain and especially with Perceval. And the many similarities between these characters are as follows:

> The gospel Simon Peter tries to walk on water and fails, the same as Simon Canaan tries to walk on water and fails. Which means that Simon Peter is likely to be Simon Canaan.
>
> Alain means 'stone' or 'rock', just as St Simon Peter and Kephas mean 'stone' or 'rock'. And Canaan was supposed to walk on the water 'as if he was on a rock'.
>
> The 'rock' was a formal title for the Grail Guardian, the keeper of the lithic Grail-stone. This was an important position, which is why St Simon Peter became the head of the Nazarene Church.
>
> The gospel Simon Peter sees a chalice and a tablecloth descending from heaven, just as the Arthurian Josephus and Peter lay a tablecloth for a Grail ceremony.
>
> Gros means 'twelve of twelve', while Simon Peter was the first of the twelve.
>
> Simon Canaan cuts off eleven of twelve heads, just as Perceval-Galahad cuts off eleven of twelve heads. And so Simon Peter Canaan is likely to be Perceval.
>
> The gospel Simon Peter Canaan became the Guardian of the Grail-stone, the Peter-Kephas, just as Perceval-Galahad became the Guardian of the Grail-stone. Which means that Simon Peter Canaan is likely to be Perceval.
>
> Perceval is a knight of the Round Table, just as Petrus-Peter is a knight of the Round Table. Which means that Perceval is likely to be Peter - and therefore the biblical Simon Peter Canaan.

These points seem to indicate that St Peter was actually Perceval the Peter, the son of Alain. And although this would appear to make the biblical St Peter much too young, there may be a solution to this generational problem, which will be explored further in Chapter XIV. Whichever is the correct Peter, these strong associations again link Bron, Alain and Perceval with the era of Joseph(us) (of Arimathaea), just as we saw in *High History*, and so these Arthurian stories are all quite firmly set within the 1st century.

But this story appears to allude to much more than that. What it appears to be saying, in its own convoluted and concealed manner, is that the gospel disciples were actually Arthurian knights. And that is what the later chapters in this book will attempt to demonstrate - that the twelve disciples of the Last Supper Table were the twelve knights of the Arthurian Round Table.

VII

History of the Holy Grail

History of the Holy Grail - Water Kayo

Having looked at some of the seemingly fanciful tangential stories within *History of the Holy Grail* and discovered some surprising real histories there, we will now move on to the book itself. *History of the Grail* is the first book of the *Vulgate Cycle,* which is a vast corpus of impenetrable Arthurian history spreading through nine volumes and some 3,500 pages of modern close-typed printing. It must have been a vast and hugely expensive undertaking, in an era when these manuscripts were hand-written on velum, and so one has to ask why any wealthy patron would want to spend so much money on such a fruitless exercise. Because it is highly likely that the number of people who have ever bothered to read the *Vulgate,* cover to cover, can be counted on both hands.

The true origins of *History of the Grail* are complex, because there are multiple claims to authorship, some more legendary than others. *History* claims that the original account of this history was in a small book, which had been given to the 'Holy Hermit' by Jesus himself back in the 1st century AD. We shall attempt to identify this Holy Hermit later in this chapter. This shadowy Holy Hermit then added various adventures from his own life to the work, and created a larger manuscript. This text eventually arrived in Normandy, presumably through the agency of Templars returning from the Near East in the early 12th century. This is a provenance not unlike the one claimed by Eschenbach for *Parzival,* which was said to have been derived from Toledo (or Edessa) and was then combined with a manuscript from Anjou in France.

It was from texts like this that had been brought back from Syrio-Judaea that Arthurian history was born, because large sections of these stories detail gospel-type events, as we have seen in the previous chapters. And this is even more true of *History of the Grail*, because the majority of this story is about Joseph of Arimathaea, the shadowy but influential aristocrat who took Jesus down from the cross in the gospel stories. And so just like *Parzival*, this great and influential corpus of Arthurian history does not start its story in the rolling shires of Britain, with a pensive King Arthur scanning the horizon for invading Saxons, it starts in 1st century Judaeo-Syria once more. And why this great obsession with 1st century Judaea within Arthurian history? Because this is where these stories came from.

These Syrio-Judaean documents were then worked on by authors like Geoffrey of Monmouth, who linked them into the known history of Britain and crafted a wonderful story from this conflated history. And then Robert Wace rewrote Monmouth's work in a clumsy and naive fashion, but did manage to mention the Round Table. Then there was Chretien de Troyes, who crafted a similar tale in his *Perceval*, but with a slightly different emphasis and a different characters. It was Chretien de Troyes, for instance, who created Sir Lancelot (but never mentions him in *Perceval*). However, it is likely that Chretien's Sir Lancelot is one and the same as Monmouth's King Lot, Malmesbury's Yder, and Eschenbach's Ither Gaheviez. So Lancelot was there all along, it is just that his character has been expanded and reworked within the *Vulgate Cycle* to become one of the major players in the drama.

The next scribe or author who reworked these manuscripts is said in most modern Arthurian literature to be Walter Map, the claimed author of much of the *Vulgate Cycle*, who may have been a squire in the court of King Henry II of England in the late 12th century. However, while Walter Map is credited as the author of *Quest for the Holy Grail*, the last line in *History of the Grail* credits Walter Kayo as the author instead. The identity of Walter of Kayo is unknown and it is unclear if he is one and the same as Walter Map, as has been assumed. Map may simply mean 'brother', and so the titles 'Map' and 'Kayo' may simply be giving the family relationship and home town of someone called Walter. Whether they are the same character or not, Walter Kayo is highly likely to have been the same as Master Kyot, who was credited as the translator of a manuscript used in *Parzival*. It was Master Kyot (Walter Kayo) who discovered an (Aramaic) manuscript written by Flegetanis of Toledo (Edessa) and translated it into Norman French. And then Eschenbach subsequently translated it into High German and used it as a foundation for his *Parzival*.

The modern translators of the *Vulgate* claim that these are early 13th century manuscripts, a date that does not match very well with the 12th century life of Walter Map. So it is likely that the original source manuscripts were reworked into the *Vulgate Cycle* at a later date. The identity of one of the later scribes and translators who created the *Vulgate* as we know it, is Robert de Boron, who is credited in chapter 27 of *History* as translating the text from Latin to Norman French. In the closing lines of *Merlin,* Robert of Boron confirms that he was merely the translator when he says: 'I Robert de Boron retell this book in the vernacular (French) according to the teachings of the Grail Books'. But rather than ploughing through Boron's impenetrable *Vulgate Cycle,* readers would be much better advised to read his *Merlin and the Grail,* which is a delightfully concise summary of most of the events in the *Vulgate Cycle.*

Modern translators of the *Vulgate Cycle* insist that *History* was written after *Quest,* even though it is presented as the first volume in the series. But it is not entirely certain that this is correct. The problem here is that the story in *Quest* constantly refers to events in *History,* and so if *Quest* really was written first then the author would have needed to deliberately leave literary 'hooks' all through his work, so that *History* could latch onto them. This seems unnecessarily complex, and it is much easier to imagine that the books were written in the order they are presented - *History, Lancelot, Merlin, Quest* and *Mort.*

The reason for this confusion, is the deliberately distorted chronology in these books. When reading these volumes in the orthodox fashion, *History* is supposed to be narrating events in the 1st century, which obviously happened long before *Quest's* supposedly 5th century Arthurian story. This is why *History* is presented as the first volume in the series. However, if *History* is read more logically and laterally, then it can be seen that it actually narrates stories about the generation that followed King Arthur, and therefore followed the story in *Quest.*

It is the distorted Arthurian chronology that is the source of this confusion. In reality, *History* (the first book) relates AD 70s material, while *Quest* (the sequel) gives us a history of the AD 60s. Chronologically, *Lancelot* and *Merlin* come in between these two books, but they are mostly flights of fanciful fiction of a highly soporific nature containing very little of interest. Although *Lancelot* does fill in some of the missing gaps about the pivotal battle between King Arthur and the Romans.

Holy Hermit

So who exactly was this semi-mythical original author of *History,* the author who is called the Holy Hermit? He is not named, just as one might expect, but we can deduce many details about his identity from the unfolding story. Either Walter Kayo or Robert de Boron is relating this story in later centuries and he says of the original author:

> The name of the author is not given in the beginning. However, the words to be said herein will permit you to know a great deal about his name. (History 1:4)

Yes, indeed, by the end of the chapter we will know a great deal about the original author, and perhaps rather more than he intended. It is said that the name of the original author cannot be given because:

> First, if he gave his name and said that through him, god had revealed such a noble and lofty story as that of the Grail, the treacherous and envious might interpret this as boastfulness.
>
> The second reason is that someone who knows him might hear his name, and thus might prize the story less, because it had been written by such a humble person.
>
> The third reason is that if there were anything improper in the story through either omissions or the naivete of later scribes who transmit it from one place to another, all the blame would be placed upon him. (History 1:4)

Although *History* will not reveal the name of the original author at this stage, the text goes on to say that no matter how much he covers up his name: 'it will be better known than he would like'. Which is quite true, as we shall see later. The book then says that the original author was: 'the most sinful of sinners' and 'the most despised person ever created' - a familiar turn of phrase that points us in the right direction from the very start.

History then switches to the first person, with the original Holy Hermit author telling the rest of the unfolding story. And he says of himself:

> 717 years after the passion of Jesus Christ it happened that I, the most sinful of sinners, was lying in a small hut ... when I awoke and saw around me such brightness ... and a man standing in front of me so handsome that his beauty could not be described by any mortal man ... he said 'be not afraid'. (History 1:5)

Here we arrive at the first test in this occult (concealed) quest. So will we fail this test, by thinking that the date was really 717 years after the crucifixion, or will we look a little deeper into the text to see what it really means? The first thing readers should note is that 717 years after the crucifixion is rather late. This would equate AD 747 according to the classical chronology or AD 787 according to the new chronology derived from the *King Jesus Trilogy*, and this is a long way removed from the classical Arthurian era which is often assumed to be the 6th century. So this new 8th century date does not link with the 1st century of Joseph of Arimathaea, who is the main hero of this manuscript; it does not link up with the Dark Ages of Arthurian history; and nor does it link in very well with the 12th and 13th century era when these manuscripts were being composed in Normandy. So why the mention of 717 years after the crucifixion?

In reality, the true question this unknown author is asking us is: 'do you understand Aramaic.' And if the answer is in the affirmative, then we will understand that numbers are words in Aramaic. And if we take the number 717 we can also derive:

700 = תש
10 = י
7 = ז

The resulting word that we can derive from the number 717 is *teshiz* תשיז. And how does this help us, readers may ask? Well, the word that the author was looking for was *teshiee* תשיע, which means 'ninth'. But the author could not write *teshiee* because this is not a valid number within the Aramaic numbering system, and so what he has done is to take the *ayin* ע at the end of *teshiee* and replaced it with the very similar-sounding *zayin* ז. Now the author did have a valid number and that number is 717, which therefore means 'ninth' in this manuscript.

The result of this lateral decypherment is that it is extremely likely that the unknown author was really talking about the 9th year after the crucifixion, rather than the 717th year. So the quote just given should really be read as:

> In the ninth year after the passion of Jesus Christ it happened that I....

And this date would represent AD 39 within the classical chronology of the New Testament, and AD 79 in the revised chronology. Surprisingly, the latter of these dates would suit the life and times of Joseph(us) of Arimathaea very well, because *History* makes Joseph(us) a colleague of Emperor Vespasian in the AD 70s. So again we see that the revised New Testament chronology is probably correct.

The reason for the Holy Hermit posing this linguistic test is probably twofold. Firstly, this conundrum establishes Aramaic-Hebrew as the underlying language of *History*, rather than Greek, Latin, Norman French or Celto-Welsh. Secondly, the author's revised 8th century chronology (if we had taken the 717 years literally) divorced the story and its author from the true era of these events. The original author did not want us to know who he really was, and his false 717 years date has neatly displaced the text from the troublesome 1st century era. And so none of the modern historians who have worked on this manuscript have ever spotted the true meaning of this story, because they have all been looking in the wrong era. And this is despite the fact that much of the story revolves around the 1st century's Joseph(us) of Arimathaea.

Inspiration

The previous quotes about the Holy Hermit author mention a 'sinner' and a 'flash of inspiration', which are very familiar turns of phrase in these investigations. In a remarkably similar fashion, Saul (Josephus) says of himself in Acts of the Apostles and his many epistles:

> This is a faithful saying, and worthy of all acceptation, that Christ Jesus came into the world to save sinners; of whom I (Saul, St Paul) am chief (sinner). (1Tim 1:15.)

> And it came to pass, that, as I (Saul, St Paul) made my journey, and was come close unto Damascus about noon, suddenly there shone from heaven a great light round about me. And I fell unto the ground, and heard a voice saying unto me, Saul, Saul, why do you persecute me? (Acts 22:6-7) (Author's brackets.)

In both cases the flash of blinding light is actually an apparition of Jesus, and he is visiting the chief of all sinners. In the gospel story Jesus visits Saul (Josephus), the scribe and priest, while in the Arthurian version he is appearing before the Holy Hermit scribe. And just as Saul (Josephus) and the Holy Hermit author of *History* were both said to be sinners, they were also both said to be great liars and boasters:

> I am forced to boast, though it is unprofitable. (2Cor 12:1 Montgomery)

> I say again, Let no man think me a fool; if otherwise, yet as a fool receive me, that I may boast myself a little. (2:Cor 11:16 KJV)

> God ... who is blessed for evermore, knows that I do not lie. (2:Cor 11:31 KJV)

> Now what I write to you, behold, before god, I do not lie. (Gal 1:20 KJV)

As we saw previously in *High History*, there are numerous links and similarities between the author of the original Arthurian manuscript and Saul-Josephus. So we have only browsed the first few pages of *History* and already it would seem likely that large chunks of this story have been influenced by or extracted from, the works of Saul-Josephus. And the many books that have been previously identified as being from the scriptorium of Saul-Josephus, include Luke, Acts, and the Epistles, plus *Jewish War, Antiquities*, and *Life*.

The account in *History* continues and Jesus, who is here called the Great Master, says that he will teach the author of *History* the secrets of everything:

> I have come here to teach you the secrets of everything you question ... I am the Great Master through whom all earthly masters know all the good they have learned ... Because I am the perfect Teacher, he who is the fountain of all knowledge, I have come to you, to teach you about the things that puzzle you. (History 1:8).

And this again is a familiar refrain. Saul-Josephus was not only branded as being the 1st century's greatest and most prolific liar, he was also deprived of the occult knowledge that he craved. He had tried to join the Nazarene Church of Jesus and James, but had been rejected, because nobody trusted this perfidious charlatan and traitor. In all his long battle with Jesus and James, the primary thing that Saul-Josephus wanted was knowledge - the secret and sacred knowledge of the Nazarene Fourth Sect. And here, quite conveniently, Jesus himself is promising the author of *History* (Saul-Josephus?) that very same knowledge.

And do remember that in Robert de Boron's *Merlin Grail*, Jesus was said to be teaching Joseph(us) of Arimathaea, rather than the Holy Hermit (p155). And remember also that in *High History* Joseph(us) of Arimathaea was so thoroughly muddled with Josephus, who was credited as the author of that manuscript, that it was impossible to know which Joseph(us) was which. In fact, *Merlin Grail* then goes well beyond the call of duty by labeling Joseph(us) of Arimathaea as the perfidious traitor instead of Judas:

> Three nights before the Passover, Christ's enemies were at the house of a man called Caiaphas, discussing how they could capture him. Joseph(us) of Arimathaea was present as they talked ... In the middle of their discussion Judas appeared, and they all fell silent believing him to be a good disciple of Jesus ... And when the Jews heard of Judas' disloyalty they were overjoyed and said: 'tell us how we can take him prisoner.' (Merlin Grail p16.) (Author's brackets.)

This is the saintly Joseph(us) of Arimathaea, who had saved Jesus from the cross, and here he is being portrayed as an arch-traitor and enemy who was trying to capture Jesus and turn him over to the Romans. Perhaps readers can appreciate the extent to which these manuscripts differ from the gospel message, and therefore how desperately heretical and dangerous they really were. But how did this great disparity between these accounts come about? And if Joseph(us) of Arimathaea was also implicated in this plot to capture Jesus, then why did Judas Iscariot take all the blame? Has Judas been made into a scapegoat? And if so, then by whom?

Once again, the most likely explanation is that Joseph(us) of Arimathaea was actually the traitorous Saul-Joseph(us) Flavius, who we know from his own writings did oppose and want to capture King Jesus-Izas (of Gamala and Edessa). And Saul-Joseph(us) of Arimathaea was able to deflect all the blame for the capture of Jesus onto Judas, instead of himself, because as the post-Revolt's chief administrator and premier historian he wrote and edited all the texts coming out of 1st century Judaea. In which case, Judas may have been innocent of all charges, and the real traitor who sold Jesus to the Romans for thirty pieces of silver was Saul-Josephus (of Arimathaea).

So we have not gone beyond the first few pages in this investigation, and already we have uncovered some New Testament chicanery to exonerate Joseph(us) of Arimathaea from Nazarene treason and incriminate Judas Iscariot instead. And we have also discovered a strong and unmistakable link between three similar characters - the Holy Hermit author of *History*; Joseph(us) of Arimathaea; and Saul-Joseph(us) Flavius. And this connection between the unnamed Holy Hermit author and Saul-Josephus the author is not simply interesting, and identical to the similar confusion we saw in *High History*, it is pivotal to the proper understanding of this text.

At present the account in *History* is thought to reside at the extreme edge of mythology, with the events it records being derived from fantasy. And yet if the author of this text was connected with or copying from Saul-Josephus, the 1st century's premier historian, then the entire account comes back to Earth with a resounding thump. For although we know that Saul-Josephus did write some fanciful accounts and was fully capable of creating a historical deception, we also know that he was a real person who wrote real history. So just as we have already seen in the previous chapter, these seemingly embellished and fanciful accounts may actually contain a kernel of real history. Furthermore, it again implies that much of the material in this semi-legendary source manuscript came from 1st century Syrio-Judaea. And since *History* touches on Arthurian history, as well as the life of Joseph(us) of Arimathaea, the stories about Arthur may also have been based upon 1st century records.

The worrying possibility that Saul-Josephus was the author of the source manuscript for *History*, has already been identified and mentioned by many venerable Arthurian scholars. And yet they swiftly rejected this possibility because, as Ernst Brugger says in his 1906 article:

> Because even if Josephus Flavius was very well known as a historian, and even much respected and held as a Christian historian, it remains striking that he could record events from Britannic history (that occurred) many centuries after his death ... I think these oddities are only a result of a confusion. [1]

And James Bruce readily agreed with this analysis in *Evolution of Arthurian Romance,* his 1928 analysis of Arthurian literature.

The reasoning here is that the author of the original source document for *History* cannot be Saul-Josephus, because the chronology will not allow it. Saul-Josephus could not be writing about a 6th century Arthur in the 1st century. However, this argument only holds true if we subscribe to the classical view that King Arthur was a 6th century king. But if Arthur was in fact a 1st century king, as all the evidence is pointing towards, then there is absolutely no problem with a 1st century Saul-Josephus being the original author of a 1st century source manuscript about a 1st century king of Syrio-Judaea.

Sacred Mountains

History then recounts that its unnamed Holy Hermit author (Saul-Josephus?) was taken up into the Third Heaven by Jesus:

> I was raised on high and taken to one of the most marvellous places that man has ever seen ... And if I said this was the Third Heaven where Saul was carried by the holy spirit, perhaps I would be telling the truth, although it would be considered boastfulness and lies. (History 1:18)

This quote is actually derived from the New Testament, where Saul (St Paul) is taken up into the Third Heaven in a very similar fashion. And so both this Holy Hermit author (Saul-Josephus?) and Saul (who is Josephus) were taken up into the Third Heaven. This Third Heaven initiation is also a component of Naassene-Ophite teachings, as we shall see in the next chapters. The seven heavens of Jewish philosophy included: the Yellum or Curtain behind which the Sun sets; the Starry Firmament upon which the stars and planets are fixed; the Clouds or Aether containing the manna of heaven; the Habitation of the heavenly Temple; the Dwelling Place of angels; the Fixed Residence where snow and hail resides; and the Araboth of justice, mercy and peace.

So both Saul (Josephus) and the Holy Hermit (Saul-Josephus?) were taken up by Jesus to see the Aether or clouds. And it would be entirely possible for someone to be above the clouds in the 1st century, if they stood on the top of a high mountain. We already know from the other books in this long series that sacred mountains were a central component of the Fourth Sect Nazarene creed. Whether it was the Temple Mount, the Great Pyramid, the great hill of Herodium-Tekoa, or the smaller hill at Sogmatar near Edessa, the focus of Nazarene ritual seems to have been centered upon a sacred hill. So if both Saul (Josephus) and this Holy Hermit author had been taken up to the top of a large sacred mount, they might well say that they had been taken to 'one of the most marvellous places that man has ever seen'. And this would be especially so if the mount in question was as imposing and sacred as the mighty Great Pyramid of Giza.

The verse that describes the gospel's Saul (Josephus) going to this Third Heaven is taken from Corinthians, which says of these events:

> I knew a man in Christ fourteen years ago ... who was taken up to the Third Heaven ... and how he was taken up into paradise, and **heard unspeakable words, which it is not lawful for a man to utter**. (2Cor 12:2-4)

These are probably the same secrets that Jesus taught to Joseph(us) of Arimathaea in *Merlin Grail*:

Fig 7.1 The crystal spheres that surrounded the Earth and held the clouds and the starry firmament of the Seven Heavens aloft.

> Jesus then **spoke other words to Joseph (of Arimathaea) which I dare not tell you**. Nor could I even if I wanted to, if I did not have the High Book in which they are written: and that is the creed of the great mystery of the Grail. (Merlin Grail p22.)

Here we see that Jesus is teaching unspeakable secrets to both Saul-Josephus and Joseph(us) of Arimathaea, as if these were two accounts of the same event. But *Merlin Grail* goes one step further than the gospels and confirms that these unspeakable secrets pertained to the Holy Grail. And so these two Joseph(us)es are being confused and conflated once more, as if they are again the same person. And although this verse from Corinthians is not explicitly saying that it was Saul (Josephus) himself who went up into the heavens, we can all see the deceit here, because as soon as Saul-Josephus mentions a 'certain man' or a 'certain place' we know that something is being hidden from us. And the minor deceit in this case, is that the 'certain man' was Saul (Josephus) himself.

The venerable theologians do not agree on their interpretation of this verse. Adam Clarke in his 1832 *Commentary on the Bible* says that this was another man, while John Gill in his 1809 *Exposition of the Old and New Testaments* says that Saul was talking about himself in the third person, to 'make himself more humble'. *History of the Grail* agrees with John Gill, and says that this was the Holy Hermit himself (ie: Saul-Josephus). But if this is so, then we may well be able to make a much better translation of this verse. The answer to this minor conundrum is given in (Saul) Josephus' *Life*, where he says of himself:

> When I was a child, and about fourteen years of age, I was commended by all for the love I had to learning; on which account the high priests and principal men of the city came then frequently to me together, in order to know my opinion about the accurate understanding of points of the law. (Josephus Life 2).

So (Saul) Josephus was a precocious child who taught theology and law to the high priests of Jerusalem, when he was just fourteen years old. Do we believe this? Do modern high priests and scientists flock to school classrooms, to receive the great wisdom of the children? Yet exactly the same thing was said of Jesus, who was an equally precocious child:

> And it came to pass, that after three days they found (a twelve-year old Jesus) in the temple, sitting in the midst of the doctors (of the law), both hearing them, and asking them questions. And all that heard him were astonished at his understanding and answers. (Luke 2:46-48) (Author's brackets.)

Let us bring these absurd boasts back down to Earth and into the realms of reality. This was not, of course, a story about the high priest of Jerusalem coming to learn points of Judaic law and scripture from a young (Saul) Josephus or Jesus, which is the ridiculous suggestion that the Church in particular wants people to believe. No, this was merely a *bar mitzvah* celebration, where the young candidate for the Judaic faith is being put to the test by the learned scholars at the Temple. And yes, perhaps even being tested by the high priest himself, if the young lad was closely connected to the aristocracy or royalty. The same happens today, in most *bar mitzvah* celebrations, where the new young man (and nowadays the young lady too), has to give a reading from the Torah and answer a question or two.

But do note that this *bar mitzvah* test was being performed on a fourteen year-old (Saul) Josephus. But if the verse from Corinthians was talking about Saul (Josephus) having a trial or test in the Third Heaven; and Josephus had his *bar mitzvah* test aged fourteen; and Saul is Josephus as we already know; then it is entirely possible that these are two accounts of one and the same event. In which case, it is likely that the verse from Corinthians was not talking about 'fourteen years ago', but rather of when Saul (Josephus) was fourteen years old. So if we understand that the 'certain man' was Saul himself, just as John Gill said, and we know that he was fourteen years old, the year of his *bar mitzvah,* then perhaps we should really read this verse as:

> I remember myself, when I was fourteen years old ... when I was taken up to the Third Heaven ... and how I was taken up into paradise, and heard unspeakable words, which it is not lawful for a man to utter. (2Cor 12:2-4)

And now perhaps we can see the truth of the matter. Saul-Josephus was such a well-connected youth that his *bar mitzvah* test was not conducted in a local synagogue. Instead, he was taken to the top of Herodium Hill south of Jerusalem. Or, more intriguingly, perhaps he was even taken to the top of the Great Pyramid, the most sacred mountain of the Jews, and the *bar mitzvah* test was conducted there. Remember that *Tempest & Exodus* has already established that the Great Pyramid was actually the Israelite's most sacred mountain - Mt Sinai. What better place could there be for a *bar mitzvah* celebration, than to be standing on the top of Mt Sinai?

Now this really would be an initiation and trial to strike fear into the heart of any pious youngster. Yes, we all know that Saul-Josephus was highly confident and ridiculously precocious, but just imagine being taken from the small and parochial Temple of Jerusalem, and then find yourself standing at the foot of the Great Pyramid - the largest man-made structure in

Fig 7.2 The new initiate gives the reading and lesson from the Torah, during his bar mitzvah. This is exactly what both Jesus and Saul-Josephus were doing, when they 'astonished the elders and rabbis' in the Temple of Jerusalem. Image courtesy of Wiki.

the world, almost to this very day. Imagine looking skywards to the very top of this enormous finely polished and bright white structure, knowing that your test of adulthood would be conducted on its summit, some 146 meters above the ground. And since the bright white Tura limestone cladding was only pillaged during the Muslim era, the Great Pyramid in the 1st century would have indeed looked like a single block of finely polished white quartz, with hardly a joint between the blocks to be seen.

In addition, just imagine that as a pious Jewish youth you knew that this was the very mountain that Moses had climbed to get his tablets of stone. And so this was the very mountain of the Judaic god, and god himself may still reside in the dark caverns located deep within the body of this vast structure. Imagine the initiate's trepidation, imagine his sphincter tightening. As *History* says of the Holy Hermit's experiences:

> I was carried to one of the most delightful places that man has ever seen, to my knowledge, for no matter how much joy any heart could think of or any tongue could speak of or any ear could hear of - one hundred thousand times as much could be found there ... And after I had looked at the marvels a long time, an

> angel (ambassador) said to me: "have you ever seen such marvels?" I replied that I never thought anything so great could exist. (History 1:8)

And if the reader has managed to climb to the top of the Great Pyramid, I am sure their reaction would be exactly the same. This is interesting, for this scenario is a real possibility, because we know that these aristocratic young lads travelled long distances in this early era. Jesus, for instance, was taken to Egypt for his education, although we are not sure what he did while he was there. And after his dramatic experience at his *bar mitzvah*, Saul-Josephus went on two very long tours across the Mediterranean, to evangelise the Nazarene Judaic and then the Simple Judaic religions. It is often assumed that Saul (Josephus) must have been an adult to do so, but it was convincingly proven in *King Jesus* that (as a conflated Saul-Josephus), he was only fifteen or so years old at the time of his first evangelical tour. But since he was already a man, having passed his *bar mitzvah* test with flying colours, he was well qualified to do so; even if he was still under the wing of his elder brother, Matthias Barnabas.

But the really interesting thing here, is that this account from *History*

Fig 7.3 The view from the top of the Great Pyramid at Giza, looking down upon the Second Pyramid and the lights of Cairo in the distance. The Third Pyramid is actually hidden from view, behind the Second Pyramid. Image courtesy Raskalov-vit.

of the Grail is adding to our knowledge of this event. Josephus (Saul) says he had a *bar mitzvah* aged fourteen; Saul (Josephus) appears to add to this account by saying he went up to the Third Heaven aged fourteen; and the Holy Hermit author of *History* not only agrees with this interpretation, he goes on to describe the vision from the top of that Third Heaven in some detail. So *History* may well contain additional biblical and historical information, within its convoluted and fantastical folds. So when the author gets to the next level (the next heaven) and describes what he saw there, perhaps this too contains elements of reality:

> There he showed me the power of the Trinity, for I saw the division of the Father, and the Son, and the Holy Spirit, so I could distinguish one person from the other. And I saw clearly how these three persons belong to one substance and one god and one power. (History 1:20)

Interesting. But is the author of *History* talking about three deities, or three pyramids? Perhaps readers can see how elements of a heretical reality can easily be hidden within these fanciful tales.

The author

The Holy Hermit author of *History* is then sent on a quest, and although the quest itself is rather pointless it ends up with Jesus tasking the author to transcribe and copy the miniature 'book of secrets'. This is the book that is said to have become the foundation for *History of the Grail*. The transcription of this little book begins with a description of the crucifixion, and the text reminds us that Jesus was very sorrowful because he had not converted very many people at that stage. But there were some secret believers and these, of course, included Joseph(us) of Arimathaea. *History* says of Joseph(us):

> The holy writing of the Grail speaks of a noble knight who lived at that time, whose name was Joseph of Arimathaea. Arimathaea was a city in the land of Ramathaim, beyond the river Jordan, and the text says it belonged to Elcan, the father of Samuel. (History 2:47)

Elcan is Elqanah, the father of the Torah's Samuel, just as it says here. But the location is more unusual. In classical scripture Elqanah was an Ephraimite, whose lands lay close to Jerusalem, and in a similar fashion Ramathaim has been identified as the town of Nevi Shmuel which is also near Jerusalem. In great contrast *History* is confidently saying that Ramathaim was located beyond the Jordan. And the probable reason for it doing so, is the close connection between these biblical aristocrats and the Kingdom of Osrhoene-Edessa, which did indeed lay beyond the Jordan.

As was explained in the previous books in this series, many of the prominent biblical locations, like the town of Bethany and the house of Simon, were located 'beyond the Jordan'. And it is possible that this description was also used as a euphemism for a location 'beyond the Euphrates'. The primary city states controlled by the biblical family were Pella, Palmyra and Edessa, and while the first of these were 'beyond the Jordan' the latter was most definitely 'beyond the Euphrates'. The significance of Pella will be discussed later.

The story then continues and says that Joseph(us) (of Arimathaea) was married and had a son. And this gives us another surprising detail that dovetails very nicely with the muddle we have already witnessed, between Saul-Josephus and Joseph(us) of Arimathaea. It is said of Joseph(us)'s son:

> Joseph of Arimathaea was in Jerusalem with his wife and a son named Josephus; not the one that scripture relies upon so often as a witness, but another one who was no less lettered. It was this Josephus who brought his father's lineage across the sea to Britain, which is now called England. (History 2:49)

One cannot help thinking of tangled webs being woven, and the resulting deceit that the clergy can no longer evade. So let us analyse this paragraph in further detail:

Firstly:
There is only one Josephus that 'scripture relies upon as a witness', and that is our favourite Judaean historian, (Saul) Josephus Flavius. It was claimed by the Church that Josephus had written the *Testimonium Flavianum*, the fraudulent description of the biblical King Jesus-Izas that was added to Josephus' *Antiquities of the Jews* at a later date. But this quote cannot be referring only to this fraudulent interpolation, because this quote says 'relied upon so often' as a witness. The *Testimonium Flavianum*, is only a couple of out-of-place paragraphs, not 'often'. So why was Josephus being described here as 'so often a witness to scripture'?

The answer, once more, is that Josephus Flavius writes copiously about Jesus of Gamala and King Izas. So Josephus Flavius is indeed a 'witness to scripture', as long as it is understood that Jesus-Izas of Gamala was actually one and the same as the biblical Jesus. In addition, Josephus Flavius also used the pseudonym 'Saul' (St Paul), which is why he is named as Saul-Josephus all the way through these books. But since Saul was the author of most of the Epistles (letters) and probably of Luke and Acts too, he was indeed a historian that 'scripture relied upon as a witness'. Once more, the evidence from *History* strongly indicates that Saul was Josephus Flavius.

Secondly:
The son of Josephus of Arimathaea was curiously called Josephus. Perhaps readers can already see why this was done. There is a huge 40-year chronological dislocation between the gospel story and historical

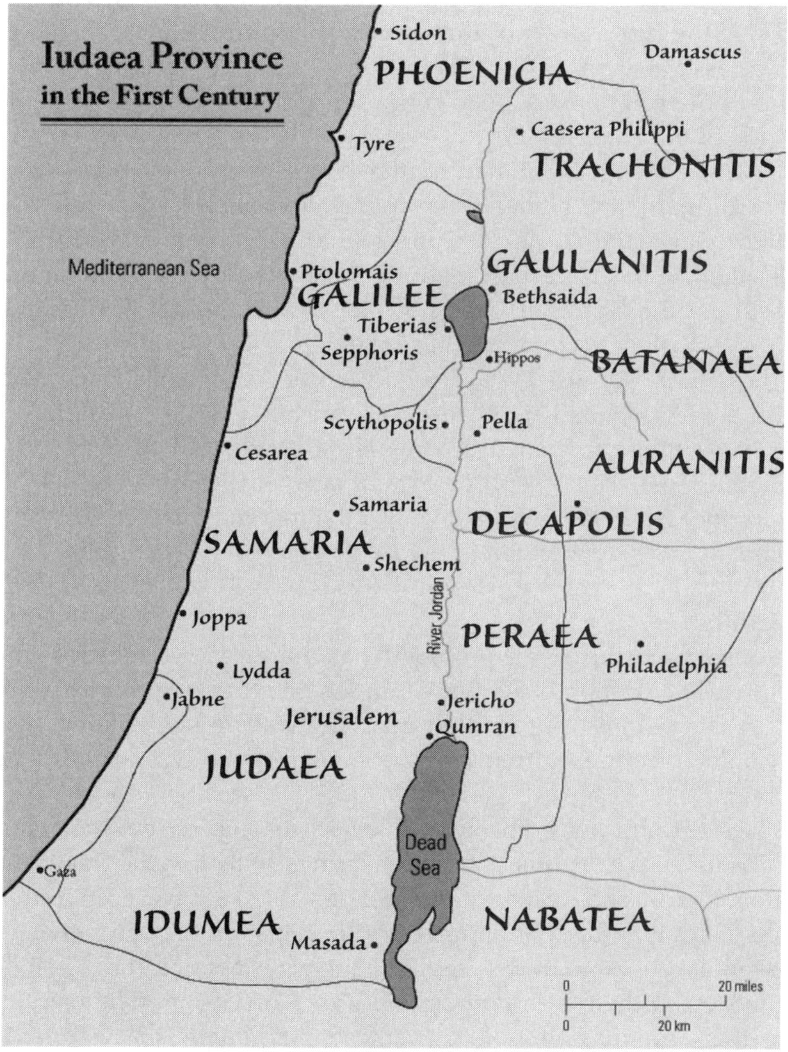

Fig 7.4
A 1st century map of Judaeo-Syria. The lands held by the Edessan royalty included Trachonitis, Gaulanitis, Batanaea, Auranitis. See also the map in fig 7.6.

reality (between the classical chronology and the revised chronology), and this great chasm has to be bridged somehow. By calling Joseph(us) of Arimathaea's son Josephus, the author of *History* has neatly achieved this, for we now have a Joseph(us) in the early 1st century and an equivalent Josephus from the same family in the late 1st century.

Thirdly:
The author of *History* is indicating that this young child called Josephus, the son of Joseph of Arimathaea, can be confused with Saul-Josephus Flavius the historian: 'not the one that scripture relies upon so often as a witness', as it says. But this Josephus-the-son was only a child in AD 70, so how can he have been confused with a 'scriptural witness' to the events of the gospels?

The answer again lies in the gospel's chronological dislocation. According to the biblical chronology, Joseph(us) of Arimathaea (the father) was active in AD 30s, and would have been very old by the AD 70s when he meets Vespasian. But it was probably well-known that Saul-Josephus (the historian) was not that old in the AD 70s when he met with Vespasian. So someone has invented a son (Josephus the son), who can easily be confused with Joseph(us) of Arimathaea (the father), and with Saul-Josephus (the historian). And readers may recall that exactly the same thing happened in *High History*, where there was a continual confusion between Joseph of Arimathaea and Josephus the Good Clerk (or scribe) who was said to have written that manuscript. And again that confusion was deliberate.

Fourthly:
We also have the small problem that the text says that Josephus (the son) was *not* Josephus Flavius - 'not the one that scripture relies upon so often as a witness, but another one who was no less lettered'. Does this invalidate the theory that Joseph of Arimathaea was actually Josephus Flavius?

Not at all. It was probably well-known that Josephus Flavius was Joseph of Arimathaea, but this association brings with it some insurmountable chronological and theological problems, as we have seen. And so the Holy Hermit author has slipped in a 'not this one ... but another', to keep Joseph(us) separate from Josephus. But why mention the possibility of a confusion, if there was no possibility of a confusion? The mere mention that this Josephus (the son) was not Josephus Flavius (the historian), means that this association *is* possible and that people ***might*** have mistaken them.

And finally:

There is the little curiosity of Epiphanius of Salamis, who says exactly the same thing about a 4th century Josephus. And so this confusion between a 1st century Josephus and a later Josephus predates the 12th century of the *Vulgate Cycle* by a long margin. In the 4th century Epiphanius wrote his *Panarion* or *Against Heresies,* in which he fulminates against the heresies of the many different sects in his and previous eras. One of these heretical sects is the Nazarene Ebionites, and he says of them that:

> They too accept the Gospel according to Matthew ... They call it, 'According to the Hebrews' and it is ... in the Jewish treasuries, I mean the treasuries at Tiberias, and is stored there secretly, as certain Jewish converts have described to me in detail ... One of them was Josephus, <u>not the ancient Josephus, the author and chronicler</u>, but Josephus of Tiberias, born during the old age of the Emperor Constantine of blessed memory.
>
> This Josephus was awarded the rank of count by the Emperor himself ... He also suffered a great deal from the Jews themselves before he came to the Emperor's notice. For this Josephus was counted as one of their men of rank ... called 'apostles.' They attend on the patriarch, and often stay with him day and night without intermission, to give him counsel and refer points of law to him. (Panarion Ebionites 3:7 - 4:2.)

And what a compendium of distortions that paragraph is! What Epiphanius is trying to say is that there was a Josephus from the 4th century who was almost exactly the same as the 1st century Josephus Flavius. So similar, in fact, that it was very easy to confuse the two, just as the opening paragraphs in *History* say about its Josephus. In comparison, these two Josephus' mentioned by Epiphanius are said to be:

1st C Josephus	**4th C Josephus**
Called Josephus Flavius	Called Josephus
From Tiberias	From Tiberias
A count or baron	A count or baron
Knighted by the emperor	Knighted by the emperor
Suffered persecution	Suffered persecution
A lawyer	A lawyer

The 1st century Josephus Flavius was the Judaean army general (or a knight) in command of Galilee in Tiberias and he suffered much persecution at the hands of the Nazarene Ebionites, who tried to end his career. (But he was persecuting the Nazarene Ebionites to an even greater degree.) Josephus was then elevated to an even higher position by Emperor Vespasian himself, which could be considered an Imperial knighthood.

The result of all this analysis is that *History* and *High History* are highly likely to be correct. Josephus the Good Clerk and Good Scribe, who wrote the original manuscript upon which most of Arthurian history was based, was actually Saul-Josephus Flavius: the manic theologian and devious historian who appears to have written, rewritten or edited so many of the texts that originated in 1st century Syrio-Judaea. And this tally now includes the secular history of Judaea, the religio-secular history of the Jews, most of the Gospels, much of the Talmud, and large sections of Arthurian history too.

So the rambling excuses in the *Vulgate Cycle,* about which Josephus is which, were probably not a 13th century Norman invention. The evidence from Epiphanius' similar confusion indicates that they go back to the very 4th century dawn of this saga, when Emperor Constantine the Great embarked upon the eradication of all these heresies, including the Arthurian heresy. It may well be that one of the Nazarene Ebionite gospels in the treasury at Tiberias, told the amazing tale of Jesus being a knight in shining armour, and this was a heresy that had to be quashed at all costs. And so just as the 1st century Queen Helena of Edessa was turned into the 4th century Queen Helena of Constantine, so the 1st century knightly King Jesus of the East was turned into a 6th century knightly King Arthur of the West.

Chronological chasms

History then goes on to relate the crucifixion story, which takes place during the rule of Pontius Pilate and high priest Caiaphas, which it would have to do in order to stay within the boundaries of the classical Christian chronology.

Joseph(us) of Arimathaea takes Jesus down from the cross, but it is not said by what authority Joseph(us) of Arimathaea was able to do this. Yet this simple act indicates that Joseph(us) was inordinately powerful. This prisoner had been sent to crucifixion by the Roman governor and the power of the mob, so who was Joseph(us) to just stroll in and overturn that judgment? (*Merlin Grail* says that Josephus of Arimathaea had been a knight employed by the Roman governor, and in the guise of Josephus Flavius that was true.) And while the gospels try to make out that Jesus was already dead by this time, the parallel story in Josephus' *Life* about King Izas-Manu being taken down from the cross, maintains that he was very much still alive (see *Life* 75).

Nevertheless, by mentioning Pontius Pilate and high priest Caiaphas, this account of the crucifixion manages to stay within the boundaries of the orthodox chronology, which insists that Jesus died in about AD 30. But this gives the author of *History* a big problem, for the rest of this story relates various meetings and discussions between Joseph(us) of Arimathaea and Vespasian or Titus in the AD 70s. Readers can perhaps see the many contortions that the earlier orthodox date for the crucifixion has created.

The author of *History* now has a real dilemma: how can Joseph(us) be an influential member of the Sanhedrin in the early AD 30s, who takes Jesus down from the cross at this time, and yet still be an influential character in the AD 70s some 40 years later? And in some of these accounts he was said to have gone on to have many adventures in Britain for a long time after that. So how is this possible? We have already seen one solution, where it was claimed that it was Joseph(us) of Arimathaea's son Josephus who went to Britain rather than Joseph(us) himself. But this still leaves us with the problem of Joseph(us) of Arimathaea being far too old when he meets with Vespasian and Titus, and so the innovative but absurd solution to this problem was to make the narrative jump 42 years in the space of one paragraph:

> Joseph(us) remained in prison, as you have heard, until 42 years had passed ... Following Nero came Titus and his son Vespasian, who was ill. In the third year of Titus' reign, Joseph(us) was freed from prison. (History 2:72) (author's brackets)

The first thing to note is that *History* has reversed the names for Titus and Vespasian. This 'error' was held up by various academics, including Professor Richard Carrier, as proof that the *Vulgate Cycle* should not be trusted as a historical source. Indeed, Richard Carrier rather turned these comments into a bitter personal attack by saying:

> Indeed, the Vulgate Cycle misidentifies Vespasian as the son of Titus, and a leper rather than the emperor. ... So you really have to get your facts straight ... Ralph Ellis is another crank. (Indeed, IMO, he is genuinely insane.) [2]

If this was not so sad, it would be funny. Here is a professor of history who does not know that the *Vulgate Cycle* uses an opposite naming convention for the Flavian emperors, to that used by modern scholarship. This is because Vespasian and Titus had exactly the same names - Titus Flavius Vespasianus - and so these names can be easily transposed. There is no historical tablet carved in stone to say that Titus Flavius Vespasianus the elder has to be called Vespasian, rather than Titus. And there is no historical tablet carved in stone to say that Titus Flavius Vespasianus the younger has to be called Titus, rather than Vespasian. These are just naming conventions to differentiate between two similar characters, and so *History of the Grail* is as correct as anyone else in the modern historical fraternity.

And the fact that *History* was simply using the opposite naming convention could not be made more plain in the quote from *History* above, which talks of Emperor Nero being followed by Titus (ie: Vespasian), who was followed by his son Vespasian (ie: Titus). This is a simple and fairly obvious transposition of names that any child of six could understand, but Professor Richard Carrier cannot. In which case the genuinely insane crank, who should really be forced to hand back his doctorate, considering the number of elementary errors he has made, is Professor Richard Carrier.

Another academic who failed to spot this nominative transposition is Professor Joanne Rittey, one of the translators of *History*. Rittey merely comments that the author of *History* was mistaken in thinking that Vespasian sacked Jerusalem. No, he was not mistaken at all, he is just calling Titus 'Vespasian' and Vespasian 'Titus', and so this Arthurian history is much more reliable than either Professor Rittey or Professor Carrier appear to assume. It is no wonder that a fresh set of eyes was required to finally see the hidden truth that lay behind Arthurian history, because modern academia is hopelessly ill-equipped to do so.

Another intriguing mystery is how Professor Rittey can devote a whole chapter on whether *History* was intended to be a romance or a historical work, and not a single paragraph on why Joseph(us) of Arimathaea was portrayed as being a contemporary of Emperor Vespasian. This represents a substantial 40-year jump in the biblical narrative, from the crucifixion to siege of Jerusalem, which must have been contrived for a reason. But why? Here we see a major chronological and political dislocation that appears to be widespread across many biblical-type texts, and yet Professor Rittey ignores it completely. Could she not see the implications of this revised chronological and political position for Joseph(us) of Arimathaea, with him becoming a 70s ally of the Romans instead of a 30s ally of Jesus? Or was she afraid of exposing it? [3]

Anyway, Joseph(us) of Arimathaea has been in prison for 42 years according to *History's* account, which would equate to a biblical crucifixion in AD 30 and a release from prison in AD 72. This would also equate well with the claim that Joseph(us) was released from prison in the 3rd year of Titus' (ie: Vespasian's) reign. But following his release Joseph(us) thinks that only three days have passed, and he has not aged at all. So the author of *History* has finally and duplicitously achieved his goal, for now Joseph(us) of Arimathaea can be middle aged in the AD 30s and also middle aged in the AD 70s. And again the only reason this entire charade has been necessary, is because of the deliberately distorted gospel chronology.

Mandylion

But we are jumping ahead here, for we have not reached the release of Joseph(us) from prison quite yet, and there are many more chronological distortions to explore before we get there.

Joseph(us) was only rediscovered, languishing in his jail, because Vespasian (ie: Titus) became ill with 'leprosy'. And do bear in mind that leprosy can refer to the scales of a fish, and so this 'infection' may have been more to do with the precessional Great Month of Pisces than a skin disease. The book *Cleopatra to Christ* has a section in Chapter VI that details the progression of these astrological Great Months, and how the leaders and monarchs of each era have sought to identify themselves with each sign of the zodiac as it passes. In the 1st century the skies above had entered the Great Month of Pisces, the fish, and so Vespasian (ie: Titus) was probably identifying himself as an initiate into these mysteries - just as Jesus did when he styled his followers as Fishers of Men.

Anyway, an old woman called Veronica came forward and said she had a cloth imprinted with the face of Jesus upon it, and this would be able to cure Vespasian (ie: Titus). This story is a retelling of the *Sudarium* or *Veil of Veronica*, which was a favorite Christian fable of the 12th century, which has spawned a myriad of relics bearing the supposed face of Jesus, none of which are remotely historic. In *History's* version of this story, the knight who is looking for this cloth arrives in Judaea during the rule of Felix. But this is a bit of a problem for orthodox Christianity, because Felix was the Roman governor of Judaea from AD 52 to 58.

> My Lord, said Vespasian (Titus) send this knight because he is from that land ... The knight went to Judaea and found a Roman by the name of Felix in charge of Judaea and Syria ... an old woman by the name of Veronica came, bringing a piece of cloth ... (she said) when I unfolded it I found Jesus' face upon it, as clear as if it has been painted on a wall ... the knight to the cloth to Vespasian (Titus) ... and as soon as Vespasian (Titus) saw the face he was more handsome and healthy than he had ever been before. (History 3:78 p20) (Author's brackets.)

In what way does this chronologically dislocated absurdity help with the release of Joseph(us) from prison in AD 72? The answer, which was not fully appreciated when these Arthurian texts were briefly analysed in *King Jesus*, is that this story has nothing to do with Vespasian or Titus at all. In fact, this is the same story narrated in both *Persian Wars* and *The Doctrine of Addai*, that was explored in the previous chapter in the section about Hippocrates. And all of these accounts are alternate renditions of the King Abgarus story, that was explored in great detail in *Jesus, King of Edessa*.

As that book explains, one of the many apocryphal Christian texts is called *The Doctrine of Addai,* and it recounts the many letters that were exchanged between Jesus in Jerusalem and King Abgarus in Edessa. And the various accounts of these letters being written contain the same old chronological problem that we have seen so many times before; because they say that these letters were being exchanged in the AD 50s, when Jesus was supposed to be quite firmly dead. The only difference is that the alternate versions of this story have changed the name of the recipient. In the Hippocrates story the news of a great healer called Jesus went to Emperor Augustus; in *Persian Wars* and *The Doctrine of Addai* the recipient of the letters and painting was King Abgarus of Edessa; while here at the beginning of *History* it is Emperor Vespasian (Titus) who receives the image of Jesus.

Anyway, on one of his many journeys to Jerusalem King Abgarus' ambassador, Hannan, drew a portrait of Jesus on a cloth and this became known in later history as the Mandylion (which may mean 'handkerchief'):

> (Jesus said to King Abgarus) I will send to you one of my disciples, who will cure the disease which you have, and restore you to health; and all who are with you he will convert to everlasting life ... Hannan ... by virtue of being the king's painter, he took and painted a likeness of Jesus with choice paints, and brought it with him to Abgar the king, his master. And when Abgar the king saw the likeness, he received it with great joy, and placed it with great honour in one of his palatial houses. (Doctrine of Addai)

Quite obviously, Veronica's cloth and the Mandylion of Edessa are the same artifact, and this explains why the *Veil of Veronica* only became famous in the 12th century, when novel Christian texts started to arrive in Europe from the Crusader East.

But the author of *History* must have spotted the many problems associated with naming King Abgarus of Edessa in his story, and so he has replaced the role of Abgarus with Vespasian (ie: Titus). Saul-Josephus Flavius did something very similar back in the 1st century, when he also expunged Edessa and its royal family from the historical record. And this has resulted in a conspiracy of silence down through the ages regarding the Edessan monarchy, which obviously included these Arthurian authors. In his many detailed works, Josephus Flavius managed to name nearly every monarch, prince, priest, pauper and pimp who ever lived in the 1st century, and yet he never mentions King Abgarus or Edessa once. Is that not strange? Actually, to clarify this assertion, he did indeed mention this royal family and royal city, but he calls them King Monobazus and Adiabene instead. But why the deceit?

What Saul-Josephus has cunningly and deliberately achieved here, is the complete and utter excision of the Edessan monarchy from history.

If readers look for Abgarus or Edessa in the works of Saul Josephus they will not find them. Conversely, if readers go and look for a real king called Monobazus in the archaeological record, they will also not find him. The only thing they will find, are some vague references within *Antiquities* and some Roman accounts to these otherwise unknown kings ruling a province called Adiabene somewhere in deepest Parthia. And to a Romo-Judaean historian like Saul-Josephus, locating the despised Edessan monarchy in deepest Parthia was as good a burying them on Mars. And because much of this monarchy's history has been relocated into deepest Parthia, readers will find precious little information about the city of Edessa either. Were it not for recent archaeology and the rediscovery of various Syriac chronicles, what would we know of the Kingdom of Edessa today?

The story of Jesus writing to King Abgarus had been a Syriac Christian tradition from the East, and Syriac Christianity had been hidden behind the divisions within Christianity that had been forged at the Council of Chalcedon in AD 451. This great schism within the Christian Church effectively separated the Roman Catholic Church and the Constantinople

Fig 7.5
(left) The Sudarium or Veil of Veronica. Hans Memling, 1470.
(right) A statue of St veronica and her veil, St Peter's.

Byzantine Church from all the Eastern Churches in Mesopotamia, and so the influence and edicts of Rome and Constantinople stopped well short of Edessa and the East. And these divisions were subsequently reinforced and made permanent by the Muslim invasion of Christian Mesopotamia in the 7th century.

The greatest opposition to the Edessan monarchy came from the Christian West, but Rome and Constantinople had no control over what the Armenio-Syriac scribes were writing out in the east of the Empire. And the Armenian chroniclers wanted to preserve some aspects of this story, because this was their history. Osrhoene-Edessa had been an eastern kingdom and King Abgarus was often regarded as being an Armenian monarch, and so some snippets of Edessan history were recorded in the East and were able to evade the censors in the West. And these apocryphal Mesopotamian texts, along with the source manuscripts for Arthurian history, only found their way back into Europe after Count Baldwin liberated Christian Edessa from Muslim occupation during the First Crusade.

Yet *History of the Grail* was still maintaining the same Catholic tradition of erasing the Kingdom of Edessa from history, even in the 13th century, by likewise deleting King Abgarus from the *Vulgate Cycle* and substituting his name with Vespasian (Titus). And this is despite the fact that the *Vulgate Cycle* is a decidedly heretical document in many other respects. One likely reason for the *Vulgate* not mentioning King Abgarus, is because the original author of the source document - Josephus the Good Clerk and son of Joseph(us) of Arimathaea - was actually Saul-Joseph(us) Flavius. So *History of the Grail* may have been following in the footsteps of Saul-Josephus by deleting King Abgarus from history, because the original author of the source document was Saul-Josephus himself.

Anyway, as soon as Vespasian (Titus) (ie: King Abgarus) had been cured of his illness, he set out for Judaea to discover everything he could about this magician and prophet called Jesus. In the real world, where it was actually King Abgarus who was being healed, it is unlikely that this could have happened. It would appear that the Romans did not trust King Abgarus and had banned him from travelling outside his small kingdom, so he could not foment an uprising. And if we equate this story to the gospel story, this is why Jesus' father disappears from the narrative so early on. In reality, many of the gospel events were happening in Judaea and Jordan, while King Abgarus was subject to strict Roman travel restrictions that prevented him travelling to Judaea. However, the Romans obviously did not ban his sons from travelling, and this is what eventually led to the Jewish Revolt.

Enquiries were made by Vespasian (Titus) and the location where Joseph(us) of Arimathaea had been imprisoned forty-two years previously was eventually discovered, and he was at last freed from prison. So the story has now arrived back in the AD 70s, and the tumultuous events of the Jewish Revolt. But when he is released from prison, Joseph(us) thinks only three days have passed and he does not look a day older. But to prove that he is Joseph(us) of Arimathaea he shows them the mark he has on his forehead. The book *Jesus, King of Edessa* explains in some detail the royal wart that was displayed on the forehead of many of these monarchs, before they emigrated to Edessa.

At last, the gospel's chronological deceit has finally been overcome. The gospel authors, under the watchful eye of Josephus Flavius himself, had wrenched the crucifixion story out of the AD 70s and placed it into the AD 30s, where it would safely distance the biblical Jesus-Izas from anything to do with the Jewish Revolt. This was done firstly, to separate Jesus from anything quite so militaristic as the Jewish Revolt; and secondly, to separate Jesus from all the characters involved in the Jewish Revolt. If the great unwashed realised that the biblical Jesus was called King Jesus Em-Manuel, while the leader of the Jewish Revolt was called King Izas Manu, they might start asking awkward questions. But with the crucifixion of Jesus safely tucked away in the AD 30s, nobody would ever know who he was.

But in order to get Joseph(us) of Arimathaea back from the AD 30s and into the AD 70s, where he really belonged, we have this crazy notion of him falling asleep for 42 years. Anyway, with the New Testament's chronological dislocation overcome, and Joseph(us) back in the AD 70s, he can now converse with Vespasian and Titus and the story can continue.

The siege

It was only after Joseph(us) of Arimathaea had been released from prison that Vespasian and Titus began the siege of Jerusalem. And in a similar fashion, Saul-Josephus had also been 'in jail' just prior to the siege of Jerusalem. And he too had been released from his jail by Vespasian. And so there is a complete agreement between *History* and *Jewish War* once more.

In *History*, three items are discussed in succession. There is a light and a voice that told Joseph(us) of Arimathaea not to be afraid, for Vespasian (Titus) would assist him; there is his rescue from a dungeon or prison after three days; and then the siege of Jerusalem begins shortly afterwards. *History* says of these three events:

> Vespasian (Titus) had himself lowered into the cell ... Once he reached the bottom he saw such a great light around him (greater than) 100 candles ... After a while he called for Joseph(us). And Joseph(us) replied: 'Good lord, who is calling me?' 'I am Vespasian (Titus)' he said 'the son of the emperor of Rome who has

> come to deliver you from prison.' (author's brackets)
>
> Meanwhile a voice came to Joseph(us) of Arimathaea saying, 'Fear not, but be confident, for earthly vengeance has come. This man Vespasian (Titus) (a Roman) will avenge you physically against your enemies. (author's brackets)
>
> Vespasian asked, 'Joseph, how long do you think you have been in prison?' Joseph(us) replied, 'My lord, I think I remained there from Friday until today, and I believe it is Sunday today.' (ie: three days)
>
> The story does not say any more except that Titus (Vespasian) and his son Vespasian (Titus) besieged Jerusalem during the year following Joseph's liberation from prison (History 3:113-114) (author's brackets)

In a suspiciously similar fashion, (Saul) Josephus Flavius says of his own experiences and imprisonment during the Jewish Revolt in Judaea during the late 60s AD:

> That night I beheld a marvellous vision ... I thought there stood by me a certain man who said, 'Cease from thy sorrows, let go all fear, for that which grieves you now will promote you to greatness. Remember that you must fight alongside the Romans'. (Josephus Life 42.)
>
> The Romans searched for Josephus ... (but) he had jumped into a deep cellar ... which could not be seen from above ground ... Thus Josephus concealed himself for two days, but on the <u>third day</u> ... he was discovered. Whereupon Vespasian sent immediately two messengers ... and ordered them to give Josephus safe conduct, and persuade him to come out. (Josephus War 3:8:1 or 3:340-344.)
>
> Now just as Vespasian returned to Caesarea, and was getting ready to march on Jerusalem. (Josephus War 4:9:2 or 4:491)

Here we have an exact equivalence between the accounts in *History* and the account of Saul-Josephus' exploits during the Jewish Revolt. Both of these characters had a vision that involved fighting alongside the Romans, both were in a dungeon for three days, both were saved by Vespasian (or Titus), and both of these events occurred just before the siege of Jerusalem. And the release of Saul-Josephus from prison is also narrated by the Roman historian Suetonius in his *Lives of the Caesars*:

> When he (Vespasian) consulted the oracle of the god of Carmel in Judaea, the lots were highly encouraging ... and one of his high-born prisoners, Josephus by name, as he was being put in chains, declared most confidently that he would

> soon be released by the same man, who would then, however, be emperor. (Lives Vespasian 5:6) (Author's brackets.)

But is Suetonius talking about Saul-Josephus, or Joseph(us) of Arimathaea? The potential for a confusion, deliberate or otherwise, is easy to see. And in narrating this very similar story about Joseph(us) being in jail for 'three days' (or 42 years), *History* obviously knows that Joseph(us) of Arimathaea and Saul-Josephus were both Judaean aristocrats from the late AD 60s who ended up working for Emperor Vespasian. And yet this assertion is interesting, for the Romans were the enemy of Jesus. So why would Joseph(us) of Arimathaea, who is supposed to be the great hero of Christianity, end up working for the enemies of Jesus? The answer once more, is that the saintly Joseph(us) of Arimathaea was actually the traitorous Saul-Josephus; and so the earlier quote from *Merlin Grail* was correct when it claimed that Joseph(us) of Arimathaea was the traitor, rather than Judas Iscariot. It would appear that Judas has been framed.

And while *History* has valiantly tried to avoid and overcome the obvious chronological chasm in these accounts, in *Merlin Grail* Robert de Boron passes straight over it as if it did not exist. Because *Merlin Grail* is a short summary of the complete *Vulgate*, Boron tells almost the same story about Vespasian (Titus) having leprosy as does *History*, but he goes on to say:

> Vespasian and Titus prepared for their journey to the land of Judaea. After their crossing they ordered Pilate to come to them ... 'I have come to avenge the death of Jesus,' Vespasian replied, 'the prophet who healed me.' Hearing this Pilate was terrified, imagining Vespasian had been told that he was responsible.' (Merlin Grail p29)

Boron then goes on to again narrate the story of Joseph being discovered in his dungeon by Vespasian (Titus). Given the historical detail that Boron has included in this condensed story, and in the rest of the *Vulgate*, it is hard to imagine that he did not know that Pontius Pilate had died in AD 37, long before Vespasian and his legions arrived in Judaea. But if Boron knew that this meeting between Pilate and Vespasian (Titus) would have been completely impossible, then why did he include it?

What Boron has probably done here, is the complete reverse of his parallel account in *History*. Faced with this chronological chasm, all of these authors had two choices: either try to explain the 40-year gap in the story, or just ignore it. In *History*, which is a much longer and more detailed account, Boron has chosen a convoluted explanation that simply serves to focus our attention on this anomaly. While in his shorter summary of these events, Boron has merely glossed right over it. But who in the 13th century, bar a few clerical scholars, would ever spot the inconsistency anyway? In many respects, the second option is much more elegant, because it does not draw attention to the problem and manages to retain some of the famous biblical characters that everyone would have been familiar with.

Evangelism

And just to finish this series of similarities between Joseph(us) of Arimathaea and Saul-Josephus Flavius, in *History* Joseph(us) is sent towards the northeast, towards the Euphrates:

> (Jesus said) When you leave Jerusalem, you will go along the road that goes to the Euphrates. And I will teach you at that time what you should do and how you should preach in the world and proclaim my name. (History 3:121)

History does not fully explain why Joseph(us) was sent towards the Euphrates, instead of taking the more conventional journey within Arthurian history that led westwards towards Britain. However, in an outburst of interconnected synchronicity Saul-Josephus does exactly the same, and is sent eastwards towards the Euphrates by Emperor Vespasian. But this time the equivalent quote in *Jewish War* tells us exactly why this happened. Saul-Josephus says of himself:

> I have proposed ... to translate those books into Greek, which I had formerly composed in the language of our country (Aramaic), and sent to the Upper Barbarians.
>
> I thought it an absurd thing to see the truth falsified in affairs of such great consequence ... while the Parthians, and the Babylonians, and the remotest Arabians, and those of our nation beyond Euphrates with the Adiabene, by my means, knew accurately both whence the war begun, what miseries it brought upon us, and after what manner it ended. (Jewish War, Preface 1&2)

In the second sentence, Saul-Josephus is telling us that the people beyond the Euphrates already knew about the Jewish Revolt. This was because Saul-Josephus had been commissioned by Emperor Vespasian to write *Jewish War* - Saul-Josephus' epic historical account of the Jewish Revolt - and send it to the rebellious Nazarene Jews beyond the Euphrates, as a warning that further revolts against Rome would not be tolerated. And so the first copies of *Jewish War* had been written in Aramaic and sent to the Parthians and the Babylonians and to 'those of our nation beyond Euphrates with the Adiabene'.

This is a phrase that did not make much sense for a long time, until the book *Jesus, King of Edessa* was finally finished, and then it became clear.

As was comprehensively proven in that book, the Adiabene were <u>not</u> a people from Arbela over in Iraq, they were the people from the Kingdom of Edessa in northern Syria. And the Edessans were proselyte Nazarene Jews, just as the Talmud explains. So yes, there were indeed 'people of our nation' (Nazarene Jews), who lived 'beyond the Euphrates' (in Edessa). And Edessa did indeed reside beyond the Euphrates, to anyone living in Judaea or Rome. And these were the first people to receive copies of Saul-Josephus' *Jewish War,* because these were the very people who had started the Jewish Revolt in the first place, as Josephus makes clear in his description of the Revolt.

And the chronology of this journey to the northeast works rather well too. According to *Quest for the Holy Grail,* which will be explored later, this expedition was mounted 42 years after the crucifixion of Jesus (the same length of time that Joseph of Arimathaea was in prison). (Quest 41:134) If the author of *Quest* understood that the crucifixion took place in AD 30, then this journey was being made in AD 72. Back in the true chronology of this era, AD 72 would have been just two years after the siege of Jerusalem had ended, and this would give Saul-Josephus (Flavius) two years to assemble and write *Jewish War* - his personal account of the events of the Jewish Revolt - and be ready to take this vast manuscript to 'those of our nation beyond the Euphrates' in the Kingdom of Edessa. This seems like an entirely reasonable and likely chronology. The Romans wanted to pacify the Edessans 'beyond the Euphrates', and so the sooner this book was sent to them, the better.

So only now - after many years of diligent study and inspired insight, that has demonstrated these are two different accounts of the same event - do we now know why *History* says that Joseph(us) of Arimathaea was sent north-eastwards towards the Euphrates and beyond. In reality, he was not being sent there by a resurrected incarnation of Jesus, as *History* maintains, but by Emperor Vespasian. And the 'preaching' that Joseph(us) was about to undertake in that region, involved taking an Aramaic copy of *Jewish War* to the people of Palmyra and Edessa, and advising them of how the Romans had just wiped Jerusalem off the face of the Earth. So this mission was not simply one of Saul-Joseph(us) (of Arimathaea) preaching the virtues of Simple Judaism to the people of Palmyra and Edessa, although he did that too as we shall see. Rather, this was more about Saul-Josephus (of Arimathaea) giving these people a dire warning delivered direct from the emperor - 'mess with Rome, and your city and your people will be destroyed.'

And if we look at the previous quotes again, we can see that it was only after Joseph(us) had returned from the Euphrates region, perhaps even a year or so later, did he then propose to translate his books into Greek. Saul-Josephus returned to Judaea to find that 'falsehoods' about the Jewish Revolt were spreading in the west of the Empire, and by falsehoods he means any account that differed from his own. And so he embarked on the onerous task of translating *Jewish War* into Greek, but since Saul-Josephus did not speak Greek very well he had to learn the language before he could undertake this great task.*

Identity

The many close connections between Joseph(us) of Arimathaea and Saul-Josephus, that we have already explored in some detail, cannot have been the result of mere plagiarism. We have already seen the following similarities:

- Joseph(us) taking King Jesus down from the cross, just as Saul-Josephus took King Izas-Jesus from the cross.
- Joseph(us) having a son called Josephus, the same name as Saul-Josephus.
- The confusion with Josephus, the son of Joseph(us), being called a 'witness to scripture', just as Saul-Josephus was a witness to scripture.
- The textural links to King Abgarus of Edessa.
- The unexplained relocation of the story in *History* and *High History* into the AD 70s, the era of Saul-Josephus Flavius.

* Various so-called 'academics' keep writing to me to say that Josephus could speak Greek perfectly well, because all his books were written in Greek. But they forget that these were originally Aramaic texts, that were translated into Greek at a later date. Josephus himself said of his translating *Antiquities*, from Aramaic to Greek:

> I grew weary and went on slowly, it being a large subject, and a difficult thing to translate our history into a foreign, and to us unaccustomed language. (Ant Preface 2)
>
> I have also taken a great deal of pains to obtain the learning of the Greeks, and understand elements of the Greek language. Although I have so long accustomed myself to speak our own tongue that I cannot pronounce Greek with sufficient exactness, for our nation does not encourage those that learn the languages of many nations. (Ant 20:11:2)

It is clear that Josephus found using Greek tedious at best, because he had not been taught it in his youth, and so he was having to learn and improve his Greek at the same time as translating his books. Josephus appears to have relied a lot on his colleague and 'publisher', Epaphroditus, to help with these translations. And do remember that *Jewish War* was written before *Antiquities*, from which the quotes above come, and so he must have really been struggling when translating *Jewish War* into Greek. So why these so-called academics think they know Josephus better than he knew himself, is beyond comprehension.

- Joseph(us) taking on the role of a nouveau-Jesus, just as Saul-Josephus craved to be the new Jesus.
- Joseph(us) being called a traitor who wanted to get Jesus arrested, just as Saul-Josephus had fought Jesus (of Gamala) and tried to arrest the disciples of Jesus.
- Joseph(us) spending just 'three days' in a prison (or 42 years) before being rescued by Vespasian, just as Saul-Josephus spent three days imprisoned before being rescued by Vespasian.
- Joseph(us)' close familiarity with Vespasian and Titus, which makes absolutely no sense in classical biblical terms, but dovetails nicely with the life of Saul-Josephus Flavius.
- Joseph(us) travelling to the Euphrates after the Jewish Revolt, just as Saul-Josephus travelled to the Euphrates after the Jewish Revolt.

So after all this evidence and all these similarities, can we now dare admit the unpalatable truth - that Joseph(us) of Arimathaea was one and the same as Saul-Josephus? Why else do we get that absurd 40-year jump in the chronology, from the 30s to the 70s? Why was there an urgent requirement to place the biblical Joseph(us) of Arimathaea into the 70s, where he could meet with Vespasian and Titus? If the crucifixion story really did take place in the 30s, then why not write about Joseph(us) setting off for Rome in the mid-30s and then to Britain in the early 50s? Surely that would have been closer to the truth, if the crucifixion really did happen in the 30s. But no, instead the authors of *History* and *Merlin Grail* desperately contort the entire story to get Joseph(us) of Arimathaea into a position where he can meet with Vespasian in AD 72 and travel to the Euphrates instead. Why?

The answer is that as Saul-Josephus, Joseph(us) (of Arimathaea) did indeed meet Vespasian. In fact, he was the Roman commander's spy, lackey and propaganda minister for three years. Saul-Josephus surrendered to Vespasian in AD 67, after the siege of Jotapata, and became the chief Jewish traitor and Roman propagandist, who was trying to get the Jews in Jerusalem to surrender. And the reason that the original Holy Hermit author of *History* felt compelled to tell us about Joseph(us)' close association with Vespasian, and contort his story to achieve this association, is because this author was Saul-Josephus himself. And Saul-Josephus was an inveterate egotist, narcissist and self-publicist, who was never going to leave himself out of the story.

Saul-Josephus was obviously very proud of his status within Roman society and his being on first-name terms with the emperor himself, and felt compelled to tell everyone about it. Having his character in this story (ie: Joseph(us) of Arimathaea) slink off to Rome in the 30s and never meet with an emperor was simply not possible. And placing the crucifixion date in the 70s was not possible either, even if it was true, because Imperial Rome had demanded an AD 30s date, to remove any traces of the Jewish Revolt from the gospels. And what Rome asked for, Rome got. And the later pope-emperors of Catholic Rome insisted on the very same amendments to the chronology, because they did not want their pauper prince of peace caught up in the Jewish Revolt either. And so the only option left open to both Saul-Josephus and to the later 13th century authors of Arthurian history, was to make Joseph(us) go to sleep for forty years.

So yes, it would appear that the otherwise unnamed Holy Hermit author of *History of the Grail* was actually Saul-Joseph(us) (of Arimathaea), just as he was in *High History*. And while it may seem hasty and perhaps lazy to ascribe yet another personality to Saul-Josephus, do remember that Josephus was the last Jew left standing after the fall of Jerusalem. It was Saul-Josephus who determined which texts survived; it was Saul-Josephus who controlled the texts that were being written; and therefore it was Saul-Josephus who controlled the historical and religions narrative. If the Knights Templar had discovered any ancient manuscripts within Christian Edessa, after its liberation from Muslim control during the First Crusade, they were likely to have been censored, influenced, penned and edited by Saul-Josephus Flavius (of Arimathaea).

Ambush Wood

So Saul-Joseph(us) of Arimathaea, his son Josephus and a large party of 75 other 'evangelists' set off towards the Euphrates, and the first city they came to was Bethany. Now while the gospels try to indicate that Bethany resided close to Jerusalem, it was proven in the previous works that it actually lay to the east of the river Jordan. So the travelogue appears to be correct so far; these evangelists are heading north-eastwards and passing the Jordan on their way to the Euphrates. One of the first places they stop for the night, is called the Wood of the Ambush, near Bethany to the east of the Jordan. But this is interesting.

We have already seen how the majority of names within these texts were derived from Hebrew-Aramaic. And if we follow this line of reasoning here, we can see that Ambush Wood results in Ets Arab עץ ארב. Now while this does mean Ambush Wood, it can also be expanded slightly to derive Erts Arabah ערץ ארבה which means 'Land of Locusts'. However, readers may recall from the *King Jesus Trilogy* that the Edessan monarchy were regularly called both 'Arabs' and 'locusts', by both Saul-Josephus and the talmudic rabbis. This derogatory title was given to them because one of the plagues of Egypt was a swarm of locusts, that came out of the east and destroyed everything in sight. And as far as Saul-Josephus and the talmudic rabbis were concerned, the Edessan monarchy had done exactly the same thing

- they had come to Judaea from the east, and their aggressive politics and elitist religion had resulted in the complete destruction of Jerusalem and its fine Temple. To the establishment, the Edessan royalty were no better than marauding locusts, and so they were mocked in this fashion in the Talmud, gospels and the works of Saul-Josephus.

Thus the Greek name that Saul-Josephus used in his *Jewish War* to describe these much-hated Edessan locusts, was Arabun Αραβων. And so the Roman historians, and the modern academics who followed in their footsteps, have all erroneously assumed that this meant that the Edessans were Arabs (Nabateans). But the Edessan royalty were not Nabatean Arabs at all, they were locusts from the east - they were an Egypto-Parthian royal family who had been exiled from Babylon to Edessa in northern Syria. But their arrival in this region eventually resulted in the destruction of Judaea.

However, in great contrast to the Romans, the author of *History* was not relying on the Greek version of *Jewish War*. Saul-Josephus' native language was Aramaic, not Greek, and the books he sent to Edessa and the East were in Aramaic. And so if the manuscripts that arrived in Normandy were from Edessa, they would have been in Aramaic.

And in Aramaic the most obvious translations for Arabah ארבה are either 'Ambush' or 'Locust'. And so the Aramaic Erts Arabah can be translated as either Ambush Wood or Land of the Locusts. What is the likelihood of this remarkable correspondence happening by chance? The book *Jesus, King of Edessa* identified the Edessans as living beyond the Euphrates, in a location mockingly known by Saul-Josephus as the Land of the Locusts. And the first place that Joseph(us) of Arimathaea and his son Josephus stop at during their journey towards the Euphrates, is the Land of the Locusts.

Woodland battle

So where, exactly, was this Ambush Wood or Land of the Locusts? *History* goes on to say that this 'wood' was also the site of the battle between King Aretas of Nabatea and Herod Antipas - the battle that was fought over the beheading of John the Baptist (or rather over Herod's divorce of the daughter of Aretas). Unfortunately we do not know where this battle took place, but we do have some information about it.

Firstly, we are told that Aretas had already had a land-dispute with Antipas over the control of Gamalitis. And although we are not exactly sure what location Saul-Josephus means by Gamala, it more often than not refers to a location to the east of Galilee and perhaps to the east of Damascus. The second clue is that Saul-Josephus says that King Aretas won this battle through:

> The treachery of some fugitives, who, though they were of the tetrarchy of Philip, joined with Aretas's army. (Antiquities 18:5:1)

In *Jesus, King of Edessa* these conveniently unnamed 'fugitives' were positively identified as being the army of King Abgarus of Edessa, because that is what the Armenian historians say. And so Saul-Josephus has deliberately deleted some key information that he did not want us to know. It is obvious that Saul-Josephus knew who these unnamed 'fugitives' were because he normally knows everything, and yet his phraseology at this point becomes deliberately vague. Certainly the Armenian historians knew who the northern contingent

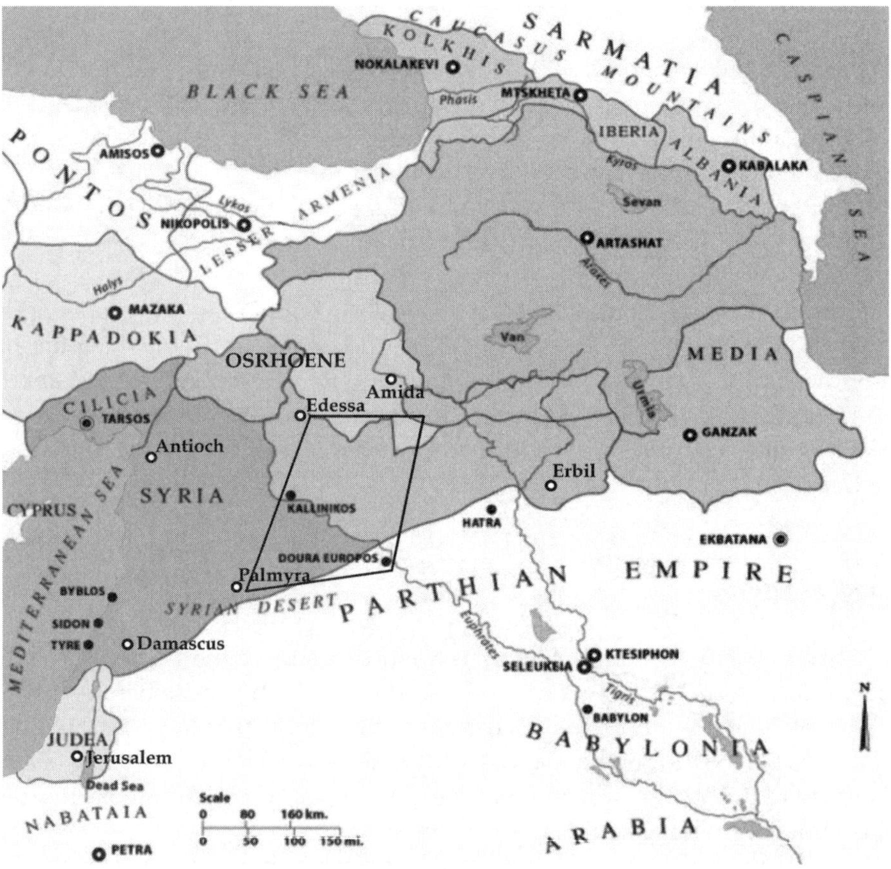

Fig 7.6
A map of the Near East showing the extent of the Osrhoene, the Kingdom of Edessa. While this may look like a very small kingdom, it is about the same size as England. And it would have been even larger if we can stretch the kingdom up to Amida and as far south as Pella, as some other reference indicate was the case. Image courtesy of Wiki.

in this battle were, so why did Saul-Josephus omit this vital information? The answer, once more, is that Saul-Josephus has deliberately deleted the Edessan kingdom and royalty from history, because his Roman patrons - the Flavian emperors - wanted to eradicate revolutionary Judaism not just from the face of the Earth, but from the pages of history too. It was the Edessan monarchy who had started the Jewish Revolt and Rome wanted to quell all further thoughts of revolt, and so Edessa became non-kingdom and their monarchs became non-people.

So here we have two good pointers towards the location of this battle. The Land of Locusts obviously refers to the Kingdom of Edessa, which ran south from Edessa to Palmyra, and may have extended even further down towards the great Decapolis cities of Philadelphia (modern Amman) and Pella. This is the eastern border region that was specifically granted to these Babylonian exiles by Herod (probably Herod Archelaus), who wanted these well-armed exiles to protect his eastern borders from incursions from Parthia. The Kingdom of Edessa had been deliberately established by Herod and Emperor Augustus as a buffer state, not simply between Judaea and Parthia, but also between Rome and Parthia. Saul-Josephus Flavius says of the resettlement of these Babylonian (Parthian) exiles:

> Herod (Archelaus), being desirous of securing himself on the side of the Trachonites (east of Damascus), resolved to build a village as large as a city for the Jews, in the middle of that country, which might make his own country difficult to be assaulted (by the Parthians). Accordingly, when he understood that there was a man that was a Jew come out of Babylon, with five hundred horsemen, all of whom could shoot their arrows as they rode on horse-back, and, with a hundred of his relations, had passed over Euphrates ... he promised to give him land in the toparchy called Batanaea ... tax-free.
>
> The Babylonian (Jew) agreed to these offers, so he took possession of the land, and built in it fortresses and a village, and named it Bathyra. Whereby this man became a safeguard to the inhabitants against the Trachonites, and preserved those Jews who came out of Babylon, to offer their sacrifices at Jerusalem, from being hurt by the Trachonite robbers. So that a great number came to him from all those parts where the ancient Jewish laws were observed, and the country became full of people, by reason of their universal freedom from taxes. (Antiquities, 7:2:1-2) (Author's brackets)

The Babylonian Jews mentioned here, are a reference to the family, courtiers and army of Queen Thea Muse Ourania, who was exiled from Parthia in AD 4 and travelled to Syria. As was related at length in *Cleopatra to Christ,* Queen Thea Muse Ourania was a direct descendent of Queen Cleopatra and Julius

Caesar, who had been married off by Emperor Augustus to King Phraates IV of Parthia. But in 2 BC Queen Ourania is said to have poisoned her husband and taken the throne of Parthia for herself and her son, Phraataces. But because of the murder of Phraates IV, Queen Ourania and her son were thrown out of Parthia in AD 4, and ended up establishing a new principality in eastern Syria. This is the event that Saul-Josephus is referring to in these paragraphs. But where in Syria did these Parthian exiles go to?

Surprisingly, from this sparse information we can satisfactorily deduce where the city mentioned here was. The first thing we are told is that this location had been a mere village and it was situated exactly between Syria and Parthia, in the lands of Batanaea and Trachonitis. Furthermore, we are also told that this was on a trade-route from Babylon to Jerusalem, a stopping place where many Babylonian Jews refreshed themselves while on pilgrimage to Jerusalem. So where was this 'village that became a city' located? At Palmyra, of course.

Palmyra was a desert village situated precisely between Damascus and the Euphrates, on one of the few trade routes that went across the Syrian desert. If a Jew wanted to travel from Babylon, where much of the Jewish population resided in this era, to Jerusalem for the Passover festival, it is more than likely that they would have travelled up the Euphrates to Doura Europos, and then across the Syrian desert to Palmyra. And the city that these Babylonian Jews built was called Bath Yra בת עירא meaning 'City of the Watchers'. Josephus may have intended to mean that this city watched over the pilgrims, as they traversed the inhospitable Syrian desert, but it is much more likely that this name referred to the Sabeans, the astronomer-priests of Syria. But the Jews of Babylon did not just traverse through Palmyra to go to Jerusalem, they also emigrated there. The previous quote says:

> So that a great number came to him from all those parts where the ancient Jewish laws were observed, and the country became full of people, by reason of their universal freedom from taxes.

It would appear that Edessa and Palmyra had become the 1st century equivalents of modern Israel, with Jews from across the region flocking to these cities because they were governed by a (Nazarene) Jewish king under Jewish (Mosaic) Law, and it was tax free: 'Never mind the barren location, look at the tax concessions.' And so Palmyra rapidly expanded to become one of the richest cities in the entire Roman Empire.

And when we come back to Joseph(us) of Arimathaea's travelogue in *History of the Grail*, if these pilgrims had just entered the Land of the Locusts (Ambush Wood), then they had just entered the Kingdom of Edessa. And they would have done so as soon as they travelled anywhere to the east

Fig 7.7
A tower-tomb of the Elabel family at Palmyra, in the eastern Syrian desert. The tomb is thought to be from the 1st century AD, and holds up to 350 burials. The platforms at the top of these towers could easily have doubled as astronomical observation points. This magnificent and irreplaceable tower was blown up by Muslim barbarians in August 2015.

It is very tragic and extremely alarming that barbarians can destroy a magnificent ancient tomb in the supposedly enlightened 21st century, in the name of their cerebrally challenged god. The current era bears all the hallmarks of the decline and fall of the Western Roman Empire in the late 5th century, when a seemingly indestructible world civilisation descended to factional barbarity within a few short decades.

of a line between Damascus and Philadelphia (Amman). And so the battle between Herod Antipas and King Aretas of Petra (and his Edessan 'fugitive' allies), must have been fought in this region - to the east of Galilee and perhaps even to the east of Damascus.

So Joseph(us) is likely to have been approaching Palmyra with his intrepid band of 75 'evangelists', but he was not doing so of his own volition but rather because Emperor Vespasian had demanded that he go there. Yet the negotiations that were about to take place in Palmyra were going to have far reaching effects upon European culture and society, because it was here in Palmyra in AD 72 that Christianity as we know it was about to be born.

VIII

City of Sarras

History of the Holy Grail - Water Kayo

While they were staying at Ambush Wood (the Land of Locusts), Joseph(us) had his people make an Ark: a wooden box to carry the Grail chalice, that had been used to collect a few drops of Jesus' blood. In effect, this was a copy of the Ark of the Covenant, because the tablets of stone in the Ark of the Covenant were directly comparable with the Holy Grail, as we shall see later. This is why the Grail Guardian was known as the Peter-Kephas, the Rock or Stone. Having constructed their new Ark, the party set off for the city of Sarras, which is said to lie between Salamander and Babylon. One presumes that Salamander is a reference to Jeru-Salem, the city that they had just come from.

The modern translator of *History* and several other academics indicate that Babylon was an ancient name for Cairo, thus placing Sarras near Egypt. However, while Babylon may have once been an alternate name for Cairo, these travellers were heading towards the Euphrates, not the Nile. Modern historians seem to have an obsession with Sarras being near Egypt, for some reason, but a location close to the Euphrates makes much more sense because the more famous city of Babylon lies in Parthia. And this is where the Babylonian Jews mentioned in *Antiquities* came from - they did not arrive in Syrio-Judaea from Egypt, they came from Babylon in modern Iraq (even though they may have been of Egyptian heritage). In addition, this is where Saul-Josephus Flavius went, while clutching his Aramaic copies of *Jewish War* - he was heading towards a location 'beyond the Euphrates', not 'beyond the Nile'.

It is possible that these references to Egypt, that modern historians have picked up upon and erroneously used, were derived from the names and heritage of the Edessan monarchy. King Abgarus V was surnamed Au Kama, meaning 'Of Egypt'. While 'King Izas-Jesus Manu was probably named after Manu, the title of the great founder-king of all nations - King Manu. As we saw in a previous work, the first king of many nations was called: Manu, Mani, Minos, and Menes, or something similar. Thus King Izas Manu VI and King Abgar bar Manu VI were probably adopting this title to allude to their Egyptian heritage. All of the Egyptian dynasties were descended from Pharaoh Mani, the first Egyptian king of Egypt. And if King Izas Manu (the Strong Manu or Great Manu) of Edessa was a direct descended of Pharaoh Mani, he would have been the foremost monarch in the entire world. As claims of royal primacy go, this one must transcend them all.

The destination for Joseph(us) and his (reluctant) 'evangelists' was Sarras, but the precise location of this city is unknown. It obviously lay near the Euphrates, on the road to Babylon, but where exactly? The 13th century author of *History* says that this name was <u>not</u> derived from Sarah, the sister-wife of Abraham. However, he goes on to say that the name for the Saracen Muslims was derived from this city, which means that these terms should have the same etymology.

The name for the Saracens is said to have been derived from *sarakenos* σαρακηνος meaning 'east' - the people from the east. But if most of the names in *History* were derived from Aramaic, then perhaps we should

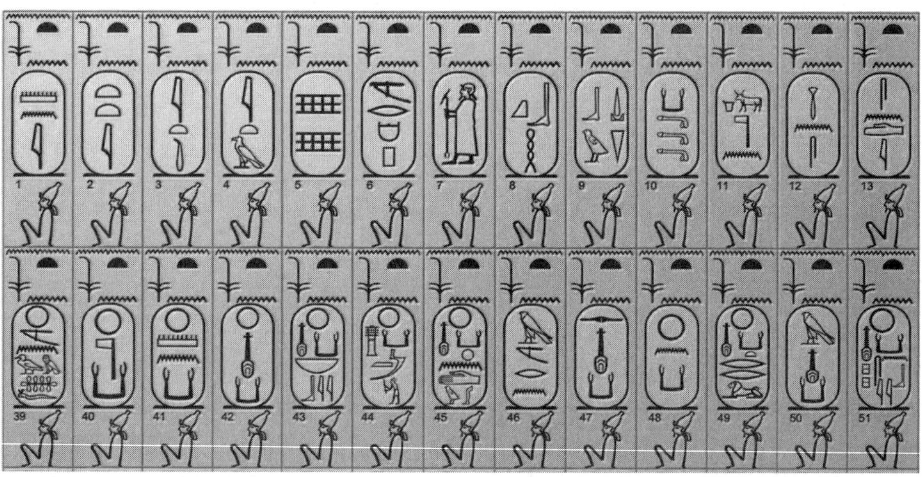

Fig 8.1
A copy of a small section of the ancient Egyptian king-list from Abydos. At the top left of this king-list is the cartouche of Pharaoh Meni, the first king of Egypt. It is entirely possible that King Izas Manu of Edessa, who was of Egyptian extract, was named after Pharaoh Mani.

be looking for a meaning for Sarras in the Aramaic. And the most obvious candidate would be *saras* סרים which means 'eunuch', and so Sarras was known, perhaps mockingly, as the City of Eunuchs. The reason for this city being closely identified with a cult of castration will become clear in later chapters. And this may also be why Saracens were similarly mocked as being eunuchs. This was not simply because the Saracens employed court eunuchs, which they certainly did, but because there was an obvious and convenient linguistic similarity between 'Saracen' and a *sarras* eunuch.

Joseph(us) then gives us another a big clue to the location of Sarras, because he says that it lay eleven days travel from Jerusalem. So how far would a band of travellers go in one day, in the 1st century AD? Luckily the answer to this is given to us by Madam Egeria, the intrepid 4th century tourist who was mentioned extensively in *Jesus, King of Edessa*. Madam Egeria said that there were 25 staging-posts between Jerusalem and Edessa. And since each staging-post was a hostelry that terminated each day's travel, we therefore know that it took 25 days to reach Edessa. And if Joseph(us) and his party had travelled for 11 days out of Jerusalem, then they would have gone about half as far. And the half-way point between Jerusalem and Edessa, while heading out towards the Euphrates, was Palmyra. This is interesting, for we have just seen evidence that the Edessan monarchy (the Babylonian Jews) founded Palmyra in the early 1st century, and now we see evidence that Joseph(us) and his party of 75 evangelists travelled to this same city to deliver his new creed of Simple Judaism, in AD 72 just after the siege of Jerusalem.

The first thing that Joseph(us) did on entering the city of Sarras, was to go to the Temple of the Sun, and if this was indeed Palmyra then the temple they went to was the magnificent Temple of Bel, which means 'Temple of the Lord'. Since this temple is adorned with many cosmological and astrological motifs it is obviously a Temple of the Cosmos, and it is hardly stretching the description to nominate this grand edifice as being the Temple of the Sun. In Palmyran theology the Sun-god was called Malakbel, meaning 'king lord' or perhaps more descriptively the 'king of the gods'. And so this temple was indeed the Temple of Malakbel, the Temple of the Lord of the Sun. Joseph(us) says of this magnificent temple:

> At the entrance to this temple there was a very high, beautiful chamber that had been built and established for the peers of the city to hold their courts of justice and business assemblies. This room was called the Seat of Judgement. (History 4:130)

This Seat of Judgement might refer to the chamber inside the temple itself, which is a large and imposing hall. One of the interesting things about the

Temple of Bel at Palmyra, is that it was surrounded by a vast colonnaded courtyard, and on each of the columns was the statue of a city official and a plaque detailing his good deeds. Not a statue of a god, as we might expect, but a statue of an aristocrat or a city official. So yes, this was not simply a temple of the priesthood, paid for by a religious poll-tax on the people, this was a temple that had been established and paid for by 'the peers of the city', just as this quote from *History* suggests. Perhaps this is why the peers of the city were able to commandeer the temple for secular purposes, because it was not just the priest's temple, it was very much a temple of the people.

The descriptions in *History* appear to be dovetailing with reality very nicely, and so this account may well be a record of a real journey to a real city - Palmyra. It would be highly unlikely that anyone could have made all of this up while sitting in a dimly-lit scriptorium in Normandy, and so this

Fig 8.2 The Temple of Bel at Palmyra, which was probably the most expensive temple in the Roman Empire. Not the largest, but the most expensive. Note that the capitals at the top of these columns are not finished. This is because the original capitals had been cast from bronze, making these columns extravagantly ornate and stupendously expensive. However, the valuable bronze capitals and soffits have long since been pillaged. The little holes all over the walls are from the pillaging of lead clamps, with most of this damage being caused during the Muslim era. The same can be seen all across the eastern and southern Mediterranean. This temple was completely destroyed in August 2015 by modern Muslim Neanderthals. There are no words to describe such barbarity, except to observe that these amoebas are a stain on humanity.

is either an account of a real journey made by a Crusader-Templar knight, or perhaps it is based upon the original journey to the 'Upper Barbarians' on the Euphrates that we know Saul-Josephus made in the early AD 70s. According to *History* Saul-Josephus was ordered to go on this journey by god, and the only minor amendment we need to make to this assertion, is that the 'god' in question was actually Emperor Vespasian. It was Vespasian who wanted a peace treaty with the Edessan monarchy (or perhaps their complete surrender), and it was Saul-Josephus who had been ordered to go and get it.

Evalach

In the great hall of the Temple of the Sun (the Temple of Bel), Joseph(us) finds a king, whose name was Evalach. Evalach is thought to be a completely mythical king of unknown provenance: a mythical king in a mythical city, which is why the *Vulgate Cycle* is regarded as a complete fantasy. However, if

Fig 8.3
The interior of the Temple of Bel, showing the large chamber which led to a smaller anti-chamber at each end. The roof of each anti-chamber is a single ornately carved megalith, and one of them displays the seven planets and twelve signs of the zodiac.

the original source for *History* was indeed an ancient text from Judaeo-Syria, then perhaps we should again search within the Aramaic for the name of this unknown king. And the result of this exploration is simply brilliant - a name and connection that makes complete sense of everything that has been explained thus far.

The surprising answer to this puzzle is that it is highly likely that 'Evalach' is an Aramaic name from the Torah. It was derived from King Amel Marduk, the son of King Nebuchadnessar of Babylon, who was called King Evilmerodach אוילמרדך in the Aramaic (in 2Ki 25:27). One cannot help thinking that the Aramaic scribes have deliberately turned the Sumerian Amel אמיל into the Aramaic Eval אויל, because this alternative spelling means 'foolish' or 'one who despises wisdom'. One of the primary goals of the Torah and Talmud was to utilise the full spectrum of inventive wordplay to praise Judaic heroes and denigrate any Judaic enemies, and here the scribes appear to have done just that. The Babylonians were the bitter enemies of the Israelites, and now their king is called Eval אויל meaning 'foolish'.

But it was not only the Torah scribes who were playing with puns and double-entendres, the Arthurian authors were quite adept at this literary technique too. And what the stupendously erudite and devious author of *History* has done here, is to leave out the 'merod' syllable and thus reduce King Eval-merod-ach down to King Evalach. To have used the name Evalmerodach would have been far too obvious and given the game away, but the shortened hypocorism has withstood the test of time and remained undecyphered for centuries.

Evalmerodach אוילמרדך
Eval-merod-ach אויל-מרד-ך

Eval-ach אויל-ך
Eval-ach אויל-ך

This naming of contemporary individuals after characters in the Torah is a standard Talmudic *pesher* technique, which serves several purposes. The primary rationale is to divine the future. If a contemporary individual has the same character or performs the same actions as a famous person in the past, the subsequent actions of that historic figure can be used to divine what the contemporary individual might do in the future. Thus the future was being divined by historical precedent, presumably on the basis that history always repeats itself. But this technique also gives the added bonus that the name of the contemporary individual is conveniently covered up, which may also be useful in certain circumstances. So the Talmud can and will say terrible things about Balaam (a character in the Book of Numbers), and nobody need know that the Talmud is actually cursing the biblical Jesus. The previous books in this series have shown many examples of this acerbic talmudic wordplay.

And so the reason for choosing the name Eval-merod-ach for this Arthurian character is twofold. Firstly it points eastwards, towards Babylon, the 'original' homelands of the Edessan monarchy. Secondly, and more importantly, there is the fact that Nebuchadnessar captured and destroyed Jerusalem in about 600 BC, and so King Evalmerodach (King Evalach) was the son of a king who had destroyed Jerusalem and its Temple. But this gives us all the requirements for a classic talmudic-style *pesher* comparison, because Jerusalem was destroyed in 597 BC and also in AD 70, just before Joseph(us) went to Sarras (Palmyra).

And having completed the exhaustive *King Jesus Trilogy,* we now know exactly who destroyed Jerusalem in AD 70: it was King Izas-Jesus Manu of Edessa - the biblical King Jesus. It was King Izas-Jesus Manu's Jewish Revolt that had attracted the Romans to Judaea, and it was King Izas-Jesus' last stand in Jerusalem that had resulted in the destruction of this city. And so it was Nebuchadnessar who destroyed the First Temple of Jerusalem, while it was King Izas-Jesus Manu who had destroyed the Second Temple. Thus we have a perfect *pesher* comparison, because King Izas-Jesus Manu, the exiled Babylonian Jew, was obviously the second-coming of King Nebuchadnessar of Babylon.

And according to the talmudic *pesher* technique, if King Izas-Jesus Manu is a 1st century counterpart of King Nebuchadnessar, then their sons should likewise be counterparts. So the son of King Izas-Jesus Manu should have been mockingly called King Evalmerodach, and he was, he was called King Eval-ach of Sarras-Palmyra. In which case, King Evalach must have been the son of King Izas-Jesus, the biblical King Jesus. So we have just discovered the son of the biblical King Jesus Izas in the Arthurian record - he was King Evalach of Sarras-Palmyra.

In addition, this acerbic wordplay follows exactly the same format, intent and purpose as the 'locust' nickname. The Edessans were called 'locusts' because the locusts of the Israelite Plagues came out of the east (from Babylon) and destroyed Egypt. And the Edessan Babylonian Jews likewise came from the East and destroyed Judaea, and so they were no better than the locusts of the Plagues. And now, in exactly the same fashion, King Evalach is being named after King Evalmerodach, the son of Nebuchadnessar, the kings who came out of Babylon in the east and destroyed Jerusalem.

Father	Known for	Son
Nebuchadnessar	Destroying Temple	King Evalmerodach
King Izas-Jesus Manu	Destroying Temple	King Eval--------ach

This is QED time once again. Quod Erat Demonstrandum: what needs to be demonstrated has indeed been demonstrated. And conclusively demonstrated and proven too - King Evalach of Sarras must have been the son of the biblical King Jesus-Izas. This nominative equivalence also demonstrates an irrefutable link between the city of Sarras (Palmyra) and the Jewish Revolt that led to the destruction of Jerusalem. And so it clearly demonstrates why Joseph(us) of Arimathaea was making this journey to Sarras (Palmyra).

Joseph(us) was Saul-Josephus, as has been demonstrated on many occasions. And Saul-Joseph(us) himself says that he went to the Euphrates to placate and subdue the Babylonian Jews of the East, to prevent any further uprisings against Rome. But the cryptic and sardonic nickname that has been given to the king of Sarras - Evalach - demonstrates that this trip was not simply being made to see the Babylonian Jews in general, but to see the son of King Izas-Jesus in particular. Which is all very interesting and informative, for we have just stumbled across direct evidence that Jesus did indeed have a son, who was the new king of Sarras-Palmyra.

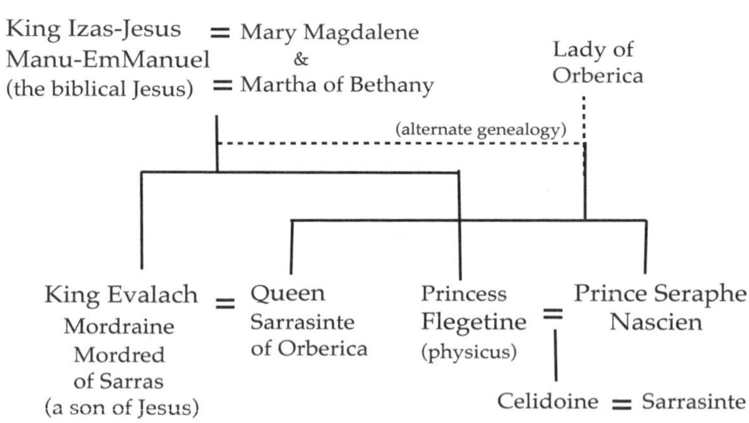

Fig 8.4
A genealogy of the royal family of Sarras, combining the biblical and Arthurian genealogy. Jesus is shown here as the father of King Evalach. The identity of Lady Orberica is unknown but she may be Martha of Bethany, Jesus' second wife. This alternate genealogy is shown in dotted lines.

King Izas-Jesus Manu of Edessa had been crucified after the siege of Jerusalem (and then reprieved by Josephus and Titus). But it was clear to the aristocracy of the Kingdom of Edessa-Osrhoene that their king was never coming back to them, for he was in prison in Rome at that time and awaiting exile to Britain. So the people of Edessa and Palmyra had been forced to crown a new king who was called King Abgar bar Manu VI of Edessa. So the Edessan succession was as follows:

King Abgarus au Kama V		AD 04 - 50
King Izas Manu bar Abgar V	(James)	AD 50 - 57
King Izas Manu bar Abgar VI	(Izas-Jesus)	AD 57 - 70
King Abgarus bar Manu VI	(Evalach)	AD 71 - 91

Arthurian history calls the new King Abgarus (VI), King Evalach, and so we now know that he was the son of the biblical King Jesus-Izas-Manu VI. And rather conveniently for this emerging theory, King Abgarus VI was crowned in AD 71, just after the Jewish Revolt had ended and just before Saul-Joseph(us) arrived in Sarras (Palmyra) in AD 72. And so we can now revise the previous table given a few paragraphs back, by including the real historical names for these monarchs.

Father	**Known for**	**Son**
Nebuchadnessar	Destroying Temple	King Evalmerodach
King Izas Manu VI	Destroying Temple	King Abgarus Manu VI

Sarras

In summary of the events thus far, we know that the era for this journey to Sarras is the early AD 70s, just after the Jewish Revolt. We also know that the Jewish Revolt had been fomented and prosecuted by King Izas-Manu VI of Edessa (the biblical King Jesus Emmanuel), because Saul-Josephus tells us so in *Jewish War*. But King Izas-Jesus lost that war with Rome, while Saul-Josephus Flavius had been the chief propaganda minister for Emperor Vespasian and therefore one of the victors. However, according to both *History* and *Jewish War*, Saul-Joseph(us) (of Arimathaea) has now been sent by Emperor Vespasian on a mission to quell further unrest in the eastern provinces, and the first city he comes to is Palmyra, because Palmyra is the closest Edessan city to Jerusalem and probably the most wealthy and influential city in the entire Kingdom of Edessa.

On entering Palmyra, Saul-Joseph(us) (of Arimathaea) meets a king called Evalach, who we now know was King Abgar Manu VI, the son of King

Izas-Jesus Manu VI. But if this is the case, then of course Emperor Vespasian would have been very concerned about the intentions of this new king. Was he a chip off the old block, and poised to launch a new assault on the formidable Roman army? Or would he admit defeat, and submit to the terms of surrender imposed by Rome?

And this scenario also gives us a very good reason why the life of King Izas-Jesus was spared, and why he was taken into exile so far from Judaea. Many readers of *King Jesus* have written to say: 'why did Vespasian not simply kill King Izas-Jesus-Manu, after the Jewish Revolt?' The answer is now obvious, for he was a valuable hostage. Saul-Josephus knew this very well, and was probably aghast to see that a Roman commander had summarily crucified King Izas-Jesus after the siege of Jerusalem. How could anyone be so politically naive and stupid? Yes, King Izas-Jesus might have been the sworn enemy of Rome, but he was also the only thing preventing another war in Syria and Judaea. So the politically astute Saul-Joseph(us) (of Arimathaea) had him immediately taken down from the cross, and luckily he survived, just as Saul-Josephus narrates in his *Life*.

No doubt the first thing that Saul-Joseph(us) (of Arimathaea) would have said to King Evalach of Sarras, the son of King Izas-Jesus, was that his father was alive and well - a few holes here and there, and a bit of a limp and a dislocated shoulder, but nevertheless alive and well. But if King Evalach dared make any military manoeuvres, his father would be crucified for a second time. It was bad enough to imagine your father being crucified once, let alone twice.

And so this was the primary reason for *History's* and *Jewish War's* account of these evangelists travelling to the city of Sarras-Pamyra, for this was less of an evangelical mission and more of a negotiated surrender and armistice. This was the equivalent of the Armistice of Compiègne, when Marshal Ferdinand Foch took the formal surrender of Germany after the First World War. But instead of the negotiations being held in a railway carriage, they were being held in the Temple of Bel in Sarras-Palmyra. Thus Saul-Joseph(us) of Arimathaea was on quite a dangerous mission into enemy territory.

The people of the Osrhoene, the Kingdom of Edessa, were the very people who had started the Jewish Revolt and this Revolt had only just ended two years previously. And while Edessa had comprehensively lost this war, there were no doubt some bellicose agitators still at large in the provinces, goading the people on to further resistance against Rome. There may have been seventy five (heavily armed) 'evangelists' in Saul-Joseph(us)'s party, but there was still a distinct possibility that the natives may turn ugly and attack them. This was not an easy diplomatic mission, by any means. In his summary of these turbulent times and the causes of the Jewish Revolt, Saul-

Josephus says this:

> At the time when this great concussion of affairs happened ... all was in disorder (in Rome) after the death of Nero ... and the opportunity this offered induced many to aim at the royal power; and the soldiery affected change, out of the hopes of getting money ...
>
> Those Jews also who were for innovations, then rose up when the times were disturbed. They were in a flourishing condition for strength and riches, because the affairs of the East were then exceeding tumultuous. Some hoped for gain, while others were afraid of loss in such troubles; for the Jews hoped that all of their nation which were beyond Euphrates would have raised an insurrection together with them. (Jewish War, Preface 2)

This is a fair summary of what actually happened. Emperor Nero had died in AD 68, and there was a great battle for the throne of Rome, with three emperors - Galba, Otho and Vitellius - coming and going within one year. Yes, Rome was in great turmoil. But the vital piece of information that all historians up until now have missed, is that the (Nazarene) Jews were involved in this very same battle for the Throne of Rome. The Jewish Revolt was not fomented to usurp the Throne of Judaea, but to commandeer the Imperial Throne of Rome. The Jews who were involved in this uprising were those 'who were for innovations', and these are explained elsewhere in Saul-Josephus' works as being the Nazarene Fourth Sect Galileans, the sect that Saul-Josephus blamed for the destruction of Jerusalem.

But note here that these Fourth Sect Nazarene Galileans were expecting help from the Nazarene Jews who lived 'beyond the Euphrates'. In classical history this is explained as being the people from Adiabene, from Arbela near Mosul in Iraq. But there is absolutely no archaeological evidence for a location or people called the Adiabene in that region, and there has been no rational explanation as to why the people of that region should have been known as Nazarene Jews. This long-standing historical conundrum, which has never before been satisfactorily explained, was solved in *Jesus, King of Edessa,* when it was explained at length that Adiabene was actually Edessa, which also lies 'beyond the Euphrates'. And yes, these people would have been considered Jews because: Queen Helena of Edessa converted to Nazarene Judaism; King Abgarus of Edessa sent famine relief to Judaea (Acts 11:28); while King Izas Manu VI was the biblical King Jesus EmManuel, who was a Nazarene.

This is why the Nazarene Jews in Judaea, who had fomented the Jewish Revolt, hoped that the Jews 'beyond the Euphrates' in Edessa (and Palmyra) would come to their aid. The Edessan king was in Judaea and had fomented a revolt, and he was hoping that the rest of his aristocracy and people would join him in this great enterprise, so he could secure all of Syrio-Judaea and then march upon Rome - just as King Arthur was said to have marched upon Rome. And perhaps some of them did join in, but obviously not enough to alter the outcome of the Jewish Revolt. Vespasian had arrived in Judaea with three legions, and these were joined by the Syrian legion and a host of auxiliaries. With these professional forces on the ground the result of the Revolt was hardly in doubt, but it was much too late for these Nazarene rebels from Edessa to back down now, as too much Roman blood had already been spilled.

And the important thing about this potted summary of the causes of the Jewish Revolt, is that the enemies of Rome were the Nazarene Fourth Sect Jews in Judaea, many of whom had been captured or killed during the siege of Jerusalem. Yet most of their ethnic and religious brethren and compatriots who lived 'beyond the Euphrates' had not entered the war, and their future intentions were in doubt. Would they stay peaceful? Would they disarm? Or would they start another Revolt against Rome? So if Saul-Joseph(us) of Arimathaea was in Palmyra (Sarras) at this time, which seems highly likely, then he was most definitely in 'enemy territory' and had every right to be concerned about this dangerous mission. Which is why he had not wanted to go in the first place:

> The lord said to (Joseph(us)): 'Fear not about this, for you only have to open your mouth and I will put into it a great abundance of words ... And I will make you my apostle ... Now go and think about doing my work, so that you may be paid as a loyal servant. And whatever menaces you receive, be not afraid, for I will watch over you and defend you. (History 4:129,130)

'God' had to ordered Joseph(us) to go to Sarras and be his ambassador, and who was Joseph(us) to refuse this divine command? Joseph(us) then complained to 'god' that he did not know what to say to these people, but 'god' said that he would tell Joseph(us) exactly what to say to them. Joseph(us) also moaned that he was afraid, but 'god' said he should not complain as he was merely a servant and was being well paid to do this dangerous work. All of which makes this 'god' sound very temporal and secular. And so if we delete 'god' from this paragraph and replace it with 'Emperor Vespasian', readers will have a very good idea of the true intent and meaning of this discussion:

> Emperor Vespasian said to Joseph(us): 'Don't worry about this mission, for I will make you my personal ambassador and tell you exactly what to say ... Now go and think about doing my work, because I am paying you handsomely to be my loyal servant and not to question my judgement and commands. And don't be

> afraid if they threaten you for I will position two legions in Damascus, not far away. (History 4:129,130.) (Reinterpreted and paraphrased.)

The meaning of this revised quote is very clear. Vespasian had saved Saul-Joseph(us) from his enemies and treated him very well, considering he was merely a Nazarene Jewish traitor. But now it was pay-back time. The quisling servant had been treated royally and paid handsomely, and now it was time for some real loyalty. Vespasian had not bought a quisling dog so that he could bark himself, and so it was time for Saul-Joseph(us) to place his neck on the block for his new master, and negotiate a surrender and peace treaty with Sarras-Palmyra.

We shall see more about Joseph(us)' fears and trepidations shortly, but the account in *History* goes on to give us some more details about King Evalach of Sarras. It is said:

> The king himself was called Evalach the Unknown. He was called the Unknown because no man knew in which country he was born, nor where he came from, nor had there been any news from anyone who had seen or heard of him in the land. (History 4:131)

This is merely a continuation of what has been said previously, about the complete excision of the Edessan royalty from the historical record. And so the reason for King Evalach being unknown, is that both Josephus and the Roman historians had deleted the Edessan monarchy from the historical record. But this was only the start of this persecution, because in the 4th century the new Catholic Church had completely changed the persona of King Evalach's father, and then disowned his son. King Evalach was the son of Jesus-Izas, as we have just seen, but according to the Catholic Church Jesus was a celibate who would not even hold hands with Mary Magdalene, let alone have carnal relations. So how could anyone claim to be a son of Jesus, when such a thing was physically impossible? Likewise, the Kingdom of Edessa never existed, so how could a son who did not exist, become the king of kingdom that did not exist? And disagreeing with this new truth was a heresy worthy of the Inquisition warming its pokers in a fire, so who was going to challenge this new truth?

And so King Evalach became a phantom monarch who ruled a phantom kingdom. He did not exist, because he could not exist, and so he became Evalach the Unknown. It was said of King Evalach that: 'no man knew in which country he was born, nor where he came from, nor had there been any news from anyone who had seen or heard of him in the land.' But Walter Kayo and Robert de Boron, the 13th century authors and translators of *History*, knew all about this heresy. Kayo could not have recorded all of this, without realising the identity of this king and the dangers associated with mentioning him. And the fact that Kayo did know the truth is given away later in the story, when Josephus the son of Joseph(us) of Arimathaea says to King Evalach:

> You believe that no-one knows who you are, or of what lineage. But I know it well, by the grace and power of the lord, from whom no secrets can be kept. (History 8:209)

The name 'Evalach', the ingenious pseudonym for the son of King Izas-Jesus, was probably coined by the quicksilver-quilled Saul-Joseph(us). But it is difficult to see Saul-Joseph(us) being the author of this sentence. Of course Saul-Joseph(us) knew who King Evalach was, because he was in Sarras-Palmyra at this time, negotiating the king's surrender, so why write something like this? This is much more likely to have been a later comment by Walter Kayo or Robert de Boron, and so it is likely that the true lineage of King Evalach was still known in the 13th century. Yes, some of the Templars who returned to Normandy in the Middle Ages knew that Jesus had a son, who had become the king of Sarras (Palmyra) in the early AD 70s. The Catholic Church accused the Knights Templar of harbouring heretical secrets, and so now we know what one of those secrets was.

Roman operations

The Jewish Revolt had officially ended in the autumn of AD 70, when Jerusalem had surrendered and its great temple been destroyed; but there were one or two ongoing Roman operations to mop up the last of the Nazarene Ebionite resistance. One of those operations was at the south end of the Dead Sea, where a band of a thousand or so rebels were holed up in the impregnable fortress of Masada, which is perched on the top of a precipitous mesa or hill. This is the same Masada that has already been tentatively identified as being Munsalvasche-Corbenic, the castle of the Holy Grail.

But were there other Roman military operations going on at this time, which have been deleted from classical history? Surprisingly, there may well have been an entire theater of operation, after the Jewish Revolt had ended, which modern history is completely unaware of. And the evidence for this again comes from *History*, where Joseph(us) says of King Evalach of Sarras (Palmyra):

> But he had been so valiant through his feats of chivalry that he had conquered all the lands up to the borders of Egypt. But he was so old he could not endure

> the effort of bearing arms. Thus he was no longer feared or dreaded, as he had been in his youth. Rather the Egyptians were warring against him and had already won a good part of the land that bordered on his. Just three days earlier, the Egyptians had defeated him in battle, and routed him from the battlefield ...
>
> Because of this (Evalach) had asked for all the wise men of his domain, for he wanted to ask their advice about how he might avenge the shame the Egyptians had done to him. (History 4:131) (Author's brackets.)

The text is confusing two kings here, the father and the son. The old king who had conquered all the lands up to the 'borders of Egypt' was Evalach's father - the biblical King Jesus-Izas Manu. But the 'Egyptians' had fought valiantly against his father, and had pushed these Nazarene Galileans all the way back to Pella to the east of the Jordan and to Sarras-Palmyra in the Syrian desert. Then we have a change in the generations, denoted by the artificial break in this paragraph. King Evalach himself had only just come to the throne of Palmyra and Edessa in AD 71, and it was now King Evalach who was asking the wise men of Sarras (Palmyra) what he should do.

But the city of Sarras has already been identified with Palmyra, and King Evalach was a Palmyro-Edessan monarch. So why was King Jesus-Izas and the army of Palmyra and Edessa, in a dispute with the Egyptians at this time? This is the late 1st century AD, and in this era Egypt was a passive Roman province that was not in a position to attack anyone. Egypt exported grain, not armies, so why does *History* mention Egypt, and why do modern historians believe this claim? It is time for another reality-check.

History of the Grail is not a mythology, it is an occult (concealed) history of the bitter aftermath of the Jewish Revolt in AD 70. However, the authors - both Saul-Joseph(us) of Arimathaea and the later Walter Kayo - have a bit of a problem here, because much of the information had either been banned by the Flavian emperors of Rome for being subversive, or was equally heretical to Catholic Christianity. Thus the text needed 'amending' every now and then to conform with the political and religious edicts of those eras.

Interestingly, these two authors, writing more than a millennium apart, were fearful of two completely different manifestations of Rome. Saul-Joseph(us) of Arimathaea was looking over his shoulder at the Flavian Emperors of Imperial Rome, who did not want King Izas-Manu VI or his sons to be mentioned in conjunction with Edessa or the Jewish Revolt. Imperial Rome wanted to quell the revolutionaries in the East, not stir things up again. Conversely, Walter Kayo was looking over his shoulder at the papal emperors of Catholic Rome, who also did not want King Izas-Jesus-Manu to be mentioned in conjunction with the Jewish Revolt. And they wanted no mention of his sons either, because Jesus was not allowed to have sons.

The new Catholic manifestation of Imperial Rome had adopted the Flavian version of Jesus and had cast it in Roman concrete, and anything that contradicted this 'approved history' was a heresy worthy of the Inquisition's barbecue being lit. The many authors and translators of *History* were treading a very narrow and precipitous path, and were desperately trying not to fall off. (Sir Lancelot had to cross a bridge as narrow as a sword, which may have been a cryptic allusion to the many problems that these author's faced.)

So the explanation for this particular quote from *History,* is that there has been a simple amendment to the text to turn 'Rome' into 'Egypt'. The Edesso-Palmyran Nazarenes had just been locked in a bitter conflict with Rome, not Egypt. Similarly, Saul-Joseph(us) had no connections whatsoever with Egypt and could not have been their ambassador. However, as the chief Judaic propaganda minister and ambassador for Emperor Vespasian, Saul-Joseph(us) was perfectly placed to negotiate with the new king of Sarras-Palmyra on the behalf of Rome. Although Rome had conclusively won the war against the Edessans, they were hardly likely to have left them alone if they thought they were intending to regroup and launch another offensive. And so Saul-Joseph(us) was in Sarras-Palmyra as the ambassador of Rome, not Egypt.

So yes, although we have no alternate information about this post-Revolt confrontation between Rome and Palmyra, because Saul-Josephus has deleted it from his history of the Jewish Revolt, it is highly likely that commander Titus sent a couple of legions to Damascus to view the situation regarding the rebels in Sarras-Palmyra. And had Titus pushed a couple of legions up through Perea (Jordan) and onto to Damascus, as *History* is indicating, it is highly likely that his troops had already experienced a few minor clashes with the Edessan army as they retreated back to Palmyra.

So why, in this case, did Rome not simply crush Sarras-Palmyra? Why was Saul-Joseph(us) of Arimathaea sent into Sarras-Palmyra as an ambassador, with just 75 'evangelists' to assist him? Surely this was a very dangerous place to be? Yes, indeed, which is why Saul-Joseph(us) did not want to go there in the first place, and why his every move in Sarras-Palmyra was made with uncharacteristic caution. But Vespasian had forced Saul-Joseph(us) to be the Roman ambassador: firstly because he spoke Aramaic and understood Nazarene-Jewish culture; secondly because Vespasian did not really care if he was lynched or not; and thirdly he was probably the only person in the Empire who could pull off such a difficult and perhaps hopeless mission. Besides, while Joseph(us)' diplomatic mission was to discuss the terms of surrender, if it failed there was always the military option.

Unfortunately for Rome, the fall of Jerusalem had not resulted in an unconditional surrender by the Edessan monarchy by any means. The Nazarene Jews were still holed up in Masada, to on the western shores of the Dead Sea, and refusing to surrender. Likewise, both Sarras-Palmyra and Edessa still harboured a large army and had also refused to surrender. And laying siege to Palmyra was problematic, to say the least. Palmyra was an oasis city that controlled the only water source for 100 km in all directions, so how were the Romans going to maintain an army in the desert without water? The Romans down at Masada had the small springs that had been previously used to supply the cisterns inside the Masada fortress, plus they had a daily donkey-train bringing water from Ein Gedi, some 20 km to the north. But at Palmyra there is absolutely nothing.

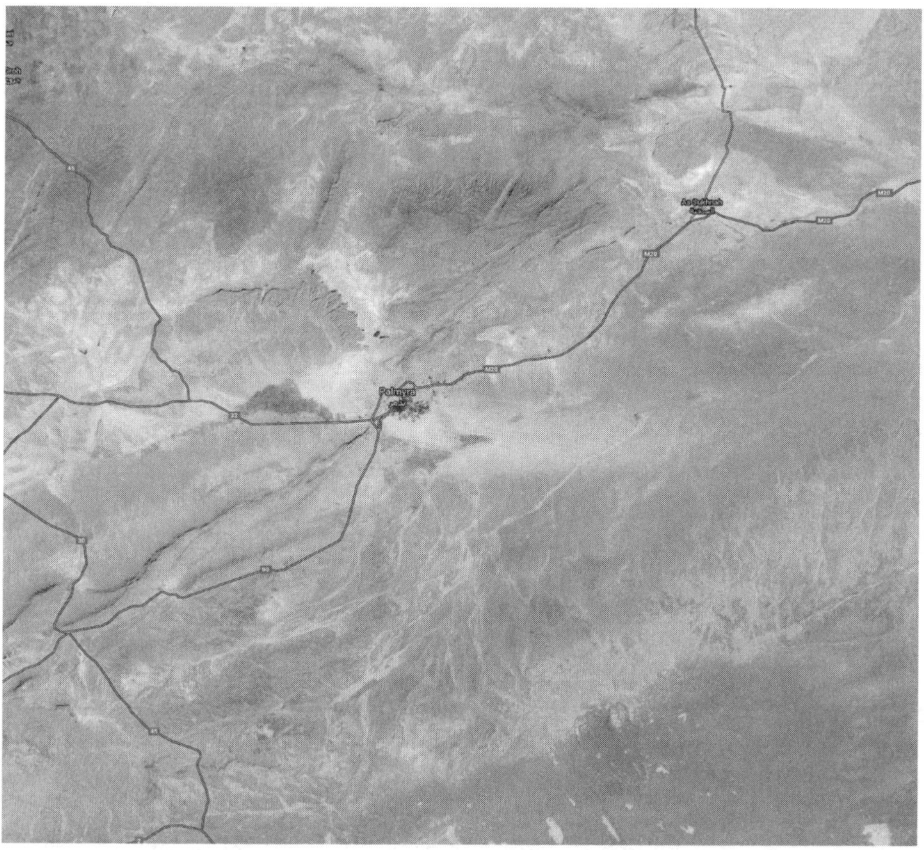

Fig 8.5
The city of Sarras-Palmyra in the center of the Syrian desert. The city was originally built without a protective wall, because the desert made the city as impregnable as island-based Knossos was during the 16th century BC. This image is 170 km across. Image courtesy of Google Maps.

Rome was not in a strong position here, but they were not about to let Edessa and Palmyra maintain an army if they suspected it would be used to cause yet more trouble on the eastern borders of the Empire. The original agreement with the Edessan monarchy was that they could keep a standing army if they protected Rome from Parthian incursions - not so that they could use that army to attack Rome itself. So this was a delicate and dangerous mission into the Palmyran lion's den, that required the ultimate in dissembling diplomats, which is exactly the role that Saul-Josephus was best suited for. But if readers still think that Saul-Joseph(us) of Arimathaea was a tranquil hermit on a peaceful evangelical mission from god, rather than on a difficult diplomatic political mission from Emperor Vespasian and Titus, just wait and hear what he had to say to the people of Sarras-Palmyra.

Anyway, being an ambassador of Rome who had been sent by Vespasian and Titus, Joseph(us) arrives in Sarras-Palmyra at a very opportune moment, for King Evalach (King Abgarus Manu VI of Edessa) is discussing their recent defeat at the hands of the 'Egyptians'. (In other words, he was discussing the recent Roman victory in the Jewish Revolt.) The king is afraid that the Egyptian (ie: Roman) army is far more numerous that his own forces, and he is afraid that 'another misfortune may befall them'. And he was correct, because half the Roman army was in Damascus at that very moment, and the emperor's envoys and ambassadors had just arrived to discuss the terms of peace.

The king's advisors all cautioned the king against continuing the war, and advised that he should seek peace. So Joseph(us) intervenes in this council of the elders, and promises the king peace and joy, and to have a victory over his enemies at the same time. But what Joseph(us) is duplicitously promising is not a military victory over the Romans, but a spiritual victory over death. Joseph(us) said:

> King, this will be advice that will bring honour to the body, and profit to the soul, for you will be honoured throughout your life and your soul will be saved after your death. (History 4:133)

Saul-Joseph(us) of Arimathaea then launches into one of his stupendously complex and rambling oratories, designed to convince his audience that male is female, up is down, black is white, and perfidy is a virtue. It is a triumph of contorted logic and literature that only Saul-Josephus Flavius could have written, which is another reason why Joseph(us) of Arimathaea and Saul-Josephus just have to be the same person. He goes on to say:

> King, I will show you how Jesus was born of a maiden without carnal relations with a man. It is true that there is only one god who made everything out

> of nothing. He was always god and will always be god, for he never had a beginning and nor can he have an end ... This god is called the faith because (Jesus) is his son, for he engendered him before the beginning of time. He did not engender him carnally but spiritually, The father was never made, created or engendered, nor was he ever born. Nor was the son ever made or created, but he was engendered by spiritual means. And he was born to the Virgin but this birth was not as a god but as a human. By this you should understand that his birth by his mother was carnal, but his birth by his father was spiritual ... so the part he had from his father never suffered death as this is the divinity that will never fail him but will endure without end. (History 4:143)

And for good measure Joseph(us) goes on to say that Mary the Virgin was impregnated by god through her ears, which is a novel proposition. (History 4:149) This must have been something Mar Addai (Thaddaeus) had read about in the *Kama Sutra*, while he was evangelising in the East. Anyway, after an hour or two of Joseph(us)' convoluted and confusing diatribe the heads of the Sarras-Palmyran aristocracy must have been spinning. But King Evalach was having none of this, and rebuts each and every claim by Joseph(us), saying:

> Are you telling me that someone who suffered the anguish of death ... is powerful enough to save me after death?
>
> How can he, who cannot protect himself from death, protect me from death?
>
> Are you really saying that he is a god because he suffered death in this way?
>
> You hold that this god, who you say was so powerful, has a father and mother?
>
> If a child were conceived without carnal relations, it would be against custom and nature.
>
> I think you are drunk, because you say one thing and then deny it afterwards.
>
> You may believe what you want, but you tell me nothing that, it would seem, can be true.
>
> (History 4: 134, 141, 151)

However, if this text had originally been written by Saul-Joseph(us), as has been suggested, readers might be wondering why King Evalach is being allowed to undermine the key tenets of Simple Judaism quite so forcefully. (Just as Simon Magus was allowed to in the *Clementine Recognitions*.) There are two likely reasons for this. Firstly, Saul-Joseph(us) was not the only author of this manuscript, as we have seen previously, and these criticisms may well be 13th century interpolations. And secondly, Saul-Joseph(us) had been told what to say by Emperor Vespasian, as we shall see again later. And Saul-Joseph(us) did not necessarily agree with many of the aspects of this new Simple Judaic creed that Vespasian had created, especially the eucharist blood rituals.

And we can be fairly certain that this rambling speech to the Sarrasan aristocracy had been written by Joseph(us) after the Jewish Revolt, because Saul's (Josephus') Epistles never mention that Mary was a virgin: not once. In fact, they never mention Mary at all. Is that not strange? One would have thought that Saul-Josephus, who was travelling across the eastern Mediterranean on two grand evangelical missionary tours during the AD 50s, might have mentioned the Virgin Mary and the reasoning for this virgin birth business. After all, the two great Christian 'proofs' that Jesus was a god are: he was born of a virgin whose name was Mary, and he died but rose again after three days. Yet the Epistles never mention Mary nor the virgin birth once, while the all-important resurrection of Jesus is mentioned just once, in 1Cor 15:4. Is that not a bit strange? Saul-Josephus was touring the Mediterranean and supposedly trying to attract new members to his new cult of virgin birth and resurrection, and yet he somehow forgets to mention all of the most central and vital aspects of his new religion. So how did that happen? *

Think about it. Those great rambling epistles or letters that were written by Saul (Josephus) and form the bulk of the New Testament, were supposed to be evangelising the merits of Simple Judaism or Christianity among the Jews and Pagans of Anatolia, and yet they never mention Mary or the full details of the crucifixion - not once. Is this not a bit strange? As was mentioned previously, within Saul's epistles there is no great lament about Jesus' unjust trial; his condemnation by those horrid Jewish people; his scourging with whips; his carrying the cross through the city; his crucifixion alongside two others; his purple robe and crown of thorns; the wound in his side; the sponge of vinegar; the lamenting women (who were all called Mary); his being taken down from the cross early; being placed in the tomb; and Mary Magdalene arriving at the tomb to find it empty. All of these dramatic and vital elements of the Christian creed are entirely missing from the epistles of Saul (Josephus).

In fact, according to the sparse testimony within the epistles, during

* As we saw in Chapter III, the eucharist is not mentioned in the Epistles either. The crucifixion is mentioned a few times, but only tangentially. And it was demonstrated in *King Jesus* that all of these oblique and fleeting references to a possible crucifixion, were either later interpolations or were talking about something else entirely and have been mistranslated.

the AD 50s there was no such thing as Christianity as we know it today. Why? Because when the epistles were written, none of this had actually happened yet. The crucifixion of King Izas Manu (the biblical King Jesus Em-Manuel) took place in the autumn of AD 70, just two years before Saul-Joseph(us) has been dispatched to Sarras-Palmyra on his diplomatic mission. And so it is only here in Sarras-Palmyra that Saul-Joseph(us) is able to launch into a great and convoluted explanation about the virgin birth and resurrection, and an equally absurd description of the Trinity. (An account that is not worth repeating here because it is utterly baffling, in a manner that only Saul-Josephus could have devised and achieved. When he is in full flow, Saul-Josephus can bring on a migraine within two or three minutes.)

So why is Saul-Joseph(us) now preaching the virgin birth, when he completely failed to do so during his AD 50s evangelical missions across the Mediterranean? The answer is obvious. This new doctrine of virgin birth, resurrection, and the cannibalistic blood-ritual of the eucharist, were all invented by Vespasian and Titus for political reasons. While the crucifixion had only just happened two years earlier, in AD 70. And Vespasian's newly invented eucharist ritual was probably based upon the standard resurrection rites of the Eleusinian mystery schools, which had been combined with the blood-rituals of Mithras. As we have already seen, before he left for Sarras-Palmyra 'god' (ie: Vespasian) said to Saul-Joseph(us):

> Fear not about this, for you only have to open your mouth and I will put into it a great abundance of words ... And I will make you my apostle ... (History 4,:129,130)

So these new elements of Roman political propaganda, which eventually became the central tenets of the Christian creed, were not a part of Saul-Josephus' original Simple Judaism. Instead they had been invented by Emperor Vespasian, and given to Saul-Joseph(us) to preach to the Nazarene rebels in Sarras-Palmyra and Edessa. And so Saul-Joseph(us) was no longer an apostle of Jesus, he was an apostle of Emperor Vespasian!

Saul-Joseph(us), ever the narcissist rationalist, probably did not believe a word of this nonsense and would have been very happy to see it challenged in later centuries, just as we see here in *History*. But the finer points of Christian doctrinal analysis were not the point of this diplomatic mission. Saul-Joseph(us) was in Sarras-Palmyra to accept the surrender of the Palmyran Edessans, and to secure a binding peace treaty of some nature. And it really did not matter if that reconciliation was brought about by guile, deception, manipulation, lies, or even by outright threats of annihilation. Titus and Vespasian wanted a disarmament and a peace deal on their terms, and it was Joseph(us)' job to get it.

What Vespasian and Titus were trying to do here, was to quell the nationalistic, separatist and militaristic creed of the Fourth Sect Nazarenes of Edessa. All the way through *Antiquities* and *Jewish War*, Saul-Josephus laments that the Fourth Sect Nazarene (the Edessans) would not accept Roman domination, Roman taxation, or any law bar their own interpretation of god's law. And they would suffer any adversity rather than admit defeat. Clearly this hard-line religion would have to be neutered, if there was ever going to be peace between Rome and Edessa. A situation not unlike the modern religio-political confrontation between West and East. But the aristocrats and advisors of Sarras-Palmyra were having none of Saul-Joseph(us) claptrap, and so a clerk of the court stood up and said:

> If the father and the son and the holy spirit were only one god, then none of the three was a complete and perfect god... (Histories 8, p52 II:198.)

Well quite. You cannot have a complete and perfect god, if he or she is split into three. Clearly, the peaceful propaganda ploy was not going according to plan here. So at this outright challenge to Vespasian's new composite Judaeo-Pagan creed, Josephus the son of Joseph(us) of Arimathaea rises to speak.

Now this is interesting, because it was obvious that father and son were actually one and the same person all along. The only reason for inventing this son called Josephus, was because of that 40-year chronological chasm that had been created by the artificially early date for the crucifixion. So to bring Saul-Joseph(us) (of Arimathaea) forward into the AD 70s era, he needed to be his own father for a while. This allowed him to be middle aged in the AD 30s and middle aged the AD 70s.* But now Joseph(us) (the father) has sat down and Josephus (the son) has stood up, and so Saul-Josephus can be himself once more. And Josephus (Saul-Josephus) can clearly see that platitudes and manipulation are simply not working here, and so he goes for the naked threat instead and says to the assembled aristocracy of Sarras-Palmyra:

> Because you have brought your false advocates against my faith, I have decided to take such great vengeance on you, that before the third day you shall fall into great misfortune ... God will punish you because you do not want to accept the faith in his glorious name.

* Saul-Joseph(us) would have been 35 years old at this time. It is likely that he did have a son, but the son who was mentioned in connection with the Jewish Revolt was only a child at this time. But this son may well have played a starring role in the later episodes of Arthurian history, where he is called Sir Galahad.

> God will show you that no creature can survive who is not prepared to follow his commandment, nor will you ever recover the great honour you are beginning to lose.
>
> You can be sure that Tholomer the fugitive, who is king of Babylonia (Parthia) has prepared his entire army and is moving against you right now. (Histories 8, II:199-200) (Author's brackets.)

And then Josephus says to the clerk who criticised him, and the new creed of virgin birth and resurrection that Vespasian had devised:

> Hear what god tells you, through his servant (ie: through Josephus): 'Because you have spoken against the one who has power over you and against all things, I will make you feel my earthly justice and suffer from it ... I will take away from you earthly speech and sight.' (Histories 8, p54 II:201.) (Author's brackets.)

Ouch. These are standard threats that playground bullies make to anyone who disagrees with them: 'if you don't agree with me, I will get my big brother (god) to hurt you in ways that you did not imagine possible.' It is the same technique that is used widely in Islam to this day, where anyone who writes a book, makes a film, or draws a cartoon that is critical of Islam, immediately receives a death-threat in the name of god. And these are real death-threats, with film producers being stabbed to death in the streets of otherwise civilised Holland, publishers being stabbed or shot in otherwise civilised Scandinavia, poets and musicians being massacred in Turkey, cartoonists being massacred in otherwise civilised Paris, and cartoonists being shot at in otherwise civilised Texas.*

This is a ruthless tactic that works, because it makes media critics and politicians fall silent, as we have all seen. The craven liberal media in the West will always champion free speech but never say anything against Islam, while simultaneously lampooning Christianity at every possible moment. But this kind of protection racketeering can only work if there really is a 'big brother' who can threaten the opposition. And in the case of Josephus (Saul-Josephus) he did indeed have a prominent and viable 'big brother' up his sleeve, which he could use to threaten the aristocrats and monarchy of Sarras-Palmyra. Like the naked threats made by Islamic radicals, Josephus (Saul-Josephus) was not

* Details about the Paris and Dallas shootings had to be added to this sentence after it was written. And no doubt this sentence will have to be updated again each year. For the Turkish murder of 35 poets and musicians, please search for the Sivas massacre.

simply relying on a belligerent god to reinforce his position, but also upon the two Roman legions who were encamped somewhere near Damascus.

And then we come to the third quote in the previous trio, which is probably the most interesting of all. This short sentence betrays the political situation at that time, and therefore tells us a great deal about the identity of King Evalach and the true identity of the city of Sarras. It says that Tholomer the king of Babylonia (Parthia) was preparing his army right at that moment, and was preparing to attack Sarras. So if we look into real history, who was the king of Babylonia (Parthia) in the AD 70s and who might he have been preparing to attack?

Interestingly, the king at this time was actually Vologases I, the son of Vonones II. It would appear that *History* has simply changed the 'V' to a 'Th', which is a common transposition between these languages. And so King Volo-gases has become King Tholo-meses or Tholo-mer. Again we can see that *History* contains real history and real information, because it is recording the correct monarchs in the correct region in the correct era.

But who were King Vologases' allies and enemies at this time? Surprisingly, considering the long-standing enmity between Parthia and Rome, at this very time point in time there were reasonably good relations between Parthia and Rome. In fact, during the Year of Four Emperors, when Vespasian was trying to decide whether to make a bid for the Throne of Rome or not, King Vologases of Parthia offered the support of his archers to Vespasian:

Fig 8.6
A coin of King Vologases I of Parthia. Most of the Parthian coins are fairly generic, but by this era the 'royal wart' is rarely displayed. See Jesus, King of Edessa for an explanation of these royal warts.

> (Vespasian's) enterprise was greatly assisted ... by the support of Licinius Mucianus (the governor of Syria), and by that of Vologesus, the Parthian king. The former - laying aside the hostility with which up to that time jealousy had obviously inspired him - promised the Syrian army. And the latter (Vologesus) promised forty thousand bowmen. (Suetonius, 8:6:4) (author's brackets)

King Vologases was sufficiently allied to Legatus Vespasian, that he had offered him an entire army. And after the Jewish Revolt had ended, King Vologases had commissioned a special gold crown in celebration of Vespasian's great victory; which was presented to Titus when he was at Zeguma, a crossing-point on the Euphrates due west of Edessa:

> Titus did not stay at Antioch, but continued his progress immediately to Zeugma, which lies upon the Euphrates, where messengers came to him from Vologeses, the king of Parthia, and brought him a crown of gold upon the victory he had gained over the Jews. Which he accepted, and feasted the king's messengers, and then went back to Antioch. (Jewish War 7:5:2)

This was the true political situation in the late 1st century AD. Parthia was obviously not terribly impressed with the Kingdom of Edessa. In fact, Parthia was such good friends with the revolutionary Edessan monarchy that they had offered Vespasian the loan of 40,000 archers to fight against them, and had congratulated Vespasian and Titus for their victory over the Edessans. So who, in the AD 70s, would the Parthian king have been more likely to attack: Rome or Edessa?

The answer is obvious. The descendants of Queen Thea Muse Ourania had carved out a small and surprisingly wealthy principality, by usurping some valuable portions of Parthian lands and negotiating its tax-free status. The Osrhoene valley between Edessa (Sanli Urfa) and Amida (Diyarbakir) had all been under Parthian control before the Edessans took it over, and the Parthians may not have been to impressed by that move. But the Edessans had just taken on the Romans in Judaea, and lost that war in spectacular fashion. The Edessans were now weakened, both economically and militarily, and they were possibly ripe for picking. All Parthia needed to do, is walk in and take over the entire region; and the only thing stopping them, was Rome. Rome may have hated the Edessans for starting a ruinous war in the eastern provinces, and they would have loved to see the Kingdom of Edessa destroyed. However, despite their burning hatred of Edessa, the Romans did not want to see a resurgent Parthia coming in and overrunning lands that Rome considered to be within their own sphere of influence.

This was political backdrop behind the threats that Josephus (Saul-Josephus) was making to King Evalach (King Abgar bar Manu VI) in

Sarras (Palmyra). Josephus was basically saying to Evalach, that if he did not disarm and agree to peace, he would allow King Tholomer-Volomer of Babylonia (King Vologases of Parthia) to stroll in and destroy all of Palmyra and Edessa.

But this was a game of bluff and double-bluff, because Rome did not really want to see King Vologases parking his Parthian army on the doorstep of Rome. So who was going to blink first - Josephus or King Evalach? Josephus (Saul-Josephus) was a complete nobody, a former princeling without a principality who had become an intellectual priest with verbal diarrhea, peddling strange ideas about virgin birth and resurrection, and insisting that Edessa adopt these stupid ideas as a part of the peace treaty with Rome. It must have been very tempting to use a standard Roman military-issue hobnail sandal and kick both Joseph(us) and Josephus out of the temple. Except, of course, that these two raving idiots appeared to have a couple of Roman legions tucked up the sleeves of their tunics, just in case things turned nasty.

The situation for the Kingdom of Edessa was not only grave, it was complexly grave too. If Edessa refused to agree terms with Rome and disarm, then Rome may send in its legions and destroy Palmyra and then Edessa too. However, Rome was now threatening to remove its legions from Syria and let King Vologases do their dirty work for them. No doubt Vologases would be in Edessa and Palmyra within a week, and wreak even more devastation than Rome would. But if they did disarm, then the Kingdom of Edessa would be completely defenceless, and forever dependent upon Rome for military protection. But what if Rome then had a political crisis, and was no longer willing or able to protect its eastern borders? Edessa would be defenceless. The needle on the Edessan political barometer was hovering somewhere between tricky and dire.

Simple Judaism

But this peace treaty was not a simple question of the Kingdom of Edessa disarming and becoming friends with Rome again. The entire reason for Vespasian and Titus sending Saul-Joseph(us) of Arimathaea as an ambassador, rather than some bumbling official from the imperial court, is that Rome did not simply want the Edessan military to be neutered - they wanted the Nazarene Ebionite religion to be neutered too. This is why Joseph(us) had launched into his great monologue about the life of Jesus, the virgin birth, and the nature of the Trinity. The Edessan monarchy did not need lessons in who King Izas Jesus (the biblical Jesus) was, for he was King Evalach's own father. They knew all about King Izas Jesus Manu from first hand.

But this was not the point. Saul-Joseph(us) had come to Palmyra to teach the people the new truth that they must now believe and teach to their children. It mattered not if they knew that Izas had only been a man - a prince and king perhaps, but still only a man - because that was the old truth. However, the new truth was the true truth, the truth according to faith rather than facts, and this was the true truth that the Palmyrans and Edessans had to recite each day on pain of death. King Izas Jesus was no longer a man, he was a god and a pauper prince of peace. Clement of Alexandria said something similar in his letter to Theodore:

> For, even if they should say something true, one who loves the truth should not, even so, agree with them. For not all true things are the truth, nor should that truth which merely seems true according to human opinions be preferred to the true truth, of that according to the faith. [1]

Now this was a very difficult demand to make of a well educated and deeply pious people. Eating humble pie and telling your children that their fathers had fought and lost a great war, is one thing. But to sit there, day after day, telling your children that black is white and up is down, is something else entirely. But there was no other option. The terms of the peace treaty with Rome could be summarised as: 'believe this and teach this to your children or you will suffer the same fate as Jerusalem.' But there was no time for discussions and debate over these unacceptable terms, because a messenger arrived with bad news:

> He knelt before the king and said: 'King Evalach, I bring you very bad news. King Tholomer (King Vologases) has entered your lands with all of his army, and has already taken your rich city Onage, and all the land around the castle of Evalachin. If he can conquer it, no castle or city will remain in all the land...' (History 8:208.) (Author's brackets.)

Unfortunately the identity of the city of Onage is unknown, and this attack does not fit into the known history of the region. However, it is entirely possible that this section of the story may be one of those strange 'back to the future' moments, just as we saw in Monmouth's account of Arthurian history. Readers might remember that when the African Muslims attacked 'Britain', this was actually a story about the Muslim invasion of the Languedoc and Aquitaine in the 8th century. And the prince who organised a Frankish army and pushed them out of Gaul was Guillaume de Gellone (William of Orange) the Prince of Orange.

Is this why the city of Onage sounds so much like the city of Orange? And is this why the Muslim king in the *Chanson de Guillaume* and

Willehalm was sometimes called Terramer? The Muslim king of this 8th century invasion was normally called Suleiman Rahman, so did this name get changed to Terramer so that it would sound like Tholomer, the *Vulgate Cycle's* name for King Vologases? There is a great deal of synergy in all of this. And do remember that *Willehalm* was written by Wolfram von Eschenbach, the author of *Parzival*; and Eschenbach credited Chretien of Troyes as the original source for this story, just as he did for *Parzival*. So again we see that the many Arthurian authors spread across Europe, were all singing from the same hymn-sheet.

William's capital city was Orange, which lay just north of Avignon on the eastern edge of the Languedoc, after which the independent Principality of Orange was named. And although the city of Orange was besieged during this Muslim invasion it never fell. And that was just as well because William's half Saracen wife was still there, defending the city. And this gives us another similarity with the account in *History*, because the wife and mother of King Evalach were both said to be from Orberica. (See fig 8.4.) Can we also see in this name a close similarity with the name of Prince Guillaume-William's wife, Princess Orable? Was Queen Orberica of Onage being linked to Princess Orable of Orange?

While this may seem like a crazy jump in the chronology and narrative, to suddenly connect 1st century in Syria with 8th century events in southern France, there is probably method in this seemingly bizarre madness. Just as in Monmouth's account, one of the primary reasons for making this connection was to link the biblical King Jesus Izas (in this case his son, Evalach) with Guillaume of Orange - because Guillaume was said to have been a descendent of Jesus. So the author of *History* may have been covertly implying that Guillaume was of the line of Jesus, and this is confirmed when Josephus the son of Joseph(us) launches into a very peculiar life-history for King Evalach of Sarras-Palmyra, saying:

> You were born ... in a very old city of France called Meaux. You were the son of a poor man who mended old shoes, just as you know. After Augustus had ruled the Roman Empire for 27 years, word spread that an man would be born who would conquer the whole world. And it was true, for Jesus ... was born in that year. (History 8:208.)

But why would anyone imagine that a 1st century king of Sarras-Palmyra in Syria had been born to a poor cobbler in northern France? Classical historians will look at this assertion and roll their eyes, but that is only because they have never understood these manuscripts or this story. They are looking at 2-down in this crossword, without having first filled in 5-across. But readers of the *King Jesus Trilogy* are at a distinct advantage, and can probably see the author's true intent; for we now have King Evalach being born in northern France, which is exactly where Guillaume Gellone-Orange was born. Guillaume is thought to have been born in Burgundy, while the town of Meaux is just north of Burgundy.

Then we have a direct and very obvious link between the birth of Evalach and the birth of Jesus, with the former being claimed as the son of a poor cobbler while the latter was said to be the son of a poor carpenter. And the reference to Jesus conquering the world is a reference to the Star Prophesy, the prophesy that Jesus would rule the entire Roman Empire, as has been explained previously. *History* then runs through an improbable tale about Rome demanding a poll tax because of the birth of Jesus, and so the young Evalach was sent from France to Rome as a part of this taxation. Much later he is sent to Syria with the Roman army, but kills one of Felix' sons and flees to King Tholomer Ceraster of Babylon. King Tholomer then attacks Sarras, which was then ruled by King Hollofernes and gives the region to Evalach as his liegeman or vassal.

Phew. What a mishmash of improbable events that is, simply to get Prince Evalach from being a pauper in France into becoming a king in eastern Syria. Not that it is important, because much of this is overtly fictional. Having said that, there are obvious historical allusions here: the poll tax is the biblical taxation under Quirinius; the killing of the son of Felix is from the story of the Old Testament Moses; while King Tholomer is King Vologases once more. And Vologases is surnamed Ceraster (Seraster or Soraster) after his religion, which was no doubt based upon Zoroastrianism; and so King Tholomer Ceraster of Babylon is King Vologases Zoroaster of Parthia.

The continuing story then gives some further pointers towards 8th century France. The great army of King Tholomer of Babylon has captured the city of Onage, and so King Evalach rides out to meet the invaders and a great battle ensues. The battle ends as the light fades, and the king retires to Castle la Choine. But the occupants will not let him in, because he was riding a Saracen horse and they mistake him for a Saracen. And so Evalach has to wait for a long time before gaining entry. This is reminiscent of Guillaume of Orange, who took his small regional army straight into battle with the army of the Muslim King Terramer. After a long fight Guillaume retires back to the city of Orange but his wife, the redoubtable Princess Orable-Giburc, does not recognise him because he is wearing Saracen armour, and so he is forced to wait before being let in.

In *History*, King Tholomer comes to besiege Castle la Choine, so King Evalach goes to Sarras for assistance. While on the way he meets his brother-in-law, Seraphe, and they retire to the city of Orcaut to gather an army. As soon as the army is assembled, they go back to attack the Parthian army and relieve the siege of Castle la Choine.

Again this is reminiscent of the account in Wolfram von Eschenbach's *Willehalm,* where King Terramer comes to besiege the city of Orange. So Guillaume goes to Lyon to get assistance from King Louis I, who again happens to be his brother-in-law through his sister, the 'Roman Queen'. At Guillaume's urging and persuasion an army is at last assembled, and they go back to attack the Muslim army and relieve the siege of the city of Orange.

And there may even be a link between Castle la Choine and the fortified city of Orange, because Choine may refer to the Latin and Hebrew Sine meaning 'China'. And the reason for *History* referring to somewhere as obscure as China, is that the orange fruit was known as the *sinasapel (chinasapel)* - the apple of China. So Castle Choine could well be Castle Orange. And so this particular chapter in *History* does appear to be based upon the history of Guillaume of Orange, as narrated in the *Chanson de Guillaume* and *Willehalm*. But since these Guillaume chansons and Arthurian histories were composed in substantially the same region and era, by the same group of authors, perhaps that is not so surprising.

And while we are looking at similarities between *History* and Wolfram von Eschenbach's manuscripts, it is worth noting that Prince Seraphe was married to King Evalach's sister, Princess Flegetine. While in Eschenbach's *Parzival,* it was claimed that the original manuscript describing the nature of the Holy Grail came from an otherwise unknown astronomer and physicus called Flegetanis of Toledo. But it was previously explained that 'Toledo' was probably a cover-story for Edessa. In which case, it is entirely possible that Eschenbach's physicus called Flegetanis of Edessa was actually a lady - Princess Flegetine, the sister of King Evalach - and her primary capital city was not Edessa but a little further to the south at Sarras-Palmyra.

It looks like we may have another direct equivalence here, between this seemingly disconnected eastern story and the family of King Arthur. Most of these histories record that Morgan le Fay (Morgane le Fay) was the muse of Merlin, and an adept sorceress in her own right. In which case, Morgan le Fay is a direct equivalent of Eschenbach's physicus: an initiate who understood the movements of the heavens and could divine the future from this knowledge. However, within the majority of Arthurian history Morgan le Fay was said to be the sister of King Arthur, while Princess Flegetine was the sister of King Evalach. But since King Evalach was the son of King Arthur-Jesus, then Princess Flegetine was Arthur's daughter. In which case, both the sister and the daughter of King Arthur-Jesus were renowned for being great physicus magicians and astronomers.

And this may also give us a possible meaning for the name of Morgan or Morgane, which has remained undecyphered thus far. Since Morgane le Fay was an mystic adept in her own right, and here she is being equated with a master physicus who understood the movements of the heavens, it is more than likely that 'Morgane' was derived from the Aramaic *mawgane* מגן meaning 'shield'. But the Aramaic *mawgane* or *magen* was not any old knight's shield, it was actually a star that became the Magen David (the Mawgane Dawveed) מגן דוד, the Star of David - a hexagram composed from two interlocking pyramids. And the reason for thinking that this star was linked to Morgane-Morgan le Fay is because this same six pointed star also became the symbol of Mary the Virgin and Mary Magdalene.

There are several interconnected explanations for this symbolism for the two Marys, but they all revolve around stellar symbolism. The primary explanation comes from the standard imagery for the Star of Venus, which was originally portrayed as an eight-pointed star. And since this stellar symbolism came from the East, it was known as the Star of Ishtar (ie Venus). But in Catholic symbolism the Venus symbol became a six-pointed star, and since Venus was closely associated with Mary the Virgin it also became known as the Marian Star. And the Marian star followed the more pronounced indents of the Star of Venus, to differentiate it from the Jewish Star of David, because the Catholic Church did not want its followers to realise that the gospel Marys were Jewish!

And so Mary the Virgin became known as the Stella Marian and thence the Stella Maris, the Sea Star, an incarnation of Venus-Aphrodite who was born in the foam of the sea. But this has not become not a maritime story all of a sudden, because the 'sea' here refers to the great sea in the heavens above, and so the Stella Maris was Venus while the foam of the sea referred to the Milky Way. But when sailors started to venerate Mary as the Sea Star,

Fig 8.7
The Persian Star of Venus or Star of Ishtar (left).
The Catholic Star of Venus and Mary, the Marian Star or Sea Star (center).
The Judaic Star of David - the Star of Mawgane or the Star of Magdalene (right).

the patron saint of mariners, they identified her with the pole star Polaris instead because that is the star they navigated by.

But it was not only Mary the Virgin who was identified with a six-pointed star, so too was Mary Magdalene, but it is likely that the latter was more closely associated with the Judaic Magen David than the Marian Star. The Star of David is formed from two superimposed pyramids and a pyramid in Aramaic is called a *magdal* מגדל, and yet a *magdal* 'tower' is also the root for Mary Magdalene's name. It is often claimed that Mary was named after a tower, but this is simply another Church deflection and deceit: a conveniently benign translation that separates Mary from both Egypt and Babylon. In reality the biblical *magdal* was more often than not a pyramid, which is why the Tower-Pyramid of Babel was called a *magdal* in Genesis 11:4 and the Pyramid of Syene-Seven was called a *magdal in* Ezra 29:10.

The Israelites had been in Egypt for 200 or 400 years, even at the insistence of the Torah itself, and so the Israelites were bound to have seen, visited and mentioned the pyramids of Egypt. How could they not? Joseph was the prime-minister of Egypt and the high priest of Heliopolis,* which was just an arrow's arc away from Giza. Are we to believe that this wealthy aristocrat never visited the Great Pyramid, even just out of curiosity? But the Israelites did mention the pyramids of Egypt, of course, and they are recorded in the Torah-Tanakh as Mt Sinai and the Pyramid of Syene-Seven, which are both references to the Great Pyramid. See *Tempest & Exodus* and *Solomon, Pharaoh of Egypt* for further details. And so we know that a *magdal* refers to a pyramid, despite its common translation into the English as a 'tower'. So Mary Magdalene was not known as Mary of the Tower, instead she held the prestigious Egyptian title of Mary of the Pyramid. And since *mari* was the Edessan title for a bishop, and Mary was portrayed in the Gnostic gospels as being the deputy of the Nazarene Church, she was probably known as the Bishop of the Pyramids.

And the point of this tangential diversion into biblical stellar-pyramid symbolism, is that Mary the Virgin and Mary Magdalene were both strongly associated with the six-pointed star of Isis-Venus-Ishtar-Astarte-Aphrodite. And now we see the distinct possibility that Morgan le Fay was

* Even as the Torah records it, the Old Testament Joseph married the daughter of the high priest of Heliopolis, owned a priest's ornamented cloak, became prime-minister of Egypt, and took a 20% tax on all of Egypt. It is axiomatic that such a thoroughly Egyptianised priestly politician and aristocrat, who was the richest man in Egypt, would have visited and mentioned the greatest wonder in the ancient world - the Giza pyramids.

also an incarnation of Venus, because she was called Morgane or Mawgane, the Judaic name for the six-pointed star of both Venus and David. And so the titles Morgane and Magdalene were two sides of the same stellar coin. The Morgan referred to a star designed from two pyramids, while the Magdal referred to those very same pyramids. In other words, two Magdals makes one Morgane. And this unification may not simply be a literary device, because the two Bethany sisters - Martha and Mary Magdalene, the two sister-wives of King Jesus - could be combined in a very similar fashion to make a unified Morgane.

But if Morgane le Fay was closely connected to Isis-Venus, then perhaps Flegetine was similarly linked to Venus, especially if Flegetine was the daughter of Morgane. (There is a suspicion that Morgane may have been the second sister-wife of Arthur, just as Jesus-Izas was probably married to both Mary and Martha.) And if we look to the Aramaic there is only one possible translation for Flegetine, and that is Peleg פלג which eventually became the Greek Falek Φαλεκ.

Aramaic	Peleg	etine
Aramaic	Pheleg	etine
Greek	Falek	etine
Norman	Fleg	etine

The Aramaic *peleg* means 'river' and 'divide in half', and this is a name or title that resonates with astrological symbolism. Remember that many of the references to rivers or seas in these texts actually refer to the heavenly seas above, and this name is no exception. The great 'river' that flows across the heavens and divides them in two is actually the Milky Way, and as we saw in *Jesus, King of Edessa,* Aphrodite was born in the foaming seas of the Milky Way. That is what her name means. In which case, the name Flegetine is directly related to the Milky Way, and therefore to the goddess Aphrodite, who eventually became the Roman Venus. And just to add to this heady mix of stellar symbolism for these princesses and queens, we shall see in Chapter X that Queen Gwenevere's name was similarly derived from the goddess Venus, but in this case from the Welsh pronunciation.

And so we have another strong connection between Arthurian and biblical history here, because the sister-wives of both of these monarchs were closely associated with Isis-Venus. The mother and wife of King Izas Jesus were incarnations of Isis-Venus, as we have just seen; while King Arthur's sister and wife, Morgane and Gwenevere, were both named after the six-pointed star of Venus. And so we may well have a direct association here, between the many queens and princesses in this story.

King	Mother-Sister	Star symbolism	Position
Jesus	Mary Virgin	Marian-Venus	?
Jesus	Mary Magdal	Magdal-Venus	physicus
Arthur	Morgan le Fay	Morgane-Venus	physicus
Arthur	Gwenevere	Gewner-Venus	physicus
son	daughter		
Evalach	Flegetine	Aphrodite-Venus	physicus

Pax Romana

The result of all these political and military threats to Sarras, from both the Romans and the Parthians, is that the ministers and advisers of Sarras agree to the terms of surrender proposed by Joseph(us) of Arimathaea, and are converted to Christianity. They then set out to another city called Orcaut to take the message of Simple Judaism there too. And if Sarras was Palmyra, and the journey of these Roman ambassadors into Edessan territory is continuing as planned, then one suspects that Orcaut is actually Orroa, Orhay or Orfa - the later names for the city of Edessa.

Josephus then goes to the main temple of Orcaut and desecrates the altar, casting out the 'devil' that inhabited the cult figures there. This devil is called Selaphas and one suspects that this has been derived from *seleph* סלף meaning 'crookedness' or 'perverseness'. Then people of Orcaut are likewise converted to Christianity:

> The king's proclamation was cried throughout the city, that all should come to the palace to hear the king's order ... that they must all go to be baptised ... Those who did not want to receive it left the country, and they fell dead as soon as they passed through the city gate. Some went out of their senses, while others were struck in the body, so that a wound was seen but not the person who did it ... but none of those who were baptised were hurt. (History 12:298)

One can sense an element of forced conversion here. King Evalach had been persuaded by Joseph(us) and Josephus (ie: Saul-Josephus) that a lasting peace with Rome was his only option and so he would have to persuade his people to be converted, by force if necessary. Rome wanted to eradicate Nazarene Judaism once and for all, and so the people would have to convert to Rome's new Simple Judaism, whether they liked it or not. And if the people objected, then the king (or Josephus) would have to send his thugs throughout the city maiming and killing all those who disagreed. It is surprising how malleable most people in a population are, when they are faced with political violence. The masses may protest that this new creed is unintelligible nonsense, but as soon their leader loses his head they will all start repeating the nonsense as if they believe it.

And then, in a triumph of propaganda worthy of Joseph Goebbels himself, the newly converted population must repeat their new belief and understanding every day, perhaps three times a day. The following is an extract from the Nicene Creed of the Catholic Church, that is chanted by Christian congregations throughout the world. And it is likely that the people of Palmyra and Edessa were forced to chant something very similar, three times a day, every day:

> I believe in one Lord Jesus Christ,
> the Only Begotten Son of God,
> born of the Father before all ages.
>
> God from God, Light from Light,
> true God from true God,
> begotten, not made, consubstantial with the Father;
> through him all things were made.
>
> For us men and for our salvation,
> he came down from heaven,
> and by the Holy Spirit was incarnate of the Virgin Mary,
> and became man.
>
> For our sake he was crucified under Pontius Pilate,
> he suffered death and was buried,
> and rose again on the third day,
> in accordance with the Scriptures.
>
> He ascended into heaven,
> and is seated at the right hand of the Father,
> He will come again in glory,
> to judge the living and the dead,
> and his kingdom will have no end.

The newly converted aristocrats of Edessa must have been rolling their eyes every time they repeated what they knew was utter balderdash, but it was better than having an arm amputated or a son taken into slavery in Rome. But then, after repeating the same nonsense a thousand times in one year, it begins to invade the mind. And then the little children start tugging at your cloak and saying: "papa, will Jesus save me from evil things too?" How does one answer that? Do you say to a child that this god-man has no power whatsoever to save anyone, and see the child burst into tears? Or does one relent and say: "yes, of course Jesus will look after you." And before you know it, the next generation has been captured by Simple Judaism: captured by the power of Rome's propaganda.

This is exactly what Emperor Vespasian wanted. This is why Vespasian had sent Saul-Josephus Flavius to the Kingdom of Edessa as his ambassador and chief propaganda minister, rather than some bumbling imperial clerk. If anyone was going to pull off this implausible task, it was the silver-tongued and quicksilver-quilled Saul-Josephus Flavius. He was not only from that region and spoke their language, he could twist any argument into so many contortions it could be made to mean whatever he liked. So Saul-Josephus (of Arimathaea) was in Sarras-Palmyra to pacify the rebellious Nazarene Babylonian Jews, to whom he was closely related. As Saul-Josephus says in the preface to his *Jewish War*:

> I thought it an absurd thing to see the truth falsified in affairs of such great consequence ... while the Parthians, and the Babylonians, and the remotest Arabians, and those of our nation beyond the Euphrates, with the Adiabene, by my means, knew accurately both whence the war begun, what miseries it brought upon us, and after what manner it ended. (Jewish War, Preface 1&2)

As Saul-Josephus says, he had already been to the 'remotest Arabians' and 'those Jews beyond the Euphrates' - to Palmyra and Edessa, which does indeed lie beyond the Euphrates. And the message he took there was what he calls (paraphrased) 'an accurate account of the Jewish Revolt and the miseries that it brought to the region'. This was the clear threat that *History's* Josephus (ie: Saul-Josephus) was bringing to Palmyra and Edessa - believe in this new Simple Judaic crap I am teaching you, or exactly the same will happen to your cities and your people.

The revolt is subdued

Both King Evalach and his brother-in-law Seraphe were then christened by Josephus. Note that Joseph(us) of Arimathaea has all but disappeared from the text now, and we are simply left with Josephus the son (ie: Saul-Josephus himself). Having both been christened, the prince and king of Sarras-Palmyra are then given baptismal names, or Christian names. Evalach is baptised as Mordrain while Seraphe is renamed Nascien, and these are names that are full of hidden meaning and strongly redolent of Arthurian history. (History 12:292-293)

The name 'Nascien' looks to be Aramaic once more, while 'Mordrain' is positively said to be Chaldean-Aramaic, but what do these names mean?

The original name given to Evalach's brother-in-law was Seraphe, which just has to be Aramaic and therefore derived from Seraphe שׂרף meaning 'serpent'. But after his baptism Seraphe was given the new Christian name, Nascien, and this is likely to have been Aramaic too. It appears to have been based upon the name for the Old Testament Nahshon נחשון, the son of Amminadab. Nascien (Naschion) and Nahshon are very similar names, so this connection is highly likely. But according to Hippolytus of Rome the latter of these names was derived from *nakhash* נחש meaning 'serpent'.[2] So Seraphe's name had not really changed at all, for he was still known as the 'serpent'.

The reason for this duplication of his name or title may be a literary device, to reinforce the links between Prince Nascien and the snake. And it may also demonstrate a close link with the Naassene Ναασσην Sect, who were also known as the Ophites Οφις - with both of these terms referring to snakes. We shall come to Hippolytus of Rome's description of the Naassene serpents later.

This connection to the Naassene Ophites is as certain as anything can be in this research, because the Torah's Nahshon נחשון was translated into the Greek as Naassone Ναασσων, and this is the name for the Naassene Sect. And Nahshon נחשון was derived from *nakhash* נחש meaning 'enchanter' or 'serpent'. The nominative progression is as follows:

Aramaic	Seraphe	שׂרף	The serpent
Aramaic	Nakhash	נחש	The serpent or enchanter
Aramaic	Nahshon	נחשון	The person
Greek	Naassone	Ναασσων	The same person
Greek	Naassene	Ναασσην	The snake sect
Aramaic	Nascien	נחשין	The new name for Seraphe

All of these terms refer to snakes or serpents, and so the Naassene sect were obviously closely linked to the symbolism of the Ophite snake. And we shall see later that the Naassene and the Nazarene of Jesus and James were one and the same sect. And since Queen Helena, King Jesus and Saul-Josephus were all said to be members of the Nazarene Sect, and all of these characters have been previously linked to Edessa and Palmyra, *History's* account of a prince of Sarras (Palmyra) being called Nahshon-Naassone is more than plausible.

Mordrain-Mordred

Then we come to the new Christian name that was given to King Evalach, and this name is much more interesting. As we have already seen, the king's original name cryptically referred to King Evalmerodach or Eval-merod-ach אויל-מרד-ך the son of King Nebuchadnessar of Babylon. And in the historical record the biblical King Evalmerodach is called King Amel Marduk, the Servant of Marduk.

But King Evalach was baptised with the Christian name Mordrain, so how was this name devised, and what does it mean? Incredibly, the conclusive answer to this is that 'Mordrain' is simply the middle syllable in the name Eval-merod-ach. This, therefore, is proof-positive that King Evalach-Mordrain was being named after King Evalmerodach, the son of King Nebuchadnessar of Babylon, because these two names dovetail together as if they had been crafted by the finest of cabinetmakers. The nominative transition is as follows:

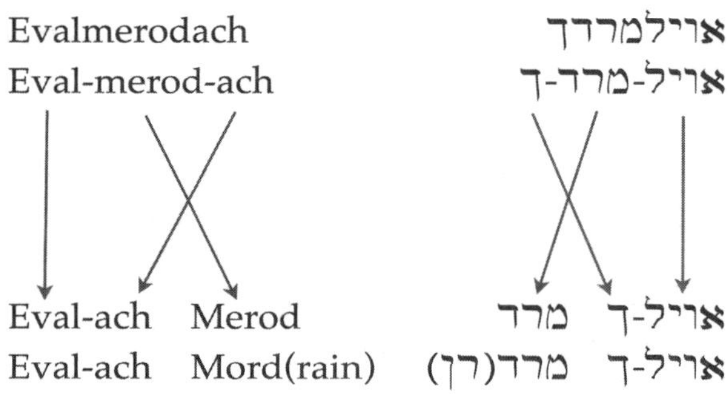

And if we look in the Aramaic there is only one meaning for Merod or Mord and that is *mord* מרד meaning 'rebellion' or 'revolt'. And this is confirmed by the biblical *Concordance,* which says that the name for King Evalmerodach was derived from Eval Merodach אויל מרדך meaning 'Man of Rebellion' or 'Servant of Rebellion'. So the new name that Evalach was given referred to the very Jewish Rebellion that his father, King Izas-Jesus, had just fought in Judaea.

And the BDB Aramaic Lexicon goes on to say that *eval* אויל means 'foolish' or 'one who despises wisdom', and so Eval Merodach really means 'Foolish Rebellion', or in full we might also derive the 'Foolish One who Despises Wisdom and Caused a Rebellion'. This truly is a hypocorism worthy of the quicksilver quilled Saul-Josephus. The author of *History* must have been rolling around the scriptorium floor, when he saw the possibilities of this *pesher* name. King Jesus-Izas was known as the Wise King who led the Jewish Revolt or Rebellion that destroyed Jerusalem, and here the author has found a son of king who destroyed Jerusalem, who was called Eval Merodach: the Foolish Rebel.

But what are the chances of this happening? How could a 13th century author of *History* manage to find such a convenient hypocorism in the Torah? The answer to this is that he probably did not, and this is yet another reason for suspecting that the original manuscript upon which all of Arthurian history is based, was written by our traitorous quicksilver-quilled friend, Saul-Josephus. And thus the origins of the *Vulgate Cycle* are not 13th century at all, but late 1st century.

Saul-Josephus would have come up against the same problem, when trying to discover this convenient pseudonym, but he had some distinct advantages over his 13th century colleagues. The consensus of modern historical and biblical opinion seems to be that the original name for this king of Babylon was Amal Marduk מרדך אמיל, with an 'm' in the first name. Note that the spelling of Marduk and Merodach remains exactly the same in the Aramaic.

Fig 8.8
An image of the Sumerian god Marduk, wearing a tunic embossed with stars and with his pet snake-dragon called Mushussu.

The second name is the god-name Marduk, meaning 'Bull of the Sun', who is said to have been a god of water and magic. But it is likely that the bull here is the constellation of Taurus, and so the 'water' in question was actually the great ocean of the cosmos in the heavens above, upon which the solar barque of the Egyptian god Ra sailed. So Marduk was the Bull of the Celestial Heavens. Note that Marduk was always associated with a pet snake-dragon, just as King Evalach is being associated with a son-in-law whose name is translated as Snake-Snake.

The first name of this king is said to be Amel meaning 'man' or 'servant', and it is likely that the original Aramaic version of this name was *amel* עמל meaning 'worker'. So King Amal Marduk was the Servant of Marduk or the Worker of Marduk. But in the Torah and in Jewish biblical tradition, the name for King Amal Marduk עמיל מרדך of Babylon has been changed into Evil Marduk אויל מרדך - the Foolish Marduk or the Foolish Rebellion. So who made this alteration to the text, and when and why was it done? The Torah had no reason to call King Amal Marduk rebellious or foolish, because Saul-Josephus says of this king:

> Nabuchodonosor ... fell sick and departed this life when he had reigned forty-three years. Whereupon his son Evilmerodach obtained the kingdom. He governed public affairs after an illegal and impure manner, and had a plot laid against him by Neriglissoor, his sister's husband, and was slain by him when he had reigned but two years. (Against Apion 1:20)

So King Amal Marduk (Evilmerodach) may have been a tyrant, but he was not a fool and nor did he lead a rebellion. In fact, it was King Amal Marduk who freed the Jewish King Jehoiachin from prison and treated him kindly, and so orthodox Judaism should have viewed Amal Marduk as a friend of Judaism. So if it was not traditional Judaism that changed Amal Marduk into Evil Marduk, then who did?

The answer lies in the history of Judaism. As was pointed out previously in this Trilogy, the Judaism we see today was not the Judaism of kings David and Solomon. Much of it was crafted during the Babylonian Exile; the very same exile during which King Jehoiachin had just been released from prison. However, there was another big change to Judaism in the 1st century AD, when much of this religion was revised by Johanan ben Zakkai, the chief rabbi who led all of Judaism after the Jewish Revolt. For instance, it was Johannan who ended the age-old Jewish tradition of animal sacrifice, which is why modern synagogues do not have a line of animals outside waiting to be slaughtered. But surprisingly, for such an influential and pivotal figure who crafted all of modern Judaism, we have no idea who Johannan was. But it was suggested in *King Jesus* that he was actually our old traitorous friend Saul-Josephus, because his escape from Jerusalem during the Jewish Revolt is strangely reminiscent of Saul-Josephus' escape from Jotapata. And so we end up with a trio of very similar people who were all working for Emperor Vespasian during and after the Jewish Revolt:

Saul-Josephus	Propagandist & historian for Emperor Vespasian
Saul-Josephus	Simple Judaic high priest for Emperor Vespasian
Joseph of Arimathaea	Simple Judaic high priest for Emperor Vespasian
Johanan ben Zakkai	Orthodox Jewish high priest for Emperor Vespasian

Remember that Saul-Josephus was not only the author of most of the New Testament, he also wrote a complete version of the Tanakh (the Old Testament), which is known as *Antiquities of the Jews*. And in writing a new version of the Tanakh, was Saul-Josephus merely the Jewish historian of Emperor Vespasian, or was he the Jewish high priest of Emperor Vespasian? It does seem that Johanan ben Zakkai and Saul-Josephus had similar lives, similar allegiances, similar roles, and created similar compositions; and so were probably the same person.

But if this is so, then this would explain all of the minor amendments to the Torah that we have seen over the course of this Trilogy. Saul-Josephus was the last Jew standing after the Jewish Revolt. And we know that he had the ear of the emperor and as many scribes as he liked, who were based at the new Jewish Sanhedrin in Jabneh, south of modern Tel Aviv. If Saul-Josephus wanted to write all of *Jewish War* and *Antiquities* he could. And in fact it was Emperor Vespasian who ordered him to write *Jewish War,* as we have already seen. And if Saul-Josephus wanted to craft a new Simple Judaism for Gentiles (Christianity), he could. In fact it was Emperor Vespasian who ordered him to write the gospels, as we have already seen, as a Rome-friendly counterbalance to the revolutionary Nazarene Ebionite sect. But what about the Torah? We know that Saul-Josephus had already written a secular version of the Torah, his *Antiquities of the Jews,* but what about the real Torah?

Surprisingly, the modern Torah in the form that we see it today, is not that old. Two of the oldest extant Hebrew bibles are the Aleppo Codex and the Leningrad Codex, which both date from about the 10th century AD. If we want to go back further into Judaic history, we have to change language, and then we have the 4th century Latin Vulgate Torah and the 2nd or 3rd century Greek Septuagint Torah. The Latin Vulgate Bible calls this son of Nebuchadnessar, King Evalmerodach, while the Greek Septuagint Bible calls him Βασιλευς Ουλαιμαραδαχ (King Eulaimaradach) - and so both of these versions are using the standard biblical spelling, instead of the historical spelling. However, all of these manuscripts were written after the 1st century, when the conflated Saul-Josephus-Johanan ben Zakkai was rewriting all the texts and all of the beliefs of Judaea. So it is entirely possible that Saul-Josephus has changed Amal Merodach עמיל מרדך into Evil Merodach אויל מרדך in the late 1st century AD, so that he could parody that name in a long-lost manuscript that eventually became Arthurian history.

This is a similar conclusion to the one made in *Jesus, King of Edessa,* where is was observed that the link between *almah* (a virgin) and Sh-Almah-th (the wife of King Abgarus of Edessa) was far too cute and convenient for coincidence. What it required is for someone to deliberately change a *bethulah,* the normal word for a virgin, into an *almah,* to make the *pesher* prophesy rhyme and work properly. And if it was Saul-Josephus in the late 1st century who wrote the original manuscript that became the Septuagint, the Vulgate and the Hebrew Codices, he could have done just that - without changing the meaning of the original text at all. And in later centuries, who would know or care that a *bethulah* virgin had become an *almah* virgin? Or that King Amalmerodach had been transformed into King Evalmerodach?

Pompeius

And if all of that was not enough rumination for the name of just one king, we have yet another confluence of names within the rest of Arthurian history. It has already been suggested that King Arthur and King Izas-Jesus were one and the same person, and yet most of the Arthurian manuscripts say that the son of King Arthur was called Mordred. So now we have a son of King Jesus-Izas called Evalach-Mordrain, and a son of King Arthur called Mordred. It looks like we have another remarkable correlation between these texts:

Volume	**The King**	**The Son**
History of Grail	(King Jesus-Izas)	Prince Mordrain-Evalach
Rest of Vulgate	King Arthur	Prince Mordred

Classical Arthurian chronology could not admit that King Evalach Mordrain was the son of King Arthur (the son of King Izas-Jesus), because King Evalach is overtly a 1st century character while King Arthur was supposed to be a 6th century character. So the pretence had to be maintained that these were two different individuals.

But most of Arthurian history was actually a 1st century story, just as *History of Kings, High History* and *Merlin Grail* have all readily admitted. So the true era for King Arthur was the late AD 60s era of the Jewish Revolt, while the era of King Evalach-Mordrain was just after the Jewish Revolt in AD 72, when Joseph(us) of Arimathaea was trying to persuade the leaders of Sarras-Palmyra to disarm and make peace. So yes, the new king of Sarras-Palmyra (Evalach-Mordrain) could well have been a son of this new 1st century incarnation of King Arthur-Jesus.

Which is probably why *Geraint and Enid,* a 12th century Welsh poem based upon Chretien of Troyes' *Erec and Enide,* calls King Arthur's son Amir. This name has also crept into the *Historia Brittonum,* in the *Miracles of Britain* section, which is thought to be a later interpolation into Nennius' chronicle:

> There is another wonder in the region ... the name of the man who is buried in the tomb was called Amir. He was the son of Arthur the soldier, and Arthur himself killed and buried him in that very place. And men come to measure the grave and find it sometimes six feet in length, sometimes nine, sometimes twelve, sometimes fifteen. (Historia Brittonum 73.)

The most obvious linguistic origin for this alternate name for Arthur's son, is from the complex nominative cypher just explained. If we allow the standard 'r' to 'l' transliteration error between Aramaic and Latin, Amir becomes Amal - the name for Amalmerodach or Evalmerodach. And so it would appear that the author of this quote knew of the link between King Evalach Mordrain of Sarras-Palmyra and the son of King Arthur-Jesus, which is one reason why this addition to *Historia Brittonum* is thought to be a later interpolation.

And the reference here to multiple measurements for Mordred's tomb, is simply a reference to the profane and sacred measurement systems that were used in this region. Most measurements were made in profane cubits of six hands, but the Egypto-Israelite priesthood had a secret and sacred measurement system that used a cubit measuring seven hands, as is made perfectly clear in Ezekiel 43:13. This seven-hand cubit was actually the thoth or royal cubit of Egypt, measuring 52.35 cm. And if one measures a tomb using a variety of measurement systems, it will appear to be a different length (a different number of cubits or feet).

And finally, in this section of sensational revelations, we must also return to the mention of King Nebuchadnessar in *Parzival*. Readers may recall that the brother of Ipomedon-Perceval was called Pompeius, and he was said to be the nephew of King Nebuchadnessar. And at long last we now know how and why the brother of Perceval could be connected with Nebuchadnessar of Babylon. He wasn't connected within real history, of course, for this Arthurian reference to the Babylonian monarchy was merely a very erudite pseudonym and concealment for the son of King Jesus-Izas. A concealment so hermetically tight that not a breath about this has leaked out for nearly 800 years.

Mordred Marduk

The confirmation that King Evalach Mordrain of Sarras was Prince Mordred, the son of King Arthur, and that this name was based upon the Torah's King Evalmerodach - can be found in Modena Cathedral in Italy. And the fact that we have to travel to 12th century Italy to discover the final proof for this interesting component of Arthurian history, demonstrates how international these accounts really are. They have very little to do with 6th century Britain, and a great deal to do with an alternate and fairly subversive history of 1st century Judaea that was rediscovered during the Crusades.

On the north side of Modena Cathedral is the Porta della Pescheria, a simple doorway containing carvings on the vault and lintel, as cathedral doorways often do. But these sculptures are interesting because they were carved by Villegmus in the early 12th century, at about the very same time that Oxford and Monmouth were writing their Arthurian manuscripts. And surprisingly, the scene they depict comes straight out of Arthurian history. The doorway is shown in fig 8.10, and even in this small-scale overview of the scene we can see depictions of six knights in traditional Norman chain-mail armour, bearing traditional Norman kite shields, and besieging a castle. The names of the knights and other characters are inscribed just above their images and these are (left, center, right):

Isdernus, Artus de Bretani, A Burmaltus
Winlogee, Mardoc
Carrado, Galvagin, Galvariun, Che

Discernible within these names are: Artus de Bretani (Arthur of Brittany), Carrado (Caradoc the Cruel), Galvagin (Gawain or Gauvain), and Che (Kay), who are all quite clearly Arthurian characters. Then there is Isdernus who must be Yder or Ydern, the son of Nut, while Galvariun may be Agravain. And then we come to the central two characters in this composition who are Winlogee (a very sad looking lady praying to god) and Mardoc (a worried looking man hanging onto the tower). A close image of them is shown in fig 8.11. And since these are Arthurian characters who are closely associated with a tower, they just have to be Gwenevere and Mordred. And so these names can be translated from the Latin as:

Ydern, Arthur of Britain, A Burmaltus (?)
Gwenevere, Mordred
Carradoc, Gawain, Agravain, Kay

The presence of Ydern and the spelling of Winlogee for Gwenevere tell us that this composition was inspired by *Yder*, a relatively obscure manuscript from western Normandy. [3] The hero of this story is a relatively unknown knight of King Arthur called Yder. He is also mentioned in Malmesbury's *Antiquities of Glastonbury*, which places this knight at the very beginning of the new Norman Arthurian history.

Within the *Vulgate*, Yder is either a knight or a duke of Cornwall, but nevertheless a very minor player in the unfolding drama. However, in *Yder* he becomes a leading knight of the Round Table who falls in love with Queen Gwenloie, who may or may not be Queen Gwenevere, the author of this story is never quite sure. But it would seem fairly certain that Gwenloie really is Gwenevere because King Arthur has his suspicions about an affair between Yder and Gwenevere, and tests the queen to see if she loved him. And then there is the comical episode where Yder throws a bear out of Queen Gwenevere's bedchamber window, into the moat below. But since King Arthur was known as the Great Bear, this incongruous 'bear' in

Gwenevere's bedroom is obviously an allusion to King Arthur himself. Such were the merry goings-on in the Arthurian court!

However, within the *Vulgate*, Queen Gwenevere's well known affair with a knight was actually with Sir Lancelot du Lac, and so the evidence from *Yder* would suggest that Yder is one and the same as Sir Lancelot. We saw a very similar scenario back in Chapter V, where Eschenbach's Prince Ither was also a favourite of Queen Gwenevere. And if Yder and Ither were the same knight then this gives us much more information about him, because the conflated Ither-Yder would have been the Red Knight who was killed by Perceval-Galahad, just as King Arthur himself ordered. And then the redheaded Perceval-Galahad took the armour of the redheaded Ither, the Red Knight, to became the new and greatly feared Red Knight.

Yet the Red Knight has already been equated with Alain li Gros, the father of Perceval. So once again we see the possibility that Alain, the father of Perceval, was actually Sir Lancelot. However, if Alain and Lancelot were the same knightly aristocrat, then this is merely the same story of 'persecution' that we saw in *High History*, where the mother of Perceval became the Queen of the Wasteland and Perceval became disinherited. And

Fig 8.10
The Porta della Pescheria on Modena Cathedral. There are six knights besieging a castle, containing a lady and a man. The knights include Artus de Bretani, Galvagin and Che.

so the reason for this persecution was not simply Perceval killing his father, but more because Ither-Yder-Lancelot-Alain had challenged the position of King Arthur and carried out a well-known affair with his wife and queen. There are not many reasons why families and kingdoms will go to war with each other, but sleeping with the king's wife is definitely one of them. We shall see more about this love-affair and feud in Chapter XIII, as it is a central topic in *Quest*.

And since the reference to Yder by Malmesbury comes nearly four decades before the first mention of Lancelot by Chretien de Troyes, it would seem that Lancelot was the new pseudonym for Yder-Ither and not the other way around. The name Ither or Yder may have been derived from Yther יתר meaning 'rich', the name for the biblical Jether or Jethro, the father-in-law of Moses. This would be an eminently suitable *pesher*-style name, as it would imply that Jesus was the new Moses and Ither-Alain was his father-in-law. The reason for Yder being renamed as Lancelot less obvious, as is the meaning of this new name. Since this new name was apparently created by Chretien it may well be Norman French, and this appears to be confirmed by the Norman prefix of *lance*, the primary weapon of Ither-Yder-Lancelot's profession. But the Norman suffix of *lot* means much the same as it does in English: either 'parcel of land', 'bundle', 'lottery' or 'fate'. Yet none of these translations results in Ither-Yder-Lancelot having a very meaningful new name.

The reason for the misspelling of the queen's name - from Gwenevere to Gwenloie in *Yder*, and then to Winlogee on the Modena sculpture - is again unknown. But it should be pointed out that Queen Gwenevere has a multitude of suffixes to her name. So although Chapter X will demonstrate that 'Gwen' refers to the goddess Venus, her precise relationship with the goddess remains unexplained. The various spelling for Gwenevere include:

Gwenevere,	Gwenhwyfar,
Gwennuuar,	Ganhumara,
Gweneuereia,	Gwenore,
Gweneuer,	Gwenievre,
Gwenloie,	Gwenlogee

The lady in the tower in this sculpture is therefore most definitely Queen Gwenevere. However, if we have a Gwenevere and a Mordred besieged in a tower, and Caradoc defending that tower, then we also know which section(s) of the Arthurian story this scene comes from. This is the account of Mordred seducing and abducting Queen Gwenevere (or perhaps even besieging Queen Gwenevere, depending on the manuscript), while Arthur was battling with the Romans. Whatever the circumstances of her 'abduction', a common theme in these histories is that Queen Gwenevere ends up being locked in a tower, just like a 6th or 1st century antecedent of Rapunzel.

But if this tower is being defended by Caradoc the Cruel, as this sculpture indicates, then this must be the Dolorous Guard - the Dolorous Tower or Castle in which Gawain had been imprisoned but released by Lancelot. And although the Dolorous Tower is not named as the tower that Mordred imprisoned Gwenevere in, she did visit this tower or castle earlier in the story.

However, it has to be observed that the story of the seduction and abduction of Gwenevere by Mordred sounds suspiciously like the seduction and 'abduction' of Gwenevere by Lancelot in *Mort.* After Lancelot defeated Caradoc, he took the Dolorous Guard (the Sorrowful Castle) for his own residence and renamed it as the Joyous Guard (the Joyous Castle). And in *Mort* we have a very similar story of Gwenevere being rescued from King Arthur by Lancelot, and taken to the Dolorous Tower. (Mort 12:126.) So the story of Mordred seducing and abducting Queen Gwenevere and taking her to a castle, is closely mirrored by this story about Lancelot 'abducting' Queen Gwenevere and taking her to the Dolorous Guard or Castle. Perhaps a reticent Arthurian author did not like the story of Arthur's son being an incestuous traitor, and so blamed this episode on Lancelot instead. We shall come across this alternative tale in Chapter XIII.

Whoever was ultimately responsible for Gwenevere's rescue or

Fig 8.11
Detail of the castle scene, showing Winlogee (Gwenevere) and Mardoc (Mordred-Marduk) in the Dolorous Tower or Dolorous Castle.

Fig 8.12
This may well be the earliest image of King Arthur-Jesus, and it is not in Wales or Normandy, but on a cathedral in Italy. Note that Arthur is the only knight not wearing armour, which is quite likely for a monarch. Instead, he wears a light tunic and an eastern-looking kilt, and is armed with a shield, lance and a Roman gladius sword.

abduction, we can now decypher the name of third knight on the left side of this sculpture, who is called A Burmaltus or A Bur Maltus. This name is not a known knight within Arthurian history, but the dots separating these short syllables are reminiscent of numismatic legends, which are always abbreviated so they can fit onto a coin. And if the same is true of this inscription, then we might derive from the Latin:

Latin	A	Bur(gus)	Mal(t)us
English	The	Castle	Evil, Sorrow, Torment

It so happens that the Dolorous Castle or Tower means 'the Castle of Sorrows', and so this supposed name for a knight may actually be the name of this castle. And the Dolorous Castle was the very same tower that Gwenevere was taken to, after her seduction and abduction by Lancelot-Mordred. In which case, the left side of this legend on the door of Modena Cathedral actually reads as:

Latin	Isdernus (et) Artus	de Bretani	a(d)	Bur(gus) Maltus
English 1	Yder and Arthur	the Briton	to the	Sorrowful Castle
English 2	Lancelot and Arthur	the Briton	to the	Dolorous Tower

The other interesting thing about this inscription is the name of the man in the Dolorous Tower. The person who seduced or abducted Gwenevere in the majority of these manuscripts was Prince Mordred, the son of Arthur. But the character in the tower in this sculpture is not being called Mordred, but Mardoc instead. So why the obvious misspelling? The answer is that this sculptor must have known his Arthurian history very well, including all the heretical elements.

As this chapter has explained at great length, Mordred, the son of King Arthur-Jesus, was actually King Evalach Mordrain of Sarras. And this alternative name for Mordred was derived from the Latinised Babylonian name Evil-**Merodach**, and the last element in this name was derived from the Sumerian god-name Marduk. Yet the man in the tower is being called Mardoc or Marduk, rather than Mordred, and so the mason who carved the Modena sculpture must have known about this connection between Evilmerodach and Mordred. In which case, we have a complete agreement between the *Vulgate Cycle* and the Modena sculpture:

Vulgate Cycle	**Sculpture**
Mordred-Marduk	Mardoc
In a tower	In a tower
Called Tower of Sorrows	Called Tower of Sorrows
With Gwenevere	With (G)Wenlogee

This is interesting. The common excuse for the name 'Mardoc' on this sculpture, is that this was a spelling mistake. But this is incorrect. In fact, the sculptor not only got the name correct, he knew a great deal more about Arthurian history than any previous modern historian. And so if the date of this sculpture is correct, and the mention of Yder would suggest that it is, then this sculptor knew that the name Mordred was derived from the Sumerian god-name Marduk nearly a century before the *Vulgate Cycle* was written.

In which case, rumours about a son of Arthur-Jesus who lived in Sarras-Palmyra and who refused to send reinforcements to Judaea, must have been swirling around much of Europe in the early 12th century, very soon after the First Crusade. And this was not simply a northern European secret from Normandy, it spanned many nations and cultures. The only difference between these many centers for Arthurian history, is that the output of romances from Normandy was more prolific and enduring than from anywhere else in Europe - including from Britain.

Mara bar Serapion

It is at about this time in the story that King Evalach Mordrain is spirited off on his wild adventure to Gibraltar, where he saw Pompey the Great defeat the Mithraic pirates, as we saw in the previous chapter. The reason for Pompey being involved in this escapade has been adequately explained, but why Evalach Mordrain (the son of Jesus) would need to witness it is not entirely clear. But while King Evalach was away on his adventure, Prince Seraphe Nascien was put into prison by a knight called Galafre. And so we end up with a prince of Sarras-Palmyra called Seraphe who is imprisoned following the Jewish Revolt and has a young son who is seven years old. Does this not sound familiar?

Readers of the previous books in this series will recall that we saw a very similar scenario of a leader who appeared to be closely connected to the Jewish Revolt who was in prison and writing to his young son. And the name of this prisoner was, of course, Mara bar Serapion; and since the 'p' and 'f' consonants are identical in Aramaic, we can also derive Mara Seraphion. But if Seraphe-Nascien and Mara Seraphion are truly the same person, then they would surely have similar concerns and views. So what, then, was Mara Seraphion writing about in his rather famous letter to his young son? Well, there are many points of interest in this letter, and we start with the following comment where Seraphion says to his son:

> When your guardian wrote me a letter, and informed me that you were very diligent in study, though so young in years, I blessed God that you, a little boy, and without a guide to direct you, had begun in good earnest. This was a comfort (that) you, little boy as you are, as displaying such greatness of mind and conscientiousness. (Letter of Mara bar Serapion)

Just as Seraphe's boy is said to be seven years old, so too is Seraphion's son of a very young age. And both boys have a private tutor, while the father is away in prison, indicating a position of great wealth and influence. Seraphion goes on to say:

> You have heard, moreover, concerning our companions, that, when they were leaving Samosata, they were distressed about it ... and said: "We are now far removed from our home, and we cannot return again to our city, or behold our people, or offer to our gods the greeting of praise." For we saw our brethren and our children captives, and we remembered our deceased companions, who were laid to rest in a foreign land. (Letter of Mara bar Serapion)

So Seraphion and his fellow prisoners came from Samosata in the Commagene. But Samosata lies barely 30 km northwest of Edessa, and it was conquered by the Romans under the command of Titus in AD 72, just two years after the Jewish Revolt. Quite obviously, this operation was a component in the mopping-up operations, following the Jewish Revolt. So this final cleansing of the Nazarene rebels by the Romans was not just being carried out down at Masada on the Dead Sea, it was also going on in northern Syria just as was proposed earlier.

And although classical history is blind to this aspect of Judaean history, the reason for these military operations in northern Syria are more than obvious. Saul-Josephus says that the Jewish Revolt was fomented and lead by the king of Adiabene; but the Armenian historians say that Queen Helena of Adiabene was actually the queen of Edessa. Ergo, one might say, the leaders of the Jewish Revolt were the king and princes of Edessa. So it would only be natural for Rome to keep up the pressure on Edessa, in any way that it could, until the region had fully disarmed and submitted itself to Roman rule. This was the reason why the Arthurian Josephus (Saul-Josephus) was leading the diplomatic mission to Sarras-Palmyra, and threatening utter destruction if the king there did not agree to Roman terms. And this is also the reason for Titus leading a military assault on Samosata, just outside Edessa.

But why did Rome invade Samosata? After all, Antiochus Epiphanes of Samosata was an ally of Rome and had sent a contingent of troops to assist Vespasian during the Jewish Revolt. So what had Antiochus done now, to earn the displeasure of Rome? Well, Saul-Josephus says:

> Cesennius Petus, who was governor of Syria at this time ... sent a letter to (Vespasian), and told him that Antiochus had resolved to rebel against the Romans; and that he had made a league with the king of Parthia to that purpose. It was therefore fit to prevent them, lest they begin such a war as may cause a general disturbance in the Roman empire. (Josephus War 7:3:3)

So Vespasian had been advised by the Syrian governor that another revolt was brewing on the eastern borders of the Empire, and Antiochus of Samosata was a party to it. But who was the 'king of Parthia' fomenting this revolt? As we have already seen, King Vologases of Parthia was on fairly good terms with Rome at the time: he had offered Vespasian troops to help him become emperor, and had made a gold crown in celebration of the destruction of the Edessan rebels in Judaea. So how, in this case, could Antiochus of Samosata have been planning a revolt with King Vologases Parthia?

The answer is obvious. The kingdom that had just waged a major revolt against Rome had been the Kingdom of Edessa, not Parthia. But since Saul-Josephus had deleted Edessa from history, so that it had become a nonexistent nation with nonexistent monarchy, he could not mention it. However, the Edessans had come from Parthia just a couple of generations ago, and so the Edessans were often referred to as Parthians, as we have seen previously. And if one travels southeastwards from Samosata the first province that will be reached is not Parthia, but Edessa. But why would Antiochus of Samosata, the king of a very small and impotent principality, have been planning to rebel against the might of Rome? Especially when the previous king of Edessa had only just demonstrated that such a policy was

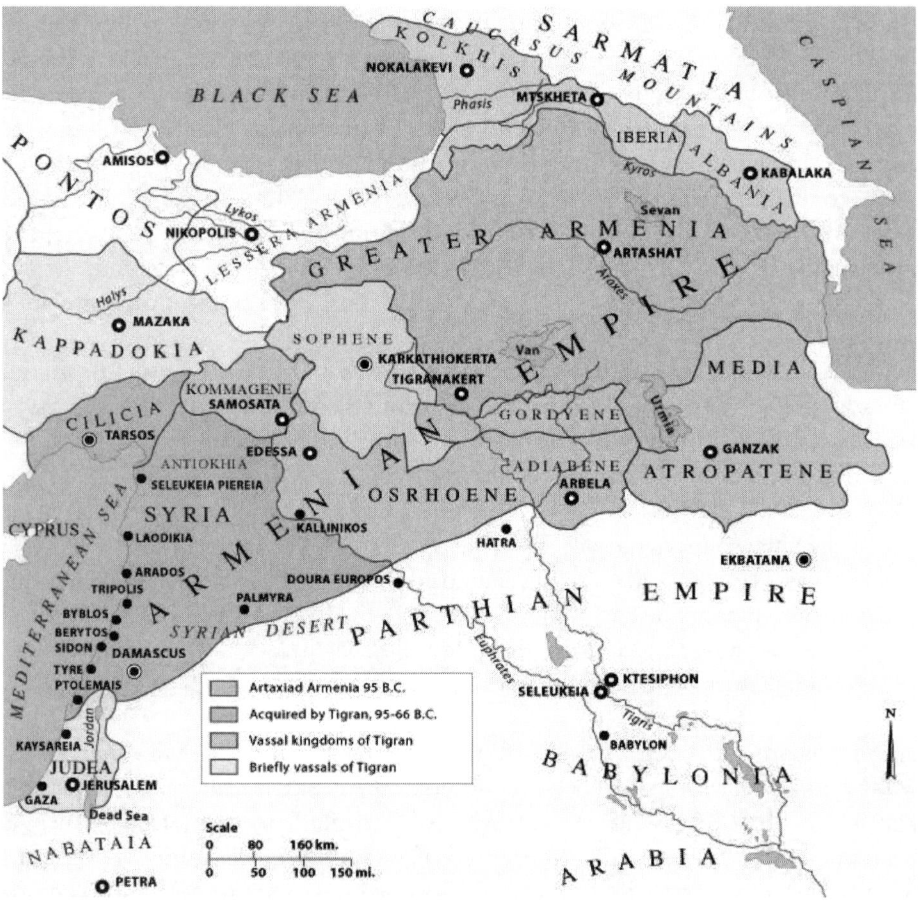

Fig 8.13
A map showing the kingdom of Osrhoene (the Kingdom of Edessa). In reality, this small kingdom stretched down at least as far as Palmyra and perhaps as far south as Pella in Perea, which lies to the south of the Sea of Galilee. Note the position of Samosata, just to the northwest of Edessa. Image courtesy of Wiki.

complete folly?

One suspects that Saul-Josephus is not being entirely honest here. Yes, the Syrian governor and the 10th legion did invade Commagene and occupy Samosata. And so Antiochus fled the region without so much as firing an arrow, because as Josephus records: 'No one of that country could so much as lift up his hand against (the Romans).' Quite obviously the prospect of any action from Samosata against the Romans was negligible, so why did Titus and the 10th legion attack this region?

The suspicion has to be that there was a marital link somewhere, between the royal houses of Commagene and Edessa. Rome was on the warpath against the royal house of Edessa, and so anyone linked with the Edessan monarchy would have come under suspicion. The story about Mara bar Seraphion appears to be closely linked with *History's* story about Seraphe-Nascien, the brother-in-law of King Evalach-Mordrain. And yet Mara bar Seraphion appears to have come from or been captured in Samosata, just to the northwest of Edessa. If we dare to link these two characters together (Seraphion and Seraphe), then of course the Romans would have wanted to capture and imprison 'Mara bar Seraphion-Seraphe-Nascien', because he was the brother-in-law of King Evalach-Mordrain, who was the son of King Izas-Jesus.

The Romans were busy hoovering up any princes who had links to the Edessan royal family. And while it may not have been prudent at this time to stroll into Palmyra or Edessa, because the Edessan monarchy still controlled a sizeable army, Titus could easily walk into Samosata and pluck a few princelings from the Edessan royal vine. Thus Seraphe-Nascien ended up in prison writing to his child from a Roman jail, just as Mara bar Seraphion was doing. In his letter, Mara bar Seraphion continues and says:

> What, again, are we to say concerning the delusion which has taken up its abode in the world? Both by reason of toil painful is the journey through it, and by its agitations are we, like a reed by the force of the wind, bent now in this direction, now in that ... Thus may you understand and see that we are walking under the guidance of delusion. (Letter of Mara bar Serapion)

The delusion mentioned here, just has to be a reference to the Simple Judaic crap that Josephus had been preaching to the people of Sarras (Palmyra). Both King Evalach-Mordrain and Prince Seraphe-Nascien said it was nonsense, and here Mara bar Seraphion claims it is all a delusion. Are they not talking about the same events here? Mara continues as says:

> Begin and tell us, O wisest of men, on which of his possessions a man can place reliance. Will you say so of abundance of riches? They are snatched away. Of

> fortresses? They are destroyed. Of cities? They are laid waste. Of greatness? It is brought down. Of magnificence? It is overthrown. Of beauty? It withers. Or of laws? They pass away. Or of poverty? It is despised. Or of children? They die. (Letter of Mara bar Serapion)

This is truly the lament of a defeated prince, who has lost everything he has worked for. Again this seems to be a commentary not simply about the fate of Samosata, but also the fate of the Kingdom of Edessa, which lay just 30 km away.

> For what benefit did the Athenians obtain by putting Socrates to death, seeing that they received as retribution for it famine and pestilence? Or the people of Samos by the burning of Pythagoras, seeing that in one hour the whole of their country was covered with sand? Or the Jews by the murder of their <u>Wise King</u>, seeing that from that very time their kingdom was driven away from them?
>
> The Athenians died by famine; and the people of Samos were covered by the sea without remedy; and the <u>Jews, brought to desolation and expelled from their kingdom</u>, are driven away into every land. (Letter of Mara bar Serapion)

What benefit did the Nazarene Edessans gain, by fomenting the Jewish Revolt? It is a moot point, for the Jews were all 'brought to desolation and

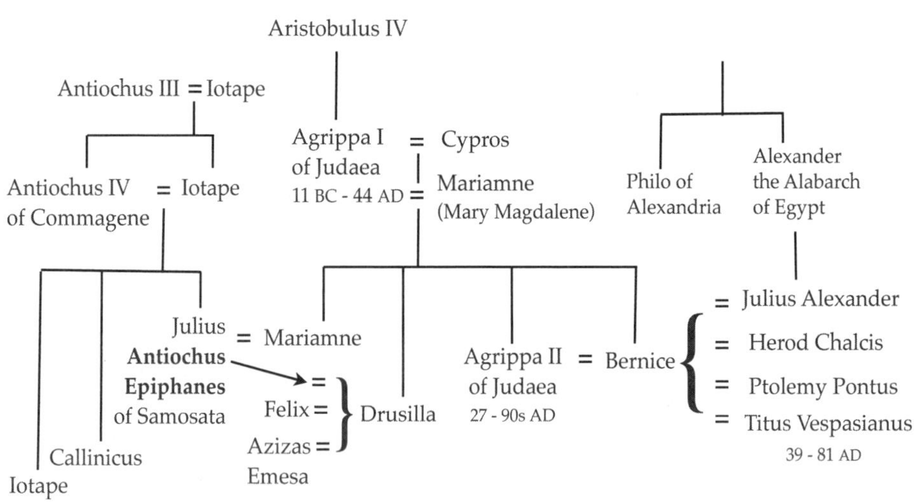

Fig 8.14
A genealogy of the interconnected royal families of Commagene and Judaea.

expelled from their kingdom', whether they were Nazarene Ebionites or not.

But for this avenue of research the benefit of this sad lament is considerable, because the Wise King mentioned here is a reference to the biblical King Jesus. But since we now know that King Jesus-Izas was actually King Izas-Manu of Edessa, and he was crucified after the Jewish Revolt, then we know that Mara bar Seraphion's letter was written after AD 70. And we also know that this must have been someone closely connected to the Edessan family, for nobody in Rome or the later Christian Church would have called Jesus the 'Wise King'.

So who was Mara bar Seraphe-Nascien, the prince who married Princess Flegetine, the sorceress sister of King Evalach and therefore the daughter of the biblical King Izas Jesus? Unfortunately we do not know much about this next generation after Jesus, because they have been deleted from just about every historical record, be that religious or secular. But bearing in mind the close connections between these royal houses we can be sure that Seraphe-Nascien was closely related the Edessan royal family, and since he was captured in Samosata he may well have been from the royal family of Commagene.

Britain and Wales

History then relates that the heroes of this story all end up in southern Britain, by various means both improbable and absurd. Joseph(us) (of Arimathaea), for instance, sails across the sea on his underpants. Once safely in Britain they set off to evangelise to the people, who are said to be both Pagan and Saracen. However, one cannot help feeling that this story is still relating events that occurred back in Judaea, and so the many battles against the 'Saracens' in Britain are probably relating stories about battles with the Romans.

Joseph(us) then receives news that the king of Hoselice had died, and the people were looking for a new king, 'for otherwise the land could quickly be devastated (without one)'. Hoselice is said to be the country of Wales in Britain, although that is not correct as we shall see. It is eventually decided that Josephus' brother, Galahad, would become the new king of Hoselice. So this Galahad was a son of Joseph(us) of Arimathaea and a brother of Josephus (the son).

Note that we are still in the 1st century here, and yet we already see the introduction of a character who appears to be identical to Sir Galahad, the saintly knight of the Round Table. And yet this is much the same as the story that we saw in *High History*, where Perceval was shown to be of the next generation to Joseph(us) of Arimathaea. See the idealised genealogy in fig 14.1. In addition, it appears that we have moved on a decade or so here.

In previous chapters Josephus (the son) was actually Saul-Josephus Flavius himself, a curious deceit that had been caused by the standard 40-year biblical chronological chasm. However, we appear to have moved on a few years and so these sons of Arimathaea called Josephus and Galahad may well be the real sons of Saul-Josephus Flavius. Although within real history the sons of Saul-Josephus are said to be called Hyrcanus, Justus and Agrippa.

The etymology of Hoselice is not given, and we shall see its true and surprising meaning in the next chapter. Unfortunately, the English translation of *History* leads us off on a tangent by saying that Hoselice was the original name for Wales, but *History* does not say 'Wales' at all. The trouble here is that the modern translators 'know' that Arthurian history is set in Britain and Wales, and so that is where they have sought to place it. But this is a huge and decidedly incorrect assumption that is guaranteed to lead us astray, which is why we have to distance ourselves from the consensus and instead look critically and rationally at the text.

Fig 8.15
The traditional image of a young redheaded Sir Galahad, as depicted by George Frederick Watts. Galahad was called the Red Knight because he wore a suit of red armour, just like Perceval in High History. But this redness is surely also a reference to the vivid red hair of both Perceval and Sir Galahad, who must be the same knight. This redness is also a reference to the redhead phenotype of the line of King David.

And if we take the dispassionate and logical approach we find that the text actually says 'Galles' rather than 'Wales', and this is something different entirely. Perhaps the first clue to Galles not being a reference to Wales is that the region was only called Galles after the coronation of Galahad, and so it is likely that the name was derived from Sir Galahad himself. In which case, the land of Hoselice was being renamed as the Land of Galahad:

> News came from the people in the kingdom of Hoselice, which was later called Wales (Galles), that they had no lord, for the king had recently died ... Once they had spoken, Josephus called his brother Galahad before him and said: 'Dear brother I am investing you with the kingdom of Hoselice, on the advice of the worthy men of this land ...' And Galahad knelt before him and received this gift. (History 38:274) (Author's brackets.)

So we are looking for a meaning for Galles, not Wales. But the original source for the name of Wales is an interesting topic in itself, for nobody seems to know for sure where this name came from. There are some who say it was derived from the Volcae or Walcae tribe of Celts, who are said to have arrived in this region in the 3rd century BC. Others say the name came from the deity Belenos, who is linked to the Syrian Baal, and Belenos became Vellaunos and eventually Wales, which all sounds rather convoluted and unconvincing. Still others say that the name was derived from the Germanic *walha* or *walsch* meaning 'foreigner', from which the Belgian Waloons were also named, and it was from this same root that the name for Wales was derived.

However, there is a much simpler source and translation than these wild suggestions. The fact of the matter is that he Latin, Spanish and French name for Wales is Galles, which only requires a 'g' to 'w' substitution to become Walles or Wales. And this is the very same consonant substitution that we saw previously, when Guillaume of Orange became William of Orange.

But was the Latin Galles a later derivation from Wales, or was it the original root for this name? Well, the French name Galles is said to be derived from Gallois, an original name for the Gaelic branch of the Celtic language. And the French *Center National de Ressources de Textualles et Lexicales* traces the name Gallois back to 1170 AD and the *Chronicle of Troyes.* And *History of the Grail* was written just a generation or two after that time. So the region called Wales was probably named after the Gallois language, in the same fashion that the Languedoc was named after its language. The nominative progression of both Galles and Guillaume are as follows:

Gallois	Guillaume
Galles	Guillaum
Walles	Willaum
Wales	William

However, even if Wales was named after the Gallois or Galles language, the proposed link between Galles-Wales and (Sir) Galahad is still not very convincing nor very illuminating. It is highly unlikely that a (Sir) Galahad who was the son of Saul-Joseph(us) (of Arimathaea) was ever given the throne of Wales in the 1st century, so why include this overtly false information? Is this merely further evidence that all of Arthurian history is entirely fictional? Yet we know that this common criticism is not correct, because we have already seen a great deal of reliable information and real history within these many manuscripts, and so the more likely and interesting alternative is that there has been yet another deliberate mistranslation here. Perhaps the text was not referring to Wales at all, but instead to something much more interesting and much more provocative.

IX

Ophites & Eunuchs

The previous chapter ended with a question-mark over the new appointment for (Sir) Galahad, because it is highly unlikely that he ever became a king of Wales in the 1st century. But if this is so then it is likely that the term Galles, as it is used in this context, has absolutely nothing to do with the Gallois-Galles-Celtic people or their language. Galles may well be a root word for Wales, but not in this case. In fact, the authors of *History* have merely used this as a convenient deflection, because they are unlikely to have wanted to divulge the true meaning of the names Galahad and Galles, and modern translators have gone along with this convenient confusion because they know no better.

For the true meaning of this quote we need to go back to the gospel's account of events in 1st century Judaea. (Sir) Galahad is the son of Saul-Joseph(us) (of Arimathaea), so this is a 1st century conundrum that requires a 1st century answer. And as we saw in the previous books, in the 1st century Jesus-Izas asked for his disciples to become eunuchs:

> All men cannot receive this saying, save they to whom it is given. For there are some eunuchs, which were so born from their mother's womb: and there are some eunuchs, which were made eunuchs of men: and there be eunuchs, which have made themselves eunuchs for the kingdom of heaven's sake. He that is able to receive it, let him receive it. (Math 19:11-12)

Jesus was asking 'those disciples who could receive it' to cut off their testicles and become eunuchs. This might seem like a surprising request for Jesus to make, and a complete diversion from the linguistic problem just posed, but bear with this explanation for a little bit longer, because there is a surprising link between Arthurian and Gospel history here.

What we need to do, in order to see this connection, is to revise and recall the true context of the New Testament story. Jesus was not a pauper carpenter, he was a prince of Egypt and Persia who had been exiled to Edessa in northern Syria. And all the great royal houses of both Egypt and Persia employed eunuchs as keepers of the king's bedchamber, for that is what eunuch means - *eune secho* ευνη σχεω or bed keeper. And the gospel verse just quoted strongly implies that Jesus also wanted some of his disciples to become eunuchs.

Making sure that only eunuchs entered the king's bedchamber was probably a prudent measure to guarantee the royal line, which is probably why this tradition started. But this access to the king's private chambers also meant that eunuchs often became the king's councilors and advisors, and therefore rose to positions of great power and influence. But eunuchs did not only become the king's courtiers, they also became the nation's high priests too. If we travel back to the lands of northern Syria, where these gospel stories were first devised, the primary goddess of Edessa was Atargatis, whose consort was Hadad. Like most goddesses, Atargatis was a fertility goddess and in Palmyra she was known as Ataratheh, a name which may have been derived from Ashtoreth and Astarte, who were both manifestations of the Egyptian Isis. And so Atargatis was another incarnation of the Egyptian Ast or Isis, the primary fertility goddess of the ancient world.

However, in Rome the syncretism or merging of the gods became an essential political tool, when other cultures were being absorbed into the Empire, and so Atargatis was linked to and became synonymous with the great Mother-Earth goddess, Cybele-Rhea (Kybele-Rhea or Mother Kybele Μητηρ Κυβελη). Cybele was also the protector of cities, which is why she wears the walls of a city as her crown, as did Atargatis on the coins of Edessa. Readers may see some Edessan coins labeled as depicting Tyche-Fortuna, but if Cybele-Atargatis was the patron deity of Edessa then this is likely to be an image of Cybele rather than Tyche.

Anyway, the point of this diversion into Syrian goddesses, is that the consort of Cybele was Attis, who had been castrated for various reasons. In honour of the castration of Attis, the high priests of Cybele were likewise castrated, and became eunuchs. So there is an obvious link here between the priests of Cybele being eunuchs and the disciples of Jesus being eunuchs. However, rather than this being incidental to Arthurian history, in the light of all the evidence presented thus far in the *King Jesus Trilogy* this cult of castration has to be a central component within this unfolding drama. King Jesus-Izas has been strongly linked to King Arthur; King Jesus-Izas was the

Fig 9.1 A coin of Cybele-Atargatis as patron goddess of Edessa, wearing the protective city-wall crown that she shared with Tyche. The bust is of Gordian III, the Roman emperor at the time this Edessan coin was minted.

king of Edessa; the patron deity of Edessa was Cybele-Atargatis; the priests of Cybele were castrated eunuchs; and in the previous quote we see that Jesus was likewise asking his priestly disciples to become eunuchs. There is a direct and unmistakable connection between all of these events.

So now at last we can tie all the lose ends of this account from *History* together, and we can begin to understand what the author was really talking about when he mentions Galles or Wales. The 'kingdom' that Galahad was about to become the leader of was called Hoselice, and it may be surprising to learn that this Arthurian name was actually derived from the Aramaic *hosawrice* הסרים meaning 'the eunuch'. Note the 'r' to 'l' transliteration once more. And this is exactly how the eunuchs mentioned in Isaiah 56:3 and Kings 2:23:11 are spelt. And so Holselice-Hosawrice was not a reference to Wales, it actually referred to the Kingdom of Eunuchs, and there is a good reason for Arthurian history mentioning this title.

We then learned in *History* that the lands of Holselice-Hosawrice were renamed as Galles, when Galahad became its leader or king. But again this name had nothing to do with a country called Wales. Instead, it was derived from the eunuch priests of Cybele who were called the Galli, Gallus or Gallae, depending on what gender these eunuchs were considered to be. So if Sir Galahad was being inaugurated as the king of Galles-Hoselice, then he was actually being crowned as the new leader of the Galli priesthood. Yes, it would appear that Sir Galli-had, the son of Saul-Joseph(us) (of Arimathaea) had accepted Jesus' invitation in Math 19:11-12 to become a castrated Galli priest of Cybele. In fact, since he was said to be the king of the Galles, then Sir Galahad must have become the high priest of the Galles.

While it would have been impossible for Saul-Joseph(us) to have become a Galli priest of Cybele, because he detested circumcision let alone castration, it is entirely possible that his son did. The members of this family were not all cut from the same piece of cloth. Remember that in *King Jesus*, a brother of Saul-Joseph(us) was positively identified as Matthias Barnabas, and yet Acts of the Apostles says of Saul and Barnabas:

> And Barnabas determined to take with them John, whose surname was Mark. But Saul thought not good to take him with them ... and the contention was so sharp between them, that they went their separate ways. And so Barnabas took Mark and sailed unto Cyprus, while Saul chose Silas. (Acts 15:37-40)

Although Saul-Josephus was a committed Romophile and semi-Gentile who hated castration, in part because castration was illegal in the Roman Empire, his brother Matthew had a different view entirely. Matthew was still a committed Nazarene, and it was the Nazarene Church of Jesus and James that was urging its members to become Galli eunuchs. And this is why Jesus-Izas was asking his disciples to become eunuchs, as we have just seen. Furthermore, we also know from Acts 1:26 that Matthias Barnabas was elected to become the new disciple, after Judas Iscariot left the Church for whatever reason. So just like Galahad, Matthias had also become elected to the priesthood (had become a disciple). Although do bear in mind that Matthias would have been of the previous generation to Galahad.

But (Sir) Galahad was not simply being promoted to the position of disciple or priest of the Nazarene Galli, he was being crowned as the new king or high priest of the Galli, and that elevated position is reflected in his new title, Galahad. The suffix to this name or title is *had* and there is only one real meaning for the Aramaic *hadd* הדר, and that is 'noble' or 'mighty'. In which case, the new title for Sir Gala-had גליל הדר would refer to the 'Great Galli' or the 'High Priest of the Galli'. This is why Galahad was known as the purest of all the knights of the Round Table and was the only knight who could sit in the Siege Perilous, the Perilous Seat. Galahad was virginal and pure, because he had set aside all earthly desires to become a castrated Nazarene monk, and the high priest of all the Galli eunuchs in Syrio-Judaea.

In addition to all of this, there is also the similar position and role of Sir Perceval to consider here. Despite what *Lancelot* and *Quest* may say, it was not only Sir Galahad who sat in the Perilous Seat, so too did Sir Perceval, as we saw previously in both *Perceval* and *Merlin Grail*. And since *Perceval* and *Merlin Grail* never mention Galahad at all, then Perceval is not simply being equated with Galahad he appears to be one and the same person. Similarly,

Quest says that of all the knights of the Round Table, only Galahad and Perceval remained virginal, and so only Galahad and Perceval were pure enough to become a Galli priest. Which is why when Perceval was about to be seduced by the devil in the form of a beautiful woman, he took his sword and wounded himself in his thighs, as we saw in Chapter VI. (Quest 32:110.) In effect, Perceval had just done what all the Galli do - he had whipped himself into a frenzy during a festival and castrated himself.

In addition, *Perceval, Merlin Grail* and *Quest* all pointedly name Perceval as 'Perceval the Welshman'. Once again this title has nothing to do with the country of Wales and everything to do with Perceval's true title. In the original Norman French, before the modern translators got hold of it and mangled it, this title was actually 'Perceval the Galles'. And since we now know that the Galles title actually refers to the Galli priesthood, then Perceval was really being called 'Perceval the Galli High Priest' or 'Perceval the Galahad'. In which case, Sir Perceval and Sir Galahad just have to be the same person, and 'Galahad' was merely the new title that was bestowed upon Perceval during his inauguration ceremony.

This rather novel and perhaps startling proposition is confirmed in both *Lancelot* and *Quest*. In the former of these two manuscripts we see a similar confusion between Sir Lancelot and Sir Galahad, with some references saying that Galahad was the son of Lancelot, while others say that Lancelot was called Galahad. The explanation for this confusion is that Lancelot was originally known as Lancelot the Galahad, but he lost the Galahad title when he had an affair with Queen Gwenevere, and the title was given to his son instead. And in this account Galahad was the son of Lancelot, not Joseph(us). (Lancelot V:149:211) And according to *Lancelot* and *Quest* this illicit and traitorous affair was begun (in his heart) on the very day that Lancelot was made a knight, and so he could only have held the Galahad title for a single day. (Quest 36:126).*

This confirms that Galahad was merely a title for the Galli high priest, and so there would have been many knights through the generations who were given the Galahad title. And this also generates a confusion for the real name of Perceval-Galahad's father:

* There is a great synergy here with High Priest Joseph-Jonathan who also became high priest for just one day, and was replaced by Matthias ben Theophilus. However, this was supposed to have happened in the AD 30s rather than the AD 60s or 70s. Has there been another chronological dislocation here? See *King Jesus* Chapter XI for details.

Son	**Father**
Galahad 1	Lancelot-Galahad
Galahad 2	Joseph(us) Arimathaea
Perceval-Galahad	Alain li Gros

Again we see that the conflation of Perceval and Galahad has generated a confusion between Lancelot, Alain and Joseph(us), who all appear to be the father of Perceval the Galahad, and this is something we shall return to later. But whoever the real father of Perceval-Galahad was, 'Galahad' must have been a formal title for the most virtuous, virginal and thence castrated knight, who spurned all sexual desires in order to become the Galli-had high priest of the Galli-Hoselice eunuchs. As Jesus-Izas said: 'he who is able to receive it, let him receive it.' But Lancelot was not very pure and virginal, and so he lost his title before his name-plate was even dry. (The knights of the Round Table all had their names written at their respective places.)

There are even some extant descriptions of these Galli ceremonies. Lucian, for instance, not only confirms that Galli priests were castrated but also describes the castration festival:

> On these days, the Galli are made. While the rest are playing flutes and performing the rites, frenzy comes upon many ... he throws off his clothes, rushes to the center with a great shout and takes up a sword and immediately castrates himself. Then (the Galli) rushes through the city holding in his hands the parts he has cut off. He takes female clothing and women's adornment from whatever house he throws these (testicles) into. [2]

This rite of castration with a sword gives us another direct link with Arthurian history. Not only have we seen how Perceval castrated himself with a sword, but one of the main titles in Arthurian history was the Wounded King, who was similarly wounded (castrated) in the thighs. So the high priest of the Galli was obviously the Arthurian Wounded King, who is normally conflated with the Fisher King and sometimes with the Holy Hermit. The Wounded King had also been injured by a sword or a lance in both of his thighs, and in many manuscripts the Wounded Fisher King is described as being old and infirm, and desperately looking for a successor. And so the Wounded Fisher King must have been the previous castrated Galli high priest, before Perceval the Galahad became the new (castrated) Fisher King. *Merlin Grail* says of this transfer of power, between the old and new Fisher Kings:

> Bron did as instructed and taught Perceval the sacred words that Joseph had taught him, which I cannot - and must not - tell you ... Then the aged Bron placed

> the vessel (the Holy Grail) in Perceval's hands ...
>
> And with that Merlin took Blaise and led him to the house of the (new) Fisher King, whose name was Perceval, and there he stayed in the company of the Grail. (Merlin Grail p155-156) (Author's brackets.)

Bron or Hebron was the grandfather of Perceval and so the title appears to have jumped a generation, from Bron to Perceval. While it is possible that a mistake has been made here, we shall see evidence in Chapter XIV that Robert de Boron may be substantially correct, because Alain only became the Grail Guardian for just one day. Whether this was a reference to Bron or Alain, the old Fisher King not only transferred the Holy Grail to his (grand) son, Perceval-Galahad, he also bequeathed him the secrets of the Grail. So it was Sir Perceval the Galahad who became the next Guardian of the Grail. And as the account of Perceval's castration in *History* makes clear, it is fairly obvious that Sir Perceval the Galahad also became the next Wounded King, the next castrated Galli high priest. And so the references to Holselice and Galles have absolutely nothing to do with a principality called Wales in Britain, and everything to do with the cult of the Galli eunuch priesthood in 1st century Syria and Judaea. [3]

The prospect of Sir Perceval-Galahad being an effeminate eunuch high priest, may seem quite fanciful. These were knights in shining armour; brave warriors who lowered their lances and charged fearlessly into battle no matter what the odds. So how could Sir Perceval-Galahad be a mincing eunuch, parading around in a pretty laced dress? Surely this entire argument is completely misguided? Think again. The fact that some of these knights were eunuchs who dressed as women, did not mean they could not also be fearsome knights of the Round Table. Saul-Josephus Flavius gives us a good account of the siege of Jerusalem during the Jewish Revolt, and then he says of the ruthless and much feared Zealots:

> These Galileans ... devoured what spoils they had taken, together with their blood, and indulged themselves in feminine wantonness ... they <u>decked their hair, and put on women's garments,</u> and were smeared with ointments; and that they might appear very comely, <u>they had paints under their eyes, and imitated not only the ornaments, but also the lusts of women</u> ... (But) while their faces looked like the faces of women, they killed with their right hands; and while their gait was effeminate, they attacked men and became warriors, and drew their swords from under their finely dyed cloaks, and ran every body through whom they alighted upon. (Josephus, War 4:9:10)

Here is the other side to these Jekyll and Hyde Galli priests. Note that these revolutionary Zealots are being called Galileans, and just like the Galli eunuchs of Syria they wore women's clothes, ornaments and make-up, and pranced around wiggling their hips and pouting their lips like a provocative and lustful woman. But then they drew their swords from under their ladies cloaks and ruthlessly slaughtered their enemies. Now that must have been a bit of a surprise to some of their victims.

It has been conveniently assumed that the Galilean title was derived from the Zealots' main base of operation, which is assumed to have been Galilee גליל to the west of the Sea of Galilee. But here we see that these effeminate Galilean Zealot warriors wore women's clothing and make up, and this can only be because they were Galli eunuchs. Likewise Jesus was often called Jesus the Galilean (Ieusous Galilaios Ιησους Γαλιλαιος), while the Nazarene Ebionites were also known as Galileans. Again, this does not refer to Jesus being born in Galilee or the Nazarenes being based in Galilee, instead it refers to King Jesus-Izas being the leader of the Galli Sect. And Jesus may well have been a Galli priest himself, for there seems to have been no prohibition on fathering a large family and then becoming a Galli eunuch in later in life. Which may be why later traditions have assumed that Jesus was a lifelong celibate. And if King Jesus-Izas was a Galli eunuch and a Fisher of Men, then there has to be a strong connection between Jesus and the Wounded Fisher King of Arthurian history. This possibility will be explored again later.

Perhaps readers can now see why is was suggested earlier that the city of Sarras (Palmyra) was named after the Aramaic *saras* סרים meaning 'eunuch'. The Galilean Galli priests were not simply based in Galilee, as the gospels try to imply, they also lived in the East, and one of their centers of influence was obviously Palmyra 'beyond the Jordan' while another was Edessa 'beyond the Euphrates'. But as we saw in the previous chapter, *History* relates that Joseph(us) of Arimathaea embarked upon a political and evangelical mission towards the Euphrates and to the city of Sarras (Palmyra), where he persuaded King Evalach-Mordrain to become a Simple Judaic 'Christian'.

History then narrates one of these absurd magical journeys, where Joseph(us) travels with 150 of his followers across the seas to 'Britain' while standing upon his undergarments, and it was only after this magical journey to 'Britain' that Sir Perceval-Galahad arrived in the Kingdom of Holselice or Wales, which was renamed as the Kingdom of Galles after he became its king. However, in *Quest*, Sir Perceval the Galahad did not become the king of Holselice-Wales, he became the king of Sarras instead. Sir Perceval-Galahad was on one of the many ships in these stories, which conveniently and magically transport the knights across land and sea to their next adventure. But the ship finally stopped and:

> When Galahad awoke, he saw before him the city of Sarras, and heard a voice which said: ... 'carry this silver table (the table of the Grail) into the city' ... When King Escorant (of Sarras) was buried, the residents of the city did not know who could be their (next) king ... They did as the voice directed and chose Galahad to be their king, despite his reluctance. When they placed the crown on his head, he was dismayed. But he realised that he must accede to their wishes, otherwise they would kill him. (Quest 84:275, 85:277) (Author's brackets.)

This is a much more likely and realistic version of this story. Sir Perceval-Galahad was not about to be become the king of Holselice or Wales, he was instead going to crowned as the king of Holselice-Sarras in Syria. And although it may not look or sound like it in the English translation, in the Aramaic Hoselice and Sarras are exactly the same name. The only difference is that Hoselice is prefixed by the definite article 'the', just as it sometimes is in the Torah:

Sarras	סרים	Eunuch
Hoselice	הסרים	The Eunuch *

Which again demonstrates that these texts were originally written in Aramaic, because this close linguistic connection between Sarras and Hoselice can only work in the Aramaic. It also demonstrates how locations and eras can be conveniently covered up in the Norman or English translations of this ancient story. A pretence has been made in *History* that Hoselice was actually Wales (Galles) in Britain, and yet this linguistic connection clearly demonstrates that Hoselice was actually Sarras: the city of Palmyra, on the road to the Euphrates.

Thus these two names are not simply the same in Aramaic, they also confirm the analysis being made in this book. Galahad (the son of Arimathaea) was being made the king of Galles-Hoselice, according to *History*; while Sir Galahad (the son of Lancelot) was being made the king of Sarras, according to *Quest*. But since Sarras and Hoselice refer to the same 'City of the Eunuchs' we can see that there was only ever one Perceval-Galahad, and he became the king and Galli high priest of Hoselice-Sarras in the AD 70s. But rather than being overjoyed about his new priestly and

* In Aramaic there is no gap between the words, and so it is spelt as *hosarice* or *hosalice*. Note also the 'r' to 'l' transposition, which is very common in these texts between Aramaic and the Latin languages.

royal status, Perceval-Galahad was very sad and only agreed to accept the royal crown on pain of death. But why the extreme reluctance? What was the problem with becoming the king of a great and wealthy city?

The obvious answer is that Sir Perceval-Galahad was not simply being crowned as the king of the City of Holselice-Sarras, he was also becoming the high priest of the Church of Holselice-Sarras - the high priest of the Galli-Eunuchs. In which case, his opulent and elaborate coronation ceremony would not only entail a crown being placed upon his ginger hair, it would also entail his ginger balls being cut off. It is no wonder that Sir Perceval-Galahad was a very reluctant monarch and only agreed to his enthronement because the alternative was death. Perhaps this is why Chretien depicted Perceval as being an ignorant country bumpkin in *Perceval,* because he had no idea what he was getting involved in.

The end result of this long diversion into the bizarre cult of the Galilean eunuchs, is that all the classical attempts at translations for the city of Sarras are incorrect. In reality Holselice, Galles and Sarras all refer to the same place and the same title, because they are all closely associated with the Galli eunuch priesthood and they all mean 'eunuch' in the Aramaic. And there may even be a nominative progression between all of these names and titles:

Name or title	Meaning	Reference
Ho-Sarrice	the eunuch	Aramaic, Torah
Hol-Salice	Wales *	History of Grail
Sarrice	eunuch	Aramaic, Torah
Sarras	Syrian city	History of Grail
Sallice	eunuch	'r' to 'l' transposition
Gallice	eunuch priest	's' to 'g' transposition
Galles	Wales *	History of Grail
Galles	eunuch priest	History of Grail

Naassene Ophites

These Galilean Zealot eunuchs were not just known as the Galli or Galles, for they had another well-known title in this era, and that was the Naassene-

* Both Ho-Salice and Gallice (Galles) were said to refer to the same location - Wales. And so Salice and Galles are firmly linked together, and the 's' to 'g' transposition is fully justified.

Ophites. This was the 'Serpent Cult' that venerated a triad of gods led by an androgynous deity known as the Primaeval Adam or Adamas. The Naassene-Ophite creed has been almost wiped from history, and we only know of their existence because some venerable Christian scholars like Irenaeus and Hippolytus tried to refute their doctrines, and in doing so preserved some of them for posterity. Most of the following comes from Hippolytus' *Philosophumena,* also known as the *Refutation of all Heresies*. Francis Legge, the translator of *Philosophumena* says of the Naassene-Ophite creed:

> The Ophites admitted the truth of the gospel narrative and asserted the existence of a supreme being endowed with the attributes of both sexes, and manifesting himself by the means of a deity called his son, who was identified with the masculine and feminine aspects of his father. This Triad the Ophites called the First Man, Second Man and the Holy Spirit. The planetary worlds were created by an inferior intermediary power called Sophia or Wisdom (a demiurge), and her son Jaldabaoth, who is said to be the god of the Jews. (Hippolytus, Refutation of Heresies note 1 p118 or n138.) (Author's brackets.)

Here we see the standard Triad or Trinity of later Christian thought, with the primary god being an androgynous being who had begotten a son and a daughter from himself. And it does makes more sense to have a singular primary deity who is androgynous, rather than the Judaeo-Christian assertion that he is male, especially if he has divine children. Below this Triad or Trinity, there are several lesser demiurge gods, two of which are called Sophia and her son Jaldabaoth. Hippolytus of Rome goes on to say of the Naassene's primary deity:

> And this man is a hermaphrodite, and is called by them Adamas. And many and various hymns are made to him ... These are the heads of very numerous discourses which (the Naassene) asserts James the brother of the Lord handed down to Mariamne. (Hippolytus, Refutation of Heresies, V:6 or n139)

This is not the Adam from the Book of Genesis but the Primaeval or Primordial Adam - the Protoanthropos (the First Man), the 'supreme being' head of the Naassene-Ophite Trinity. This Adam is the equivalent of the Egyptian Atum, who inseminated and created the lower-order demiurge creator-demigods, who in turn created the world and mankind. And the similar name might suggest a common origin for this Naassene mythology. Hippolytus sees Adamas as a counterpart of the Greek Attis, the eunuch partner of Cybele, even though Attis was only a minor godlet rather than being the great creator god. This is presumably because Attis is similarly androgynous (actually a eunuch). And while traditional history does not make this connection, it has been suggested in the previous books in this series that the concept and history of a Primaeval androgyne (or maybe a eunuch) was also based upon the history of Pharaoh Akhenaton.

As we saw in *Eden in Egypt*, it was the history of Akhenaton and Nefertiti that was the foundation for the Torah's mythology of Adam and Eve, while Akhenaton's Hymn to the Aten became the basis for the Genesis creation myth. But if this is true, then Pharaoh Akhenaton is directly comparable with the biblical Adam, and may even have even been called 'Adam' by his followers. But if it was known that Akhenaton was regularly portrayed as an androgynous eunuch, it is not so surprising that a tradition evolved that said the First Adam or Primaeval Adam was androgynous. Hippolytus says that Adamas is masculo-feminine, and then goes on to describe Attis, who he claims to be a Greek equivalent of Adamas, as being:

> For Attis is castrated, he says. That is, he has changed over from the earthly parts of the lower creation to the eternal substance on high, where, he says, there is nether male nor female, but a new creature, a new Man who is masculo-feminine. (Hippolytus, Refutation of Heresies, V:7 or n146)

By becoming castrated, Attis had presumably joined company with the greater gods in the heavens above, and become masculo-feminine. So the Primaeval Adamas was not a hermaphrodite, it was more accurately described as androgynous with indeterminate characteristics indicating both a

Fig 9.2
Pharaoh Akhenaton portrayed as an androgynous eunuch or hijra. Did the concept of a Primaeval Adam come from these sexless depictions of Akhenaton.

male and female gender, or perhaps sexless with no gender characteristics at all. But is that not what we also see in the statuary of Akhenaton - a new creature that is 'neither male nor female, but rather masculo-feminine'? Look at the wide hips, slight bust, lack of genitals, plus the masculine beard. Is Pharaoh Akhenaton not being depicted here as the androgynous Primaeval Adamas of the Naassene Ophite creed?

Since John the Baptist, Simon Magus and King Izas-Jesus all studied in Alexandria, in Egypt, it is entirely possible that the traditions of the Naassene-Ophites came from Egypt. And we shall see more evidence for this claim shortly. And who within Egyptian history would be the most likely founder of an androgynous masculo-feminine creed? Well, the Egyptian monarch who has weaved his way in and out of the narrative within all of these books, is Pharaoh Akhenaton. It was Akhenaton and his brother Tuth-Moses (Aaron and his brother Moses) who led the second Israelite Exodus out of Egypt, and it was Pharaoh Akhenaton who created modern monotheism, based upon his Aten god, which then became the Israelite god Adon (the alternate name for Yahweh). And so the most likely founder of the Naassene-Ophite creed is Akhenaton himself.

There is even a direct link between the names of these two deities. It has been positively demonstrated in the previous books that the Aten god of Akhenaton became the Adon god of the Torah, the name that is translated in English Bibles as 'Lord God'. The 't' consonant often becomes a 'd' when translating between Egyptian and Aramaic, and so Aton can become Adon. This transposition can even happen just within the Egyptian language, where the Aten god is sometimes spelt as Adjon  instead of Aten . And yet it is only one step further to proceed from Adon אדן to Adam אדם. And this slight transcription error is all the more likely, considering that in the Egyptian the Sun-god can be separated into opposite aspects of rising (Ten 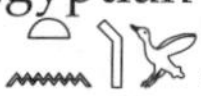) and setting (Tem ). And we know from the Hymn to the Aten that the Aten was generally considered to be a god of the sunrise, and so we possibly see here the two diametrically opposed aspects of the Aten-Aden-Eden (sunrise) and the Atum-Adem-Adam (sunset).

But Akhenaton was not the creator-god himself, as that role was taken by the heavenly Aten, who was depicted as a sun-disk. In which case, perhaps there were two Adams within the Naassene Triad or Trinity. The Primaeval Adamas is likely to have been the Egypto-Judaic god Atum-Aten-Adon, but the son of the Primaeval Adamas may have also been called Adamas or Adam. And so we see the Egyptian first son of god being called Akhenaton, and the biblical first son of god being called Adam. And we know that Akhenaton was sometimes known as Adam, because he and Nefertiti are depicted naked within the Garden of Aten-Aden, just as Adam and Eve are depicted naked within the Garden of Aden-Eden. And since

Akhenaton's god Aten-Aden is spelt with the softer reed-glyph, this name is much more likely to have been pronounced as Eyden or Eden.

And so Akhenaton and Nefertiti, as the son and daughter of the Primaeval Adamas, had themselves depicted in the appearance and image of Adamas. And for whatever reason, they thought that the Primaeval Adamas had not only androgynous features, but grossly extended bodily features too. Thus we see both Akhenaton and Nefertiti with thick thighs, wide hips, tiny waists, a slight bust and an elongated head with heavily distorted facial features.

These curious bodily features were not caused by a disease, as many Egyptologists have suggested. Although many of the Amarna royalty did have conical skulls through cranial binding in infancy, as the CAT-scans of Pharaoh Tutankhamen demonstrate, they did not have distorted facial features. There are many sculptures of Akhenaton, Nefertiti and their daughters that depict them as being entirely normal, and so we know that these distorted features were merely an artistic fashion. But why did Akhenaton order his artists and sculptors to depict such misshapen bodies and features? The answer once more, is that this is what the Primaeval Adamas was supposed to have looked like. The Primaeval Adamas was a god, and thus not of this Earth. It was a bipedal humanoid creature for sure, but quite different in many other respects to humankind, and Pharaoh Akhenaton wanted to recreate those peculiar features in his sculptures.

Fig 9.3
Pharaoh Akhenaton and one of his daughters, praying to the Aten-Adamas (Atemas). Note their distended bodies and features.

And while this diversion

into Egyptian history may seem strange, do remember that in the previous quotes Hippolytus said that these traditions and doctrines were handed down from James to Mariamne. And this just has to be a reference to James the brother of Jesus, and Mary Magdalene. Since this assertion is rather heretical, the *Catholic Encyclopaedia* tries to deflect this by saying that this Mariamne was an unknown acolyte of James the Just. But since we know from the Nag Hammadi Gnostic gospels that Mary Magdalene became the leader of the Nazarene Church after the crucifixion of Jesus, this Mariamne just has to be a reference to Mary Magdalene herself. And the Nassene Ophite traditions that Jesus-Izas handed down to Mary Magdalene, included the history of the Primaeval Adam and the creed of the Galli eunuchs.

Fig 9.4
Portrait of Pharaoh Akhenaton showing his deliberately distorted facial features. This is what the Primaeval Adamas is supposed to have looked like. Image from the Neues Museum, Berlin.

And it was not just the 1st century disciples of Jesus and James who became Galli eunuchs, so too did Emperor Elagabalus of Rome in the early 3rd century AD, as was explained within previous books in this Trilogy. And this demonstrates that he too was a Naassene Galli high priest. But Elagabalus came from Syria, and so it is likely that he was raised into exactly these same traditions, some 150 years after the Galli disciples of Jesus and James.

Hippolytus then says that the Naassene were also well acquainted with the Egyptian cult of Isis and Osiris, and gives a good summary of the loss of Osiris' penis. But since both Jesus and John the Baptist studied in Alexandria, it is not so surprising that they should have been familiar with these Osirian fertility rites.[4] The Naassene Ophite creed then makes a curious pun on the name for the Primaeval Adam and says that the Adamas was the 'stone that became the corner-stone, the head of the corner'. This quote is taken from both Psalms 118:22 and Matthew 21:42, and may be a play on words between *eben* אבן and *eden* אדן meaning 'stone' and 'foundation' respectively. More importantly, this is also a direct reference to Jesus-Izas, who was also called the 'rejected stone' who became the 'head of the corner', and so the Naassene Ophites were obviously trying to make a direct link here, between the Primaeval Adam and Jesus-Izas.

The serpent

And finally, we come to the true meaning of the Naassene Ophite serpent symbolism, a meaning that has never been decyphered before but explains all we need to know about this sect and its close links with the Egypto-Judaic Nazarene sect of Jesus and James. This section in *Refutation of Heresies* first describes the great mother goddess, Cybele, and remember that Cybele-Atargatis was the patron goddess of Edessa. It then appears to describe a class of initiate who remain as virgins and 'perform as if they were castrated Galli priests', but were not actually eunuchs. The paragraph then says:

> It is time to approach ... those who have dared sing the praises of the Serpent ... Therefore the priests and chief of the doctrine were the first who were called Naassenes, for the Serpent is called thus in the Hebrew tongue. Afterwards they called themselves Gnostics.
>
> But they worship none other than the Naas, calling themselves the Naassenes. But Naas is the serpent, from whom he says all the temples are called Naos ... But they say the serpent is the watery substance ... and no being ... can be made without him ... And he is good and contains all things within him as in the horn of the one-horned bull (the cornucopia) ... as if he went forth from Eden and cut himself into four heads. (Hippolytus, Refutation of Heresies, V:6 or n139; V:9 or n178) (Author's brackets.)

So the Gnostics were the Naassene, the sect who used the serpent as their primary symbol, and they appear to be closely linked to the Nazarene. And there is a nice allegorical story in the Talmud that demonstrates that the Nazarene leaders of the Jewish Revolt utilised this same serpent symbolism.

The following conversation is between Rabbi Johanan ben Zakkai and Vespasian in the final months of the Jewish Revolt. Johanan ben Zakkai is an unknown rabbi who became the leader of all Judaism after the Jewish Revolt, and for many reasons he has already been closely linked with Saul-Josephus. Anyway, Johanan ben Zakkai had just escaped from the siege of Jerusalem by pretending to be dead in a coffin. But commander Vespasian chides him for not coming over to the Romans sooner, and their conversation is as follows:

> (Johannan said) 'I did not come to you till now, (because) the *biryoni* among us did not let me.' Vespasian said to him: 'If there is a jar of honey round which a serpent is wound, would they not break the jar to get rid of the serpent?' Johannan could give no answer. But ... he ought to have said to (Vespasian): 'He should take a pair of tongs and grip the snake and kill it, and leave the jar intact.' (Gittin 56b) (Author's brackets.)

As usual the Talmud is all written in code, but thankfully this particular cypher is quite easy to solve. In this quote Vespasian is saying that if a serpent had a jar of honey in its grip, you might be forced to break the jar in order to kill the snake. And if we decypher this allegorical statement, the jar of honey is obviously a reference to Jerusalem, while the snakes that were holding it in their grip were the Nazarene Zealot Galileans. The *birioni* is a common reference for the Zealots. Vespasian is excusing himself for destroying Jerusalem, by saying that he had been forced to break the jar of honey (Jerusalem) in order to kill the serpent (the Naassene-Nazarene rebels). And this is a positive confirmation that the Nazarene were known in this era as Naassene-Ophite 'serpents'. But the advice of the sages in later years, was that Vespasian should have used a pair of tongs to kill the serpent (the Nazarene-Naassene-Ophites), while leaving the jar of honey (Jerusalem) intact.

Then we come to the description of Naas and Eden, in the previous quote from *Refutation of Heresies*. So why is this sacred serpent-snake of the Naassene said to be a watery substance, rather than something desiccated and scaly? The surprising answer to this lies in the description that this serpent was divided into four heads or branches - because this is exactly the same as the Torah's description of the river that ran through Eden. Quite obviously, the Naass-Nachash serpent of the Naassene-Nazarene Sect was not a small reptile, but a vast serpentine river - the very same river that ran through Eden and was then divided into four heads. The Book of Genesis says of this great river:

> And a river went out of Eden to water the garden; and from thence it was parted, and became into four heads. (Genesis 2:10)

And just in case the reader did not understand this obvious connection, *Refutation of Heresies* goes on to describe the four branches of the Eden river, just as they are given in Genesis. So the Naassene snake was not the snake that tempted Eve, it was the serpentine snake of the great river that ran through Eden. But what no other historian or theologian had understood before now, is where that river was really located and therefore what form of belief system the Naassene doctrine was founded upon.

The true location for the river of Eden was exposed many years ago in *Eden in Egypt*. There is only one river in this region that runs through a garden and then is divided into four heads or branches, and that is the Nile. The Nile ran past the Garden of the Aten or Eten (the Garden of Eden), which was located at Akhenaton's capital city of Amarna, and when the river reached Giza it was parted into four heads or branches. Note that the real Garden of Eden was not simply the strip-oasis of the Nile valley, it was more specifically the garden dedicated to Pharaoh Akhenaton's god, the Aten or Eten. Thus the Garden of Eden was actually the Garden of Eten, the garden dedicated to the god Aten or Eten.

From this novel explanation it can now be seen that: Eden was in Egypt; the Eden river was the Nile; and so the Naassene 'snake' was actually a reference to the river Nile. And the Nile does indeed look like an Egyptian cobra, with its long sinusoidal body winding through the eastern Sahara desert, and the flared delta region in the north representing the head of this terrestrial cobra. Which is why the Naassene creed then goes on to identify the four branches (or heads) of the Eden river with a head:

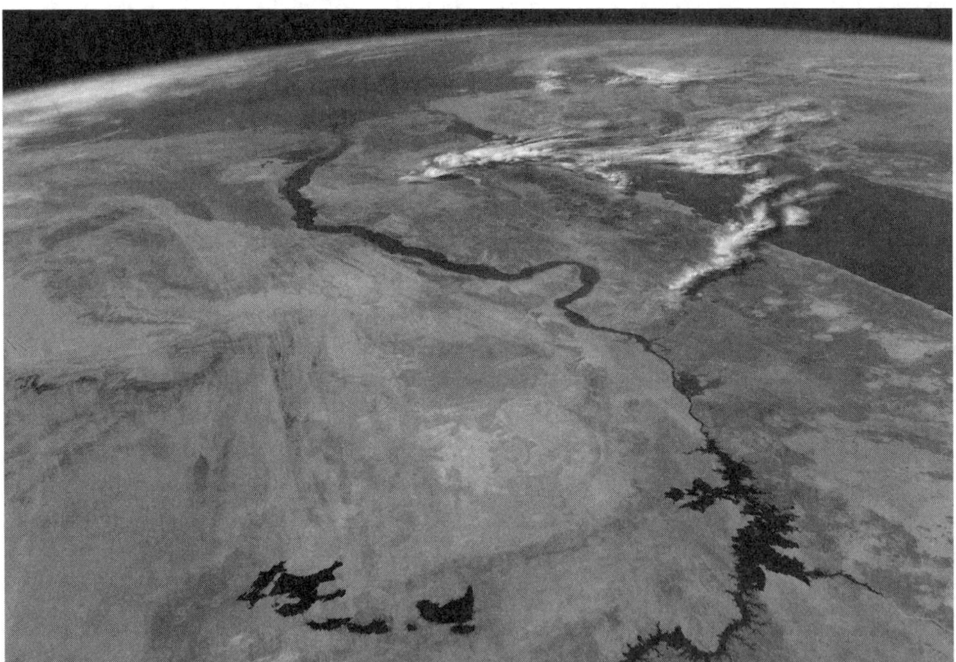

Fig 9.5 The serpentine course of the river Nile through Egypt. This was the Naass-Ophis 'snake' that was venerated by the Naassene-Ophites, whose body split into four branches or heads when it reached the Nile Delta. The Nile Delta is the dark (green) area at the top of this satellite image.

> But Eden, they say, is the brain, as it were bound and enlaced in the surrounding coverings as in the heavens. And they consider man as far as the head alone to be Paradise. Therefore 'the river that came forth from Eden' - that is from the brain - they think 'is separated into four heads ....' (Hippolytus, Refutation of Heresies, V:9 or n178-179)

So the Nile Delta is the brain, and that is exactly where the brain of this terrestrial snake would be: in the Nile Delta. And yes, this brain or head of the snake was indeed paradise - the 'land of milk and honey' - because that is where the Israelites lived for many centuries. As was narrated in *Solomon, Pharaoh of Egypt*, the United Monarchy of kings David and Solomon had their capital city at Zoan (Tanis) rather than Zion (Jerusalem). These monarchs may have controlled all of Judaea and Israel, just as the biblical books of Kings and Chronicles relate, but their capital city and their great temple were firmly located at Tanis in the Nile Delta. And they are still there today, if the Muslim Neanderthals in ISIS have not destroyed them.

And when the Naassene creed says that Eden is a brain 'bound and enlaced in coverings as in the heavens', we even have a very famous painting of this description. It is the *Creation of Adam* by Michelangelo. This very famous painting depicts god as being enveloped in the folds of a red cloth that happen to look exactly like a human brain. But this is no earthly brain, for it is the very brain in the heavens that surrounds god himself in the heavens above. And so the Naassene creed goes on to say:

> But the seven-robed nature (of Isis), encircled and arrayed with seven mantles of ethereal texture (for so they call the planetary stars, allegorizing them as ethereal robes) is as it were the changeable generation ... And this, they say, is what is declared in Scripture: 'The just will fall seven times, and rise again.' For these falls are the changes of the stars, moved by god who puts all things in motion. (Hippolytus Refutation of Heresies 5:2) (See Proverbs 24:16 and Luke 17:4 for these 'seven-fold falls'.) (Author's brackets.)

The fall and rise of the stars mentioned here has to be a description of the precessional Great Months, that last for some 2,140 years each. So Michelangelo's folded ruby-red robes encircling the figure of god are not simply a depiction of a human brain, they are also the 'seven-robed nature of the planetary stars, bound and enlaced in the surrounding coverings as in the heavens', as is described in Naassene theology. And this is interesting, for it means that Michelangelo and his patrons must have been familiar with the Naassene creed, sufficiently so to want to preserve elements of it in Rome itself.

This is the essence of the Naassene Sect, a sect that venerated the Nile river as being sacred. But in doing so they have exposed the true roots of Naassene beliefs, which must therefore have been strongly linked to Egypt and to the ancient belief systems of that region. And since the Giza plateau stands at the neck of the Nile, where it divides into four heads, no doubt some of those beliefs revolved (quite literally) around the sacred rites of the Giza priesthood.

This is why Saul-Josephus had his *bar mitzvah* at the top of the Great Pyramid, as was discussed in a previous chapter. The Great Pyramid was not only the Israelite's most sacred mountain, Mt Sinai, it is also situated on the neck of the Naassene snake - the river Nile. So Saul-Josephus' very exclusive *bar mitzvah* was not simply an induction into Judaic adulthood, it was also an initiation into Naassene philosophy. Saul-Josephus was a Nazarene-Naassene follower, as it says in Acts 24:5, and this is why he was being taken up into the third level of the seven heavens - the seven ethereal robes of the Naassene heavenly brain.

The Dyke

A tentative confirmation of these arguments can be seen in modern England, where there is a similar sinusoidal structure on the borders of England and Wales. This is Offa's Dyke, a great earthwork defensive system that runs

Fig 9.6
The Creation of Adam, by Michelangelo. Look at the shape of the surrounding red robes. As the Naassene creed says: 'the brain, as it were bound and enlaced in the surrounding coverings as in the heavens'.

from north to south along the borders of wales for up to 240 km, according to some of the older claims, or just 100 km according to more recent estimates.

Surprisingly for such a large civil engineering project, the monarch or leader who conceived and created this great project, and thus the era of its construction, are completely unknown. A monk by the name of Asser, who wrote a biography of King Alfred the Great, claimed that the dyke was constructed by King Offa in the 8th century, a claim that has endured to this day:

> A certain vigorous king called Offa ... had a great dyke built between Wales and Mercia from sea to sea. (Asser, Alfred the Great, ch14, p71.)

King Offa was a real monarch of Mercia, the English Midlands, and he was rich and powerful enough to issue silver and gold coinage. But did this Dark Age king have sufficient wealth, resources and spare manpower to create a defensive work that ran for up to 240 km (or 100 km) along the borders of Wales? Surely not.

And while wrenching this great defensive work away from the reign of King Offa may seem a bit radical, recent archaeology supports this proposal. One of the many downsides of the recent mass immigration into Britain is the introduction of a whole raft of people who know nothing of the history and heritage of Britain and its people. And the result of this ignorance was that someone carved a roadway right through Offa's Dyke, thinking it was just a mound of earth, and completely destroyed that section. The only fortunate thing about this minor tragedy is that it exposed some of the original grass turves from when the dyke was built, and the radio-carbon dating of these organic remains suggested that the dyke was centuries earlier than the reign of King Offa. But if this dyke did not belong to King Offa, then who built it?

The alternative suggestion is that this great engineering project was actually Roman, not Anglo-Saxon. Now this was an era when great civil engineering projects like this were readily achievable, as is amply demonstrated by the Hadrian and Antonine Walls, which stretch from coast to coast along the borders of Scotland. And these were not simply earthen structures, presumably with a wooden palisade on the top, these were great stone walls 3 meters wide and six meters high with a commanding walkway along the top and small fortresses every mile.

And it is from this richer and more productive Roman era that we find another description of a great defensive work being constructed. The Roman historian Eutropius says of the relatively unknown wall constructed by Emperor Septimius Severus:

> (Severus) had his most recent war in Britain, and to fortify the conquered provinces with all security, he built a wall for 133 miles from sea to sea. He died at York, a reasonably old man, in the sixteenth year and third month of his reign. (Historiae Romanae Breviarium, viii 19.1)

The *Historia Augusta* agrees that Severus built a great wall. And although one has to be careful about the *Historia Augusta,* because it contains satire as well as history, there is no reason why a comment about a mundane defensive wall should have been invented:

> (Severus) built a wall across the island of Britain from sea to sea, and thus made the province secure - the crowning glory of his reign. In recognition thereof he was given the name Britannicus. (Historia Augusta, Life of Severus, 18:2, written around AD 395)

Septimius Severus was a Roman Emperor of the late second and early 3rd century AD, and he did indeed do a considerable amount of campaigning in

Fig 9.7 Offa's Dyke on the borders of England and Wales, an earthen rampart that winds is way across the countryside like an earthen snake for 100 km or perhaps even 240 km. This was actually the Severan Wall. Image courtesy of Jim Saunders; nature photographer and author of 'Offa's Dyke': www.jimsaunders.co.uk

Britain. And although Cassius Dio does not mention it, he obviously built a wall of some nature. But which one? Geoffrey of Monmouth claimed that the Severan wall stretched from Deira, or northwest England, to Albany, which is an archaic name for Scotland (5:2, 7:10). It is often presumed that this is a reference to the Antonine Wall, which lies to the north of Hadrian's Wall. But the Antonine wall was quite certainly constructed by Emperor Antoninus Pius in the mid 2nd century, and so Monmouth must be incorrect. Furthermore, the description of the Severan wall that we have from the Venerable Bede, who was writing before Monmouth, does not give the same details. Bede says:

> In the year of our lord 189, Severus became Emperor ... He thought fit to divide that part of the island that he recovered from the other unconquered nations - not with a wall as some have imagined but with a rampart, for a wall is made of stones. A rampart for which camps are fortified to repel enemies is made of sods cut out of the ground and raised high above the ground like a wall, having in front of it a trench from whence the sods were taken, with strong stakes of wood fitted above it. Thus Severus drew a great trench and rampart fortified with several towers from sea to sea. (Ecclesiastical History, 1:4)

So the Severan Wall was actually an earthen wall with a ditch in front of it and wooden stakes behind, and it was built from 'sea to sea'. But which seas? Monmouth has obviously guessed that this wall was built between Britain and Scotland, but the attributions for the Hadrian and Antonine walls are quite certain, and so we can discount those constructions as belonging to Severus. And this leaves us with Offa's Dyke, which is a 'trench from whence the sods were taken with strong stakes of wood fitted above ... from sea to sea'. And this wall does extend from sea to sea because it starts on the Bristol Channel and runs north to the Dee Estuary, along the borders of modern England and Wales.

The scientific and historical evidence strongly suggests that Offa's Dyke is the Severan Wall, and so one wonders why this fortification was ever claimed to be the dyke of King Offa. Of course, there is the curious name of this fortification, which appears to link the dyke with King Offa. But did the dyke get its name from the king, as one might naturally expect, or did the dyke become linked to the king because of its name. And while the latter option may seem improbable, it is likely to be the correct answer to this conundrum. In fact, the true reason for the Severan Wall being called the Offa Wall is twofold.

Firstly, the wall wound its way across the countryside like a huge great serpent, just as the river Nile snaked across the eastern end of the Sahara desert in exactly the same manner. And a snake in the Greek is an *ophis* οφις. And so this was not King Offa's Dyke at all, it was the Offis Dyke or Ophis Dyke - the Serpent Dyke. The Ophis Dyke only became linked to King Offa in later centuries, because it had a similar name to the Mercian king. (Perhaps the Mercian king was similarly named after a serpent.)

The second reason for connecting this dyke with a serpent, is that Septimius Severus was an emperor from Leptis Magna in modern Libya, but he married the indomitable Julia Domna from Emesa in Syria, modern

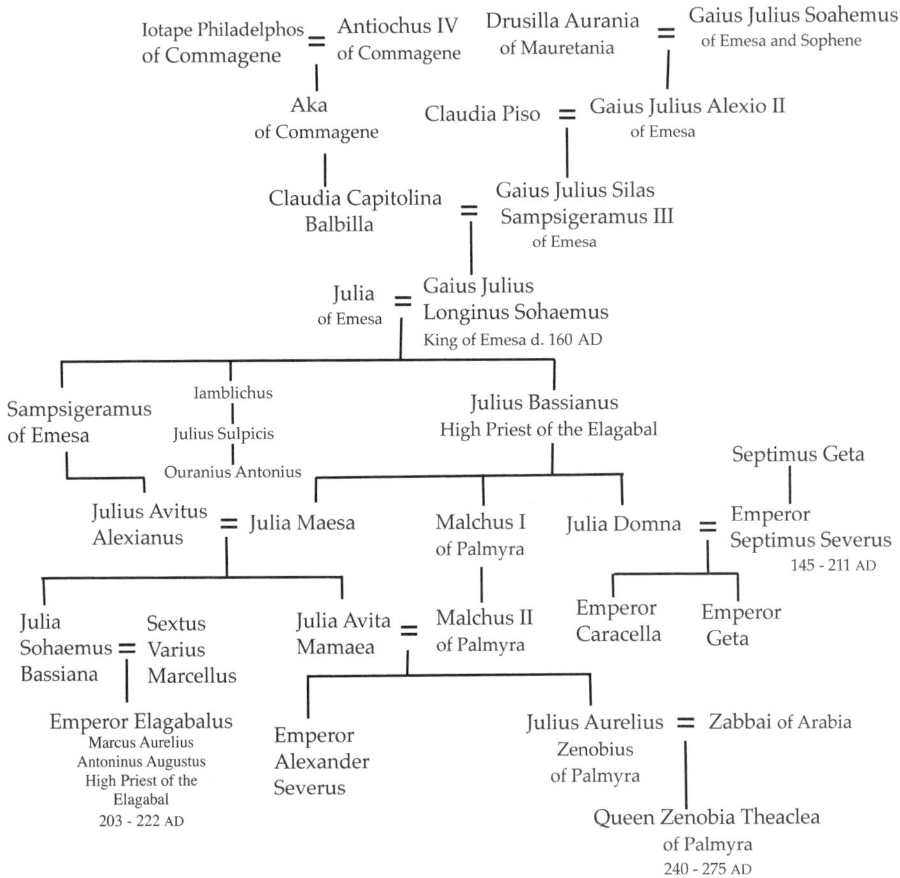

Fig 9.8
Genealogy of Septimius Severus and Julia Domna. Note that their family governed not only Emesa in Syria, but also Palmyra. Note also the genealogical links with Mauretania, Commagene and if we go back a little further, with Edessa too.
This family was also the Guardian of the Elagabal omphalos stone, the Holy Grail, in the 3rd century. Emperor Elagabalus took this sacred Grail-stone to Rome, but it is not known what happened to it afterwards. Previous books in this series have speculated that it was taken to Chester in Britain.

Homms. Julia Domna was a direct descendent of the Sampsiceramids, the priest-kings of Emesa, the royal family who venerated the Elagabal - the meteoric omphalos stone that was discussed at length in the previous books. The name for Sampsigeramus I (Σαμψιγεραμος) may be a protraction the name Sampson Σαμψων, the Greek rendering of the Israelite hero. The Aramaic Samson שמשון means 'Likeness of the Sun', while Samsigeram גרם שמשי may mean 'Bones of the Sun' and imply 'Strength of the Sun'. (Samson is pronounced as Sampson in the Greek.)

The father of Sampsigeramus I was Aziz, who was also known as Azizus the Arab, or Azizus the Phylarch of the Arabs. [5] And so we are back to the same terminology we have seen so many times before. The kings of Edessa were also called Arabs by Roman historians, and this has been taken by modern historians to mean that they were Nabatean or Arabian Bedouin, just as is being claimed for the Sampsigeramid kings of Emesa. But this was not the true meaning at all. Saul-Josephus had denigrated these people as 'locusts', because they had arrived from the east and destroyed Judaea - just like the locusts of the biblical Plagues had similarly come from the east and destroyed Egypt. And a locust in Aramaic is an *arabeh* ארבה, an Arab. In which case, it would seem likely that the Sampsigeramid monarchs of Emesa and the Abgarid monarchs of Edessa were closely related, and so they were all branded and stigmatised with the same derogatory title.

And do note that the name for Azizus (Az-Izus), the father of Sampsigeramus I, is significantly similar to the name for King Izas-Jesus of Edessa (the biblical Jesus). And this seems especially so in the Aramaic. All the Torah characters whose names begin with a Latinised 'Az' are spelt in the Aramaic with a prefixed עז, and so the name Azizus must have been spelt as עזיזוז. But as we saw in a previous chapter, a possible Aramaic spelling and meaning for the name of King Izas was Izuws עזוז meaning 'strong' or 'mighty'. And so Azizus עזיזוז is simply a superlative of that, meaning 'strong strong' or 'very strong'. Again, it seems highly likely that there was a close family relationship between the Edessan and Emesan dynasties.

And if the links between Emesa and Edessa appear close at this point, they are about to become closer still. Emperor Severus' wife was Julia Domna, and they had two sons, Emperor Caracalla and Emperor Geta. But Julia's sister was Julia Maesa, the grandmother of Emperor Elagabalus and Emperor Alexander Severus.

Readers may remember Emperor Elagabalus from the book *King Jesus*. He was the slightly deranged emperor who was the high priest of the Elagabal omphalos stone, and had an operation in an attempt to turn himself into a woman. But now we can see exactly what Emperor Elagabalus was trying to do with this castration-type operation. He was obviously attempting to become a eunuch or an androgyne so that he could become a Galli high priest, just as Sir Perceval the Galahad (Galli-had) had likewise done in Arthurian history. Yet the biblical Jesus-Izas also asked his disciples to become eunuchs for his very similar Galilean sect (the Galli-lean sect). And the capital city of Jesus-Izas' small kingdom was Edessa in northern Syria, while Emperor Elagabalus came from Emesa in Syria.

And if Emperor Elagabalus was a Galli high priest, then it is also clear that these Galli high priests must have venerated the conical omphalos stone - the Elagabal. The Elagabal was the primary cult object of Emperor Elagabalus and therefore of the Galli priesthood, while in *Merlin Grail* Sir Perceval the Galahad had became the Guardian of the Holy Grail. And yet the Holy Grail was not simply a golden chalice or even just a bloodline, it was also described in Wolfram von Eschenbach's *Parzival* as being a stone.

> Many a valiant (knight) resides by the Grail at Munsalvasche ... they live by a stone whose nature is pure. If you know nothing of it, it shall be named for you here: it is called Lapsit Exillis. By that stone's power the Phoenix burns away, turning to ashes, yet those ashes bring it back to life ... that stone is also called the Grail. (Parzival, ch 9.)

So the Holy Grail of Arthurian history can also be seen as a stone, which was strongly associated with the Phoenix. And yet the sacred Elagabal stone of Emperor Elagabalus was always embossed with the symbol of the

Fig 9.11
The conical omphalos stone known as the Elagabal, on a gold coin of Elagabalus. The stone is embossed with an image of the Phoenix, and is being drawn around the city of Rome in a quadriga chariot.

Phoenix, as can be seen in fig 9.11. And so Arthurian history and Roman history dovetail once more at this point, because the Elagabal stone is quite obviously one of the aspects or manifestations of the Arthurian Holy Grail. The Grail is a multi-faceted concept and artifact, and here is one of those facets displayed for everyone to see in black and white (or in gold, if viewed on a tablet). This small conical stone is the Holy Grail, the sacred talisman that permeates so many ancient mythologies.

So the lithic (stone) aspect of the Holy Grail was once a real artifact, that could be paraded around Rome in a *quadriga* chariot. This was the lithic form of the Holy Grail that had been guarded and maintained by the Galli high priesthood, by the knights of the Round Table, by the Grail princesses, and even by Emperor Elagabalus. So the Holy Grail is not a mythology, it was once a real component within the real history of the Roman Empire, but it is now a lost and largely forgotten artifact and history that has faded into the mists of time.

It was demonstrated in *Jesus, King of Edessa* that this sacred conical stone that Emperor Elagabalus venerated, was the very same sacred conical stone that the biblical Jacob venerated when he was near Harran just south

Fig 9.12
The conical hill at Sogmatar near Edessa. The Ark of the Covenant and its sacred stone(s) are said to have been located here in the 2nd century AD.

of Edessa - the 'pillow' or stone that Jacob anointed with oil. But it was also demonstrated in that book that Jacob's 'ladder', which was in the same location as the sacred stone, was actually a reference to the sacred hill at Sogmatar near Harran, which was also the necropolis of the Edessan monarchy. And it was further demonstrated that - after many long and eventful travels - Jacob's sacred conical stone was relocated back at Sogmatar once again in the 1st and 2nd centuries AD, by the Edessan monarchy. And the Ark of the Covenant was also installed upon the hill at Sogmatar, as the coins of King Wael clearly demonstrate. And so now we can see a complete conflation of traditions, creeds, artifacts and events, between Edessa and Emesa. And these include:

Edessa	**Emesa**
Sacred conical hill at Sogmatar	Sacred conical hill at Shmemis
Sacred conical stone at Sogmatar	Sacred conical stone, the Elagabal
Galli eunuch priesthood	Galli eunuch priesthood and emperor
Known as Arabs by the Romans	Known as Arabs by the Romans
Members of the Naassene Nazarene	Members of the Naassene Nazarene
The royal name Izas	The royal name Izizus
The royal name Sampson	The royal name Sampson

Fig 9.13
The conical hilltop fortress of Shmemis, just east of Hama in Syria. The fortress on the top of this volcano is thought to have originally been constructed by Sampsiceramus I.

Thus is it likely that these were two strands of the same royal family, who were living in close proximity to one another in Syria.

And after this lengthy interlude, we must return now to the original question, of why Offa's Dyke was given this name. We have already established that the dyke was most probably built by Emperor Septimius Severus in the early 3rd century AD. And Septimius Severus does have a strong link with Britain and Arthurian history, because he died in York in AD 211 just as Emperor Constantius died in York in AD 306. And the great nephew of Septimius Severus was Emperor Elagabalus, who was a Galli-Galles high priest of the Elagabal, the sacred conical Arthurian Grail-stone. And the Galli-Galles were the high priests of the Naassene-Nazarene sect, or the Galileans (Galli-leans) as they are known in the New Testament gospels. Yet the Naassene-Nazarenes were simply the Aramaic names for this sect, while in the Greek they were more often known as the Ophites - the 'Serpent River Sect'.

And this may well be why the Severan Wall was called Offa's Dyke. It not only resembled a great serpent winding its way through the countryside, it was also built by a Roman imperial family who were

Fig 9.14
The conical hilltop fortress of Herodium (Tekoa) just south of Jerusalem. The fortress on the top of this mesa was rebuilt by Herod the Great. This is a natural mesa that has been artificially made to appear conical.

very closely connected to the Naassene-Ophite creed. Julia Domna was a daughter of the high priests of the Elagabal Holy Grail, who were obviously Naassene-Ophites; while her great nephew became Emperor of Rome and a castrated Galli-Galles high priest of the Elagabal Holy Grail. Because of these connections Julia became closely associated with the snake, with many of her coins bearing the image of the Ophite snake. And so it is hardly surprising that a great sinusoidal earthen rampart built by Septimius Severus, the husband of Julia Domna, should become known as the Ophite Dyke, or Offa Dyke.

Seraphe-Nascien

Fig 9.15
Two coins of Julia Domna, showing her close affinity with serpent imagery.
The upper coin is said to be an Agathodaemon, a good-luck charm. But this is more likely to be an image of the Shining Serpent - the Sun-god Helios in the image of a serpent, which is why the serpent wears a Sun-halo. The lower coin shows two winged serpents pulling a god in a chariot. The god is said to be Demeter, but the god in a chariot wearing a radiant halo is normally an image of Helios, the Sun-god.

The Naassene-Nazarene were also the sect that Prince Seraphe-Nascien of Sarras was strongly linked to earlier in this chapter. The Naassene were the 'Serpent River Sect' while the name for Seraphe-Nascien, the brother-in-law of King Evalach, was 'Serpent-Serpent'. And because of the strong links that exist between Sarras-Palmyra, Queen Helena of Edessa, and King Izas-Jesus, a very strong argument can be made that the Nazarene and the Naassene sects were one and the same sect.

But before we do so, perhaps we should look again at why the Church of Jesus and James can be equated with the Nazarene sect. As we saw in previous works, both Jesus-Izas and Saul were known as Nazarenes in the gospels. And so the 4th century Epiphanius of Salamis says of the Nazarenes:

> As I have indicated, everyone called the Christians 'Nazoreans.' As they say when accusing Paul (Saul) the apostle, 'We have found this man a ... ring-leader of the sect of the Nazoreans' ... And no wonder the apostle admitted to being a Nazorean. In those days everyone called Christians (by this name) ... for there was no other usage of the name at the time. (Panarion 29:6:2, 5) (Author's brackets.)

So all of the early Christians were known as Nazarenes 'for there was no other usage of the name at the time'. This was not because Jesus came from the town of Nazareth, as Epiphanius and Math 2:23 maintain, for that town did not exist in the 1st century. As Acts 24:5 clearly says, Saul (Josephus) was accused of being from the Nazarene sect, not from the city of Nazareth, and the Nazarene were an influential Judaic sect that long predated the gospel era.

In fact, the name for the Nazarene sect was derived from a surprising yet familiar source - it came from the Aramaic *mazaroth* מזרות or *nazaroth* נזרות meaning 'zodiac'. So Jesus-Izas, James and Saul (Josephus) were all from the Zodiac sect, or perhaps the Astronomer sect of Judaism. So the Nazarene Ebionites were not Christians by any stretch of the imagination, they were proselyte Jews who were closely linked with the Sabaean astronomers of Syria. And Epiphanius himself makes this distinction between the Simple Judaic and Orthodox Judaic aspect of these sect quite clear:

> The (Nazarene) are different from Jews, and different from Christians, only in the following ways. They disagree with Jews because of their belief in Christ; but they are not in accord with Christians because they are still fettered by the Law, circumcision, the Sabbath, and the rest. (Panarion 29:7:5)

Which is a succinct and accurate summary of the differences between these three sects. The Nazarene astronomers were proselyte Jewish, and yet they still venerated Jesus the christ (Jesus the king) because he had been their secular king. This is not to say that they venerated Jesus-Izas as a god who had the same standing as Aton, Helios or Yahweh, but honoured Jesus-Izas as their former monarch. Although it has to be acknowledged that most Egyptian pharaohs and Roman emperors were venerated as demi-gods at some point in their lives, and so there may have been a small element of worship within the Nazarene veneration of Jesus-Izas. Hence we have Emperor Vespasian's famous last words, which are reputed to have been: '*vae, puto deus fio*' or 'alas, I think I becoming a god...'

Jewish astronomers

And don't be led into thinking that Orthodox Judaism and astronomy-astrology are mutually exclusive creeds and doctrines. Several allusions to Judaic astrology within the Bible have already been discussed in previous works, and here are some more. The following verses are from the Book of Job, and they quite overtly refer to precessional astrology.

> Can you bind the sweet influences of Pleiades, or loosen the bands of Orion?
> Can you bring forth Mazzaroth in season? Or guide Arcturus with his sons?
> Do you know the ordinances of heaven? Can you set its dominion on the earth?
> (Job 38:31-33)

Where the King James Bible derives its 'sweet influences' from is anyone's guess, perhaps the monthly delivery of narcotics had arrived in the Church's publishing house that day. Anyway, a much more literal translation of these verses results in something much simpler and more logical. When translated from the Aramaic these verses simply say:

> Tighten the bonds of the Pleiades, and loosen the bonds of Orion.
> Bring the seasons from the Zodiac, and guide the sons of Ursa Major.
> Know the laws of heaven, that make the rules on Earth.

The zodiac above did indeed bring the seasons on the Earth below and govern their movement, which is why all the Syrio-Judaean zodiacs were marked out in each corner with the appropriate seasons. And the reference here to the sons of Ursa Major again confirms that Uwth does refers to Ursa Major. There is only one constellation that has twelve sons and that is Ursa Major, which sits in the middle of the zodiac surrounded by its twelve constellations of the zodiac. The images of the zodiac in fig 1.3 and 14.6 show this arrangement quite clearly.

The Book of Job obviously delights in its astronomical knowledge, for it contains a few verses like this. The next example is perhaps a little more complicated for it says:

> Which shakes the earth out of her place, and the pillars tremble.
> Which commands the sun not to rise; and seals up the stars.
> Which alone spreads out the heavens, and treads upon the (high) sea.
> Which makes Arcturus, Orion, and Pleiades, and the chambers of the south.
> Which does great things beyond discovery. Yes, and wonders without number.
> (Job 9:6-9) (Author's brackets.)

While these verses are obviously something to do with astronomy or astrology, the translation that has been made is so poor that it is difficult to understand the meaning. The problem is that the translator knew nothing about the precession of the equinox, and so the result is the equivalent of a poet trying to make sense a scientific paper on nuclear physics. As one might expect, the result is garbled and confusing. For example, most of the venerable theologians interpret the first verse here as referring to an earthquake, which is not even remotely correct and destroys the meaning of the subsequent verses from the very outset.

In reality, this first verse is referring to the precession of the equinox. The crucial difference is the translation of the *macomah amudah* ועמודיה ממקומה meaning the 'standing place of a pillar'. This description has a close affinity with the stylite priests, who used to stand on top of pillars all across the Near East in the early centuries AD. Daniel the Stylite is perhaps the most famous of these stylite priests. But what does the 'stylite pillar' or the 'standing pillar' represent? This did seem like a mystery for some time, but in the context of astronomy it just has to refer to the axle-shaft of the Earth, as it was called by the Greeks - the Earth's axis. The Greeks and others viewed the heavens as rotating about an axle-shaft, and this 'standing pillar' is the axle of the Earth, around which the heavens appear to rotate. But the Earth's axis is not static, it is shaken or moved out of place during the precession of the equinox, as the diagrams in Chapter XIV will demonstrate, and this is what is meant by the 'pillars trembling'.

The third verse is sometimes translated as the 'waves of the sea', but waves are not mentioned here at all. It actually says the 'high sea' which is quite different, and the reference is again astronomical. The 'sea' refers to the cosmos, the watery abyss upon which the solar-boat of Aton-Ra sailed, and so this reference is actually to the high seas above - the 'heavenly seas'. And finally we get to the verse mentioning the 'chambers of the south', which is actually a reference to the twelve houses of the zodiac. And just as this verse says, the houses of the zodiac do rise in the southerly heavens rather than in the north. And so a very literal translation of these same verses in an astronomical context might be:

> Shake the Earth's axle-shaft and make it tremble.
> Command the Sun not to rise behind the seals of the stars.
> Spread the heaven's spokes, and they stride over the celestial seas.
> Ursa Major: make a house in the south for Orion and Pleiades.
> Make great beyond discovery, make wondrous beyond number.

This is quite obviously a commentary on the precession of the equinox. The Earth's axis does indeed shake and tremble, just as the axle or axis of a child's spinning top will 'shake and tremble' as it spirals around and around according to the laws of precession. And as the Earth precesses and rotates through its 25,680-year Great Year, the spokes of the heavens - the twelve spokes that delineate the twelve houses of the zodiac - will indeed stride over the heavens or the celestial seas above. And finally we have another confirmation that the Aramaic Awsh עוש or Uwth עות refers to Ursa Major. There were only two arbiters or ring-masters of the heavens, and they were Ursa Major and Orion. And since we see Orion being told to go to his house in the south, the ring-master in question here must be Ursa Major - King Uwther or King Arthur.

All of which proves that the standard Judaic Torah does contain a number of references to astronomy and the precessional zodiac, if anyone could be bothered to translate these books properly. And so for many reasons we know that the members of the Ebionite Church of Jesus and James were Nazarene astronomers, and closely linked to the Sabaean astronomers of the Osrhoene, the Kingdom of Edessa. But were they also Naassene serpentists? Well, the many similarities between these two sects now include:

The Naassene were circumcised Jews from east of the Jordan.
The Nazarene were circumcised Jews from Pella, east of the Jordan.

The Naassene were against roast sacrifices.
Jesus drove the animals out of the Temple in Math 21:12.

The Naassene agreed with the gospels.
Jesus the Nazarene was a central character within the gospels.

The Naassene priests were Galli eunuchs.
Jesus the Nazarene asked for his disciples to become eunuchs.

The Mother Goddess of the Naassene was Cybele
The patron goddess of Edessa was Cybele-Atargatis.

King Jesus-Izas and Queen Helena both came from Edessa.

Nascien was a Naassene 'serpent' from Sarras (Palmyra).
King Jesus was a Nazarene and possibly the father-in-law of Nascien.

King Izas-Jesus was educated in Alexandria in Egypt.
The name for the Naassene comes from the 'serpent' Nile.

But if the Naassene and the Nazarene sects were one and the same, and they were intimately linked to the veneration of the zodiac, then the probability that the Nazarene Church of Jesus and James were led by a Galli eunuch priest is looking increasingly likely. In which case King Izas-Jesus, as one of the leaders of the Nazarene-Galilean Fourth Sect, may well have become a Galli-Galles eunuch himself. And if this is so, then he was directly comparable to the Arthurian Wounded Fisher King. King Izas-Jesus was called Jesus the Galilean (Ieusous Galilaios Ιησους Γαλιλαιος) in Math 26:69, and rather than this referring to Jesus being born in Galilee it is much more likely that this is a reference to the Galli-Galles sect. Jesus the Galilean really means Jesus the Galli-Galles eunuch, or Jesus the Wounded Fisher King. But each generation within this Judaeo-Arthurian history would have had its own Wounded Fisher King, and the next in line for this ceremony and title was the rather reluctant Sir Perceval-Galahad.

Gilead Galileans

The title for these priestly Galli-Galles eunuchs is also quite interesting, because again it would appear that nobody knows where this title was derived from. We now know that it had nothing to do with Wales or the Gallois-Celtic language, so where did it come from? According to the many varied claims that have been made, it was either derived from a King Gallus mentioned by Ovid; or maybe from the Gallus river in Phrygia; or perhaps it came from the Galli Gauls. But why would the priests of an eastern cult of Cybele-Atargatis in Syria be named after the northern Gauls or after a river in Phrygia? This is hardly an etymology that makes sense.

But since the primary of icons of veneration for these Galli priests were the Elagabal omphalos stone and the zodiac, and we shall see more evidence for this in Chapter XII, there is a much better etymological root for the Galli-Galles that utilizes all the information now available. This alternative root is the Aramaic word *gal* גל, which is related to all things circular. It is from *gal* that the name for Galilee was derived, which is pronounced as *galiyl* גליל in the Hebrew-Aramaic and means 'circle'. And these Galli priests were often called Galileans, as we have seen. But did this name refer to the region called Galilee, or did it refer to another type of circle altogether? Surprisingly, the latter is the correct answer.

As was narrated in the previous books in this series, if readers walk four furlongs south from the old city wall of Tiberias in Galilee, they will come to the archaeological site of Hamat Teverya (the Hot Springs of Tiberias). Here, in the Hamat synagogue, is one of the most detailed and accurate precessional zodiacs in all of Syrio-Judaea, a zodiac that will become central to the story in later chapters. If we are looking for the original Galli-Had גליל הדר, the original 'Great Circle' of the Galli Priesthood, there are none finer than the zodiac at Hamat Teverya. So yes, Sir Galahad's name translates not simply as 'Great Galli', referring to the Galli priesthood, it is also symbolic of 'Great Circle' that the Galli priesthood venerated.

But this zodiac is not the only great circle that the Nazarene Galli priesthood venerated, for it is merely an earthy representation of that

Fig 9.16
The precessional zodiac at Hamat Teverya, on the shores of the Sea of Galilee. This zodiac was not simply a galyl (a circle) itself, it also represented the Great Circle (the Galli-Had) in the heavens above. Note that the annual seasons are marked out at the four corners of this zodiac.

much Greater Circle in the heavens above, from which the Elagabal stone fell in great antiquity. The real Great Circle of the Galli priesthood was the zodiacal sphere that serenely rotates around the Earth in its curious treble motion - the daily, seasonal and millennial dance of the constellations in the heavens above. And it was the millennial motion of the Great Circle that produced the precessional Great Month (of about 2,140 years) and the precessional Great Year (of about 25,680 years), when the Elagabal - the Primaeval Mound or Primaeval Egg of the Phoenix - heralded in a new cosmic era. Everything about this huge circle in the heavens was of great magnitude and of great import.

Thus the Naassene-Nazarene Galli were the Nile-Serpent sect who venerated the precessional zodiac and the sacred Grail-stone, and one of their primary religious sites was at Hamat Teverya on the shores of the Sea of Galilee.

Fig 9.17
The traditional image of a young redheaded Sir Galahad, as depicted by George Frederick Watts. Galahad was called the Red Knight because he wore a suit of red armour. But after he became the high priest of the Galli he would have worn a brightly coloured woman's dress, just as Christian bishops do to this day.

Title	**Meaning**
Naassene	Serpent-Nile
Nazarene	Zodiac
Galli	Circle

However in the light of this revolutionary (sic) new evidence, it is likely that our entire perception of Arthurian history needs a radical overhaul. Contrary to the image we normally have, of the knightly Sir Perceval-Galahad dressed in a shining suit of red armour* astride a powerful charger and holding a lance and shield, it would appear that Sir Perceval Galahad was actually a castrated Galli priest, who were famed for their flamboyant women's dresses.

In his new role as a Galli eunuch high priest, Sir Perceval Galahad would have worn gaily-coloured women's clothes, sparkling jewellery, garish lipstick, kohl eye-shadow, blusher and sweet perfume. Such a spectacle may be a world away from our traditional perception of Arthurian courtly life, but this is exactly what the ancient texts say. Let us remind ourselves what Saul-Josephus said about the Galli priests of the 1st century, during the Jewish Revolt:

Fig 9.18
Contrary to the classical view of Sir Galahad in the previous image, it is much more likely that Sir Perceval-Galahad dressed like these Hijra eunuchs from India. Note that two of these Hijra wear a crown that mimics the shape of the city-wall crown worn by the goddess Cybele-Atargatis. Although it should be stressed that a Nazarene Ebionite would not have worn dresses quite as revealing as these. The dresses that Sir Galahad wore would have been more like those depicted in the next diagram.

> These Galileans ... indulged themselves in feminine wantonness ... they decked their hair, and put on women's garments, and were smeared with ointments; and that they might appear very comely, they had paints under their eyes, and imitated not only the ornaments, but also the lusts of women ... (Josephus, War 4:9:10)

Earlier in this chapter we saw that Jesus asked his disciples to become Galli eunuchs, while Joseph(us) (the son of Arimathaea), had asked Galahad to become the king or high priest of the Galles. But this had nothing whatsoever to do with a principality called Wales in northwest Europe; instead, Sir Perceval Galli-had was being (very reluctantly) inaugurated as the high priest of the castrated Galli priests of Cybele-Atargatis. And so Sir Perceval Galahad slipped on a brightly coloured frock, perhaps containing false breasts, applied some blusher, kohl eye-shadow and lipstick, and became High Priest Perceval

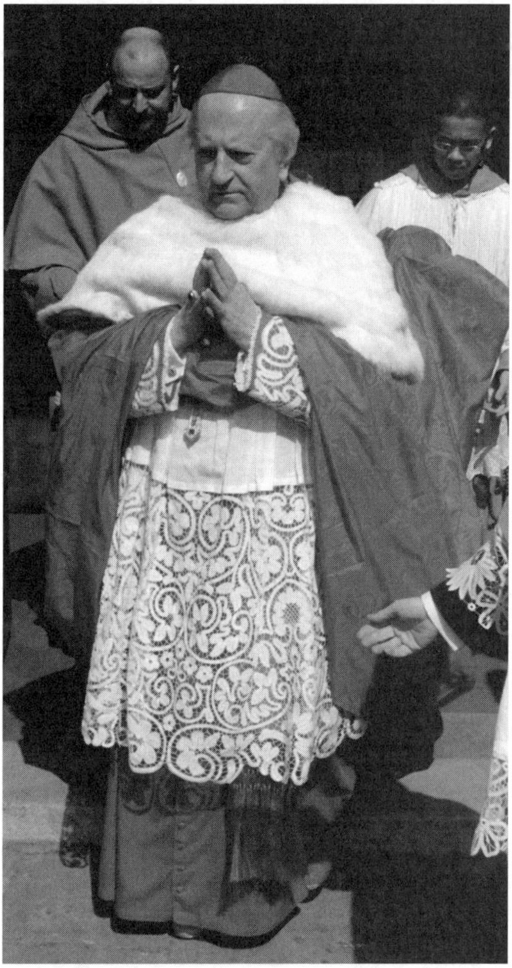

Fig 9.21
Not much has changed, over the last two millennia. Catholic cardinals and bishops are still old men wearing red dresses with a frilly white petticoat. It is not said if cardinals are still castrated, but the goings-on in the Catholic Church would suggest not. It is also not said if cardinals still carry swords under their cassocks, to kill their enemies just as Sir Perceval the Galahad would have done. But if they do, then an inquisitive choir-boy might rightly ask: "Is that a sword under your cassock or are you......"

* A common complaint within Arthurian history is that these suits of armour were often rusty, and the knights were red with rust after a whole day wearing it. It was probably difficult to keep chain mail polished and free of rust.

the Galahad. And then, as we saw in a previous quote, he would draw his sword from under his dress, and cut his enemies in two.

Interestingly, while Lucian and Saul-Josephus inform us that the Galli high priest would have worn a woman's dress and make-up, it is *Quest* that tells us the colour of these dresses - red:

> Just as our lord appeared in the form of fire, so too did the Good Knight appear in red armour, the colour of fire. (Quest 22:78.)

The Good Knight is Sir Perceval in all the early Arthurian manuscripts, but becomes Sir Galahad in the *Vulgate Cycle*. And where it says 'armour' here, read 'dress' instead. And this tradition of the high priest of the Galli wearing a red dress is still with us in the modern era, where Catholic bishops wear red dresses with pretty lace petticoats and cardinals wear scarlet dresses with pretty lace petticoats. And so the modern bishop or cardinal of the Catholic Church, is wearing exactly the same uniform as Sir Perceval the Galahad.

X

We Three Kings of the Orient

Within the many different Arthurian genealogies, we appear to have three royal or aristocratic brothers, King Pelles, King Fisher and King Pellehan, who are also known as the Wounded King, the Hermit King and Alain li Gros. And when we turn to the Talmud we find a similar trio of prominent wealthy aristocrats during the Jewish Revolt, who were called Kalba Shabua, Nakdimon ben Gurion, and Ben Zizit Hakeseth. And in a similar fashion, the gospels mention the visit of three wise men or kings to the birth of King Jesus-Izas. So are there any similarities or connections between these three groups of three kings or aristocrats?

Regards the gospel's aristocrats Matthew chapter two is the only account we have of these 'wise men' and they were actually called Magi Μαγοι, the priestly astrologers and king-makers from the east. Their precise number is unknown and it is only presumed that there were three Magi because they brought three gifts. And while the popular view is that the Magi must have travelled all the way from Parthia to get to the birth of Jesus-Izas in Syrio-Judaea, the primary pupil of John the Baptist was Simon Magus who was also a *magos* μαγος, or a magician μαγευω as he is called in Acts 8:9. And so the Three Magi did not need to come all the way from Parthia to visit the birth of Jesus-Izas, because some of them may well have been living in Syrio-Judaea. And if these local *magi* were connected to the Edessan monarchy in any way, they would have been of Egypto-Parthian heritage and therefore considered to be from the east. Certainly the Edessan royalty would have worn the same Eastern clothing that the Magi are often depicted as wearing.

Fig 10.1
The Three Magi bring gifts to the birth of King Jesus-Izas. A 6th century mosaic from the Basilica of St Apollinare Nuovo, Ravenna. Note the names above the Magi, and their standard Parthian dress, with leggings, capes and a red Phrygian cap. This is exactly the same clothing that the Edessan monarchy wore, as was demonstrated in 'Jesus, King of Edessa'.

The Magi are not named in the gospels, but a very old tradition says that they were called Balthasar, Caspar and Melchior. Since Saul-Joseph(us) was the editor-in-chief of the New Testament, and he readily admits to struggling with the Greek language, it is likely that these names will be Aramaic rather than Greek. Yet these 'names' appear to be titles that betray the wealthy and aristocratic background of these Magi, rather than their wisdom, knowledge and expertise at sorcery. They are the titles of royal aristocrats, rather than monks in bare feet and tattered habits:

Name	Aramaic	Aramaic	Description
Belthasar	Bel Azar	בל אצר	Lord of the Treasure
Caspar	Gizbar	גזבר	Treasurer
Melchior	Malchus	מלכוס	King

Balthasar or Baltshassar בלטשאצר was also the name of the Torah's Daniel, when he worked as a governor for a Babylonian king of the same name. So in a similar fashion to the son of Jesus-Izas, who took the name of the Babylonian prince Evalach Mordrain (Evalmerodach), Daniel did exactly the same. The story of Esther and Daniel-Baltshassar in Babylon is related in *Solomon, Pharaoh of Egypt*, and it is an interesting tale that highlights the very strong ties that existed between the Israelite-Jews and Babylon-Iraq, which is glossed over in modern news reporting from the region. In truth, the Jewish people were a substantial proportion of the Babylonian-Iraqi population for 2,400 years, until the great exile in 1947.

Malchus was also the name of the 'servant of the high priest' who had his 'ear' chopped off by Simon Peter, as was related in Chapter VI. This would have been a later Malchus, but the usage of this name or title in Judaea does demonstrate that this was not simply a Parthian title. And when writing of Prester John, who we last saw in Chapter V, Otto von Freising says:

> It is reported that he (Prester John) is the descendant of those Magi of old who are mentioned in the Gospel, and to rule over the same nations as they did, enjoying such glory and prosperity that he uses no sceptre but one of emerald. [1]

And if we wish to equate these three Magi with the three main kings of Arthurian history, then this would make sense. Prester John was the son of Feirefiz, who was the son of Gahmuret, who is the equivalent of *Perceval's* Alain li Gros or the *Vulgate's* King Pellehan. In which case, we might speculate that the Three Wise Men or Three Kings who were said to have come to the birth of Jesus-Izas from the East were in Arthurian terms King Pelles, King Fisher and King Pellehan. Or in Talmudic terms, Kalba Shabua, Nakdimon and Zizit Hakeseth.

However, when attempting to make any such comparison there is still the standard biblical chronological chasm to deal with. In the earlier Arthurian manuscripts the three main monarchs appear to be of the same generation as King Arthur-Jesus, but in the *Vulgate* they are definitely of the previous generation to Arthur. Bearing this confusion in mind, we shall nevertheless struggle on and discover that these three brother-kings are named in the various manuscripts as:

Source	**Aristocrat 1**	**Aristocrat 2**	**Aristocrat 3**
Monmouth	Uther ben Dragon	Constant the Monk	Aurelius Ambrosius
Perceval	King Pelles (Wounded Fisher)	King Hermit	Alain li Gros

High History	Fisher King King Pelles	(Hermit King)	Alain li Gros
Parzival	Anfortas Wounded King	Trevrizent The Hermit	Gahmuret
History-Quest	King Pelles Fisher King	......	King Pellehan Wounded King
Merlin	King Pelles	King Pellehan Wounded King	Fisher King Alan li Gros
Post Vulgate	King Pelles	King Pellehan	Garlon

Most of these monarchs are equivalents of each other, but can they be directly equated with the three semi-historical aristocrats mentioned in the accounts of the Talmud?

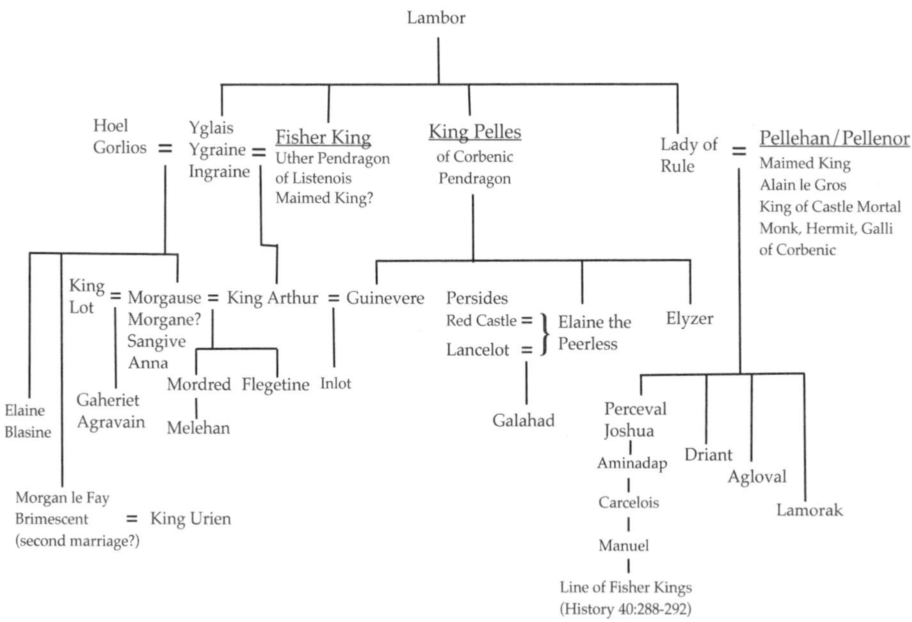

Fig 10.2 A genealogy of the Grail family, taken from both 'Merlin' and 'Lancelot', highlighting the three primary Arthurian brothers: Uther Pendragon, King Pelles, and Pellehan. Some of the other genealogies indicate that the Fisher King was King Pellehan and that King Pelles was the father of King Arthur; and in this case, King Pelles would become the equivalent of Uther Pendragon. And just to add to the confusion, many of these genealogies indicate that King Arthur was of the same generation as King Pelles.

Fisher King

King Pelles and Uther Pendragon have been listed in the table above as being possibly the same person, because in *History* and *Quest* King Pelles, the Fisher King, is the father of King Arthur. Meanwhile, in Monmouth's *History of Kings* it is Uther Pendragon who is the father of King Arthur. Ergo, one might say, Uther Pendragon, King Pelles and the Fisher King should be the same person. But just to be contrarian, *Merlin Grail* and *Merlin* say that the Fisher King title was held by Bron, Alain-Pellehan and then Perceval. The Fisher King is a title that is normally passed from father to son, but it may well have been usurped by the family of Alain-Pellehan, as we shall see later.

However, it is likely that the Fisher and Pendragon titles were originally linked, and we can probably see this connection in the description of the latter. Geoffrey of Monmouth says in *History of Kings* 8:17 that the Pendragon title means 'Dragon's Head', and it was said to have been derived from the appearance of a comet in the night sky that looked like a dragon. And this dramatic sign in the heavens signified the birth of a son and daughter, Arthur and Gwenevere(?), 'whose sons and grandsons would hold the kingdom of Britain in succession'. *

> There appeared a star of marvelous size and brightness, stretching forth one ray whereon was a ball of fire spreading forth in the likeness of a dragon. And from the mouth of the dragon issued forth two rays ... reaching beyond the regions of Gaul ... and towards the Irish Sea ... The ray towards Gaul portended that a son shall be born ... and the other ray signified a daughter ... (History of Kings VIII:14)

King Arthur and his sister were born under a special star that looked like a dragon; and since it would appear that King Arthur married his sister, Princess Gwenevere, these cosmic siblings were destined to be the joint king and queen of the realm. However, Jesus was also born under the Eastern Star and married his sister Mary Magdalene, as has been explained previously, and so the birth legends of Arthur and Jesus are very similar. The star that Jesus was born under is likely to have been a reference to the Star of Venus, the Marian Star that was strongly linked with Mary the Virgin:

* Monmouth is not clear about the identity of Arthur's sister. She is called Anna, the wife of King Lot, while Gwenevere is simply an aristocratic lady of Roman heritage. But other Arthurian histories say that Gwenevere was Arthur's sister, and therefore Arthur had married his sister in the traditional Judaeo-Egyptian tradition, just like King Agrippa II of Judaea, Simon Magus of Judaea, and King Abgarus Monobazus of Edessa.

> There came Magi from Parthia to Jerusalem, saying: 'Where is he that is born King of the Jews? For we have seen his star in the east, and are come to worship him.' Math 2:1-2

Gwenevere and Venus

As we saw in Chapter VIII, there is a very strong link between the goddess Venus and Mary the Virgin and Mary Magdalene, because both of these princesses were venerated as incarnations of the archetypal fertility goddess: Astarte, Astoreth, Ishtar, or Aphrodite. These goddesses were all manifestations of the Egyptian Isis or Ast , and were all linked with and symbolised by the Eastern Star, Venus . We have seen this connection many times previously in the *King Jesus Trilogy*, where Mary the Virgin was often portrayed in Renaissance art as an incarnation of Venus-Aphrodite or displaying the star of Venus-Isis on her robes. And this allows us to take the associations between these Marys and Arthurian history one stage further, because there is also a very strong nominative connection between Venus-Isis and Queen Gwenevere.

The name 'Gwenevere' is often translated as meaning 'white'. But this is incorrect and the true but previously unnoticed connection with Venus-Isis can be demonstrated via the days of the week. The English for 'Friday' was derived from the goddess Frigg or Friya, the Norse wife of Odin, whose name comes from *frigg* meaning 'beloved'. This gives us the Anglo-Norse word Frigg-day or Friya-day, which became the English 'Friday'. However, since Frigg was the Norse goddess of love, she was traditionally seen to be the direct equivalent of Venus-Isis. In which case, the Norse trinity of Odin, Frigg and Thor appear to be remarkably cognate with the Egyptian trinity of Osiris, Isis and Horus, and the Christian Trinity of God, Mary and Jesus.

So far, so good. But if we return to the analysis of Friyaday or Friday, and remember that Venus was called Veneris in Latin, we can see a direct connection between the 5th day of the week and the Eastern goddess of love and fertility in many languages:

Language	5th Day	Goddess	Attributes
English	Fri-day	Frigg-Friya	goddess of love (Venus)
German	Frei-tag	Frigg-Friya	goddess of love (Venus)
Latin	Dies Veneris	Venus	goddess of love
French	Vendre-di	Venus	goddess of love
Italian	Vener-di	Venus	goddess of love
Welsh	Dydd Gwener	Gwene	goddess of love (Venus)

It looks like Friday has long been considered to be the sacred day of Venus-Isis-Aphrodite, across many cultures and languages. And if the Welsh name for Friday is Dydd Gwener, then surely Gwener must be the Welsh pronunciation for Venus-Isis. And this is exactly what William Spurrell's 1848 Welsh-English dictionary says - **Gwener means 'Venus'**. And if we drop the prefixed 'g' and remember that the Latin 'v' often becomes an Anglo-Saxon 'w' (just like 'vespa' becomes 'wasp'), it is apparent that the Welsh Gwener is merely a poor rendition of the original Latin pronunciation:

Welsh	Gwener
	Wener
	Vener
Latin	Veneris
English	Venus

Once again we see that large segments of the Celto-Welsh languages are simply peculiar pronunciations of Latin and Greek. And in this case, it has been proven beyond doubt that Gwener is a reference to the goddess Venus-Isis. So the end result of this tangential investigation is that it is highly unlikely that Queen Gwenevere was named after a simple colour. Instead, she was bore the illustrious name of the goddess Isis-Venus, or was possibly even considered to be an incarnation of Isis-Venus herself, and her special veneration day was Gwener-dydd, Gwenerdi, Venerdi, Vendredi, or Friday.

In which case, we have now arrived back at the same point where this investigation first started. The birth legends of Arthur and Jesus appear to be very similar, with both being born under the symbolism of a star. In the case of Jesus, that star symbolism was due to Mary the Virgin (and Mary Magdalene) being an incarnation of Venus-Isis. But now we see that Queen Gwenevere was also an incarnation of Venus-Isis, and so these two sibling royal marriages now appear to be almost identical, with both Arthur and Jesus marrying sisterly incarnations of Venus: Gwenevere and Mary.

So was 'Gwenevere' simply a Latino-Welsh pseudonym for Mary Magdalene? As we saw in fig 8.7, Mary Magdalene was strongly connected to the Star of Venus via her Magdalene title referring to a pyramid - the double pyramid that forms the outline of the Magen Star or Mawgane Star of Venus. And this is a name that strongly links Mary Magdalene with Arthur's other sister, Morgane le Fay. And yet this is not all, for there are more similarities and connections to consider. Just as the Arthurian Star Prophesy signalled that Arthur and Gwenevere would rule a great kingdom, so the biblical and Judaean Star Prophesy signalled that Jesus and Mary Magdalene would also rule the whole world. The Roman historian Tacitus says of this Judaic prophesy:

> In most (Jews) there was a firm persuasion, that in the ancient records of their priests was contained a prediction of how at this very time the East was to grow powerful, and rulers coming from Judaea were to acquire a universal empire. These prophesies had pointed to Vespasian and Titus, but the common (Jewish) people had interpreted these mighty destinies of themselves. (Tacitus, Histories, 5:13) (Author's brackets.)

This was the Judaic Star Prophesy from Numbers 24:17, that was being used in the 1st century to hail a new King of the Jews and a new Judaeo-Nazarene emperor of Rome. And it was the supporters of Jesus who were promoting this prophesy, so that their leader could fulfill his destiny. And this is why they proclaimed that Jesus-Izas had been born under the Eastern Star of Venus-Isis. And the result of all these deliberations is that we now have multiple correlations between two very similar royal couples:

Jesus was a king born under a star
Arthur was a king born under a star

Mary Mag was an incarnation of Venus
Gwenevere was an incarnation of Venus

Jesus married his sister
Arthur married his sister

Jesus was a 1st century monarch (Math 2:2)
Arthur was a 1st century monarch (*High History*)

Jesus was destined to rule world (Math 2:6)
Arthur was destined to rule world

Jesus had a tax-dispute with Rome (Mk 12:17)
Arthur had a tax-dispute with Rome

Jesus fought a war with Rome (Mk 15:7)
Arthur fought a war with Rome

Fisher King and Uther Pendragon

But it is not only the name for Queen Gwenevere that has been mistranslated by previous researchers, so too has the name for Uther Pendragon. And yet these translations are key elements within this investigation. Uther Pendragon was said to be father of King Arthur, so how can we discover the true roots of Arthurian history unless we understand what his name really means? It is often claimed that 'Uther' was derived from the Welsh meaning 'terrible', resulting in the unsatisfactory name: 'Terrible Head of a Dragon'. But since Arthur's name is said to have been derived from a bear, then why not Uther's too? After all, in comparison with some of the bastardised names in these manuscripts, the difference between 'Arthur' and 'Uther' is minimal. In which case, Uther's full name would become 'Bear Head Dragon' or perhaps 'Bear Chief Dragon'.

While these translations are possible the resulting name is not entirely satisfactory. What exactly does a 'Bear Chief Dragon' refer to? Actually, the correct answer to Uther's name was given in Chapter I, where it was observed that the name Arth or Uwth was Aramaic, and referred to Ursa Major, the Great Bear. There are three elements to Uther's title, and if we use Aramaic as our root language we can derive the following:

Name	Aramaic		Meaning
Uther	*uwth-uwsh*	עות-עוש	Ursa Major or Great Bear*
Pen	*penah*	פנה	face (head?)
Dragon	*dagown*	דגון	fish or dragon

Just in case readers are wondering, most of these terms have migrated into the Latin, and so this translation works there too. The Aramaic Uwth or Uwsh has become the Latin *ursa* meaning 'female bear', which is where the Latin name Ursa Major comes from. But the Latin Vulgate Bible has chosen to translate the Aramaic Uwth as Arcturus, which has come from the Greek *arktos* αρκτος meaning 'bear'. The Greek *arktos* is also the root for the Latin Arcticus and the English Arctic, and so the northern polar lands were named after the northern constellation. So the equivalent translations for Uther Pendragon's name from the Latin would be:

Name	Latin	Meaning
Uther	*ursa*	Arcturus or Ursa Major
Pen	*princep?*	chief
Dragon	*draconem*	dragon

Note that when this name is translated from the Aramaic to the Latin, the import of Uther's name remains very much the same - he was still named

* Note that Ursa Major was originally a hippopotamus, in the Ptolemaic Egyptian zodiac of Dendera. Not knowing what a hippo was, the Greeks and Romans substituted the hippo with image of a bear. See fig 10.9 for an illustration.

as the Head Dragon. However, if 'Uther' refers to a constellation rather than an animal, then perhaps the Dragon title should do likewise and refer to the constellation Draco. But this would result in a rather meaningless title that invoked two constellations simultaneously - something like 'Ursa Major head of Draco'.

The answer to this confusion comes from both Walter Oxford and Robert Boron, which is a good illustration of why we need to use more than one manuscript to decypher this Arthurian mystery. The first and most important step in this new translation comes from Jesus College Manuscripts 61 and 28, which are 15th and 17th century copies of the original 12th century Welsh *Brut Oxford*. And these are among the earliest extant references to Uther Pendragon that we have. However, there is a strange oddity in these manuscripts that is not often mentioned, and that is the fact that the name for Uther in the Welsh versions of *Brut Oxford* is not given as Ythr Pendragwn, it is actually written as Ythyr ben Dragown.[2] See the images in fig 10.3 for confirmation.

So the Pen was originally a Ben, and it was a separate preposition or noun. But that small change can make a considerable difference to this royal title. If the 'ben' in this Welsh manuscript had been taken straight from the Aramaic, as was the rest of this title, then this just has to be the standard Aramaic patronymic meaning 'son of'. This would make a great deal of sense because patronymics were very common in names of this era, from the Scottish 'mac' (MacDonald), to the Norman 'fiz' (Fitzgerald or Feirefiz), and the Irish 'o' (O'Reilly), the addition of the father's name was very important in many families. And especially within aristocratic families, who had a heritage to maintain. And this is a very ancient tradition that probably springs from the royal names of Egypt, where the pharaoh was given what might be called a theonym - the name of his spiritual god-father.

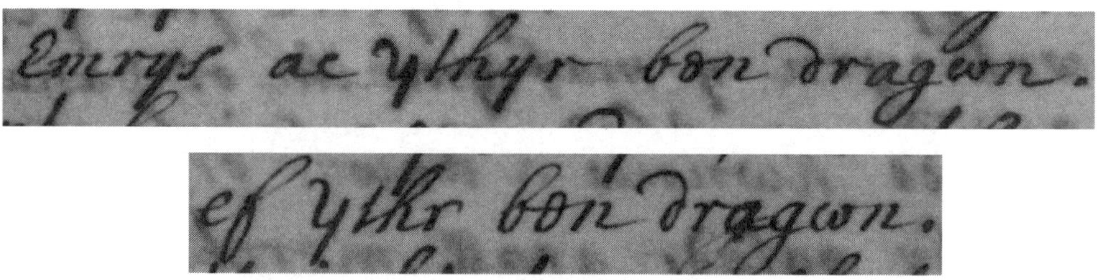

Fig 10.3
Two references to Ythr ben Dragown in Brut Oxford. Note that the central noun is definitely a 'ben' rather than a 'pen' - a 'son' and not a 'head'. Images from Jesus College Manuscript XXVIII at Oxford University, which is a 1695 copy of the original made by Hugh Jones of the Ashmolean Museum.

Ramesses	Ra-Moses	Son of the Sun-god, Ra
Tuthmoses	Tuth-Moses	Son of the Moon-god, Thoth

Being a king, Uther's patronymic name is again likely to refer to something cosmic, rather than his mortal father, and so the true origin of Uther **ben** Dragon may not refer to a 'Son of a Dragon' but rather to a 'Son of Dragon Constellation'. However, there is one important additional step that needs to be taken in this decypherment. If we take the Greek *drakon* δρακων meaning 'dragon' or 'sea monster' and translate it into Aramaic, we find that the Aramaic *dagown* דגון is more of a 'fish' than a 'dragon'. The Philistine's fish-god, for instance, was called Dagown in 1Samuel 5:2-5. This final clarification gives us a new revised meaning for Uther's name, and so the equivalent translations from the Aramaic would be:

Name	Aramaic		Meaning
Uther	*uwth-uwsh*	עות-עוש	Ursa Major
ben	*ben*	בן	son
Dragon	*dagown*	דגון	fish (or Pisces)

Now this is a translation that makes much more sense. The suggestion that Uther's Dragon-title was a stellar symbol was correct, but the portentous sign that appeared in the heavens above in the 1st century was not Draco, it was actually the constellation of Pisces. In which case, the 'two rays' that were said to emanate from this cometary dragon-fish, were actually the 'two rays' that form outline of the constellation of Pisces. In fact, the description in the previous quote from *History of Kings* is so perfect, it is as if Monmouth was looking at a symbolic depiction of the constellation of Pisces, like the one in fig 10.4, and trying to describe it. And we know that this 'two ray' design for Pisces is a very ancient depiction, because the 1st century BC zodiac at Dendera in Egypt displays this exact same layout, as can be seen in figs 10.9 and 10.10.

More importantly, the foremost constellation of interest in the 1st century, and within all of Arthurian and gospel history, was not Draco the dragon, but Pisces the fish. As we have already seen, all of the main events within Arthurian and gospel history took place in the 1st century AD, and yet this was the very era when the constellations moved away from the Great Month of Aries and towards the Great Month of Pisces. So the title for Uther ben Dragown refers to this king being the Son of Pisces - the first king of the new Great Month of Pisces.

This is why King Uther ben Dragown became the first of the famous Fisher Kings within Arthurian traditions, because he was the first king of Pisces. And in the equivalent gospel traditions Jesus-Izas adopted a very similar title and became the first of the Fishers of Men. In reality, both of these 1st century monarchs were being identified with the Great Month of Pisces, and it is the steady and predictable movement of the heavens within precession that gives us a secure astronomical date for their births and reigns. The Great Month of Aries ceded to the Great Month of Pisces in about AD 10, and so the infant Jesus and the infant Arthur must both have been born in the very early 1st century AD.

Since the appearance of the new Great Month of Pisces (the Arthurian dual-rayed 'comet') signalled this momentous change in the heavens, this should really have made the birth of King Arthur the primary celebration, and therefore made King Arthur the first ben Dragown or son of Pisces, not Uther. However, since this momentous event took place during the reign of King Uther, it would not be so surprising that he too claimed to be the first ben Dragown - the first of the Fisher Kings or Kings of Pisces. However, if we were to be even more radical, and say that Uther and Arthur were the same

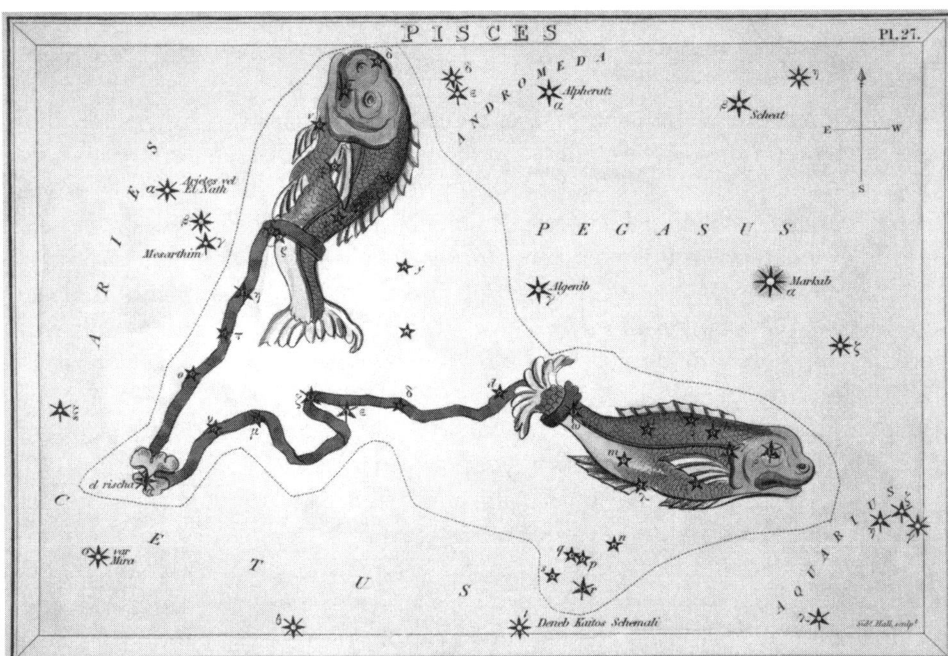

Fig 10.4
The 'two rays' of Uther's cosmic dragon or fish, were actually the 'two rays' that emanate from the constellation of Pisces. In which case, the Arthurian stellar symbol was not a comet, but the first appearance of the constellation of Pisces. The new precessional Great Month of Pisces commenced in about AD 10, and so this cosmic symbolism dates Arthur's birth to the early 1st century.

individual, then Arthur ben Dragown would indeed have been the first of the Fisher Kings, and born in the early 1st century just as Jesus-Izas was.

And while these interconnected explanations are cogent and make sense of the information available, there is one more hurdle to cross. While the 'Son of Pisces' translation for ben Dragown is fairly secure and meaningful, the full title for Uther ben Dragown or Arthur ben Dragown appears to mean 'Ursa Major son of Pisces', which does not make much sense. Why would a king be named after two constellations?

The answer is that we may be reading this title the wrong way around - perhaps Uther was the patronymic rather than Dragown. The reason for thinking this is that the ring-master of the cosmos and zodiac was Ursa Major, and this central father-figure of the zodiac had twelve subordinate sons, which were the twelve signs of the zodiac residing in their twelve separate houses. So just as Jesus had twelve disciples, and Arthur had twelve knights, and Bron-Hebron had twelve sons, so too was Ursa Major encircled by twelve constellation-sons. So perhaps we should read this Arthurian name as Dragown ben Uther (Pisces the son of Ursa Major), rather than Uther ben Dragown (Ursa Major the son of Pisces).

However, the Arthurian Uther may not have been the only king with

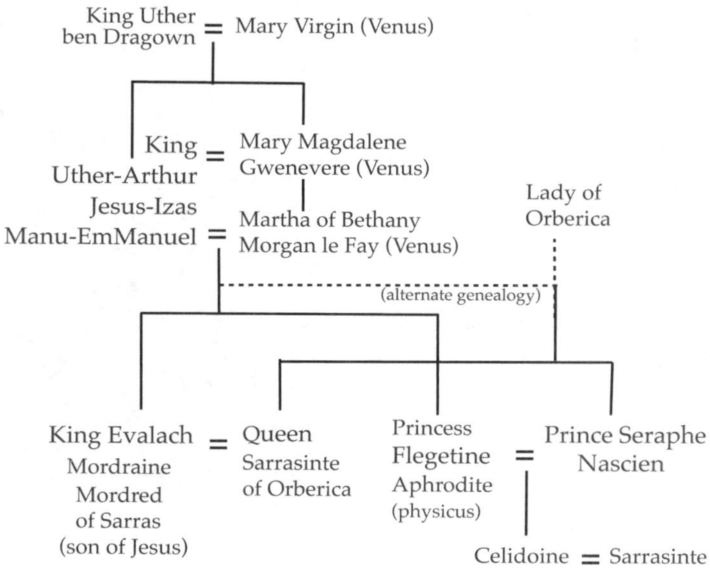

Fig 10.5
A revised genealogy of the Arthurian Sarras monarchy, taking into account the new links between Jesus and Arthur, and therefore also between Mary-Martha and Gwenevere-Morgan.

this name or title in this region and era. If Arthurian history was largely based upon the royal family of Edessa, then the name Uther may well have been Edessan and may have been used by other monarchs in this region. One of the neighbouring city states who followed these same traditions may well have been the principality of Hatra in Mesopotamia. The 2nd century kings of Hatra not only claimed a lineage from the Edessan monarchy they also wore a very similar crown, as reader Mike Ross has pointed out. And one of the more famous of the kings of Hatra was called Uthal. And since the 'l' to 'r' transliteration is one of the most common between Aramaic and Latin, King Uthal could easily be pronounced as King Uthar. In which case, the prestigious Uther title may well have been claimed by several monarchs in this region, because it honoured the central and therefore the most important constellation in the night sky - Ursa Major.

However, any research on the possible connections between the kings of Hatra and Arthurian history are now going to be severely hampered, because this very same statue has just been destroyed by the mindless Neanderthals of Islam. When it was observed in *Jesus, King of Edessa* that the mosaics recently discovered in Edessa only had a slim chance of survival in Muslim lands, this casual but accurate observation was widely criticised. However, the widespread destruction we have recently seen across fundamentalist controlled Egypt, Libya, Tunisia, Syria, and Iraq has demonstrated once more that this great series of books will not hide from the truth. It would be very easy and much safer to narrate sweet platitudes about the fundamental nature of Islam, just as our media and politicians regularly do, but that would be deceitful.

Fig 10.6
A statue of King Uthal of Hatra, which was displayed in the Mosul museum until it was destroyed by Muslim barbarians. His name and crown are reminiscent of Arthurian and Edessan traditions.

Talmud aristocrats

In previous chapters we have seen

good evidence that Arthurian history and the gospels are often singing from the same hymn-sheet. And if this is so, we may well have several alternate records and histories which we can explore, in order to further identity these Arthurian monarchs. These include the New Testament stories, the Talmud's version of these events, and even the historical accounts of Saul-Josephus Flavius. And it is entirely possible that we might find some common ground and agreement between this seemingly diverse array of accounts.

The starting point for this alternative investigation will be the Talmud, which contains a surprising amount of material about events in 1st century Judaea. And when we turn to the Talmud's account of the Jewish Revolt, we do indeed find three influential aristocrats who stand out as being very similar to Pelles, Pellehan and the Fisher King. These three aristocrats should really have been central to the story that has already been recounted within the *King Jesus Trilogy*, but because they have never been fully identified before, they have remained on the sidelines of this story. And yet there seems to be something familiar about them. They are called:

Name	Kalba Shabua	Nakdimon ben Gurion	Ben Zizit Hakeseth
Meaning	Dog Star	Victory of the People (Boethus or Boni)	Cushions and Tassels

Fig 10.7
Muslim barbarians destroying that very same statue of King Uthal of Hatra. The museum curator has since said that this statue was only a plaster copy of the original. Let us hope he is right about that. (Perhaps he should not have said anything, until this uprising is quashed.)

These three aristocrats were said to be the richest men in Judaea, and they controlled so much of the trade in food, wine, oil and wood, that they boasted that they could resist a siege of Jerusalem for 21 years. The provider of wood was said to be the most generous because it took 60 times the storage space to keep the wood, in comparison to grain or oil. So the provider of the city's wood was the equivalent of today's oil barons, for no society can operate without energy - not only the energy for cooking and heating, but also the energy to power industry and to make the vital industrial items fabricated from metal, pottery, brick and glass. The Talmud says of these wealthy aristocrats, in the late AD 60s:

> (God) then sent against them Vespasian the Caesar who came and besieged Jerusalem for three years. There were in it three men of great wealth, Nakdimon b. Gorion, Ben Kalba Shabua and Ben Zizit Hakeseth. One of these said to the people of Jerusalem, I will keep them in wheat and barley. A second said, I will keep them in wine, oil and salt. The third said, I will keep them in wood. The Rabbis considered the offer of wood the most generous (because) a storehouse of wheat requires sixty stores of wood. These men were in a position to keep the city for twenty-one years. (Gittin 56a)

In addition, Professor Eisenman has identified Nakdimon ben Gorion with Simon Boethus, because they appear to have the same daughter(s). So let us have a look at these three aristocrats in more detail and see if we can at last decypher their true identities, and their relationships to the biblical and Arthurian family trees.

Nicodemus Nakdimon

The New Testament has a few problems with the Talmud's account of Nakdimon. Firstly, he is an exceedingly rich aristocrat who has been closely linked with the gospel's equally rich aristocrat called Nicodemus: the neo-disciple who brought 100 'pounds' (about 34 kilos) of resins and spices (myrrh and aloes) to embalm Jesus' body after the crucifixion (Joh 19:39). This was an inordinate amount of expensive resins, enough according to the venerable theologian Adam Clarke to embalm 10 bodies rather than one. And this demonstrates how wealthy the gospel's Nicodemus really was. Clarke goes onto say of the gospel's Nicodemus:

> He was one of the members of the grand Sanhedrin; for such were ordinarily styled rulers among the Jews. Nicodemus, the son of Gorion, is mentioned in the

> Jewish writings, who lived in the time of Vespasian, and was reputed to be so rich that he could support all the inhabitants of Jerusalem for (twenty one) years. (Adam Clarke, 1832 Commentary on the Bible) (Author's brackets.)

The first problem with this quote, is that Adam Clarke is specifically linking the gospel's Nicodemus with the Talmud's Nakdimon - the rich aristocrat just mentioned who could 'support all the inhabitants of Jerusalem for 21 years'. But how was Nicodemus able to be so wealthy and influential in AD 30, at the time of the classical crucifixion scene, and then an equally wealthy and influential contemporary of Vespasian in AD 70? Forty years was a very long time to be at the peak of your power in the 1st century AD.

The answer to this is the standard chronological chasm we have seen many times before, because in reality all of the gospel events actually happened in the AD 60s rather than the AD 30s. And so we see here exactly the same chronological chasm that Joseph(us) of Arimathaea had to cross, in the account narrated by *History* in Chapter VII. In the case of Joseph(us) the *Vulgate's* inventive authors made him go to sleep for 42 years, while Adam Clarke has not even attempted an excuse for how Nakdimon-Nicodemus could bridge this same 40-year gap.

But whatever excuses are devised, these two aristocrats appear to have crossed this same chasm together. According to the gospels, Joseph(us) of Arimathaea and Nicodemus-Nakdimon were colleagues who were both involved in the 'burial' of Jesus after his crucifixion. However, according to a combination of the Talmud and Arthurian history, Joseph(us) of Arimathaea and Nicodemus-Nakdimon were also colleagues who were both involved in the Jewish Revolt. More importantly, they were both involved on the Roman side and became colleagues of Emperor Vespasian after the Revolt. So the AD 30s Josephus and Nicodemus were most certainly the same as the AD 70s Joseph(us) and Nicodemus, and this is a problem for the classical account of these events. However, if we use the revised chronology, and set Izas-Jesus' life and crucifixion into the late 60s and early 70s, just as Saul-Josephus narrates in his *Life*, then these aristocrats do not have to be colleagues at the peak of their power for 40 years or more.

And if we look for historical equivalents to Joseph(us) of Arimathaea and Nicodemus-Nakdimon, then they must surely be related in some manner to Saul-Josephus Flavius. Just like these two biblical Judaean aristocrats, Saul-Josephus was also a Jewish aristocrat who became a colleague of Vespasian after the Jewish Revolt and worked for the Romans. So if Joseph(us) and Nicodemus were working for Vespasian in AD 70, as Arthurian history relates, and Saul-Josephus was also working for Vespasian in AD 70, as classical history tells us, then all 'three' of these aristocrats must have been contemporaries and colleagues in the 70s. So why do none of these histories tell us that? Where is the account of Joseph(us) of Arimathaea having a meeting or meal with Saul-Josephus?

The answer is that none of these authors wanted us to know who Josephus Flavius really was, and what he was called in other accounts of this era. Remember that it was Saul-Josephus Flavius who took the three crucified leaders of the Jewish Revolt down from their crosses, after Jerusalem fell to the Romans in AD 70. So just as Joseph(us) and Nicodemus were taking an important rebel king down from his cross - one of three crucified rebels - Saul-Josephus was doing something remarkably similar. And the king who Joseph(us) and Nicodemus saved was called Jesus EmManuel, while the king who Saul-Josephus saved was called Izas Manu of Edessa. Once again we see an extraordinarily close connection between the lives of Joseph(us) of Arimathaea and Saul-Josephus, as if they were the same person. Which they were. But now we see that Nicodemus-Nakdimon was also closely linked to this conflated Saul-Joseph(us) (of Arimathaea).

The second problem with this quote by Adam Clarke, is why the orthodox Jesus-the-pauper-carpenter character was surrounded by so many rich and powerful men, who were leaders of the Sanhedrin and active during the Jewish Revolt. Rich and powerful leaders like Gamaliel (Acts 5:34), Joseph(us) of Arimathaea (Joh 19:38), and Nakdimon-Nicodemus (Joh 3:1). And the twin problems that Nicodemus-Nakdimon brought to the gospel story were so contentious that he was completely deleted from the Synoptic Gospels, even though he was the sympathetic neo-apostle who was going to pay for Jesus' burial. And so we are left with five short references to him in the Gospel of John, but these do not give us any idea of who he really was:

> There was a man of the Pharisees, named Nicodemus, a ruler of the Jews. The same came to Jesus by night, and said unto him, Rabbi, we know that thou art a teacher come from God: for no man can do the miracles that you do, except if god is with him. (John 3:1-2)

But Nicodemus was not an immediate convert to this new Fourth Sect Nazarene creed. In reply to Jesus' teachings he says:

> How can a man be born when he is old? Can he enter a second time into his mother's womb, and be born? (John 3:4)
>
> Nicodemus answered and said unto him, How can these things be? (John 3:9)

Nicodemus was therefore a very rich member of the Jerusalem Sanhedrin who was sympathetic to Nazarene Judaism, but hardly the most enthusiastic of converts. In fact, Nicodemus sounds like another version of Simon

Magus or Saul-Josephus, who were also sceptical about many aspects of the Nazarene Ebionite creed.

So does this narrow down his identity in the historical record at all? Unfortunately, not by much, because although Nicodemus was obviously closely associated with Joseph(us) of Arimathaea and the story of Jesus' crucifixion, his name was merely a nickname or a pseudonym derived from the Greek Nikos-Demos Νικος-Δημος meaning 'Victory of the People'. But this is a highly unlikely title for a Judaean aristocrat, who would have been an Aramaic-speaking Orthodox or Nazarene Jew rather than a Greek Gentile. And so this name has to be a humorous or perhaps ironic hypocorism, created at a later date by a Greek scribe for the Greek versions of the gospels.

However, if we turn to the Talmud we find a similar character called Nakdimon נקדימון. And as we have seen, Adam Clarke and the *Jewish Encyclopaedia* both readily admit that the Talmud's Nakdimon and the gospel's Nicodemus were the same person. Again this admission is surprising, considering the almost 40-year chasm that lies between these 'two' eras in his life, when using the classical chronology. The meaning of Nakdimon's Aramaic name is similarly obscured, because the Talmud merely gives two *pesher* interpretations that don't make much sense:

> A Tanna (Taanith 19b) taught that just as the sun stood still for Joshua, so did the sun stand still for Moses and for Nakdimon b. Gorion. (Aboda Zara 25a)

> Nakdimon b. Gorion was so called because the sun continued shining for his sake. (Gittin 56a)

The reference to the Sun standing still, points us towards a very famous verse in the Book of Joshua that most people in this era would have known about. The patriarch Joshua and his Gibeon allies were in a battle with the five kings of the Amorites and needed more time to finish the fight. So instead of helping Joshua militarily, god decides to make the day longer so the fight could continue. The god of the Jews never considers the most rational solution to a problem, and invariably comes up with some absurdly convoluted compromise. The original verse says:

> Then said Joshua to the Lord ... in the sight of (the Children of) Israel, 'You the Sun, stand still upon Gibeon. And you the Moon, (stand still) in the depths of Ayilon.' (Joshua 10:12)

However, in Nakdimon's case god made the Sun stand still so that he could win a bet over the lease of twelve wells - which seems like an inordinate waste of a supreme being's time and energy. But the Judaic god is like that sometimes: 'never mind the 350,000 people about to die in a tsunami, I have to save this guy from losing money in a bet...' Although in more rational terms the Talmud's description of the Sun 'setting' and then suddenly 'reappearing' during this bet sounds suspiciously like a solar eclipse in the evening. Anyway, one of the Talmud's *peshers* claims that the name Nakdimon was derived from the Aramaic *nakad* meaning 'shine', while the other claims it came from *kadima* meaning 'hasten'. But the Sun did not hasten, it either stood still or went backwards, and so these particular *pesher* interpretations are contrived and worthless.

A much more likely translation can be seen if we look at the name of the father of Alain li Gros, who was direct relative of Nakdimon and is alternately called Bron or Hebron. In *Merlin Grail* Bron-Hebron was the next Guardian of the Grail after Joseph(us) (of Arimathaea), and so the reason for choosing the name 'Hebron' is more than obvious. This is a classic example of Judaic *pesher*: looking to the Torah or Tanakh to find similar people with similar lives, and using them to either predict the future or conceal the present.

In this particular case there is only one Hebron in the Tanakh, and he is the son of Kohath and the brother of Uzziel or Izziel (Num 3:19). And the reason for picking this character as a pseudonym is that Izziel עזיאל has almost the same spelling as Izas-Jesus עזוז, and he was also the Guardian of the Ark of the Covenant (Num 3:30). So this *pesher* verse is deliberately conflating the Guardian of the Holy Grail with the Guardian of the Ark, as if they were the same relic, which they probably were. And it is likewise deliberately conflating Joseph(us) of Arimathaea with Izziel. (Josephus of Arimathaea was said to be the brother-in-law of Hebron-Bron, just as Izziel was the brother of Hebron.)

The great goal in life for Saul-Josephus (of Arimathaea) was to usurp the role of the gospel Jesus-Izas, and here he appears to have done just that. He is modeling himself on the Tanakh's Izziel (the Guardian of the Ark-Grail), so that he can pretend to be the new Izas-Jesus (and the Guardian of the Ark and Grail), and bequeath this holy relic to the next generation - Bron or Hebron:

Source	Character	Role
Arthurian	Joseph(us)	Guardian of Holy Grail
Arthurian	Hebron-Bron	brother-in-law of Joseph(us) (who wanted to be Jesus)
Tanakh	Izziel	Guardian of Ark of the Covenant
Tanakh	Hebron	bother of Izziel (sounds like Izas-Jesus)

And having discovered a great deal about Hebron-Bron, we can now decypher a great deal more about Nakdimon too. Because according to *High History*, Nakdimon was directly related to or perhaps the same as Hebron-Bron, who became the new Guardian of the Grail:

> Good Knight (Perceval) was he of right, for he was of the lineage of Joseph of Abarimacie (Arimathea) ... Yglais was his mother's name, and King Fisherman was his uncle ... The head of the lineage on his father's side was named Nichodemus. (High History chI:I) (Author's brackets.)

Perceval was the son of Alain li Gros (Pellehan), who was the son of Hebron-Bron-Hebron. So *High History* has already made it clear that Alain li Gros and his sons, Perceval and Feirefiz, were descended in some manner from Nakdimon-Nicodemus. Once again we see that all these manuscripts and authors are singing from the same hymn-sheet. But now we can include the Talmud in this literary choir too, because the rabbis go on to declare that Nakdimon was actually called Buni or Boni:

> We have learned in a Boraitha: His name was not Nakdimon, but Boni, and he was called Nakdimon because on his account the sun hastened. (Taanith 21a)

It is likely that the name Buni or Boni is the original Aramaic name for Nakdimon, upon which the distorted Arthurian *pesher* name of Bron or Hebron was based. And so the New Testament Nicodemus-Nakdimon was actually the Arthurian Bron or Hebron, the grandfather of Perceval. Nakdimon-Boni only became known as Nakdimon-Bron so that he could be positively confirmed as the Guardian of the Ark and the Grail, to confirm to those 'with ears to hear and eyes to see' * that the Ark of the Covenant and the Holy Grail were one and the same artifact. And they were the same, because the Ark was merely the Bethel-box: a 'House of God' that contained the Grail-stone. And so the Guardian of the Ark was also the Guardian of the Grail that resided inside the Ark. But it is likely that the original Ark of the Covenant had been lost, because when Joseph(us) went to Sarras he was instructed to make a new Ark. God said to Joseph(us):

> Before you leave this wood, you shall make an Ark for my chalice (the Grail) ... And when you wish to speak to me, open the Ark wherever you may be, so that only you and your son Josephus see the chalice. (History 4:127.) (Author's brackets.)

* A biblical quote from Ezek 12:2 and Mark 8:18.

So the Arthurian Holy Grail-chalice resided inside the Ark of Joseph(us), which was a copy of the original Ark of the Covenant. Although it is entirely possible that Joseph(us) was merely making a duplicate Ark, to increase his prestige and authority, while the original Ark remained in another location (Masada, Palmyra or Sogmatar). As we shall see in Chapter XII, the Grail was not simply a chalice or a bloodline, it was also a stone. And so the Arthurian Grail-stone was placed inside the Ark of Joseph(us), just as Moses placed his two Holy-stones inscribed with the Ten Commandments inside the Ark of the Covenant. (See Exodus 24 or Deuteronomy 10.) No doubt Saul-Joseph(us) (of Arimathaea) was triumphant at this time, for he had not only usurped the majesty and glory of Jesus, he had also become the new Moses, leading his people across the Syrian desert to Sarras-Palmyra.

The Talmud's conflation of the biblical Nakdimon-Nicodemus with the Arthurian Bron-Hebron, would make Nakdimon the father of Alain li Gros and the grandfather of Perceval and Feirefiz, as can be seen in the idealised genealogies in figs 13.6 and 13.7. And if Nakdimon was a *pesher* analogue of Hebron, then it is likely that his new nickname was derived from *nakad* נקד meaning 'piebald sheep' and *imon* ימין meaning 'south' or the 'southern quadrant in the sky'. And the resulting translation is astrological, as one might expect by now. The reference to 'piebald sheep' probably refers to the constellation of Aries, because in the 1st century era the Great Month of Aries was giving way to the Great Month of Pisces. So Nakdimon-Nicodemus was the last of the Ram Kings of Aries before the rise of the Arthurian Fisher Kings of Pisces. And this is more or less what Arthurian history relates, that Nicodemus was of the previous generation to the Fisher King, who is linked to either King Pelles or to King Pellehan-Alain.

And the reason for the suffix *imon* meaning 'south', is because during the Exodus the family of the Old Testament Izziel and Hebron were given the tent on the south side (or right side) of the Tabernacle (Num 3:29). However, the imagery of the twelve tents of the tribes of Israel surrounding the central Tabernacle, was actually another portrayal of the twelve 'houses' of the constellations of the precessional zodiac. And so the tent of the family of Izziel and Hebron represented the 'house' of the constellation that lay to the right side or south side of this Tabernacle-zodiac. And this description equates well with the positions of the constellations at the time of the Exodus.

The book *Tempest & Exodus* has equated the Israelite Exodus with the precessional change between the Great Month of Taurus and the Great Month of Aries (and with the eruption of Thera that happened at about that same time). This dates the first Great Exodus to about 1580 BC. If the Israelites had laid out the design of their Tabernacle-zodiac according to the positions of the zodiac constellations at the vernal or spring equinox in that era, then the result would be the zodiac in fig 10.8. The primary viewing orientation in astrological astronomy is to the east at the vernal or spring equinox, as shown in this diagram, which is why the Aramaic word *imon* or *timon* means both 'south' and 'right side'. And so if we look to the east at the spring equinox in about 1600 BC, we see that the constellation of Aries the ram is indeed on the south or right side.

And the 'piebald' description for Nakdimon-Nicodemus also makes a degree of sense in Arthurian terms. Firstly, this side of the Arthurian family had a well-known piebald descendent, according to Eschenbach's *Parzival,* because Feirefiz was the piebald son of Alain li Gros who looked like a magpie. And secondly the patriarch Jacob had similarly piebald sheep, which is why black and white sheep are still called Jacob's Sheep. But since this piebald colouring was closely connected to Aries and the zodiac, it is likely that this name has less to do with skin pigmentation and more to do with a solar-lunar conjunction within the constellation of Aries.

Within the dualist theology of Egypt, from which many of these concepts originated, the Sun and Moon were said to be white and black - complementary but contrasting dualist opposites. Thus the sexual union between the white Gahmuret-Alain and the black Belacane, the parents of the piebald Feirefiz, may well be an occult (hidden) allusion to the syzygy conjunction between the white Sun and the black Moon. In Egyptian theology, the Moon is seen to be dimmer than the Sun and it waxes and

Fig 10.8
The zodiac, looking east at the vernal equinox dawn in 1750 BC, when Taurus changed to Aries. Note that Aries lies on the right or south side of the primary viewing orientation for precessional astrology, which is east.

As the centuries roll by, this precessional zodiac will slowly turn anti-clockwise. And in AD10 the vertical position would mark the conjunction-line between Aries and Pisces, instead of Taurus and Aries.

wanes, so the Sun was said to be 'white' while the Moon was its dualist opposite and 'black'. In addition, the Sun was said to be the stable male while the Moon was its dualist opposite, the changeable female with a physiology that matched the cycles of the Moon, and so this allegorical story works on all levels. But this does not necessarily mean that this story was entirely cosmic and these princes and kings did not exist. The royalty of this era took on the role of the Sun-god and Moon-goddess, and so a royal marriage and its sacred consummation could be seen as a celestial syzygy conjunction - the Sun and Moon eclipsing in *flagrante delicto* in the heavens above.

Dendera zodiac

The evidence thus far indicates that the name for Nakdimon was something to do with this aristocrat being the last King of Aries, before the new King of Pisces was crowned. And it may well be that the signal for the change in the Great Months is a Solar-Lunar conjunction and eclipse in the correct era and constellation, which is why the patriarch Jacob ended up with piebald sheep when the Great Month of Taurus changed to the Great Month of Aries. See the book *Jesus, Last of the Pharaohs* for a detailed explanation of the precessional-astrological symbolism within the patriarch Joseph's discussion with pharaoh about bulls and sheep (Taurus and Aries).

Further evidence for the new Great Month being initiated by an eclipse comes from the magnificent zodiac at Dendera in Egypt, which is now in the Louvre Museum. This magnificent Greco-Egyptian zodiac, which is a 1st century Ptolemaic carving rather than being truly ancient, depicts the standard symbols of the constellations that are familiar to modern astrology. The only exception is the central constellation facing Leo and Cancer and with its back to Capricorn and Sagittarius, which must therefore be Ursa Major, the Great Bear. But on the Dendera zodiac this large animal is actually the standard depiction of the Nile-god Hapi, in the guise of a hippopotamus. It would appear that as depictions of this Egyptian zodiac spread to the more northerly regions of Europe, the locals there had never seen a hippopotamus and presumed that this large animal walking on its hind legs must be a bear. And so the constellation of Hapi Major, the Great Hippo, became Ursa Major, the Great Bear. And had this change not happened, then King Arthur would have been called King Hippo instead.

Perhaps this is another reason for the story about Hippocrates in Rome, in Chapter VI. We saw there how the name Hippocrates could be translated into the Aramaic as Iz-sus meaning 'Powerful Horse', and this being a convenient pseudonym for King Izas Jesus. However, if the constellation of Ursa Major the Great Bear was originally Hippo Major, the

Great Hippo, then Hippocrates would have been a convenient and decidedly covert pseudonym for King Arthur. So the Hippocrates story in Chapter VI works for King Jesus-Arthur in both of these languages and traditions. This may imply that 'Hippocrates' was a well-known title for anyone who was considered to be the ring-master and governor of the heavens - the great sage and Herculean Ursa Major character who took on the role of the central constellation of the zodiac:

Language	**Constellation**	**Meaning**	**Name**
Latin	Ursa Major	Great Bear	Arthur
Egypto-Greek	Hapi Kratos	Great Hippo	Happicrates
Greek	Hippo Kratos	Great Horse	Hippocrates
Aramaic	Iz Sus	Great Horse	Jesus

From the layout of the Dendera zodiac in we can see that this is definitely a precessional zodiac, because the primary zodiac symbols are all displaced to one side. So if we draw a circle around them, like the top-right red circle in fig 10.9, the circle is very asymmetric to the main layout of this composition. And if we draw this circle's asymmetric twin, depicted here with the bottom-left blue circle, we end up with two intersecting circles. These are the standard celestial and ecliptic perimeter circles that form the basis of precession, and are displayed on any good stellar planisphere.

These are the big brothers of the circles that we saw in fig 3.8. They intersect more here because the wheels in fig 3.8 were not drawn to their full extent, and the circles drawn on the Dendera zodiac are actually the celestial and ecliptic perimeters or planes, rather than the smaller axis circles. The two types of concentric circles in the heavens are shown more clearly in fig 14.14. And the Dendera circles intersect more than the actual celestial and ecliptic perimeters in fig 14.14, because the sculptor has used a 1/4 displacement ratio between the circles, rather than the proper 1/8 displacement. Presumably this was done to highlight the difference between these circles. However, having made this artistic change the designer has rather cramped the central constellations that lie inside the arcuate or ellipse, resulting in some changes in constellation positions. Likewise, we can see that because Leo is such a long symbol to draw, it has displaced Cancer inside the zodiac perimeter circle (the ecliptic circle).

The central axis of the Dendera zodiac is exactly the same as on the Hamat Teverya zodiac, in fig 12.12. The vertical axis (as shown here) bisects the constellations of Aries and Pisces, indicating the start of a new Great Year and therefore a precessional date of about AD 10, which is presumably when this zodiac was constructed. The illustration here has been reversed, with Aries on the left and Pisces on the right, to match the design and layout of the Hamat zodiac. Some planispheres have the constellations the other way around, because they expect the viewer to be looking up to the heavens. The Dendera zodiac was depicted like this because it was recessed into the ceiling of the temple, but the Hamat zodiac is on the floor and so the constellations are depicted the other way around.

The strange thing about the Dendera zodiac is that although it is

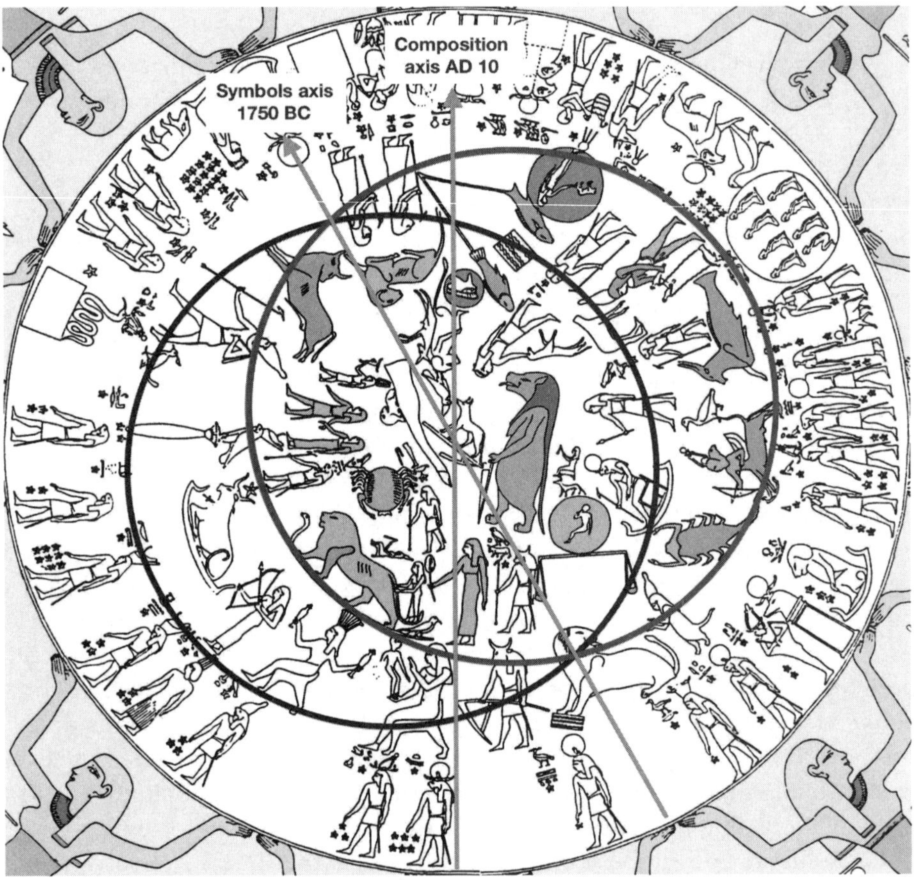

Fig 10.9
The Dendera zodiac, with the zodiac constellations highlighted. The central top-bottom axis is the same as on the Hamat Teverya zodiac in fig 12.12, suggesting a date of AD 10. However, the two circles are the ecliptic plane (red right) and the celestial plane (blue left). The top-left crossing point is between Taurus and Aries, and therefore marks the new Great Month of Aries in 1750 BC. Note the Sun and Moon in syzygy conjunction either side of Pisces, which suggests an eclipse in the constellation of Pisces. The Dendera zodiac is on the ceiling of the temple, and therefore normally shows a reversed layout to the one displayed on the floor at Hamat Teverya.

physically orientated with an precessional early 1st century date - with the axis of the entire zodiac composition aligned with a centerline through Aries and Pisces - the layout of the zodiac symbols themselves are marking a much earlier date. The two circles marked on this zodiac are the celestial and ecliptic planes or perimeters, as we have seen, and in astronomy the spring crossing point where these circles meet is called the vernal point. In the yearly cycle the vernal point marks the spring equinox on March 21st, which is when these precessional observations are made. But in the precessional cycle, the same spring crossing point marks the precessional era or date for the entire zodiac.

On the Dendera zodiac we can see that the spring crossing point is exactly aligned between the constellations of Taurus and Aries. This is marked by the orange arrow that is displaced anti-clockwise from the vertical. The strange thing about this layout, is that this is the exact location the vernal point would be in during precessional change from the Great Month of Taurus to the Great Month of Aries. And this marks a precessional date of 1750 BC. So the Dendera zodiac was certainly constructed in the early 1st century AD or BC, because the entire composition is aligned with the conjunction between Aries and Pisces; but the layout of the zodiac marks the turn of the previous Great Month, between Taurus and Aries. Why this has been done, is a bit of a mystery.

However, this is very similar to the cult of Mithras in Chapter VI, which was also shown to be an entire Great Month out of date. And it is also very similar to modern astrology, which is again an entire Great Month out of date. So here we have three precessional astrological fraternities, and all of their zodiacs are one precessional month out of date. Is this how precessional astrology is supposed to work? Is the previous layout of the zodiac maintained, until the Great Month changes nearly 2,000 years later? Just for reader's interest, the Voyager 4.0 planisphere dates for the precessional Great Months are as follows:

Great Month of Pisces	0010 AD	to	2500 AD	
Great Month of Aries	1750 BC	to	0010 AD	*
Great Month of Taurus	4500 BC	to	1750 BC	

The other interesting observation about the Dendera zodiac, which is probably more pertinent to Arthurian research, is that either side of the two arms of Pisces there are two circles. The larger circle contains an image of Isis and a baboon (Thoth), which clearly indicates that this is the Moon; while the smaller circle contains the Eye of Horus, representing the Sun. So this zodiac is clearly illustrating the Sun and Moon in syzygy conjunction with Pisces.** Since this conjunction is in Pisces, one presumes it is marking the 1st century construction era of this precessional zodiac, when Aries was about to cede its dominant position to Pisces. And presumably this was not any old syzygy conjunction with Pisces, but an actual solar eclipse within Pisces. And this will have to be a solar eclipse, rather than a lunar eclipse, because the Sun and Moon are depicted in the same constellation.

If we now search for solar eclipses that took place in the constellation of Pisces (ie: in March) in the early 1st century, that were visible in Egypt, there are not that many to choose from. They include:

7th	March	50	BC
28th	March	05	AD
19th	March	52	AD
20th	March	71	AD [3]

Depending on how good the Egyptians and Nazarene Jews were at predicting solar eclipses, and where they drew the boundary-line between Aries and Pisces, they would most likely have chosen AD 5 as being the closest Piscean solar eclipse to the start of the new Great Month of Pisces. So if this cosmic solar-lunar consummation of a celestial and royal marriage was important in deciding the boundary changes between the Great Months, then the Great Month of Aries must have turned into the Great Month of Pisces in AD 5. And if this conjunction simultaneously marked the birth of a special royal son and daughter, they too would have been born in AD 5. And the closest

Fig 10.10
An enlargement of the actual Dendera zodiac, showing the circles of the Sun and Moon at the ends of the 'two rays' of Pisces (as Monmouth describes them). The larger circle symbolises the Arthurian Moon-daughter, while the smaller circle represents the Sun-son, or King Arthur-Jesus.

royal Egypto-Nazarene birth to AD 5 would have been the biblical nativity of Prince Jesus-Izas-Arthur (and possibly Mary Magdalene), who would have become the first of the Fisher kings and queens. And this is why *History of Kings* says of King Arthur's birth:

> There appeared a star of marvelous size and brightness ... in the likeness of Pisces. And from the mouth of Pisces issued forth two rays ... (One) ray ... portended that a son shall be born ... and the other ray signified a daughter. (History of Kings VIII:14) (With 'dragon' changed to 'Pisces'.)

The two rays of Pisces can be clearly seen on the 1st century Dendera zodiac in fig 10.10. And since the Sun is male and the Moon is female, we have here an unmistakable depiction of a son and daughter being born at the ends of the two rays of the constellation of Pisces, just as this quote says. One ray terminates in a (larger) Moon-daughter while the other ray terminates in a (smaller) Sun-son. Again, it is almost as if Monmouth is looking at the Dendera zodiac and trying to describe what he sees. And this is interesting, because it suggests that this accurate description came directly from the Dendera zodiac. But if so, then a Crusader knight must have been to Dendera in Egypt in a very early era. Monmouth was writing his manuscript in 1135, while King Amalric I of Jerusalem did not liberate Egypt until 1163. Which suggests that a party of knights or pilgrims had already negotiated a trip into Fatimid Egypt in the early 12th century, prior to the liberation of Christian Coptic Egypt from Muslim subjugation.

So the great portent in the heavens that marked the birth of King Arthur-Jesus was actually the precessional movement from the Great Month of Aries to the new Great Month of Pisces. And this was accompanied by a solar eclipse: a daughter-son syzygy eclipse in the constellation of Pisces. And this gives us a rather precise date for this royal birth of AD 5. And if this event was all planned down to the last detail, and included a small deceit by the priesthood and physicians involved in this royal birth, we might further narrow this date down to 28th March AD 5. And the special prince who was subsequently said to have been born under the eastern star on 28th March AD 5 was King Izas-Jesus (ie: King Arthur-Jesus).

This eastern star was actually Venus, and although it rose in the east the biblical Magi followed it to its destination, which would have been in the

* The constellations are all different sizes and so the Great Months are of different lengths. The constellation of Aries is quite small, and so the Great Month of Aries was only 1,760 years long, instead of the average length of 2,140 years.

** Syzygy refers to a solar-lunar conjunction, normally during an eclipse.

west. And it so happens that the solar eclipse in AD 5 was a sunset eclipse in the west, and it was in a very close conjunction with Venus. Venus would not have been visible until the eclipse began, but would have suddenly blazed into view as the skies darkened - the Eastern Star setting in the west. And this would have been most unusual, because you cannot normally see Venus when it is in conjunction with the blazing Sun. But this was a very rare eclipse where the darkened skies meant that Venus could be clearly seen, right next to a Sun that was in *flagrante delicto* with its lunar consort.

And since this particular eclipse was an evening eclipse, it would also recreate the circumstances of Nakdimon-Nicodemus's celestial trick, where he was supposed to have made the Sun stand still or run backwards. It was claimed in Talmud *Ta'anit* 19b-20a that the Sun had set before it had begun to rain, and so the day had already finished and Nakdimon had lost his bet with a Gentile about water in some wells. But after it stopped raining the Sun suddenly came back out again, and so the day was not over and Nakdimon had won his bet. So an improbable story was devised that Nakdimon had asked god to make the Earth stop turning or the Sun to go backwards. And some Jewish fundamentalists still believe these absurd fabrications, and set school homework for kids asking questions about it. And yet if we disregard the usual religious fantasy, this very same scenario could indeed have happened during this late evening eclipse.

If the sky was overcast, so the Sun could not be clearly seen, the sky would have been darkened by the eclipse about 30 minutes before the normal sunset and it would have looked like the Sun had already set. The eclipse ended 45 minutes after sunset, and so the sky might well have brightened again after the Sun had been seen to set. This display would not have been very dramatic at sea level in Judaea, but if this wager had been discussed further west in Libya or Tunisia, the end of the eclipse and the re-brightening of the sky would have been clearly visible, and so this was indeed a day with two sunsets. In which case, this unlikely story was not about the intervention of god in the paltry affairs of man, it was really about a knowledgeable Nazarene astronomer winning a bet against an unenlightened Gentile.

Nicolaitans

There is another possible reference to Nicodemus within the gospels that may help confirm his identity, and that is the reference to someone called Nicolas in Acts of the Apostles. In these verses, the disciples are complaining that they have to do menial tasks like serving at the table, just as monks in a monastery would have to do, when they should be out evangelising. So they appointed several (rich) deacons to look after the administration of the Church, and these included someone called Nicolas:

> And the saying pleased the whole multitude: and they chose Stephen, a man full of faith and of the Holy Ghost, and Philip, and Prochorus, and Nicanor, and Timon, and Parmenas, and Nicolas a proselyte of Antioch. (Acts 6:5)

The biblical *Concordance* says that Nicolas is merely an alternate form of the Greek Nicodemus. The name was derived from Nikos Laos Νικος λαος which means 'Victory of the People', the same as Nicodemus.

However, if these two similar characters were the same person, then we can see here that Nicodemus must have been a proselyte (a convert to Judaism) from Antioch, who became a deacon of the Church. Now this is interesting, for we have already uncovered and discussed the famous proselytes from Antioch in previous works, and the most famous of the proselyte Jews from Antioch included most of the members of the royal family of Edessa, with Queen Helena as their proselyte matriarch. And since Nicodemus was the person in charge of embalming, according to the Gospel of John, he must have been a deacon in the Church of Jesus and James. The only difference to the story being told here in Acts, is that in reality this family were proselyte converts to Nazarene Judaism rather than Orthodox Judaism, and they actually came from Antioch-Edessa rather than Antioch-Orontes.

In which case, the gospel's Nicodemus is getting ever-closer to the story we are familiar with - the history of the royal family from Antioch-Edessa fomenting and prosecuting the Jewish Revolt. But if this is so, then this same royal family became despised after Jerusalem and its Temple had been destroyed in AD 70, according to the historical and talmudic accounts. So did Nicodemus-Nicolas suffer the same fate as the Edessan royalty? Was he too despised? Well, in Revelations we do see that orthodox opinion turned against Nicodemus. The author of this part of Revelations - who sounds remarkably similar to Saul-Josephus writing his epistles - writes to the angels (the ministers) of Saul-Josephus' Simple Judaic communities in Anatolia and scolds them yet again. They must have dreaded the arrival of every new letter from Judaea:

> Unto the angel (minister) of the church of Ephesus write this: '... I know your works and your labor and your patience, and how you cannot not bear those who are evil; and how you have examined those who that say they are apostles and are not, and you have found them to be liars ... repent, or else I will come unto you quickly and remove your candlesticks ... But this you do have, that you hate the creed of the Nicolaitans, which I also hate. (Rev 2:1-6)

> And to the angel (minister) of the church in Pergamos write: '... you have there

> some who hold to the doctrine of Balaam, who taught Balak to cast a stumbling block before the children of Israel, to eat things sacrificed unto idols, and to commit fornication. And you also have them that hold the doctrine of the Nicolaitans, which thing I hate. Repent, or else I will come unto thee quickly, and will fight against them with the sword of my mouth. (Rev 2:12-16)

So who were these Nicolaitans, who (Saul-Josephus?) so despised in the post-Revolt era? Adam Clarke says that they were:

> These were ... a sect of the Gnostics, who taught the most impure doctrines, and followed the most impure practices. They are supposed to have derived their origin from Nicolas, one of the seven deacons mentioned Ac 6:5. The Nicolaitans taught the community of wives, that adultery and fornication were things indifferent. (Commentary on the Bible, 1832)

As Clarke says, the Nicolaitans were supposed to be followers of Nicolas, the very same Nicolas from Acts 6:5 who we have already closely linked with Nicodemus-Nakdimon. And yes, if the Nicolaitans indulged in the Egypto-Nazarene custom of incest, as did many of these Egypto-Judaean royal families, then they would indeed have had consanguinity rules that strongly conflicted with the new rules and regulations that Saul-Josephus had crafted within Simple Judaism.

As can be seen, the author of Revelations hates the creed of the Nicolaitans (the Church of Nicodemus) with a passion, and if this author had been Saul-Josephus then we know exactly why this should be so. Saul-Josephus was the Nazarene traitor who worked with the Romans to oppose and destroy the Nazarene Church, and so if any elements of those teachings still resided in Anatolia, then Saul-Josephus was going to root them out and destroy them - just as he was rooting them out and destroying the same creed over in Sarras-Palmyra.

These quotes also say that in Pergamos (Pergamon in northwest Turkey) there were still 'some who hold to the doctrine of Balaam'. But as we have seen in previous works, Balaam was commonly used in the Talmud as a covert reference to Jesus-Izas. And yes, the Nazarene Church of Jesus and James did use idols, just as the Catholic Church does today, and there were many references in these ancient texts to the cult of the Hieros Gamos Ηεροϛ Γαμοϛ or the Sacred Marriage.

But this quote comes from the post-Revolt era and Saul-Josephus was in the process of destroying anything and everything that had any connection to the vanquished King Izas-Jesus of Palmyra and Edessa. And so the author of these quotes (Saul-Josephus?) threatens to take the candlesticks from the Church at Ephesus, if they do not repent and agree to his demands! And while this threat sounds rather humorous it would have been quite a severe punishment, because no services could be held without the candlesticks being present. So the threat being made here is to excommunicate this Church and all its ministers, making them both heretics and unemployed. And so these bishops did the same as all salarymen do when faced with unemployment, they ~~stood up to their bullying manager and told him where to go~~. Actually, they did what the majority of people will do in this situation: they cravenly did as they were told and deleted anything to do with the creed of Nicodemus and King Izas-Jesus-Balaam. There was only one creed in town now, and it was a case of either adopting it or jumping on the next ship to an uncertain future in some far-flung land.

But do notice how this research has drifted so easily back to Judaea and the events of the Jewish Revolt. Only a few pages ago we were talking about Nicodemus being strongly linked to the father of Perceval-Galahad, and suddenly we are back to the aftermath of the Jewish Revolt and the supporters of the Nazarene Church of Jesus being persecuted by Saul-Josephus. So these verses in Revelations were not an account of an impoverished hermit-like Saul-Josephus sitting in the new Sanhedrin in Jabneh, after the Jewish Revolt, and writing threatening letters to communities all across Anatolia. What would that do? Who would take any notice? Instead, this was a confident Saul-Josephus who was the right-hand man of Emperor Vespasian, and therefore the master of all the Jewish and pseudo-Jewish congregations in the Roman East.

If Saul-Josephus was writing letters in this era, we can be sure that they were being delivered to these Anatolian Churches by a centurion and a small detachment from the legions. The fully armed centurion in his shining armour would stand to attention, salute, and hand the letter to the bishop while crisply barking: "A letter from the emperor's representative in Judaea - Sahh!" "Do you have any questions - Sahh!" There were no questions and the priest did exactly as he was told. And no spoons were discovered in the church either. *

Marie Antoinette

There are some further references to Nicodemus in the Talmud, which will support and clarify the hazy historical picture that is being painted here. The first of these quotes illustrates the great wealth that Nakdimon-Nicodemus had, before the Jewish Revolt:

* Please see the film *Life of Brian*.

> When the sages granted the daughter** of Nakdimon b. Gorion a weekly allowance of two *seahs* of wine for her puddings she said to them, 'May you grant such allowances to your daughters'. (Kethuboth 65a)

A *seah* is said to be seven liters, and so the daughter (in-law) of Nicodemus was receiving 14 liters of wine daily. And she blithely presumed that the other rabbis could afford to give the same allowance to their daughters. So this quote reads a little like Marie Antoinette's famous *faux pas*. Jean Rousseau said of this in his *Confessions*:

> Finally I recalled the temporary solution of a great princess, who was told that the peasants had no bread and who responded: 'Let them eat *brioche*.' [4]

But *brioche* is a much more expensive sweet-bread not unlike a cake, which the peasants could never have afforded. Rousseau does not clarify which princess said this, but it has been presumed to be Marie Antoinette. And the comment about the haughty daughter of Nikadimon was included in the Talmud for the very same reason - to demonstrate how out of touch with the common people this aristocratic Syrio-Judaean family were. But do remember that this is an account recorded by the victors in this civil war, and therefore by the enemies of this family. The truth is likely to reside somewhere in between this account, and the gospel view of a movement that was more in touch with the needs of the people.

There is a similar comment about this same haughty daughter of Nicodemus-Nakdimon in Kethuboth 66b, where she was said to have received 400 gold coins just for her perfume basket:

> It once happened that the daughter of Nakdimon b. Gorion was granted by the sage an allowance of four hundred gold coins in respect of her perfume basket for that particular day, and she said to them, 'May you grant such allowances for your own daughters!' And they answered after her: Amen (to that). (Kethuboth 66b) (Author's brackets.)

The reply: 'Amen (to that)!' is deliberately contemptuous. One can almost see the little 'thinks bubble' over the rabbi's head saying: "what planet is this woman on?" And a strikingly similar point is made in the gospels where

** This reference actually says that this lady was the daughter-in-law of Nakdimon, whereas the other quotes say she was the daughter. The balance of probabilities is that she was the daughter.

another rich princess, Mary Magdalene, uses an equally expensive 'perfume basket' to anoint Jesus:

> Then took Mary a pound of ointment of spikenard, very costly, and anointed the feet of Jesus ... Then said Judas Iscariot: "Why was not this ointment sold for three hundred denari (pence), and given to the poor?" (John 12:3-5.)

So the Talmud's pampered princess received a perfume basket worth 400 gold *denarii*, while Mary Magdalene's spikenard was worth about 300 *denarii*. And since it will be demonstrated shortly that the daughter of Nicodemus-Nakdimon was also called Mary, these seemingly diverse accounts appear to be rapidly merging. These were probably two separate accounts of the same expensive perfume. And this was indeed an inordinate amount of money to spend on perfume, because an allowance of 400 gold *denarii* was the equivalent of 110 years pay for a skilled artisan in the 1st century, or the equivalent of $8 million at today's values. (With 1st century labourers often working longer hours. See the labour-rates comparison in the following pages.)

And perhaps it should be pointed out that Judas' well-meaning socialist philanthropy would have flooded the market with spikenard and removed its largest customer from the market, thereby reducing the price of these valuable fragrances by about two thirds. And this would have resulted in widespread unemployment, hardship and poverty throughout the spikenard farming regions in India and China, and also among the caravan traders who brought these inordinately expensive aromatics, spices and silks all the way to Judaea and Rome.

This is the status and wealth that this group of wealthy aristocrats had, before the Jewish Revolt impoverished them. And this is the same status and wealth that Mary Magdalene and Jesus obviously had, before the Jewish Revolt impoverished them. Yes, by the admission of the very gospels themselves, Mary Magdalene and the Nazarene Church were inordinately wealthy. And so this second Marie Antoinette moment has been included in the Talmud's critical texts in order to build up the wealth and arrogance of this princess, in order to make her fall appear even more dramatic. As we all know, wealth can be a fickle thing, especially if one chooses to pick a fight with Rome. And so after the Jewish Revolt we find that the house of Nakdimon-Nicodemus had been laid low - so low that the wealthy Marie Antoinette-style daughter of Nicodemus could not be recognised among the starving refugees living in the ruins of Jerusalem.

> It once happened that Rabbi Johanan b. Zakkai left Jerusalem riding upon an ass, while his disciples followed him, and he saw a girl picking barley grains in

> the dung of Arab cattle. As soon as she saw him she wrapped herself with her hair and stood before him. 'Master', she said to him, 'feed me'. 'My daughter', he asked her, 'who are you?' 'I am', she replied, 'the daughter of Nakdimon b. Gorion'.
>
> 'My daughter', he said to her, 'what has become of the wealth of your father's house?' 'Master', she answered him, 'is there not a proverb current in Jerusalem: 'The salt of money is diminution?' 'And where, the Master asked, is the wealth of your father-in-law's house?' 'The one', she replied, 'came and destroyed the other'.
>
> 'Do you remember, Master', she said to him, 'when you signed my *kethubah*?' 'I remember', he said to his disciples, 'that when I signed the *kethubah* of this [unfortunate woman], I read therein "A million gold *denarii* from her father's house" besides [the amount] from her father-in-law's house'. Thereupon R. Johanan b. Zakkai wept. (Kethuboth 66b)

A sad tale indeed. Here is a lady who was given a *kethubah* bride price that was considerably in excess of a million gold *denarii*. (A *kethubah* is a complete marriage contract, including all financial arrangements. And in this instance the lucky couple received money from both parents.) Of course this million gold *denarii* marriage gift may be an exaggeration, but it would still represent quite a fortune even if it was divided by ten.

A gold *denarii* is an *aureus*, and in the 1st century an *aureus* is said to have weighed about 7 gm of pure 24 carat gold. This would mean that this million *denarii* bridal gift weighed in at 7 tonnes of gold, which is unlikely but always possible. At today's gold price of $40 a gram ($1,240 a troy ounce),* an *aureus* was worth $280, and therefore the daughter's million gold *denarii* bride-price was worth about $280 million. But this is not a true valuation of this *kethubah* gift, because the value of gold has slipped a great deal over the last 2,000 years. A much better and truer valuation can be obtained by the equivalent labour rates. Money is merely the value of human endeavour (labour, and the products of that labour), rather than the arbitrary value of gold in your pocket, and these two values do not always keep in step with each other.

According to Matthew 20:2 a labourer's wage was a silver *denarii* a day, which equates quite well with what we know about the pay of Roman soldiers. A silver *denarii* of the same size as the 7 gm gold *aureus* would weigh

* At the time of writing the bullion prices were:
Gold price: $40.0 /gm or $1,240 /tr oz
Silver price: $00.55 /gm or $17 /tr oz

3.8 gms, which equates quite well with the weights of 1st century silver coins. And this seemingly expensive silver *denarii* would be worth just $2.05 at today's values. And since these 1st century workers would have laboured ten hours a day over a six-day working week, their monthly wage would have been 26 silver *denarii*, while their annual wage would have been 310 silver *denarii*. (Or 25 per month and 300 per year for ease of calculation.)

However, if we look at modern labour rates for a comparison, the American Bureau of Labor Statistics says that the median labour-rate for construction workers (bricklayers, plasterers, electricians, carpenters, and plumbers) in 2013 was about $24:00 an hour. This gives us $240 a day and $6,000 per month, for a 1st century 60-hour working week. And since 1st century Judaeans also paid taxes on their wages - via the annual pol-tax, temple tithes, and the many import duties and transport taxes on goods - this modern wage is a reasonable equivalent of the gospel's artisan getting a silver *denarii* a day. This means that a 1st century silver *denarii* should be worth about $240 in modern terms, rather than the $2 suggested by the modern silver bullion price. Thus the value of silver has slipped about 120-fold over the last 2,000 years, from its 1st century equivalent work-value.

However, the value of gold has not fared quite so badly. The 1st century silver-gold exchange rate was 25 silver *denarii* to one gold *aureus*. And so the same 1st century worker would have earned the equivalent of one gold *aureus* per month (roughly 25 days work in a month). If the modern work-value is $6,000 a month, as was calculated above, and the modern gold *aureus* value is $280, then the value of gold has decreased only 21-fold over the same 2,000 year period.

Precious metal	**weight gms**	**old hours work**	**modern work**	**modern value ($)**	**depreciation in value**
Gold	7.0	250 hrs	11.6 hrs	280	21-fold
Silver	3.8	10 hrs	0.08 hrs	2	120-fold

While gold has only depreciated 21-fold against modern work-rates, silver has depreciated 120-fold. But ordinary 1st century workers were paid in silver, not gold, because gold coinage was primarily reserved for Imperial taxes. So perhaps it should be the silver value and the silver depreciation that is the most representative here. Having said that, perhaps the fairest comparison would be an average of the modern value of these two precious metals, which works out at roughly a 70-fold depreciation in bullion values since the 1st century.

In which case, the true value of a 1st century gold *aureus* would not be $280, it would be closer to $20,000 in today's fiat money. This $20,000 value is a reflection of the ability of these gold coins to purchase skilled labour, and therefore purchase the goods and services that these skilled artisans provided. Thus the 1st century gold price was roughly $2,850 a gram or $88,500 a troy ounce, in today's fiat paper-money terms. So the million *aureus* bridal gift for Nakdimon-Nicodemus' daughter was not worth $280 million in today's money, it was worth more like $20 billion. And remember that this was not the value of the wealth controlled by this family, this was just the amount they paid to celebrate and seal the marriage of their daughter. So if this family had given 5% of their entire wealth to secure this prestigious marriage, then their total personal wealth was more like $400 billion. So the Nicodemus family were considerably more wealthy than today's Bill Gates and Warren Buffet, let alone impoverished paupers like Elon Musk and Jeff Bezos.

And who was the groom who secured such a prized wife? Well, the Talmud records that the pampered Marie Antoinette daughter of Nakdimon-Nicodemus married Jesus of Gamala, who was the high priest of Jerusalem in the early AD 60s. However, during the Jewish Revolt this same Jesus of Gamala also became a revolutionary rebel commander in Galilee, who commanded 600 rebel fishermen. And as the leader of the Jewish Revolt he fought many running battles with Saul-Josephus Flavius, during the time when the latter was the Jewish army commander in charge of Galilee.

It was because of these many similarities that it was claimed in *Jesus, Last of the Pharaohs,* that Jesus of Gamala was the biblical King Jesus-Izas (of Edessa). Which is why the famous quote in Acts of the Apostles has Jesus exclaiming: 'Saul, Saul, why are you persecuting me?' (Acts 26:14.) This was Saul-Josephus persecuting the biblical Jesus-Izas of Gamala in the late 60s, at the outbreak of the Jewish Revolt. So now we can see who the two opponents in this trial of strength and resolve really were. There is Saul-Josephus (St Paul) and his Simple Judaic Church on the one side, and Jesus-Izas of Gamala (the biblical Jesus) on the other. The enmity between these two opponents was deep and ultimately unresolvable, and Acts of the Apostles says of this family feud:

> And Saul, yet breathing out threatenings and slaughter against the disciples of the Lord, went unto the high priest and asked for a warrant (authorisation) ... that if he found any ... he might bring them bound unto Jerusalem. (Acts 9:1)

Yet Acts never explains how a simple priest and evangelist like Saul received this authorisation. Who was Saul, to become the official 'chief of police' in the region, arresting members of the Nazarene Ebionite Church and throwing them into prison? The answer is that he was Josephus Flavius, as has been explained many times previously, and Josephus did indeed become the army commander in charge of Galilee and did indeed persecute Jesus (of Gamala), just as he himself relates in *Jewish War*.

It was because of this open warfare between these two sects, and the very different teachings that they espoused, that the Nazarene Ebionite Church rejected anything and everything to do with Saul-Paul (ie: Saul-Josephus). Some theologians call the Nazarene Ebionites 'Jewish Christians', but this is a (deliberately) confusing term. It was Saul (St Paul) who had created Simple Judaic Christianity, not Jesus and James, and the open warfare between these two sects clearly demonstrates that the Nazarene Church of Jesus and James had become completely disconnected from Saul-Josephus' Simple Judaic Christian sect. Yes, Simple Judaism had originally been officially sanctioned by James the Just, as we saw in Chapter III, but it had grown so powerful and so far apart, that it was now an aggressive competitor creed that sought to expunge its parent.

If only more modern Christians would realise that they are following the religion of the enemy of the Nazarene Ebionites, and the enemy of Jesus and James. In fact, this was a religion that Jesus-Izas had rejected, opposed and bitterly fought. Boulanger, one of the many venerable early 19th century theologians who understood so much more than modern academics, said of the origins of the Christians and Nazarene:

> Generally speaking it is St Paul (Saul), or the author of the epistles that are attributed to him, that aught to be regarded as the true founder of Christian theology.
>
> The Ebionites or Nazarenes who, as we shall soon see, were the first Christians, rejected all the epistles of St Paul and regarded him as an imposter and hypocrite.
>
> Moreover, Eusebius and St Epiphanius inform us that St Paul (Saul) was regarded as an apostate, an impostor and an enemy by the Ebionites, that is to say by the first faithful (the first Nazarene Christians). [5] (Author's brackets.)

As can be seen, it has been known for a very long time that Christianity has nothing to do with Jesus-Izas, or the Nazarene Church of Jesus-Izas. And so even Boulanger's use of the term 'Christian' is incorrect here, because the Nazarene Ebionites were Egypto-Gnostics and proselyte Jews, not Christians. The Nazarene Ebionites can hardly be called Christians, if they rejected half of the New Testament (all of the Epistles and possibly Acts and Luke too). In reality Christianity was founded by the enemy of Jesus, and so modern Christians are all following the wrong religion. In fact, the error that Christians are making is so great, that reading the gospels is a bit like reading a biography of Winston Churchill written by Adolf Hitler. Yes, their error is that stark.

Kalba Shabua

Kalba Shabua was another of the three wealthiest people in Judaea, just before the Jewish Revolt, and once again we don't exactly know who Kalba Shabua really was. The translations for this name that are given in the Talmud are merely humourous hypocorisms once more, so these do not explain too much either.

The Talmud claims that Kalba Shabua meant 'Satisfied Dog', because guests went to his house as hungry as a dog (*keleb* כלב) and came out full (*saba* שׂבע). But this is merely a humorous play on words, for no powerful Syrio-Judaean aristocrat would ever have been named 'Satisfied Dog'. It is much more likely that the title for Kalba Shabua was devised from a quite different talmudic *pesher*, and the prophesy that these inventive scribes discovered involved Kaleb כלב or Kalba כלבי, who was the spy (and his family) who saw the Promised Land and urged Moses and the people to capture it (Num 13:30). The Promised Land was said to be Judaea and Jerusalem, and Kaleb the spy was urging the Israelite leadership to attack the region and take control of it straight away.

The correlation between this Old Testament *pesher* prophesy and the events of the Jewish Revolt are inescapable. Whatever Kalba Shabua's real name was, it is likely that he was being renamed after an Israelite commander who urged the Israelites to take control of Judaea and Jerusalem, and that is exactly what the Nazarene royal family of Edessa were doing in the late AD 60s. And the point of making this *pesher* prophesy was that the Old Testament Kaleb was successful in his endeavour, and surely if Kalba Shabua was named after Kaleb then he would be successful too. This was the whole point of talmudic *pesher*, it was designed to predict and perhaps even influence an uncertain future.

But where did the influential families of Kalba Shabua and Nicodemus originate from? Were they really connected to the royal family of Edessa, as has been suggested here? We know that they lived in Jerusalem in the mid to late 1st century, but did they originate from Judaea or from elsewhere? The answer to this question can be found on the Palmyran altar in the Capitoline Museum in Rome, which is inscribed with two very interesting dedications. The two texts are in Latin and Palmrene Aramaic and they say, together with their English translations: [6]

Latin:

Soli sanctissimo sacrum.
Ti. Claudius Felix et Claudia Helpis et Ti. Claudius Alypus filius eorum votum solverunt libens merito Calbienses de cohorte III.

Dedicated to the holy Sun.

> Tiberius Claudius Felix and Claudia Helpis and their son Tiberius Claudius Alypus gratefully offer in fulfillment of a vow (to the Sun-god) who has earned it. The Third Cohort of Calbienses.
>
> **Palmrene:**
>
> Alta dh lmlkbl wlalhy tdmr qrb thbrys qlwdys plqs wtdmrya lalhyhn shlm
>
> This is the Altar that Tiberius Claudius Felix and the Tadmorians offered to Malakbel and the gods of Palmyra. To their gods. Peace.

The date of this dedication is unknown, and is largely irrelevant as the same Palmyran families kept their traditions and positions of power for two or more centuries. The intent of the dedication is the same in both languages, but readers can probably see some major differences in style and presentation between the two. These include the Roman Sun-god Sol becoming the Palmyran Sun-god Malakbel, and the Calbienses becoming the Tadmorians. And while we don't know who the Calbienses were, we do know from the Talmud that the Tadmorians were the Palmyrans. And so the Calbienses must be linked to Palmyra in some fashion.

These differences, and the difficulty in understanding the meaning of 'Calbienses' have induced some scholars to think that these are two different inscriptions, so that the reference to Calbienses can be separated from Palmyra. George Houston took this to its ultimate conclusion in arguing that the 'Calbienses of cohort III' was the address of their apartment block in Rome. But this has to be a good contender for the silliest suggestion ever from humanities academia, for who puts their home address on a sacred dedication to the Sun-god? If the monument had also included their post-code and phone number, we might be more convinced!

The answer to this minor but nevertheless pivotal conundrum, is that the Calbienses were the wealthy and influential Palmyran family called the Bene Kalba, just as Javier Teixidor suggested in *The Pantheon of Palmyra* (p47). The name 'Bene' is being used here to denote the 'Sons of', which referred to the entire family of the Kalba and was a common prefixed title in Palmyra. However, what has not been suggested previously is that it is highly likely that the Palmrene family called Bene Kalba and the Judaean aristocrat called Kalba Shabua were closely related - they were a part of the same family. So it is highly likely that the Talmud's rich aristocrat called Kalba Shabua came from Palmyra.

And lastly we come to the interesting question of what is called here the 'Third Cohort of Calbienses'. The Calbienses (Kalb-ienses) have been linked to the Palmyran family of Bene Kalba, and therefore linked to Kalba Shabua himself. But the end of the dedication on this altar said that this was the Third Cohort of Calbienses and therefore the Third Cohort of Bene Kalba

Shabua. But why was the family of the Bene Kalba Shabua being given a pseudo-military rank? The answer may be that these Syrio-Judaean aristocrats appear to be closely linked to Arthurian history, and the princes of Syrio-Judaea were also knights of the realm - they were aristocratic knights in shining armour just like Sir Lancelot and Sir Perceval Galahad. In which case, the caption reading 'Third Cohort of Calbienses' may simply refer to the Kalba Clan being Third Cohort in the Palmyran military, the third place at the Syrio-Judaean Round Table.

Fig 10.11
The Palmyran altar from the Capitoline Museum, dedicated to Malakbel by the Calbienses Palmyrans.

Once again we appear to see yet more links between Arthurian history and the influential city of Palmyra. It has already been convincingly demonstrated that King Evalach-Mordrain (the son of King Arthur-Jesus) was the king of Palmyra in the years just after the Jewish Revolt. But here in the Talmud we appear to have a reference to the aristocrats who ruled Palmyra in the years just before the Jewish Revolt. And so the three wealthy aristocrats and princes from the Talmud and the three wealthy kings from Arthurian history appear to be closely related - King Pelles and King Pellehan must have been related to Nakdimon-Nicodemus and Kalba Shabua, just as *High History* claimed.

Ben Zizit Hakeseth

The last of these three wealthy Judaean aristocrats is Ben Hakeseth. Much less is said and known about Ben Zizit Hakeseth, perhaps because he was the most Romanised and therefore the least liked of these three aristocrats. The Talmud says of Zizit Hakeseth:

> Ben Zizit Hakeseth was so called because his fringes (*zizith*) used to trail on cushions (*keseth*). Others say he derived the name from the fact that his seat (*kise*) was among those of the nobility of Rome. (Gittin 56a) (Author's brackets.)

This wordplay comes from Zizith *tsitsith* ציצת meaning 'tassel', Ha-keseth *h-kisa* ה-כסא meaning 'the seat', and Ha-keseth *h-kiseth* ה-כסת meaning 'the pillow' or 'phylactery box'. So it would appear that Ben Zizit Hakeseth must have been a figure of fun in rabbinical circles. He dressed flamboyantly, wearing very long *tsitsith* tassels that trailed on sumptuous cushions, and his seat was inordinately large and uncomfortably close to the Romans. But these were merely witty *double entendres* for satirists, including the biblical Jesus as we shall see shortly, and so we know how the name for Ben Zizit Hakeseth was pronounced but not what it really means.

But if the Talmud's translation of 'tassels and pillows' is merely wordplay, perhaps a better translation involving fabrics and tassels would be Tsitsyth Ha-Kaseth ציצת כסת, which refers to the 'tassels on a diadema headband'. As we saw in the previous books in this series, the kings of Greece, Parthia and also Edessa, often wore a diadema headband instead of a crown. These diadema headbands were made of silk, and were therefore very expensive and probably quite colourful too, and the tassel endings of these headbands trailed down the king's back as can be seen on the coins in fig 10.12. And while 'tassels and pillows' might not be a suitable name for a Judaean aristocrat, a 'diadema headband' may be more so. It would be similar to having the title Stephen Στεφανος meaning 'crowned', and would have alluded to his royal status.

However, these *zizith* tassels and *h-kiseth* phylacteries give us a very surprising link to the gospel stories once more. We have already seen a great deal of evidence for a feud within this extended royal family, with Alain li Gros and Perceval-Galahad being dispossessed from their lands by King Arthur. But if King Arthur was the biblical King Jesus-Izas, as appears highly likely, then surely we should find similar evidence within the gospels of King Jesus-Izas being highly critical of one of these three Judaean aristocrats. Surprisingly, we can. In Matthew 23:1-6 Jesus himself heavily criticizes Zizit Hakeseth for being out of touch with reality and out of touch with the needs of the common people:

> Jesus said to the multitude ... The scribes and the Pharisees ... bind heavy burdens ... and lay them on men's shoulders; but they themselves will not move them with one of their fingers. And all their works they do so they can be seen by men (and not by god). They enlarge their phylacteries, and lengthen the tassels on their garments. And they love the uppermost rooms at feasts, and the chief seats in the synagogues. (Matthew 23:1-6) (author's brackets)

Anyone listening to Jesus-Izas' speech who had a passing understanding of Aramaic and knew that there was a leading Palmyro-Judaean aristocrat by the name of Zizit Hakeseth, would be choking on their pretzels at this point in the sermon. They would immediately know that this was a direct and damming criticism of this very person, and might be very surprised about Jesus-Izas using such forthright language. Jesus-Izas is using the Talmud's standard wordplay to condemn Zizit Hakeseth, by saying that these wealthy aristocrats place burdens on the backs of the common people. But in their personal life they flaunt their great wealth and high positions by having:

Long tassels on their garments	...	Zizit
Large phylactery boxes on their heads	...	Ha-Keseth
Claiming the chief seat in the synagogue	...	Ha-Kesa

Ouch! King Izas-Jesus was really going for the jugular here - he and Ben Zizit Hakeseth were obviously not on speaking terms at this time. In fact, it is entirely possible that the nicknames given in the Talmud's version were direct quotations from the gospels, and so the unmentioned critic of Zizit Hakeseth was probably Jesus-Izas himself. And so this gospel verse is interesting for

Fig 10.12 Two coins depicting kings wearing a silk diadema headband, with the loose tassels flowing down behind their backs. Left is King Phraates IV of Parthia. Right is a King Abgarus of Edessa, who also wears a domed crown of thorns on top of his diadema headband.

The diadema headband and royal wart of these Parthian and Edessan monarchs may have been a discrete equivalent of the Jewish phylactery box tied around the forehead. If one wished to disguise an Egypto-Jewish heritage and yet continue some of its ancient traditions, this would be an ideal method of concealment. The royal wart of Phraates IV can be seen on the side of his forehead.

many reasons.

Firstly, it confirms that the gospels and the Talmud were singing from the same hymn-sheet once again. So the gospel authors were not making this up, and there really was a wealthy Judaean aristocrat in this era who was called Ben Zizit Hakeseth, and he was popularly known and lampooned by these 'tassel and phylactery' nicknames. Secondly, it again demonstrates that the gospel events all took place in the late AD 60s. King Jesus-Izas is clearly criticizing Zizit Hakeseth in this biblical verse, and yet Zizit Hakeseth is most definitely a character from the late 60s and the events of the Jewish Revolt, just as the Talmud asserts. Ergo: Jesus-Izas was alive and well in the 60s.

We have seen this chronological dislocation or chasm many times before, of course, with Jesus complaining about the death of Zacharias and talking about Jerusalem being surrounded by a trench, which are also AD 60s characters and events. Quite clearly the gospel story was set in the turbulent 60s, rather than the relative calm of the 30s. But it was very difficult for the gospel authors to tie up these many historical lose ends and deceitfully

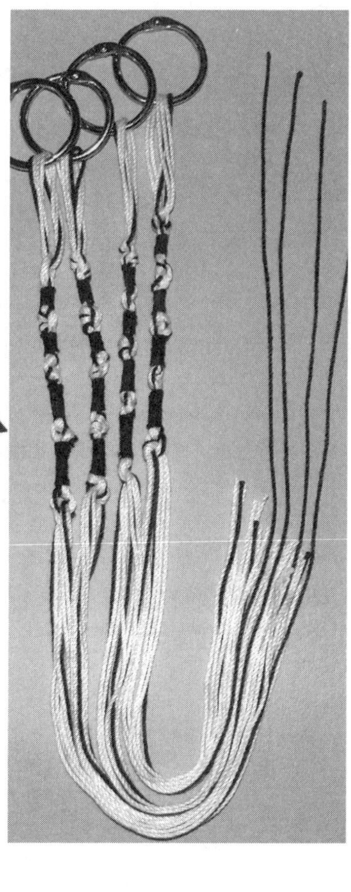

Fig 10.13

(left) Two keseth phylactery boxes, that contain parchments with verses from the Torah and are worn on the arm and forehead.

(right) Blue and white zizit or tsitsith tassels, which are attached to garments or prayer-shawls. These are the original 'knotted hanky', and the knots are supposed to remind you of god's commandments. This ancient tradition is said to be derived from the Egyptian priesthood.

place them all back into the 30s. How could they place Zacharias and Zizit Hakeseth into the 30s, when everyone knew that these aristocrats lived in the 60s?

And the gospel authors probably had no idea what the Talmud's rabbis and scribes would be writing, especially the ones living in Pumbeditha in Mesopotamia (modern Fallujah), where the Babylonian Talmud was written. So they had no easy mechanism for checking for contradictions between these two records, and many chronological contradictions inevitably slipped through the censor's net. But Jesus was hardly one to complain about the excesses of Zizit Hakeseth, as he himself had been branded as a glutton and a drunkard who consorted with tax-collectors and sinners, during previous years (Math 9:10, 11:19). And it was the imperious Mary-Martha Boethus, the daughter of Nakdimon-Nicodemus, who received a million gold *denarii* bride-price and bought (or bribed) the position of high priest for Jesus of Gamala (the biblical King Jesus-Izas).

However, if Jesus was going to win the Imperial popularity contest and become the next emperor or Rome, he was going to have to go on a public relations charm offensive, and this meant understanding the needs of the common man and appearing to be generous and charitable. In modern presidential terms, Jesus was going to have to kiss a few babies and promise to reduce the tax on ball-games and beer. Perhaps the overt opulence of Zizit Hakeseth and his close association with the Romans was not assisting the revolutionary cause, which is why he received this damning condemnation from Jesus. If Jesus was going to win this popularity contest, he was going to have to distance himself from his rich relations, and ally himself more with the common man. And this is exactly what Saul-Josephus said happened just before the Jewish Revolt:

> And concerning these things ... the Sadducees are able to persuade none but the rich, and do not have the populace groveling to them. But the Pharisees have the multitude on their side. (Ant 13:10:6)

> But this doctrine (of the Sadducees) is received only by a few, mostly by those of the greatest nobility. But they are able to do almost nothing of themselves; for when they become magistrates, as they are unwillingly and by force sometimes they are obliged to be, they become enthusiasts of the beliefs of the Pharisees - because the multitude would not otherwise accept them. (Ant 18:1:4)

Jesus-Izas was a Sadducee, and we know this because his brother was called James the Just by many of the Church fathers, including Epiphanius, Eusebius and Hegesippus. But the Greek Justus Ιουστος was derived from the Hebrew Zadok צדוק meaning 'just' or 'righteous'. And it was from the

Zadok 'righteous' or Sadok Σαδωκ 'righteous', that the sect of the Sadducees Σαδδουκαιος gained their title. There are various modern Christian groups who desperately try to make Jesus a Pharisee, a man of the people, because it is a bit embarrassing to admit that Jesus-Izas was a member of the aristocratic Sadducee sect. But the gospels are filled with examples of Pharisees condemning Jesus and Jesus condemning the Pharisees, and so it is highly unlikely that Jesus was ever attached to the Pharisee sect. See the great list of criticism of the Pharisees in Matthew 23.

But just as Saul-Josephus says in the previous quotes, in order to gain popularity the Sadducees were having to (pretend to) embrace Pharisee doctrines, to make themselves more popular with the common people. Armies and revolutions need foot-soldiers, as well as commanders. And this is exactly what Jesus was doing by condemning Zizit Hakeseth in such forthright terms - he was distancing himself from the wealth and luxury of these Syrio-Judaean aristocrats and the 'Marie Antoinette' style indiscretions of his own wife, Mary-Martha of Boethus Nicodemus, and pretending to be a champion of the common people.

Simon Boethus

As was briefly mentioned previously, in his seminal works on 1st century Judaea, Professor Robert Eisenman has identified Nicodemus with another rich aristocrat called Simon Boethus. Which means that the pampered Marie Antoinette princess(es) of Nicodemus were actually the rich daughters known as Mary and Martha Boethus. But Eisenman also equates Mary and Martha of Simon Boethus with the biblical Bethany sisters, the Mary and Martha who lived at the house of Simon. In which case, the biblical house of Simon in Bethany was actually owned by Simon Boethus, the rich aristocrat and father of the pampered Mari Antoinette princess(es). And since Mary Boethus is better known in the gospel stories as Mary Magdalene, it is likely that this Mari Antoinette princess was Mary Magdalene herself.

Eisenman prefers to say that the lives of Mary and Martha of Bethany were modeled upon Mary and Martha Boethus, rather than them being the same ladies. No doubt he does so because he can clearly see the chronological chasm looming before him once more, and all the many pitfalls associated with this vast crevasse - because if these two pairs of ladies were the one and the same, then Jesus would have to have been alive and well in the AD 60s. It is much less controversial for Eisenman to separate them, and say that the gospel authors based the life of the Bethany sisters upon the real lives of the Boethus sisters, than get into heated discussions with irate Christian fundamentalists about Jesus not dying in AD 30.

However, if we are prepared to accept that these two pairs of ladies were the same princesses, there is a lot more evidence we can use to confirm this suggestion - evidence that Eisenman cannot and will not accept. One of the most interesting aspects about this alternate line of evidence is that the Talmud closely associates Mary and Martha, the daughters of Simon Boethus, with Jesus of Gamala. And yet the previous books in this series have amply demonstrated that this same Jesus of Gamala was actually King Izas-Jesus au Kama of Edessa - the biblical Jesus. The Talmud says of this Jesus of Gama-Kama(la):

> A priest who was betrothed (to a) widow, and was subsequently appointed high priest, may consummate the marriage. It once happened with Jesus ben Gamala that he was betrothed to Martha the daughter of Boethus, and the king appointed him high priest. And he nevertheless consummated the marriage. (Yebamoth 61a)

The Talmud tends to conflate and confuse Mary and Martha Boethus into one lady, probably because Jesus-Izas married both of these sisters, just as the Talmud commands. This quote says that Jesus of Gamala married Martha (Mary) Boethus (of Bethany) and became the high priest of Jerusalem, but that he still consummated the marriage. This suggests that Martha (Mary) was a widow, and we shall see why that may have been so shortly. And Jesus not only married Mary (Magdalene-Boethus), it was this same Mary who bribed King Agrippa II to arrange the position of high priest for her new husband, in about AD 63:

> I see here a conspiracy for ... Martha the daughter of Boethus brought to King Jannai a *tarkab* of *denarii,* before he gave an appointment to Jesus ben Gamala among the high priests. (Yebamoth 61a)

King Jannai is often a reference to King Agrippa II in the Talmud, as seems most likely here. And this *tarkab* of *denarii* represents a great deal of money. A *tarkab* is known to be two *kabs*, and a *kab* is four *logs*. The *Oxford Biblical Studies Online* says a *log* measures 0.32 liters, while the *Jewish Encyclopaedia* says that a *log* is 0.50 liters. Thus a *kab* is either 1.3 liters or 2.0 liters, while a *tarkab* is either 2.6 liters or 4.0 liters. This is a smaller volume than is given in the talmudic notes, but nevertheless a reasonable amount of coinage. If we deduct 20% from this volume, for the coins not fully fitting the container, this would equate to between 2 kg and 3.6 kg of water-equivalent; and this would give a weight of between 21 kg to 37 kg of silver (the specific gravity of silver being 10.5). However, the previous quotes about this same wealthy and pamper princess of Simon Boethus were talking about gold *denarii*, not silver *denarii,* and in this case this same *tarkab* of *denarii* would then equate to between 38 kg and 70 kg of gold (the specific gravity of gold being 19.3).

This is quite a fortune to purchase the high priesthood for your husband - somewhere between $2.2 billion and $4.0 billion in today's fiat money, according to the previous calculations. But since Mary (or Martha) of Boethus had already received a wedding gift of 7 tonnes of gold, perhaps she could easily afford to spend 1% of this marriage allowance on her husband's future career as the high priest of Jerusalem. And this was probably money well spent, because the Jerusalem priesthood levied temple taxes and controlled the sale of sacrificial animals, and so they were able to earn substantial amounts of money each year from the gullible population. Although do remember that Jesus had already driven the sacrificial animals and the money lenders from the Temple, and so he had already reduced this priestly revenue stream (John 2:15). And perhaps it is worth having a quick reminder at this point, that this Mary Boethus was Mary Magdalene and this was the magnitude of her inordinate wealth. Perhaps it is not so surprising that the 13th century *Golden Legend* describes Mary Magdalene as a princess who owned a castle in Judaea (G.L. 36).

While Jesus of Gamala became high priest in the early AD 60s, the Talmud also records that Simon Boethus (his father or father-in-law) had become high priest of Jerusalem in the AD 40s. This is confirmed by Saul-Josephus who says of Simon:

> And when Agrippa (II) had entirely finished all the duties of the Divine worship, he removed Theophilus, the son of Ananus, from the high priesthood, and bestowed that honor of his on Simon the son of Boethus, whose name was also Cantheras whose daughter king Herod married, as I have related above. Simon, therefore, had the [high] priesthood with his brethren, and with his father (Ant 19:6:2)

This was Herod Agrippa II in AD 44, sorting out the affairs of his small principality after the death of his father, Herod Agrippa I. Agrippa made a change in the high priesthood of Jerusalem, as often happens when there is a change in the political or monarchal administration, deposing Theophilus and installing Simon ben Boethus instead (ie: Nakdimon-Nicodemus).

Note also that a Herod had married the daughter of Simon Boethus. This generic 'Herod' title is slightly confusing, but it must be a reference to Herod Agrippa I (the father of Herod Agrippa II) who had just died, just as the quote implies. If so, then this daughter of Simon Boethus would have now been a widow. But the most famous daughter of Simon Boethus was Mary (Martha) Boethus (ie: Mary Magdalene), the princess who married Jesus of Gamala (the biblical Jesus). And this is why the previous quotes implied that the daughter of Boethus was a widow, because she had been married to King Agrippa I and upon his death she was now marrying Jesus-Izas of Gamala-Kama(la).

There is a striking agreement here, between the records of Saul-Josephus and the Talmud, which suggests that the Talmud is recording real historical accounts, just as Arthurian history is also giving us real historical information. And the Talmud's slight confusion between Mary and Martha of Bethany-Boethus was caused by the biblical Jesus marrying both of these sisters:

> The high priest must be married; (but) to guard against contingencies it was proposed to hold a second wife in readiness immediately before the Day of Atonement. (II Yoma i.)

So Mary and Martha of Bethany-Boethus not only shared the same house they probably shared the same husband, which might explain the slight contention that we see between these two sisters in the gospel accounts. Even the name for Martha מרתא, which means 'mistress', would suggest a second wife for Jesus. And not surprisingly, given their close relationship to Simon Boethus-Nicodemus, these two biblical sisters lived in the house of Simon (Boethus). And this dual sisterly betrothal is strangely reminiscent of the accounts we have already seen within Arthurian history about King Arthur, and so the famous royal threesome from the 1st century appears to be named as either:

King	**Queen**	**Symbol**	**Goddess**
Arthur	Gwenevere	Marian Star	Venus
Arthur	Morgaine le Fay	Magan Star	Venus
or			
Jesus-Izas	Mary Magdalene	Magan Star	Venus
Jesus-Izas	Martha	?	?

However, there is one further difficulty to resolve with regard to Mary and Martha, and that is the peculiar account by Saul-Josephus that one of these daughters of Simon Boethus married Herod the Great:

> There was one Simon, a citizen of Jerusalem, the son of Boethus, a citizen of Alexandria, and a priest of great note there; this man had a daughter, who was esteemed the most beautiful woman of that time; and when the people of Jerusalem began to speak much in her commendation, it happened that Herod (the Great) was much effected with what was said of her ... so he thought it best to take the damsel to wife. (Ant 15:9:3) (Author's bracket.)

Now this claim is a bit of an oddity that has caused a lot of head-scratching in academic circles, because this account is talking about the 1st century BC, and it is therefore quite obviously out of place. Daniel Schwartz says of this anomaly:

> A chronological problem must be mentioned here: Simon Boethus was appointed to the high priesthood in 23 BC and at that time he had a marriageable daughter. It is possible that he had a son capable of being appointed to the high priesthood sixty years later (or 80 years later) ... but the less likely that appears. (The Last King of Judaea, Daniel Schwartz. p87.) (Author's brackets.)

There is a huge chronological problem with Saul-Josephus' assertion here, just as Schwartz says, and it only gets worse if we read these quotes in *Antiquities* more literally. The Simon Boethus in 19:6:2, as quoted above, is actually the same person as the Simon Boethus in 15:9:3, and so the same aristocrat is being given the high priesthood some 67 years apart. And Jesus of Gamala was marrying the daughter of this Simon in the AD 40s, when Simon must have been about 100 years old by that time. There is clearly an error in the chronology here, and it is the very same error we have seen so many times before. Daniel Schwartz has also recognised this problem, but not the simple solution to it, and so he embarks upon various alternate scenarios about Simon Cantheras perhaps being the son of Simon Boethus and the like.

In reality the problem and the solution are very simple. As we have seen before, the life of the biblical Jesus (Jesus-Izas of Gamala) has been dragged back into the past by 40 years, from the AD 70s to the AD 30s, to distance him from the turbulent times of the Jewish Revolt. And so anyone connected with Jesus has had their life distorted accordingly. In this case, one of the scribes working on Josephus' text must have known that Jesus of Gamala and his new wife Mary (Martha) Boethus were closely connected to the biblical story, and so they could not have been marrying in the AD 40s, a decade after Jesus had supposedly died.

And so the dutiful scribes have shoved the previous quote from *Antiquities* into completely the wrong section of the manuscript. The daughter of Simon Boethus actually married Herod Agrippa I, but knowing that this was not compatible with the biblical chronology the life of this daughter had to be moved into the past. And the simple solution the scribe employed was to utilise the standard confusion with the generic title 'Herod', and deliberately confused Herod Agrippa I with Herod the Great. In a literary instant, the life of Mary-Martha Boethus was conveniently transported some 50 years back into the past.

The solution to the chronological problem that these scribes have created is therefore very simple. All we need to do is bring the quote in 15:9:3 forward in time, and place it at the end of the life of Herod Agrippa I. Having done so, we then see that it was Herod Agrippa I who had the infatuation with Mary (Martha) Boethus and married her, and not Herod the Great. And Simon Boethus was probably very happy with this match, because King Agrippa I was now his brother-in-law, and the king gave Simon Boethus the high priesthood as a consequence of this marriage.

This is why we see the improbable spectacle of High Priest Simon Boethus being replaced by a High Priest Matthias who lasts for one year, plus a High Priest Joseph or Jonathan who only lasted for just one day.* And this same sequence of events happens during the reign of both Herod the Great and Herod Agrippa II. Again, the most likely cause of this improbable similarity is a duplication of these events, and so the Simon Boethus mentioned at the time of Herod the Great should be deleted completely. The result of this amendment is that Simon Boethus would indeed have had two terms in office, just as the priestly records maintain, but these were under kings Agrippa I and Agrippa II. And so the quote we saw previously should actually read as:

> King Agrippa II ... removed Theophilus, the son of Ananus, from the high priesthood, and bestowed that honor of his on Simon the son of Boethus ... whose daughter had married King Herod Agrippa I. (Ant 19:6:2, but corrected and clarified)

So who, in the historical record, was this secretive daughter of Simon Boethus the high priest who married Herod Agrippa I? Well now these two chronologically displaced quotes about Simon Boethus have been conjoined, her name is given to us in *Antiquities* 18:5:4, and in this earlier 'out of place' quote she is called Mariamne. And so it is fairly certain that this was the same Miriamne or Mary Boethus who married King Agrippa I according to Josephus, and then married Jesus of Gamala according to the Talmud. And in the gospel stories she was known as Mary Magdalene, and she lived at the house of Simon.

And since Agrippa I's reign was fairly short, we can place these events upon a fairly secure time-line. Mary (Mariamne) must have married Agrippa I in about AD 42, and then married Jesus of Gamala sometime after

* Note also the similarity with Lancelot, who also became high priest (the Galahad) for just one day. In the case of Lancelot, he lost his position because he consummated an affair with Queen Gwenevere on that day.

her first husband had died in AD 43. And if Mary had been about 18 years old when she married Agrippa I, then she would have been about 44 years old when the Jewish Revolt started. So according to the chronology outlined here, Mary was plainly of a suitable age to have anointed her husband as the king of the Jews at the house of Simon in the mid 60s, and to see her husband crucified in the Kidron Valley in AD 70.

Judaeo-Arthurian aristocrats

This chapter has explored the identity of these Syrio-Judaean aristocrats at great length. And we appear to have three (brother) aristocrats in the Judaean record and three similar brother princes in the Arthurian record. So were these brothers in any way related to each other? Surprisingly, it is entirely possible that they were, and bearing in mind the available data the best guesses for their Arthurian identities are:

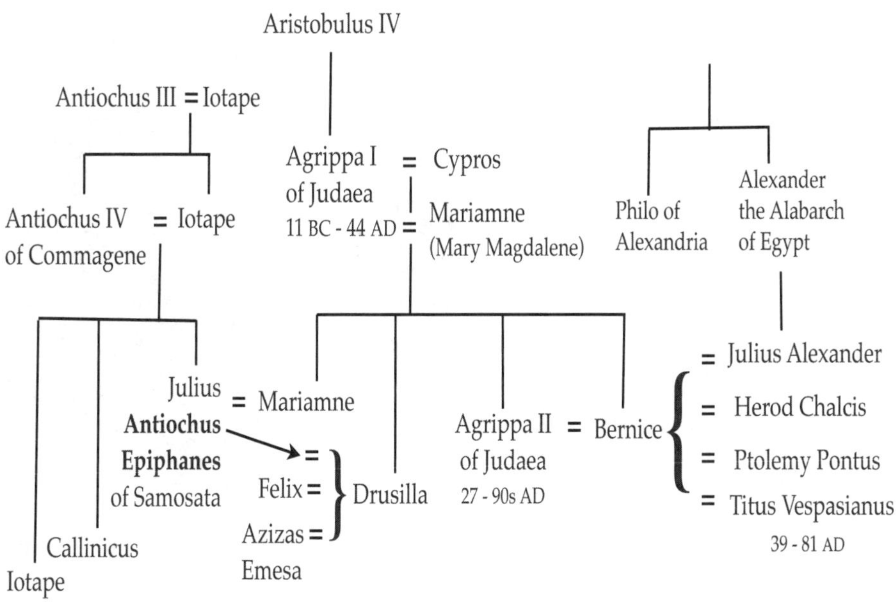

Fig 10.14
A genealogy of King Agrippa I, showing the king's short marriage to Miriamne (Mary Magdalene). The fact that these princesses did get betrothed to many aristocratic or princely partners, is demonstrated by the multiple husbands of Berenice and Drusilla.

Nicodemus - Bron:

Nicodemus has been identified as the father of Alain li Gros, because that is what *High History* appears to claim as we saw in Chapter III. Thus Nicodemus would be the equivalent of the character called Bron or Hebron in *Merlin Grail*, and this is confirmed when the Talmud calls Nicodemus Boni. So the real name of Nicodemus was Boni, from which Arthurian history has derived the names Bron and possibly also Ban. (We shall come across King Ban in later chapters.)

And it may or may not be significant that the tutor of (Saul) Josephus Flavius in the historical record was a wise old sage called Banus. If this famous Banus can be equated with the Talmudic Boni and the Arthurian Bron or Ban, then Saul-Josephus was tutored by Nicodemus. And it was demonstrated in Chapter VI that Sir Perceval-Galahad was actually St Simon Peter Kephas, the disciple of Jesus and a father of the Christian Church. This would mean that the biblical Nicodemus was not only the father of the Arthurian Alain li Gros, but also the grandfather of St Peter.

Kalba Shabua - Pelles, Jesus:

Kalba Shabua was named after the Israelite leader who advised taking control of Judaea and Jerusalem, and in terms of AD 60s events this must refer to the leader of the Jewish Revolt. And the leaders of the Jewish Revolt included King Izas-Manu au Kama VI, who is otherwise known as the biblical Jesus, and his brotherly disciples.

Fig 10.15
An image of Mariamne (Mary Magdalene) from the 16th century Promptuarii book of iconography. Note that the artist has managed to give Miriamne the very distinctive straight nose of the Edessan monarchy. The French icon, Marianne, was given the same straight nose, as we saw previously.

Zizit Hakeseth and Alain

Zizit Hakeseth was heavily criticised by King Jesus-Izas for having huge tassels and phylactery boxes, and being on rather good terms with the Romans. And if King Arthur is King Jesus, then this Judaean aristocrat called Zizit Hakeseth would also have been the enemy of King Arthur. And the Arthurian aristocrat who was on the receiving end of the most criticism and 'persecution' was Alain li Gros. So of all these

> three royal aristocrats, Zizit Hakeseth just has to be Alain li Gros. Alain was also identified as the father of the gospel St Simon Peter-Perceval. And so this animosity between Jesus and the family of Alain and Perceval is similarly reflected in the gospels, when Jesus branded St Peter as being an incarnation of Satan (Math 4:10 and Luke 4:8).

In conclusion, the possibility exists that the three aristocrats from Arthurian history can be found in the history of the Jewish Revolt. And while the following are not fully confirmed identifications, these three aristocrats could well be identified as follows. The three layers in each identification are: Talmudic, Arthurian, and gospel:

Aristocrat 1
Nakdimon Boni Boethus
Embalming spices

Bron-Hebron

Nicodemus
Pro-Roman?

Aristocrat 2	**Aristocrat 3**
Kalba Shabua Leader of Revolt	Zizit Hakeseth Tassels and Seat
King Pelles Fisher King? King Arthur	King Pellehan Alain li Gros The Monk?
King Jesus-Izas Pro-Revolt	St Simon Peter Pro-Roman?

XI

Lancelot

Lancelot - Walter Map
Books 3-5 of the *Vulgate Cycle* or *Lancelot Grail*

The most formidable challenge in any investigation of the *Vulgate Cycle* is *Lancelot*, because it runs to six books in three volumes, totalling about 1,300 pages. It is a daunting prospect, especially as much of the prose is convoluted and rambling drivel. As the learned linguists who translated these books said, the *Vulgate Cycle*:

> ... is a literary dungheap in which one might locate a few textual diamonds.
> Albert Pauphilet, 1918.
>
> ... is one of the most disjointed European literary works ever written.
> J Bruce, 1923.
>
> ... has a highly repetitive narrative structure that creates a monotony bordering on the offensive.
> Ferdinand Lot, 1954.
>
> ... lacks focus, rambles, gives you a headache and puts you to sleep.
> Jane Burns 1993.

Quite! This somewhat tedious story is mainly about a dispute between the kingdoms and families of King Bors of Gaunes and King Ban of Benoic on the one side, and a usurping foreigner called King Claudas on the other. King Claudas was allied to the Romans, and the result of the initial struggle at the beginning of *Lancelot* is that the sons of Bors and Ban are all dispossessed from their lands.

The sons of King Bors and King Ban are the famous Arthurian knights we already know about: Bors and Lionel plus Lancelot and Hector. Note that Lancelot is the son of King Ban here, while Alain li Gros was said to be the son of Boni (Bron). And in a similar fashion some of these manuscripts say that Perceval-Galahad was the son of Sir Lancelot, instead of the son of Alain li Gros. And so we have the same (troublesome) conflation of fathers, and the same sad lament about the dispossession of Perceval-Galahad that we saw in *High History*. But this time the dispossession is at the hands of an invading monarch - King Claudas. But was this an invasion of 6th century Britain, or 1st century Syrio-Judaea?

Claudas

Surprisingly, *Lancelot* starts to mirror the accounts of Saul-Josephus' *Jewish War* from the very outset. All we need to do in order to see true import of this story, is to: bear in mind that a name like Claudas is probably Roman; that King Claudas appears to be a contemporary of Monmouth's Lucius Hiberius, who was an AD 60s character; that the Roman legions arrived in Judaea in AD 66 to quell a major revolt in the eastern provinces; and that they were greatly assisted by a Jewish traitor (ie: Saul-Josephus). So rather than this being an impossible account of 6th century Britain, when the Western Roman Empire no longer existed, this story is probably set in AD 66, and details the well-known history of the Roman 'invasion' of Judaea by Legatus Vespasian and his son Titus.

And if this story really was about 1st century Judaeo-Syria, then we need to adjust the geography in the same fashion as previous chapters. The authors of the *Vulgate Cycle* could not admit that they were relating events that strongly conflicted with the standard gospel story, and so they simply relocated Judaeo-Syria into northern Europe. It was a simple and effective adjustment that has stood the test of time for many centuries.

So it will be assumed here that Logres-Britain actually refers to the lands east of the Jordan and east of the Euphrates - the lands of the Edessan monarchy which included Osrhoene, Batanaea, Aurania and Perea. In a similar fashion, Gaul-France actually refers to the lands west of the Jordan and Euphrates, including all of Judaea and much of western Syria. In this new relocated story Gaul-France (ie: Judaea and western Syria) was indeed subordinate to Rome at this time, just as *Lancelot* relates. While the lands of Logres-England (ie: Perea, Batanaea, Aurania and Osrhoene) to the east of the Jordan and Euphrates were semi-autonomous principalities that were supposed to send tribute to Rome, but had refused to do so.

The story of Claudas starts with a long and rambling story about the capture of the two sons of King Bors, which gives us some good descriptions of King Claudas. There are some minor battles and then we arrive in what appears to be the AD 60s, and the era of the Jewish Revolt. It will be assumed here that King Claudas is a generic name for both Vespasian and his son Titus, and the reason that the name Claudas was chosen is because of the standard chronological dislocation or chasm. It just so happens that if we jump back into the AD 40s, when Legatus Vespasian invaded Britain, he did so under the command of an emperor called Claudius:

> The pride (of Arviragus) did wax so great as that he despised Roman power, and was minded to no longer be bound by homage to the Senate ... Upon hearing this news, Vespasian was sent by Claudius either to bring about a reconciliation with Arviragus or to reimpose his subjugation to the Romans. (History of Kings 4:16.) (Author's brackets.)

This is actually an account of the second landing of the Roman army in Britain in the AD 40s, under the command of Legatus Vespasian and Emperor Claudius, rather than the landing of the Roman army in Judaea in the AD 60s under the command of Legatus Vespasian and Emperor Nero. But who in the 13th century would really know the difference? And the result of this deliberate and highly convenient confusion between the two Roman invasions commanded by Vespasian, is that the Roman commanders of the invasion force landing in Syrio-Judaea in AD 67 could easily be said to be King Claudius (Claudas) and Vespasian, rather than King Nero and Vespasian.

And so when a consul by the name of Pontus Anthony arrives from Rome to assist King Claudas (ie: Vespasian), we can safely assume that this was actually Marcus Antonius Julianus, who arrived in Judaea alongside Vespasian and Titus and became the new governor of Judaea during the Jewish Revolt. King Claudas and Anthony take all of King Ban's lands, except for the city of 'Trebe', which was too well fortified. This equates well with the opening skirmishes in the Jewish Revolt, where Vespasian and Titus defeat and destroy several cities including Jotapata and Gamala, while Tiberius was spared.

King Ban withdraws to Trebe, where he finds King Bors dying. Claudas (Vespasian) proposes that Ban surrenders the city or castle to him, and he will give it back to him if he swears to be his liegeman or vassal. King Ban refuses and decides to go to in person to see King Arthur in Logres (Edessa or Palmyra) to ask for military assistance. But his traitorous seneschal (a courtier or minister) goes to see Claudas privately. Claudas offers this unknown seneschal rule over the entire kingdom if he surrenders the city to Claudas, and the seneschal agrees. Accordingly, the traitorous seneschal leaves the city gates open for Claudas and the Romans to enter and capture the city. But the plan nearly backfires when Banin, the godson of King Ban, sees the Romans coming. But they are already in the gate and securing the walls, so Banin shouts to the traitorous seneschal:

> Murderer, Bastard. You are the man responsible for all this. You have betrayed your rightful lord, who raised you to great power, and now you have robbed him of all hope of regaining his lands. May you come to the same end as Judas. (Lancelot 2:15)

This again accords well with the initial events of the Jewish Revolt, where Saul-Josephus was also a traitorous governor (of Galilee). And in a similar fashion to this traitorous seneschal, Saul-Josephus also (reluctantly) fought against the Romans until he found himself cornered in a fortified city, in this case Jotapata. He then surrendered, changed sides and fought alongside the Romans.

Are these the same events? Is the traitorous seneschal who surrendered to Claudas actually Saul-Josephus who surrendered to Vespasian and Titus? Did Saul-Josephus sell out his own family to the Romans, in order to become the vassal prince of Vespasian and Titus, and therefore the lord of all Judaea? Or was Saul-Josephus more like Sir Perceval-Galahad, who had already been dispossessed by the internal feud between these families, and was looking to use the Romans to regain his inheritance? Both of these scenarios are entirely possible, for we know that Saul-Josephus joined the Romans under Vespasian and Titus as a Jewish traitor, and after the Jewish Revolt he became a Roman vassal 'prince' of Rome and the *de-facto* lord of all of Judaea.

As to Saul-Josephus' own father, throughout all of Josephus' works we only hear of his family twice - once when it is said that they were in prison in Jerusalem, and once again when his father wrote a letter to Josephus. Interestingly, the letter was sent while Josephus was the Jewish commander of Galilee, and it urged Josephus to surrender to the (Rome-friendly) Jewish authorities in Jerusalem. And the rebel forces that the Jerusalem authorities paid to disarm Saul-Josephus, included the army of Jesus of Gamala (ie: the biblical King Jesus-Izas). The rapidly shifting allegiances in the Jewish Revolt were and still are highly confusing. (War 5:13:1, Life 41).

Physique

Lancelot then describes King Claudas in greater detail, and this gives us a much better idea of who he really was. He has a son called Dorin, an arrogant youth who Claudas distrusted and refused to make a knight. And we might easily equate such a boorish youth with Vespasian's younger son, Domitian. Claudas is said to be the most miserly king in the world, and in comparison to Nero, Vespasian was indeed parsimonious. Even when he was a governor of North Africa he made no money from the appointment, which was most unusual for Roman governors.

It is said that Claudas had only been in love once, which again suits an association with Vespasian, who only married once and only had one mistress after his wife died. And finally we have a description of Claudas' physique. He is said to be a great bull of a man, of intimidating size with a handsome chest and a broad face. He has a short and twisted nose, widely space eyes, reddish hair and a thick neck. (Lancelot 8:54) Is this not a perfect description of both Vespasian and Titus? Look at the busts that follow. Are these not the features of a father and son who have a broad face, a thick neck and widely spaced eyes? Is Claudas not a generic name for both Vespasian and Titus?

Claudas and Arthur

We then have a hiatus in the hostilities between King Claudas and King

Fig 11.1 Emperors Vespasian (left) and Titus (right). Note their intimidating size with a handsome chest, broad face, widely space eyes, and a thick neck. The composite Vespasian-Titus appears to be the exactly the same as King Claudas. And we can probably see from these busts that there was no maternal infidelity within the Flavian family!

Arthur's forces, for two years. And again this equates quite well with the history of the region, because all Roman hostilities in Judaea were put on hold during the tumultuous Year of Four Emperors. So nothing happened in Judaea from June of AD 68 to the early spring of AD 70, a period of nearly two years.

During this time, King Claudas decides to go to the court of King Arthur in disguise, to spy on his opponent and see why this famous monarch was being hailed as such a noble and wise king. Claudas takes a local liegeman who can speak the language of the 'Britons', but he turns out to be a particularly rebellious liegeman who ends up declaring that he could not support King Claudas if he declared war on King Arthur. However, he graciously said that he would defend Claudas, his liege, if he was attacked. Such a generous liegeman. This causes some contention between them, with the king accusing his servant of treachery and a fight nearly breaking out. So did anything like this ever happen in the historical record? Would Vespasian or Titus ever have journeyed incognito to Palmyra or Edessa, to spy on King Izas-Jesus-Manu? While such a suggestion may seem unlikely and even outrageous, we have already seen in *Jesus, King of Edessa*, that something very much like this did indeed happen.

During the two-year hiatus in hostilities in Judaea, Titus had been sent to Rome by his father Vespasian, to strike a deal with the new and fleeting Emperor Vitellius - the emperor who Vespasian eventually defeated and deposed. Vespasian was becoming rather powerful in the East, and wanted to secure a high position for himself in this new Roman administration. These talks obviously came to nothing, but on his return Titus took the opportunity to visit Rhodes and Cyprus. And then he went to Syria to see what Tacitus calls the Paphian Venus - the Aerian omphalos stone of Venus.

Now this travelogue is odd, as the Paphian omphalos stone was located in a temple at Paphos in Cyprus and not in Syria, and so it is often presumed that the itinerary of Titus' journey has been recorded incorrectly. However, it is unlikely that Titus would have wanted to see the misshapen lump of granite that is the Paphian omphalos. Had Titus wanted to see the real omphalos, the famed Elagabal omphalos of Syria, he would have needed to travel to Edessa, because in this era the Elagabal was probably located at Sogmatar, the Edessan necropolis (it certainly was in the 2nd century). And Edessa was in Syria, just as this travelogue maintains.

It would appear that the account in *Lancelot* is correct, King Claudas (ie: Titus) did indeed go to Edessa to spy upon his enemy. But the king he was spying upon was not King Arthur, as such, it was King Izas-Manu au Kama VI of Edessa (who was King Arthur). And it was King Izas-Manu of Edessa who led the Jewish Revolt and was captured and crucified after the siege of Jerusalem, just as Saul-Josephus records in his *Jewish War* and *Life*. And yes,

Titus would have required an Aramaic-speaking Nazarene Jew as his servant and guide, if he was going to successfully maintain his cover in Edessa. And who better to take with him than Saul-Josephus, the quisling Jew who was now a commander and propaganda minister in the Roman army. But if Saul-Josephus had been the liegeman of Titus, it is no wonder that Titus was forced to accuse him of treachery and siding with King Izas-Manu, for Saul-Josephus bore allegiances to both sides in this dispute just as the liegeman in *Lancelot* did. (Lancelot 8:65)

Lancelot then goes off into a soporific morass of questing and courtly love which lasts for some 900 or more pages. The next time we hit anything remotely historical in this manuscript, is when we return to what appears to be the central topic of this story - the battles between Claudas (Vespasian and Titus) and the monarchs of Logres and Gaunes. In fact, *Lancelot* appears to be a short 50-page account of the Jewish Revolt immersed within 1,250 pages of padding, to keep the Inquisition away. The story about King Claudas is rejoined with an account of a lady courier trying to deliver a message to the two lost princes of Logres, who are being sheltered by Pharian, who may be King Agrippa. She is captured by King Claudas' men and searched for her letter, but her dwarf had already thrown it into some water. But she is imprisoned in a tower, nonetheless.

In return, King Claudas (Vespasian or Titus) sends two messengers to Logres, to spy upon King Arthur once more. When the spies get to Carduel, where Arthur is holding court, they are amazed at the richness of the celebrations and the largesse being dispensed to the courtiers, for they had never seen the parsimonious King Claudas (Vespasian or Titus) hold such a rich court. And that is probably true. Vespasian was a soldier, not a monarch, whose life had been spent in frugal army camps on the fringes of the Empire. It is unlikely that Vespasian ever indulged in the excesses of monarchs and emperors like Arthur and Nero. Indeed, when Vespasian felt like throwing money around he did not spend it upon himself, as Nero had done with his lavish palace in Rome, he built the Colosseum instead - a monument of pleasure for the people of Rome.

The messengers of King Claudas (Vespasian) were so impressed with wealth the and chivalry of Arthur's court that one of them declares he will never leave this court, while the other departs immediately and goes to report back to Claudas. Eventually Queen Gwenevere finds out who this spy is, and he is asked about the lady messenger that King Arthur had sent to Gaunes. Upon discovering that she is imprisoned in a tower Gwenevere orders the spy to take a letter to King Claudas, demanding the release of her messenger and threatening retribution if he does not comply. The messenger takes the letter to King Claudas, who is outraged and writes back to Gwenevere that he will not let the lady messenger go, and will dishonour her instead. These communications are inconclusive, but it is interesting to see the number of spies and ambassadors that were shuttling back and forth between these two nations, during this time of great political tension.

Claudas and Claudin

Having suffered King Claudas (Vespasian and Titus) in their lands for a couple of years, Bors and Ban and the other the princes of Logres and Gaunes decide to go to war with Claudas. King Claudas of Rome is concerned by these developments in Logres and asks his minister for advice. The seneschal advises that Claudas is in a very strong position, because he owns lands that stretch from Greece to Gaul. This is an interesting comment, because the only ruler who owned lands stretching from Greece to Gaul at this time was the Emperor of Rome. But King Claudas is obviously not the emperor himself, because the seneschal then advises Claudas to send a letter to the emperor to ask for assistance. And so these two comments together accord very well with the contention here that King Claudas is actually Vespasian, who was only an army commander at this time.

And then the author of *Lancelot* completely confuses the chronology once more by saying that this letter was sent to Emperor Tiberius. So having vainly tried to imply that this was actually the 6th century era of classical Arthurian history, *Lancelot* now plunges us back into the mid 1st century of Emperor Tiberius, who reigned from AD 14 to 37. This strange choice of era was obviously influenced by the standard chronological chasm. The looming battle between King Claudas (Vespasian) and King Arthur (King Jesus-Izas) was obviously an account of the Jewish Revolt. And according to the classical biblical chronology the revolt that King Jesus-Izas was involved in must have taken place in the 30s, not the 60s. Thus *Lancelot* completely confuses the chronology by mentioning Emperor Tiberius. Anyway, this letter is sent to the emperor in Rome, who would in reality have been Nero, but King Claudas is still anxious about the situation because:

> Claudas took council with his people and said: "What can I do about my men of this land? I very much fear that they will desert me at the last (minute) and betray me, because I am not their natural lord. I beg of you, advise me what to do." (Lancelot 171:41)

And this was a real worry for King Claudas (Vespasian-Titus), because at least half of his forces were local. Vespasian had landed in Syria with legions X Fretensis and V Macedonica, while Titus had arrived from Alexandria with XV Apollinaris. But the rest of his troops were gathered from the remains of the Syrian legion, and from the armies of King Agrippa II and King Sohemus of Emesa. And there was even a small force from Samosata in the Commagene, as we have seen previously. Would all these troops remain loyal, when they started fighting against the Jews of Judaea? Where did their true allegiances lie? Were these troops Greek Gentiles, Syrian Sabaeans, or Jews?

A nephew of Claudas advised him to rid himself of all the locals who wanted to leave Gaunes, because they were not going to be loyal. This Claudas does. And so many people (and soldiers?) do indeed flee from Gaunes and Benoic ahead of the looming battle, in an event that appears to be very similar to the historical 'Flight to Pella' of the Nazarene Ebionites. Then King Claudas appoints a new commander:

> And because there was no man in all the world in whom (King Claudas) could trust as much as one of his sons, who was a very worthy knight, he entrusted him with the lordship of his people, and second only to King Claudas himself ... That knight was ... so young that he was not yet 27 years old, and his name was Claudas the Younger. And because they did not want to call him by the same name as his father, they called him Claudin. (Lancelot 171:48)

And this is absolutely correct. In the historical record Vespasian did indeed appoint his son Titus as his second in command, despite there being many able Roman commanders in Judaea who could have been promoted to this position. So Claudin, the worthy knight and son of Claudas, was actually called Titus. And yes, Titus was exactly 27 years old at the start of the Jewish Revolt when he was given command of legion XV Apollinaris, just as this account says.

And note that there is a confusion of names here, between father and son. This is because both father and son had the same names - Titus Flavius Vespasianus - and so a convention had to be agreed upon to differentiate between the two. In *Lancelot* they chose the names Claudas and Claudin, while in modern history we have chosen Vespasian and Titus to differentiate between father and son. However, as we saw earlier *History of the Grail* reverses the modern naming convention; and this lured Professor Richard Carrier into making a complete fool of himself, by his not spotting and understanding this very simple transposition.

In the continuing story, King Claudas continues fortifying and stocking his castles and cities. Then his messenger finally comes back from Rome with bad news:

> "My Lord, Tiberius Caesar, the emperor of Rome had died just recently on St John's day, and so I found them all downcast when I got there." ... Because they don't yet have a new emperor, they inform you that this winter they will send

> you the chief consul of Rome with as great a force of men as they can assemble. Be informed that if you can wait until then, you will have no fear of King Arthur. (Lancelot 171:49)

This is another very telling passage. Again this account is correct in almost all respects, but only if we set the story in the AD 60s. When the throne of Rome went from Emperor Tiberius to Emperor Caligula, the throne was empty for twelve days. Between Caligula and Claudius the throne was reoccupied the next day, just as it was between Claudius and Nero. The only time we see an unoccupied throne in Rome is between emperors Nero and Vespasian. And this was indeed a significant event worth recording, because the throne was effectively empty for a whole year - the Year of Four Emperors. In addition, Nero is said to have died on the 9th June, while St John's feast day is the summer solstice on 24th June, so the date is almost correct too.

So just as *Lancelot* says, there was indeed a hiatus in all military operations in the middle of the Jewish Revolt, during the Year of Four Emperors. And Vespasian did indeed send to Rome for further instructions, but received no replies or reinforcements because the throne of Rome was empty. In fact, the war against the Nazarene Ebionite rebels only resumed after Vespasian himself had accepted the Imperial Purple and had become the new emperor.

War clouds

King Arthur convenes a gathering of the clans in Logres, at which the majority of princes and leaders press for renewed military action against King Claudas and Prince Claudin. King Arthur agrees, but in his battle plan he sends out the armies of Brandegorre, Bademagu, Caradoc and Cabarentin, while the forces of Lancelot and Arthur remain behind. But just as this confederated force sets out from Logres, word comes to them that King Claudas has gone to Rome.

> They had some news destined to make them very glad ... 'My lord ... you can now pass through Gaul, for the lord (Claudas) has gone to Rome, two months or more ago, and many say he is dead.' (Lancelot 173:70)

Again this is substantially correct. Vespasian travelled to Alexandria in the July of AD 69, and did not come back to Judaea until early AD 70 (the dates vary slightly, in the various accounts). And at some point during this same period, Titus had sailed to Rome to see if he could strike a deal with the short-lived Emperor Vitellius, before travelling onto Syria. So yes, King Claudas and Prince Claudin had both left the field of battle for some considerable time during AD 69, which may have cheered rebel spirits considerably. Just replace 'King Claudas' with 'Vespasian' or 'Titus' in this quote, and it makes perfect historical sense.

And it is not surprising that many of the rebels thought Vespasian (or Titus) may be dead. This was the Year of Four Emperors and three emperors had already been murdered during this turbulent time. The odds of Vespasian surviving his bid for the throne of Rome were slim to non-existent, and a rumour that he was dead was good for rebel morale. The story in *Lancelot* then says that Claudas came back to 'Gaul' to continue the battle, which agrees well with Vespasian's late AD 69 visit to Alexandria to secure the Egyptian grain supplies.

The army from Logres then set off for 'Gaul' and eventually came to a castle called Pagon, which they easily defeat. Some of the defenders escape and receive news that King Claudas had arrived to protect the castle, which had already been taken. Claudas decides to make a night attack on the Logres army. One presumes this is quite a small castle or town, because most of the Logres army are camped outside and the night attack catches them all by surprise. So there is a great slaughter of the Arthurian army, and King Claudas and Prince Claudin take no less than 700 prisoners.

This account is interesting on many levels. Firstly, it is hardly the fictional story we might imagine, of a heroic King Arthur and his army casting aside all the forces of evil that they encounter. Having had a minor victory against a small fortification, a large proportion of the Arthurian army is killed and captured by the superior tactics of King Claudas (Vespasian). When looking at the historical version of this history in AD 60s Judaea, it is not clear if this battle is mentioned by Saul-Josephus. There were still some small skirmishes going on in and around Judaea at this time and so one possibility is that this was a reference to the rebel leader Simon taking Hebron and the Roman commander Cerealis retaking the city.

There then follows a set piece battle between the armies of Logres and King Claudas, a battle that is firmly set in the crusading Middle Ages despite the overtly 1st century era that the author is trying to describe. It is a melee of knights in shining armour charging with lances lowered to impale the opposition, which was not how battles were fought in the 1st century. Although do bear in mind that all the commanders involved in the Jewish Revolt would have worn standard Roman armour, which was indeed metallic and probably shining. And there would have been large detachments of cavalry on both sides too, but without the lances.

There is also a great deal of Hollywood-style single combat between the commanders of these armies, which is highly unlikely in the extreme. Roman military tactics placed a great emphasis on maintaining the line, with interlocked shields for protection and short stabbing swords to pierce the enemy who were pressed against those shields. The only time when single combat would take place is when the formation had been broken and the battle was all but over. Although it is possible that detachments of opposing cavalry got involved in more of a melee-style combat. Anyway, this particular battle goes on all day, but proves to be inconclusive. And because so many commanders had been captured on each side, an exchange of prisoners is arranged in the evening.

In a reversal of the historical situation, King Claudas (Vespasian-Titus) finds himself besieged in Tower Castle, by the army of Logres. Claudas sends to Rome for reinforcements, who attack the army of Logres as soon as they arrive. The Arthurian besiegers are beaten back by this onslaught, and send to Arthur for reinforcements. Arthur gathers his remaining forces together and invades Gaul, and has some difficulty in establishing his authority in the region. Then, right in the middle of this great war, King Claudas again decides to pack his bags and go back to Rome. Claudas says to his squire:

> Go back to Gaunes and tell those you find that I am going to the Emperor in Rome, and they are to manage as best they can, for they will no longer be helped by me. Be assured that I would never have given up if I thought I could make peace with Arthur and Lancelot. (Lancelot 176:166)

While the prospect of a king leaving the battlefield and going to Rome for a second time might sound improbable, this is exactly what happened in the real history of this conflict. We have already seen the departure of Vespasian to Alexandria in AD 69, to secure the Egyptian grain supplies. And now that the turbulent Year of Four Emperors was at last coming to a conclusion, and Vespasian was being hailed as the popular new emperor, he did indeed sail to Rome. Vespasian departed from Judaea in the spring of AD 70, and left the siege of Jerusalem and the final battles in Judaea to his son, Titus. According to Saul-Josephus, the siege of Jerusalem ended in Gorpiaios or August, and it was Titus who directed the final weeks of the siege.

Thus just as King Claudas leaves the battle to his son, Prince Claudin, so too did Vespasian leave the battle to his son, Titus. The only difference between these two parallel stories, is that *Lancelot* says that Prince Claudin surrendered to King Arthur, and so it is Arthur who is the victor rather than Titus or Vespasian. And while this ending to the story is a deliberate reversal of reality, it is hard to see what else the author of *Lancelot* could have done with his narrative. King Arthur was the great hero-figure, and it would ruin the whole point of the story to see the hero defeated and carted off to prison in Rome.

And while the gospels managed to get away with this very same tragic twist to the end of the story, if *Lancelot* had similarly said that King Arthur had been captured and crucified it would have given the entire game away - it would be obvious that King Arthur was a pseudonym for King Jesus. So the only other option open to the author, was to have Prince Claudin (Titus) surrender, and for King Arthur (King Jesus-Izas) to become the victor. But the duplicity in the story is easy to see, for Claudin (Titus) does not suffer imprisonment, trial or execution. Instead, the story simply forgets about this little incident completely, and moves on.

XII

The Grail Quest

Quest for the Holy Grail - Walter Map
Book 6 of the *Vulgate Cycle* or *Lancelot Grail*

Within *Quest for the Holy Grail (Quest)* and *Death of Arthur* (*Mort*) it is claimed that the author was Water Map; and it is also recorded that these books were written for Henry II Plantagenet, who was king of England from 1154 to 1189. This claim would match the known life of Walter Map, who is said to have been a minor courtier and adviser in the court of Henry II. But as we saw in the chapter on *History of the Grail,* this assertion does not match very well with the orthodox 1220s date for the composition of these manuscripts.

Quest is yet another an account of courtly love, questing and strange visions that are translated into morality tales. Nothing is quite as it seems, and everything is a portent for the future or an explanation of the past. But thankfully these soporific sections of the story are rather shorter than in *Lancelot*. This chapter will also use a few extracts from the *Post Vulgate* series, *Post Quest* and *Post Mort,* which are later expanded renditions of the same story with a few minor alterations.

The *Post Vulgate* books introduce a few new characters, like Tristan, and expand some events, like Prince Claudin's spying mission to Camelot. They also exaggerate the story with shocking and gory details, like Eric killing his sister (ch 115); King Arthur raping a girl (ch 123); and Mordred, Arthur's son, raping and beheading a girl (ch 112). It is not clear if these are scandalous events that *Quest* deliberately left out of the story, or dramatic embellishments in the later works to spice up the story. But in general it has to be said that the *Post Vulgate* series contain a lot less historical information than the earlier works. The same can be said of Thomas Malory's *The Death of Arthur*, which seems to have no clue whatsoever about the secret historical story that underlies these works.

The narrative in *Quest* superficially masquerades as a sacred quest to find the Holy Grail. But since the knights of the Round Table all saw the Holy Grail at Camelot before they set off on their quest, the entire escapade seems fairly pointless to the untrained eye. At the very beginning of the story the knights gather at the Round Table to witness the Grail procession:

> Then the Holy Grail entered the room, covered with a white silk cloth, but nobody could see who carried it. It entered through the main door of the hall. And as soon as it arrived, the room was filled with a delicious fragrance, as every earthly spice had been strewn there. The Grail travelled through the room and around the dias. And as it passed, each place setting was filled with the food each occupant most desired. When everyone was served, the Grail left in such a way that no one knew what became of it, nor did they see where it went. (Quest, 5:15)

This description poses two obvious questions. Why would these knights bother go on a quest to find the Holy Grail, when it was right there in front of them just a moment ago. And what exactly was this mysterious Grail, that was covered in white silk and glided effortlessly through the great hall serving each of the knights with their favourite foods?

In fact, the first question may eventually lead us towards the answer for the second, so what exactly was this quest all about? How can the knights go on a quest to find something they have already seen? But did anyone see it? The whole point about the nebulous descriptions of the Holy Grail in *Quest*, is that everyone saw the Grail as an artifact, because it was right in front of them, but nobody recognised it or understood what it was. Therefore, the quest for the Holy Grail is a not so much a search for a physical artifact, a golden chalice, but a search for the meaning of that artifact - a search for an answer to what they saw.

And then the knights all go off in different directions, looking for the Holy Grail. Again, the meaning of this description is clear. Recognising and understanding the Holy Grail was not supposed to be a group exercise, with the twelve knights of the Round Table riding line-abreast to the next castle or hermitage to seek a real golden chalice studded with gems. Quite the reverse. The Grail quest was a personal adventure and a personal experience, to be resolved by your own thoughts and by amending your own perspective and world-view. The Grail may present itself to a knight on several occasions during his quest, as we shall see, but only the most perfect of knights would ever recognise it, let alone comprehend its true meaning and understand its true value.

And if the quest itself was cryptic, then so too were the descriptions of the Grail. The descriptions in *Quest* are merely teasers to intrigue the reader and whet the appetite for more information - information that for many readers never arrives. It is quite possible that the vast majority of readers of *Quest* never discovered what the Grail was, or even what the quest itself represented, and must have been left deeply dissatisfied with the whole concept of the Grail Romance. But that was the whole point of the *Vulgate Cycle* - readers were not meant to understand the story unless they had been guided towards the explanation. This not only kept the secrets secret, it also proved to the initiate that there was hidden information to be found, if they persevered in their esoteric studies. All the uninitiated would come away with, was the description in *Lancelot* that says:

> The Holy Grail is the vessel in which Jesus ate the lamb with his disciples in the house of Simon the Leper. Joseph of Arimathaea brought it to the kingdom of Logres, and since then it has continued to produce miracles ... and King Pelles and all his household are still fed by it every day. (Lancelot VI:177:205)

This was the traditional conception and understanding of the Grail, that it was a sacred chalice of some nature; used either as a serving dish for the disciples at the Last Supper, or to collect drops of blood from Jesus during the crucifixion. No doubt this belief was reinforced by sculptures of the original Last Supper scene from the east of the Romo-Byzantine Empire, especially from Palmyra, where the deceased aristocrat was always portrayed lounging on plump cushions and eating or drinking from a wide-brimmed chalice. The tomb of Yahai in Palmyra is a good illustration of this scene, with Yahai holding his wide-brimmed Grail chalice. And do remember that this is a Last Supper scene, in the afterlife, just as the scene with Jesus-Izas and his disciples in the gospels is also described as a Last Supper.

The Grail itself is a multifaceted artifact with many attributes, aspects, characteristics and meanings, and so this golden chalice-style manifestation of the Grail is not the Holy Grail that is described in *Quest*. The Grail in *Quest* is much more esoteric and much more historically and culturally significant than a mere chalice, just as *Quest* plainly states when it says:

> But the observers were so deceived that they couldn't see the Grail clearly, and its true form remained hidden from them. (Quest 5:16)

> Even if the Grail appeared before you, I don't think you could see it any more than a blind man could see a sword in front of his face. (Quest 35:123)

> This is not a quest for earthly goods. Rather it should be understood as the

Fig 12.1 The tomb of Yahai, in Palmyra. Note the reclining positions and the sacred grail chalice, all of which is very reminiscent of the biblical Last Supper, and of the Grail quest.

> search for the great secrets of our Lord (Jesus) ... The Lord will show this knight the great wonders of the Holy Grail and allow him to contemplate what mortal hearts could never imagine. (Quest 6:19)

It would seem that the Grail is so difficult to comprehend that most people cannot see it even when it appears right in front of them, just as the knights seated around the Round Table also failed to understand what the Grail was. And this is not because the Grail is incomprehensible, it is because most people are looking for the wrong thing. The uninitiated are like children desperately looking for Father Christmas, when their parents are standing right in front of them.

The second quote here clarifies the situation slightly, by saying that this is an esoteric quest for the 'secrets of our Lord' - secrets that are so divergent from the gospel narrative and normal expectations, that most people could not imagine such things. Or even if they could imagine such things, they would purge them from their minds because they appeared to be dangerously heretical. In an era when Christianity ruled the hearts and minds of almost everyone in Europe, the possibility that many of the teachings of the Church were completely false would be very shocking indeed. So shocking, they would be inconceivable to most people. Even in today's supposedly enlightened world, when devout theists hear about Jesus actually being a king of Edessa they invariably put their fingers in their ears and start shouting: 'la, la, la, I cannot hear you...' It is not that they cannot understand, it is that they do not want to understand. As the age-old adage says: 'there are none so blind as those who ***will*** not see'.

But in what manner can a 'Holy Grail' undermine the central teachings and tenets of the Christian Church? What is the answer to the mystery of this secretive, occult (hidden), and highly esoteric Grail that is being described in *Quest*? Unfortunately, *Quest* only gives us a few tantalising clues, and the complete answer does not arrive until we read *Mort*. Again the reader is being tested, to see if they will give up early and move onto other topics and interests, for only those who persevere will ever see the Grail.

The next tangential hint to the true nature of the Grail comes when

Fig 12.2 The Holy Grail envisioned as a ciborium chalice held aloft by two angels. There are 24 knights around this table, indicating that this is the Round Table of Joseph(us), rather than the Round Table of Arthur. This image is taken from BNF 112, one of the original manuscripts of the Vulgate Cycle. Clearly the illustrations in these manuscripts were not designed to clarify the true nature of the Grail. Do note that there is space for a chair in the very center of the this table, where the king may have actually sat.

Lancelot is on his quest to find the Holy Grail and meets a young lady on a white palfrey, a ladies' horse:

> After vespers (Lancelot) met a young woman on a white palfrey. She greeted Lancelot and asked: "where are you going?" "I don't know, lady," he replied ... I have no idea where I might find what I am looking for."
>
> "I know what you are looking for," she replied. "You were closer to it earlier than you are now, and yet you are also closer to it now than you have ever been..." "Lady," answered Lancelot, "the two phrases you have just uttered seem to contradict each other." "That does not matter," she replied. It will become clear to you in time..." (Quest 38:130)

The unnamed lady is speaking about the Grail, of course. And when she says: "You were closer to it earlier than you are now," she is referring to the banquet at Camelot, where the knights had been served by the Grail but never truly saw it or understood it. So Lancelot has been close to the Grail twice, once at the Grail banquet and once again when he sees a beautiful lady, and yet on both occasions he fails to properly see this holy chalice. So what was this mysterious Grail?

We need to plough through the manuscripts and onto to *Mort,* the next book in the series, before the answer to the young lady's riddle can be found. And the answer lies in another description of the Grail banquet, where the apparition that accompanies the Grail is described in more detail:

> Once they were seated at table, the maiden came slowly and humbly into the palace, carrying the Holy Grail in her hands. When Bors saw the holy vessel he adored it profoundly, bowing in front of it with weeping and tears ... As soon as the maiden had gone once round the palace, the tables were suddenly filled with every good food in the world. (Lancelot V:152:271.)

On this occasion the Holy Grail does not float around the room unaided, it is held aloft by a young lady. So now we have a good idea why the white silk and sweet perfume were mentioned previously, because the young lady was wearing them. So the focus of attention is moving away from the chalice and towards the young lady. This description is duplicated and expanded upon in Wolfram von Eschenbach's *Parzival,* where it is said:

> The heathen (Feirefiz) asked for knowledge: what made the empty golden dishes become full? Then spoke Anfortas (the Wounded Fisher King): 'My lord, do you see the Grail lying before you?' The many-coloured heathen said: 'I see nothing except a green cloth. My young lady brought that to us, who stands here before us, wearing a crown. Her looks go to my heart.' (Parzival, bk 16.) (Author's brackets.)

So now the young lady who holds the Grail wears a crown and holds a green cloth. But still the knight - this time the piebald Feirefiz - cannot see exactly what the Grail is, even though it is right in front of him.

And then we have a story in *Mort,* where the knights of the Round Table travel to Winchester to attend a jousting tournament. On the way back to Castle Corbenic they stop for the night at Castle Escalot, which sounds like a small fortified manor house. Here, they are served by the beautiful daughter of the lord of the manor:

> When the knights had sat down to eat, the young woman served them. At that time in the kingdom of Logres there was a custom that if a wandering knight came to the home of any noble man, and there was a maiden there, she should serve them. And the more noble she was, the more she was obligated to serve and not sit down to eat before the knights had finished. (*Mort* ch2 n 23)

Here we have exactly the same scenario as before: a banquet served by a beautiful young lady of noble heritage and standing. But here there is no Grail to distract our attention, just the young lady. And she is compelled to serve the tables of these princely knights, no matter how noble or royal she is.

And so here we have several concise, cryptic and yet very clear explanations of what this aspect of the Holy Grail really was, and so the reader can now resolve this millennial riddle of the identity of the Holy Grail. And the answer is that the self-propelled Holy Grail dressed in white silk and wearing a crown, that filled the room with perfume and served the knights of the Round Table with food, was actually a young lady: a princess.

And the reason for the *Mort's* unlikely assertion that even the most noble of ladies were forced to serve at table, is to confirm that no matter how lofty, aristocratic or royal this young lady was, she was still obliged to serve the knights. So the Grail lady was not any busty young serving wench, she was of noble blood, and probably the most noble and aristocratic princess in King Arthur's court at Corbenic. And so the young Princess of the Grail just has to be a daughter of King Arthur and Queen Gwenevere.

And there is a delightfully cryptic allusion to the true Grail being a princess in *Post Merlin*. Wolfram von Eschenbach mentions that another facet of the Holy Grail is a sacred stone, as has been mentioned previously. This sacred Grail-stone is closely linked to the sacred omphalos stones of Greece and Syria, and also to the story of the Sword in the Stone. So the stone that Excalibur gets stuck in, is just one feature of the multi-faceted Holy Grail. But *Post Merlin* completely turns this sword and stone scenario completely around, and says that the sword got stuck upon a princess instead:

> My lady of the Isle of Avalon sends me to you, king, so I may obtain your help ... king, there is a sword that I have girded around me; but know that I cannot do anything with it (not) drawing it from the scabbard nor ungirding it from around me... (Post Merlin 8:123-124)

This magical sword is, of course, Excalibur or Caliburn. And this is a name that was derived from the Aramaic once more, just as we might expect. In the Torah a sword is called a *careb* חרב, and if we apply the standard 'r' to 'l' transliteration we derive Caleb or Calib(urn).

But in this story Excalibur is not stuck in a stone, it is stuck on a princess. And only the best and most virtuous knight in the land can remove the sword from her body, just as only Arthur or Galahad could take Excalibur from the stone. So the standard Excalibur story has been deliberately turned around, so that the sacred Holy Grail stone from *Parzival* has become a sacred Holy Grail princess. And since this sword is Excalibur, which was forged in Avalon, this distressed princess has come from the Lady of the Lake - the Lady of the Isle of Avalon, who is sometimes said to be Morgan le Fay, the sorceress sister of King Arthur. And so this sacred quest was being devised by Arthur's own sister. And in a final version of this story, *High History* says that the sword was stuck in a pillar and the prize was a princess:

> The daughter of the lord of the castle is the fairest in the world that is known in any kingdom, and she must be offered as a wife to all knights that enter within. He that can draw a sword that is fixed in a column in the middle of the hall, he shall have her as of right ... And he showed him (Lancelot) the sword that was (stuck in) the column, all inlaid with gold ... As soon as (Lancelot) touched it, the sword drew forthwith such a wrench that the column shook. (High History 24:2, 5)

The many descriptions of the Holy Grail invariably have it closely linked to a young princess. And so the chalice was merely a deliberate distraction, to take our attention away from the answer to this facet of the quest. The chalice was the equivalent of a magician clicking the fingers of his left hand, so we do not notice his right hand removing our watch or wallet. And this was a simple but effective distraction that has stood the test of time, for very few people have ever realised that the Holy Grail was actually the princess herself. So when Feirefiz says he cannot see the Grail, only a pretty princess holding a green cloth, the other knights must have been biting their lips to stifle their amusement - because the Grail was the princess herself.

But if the Holy Grail was actually a princess, then we can also decypher the confusing and contradictory answers given to Lancelot by the lady on the white palfrey. She said to Lancelot:

> "You were closer to it earlier than you are now, and yet you are also closer to it now than you have ever been..."

Lancelot had been closer to the Holy Grail at Camelot, because at least on that occasion he knew that he was looking at the Grail - even if he did not recognise or understand it. Lancelot was looking for a magical chalice, but all he could see was the princess. One can even imagine an uninitiated knight of the Round Table asking the princess to step to one side, so they might see the Grail more clearly, and receiving a sweet and knowing smile in return.

But when Lancelot spoke to the young lady on the white palfrey he did not even realise he was in the presence of the Grail, and yet he was standing much closer to the Grail Princess there than he had been at Camelot. So yes, the Grail Princess on the white horse was quite correct, and her cryptic answers were not contradictory at all. Lancelot was cognitively closer to the Grail at Camelot, but physically closer to the Grail Princess on the white palfrey. And this is how convoluted the story in *Quest* is, and how closely we must look in order to understand it.

And so when the *Vulgate* says that the Grail princess was holding the Grail, it probably meant that she was clasping her abdomen with both hands, for the true Grail was a bloodline that resided within her womb. In antiquity the womb was always represented by the V symbol, the symbol of the chalice, and this was an age-old tradition derived from ancient Egypt, as was discussed in *King Jesus*.

And if one of the facets of the Grail was the royal womb, and therefore a royal bloodline, then there must have been a succession of Holy Grails throughout the generations. And we see this succession of Grails within *Lancelot*, where the daughter of King Pelles (the sister of King Arthur), became a holder of the Grail. This was probably Princess Gwenevere herself, just as *Merlin* says (Merlin 42:346). But Princess Gwenevere would have renounced her position when she got married and lost her virginity, and so the holder of the Grail became her cousin, a niece of King Pelles (Lancelot V:152:270). Later, the position of the Grail went to a daughter of King Arthur and Queen Gwenevere, and so this third Grail Princess was a granddaughter of King Pelles. And so on through the many generations and into the modern era.

And so the primary aspect of this many-faceted concept of the Holy Grail was actually a princess, and the royal bloodline that she bore within her womb. And this is why the San Greal (the Holy Grail) could be deliberately transformed into the Sang Real (the Royal Blood), because the Holy Grail was a royal bloodline. More precisely it was the royal bloodline of King Jesus-Izas, which did survive the 1st century but only just. But this amusing literary allusion to a royal bloodline is not a modern concept derived from the bestselling book *Holy Blood Holy Grail*, it is a concept that goes back to the very beginnings of Arthurian history.

Witty or secretive wordplay is one of the central features of any ancient manuscript. Presumably the scribes of the era were very proud of their skills, which few other people possessed, and were delighted that they could pass secrets to each other in otherwise boring old texts. And then we have the Talmud, which used the same literary technique to pour bile and scorn upon the enemies of Judaism, while covering up who they were talking about, and we have seen many examples of this in the previous books in this series. But there is no reason to think that the Arthurian scribes and chroniclers were any different.

And we know that these authors used wordplay to disguise the Grail, because *Merlin Grail* calls it 'the dish that delights'. This is a play on words derived from the Norman French *agreer* and the Latin *ad gratus* meaning 'to delight', from which we also derive the English 'agree'. The delightful Greer is supposed to sound like the holy Greal, which is all very witty. But the San Greal vs Sang Real (Holy Grail vs Royal Blood) wordplay was also used in this same early era, and the 1917 *Catholic Encyclopaedia* says of this deliberate wordplay:

> The explanation of San Greal as Sang Real (kingly blood) was not current until the later Middle Ages.

The bards of the Middle Ages would have derived this wordplay not only from the legends of the New Testament family surviving the many Roman pogroms against them, but also from *High History* which describes the Holy Grail as the vessel that Joseph of Arimathaea used to collect the blood of Jesus. In *High History* an unnamed master of a castle says of the Holy Grail:

> 'I saw the Graal,' said the Master, 'where Joseph, that was the uncle (nephew) of King Fisherman, collected therein the blood of Jesus Christ. Know that I am well acquainted with all your (Perceval's) lineage, and of what folk you were born.' (High History 35:7) (Author's brackets.)

The Grail was therefore the vessel that held the blood of Christ, and it was directly connected to Perceval's lineage. And so even within *High History* we can see the beginnings of the San Greal to Sang Real wordplay. The San Greal collects the royal blood of Jesus-Izas, and so the San Greal is the Sang Real - the Holy Grail captures the Royal Blood.

The Grail stone

Yet the mystery of the Holy Grail goes even deeper that this. While the Grail was often seen as a chalice and only occasionally recognised as a covert reference to a bloodline, it was also said to be a sacred stone. In *Parzival* the Holy Grail was said to be a sacred stone called Lapsit Exillis, meaning 'Stone from Heaven'. And although this translation for the name is much disputed, this is exactly what Wolfram says this stone was, as we shall see. And the Grail stone was also closely linked to the sacred Phoenix, because Eschenbach says of the Grail:

> It is called Lapsit Exillis. By that stone's power the Phoenix burns away, turning to ashes, yet those ashes bring it back to life ... that stone is also called the Grail. The Grail allows all animals that live under the sky to multiply ... it gives sustenance to the brotherhood of knights ... (Parzival 3500 of 7000)

Surprisingly, we know that Eschenbach is giving us true facts here, as far as such assertions can be known as true facts, because we have an image of this very stone dating from the 3rd century. This is the Grail-stone of Emperor Elagabalus, which was known as the Elagabal and translates as the 'Sun-god Mound' or 'Sun-god Mountain'. And while this descriptive name may sound confusing, it simply refers to the Egyptian concept of the Primeval Mound (see the book *King Jesus* for details).

Fig 12.3 The Holy Grail-stone had the image of the Phoenix embossed upon it, back in the 3rd century AD. So Wolfram's description of the lithic Holy Grail was correct.

The Elagabal Grail-stone was a real artifact that Emperor Elagabalus used to place in a chariot and take on processions around Rome. And this sacred stone was so intimately associated with the Phoenix that it had an image of this fiery avian embossed upon it. Yet the coin of Elagabalus predates Wolfram von Eschenbach's similar description of the Grail-stone by a thousand years. And since it is highly unlikely that Eschenbach ever saw a coin of Emperor Elagabalus, we know that an oral or literary tradition had maintained the link between the Grail-stone and the Phoenix for all of this time. The history and travelogue of this particular sacred omphalos stone is explored in some detail in the *King Jesus Trilogy*, and it is an interesting story it its own right.

The connection between this sacred omphalos stone and the Grail princesses, is that a select royal family were chosen to look after this sacred Grail stone. And that family line passed through the first Fisher King, King Pelles, and thence to King Arthur-Jesus and beyond to the line of the Fisher Kings. This was the Grail family, that had been entrusted with guarding the sacred stone through the millennia, and the chief priest entrusted to be the Guardian of the Grail-stone was the Peter-Kephas, the Stone-Stone. And as we saw in Chapter VI, one of those guardians was the biblical St Simon Peter Kephas, who was appointed as the Guardian of the Grail by Jesus-Izas himself. And if the first St Peter was Bron-Hebron, as will be demonstrated again in a later chapter, then the next Grail Guardian was Sir Perceval-Galahad.

Perhaps the best description of this interconnected relationship between the Grail stone and the Grail family comes from Wolfram von Eschenbach, who says the source for his information was Master Kyot. This otherwise unknown Kyot was probably Walter Kayo, the claimed author of *History of the Grail*, and Kayo claimed that he received the information from Flegetanis of Toledo (or Edessa). However, as we saw earlier, this same physicus called Flegetanis may well have been King Evalach Mordrain's sister, Princess Flegetine, who was therefore King Jesus-Arthur's daughter. This would agree with the description in *Lancelot*, where one of the princesses of the Holy Grail was a daughter of King Arthur and Queen Gwenevere. And so perhaps we can now name this daughter as being Princess Flegetine of Palmyra - the princess who, as we saw in Chapter VIII, was named after the Milky Way and therefore after Venus-Aphrodite.

And so there is a claimed line of transmission that takes this information and knowledge about the Grail-stone all the way back to the 1st century family of Jesus. Within Eschenbach's *Parzival* this 1st century princess called Flegetanis is said to have been an astronomer who:

> ...was able to define the regression of each planet and its return, and how long each revolves in its orbit before it stands its mark again. All humankind are

> affected by the revolutions of the planets. With his (her) own eyes Flegetanis saw, and spoke of it reverentially, hidden secrets in the constellations. (Parzival 3380 of 7000) (Author's brackets.)

One of the central tenets of this esoteric Gnostic religion was obviously astronomy and the workings of the cosmos, and this is why so much obscure astrology and astronomy will be discussed in Chapter XIV. This seeming diversion into esoterica is not incidental to the Arthurian story, it is the central foundation upon which this belief system and story was constructed. But the wise Flegetanis-Flegetine did not just know about the revolutions of the planets. Since she was herself the Grail Princess, it is not so surprising that she also understood the true nature and origins of the Holy Grail. And surprisingly, the Grail was not a chalice, nor was it simply a bloodline, and it wasn't even a fiery meteorite that had once flamed through the skies of ancient Egypt. No, the stone of the Holy Grail had come from what can only be described as a party of 'extraterrestrials':

> A party (of angels or ambassadors) had left it (the Grail-stone) on Earth and then they rose high above the stars, as if their innocence drew them back again. Afterwards a (royal) progeny bred to a pure life had the duty of keeping it. Those humans who are summoned to the Grail are ever worthy ... Since that time the Stone has been in the care of those whom god appointed to it, and to whom he sent his angel (messenger). This is how matters stand regarding the Grail. (Parzival 3400, of 7000) (Author's brackets.)

So Eschenbach, writing in the early 13th century, believed that something akin to a party of alien spacemen had left the Holy Grail on Earth, and created a special royal family to look after it. And this is why the translation of Lapsit Exillis as the 'Stone from Heaven' is correct, because this stone did indeed come from the heavens above. But this leaves us with an interesting question. If Eschenbach can be correct about the Holy Grail being a stone that was closely associated with the Phoenix, a history that had been accurately maintained for more than a thousand years, could he also be correct about the origins of the Grail? Was the Holy Grail simply a meteorite that had streaked through the skies above, to land with a resounding thud in some soft earth? Or was it a special stone with unique properties and capabilities, which had been brought to Earth by a group of alien beings?

The Grail Quest

Having witnessed the Holy Grail at Castle Corbenic, the knights of the Round

Table then go off on a quest to find the Holy Grail. As has already been explained, this makes little or no sense in terms of finding an object - some kind of grail chalice - and so the real quest that the knights and Arthurian readers are challenged with, is not to find the Holy Grail but to find out what it represents. This was the vital question that Perceval forgot to ask, when he saw the Grail at the castle of the Fisher King.

Readers of *Quest* then have to move through a quagmire of absurd jousting and questing, most of which makes no sense whatsoever in terms of trying to find an artifact, to find the answer they are looking for. As *Quest* itself says:

> Until the Lord sends this man among them (ie: Sir Galahad) with a suddenness that will take them by surprise, the members of the Round Table will waste their time searching for the Holy Grail. (Quest 22:77)

Quite obviously, the search for a golden chalice is a worthless enterprise born of ignorance. The true esoteric Grail is a conical stone, guarded and tended by a royal princess of the Grail bloodline. And so most of the questing in *Quest* is merely tales of knightly chivalry and glory, that are translated into morality tales of how to be an upright and upstanding person and follow the chivalrous code of an honourable knight. And if one falls below the expected standards, as Sir Lancelot does with his love for Queen Gwenevere, then the knight must confess and repent his sins and turn over a new leaf in life. And while this is all a wonderful morality tale, it does not tell the reader much about what this mysterious Holy Grail might be, nor where it is located.

Many readers may give up at this juncture wondering what the story is all about, and what the point of continuing is. And perhaps that is the intention of the author of *Quest*, for only the worthy who persevere and continue with *Mort* will ever get close to the truth. This was also a necessary safety measure, because although the Catholic Inquisition could and would burn heretics to death for many sins, searching for a sacred golden cup associated with Jesus was not one of them. After all, the Catholic Church had been venerating and selling bits of the true cross and the bones of various saints for centuries, so one more holy relic was hardly something the Church could get too animated about. As long as the Church did not realise that the San Grail chalice was a Sang Real princess, the authors of the *Vulgate Cycle* were fairly safe from persecution.

However, the persistent and initiated reader will eventually discover that the Holy Grail is a sacred stone, cared for and protected by an Arthurian princess and her knights. But only the truly worthy will then put two and two together, and realise that the Knight of the Grail-stone is the Peter, the Rock or Stone. And even if they did so, only those blessed of logic, reason and independent mind would understand that the gospel St Peter had also been a Guardian of the Grail-stone.

But none of this inner enlightenment tells us very much about where and when these events took place. As we saw in Chapter VI, *Parzival* claimed that in the mid 1st century the Grail-stone resided at Corbenic, which was identified as being Masada on the shores of the Dead Sea. Conversely, the previous books in this series demonstrated that by the 2nd century this same sacred stone had been relocated to Sogmatar near Edessa, while in the 3rd century it may have been taken to Fortress Dewa in Britain. But what about the late 1st century, after the Jewish Revolt, where was the princess and her sacred Grail-stone located at that time? *Merlin Grail* says that the Grail-stone was taken to the west, presumably to Britain, but here in *Quest* it says that the Grail was to be found in Sarras. *Quest* says of Perceval's mortally wounded sister and the Grail:

> (Perceval's sister said) Be assured that when you come to the city of Sarras, where you will go in search of the Holy Grail, you will find that I am already there, at the foot of the tower. (Quest 75:241)

> Now (Josephus) took the Grail to Galahad ... (the Grail) is the chalice from which Jesus ate the lamb with his disciples ... But you have not seen it as fully as you will. Do you know where this event will take place? In the city of Sarras, in the spiritual place. Quest 82:270) (Author's brackets)

If the Holy Grail-stone had been kept secure in the 'impregnable' fortress of Masada, during the Jewish Revolt, it was certainly not there in the late 1st century. Masada had been besieged by the Romans in AD 73, and through their usual tireless energy and unbeatable organisation the Romans had constructed a ramp to raise siege engines up to the precipitous walls of this great fortress. Probably to the surprise of everyone, the impregnable fortress of Masada fell to the Romans that same year, and so the Grail would have needed moving somewhere safer. And this would not have been an easy task, because the Romans had built a wall all the way around Masada to prevent the rebels from leaving. But if it had been possible to sneak through the Roman lines, perhaps via a tunnel somewhere, it would make sense to take the Grail-stone to Sarras-Palmyra as this city was still in rebel hands.

Perceval's sister died shortly after the quotes just given, so the reason that she would be found at the foot of a tower in Sarras is because the dead of Sarras-Palmyra were buried in great funerary towers, as can be seen in fig 12.4. So the text is quite correct again, if we understand its meaning, for the recently deceased daughter of a noble from Palmyra would indeed have been found in the antechamber of a tall funerary tower. Incidentally, the text then says that both Perceval and Galahad (Perceval-Galahad) were buried in the same tower, so perhaps one of the burial busts from these towers mentions a Galli priest called Perceval the Galahad.

Perceval and Lancelot

In amongst the many fanciful questing stories in *Quest* there are some interesting details that are worth mentioning. One of these is the story that mentions Perceval and Galahad together, and so they are now two separate knights rather than the same person. However, these 'two' knights may not be quite so separate as they at first appear. Firstly, they seem to be half-brothers. Secondly, Perceval always rides with Lancelot, and yet Lancelot is the father of Galahad. Thirdly, these 'brother' knights, Perceval and Galahad, are destined to share the same tomb. Fourthly, Perceval is called

Fig 12.4 One of the great funerary towers at Palmyra (Sarras). The sister of Perceval, who had just died, said she would be found in a tower like this one.

Fig 12.5 Two of the funerary busts from the tower-tombs in Palmyra. These lavish tombs and their depictions of the deceased dripping with jewellery, demonstrate the great wealth of Palmyra in the 1st and 2nd centuries.

the Welshman on several occasions in *Quest*, but the original term being used here before it was mistranslated is 'Galles'. And finally, in chapter 32, Perceval takes his sword and castrates himself, rather than lose his virginity.

However, if Perceval was called Perceval the Galles, and he castrated himself just like a Galli priest, then we can be fairly certain that Perceval the Galles was actually Perceval the Galli high priest, or Perceval the Galli-had. Once again we can see that the 'two' brothers are probably the same person, and Perceval was called Perceval the Galahad. And the reason for separating the two names and personalities here, is because we now have Lancelot in the genealogy, who did not exist in many of the previous manuscripts. It was probably easier to separate the fathers of Perceval-Galahad into Lancelot and Pellehan-Alain, than try to explain exactly who Lancelot really was. The idealised genealogy in 13.6 attempts to place Sir Lancelot back within the heart of this family, with a singular Perceval-Galahad as his son.

Quest also dwells on the illicit affair between Lancelot and Queen Gwenevere, the wife of King Arthur. In fact this becomes a central topic of the manuscript, as Lancelot appears to confess this affair to every priest or hermit he meets on his questing travels (Quest 17:66). But the author of *Quest* has a problem with this marital infidelity, and has had to separate it into two separate events and two separate affairs. Firstly it is said that Lancelot had slept with the 'daughter of the Rich Fisher King' or the 'daughter of King Pelles', and the fruit of that illicit union was Sir Galahad (Quest 6:20; 42:138). This quite incidentally confirms that King Pelles and the Fisher King were the same person, according to *Quest's* version of the Arthurian genealogy. But the story then goes on to say that Lancelot's great love was actually Queen Gwenevere (Quest 17:66). But since Sir Galahad-Perceval became the Perfect Knight and the Good Knight - the only knight of the Round Table who could sit in the Perilous Seat - then surely the mother of such a fine knight would have to be the most senior daughter of King Pelles. Queen Gwenevere is often said to have been the most famous daughter of King Pelles, and so the daughter who was the mother of Galahad-Perceval must have surely been Gwenevere herself.

In which case, the problems that these authors were struggling with here, were twofold. Firstly, if Lancelot was the father of Perceval-Galahad, who is normally said to be the son of King Pellehan-Alain, then Gwenevere was having an affair with King Pellehan-Alain's side of this family. And so this affair may have been the main reason for the family feud that tore this family apart, and dispossessed Perceval from his lands and turned them into a wasteland.

The second problem is that the two daughters of King Pelles that Lancelot was having affairs with, are likely to have been the two wives of King Arthur. And so the reason for covering this up, is to prevent readers from knowing that King Arthur had married two of his sisters. In the gospel accounts these two sisters were Mary and Martha of Bethany, the two sister-wives of King Jesus-Izas. And while a sibling marriage was certainly worthy of concealing, it is also setting quite a trend, because King Agrippa II, Simon Magus, King Monobazus and possibly King Izas-Jesus himself, all married their sisters. And Saul-Josephus also asked to marry his sister in 1Cor 9:5. (See Chapter I in *Mary Magdalene, Princess of Orange*.) And now it would appear that King Arthur did likewise.

But the deliberate obfuscation of this incestuous marriage is slightly odd. Why would the author of a purely fictional story want to cover up this sibling union? Why include it in the first place, if it cannot be mentioned? The author's reluctance to deal with this situation honestly, strongly indicates that *Quest* was based upon a real story. And since the author could not change the historical events that had already transpired, all he could do its side-step the issue and cover it up, by not mentioning who the unnamed 'daughter of King Pelles' really was.

Numeric cypher

We then come across another of those chronological cyphers, just like the one that we saw in *History of the Grail* in Chapter VII. *Quest* says of the era of the Round Table:

> Four hundred and fifty four years have passed since the passion of Christ, (before) this seat will find its master. (Quest 1:4)

The seat in question was the Perilous Seat on the Round Table of King Arthur. In previous manuscripts, the knight who eventually claimed that seat was said to be Perceval, but here in *Quest* it is taken by Sir Galahad, the Perfect Knight and Good Knight. So the author of *Quest* has attempted to place a 454 year interlude between the crucifixion and the events in this story, and this would place these events in the 480s according to the orthodox biblical chronology or the 520s according to the revised chronology. However, as we saw back in Chapters I & II, it would be impossible to have a wealthy King Arthur threatening Rome in this late era. The Western Roman Empire fell in 480, and so there was no Rome for King Arthur to have a dispute with, let alone invade.

But this results in a further chronological muddle. This story is now supposedly set in the 6th century, and recalling historical events that happened in the 1st century, more than 400 years before this time. However, in chapter 80 of *Quest* King Evalach of Sarras dies in the arms of Sir Galahad; while in chapter 85 Sir Galahad meets Josephus, the son of Joseph of Arimathaea. But both King Evalach and Josephus (the son) are 1st century characters, so how can a 5th or 6th century Perceval-Galahad possibly meet them?

Unlike *History* and *High History*, which were overtly and unashamedly 1st century stories, the account narrated in *Quest* is deeply contradictory from beginning to end. Even a cursory reading will demonstrate a deliberate dislocation within the chronology, which was presumably crafted to separate the era of King Arthur from the 1st century era of the gospel stories. And so this addition of a very precise 454 years to the chronology is not only peculiar, it is very similar to the addition of the very precise 717 years that we saw in *History of the Grail*.

But it was demonstrated in Chapter VII that this 717 years was actually a cypher created from the Aramaic numerical system, which actually referred to the 9th year. And so by using the very same rules for the Aramaic numbering system, perhaps we can find yet another code within this 454 year interpolation into the chronology. And if we apply the same methodology, we find that 454 equates to the following consonants:

400 = ת
50 = נ
4 = ד

The resulting word we can derive from the number 454 is therefore *tanad* תנד which is fairly unhelpful and meaningless. But again the Aramaic numbering system is not as flexible as the author would like, and the word that he was looking for was actually *tanan* תנן, which means the 2nd. But the author could not write *tanan* because this is not a valid number within the Aramaic numbering system, and so he has taken the *nun* ן at the end of *tanan* and replaced it with the very similar looking *daled* ד. Now the author did have a valid number, and that number is 454, which was supposed to represent the 2nd. So the sentence quoted earlier was supposed to be read as:

> In the second year after the passion of Christ, this seat will find its master. (Quest 1:4)

Now that makes much more sense. Under the revised gospel chronology, the crucifixion was in AD 70 and so this places Galahad's acceptance of the Perilous Seat at the Round Table of King Arthur in AD 72. So this is now

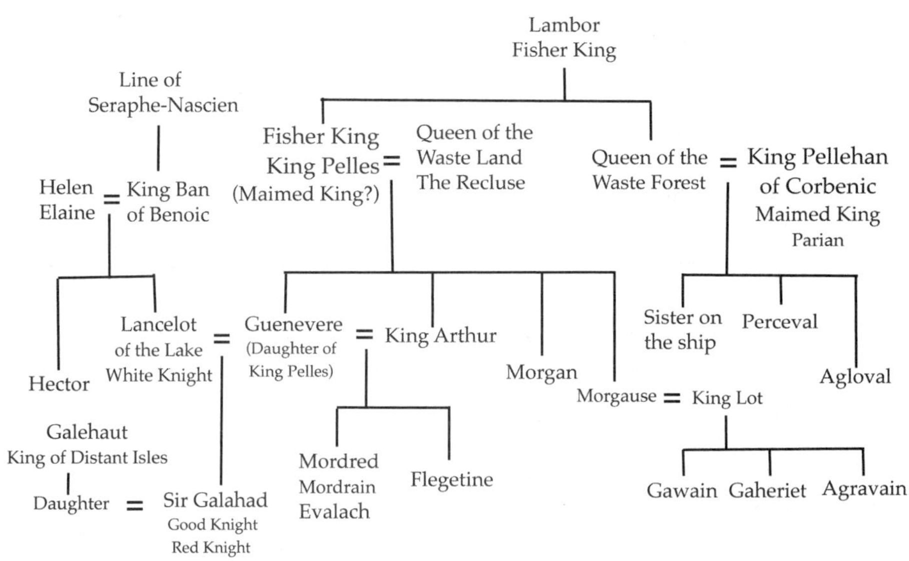

Fig 12.6
The genealogy of the Grail family as given in 'Quest for the Holy Grail'. Note that this genealogy takes Perceval away from being a son of King Pellehan-Alain. The genealogies in Chapter XIII restore Perceval to the correct side, by placing Lancelot on King Pellehan's side of the family.

a 1st century story, rather than a 5th or 6th century story; and so there is no problem with Sir Galahad going to the city of Sarras and meeting King Evalach and Joseph(us) of Arimathaea, because they now live in the same era. King Evalach was king of Sarras in AD 72 when Joseph(us) visited the city, and Sir Perceval-Galahad took up his knightly position in the Perilous Seat in that very same year.

And the assertion that King Evalach died in the arms of Sir (Perceval) Galahad would also make chronological sense, because according to this new genealogy Evalach was Galahad's cousin or great cousin. And Sir (Perceval) Galahad became the king of Sarras-Palmyra shortly after King Evalach. And so the two chronological quizzes in *History* and *Quest* match each other very well. Sir Perceval-Galahad travelled to Sarras in the 2nd year (454 years) after the crucifixion, or AD 72. While this story was narrated to or written by Saul-Josephus, the original author of *History,* in the 9th year (717 years) after the crucifixion, or AD 79.

This also clarifies and confirms the conflation of the 'two' Galahads. Both Joseph(us) of Arimathaea and Lancelot had a son called Galahad, but they cannot be the same person, according to the classical interpretation of *Quest,* because the later Galahad lived 454 years after the crucifixion. However, now that the chronology has been readjusted to just 2 years after the crucifixion, and Sir Galahad was therefore a 1st century character who travelled to the city of Sarras to see King Evalach and Joseph(us) of Arimathaea, these two Galahads can easily be the same person.

This is why there was a confusion between Sarras and Hoselice, as we saw in Chapter IX. Galahad (the son of Arimathaea) was being made the king of Hoselice, according to *History,* while Sir Galahad (the son of Lancelot) was being made the king of Sarras, according to *Quest*. But Sarras and Hoselice are the same name for the same 'City of the Eunuchs', with Hoselice merely having a prefixed definite article: 'the'. So there was only ever one Perceval-Galahad and he became the king and high priest of Sarras-Hoselice in the AD 70s. And this is further confirmed by the author of *Quest* when he has Josephus (the son of Arimathaea who is the brother of Galahad), say to Sir Galahad at his death:

> Do you know why (god) has sent me? Because you are like me in two ways: you witnessed the mysteries of the Holy Grail, as I did, and you are a virgin, as I am. It is therefore fitting that we should be together. (Quest 85: 278)

The sentence almost reads as if the author is imploring us to understand that the famous Sir Galahad was Galahad, the brother of Josephus and son of Arimathaea. They are so alike because they are brothers, and so in the following genealogy they are shown as half-brothers. And so in the tomb scene in chapter 80 of *Quest*, Sir Galahad was looking at his own tomb, which lies in Sarras. And yes, these tombs were ordered and made well in advance, because it took so long to make them and life-expectancies in this era were so uncertain, and so Sir Galahad could easily inspect the construction progress of his own tomb. And if Sarras is Palmyra, as appears very likely, then the tomb of Sir Galahad will be found in the oasis city of Palmyra in the Syrian desert. As long as the modern Muslim Neanderthals in Syria have not destroyed Palmyra, of course. *

We now have two family trees that contain a common Sir Galahad, and so these two families are demanding an amalgamation. This requires making Josephus (the son of Arimathaea) into a brother of Sir Galahad, and in turn this demands that Lancelot and Joseph(us) of Arimathaea become the same person. And while it may seem absurd to equate a cerebral theologian and author like Saul-Josephus with a brave knight in shining armour like Sir Lancelot, do remember that Saul-Josephus had been the Jewish army

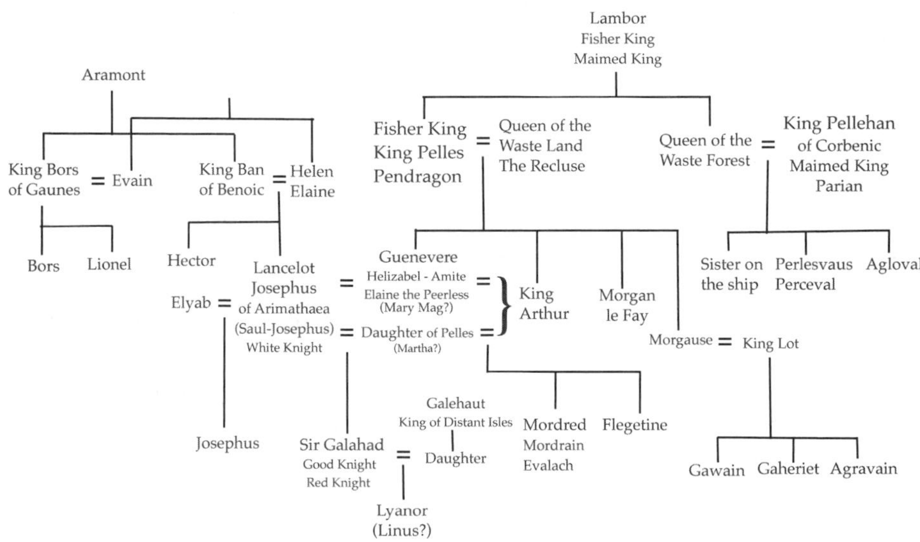

Fig 12.7 A revised genealogy from Quest, demonstrating the difference if Josephus and Sir Galahad were brothers (they are shown as half-brothers here). This conflation does mean that Lancelot and Joseph of Arimathaea have to be the same person. But since Lancelot is never mentioned in the early manuscripts, that is entirely possible.

Note that Perceval is still on a separate family line in this genealogy. It is difficult to link Perceval and Galahad in this genealogy, if the father of Galahad is Josephus-Lancelot, but fig 13.6 will attempt to do this.

commander in control of Galilee, who fought many battles in the region before surrendering to Legatus Vespasian. And within the Roman army Saul-Josephus again became an army commander and propaganda minister. So for all the many faults and fractures in Saul-Josephus' character, he had already proved himself to be a brave and valiant (but highly duplicitous and manipulative) knight in shining armour.

And since this is the Roman 1st century, it is likely that Saul-Josephus did indeed wear a suit of shining armour of the Roman variety, just as all the Judaean and Palmyran commanders did. Interestingly, the main base of operations for Saul-Josephus during his time as an army commander was Tiberias on the shores of the Sea of Galilee. Was this why Lancelot was called 'Lancelot of the Lake'? Was the lake in question the Sea of Galilee, or was it something more celestial and Elysian? And did Joseph(us) (Lancelot) sire a son with the wife of King Jesus-Izas (King Arthur), and cause an irrevocable split within this royal family? There is no hard evidence for this speculation, that Lancelot was Saul-Josephus, but it is an interesting suggestion that resolves many issues within this genealogy (and creates many others besides).

The Round Tables

Another interesting story in *Quest*, is the account of the three sacred tables. It is Perceval's aunt, who we can safely assume is the wife of King Pelles, who narrates this story.

The first round table was the table of the Last Supper, where Jesus-Izas ate with his disciples 'on several occasions' according to *Quest* (Quest 21:74). The second round table was the table of the Holy Grail, which was constructed by Joseph(us) of Arimathaea. While the third round table was

* Apologists in the Western media will claim that Islam is incidental to the destruction of history by ISIS and the Taliban, rather than being causal. However, these iconoclastic Neanderthals are citing Islamic scripture as the reason for this destruction, and their reasoning is not being challenged or refuted by mainstream Islam. And of course Islamic scholars cannot challenge it, because the Neanderthals are correct and are following the true creed of Islam to the letter. The verses often quoted are Koran 5:90, 17:81, 21:53-55, 37:22-23, and 37:85, and also Bukhari 2.671, 3.658, 5.583-4, 6.244, and 6.442 from the Hadith. The Hadith quotes narrate the history of Muhummad destroying the 360 idols in the Ka'ba, when Mecca was captured in 631. And since Muhummad is the perfect man, perfect guide, perfect example, and perfect paedophile, then all good Muslims are compelled to follow his perfect example.

the table of King Arthur-Jesus. And we know that this was supposed to be a succession of identical tables with the same symbology because *Quest* says:

> You know that since the time of Jesus, the world has seen three famous tables. The first was the table where Jesus ate on several occasions with the disciples. This table sustained the body and soul ... After this another table was made that resembled the first and preserved its memory. It was a table of the Holy Grail, which was responsible for the great miracles that took place at the time of Joseph of Arimathaea ... After the Table of the Holy Grail there came the Round Table, established according to Merlin's advice and laden with symbolic meaning. Quest 21:74-76.) (Author's brackets.)

The description of how the table of the Last Supper 'sustained the body and soul' is actually a description of the procession of the Holy Grail, and so we know from this description that the Holy Grail was present at the Last Supper of Jesus and his disciples. The second table was a copy of this table that 'preserved it memory', and so one presumes that it was identical in all respects - including its design, carpentry and any symbolic artwork on its surface. The third table was the Arthurian Round Table, and if the 'memory' of the Last Supper table was so important that it needed preserving then it is likely that the third table also preserved this tradition and was made in exactly the same style and fashion. Thus the Last Supper table of Jesus and his twelve disciples must have been a round table.

Merlin Grail says much the same thing, when it asserts that it was actually Jesus who ordered these three tables to be made, during the Last Supper meeting at Simon's house in Bethany:

> (Jesus said) 'I took the Last Supper at the house of Simon ... As I said at that table, several tables will be established in my service, to make a sacrament to my name, which will be a reminder of the cross.'
>
> 'As I sat at the Table of the Last Supper at Simon's house,' said (Jesus) ... 'make another in its name; and when you (Joseph) have made it summon your brother Bron ... and bid him to go fishing and bring you the first fish he catches.'
>
> (Merlin said to Uther ben Dragown) At the second table they called the vessel that bestowed this grace the Grail. If you trust my advice, you will establish a third table in the name of the trinity, which these three tables will signify.
>
> Merlin said to Arthur: "Your Father Uther was a most worthy man, and in his time the Round Table was established, which was made to symbolise the table at which our lord sat on the Thursday, when he said that Judas would betray him. It was made too, as a reference to the table that Joseph of Arimathaea, which was established for the Grail." (Merlin Grail p22, 35, 92, 112.) (Author's brackets.)

Again we have an account of the tradition of three tables, and here it is clear that they are all based upon the same design and served the same purpose. And the cross here is not the instrument of Roman torture, but the cross of the zodiac: the cross that divides up the four segments of the zodiac and therefore the four annual seasons. It is also interesting that *Merlin Grail* says that the third table was not actually King Arthur's table but rather the table of his father, Uther ben Dragown. The succession of these semi-sacred tables is therefore as follows:

Round Table - 1	Jesus-Izas and his twelve disciples.
Round Table - 2	Joseph(us) and his twenty-four disciple-knights.
Round Table - 3a	Uther ben Dragown and his twelve knights
Round Table - 3b	King Arthur and his twelve knights.
Round Table - 4a	King Edward I and his twenty-four courtiers.
Round Table - 4b	King Henry VIII and his twenty-four courtiers.

Interestingly, *Merlin Grail* suggests that the second table was made in Sarras-Palmyra, rather than in Britain (p113). And since there is (was) a large zodiac on the ceiling of the Temple of Bel in Palmyra, the presence of a zodiac table there would make sense.

Quest says that the Perilous Seat at the second table was reserved for Josephus, the son of Joseph(us) of Arimathaea. This was the seat that had originally been occupied either by King Jesus-Izas or by Judas Iscariot, depending upon the manuscript. But the Perilous Seat on the third table was reserved for either Perceval or Galahad (Perceval-Galahad). And since Joseph(us) of Arimathaea had a son called Galahad, as we have seen, this again indicates that Sir Perceval-Galahad and Josephus (the son) were brothers, and it also indicates that the table of King Jesus and the table of King Arthur were one and the same. Because of this shift in the chronology, the revised order for the construction of these Round Tables would therefore be:

Round Table - 1	Jesus-Arthur and his twelve disciple-knights.
Round Table - 2	Joseph(us) and his twenty-four disciple-knights.
Round Table - 4a	King Edward I and his twenty-four courtiers.
Round Table - 4b	King Henry VIII and his twenty-four courtiers.

Winchester

There was one other Round Table in this great tradition, and that is the 'fourth table' of Winchester. This great Round Table is said to have been made for King Edward I and dates from the late 13th century. The artwork divides the table into twenty four segments instead of twelve, just as Joseph(us) (of Arimathaea's) second table was similarly divided into twenty four segments. The present artwork is 16th century Tudor, but now that techniques are available that can see under the surface layers of a painting, it would be interesting to see what underlies this Tudor artwork. Could the original layout of the Winchester table have been of a zodiac, just like the layout we see at Hamat Teverya? Is the red Tudor rose at the center of this table actually a Sun-symbol, surrounded by places for each knightly constellation of the zodiac? The *Vulgate Cycle* was being composed at about the same time the Winchester table was being assembled, so it would be interesting to see if the original artwork contained any other symbolic connections with Arthurian history.

Fig 12.8 The 13th century Round Table of Winchester is a copy of the Arthurian original, and thought to have been constructed during the reign of Edward I. The artwork is Tudor.

If the twelve or twenty-four segment layout on all of these Round Tables was based upon the symbology of the zodiac, then the twelve disciple-knights seated around the table would all be associated with one of the astrological constellations. And presumably a constellation would be chosen that met the character or role of that particular knight, so an enthusiastic zealot might be given Aries, for instance. So the original table of the Last Supper may well have depicted the twelve constellations, exactly like the Hamat Teverya zodiac. It is even possible that the biblical disciples sometimes sat around the Hamat zodiac itself, if it was permitted to use this room for meetings and dining. The traditions from Rome and the description from the gospels indicate that the disciples would have lounged on couches and cushions to eat, rather than sitting at a table, and so the twelve disciples could have placed their couches around the zodiac and had their meal right there on the floor of this synagogue.

And Jesus-Izas, as the leader and Sun-god figure of the twelve disciple-knights of this Last Supper Round Table, would have sat in the center of the zodiac, just as Helios is depicted in the center of the Hamat zodiac. Jesus-Izas was the leader of the Nazarene Ebionite Church and the name for the Nazarene was taken in part from the Aramaic *mazzaroth* מזרות or even *nazzaroth* נזרות meaning 'zodiac'. And so surely the leader of the Zodiac Church would have sat in the center of the zodiac. The suggestion that the king (Arthur-Jesus) sat in the center of the Round Table drew some muffled laughter when it was first proposed in *King Jesus*, for who would design a table with a seat in the middle? However, *History* does say that:

> It was Friday, and that day Bron was sitting next to Josephus (son of Arimathaea) at the table of the Holy Grail. Between them, at the very middle of the table, there was easily enough space to put a man's chair. When Peter, a relative of Josephus, saw this empty place he said to Josephus: "my lord, why don't you call someone there?"
>
> "My good friend, this space is to stay empty. No one may sit there who is not worthier than all the others ... It serves as an important symbol, for you should understand that it symbolises the place where Jesus Christ sat at the holy table at the Last Supper. That place is empty because it awaits its master. (History 34:199) (Author's brackets.)

This was the Perilous Seat, the seat that nobody could occupy without fear of death. And the worthy master that it waited for was the young Sir Perceval-Galahad, who was a Galli high priest just like Jesus had been. Although in *Quest*, it was Josephus (son of Arimathaea) who claimed he was the master of this seat.

But note the position of this Perilous Seat, which lay at the very middle of the Round Table. It is claimed that this seat was located between Bron and Josephus, and yet still somehow at the 'middle of the table'. But the whole point of a Round Table is that there is no 'middle': there is no seat at the head of the table, and no seat in the middle either. The only seat at the middle of the table was the seat in the very center of this table - the position of the rose on the Winchester table or the position of Helios on the Hamat Teverya zodiac. It is likely that there has been a mistranslation here, by the 13th century authors.

Think about it. If Jesus-Arthur had twelve disciple-knights, then there must have been thirteen places at this table, just as it says in *Merlin Grail* (p116). So is this table going to be divided up into a decidedly awkward thirteen segments, that do not match the layout of a zodiac whatsoever? Or will it instead be divided into twelve segments, with the thirteenth at the very center? The image in fig 12.2, which comes from an illustration in the *Vulgate*, demonstrates that there was a void in the center of the table for the 13th place-setting, where the monarch (King Arthur-Izas) could have sat. And in taking this central position, the king becomes the Sun or the constellation of Ursa Major, surrounded by his twelve constellation disciple-knights. He becomes the Great Bear or the Great Arthur.

And this confederacy of disciple-knights would have known all about the design of these zodiacs, because they were all from Judaea and may well have sat at the original table-zodiac at Hamat Teverya. *History* says of this very meeting, where the history of these three tables was discussed:

> Twenty-four people were at this discussion, all from the land of Jerusalem. (History 34:200)

Although the design of these tables was therefore based upon the Judaean Last Supper original, Josephus (the son) considered himself to be greater than Jesus and so he had twenty-four disciple-knights arranged around his zodiac table instead of twelve. Another interesting comparison between the Round Table and the Hamat zodiac, is the assertion in *Quest* that the Round Table had columns between each place-setting at the table.

> In the meadow that you saw, there was a rack (for hay). We should understand the rack to be the Round Table. For just as the rack has rods separating the compartments, so the Round Table has columns separating each seat from the next. (Quest 49:156) (Author's brackets.)

It is difficult to imagine the design and purpose of these twelve columns placed around the perimeter of a table, that separated each knight. Were they free-standing columns and liable to be knocked over, or where they simply drawn onto the table? And what purpose did they serve? The possibilities and permutations are endless, and therefore inconclusive. But we may have a 1st century illustration of what these pillars looked like, which may solve this minor conundrum.

Readers may recall that the twelve segments for the twelve disciple-constellations on the Hamat zodiac, are separated by twelve serpentine decorations resembling pillars, as can be seen in fig 12.12. Are these the 'columns' on the Round Table, that looked like the compartment rods on a circular hay-rack? And while this suggested astrological symbolism for the Round Table may still seem like speculation to some, *Quest's* description of the Arthurian Round Table appears to confirm these speculations by saying:

> The name 'Round Table' signifies the round shape of the Earth and the disposition of the planets and other elements in the firmament, where one sees stars and other heavenly bodies. One can thus rightly assert that the Round Table represents the world. (Quest 21:76)

Fig 12.11 A modern circular hay-rack, showing the 'pillars' that divide up the rack. The pillars are there not simply to keep the hay in the rack, but also to stop the animals fighting each other over the food.

The firmament is the 'celestial sphere' in the heavens above, that is punctuated and dotted with the stars and planets. So the Arthurian Round Table represents the Earth and the stars; and if we depict the Earth and its surrounding planets and constellations on a piece of paper, we have just drawn a zodiac.

And when the text says that the 'Round Table represents the world', it is not meaning that it represents the Earth. Almost every time that the term 'world' in used in English translations of the gospels, the word it is translating is actually *kosmos* κοσμος. And while *kosmos* may refer to the world, it more accurately describes what the Thayer Greek dictionary calls 'the universe and the circle of the earth'. And this is how we understand the term today, the *kosmos* is the cosmos: the universe. Therefore the last sentence

Fig 12.12 The precessional zodiac at Hamat Teverya on the shores of the Sea of Galilee. The position of Jesus-Izas and Sir Perceval-Galahad is the central position, occupied here by Helios, who holds the blue-green Earth in his (gravitational) grasp. Note the pillars or columns that separate each constellation. Are these pillars the same 'columns' that Quest is describing on the Arthurian Round Table?

in this quote is better translated as:

> One can thus rightly assert that the Round Table represents the universe (and the twelve constellations around that universe).

It has sometimes been argued that the 'round shape of the Earth' mentioned here refers to the circular maps of the world that were produced in the Medieval era. The 13th century Mappa Mundi (Map of the World) in Hereford Cathedral is a good example of these circular maps, and a reproduction of this Mappa Mundi is shown in fig 14.9. However, if the Arthurian table was based upon the knowledge and wisdom of the Gnostics who created the Hamat zodiac on the shores of the Sea of Galilee, it is highly unlikely that they would have been creating something as rudimentary as a Mappa Mundi. And the evidence for this assertion lies on the Hamat zodiac, for Helios is holding the Earth in his (gravitational) grasp, and the Earth is displayed here as a blue and green sphere.

Any organisation or sect that knew the Earth was a blue-green sphere that circled around the Sun (Helios), would not have been creating a Mappa Mundi. And according to *Quest*, that knowledge was held by the kings and princes of Sarras (Palmyra):

> Seraphe-Nascien ... knew the paths of the stars and planets and the configuration of the firmament as well or even better than the philosophers did. Because he was so learned in science he appeared to be surrounded by stars ... He was truly a source of science and knowledge, from which one could derive all the principles and moving force of the divinity. (Quest 41:135)

Considering the fact that the *Vulgate Cycle* was written in an overtly Christian era, it is odd that it should claim that the foundations and fundamentals of science and astronomy were held in Sarras, rather than Jerusalem. And the description of Seraphe-Nascien being 'surrounded by stars' might suggest that he was an heir to the central position on the Round Table-zodiac, where he would indeed have been surrounded by the stars of the constellations. Perhaps Seraphe-Nascien also sat in the Perilous Seat, just like Jesus, Joseph(us), and Sir Perceval Galahad.

Note also that Wolfram von Eschenbach claimed that the primary physicus or astronomer who preserved these secrets for future generations was Flegetanis of Toledo (Edessa), who has already been identified as Princess Flegetine of Sarras (Palmyra). But now we see that another famous physicus-astronomer of the Nazarene Ebionites was Prince Seraphe-Nascien of Sarras. However, since Prince Seraphe-Nascien was married to Princess Flegetine, and she was the daughter of King Jesus-Izas, this all makes sense.

Just as Mary Magdalene was supposed to have held the Gnostic knowledge of the Nazarene sect after the death of Jesus, so too would Princess Flegetine have held the scientific and astronomical knowledge of the Nazarene after the death of Seraphe-Nascien. And history records that there was a famous female physicus in this era who was involved in the Jewish Revolt, because Saul-Josephus says:

> Now there was one Joseph, the son of a female physician, who excited a great many young men to join with them. He persuaded (the people of Gamala) to revolt from the king and take up arms. (Life 185)

This was in the 60s, just prior to the Jewish Revolt, and the son of a female physician was leading the revolution. And the term being used for physician is *magus*, the same as the three Magi, which confirms that these 'physicians' studied the motions of the stars more than they did medicine. And as we have seen, the biblical Magi are highly likely to have been linked with the ex-Parthian royal family living in Edessa. And while the era of this particular quote does not suit Princess Flegetine so well, it would suit the era of Mary the Virgin or Mary Magdalene very nicely. And one of the elder Mary's sons was indeed called Joset, the short form of Joseph.

This tradition and name and for these Parthio-Edessan *magii*-physicians may well have lived on into 15th century Florence, and the rise of the Renaissance House of Medici. In his book *The Master Game* Robert Bauval observes that *medici* means 'physician' and so the Medici family were probably medical doctors. But Bauval is singularly ill equipped to divine the esoteric truth. He professes arcane knowledge but invariably leads his readers completely astray, just as he did with his demonstrably false Orion star-pointing theory.* Actually, it is much more likely that the name for the Medici was derived from the Medes, from the Parthians and therefore from the family of Queen Thea Muse Ourania of Parthia and Edessa. Renaud de Beaune, the 16th century archbishop of Bourges in the Loire Valley, gave a funerary oration to Catherine of France saying:

> In the time of the great king of Gaul, <u>Brennius</u>, he led his army all over Italy,

* Please see *K2, Quest of the Gods*, Chapter VI. The correlation with Orion is correct, but the star pointing theory is most certainly not. The angles of elevation of the small shafts in the Great Pyramid are based upon Pi. These shaft angles cannot be based on a fixed mathematical constant, Pi, and still have the freedom to point at particular stars in any particular era. The whole star pointing theory is a crock of Bauval's devising.

> Greece and the East. With him in his company were two noblemen of France, one called Felonius the other Bono ... They came into the land of Medes which is close to Lydia and Persia. And having made several conquests and achieved great victories, finally withdrew and hoped to pass through Italy to return to France. Felonius rested in a place located along the river of Arne, that he knew was quite beautiful and delectable ... and built there a city, which today is Florence. And his companion Bono built the city of Bononia, called Bologne (Bologna) ... Because the conquests and victories of Felonius had been in the country of the Medes, he was called Medicus and this surname remains in the family. [1] (Author's brackets.)

Being a funerary oration this story may well be apocryphal in some respects, but it actually makes a great deal of sense. Firstly we find ourselves way back in Geoffrey of Monmouth's story of Brennius and Belinus (Brennius and Felinus), and their invasion of Rome. Note the 'b' to 'f' transliteration, the same as with Boucaire and Foucaire. And Bono-Boni is the original name for Nicodemus. And so much of this quote has been taken from what became Arthurian history. And then we have the story of the Medici family being named after the lands of the Medes - the lands of Persia-Parthia.

It is highly unlikely in the extreme that the 4th century BC King Brennius of Gaul ever went to Parthia. But what this story is actually doing, by invoking the history of Brennius and Belinus, is deliberately linking Arthurian history with Parthia (the Medes) once more. And the famous family who came out of Parthia in the 1st century AD and settled in Edessa would not only have been called 'Medes', because they were Babylonian Jews from Media or Parthia, they would also have been called physicus or physicians. The Magi physicians were the Parthio-Medes priests, astrologers and king-makers, and they came to see the birth of King Jesus-Izas. And so there was a royal family who would have combined the name Medes and the profession of Magi physicus 'doctors', and that was the Edessan royal family.

And any descendents of this illustrious Medes-Magi royal family from Edessa would have been: greatly interested in religious esoterica; supremely eclectic in their literature; closely involved in banking; deeply heretical in their beliefs; and eager to undermine the Catholic Church in any way that they possibly could - especially by placing heretical symbolism within the heart of Catholic Rome. And they would have required the finest craftsmen to create heretical artworks of the caliber of the 1st century Hamat Teverya zodiac: gifted artisans like the Medici's Michelangelo and Leonardo da Vinci. In fact, the proposed descendents of the royal House of Edessa would have been indistinguishable from the 15th century House of Medici, who were so closely linked to the Renaissance and Reformation movements. So was the Medici family name derived from the Babylonian Medes and Magi of Edessa? It is a logical possibility that is certainly worthy of further research.

Turning table

As the guardians of much archaic arcane knowledge, these Gnostic Magi royal families of the East would not have been creating something as rudimentary as a Mappa Mundi. What they would have been creating is a Round Table depicting a central Sun-figure or Ursa Major figure, surrounded by the twelve astrological constellations - a king 'surrounded by stars', just as Seraphe-Nascien was described. And separating these twelve knightly constellations into their respective houses would have been twelve 'pillars', just as we see on the Hamat zodiac. Is this evidence that the author of *Quest* knew of the Hamat zodiac? *Quest* was written during the Crusader era, when Templar Knights would have been returning from the Holy Lands. So did these knights bring home first-hand descriptions of this very zodiac, or did

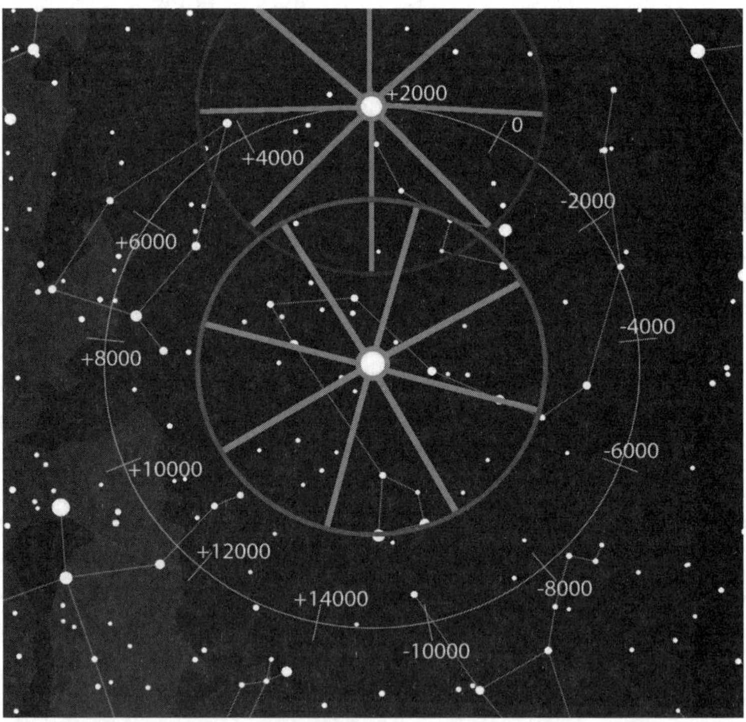

Fig 12.13 The two great wheels of King Arthur's cosmic cart, in the heavens above. The blue wheel is attached to the celestial axle or pole, and rotates daily. The red wheel is attached to the ecliptic axle or pole, and the blue wheel circulates anti-clockwise around the red wheel once every 25,680 years. The numbers are years AD and BC.

traditions and manuscripts still exist that described King Jesus-Izas' famous Last Supper Round Table?

Furthermore, as we saw in previous chapters the Hamat zodiac is not a static feature merely for decoration, it was a graphic representation of the two great wheels of the Cosmos, the two wheels that formed what became known as King Arthur's Cosmic Cart. Those two great wheels in the heavens above revolve around the celestial pole and the ecliptic pole, and they drive the days, seasons, years, and millennia. And they not only count off the seasons and years, they also measure the Great Months and the Great Years, which are 2,140 and 25,680 years long respectively. In which case, a truly representative Round Table, a table that symbolised the inner working of Arthur's Cosmic Cart, would surely be made to rotate - so that the changing of the constellations could be demonstrated and understood by the twelve knightly-disciples sitting or lounging at this table. And this may well be what the Arthurian Round Table actually did, for Beroul says in *Tristan et Iseut*:

> *A un pastor qui chalemele*
> *A demandé ou est le rois.*
> *Sire, fait il, 'Il sit au dois,*
> *Ja verroiz la Table Reonde,*
> *Qui tournoie come le monde,*
> *Sa mesnie sit anviron.'*
>
> And a priest who ......
> Asked where is the king.
> Sire, it is made, 'He must sit,
> Already we see the Round Table,
> Which turns like the world,
> And his followers sit around.'

It is not certain where Beroul got this idea of a table that turned with the world from, as none of the other manuscripts mention it. But it is hardly something that an author would devise *de novo,* because who would imagine that a table turned, had they not been told about this possibility? So it is likely that the Round Table did indeed turn, as that was the whole point of creating a table designed to mimic a precessionary zodiac, and a tradition of this function was transmitted along with the source manuscript for these Norman Arthurian stories. And we know that there was a much larger and more ambitious 'table' that turned like the world or heavens in this very era, because we have similar descriptions of Emperor Nero's ingenious rotating cosmos.

We do not know too much about the level of astronomical-astrological knowledge within Rome: whether they venerated the millennial precessional zodiac or whether they only knew of the annual zodiac. The cult of Roman Mithras, for instance, was nearly two thousand years out of date according to the precessional zodiac, because it was symbolic of the ending of the previous Great Month of Taurus. Nevertheless, the Romans did look to the heavens above and venerated the movements of the cosmos, and we know this because of Nero's rotating cosmic dining room. Suetonius says of Nero's great new palace:

> Its vestibule was large enough to contain a colossal statue of the emperor a hundred and twenty feet high, and it was so extensive that it had a triple colonnade a mile long. There was a pond too, like a sea, surrounded with buildings to represent cities ... The main banquet hall was circular and constantly revolved day and night, like the heavens. (Suetonius Life of Nero, 31.1-2)

This being the megalomaniacal Nero, he had not designed something as trivial as a mere rotating table, he had commissioned a *coenatio rotunda*, an entire rotating dining room. Here, the assembled guests could sit at their leisure, and watch the starry firmament rotate above their heads, which

Fig 12.14 The central pillar, upon which Nero's cosmic rotating dining room is thought to have rested. The top of the pillar has holes in which spherical bearings may have sat.

was no doubt accurately painted on the ceiling or perhaps depicted with hundreds of small lamps. This was not Arthur's Round Zodiac Table, this was Nero's Rotating Zodiac Room.

And in Syrio-Judaea the tradition of the round zodiac 'table' was continued well into the Christian era, and we know this because of the wonderful mosaic in the Lady Mary monastery at Beit Shean, just south of the Sea of Galilee. There, on the floor of the central cloister in this monastery, there is what can only be described as a zodiac. But this is not overtly a zodiac, because the individual constellations have been replaced by the twelve months of the year. And the modern names of the months are still recognisable on this very early circular calendar, which names Aprilios, Maios, Oktobrios, Noembros etc.

But these months of the year are merely proxies or substitutes for the constellations. There are twelve months just as there are twelve constellations of the zodiac, and they all rotate in concert with one another during the year. But a circular calendar of months does not need any central motif, for there is no 'center' to an annual calendar. And yet on the Lady Mary calendar there

Fig 12.15 The calendrical zodiac at Beit Shean. Here, the zodiac is now fully Christianised, with the Sun and Moon (Jesus and Mary) in the center, surrounded by twelve male disciples (months of the year or constellations of the zodiac). But the central couple are not simply Jesus and Mary, they are also Arthur and Gwenevere.

is a central image of Helios and Selene, the Sun and Moon. So what we have at Beit Shean is a covert zodiac, designed to suit Christian sensitivities and avoid the hot pokers of any forerunner of the Catholic Inquisition. So this is a Christian-friendly zodiac, in which the twelve signs of the zodiac have not simply become months of the year they have also become twelve men or disciples. *

Then there is the center of the Beit Shean zodiac, which depicts a man and woman as Helios and Selene, the Sun and Moon, in syzygy (in conjunction). But who would be the central two figures on a Christianized calendar-zodiac, surrounded by twelve disciples? This just has to be an image of Jesus-Izas and Mary Magdalene. This calendrical zodiac is the central image on the floor of the floor of a Christian monastery, a vast mosaic that reaches across the entire width of the central cloister. The complete mosaic depicts numerous birds, fruits, and exotic animals and measures some 15 x 8 meters, while the central calendrical zodiac measures about 5 meters in diameter. However, if we entered a monastery and saw a large depiction of a king and queen wearing radiant halo-crowns, surrounded by twelve men, who could this possibly represent? It could only be an image of Jesus and Mary surrounded by the twelve disciples. It can be nothing else.

The Catholic Church may have preferred this to be an image of Jesus and Mary the Virgin, perhaps with a little less solar and lunar symbology than we see here, but nevertheless this imagery would be acceptable to many of the Christian sects that allow the breaking of the second of the Ten Commandments. However, if we look a little closer, what we actually see on this zodiac is Helios and Selene in syzygy - in divine conjunction - which depicts the age-old sexual union of the planetary gods. And so this could not have been seen as an image of Jesus and Mary his mother, it was most definitely a portrait of Jesus and his syzygy partner, Mary Magdalene. And so this mosaic actually depicts Jesus and Mary in *flagrante delicto* on the floor of a monastery cloister, which is a boldly heretical depiction to say the least.

* Some of the damage on this zodiac is obviously deliberate. The disciple-month of September has been literally defaced, but which of the twelve disciples would have been hated so much, that someone would want to hack out his face? The answer, surely, is Judas Iscariot, and so Judas must be the month of September. Similarly, the disciple-month of May has had his eyes cut out, which may be a reference to the doubting Thomas not being able to recognise Jesus after the crucifixion.

XIII

Death of Arthur

Quest for the Holy Grail - Walter Map
Book 6 of the *Vulgate Cycle* or *Lancelot Grail*
Mort Artu - Death of Arthur - Walter Map
Book 7 of the *Vulgate Cycle* or *Lancelot Grail*

If these Grail stories were closely related to Syrio-Judaea, and to the events of the Jewish Revolt in AD 66-70, then perhaps this can also explain the many references to a wasteland. This is a constant theme throughout these manuscripts, with either the wife of King Pelles or the wife of Alain li Gros (Pellehan) being called the Queen of the Wasteland. In *Quest*, the reason for the region becoming a wasteland is explained when the 'reclusive lady' speaks to Perceval:

> I am your aunt and you are my nephew. Don't let my humble surroundings confuse you. Be assured that I was formerly the Queen of the Wasteland ... I was one of the richest women in the world. However, my wealth never pleased me or suited me as much as the poverty I now experience. (Quest 20:73)

The aunt of Perceval was the wife of King Pelles, who had been called the Queen of the Wasteland but was now being called 'the recluse'. She was once very rich, and being the wife of Pelles and the Queen of Logres she probably was, because King Pelles was known as the rich Fisher King in this story. But how did this wealthy monarch become the Queen of the Wasteland? It is only when we get to chapter 66 in *Quest* that these events are explained more fully, and we find ourselves back with the same story that was narrated in *History of Kings* about the battle between the Arthurian knights and Varlan, the governor of Syria (ie: Publius Quintilius Varus). In this version of the story the Arthurian king is called Lambor, who is father of King Pelles (the Wounded King in this account):

> A bloody war was raging between King Lambor the father of the man called the Wounded King, and King Varlan ... One day it happened that King Lambor and King Varlan assembled their armies ... King Varlan was losing the fight and realised his defeat and began to fear for his life ... He found the sword (the sword of the strange straps) and withdrew it from the scabbard ... When King Varlan saw King Lambor he raised his sword and struck his helmet so hard that he split the king and his horse clean in two. This was the first blow struck by this sword in the kingdom of Logres, and it resulted in pestilence and persecution in both kingdoms ... From that time on no wheat grew, no tree gave fruit, and very few fish were found in the sea. For this reason the two kingdoms were known as the Waste Land. (Quest 66:204; History 40:293) (Author's brackets.)

The modern translators of *Quest* say that the Maimed or Wounded King is King Pellehan, because that is what *Parzival* and *Merlin* say, but *Quest* is not entirely clear about this. In this story the Queen of the Wasteland is the aunt of Perceval, not his mother. Similarly, the Wounded King is said to be the King of Corbenic (23:79), but in *Quest* it is King Pelles who appears to be most closely connected to Corbenic. And Corbenic has to be associated with the kingdom of the Wasteland because *coreb* חרב means 'wasteland'. This may be why we see a close association between the castles of Camelot and Corbenic, it was called Camelot before the kingdom was destroyed and Corbenic afterwards. One solution to this continual confusion between King Pelles and Pellehan-Alain, is to speculate that there was only one primary king with two wives, and so all of the next generation were half-brothers instead of cousins. This option is explored in fig 13.7.

Alternatively, we may again be seeing the two conflicting viewpoints from which these manuscripts were written, as was speculated with the obvious differences between *High History* and *Perceval*. In *High History* we saw Perceval complaining bitterly about his own mother being made the Queen of the Wasteland, because she was being attacked by King Arthur's forces. But in *Perceval* the queen does not become impoverished, while in *Quest* it is the wife of King Pelles who falls from grace, because of the actions of Varlan who is a Roman governor (ie: Publius Quintilius Varus). But of course both of these claims are correct, because the family of Perceval and Joseph(us) had been dispossessed from their lands before the Jewish Revolt, while the family of King Pelles-Arthur-Jesus were dispossessed after the Jewish Revolt. So these authors were free to take their pick from these two families and their respective wastelands, depending upon their allegiances and point of view.

The story of this battle in *Quest* and *Lancelot* is essentially the same as in *History of Kings*, but these new versions contain additional details that give us a better understanding of this conflict. As we saw in Chapter II, Saul-Josephus Flavius has used Governor Quintilius Varus (or Varus) as a pseudonym for Governor Caius Cestius Gallus, and this is why *Quest, Lancelot* and *Jewish War* all use a name that is very similar to 'Varus'. However, Geoffrey of Monmouth knew a great deal more about this literary deceit and so he has used the conflated pseudonym Caius Quintilanus, which is a deliberate combination of **Caius** Cestius Gallus and **Quintilius** Varus. So the various names of the governor-antagonist in this battle was:

Governor of Syria 64-67 AD	**Caius** Cestius Gallus
Governor of Syria 7-4 BC	<u>Quintilius</u> Varus
Geoffrey Monmouth	**Caius** <u>Quintilanus</u>
Saul-Josephus	Varus
Quest for Holy Grail	Varlan
Lancelot	Vadalon

So *Quest* is blaming Varlan (Cestius Gallus) for turning Syria and Judaea into a wasteland. But how can this be? Surely the battle between the rebel forces of King Izas-Jesus and Varlan (Cestius Gallus) was a great victory for the rebels, not a defeat. If anything, it was Legatus Vespasian who subsequently destroyed Judaea, not Varlan (Cestius Gallus). Well yes, but it was actually the actions of Cestius Gallus that started the Jewish Revolt in the first place. Saul-Josephus does not really mention this, and places the blame squarely upon the Nazarene Jewish rebels, but the many versions of this story in Arthurian history all agree that the rebels were provoked. And if this is true, then Arthurian history is a real historical resource that can add to our understanding of these events, because much of Arthurian history comes from an alternate perspective to the pro-Roman view that Saul-Josephus was preaching.

Anyway, the standard story of the Jewish Revolt is that the Jews were revolting, and Cestius Gallus (Varus-Varlan) marched his legions from Syria to Jerusalem to put down the revolt. But his legions got caught out in street-fighting, and during their retreat and subsequent rout the majority were slaughtered. Thus the rebel Jews were entirely responsible for the Jewish Revolt, because they attacked the innocent Romans. However, as with all political and military incidents there was a back-story to these highly politicised events, and that concerned the poor governorship of Judaea.

The Jewish authorities had long complained about the brutality of Gessius Florus, the Roman governor of Judaea from AD 64 - 66. So King

Agrippa II of Judaea and Syria went to see Cestius Gallus (Varus-Varlan) at Caesarea, to complain about Florus' abuse of power. In fact, according to Saul-Josephus there were many in Judaea who thought that Florus was deliberately trying to stir up a revolt in Judaea, so that he could slaughter the Jews and yet blame them for starting the war.

> Florus contrived another way to oblige the Jews to begin the war (revolt), and sent to Cestius falsely accusing the Jews of revolting ... But the governors of Jerusalem were not silent upon this occasion, and wrote to Cestius, as did Bernice also, about the illegal practices of which Florus had been guilty against the city. (War 2:16:1) (Note: Berenice was the sister-wife of King Agrippa II.)

But Florus was half right about the Jews revolting, because his oppressive rule had already started disturbances in Judaea and there was also an open revolt of the Jews down in Alexandria in Egypt. One can imagine that Cestius Gallus (Varus-Varlan) did not exactly view the Jews as a completely innocent party in all of this. The Jews had always been a rebellious people, unlike the Egyptians for instance, and Rome needed to maintain control of the region. And the ruling clique of any administration always has to close ranks and present a unified face, otherwise revolts and rebellions would break out all the time. And so Cestius Gallus (Varus-Varlan) did nothing about the oppressive rule of governor Florus. The result of this inaction was that the rebels upped the stakes by capturing the Roman garrison in Jerusalem, and took over the palace of Herod.

One of those who was besieged by the rebels in Jerusalem was Philip of Gamala, the son of James, the brother of Jesus (of Gamala). A rumour was spread that Philip had sided with the rebels, rather than being besieged by them, and so therefore he must have revolted against the Romans. And if this was true then his city and people, the Babylonian Jews of the Osrhoene, could be subject to Roman attack and retribution (Philip controlled one of the Edessan cities). Philip was busy sending ambassadors to King Agrippa to say he had not revolted, but someone called Varus (ie: Cestius Gallus) killed both of these ambassadors, to prevent Agrippa from knowing of this. Then Varus (Cestius Gallus) sent ambassadors to the Babylonian Jews in eastern Syrio-Judaea to tell them to lay down their arms, and to send seventy of their principle men to see him immediately. This they did, but when the seventy ambassadors arrived at these negotiations, Varus (Cestius Gallus) killed them all (except for one who escaped).

Much of this account has already been narrated in Chapter II of this book and Chapter VII of *King Jesus*, and so there is no point spending too much time on the details of this ambassadorial saga. Suffice it to say that this was such a major issue in Judaea at this time, that it was not only recounted in *Jewish War* and in *Life*, but it also found its way into Arthurian history and into the gospels, where it became the parable of the vineyard owner (Mt 21:33-41, Mk 12:1-9, Lu 20:9-16). In this parable, the landlord went away to a far country and so his vineyard was left in the control of a wicked tenant, who refused to pay his rent. And when the landlord sent his ambassadors to see the wicked tenant, he killed them. So the owner then sent his own son to sort out these debts, and the tenant killed him too. And the moral that the biblical Jesus-Izas drew from this sad story was that:

> (The landlord) will come and destroy the tenant, and will give the vineyard to others. (Mark 12:9.)
>
> (The landlord) will miserably destroy those wicked men, and will let out his vineyard to other tenants, who shall render him the fruits in their seasons (ie: render him the taxes from the land). (Matthew 21:41.) (Author's brackets.)

As we have seen many times before, the primary focus of Jesus' teachings were diametrically opposed to the versions that the Church now preaches from its pulpits. In this case, Jesus was not concerned about the rights of the poor and disenfranchised, but instead of the legal right of landlords to kill their tenants if they do not pay their rent, and to lease their lands out to more compliant tenants. Yes, the main concern of Jesus was not poor labourers and farmers, but the rights of rich absentee landowners who were demanding their rent.

However, the true meaning of this parable goes much deeper than a simple story about a landlord demanding rent from a tenant. And in order to understand its true meaning we need to understand once more that Jesus was not a pauper artisan but a prince and king - King Izas-Jesus of Edessa. In reality, this parable was complaining about Romans living on Judaeo-Edessan lands, the lands of King Izas-Jesus of Edessa, and not paying any taxes. In fact, the situation was even worse than this, because the Romans were demanding taxes from King Izas-Jesus of Edessa. But what kind of stupid tenant demands rent from the landlord!

This was the underlying political message that Jesus' parable was trying to convey; it was merely a simplistic but no doubt successful justification for waging war on the Romans - the war of the Jewish Revolt. This is the revolutionary political message that the Gospels were sending, before it was covered with several layers of fairy-dust and icing-sugar, and reworked into the semi-fictional story we see today. What King Jesus-Izas was really saying here, is that the Roman governor Gallus-Varus was acting unreasonably in not paying rent for living on Nazarene Jewish land (and demanding taxes from Jesus-Izas instead). And he had acted unreasonably and unlawfully in murdering the ambassadors who had been sent to him (to ask for that rent).

In which case, all we need to do in order to understand this parable is to replace 'tenant' with 'Romans', and to replace 'landlord' with 'King Jesus-Izas' himself. And now the parable will make perfect sense - including that surprisingly brutal and bloodthirsty conclusion. And so the two short gospel verses just given should be rewritten to read:

> The moral of this biblical story is that the Romans were living on Judaeo-Edessan lands (the lands of King Izas-Jesus), and not paying their taxes.
>
> So the Edessan king will miserably destroy those wicked Romans, and will let out his lands to better tenants, who shall render the taxes and tribute that are due. (Based upon Matthew, Mark and Luke.)

This is the gospel version of these events, but now we see that Arthurian history is relating the exactly same story. In *Quest*, King Varlan (Varus-Gallus) was in a battle with King Lambor. Varlan was losing the fight, just as Cestius Gallus-Varus lost the battle against the Jewish rebels. But then Varlan-Varus (Cestius-Gallus) came upon King Lambor with the 'sword of the strange straps' and split the king and his horse in two. And so the meaning of this is clear - the Dolorous Stroke or Sorrowful Stroke from this semi-magical sword had split the nation in two and caused a civil war. And that is exactly what happened.

But this was no longer an internal civil war within Judaea. An entire Roman army had been wiped out, and so as sure as night becomes day, the Romans would arrive with more legions, and there would be a war with Rome. But the Dolorous Stroke that Varlan-Varus (Cestius-Gallus) had delivered had divided the nation right down the middle, and so the resulting Jewish Revolt became a three- or four-way civil war, with the Orthodox Jews, Nazarene Jews and Gentile Greeks of Judaea all fighting each other, while the Romans were somewhere in the middle trying to restore order.

So the Arthurian version of this event is correct, for Varlan-Varus (Cestius-Gallus) did indeed split the nation in two when his ill-fated expedition to Judaea to restore order resulted in the annihilation of his Roman army. But the crucial thing that we cannot derive from reading Josephus and the gospels, is that this conflict was caused by a series of needless events that ratcheted up the tension, while absolutely no effort was made to defuse the situation. These included a rumour that King Agrippa had been captured, and a princess who had been locked in iron bands. But the event that stands out as being most significant is when Varlan-Varus (Cestius Gallus) had requested seventy of the leading men of the Babylonian Jews (of

Edessa and Palmyra) to attend his court. But following a barbed exchange of words a fight erupted, and most or all of these high ranking ambassadors had been slaughtered. There are a few fundamental conventions in international diplomatic relations, that have been a constant throughout the history of human civilisation, and killing the ambassadors from another king or nation is not one of them.

One suspects that Cestius Gallus was taking his uncompromising stance from the utter defeat of Queen Boudica at the Battle of Watling Street in Britain, which happened just five years prior to these events. But if Cestius Gallus thought he could treat the Babylonian Jews in the same fashion that Gaius Paulinus had treated the Britons, he was very much mistaken. The Nazarene Ebionites of Edessa and Palmyra were not woad-adorned axe-wielding tribesmen from the fringes of the Empire, and nor were they pious and cerebral Orthodox Jews nodding before a wall of the Temple in Jerusalem. Instead, these were the descendents of a royal family from Parthia and Egypt who had brought the feared Parthian cavalry with them, when they had been exiled to Syria just sixty years previously. This was the same swift cavalry that had already wiped out two entire Roman armies, under the command of Crassus and then Mark Antony, so they were not the kind of forces Cestius Gallus should have been taking on with a single undermanned and inexperienced local legion.

Agrippa II

The fact that the *Vulgate Cycle* is relating this particular battle in Judaea, and not any old battle from the thousands throughout history, can be seen in another version of this same story, this time from *Lancelot*. In this alternate version the names and events have changed slightly, with some interesting results. The section will be quoted at length, because it contains some interesting information:

> Exactly one year ago King Vadalon, the brother of the king of North Wales, besieged my father King Agrippes at Mabon Rock, because he said my father had killed one of his brothers. After imprisoning my brother inside by using the force of his brother, a king of North Wales, he blockaded our castle and cut off our food supply for three days. It was so intensely hot that all the springs in out country had dried up, except for a fountain that supplied the enemy camp. If that spring failed they would have to give up the siege.
>
> I told myself that I could surely kill our enemies by poisoning the spring's water; and that is what I did ... In three days more than 500 died, so they abandoned the siege and returned to their country. When (Vadalon) found out he

> became crazed with grief and announced that he would never be happy until he had taken his revenge ... Afterwards I happened to be riding through the territory of the king I told you about, I was captured and brought before him. When he saw me, he said if he killed me he would never be avenged, because this would be too quick. So he had two iron bands bound tightly around me ... I was in so much pain that I would rather be dead and I said in front of his entire court: "King Vadalon, do you think you have had your revenge on me?" (Lancelot IV 118:172-173)

The name Vadalon is a corruption of Varlan, with the Aramaic 'r' being mistaken for a 'd', as it often is. Take away that common transcription error and Vadalon ודלן becomes Varalon or Varlan ורלן, and so this quote is about the same person and the same events. Notice how the spelling of this name barely changes in the Hebrew-Aramaic, which is a good indication that this name was indeed originally Aramaic rather than Latin or Norman French.

And the proof that this was not a story about events in North Wales is given in the description here that the land was too hot and all the springs had all dried up. In Wales? Really? Every rock you kick over in Wales reveals yet another spring, at any time of year. This cannot have been a story about Wales, instead it was a story about Judaea where the land can get exceedingly hot and dry and poisoning a spring might well be a successful tactic. We can see the same type of muddled deception in a relatively unknown Arthurian manuscript called *Roman de Fergus*. The hero of this story, Fergus, is a rustic fool who becomes a knight of King Arthur, and he is a direct equivalent of Chretien's Perceval in all respects. It is exactly the same story, recast into a Scottish setting. But then Fergus rides to the Black Mountain in Scotland and ties his horse to an olive tree. In Scotland?

In *Lancelot* we then have the name of the father of this princess, who is called King Agrippes. A King Agrippes of Wales? Really? In reality, this can only be a reference to King Agrippa II, who did indeed travel to meet Varus-Varlan (Cestius Gallus) in Caesarea, to discuss the harsh rule of Gessius Florus. And in the accounts of (Saul) Josephus, a rumour was spread that Varus-Gallus had killed the king. In the following quote, the seventy ambassadors from the Babylonian Jews at Ecbatana had gone to meet with Varus-Gallus and:

> Varus met them with the king's army, and slew them all ... and made an expedition against the Jews of Ecbatana ... When Philip (of Gamala) was informed of these things, he also came to the citadel of Gamala. And the people cried aloud, and urged him to resume the government, and to make an expedition against Varus, and the Syrians of Caesarea, for it was reported that they had slain the king. (Agrippa) But Philip restrained their zeal ... and told them how powerful the

> Romans were, and said it was not for their advantage to make war with them. (Life 11) (Author's brackets.)

The account in *Lancelot* appears to be correct - the rumour swirling around Judaea at this time was that the king (Agrippa II) had been slain by Varus-Gallus, the Roman governor. And so once again we see that these were actually 1st century events that took place in Syrio-Judaea.

Throne of Rome

This slaughter of the ambassadors at the peace negotiations has already been explored in Geoffrey of Monmouth's *History of Kings*, in Chapter II. But Monmouth's account continues and gives us some further details about the ensuing battle in some detail, and this gives us yet another view of this major and pivotal military engagement that started the entire Jewish Revolt.

The remains of the Roman and Arthurian delegations retreat from the melee at the conference, back to their respective armies. A battle ensues, in which the Arthurians get the upper hand. They then take their Roman captives back to 'Paris', but they are attacked en-route by the Romans. But Arthurian reinforcements arrive and put the Romans to flight. King Arthur then says to his men:

> The Romans have taken refuge with shame in the city over there. At this moment they are ready to issue forth on a march to Autun. They must pass through this valley, and here we shall fall upon them where they least expect it, and you may slaughter them like sheep. (History of Kings Bk X ch7)

And this is more or less what Saul-Josephus says about the same battle in Judaea. Cestius Gallus (Varus) initially gets trapped in Jerusalem, and has to withdraw. He eventually gets to the Roman camp at Gabao, but sees ever more of the enemy gathering day by day. Unable to stay in this small camp indefinitely, he breaks camp and marches to Bethoron, heading west through the Judaean highlands to reach the plains on the Mediterranean coast. However, calamity is about to strike in the valleys and gorges around Bethoron.

> (Cestius Gallus) then made his army march on as far as Bethoron. Now the Jews did not so much press upon them when they were in large open places; but when they were penned up in their descent through narrow passages, some of them got in front and hindered them while others thrust at the rear. And the whole multitude extended themselves over against the neck of the passage, and covered the Roman army with their darts.

> The ascents were so high, that the (Roman) cavalry were not able to march against the enemy. The precipices also and valleys into which they frequently fell, and tumbled down, were such on each side of them, that there was neither place for their flight, nor any contrivance could be thought of for their defence. Until the distress they were in was so great that they betook themselves to lamentations ... Indeed, things were come to such a pass, that the Jews had almost taken Cestius' entire army prisoner, had not the night come on. (Jewish War 2:19:7-8)

As Geoffrey Monmouth has just explained, the Arthurian-Nazarene forces were going to strike the Roman Army of Cestius Gallus (Varus) as it moved through the passes in the Judaean highlands, before they got to the safety of the western plains. And this is exactly what Saul-Josephus said happened, and so the rebels managed to wipe out the best part of an entire legion.

But why had King Jesus-Izas-Arthur decided to pick a fight with Rome? Was this bold strategy just because Rome had demanded tribute (taxes) from the Edessan royalty, or was there more to it than that? Once again the answers are to be found within Arthurian history, rather than Saul-Josephus' biased Romanised history. In *History of Kings* King Arthur addresses his men and says:

> As soon as we have put them (the Roman army) to rout, we shall start forthwith to Rome. For us to march upon Rome is to take it and possess it. Yours shall be the gold, the towns and cities, and all the riches of the vanquished. (History of Kings Bk X ch7)

> The messengers did their work and assembled such a massive army ... that numbered more than a hundred thousand ... (Gawain and Kay said) 'King Arthur ... if you shared our heart we would conquer France and Rome ... we would have you bear the crown as far as Jerusalem and you would be the lord of the world.' (Merlin Grail p157) (Author's brackets.)

So the wider objective of this Judaeo-Arthurian revolt was not the throne of Judaea in Jerusalem, it was to place King Arthur (King Jesus-Izas) on the Throne of Rome as the emperor of the whole Roman Empire. This is exactly what has already been suggested in both *King Jesus* and *Jesus, King of Edessa*, but here we have the Arthurian authors fully supporting and confirming that claim. King Jesus-Izas (Arthur) was not really interested in Judaea, for that small provincial backwater was merely a stepping-stone on the road to the heart of the Empire. The real goal was the Throne of Rome itself. Even the gospels know this, which is why King Jesus-Izas was taken for crucifixion wearing the Edessan crown of thorns and the Imperial Purple - the cloak of a Roman emperor:

> And the soldiers platted a crown of thorns, and put it on his head, and they put on him a purple robe ... Then came Jesus forward, wearing the crown of thorns, and the purple robe. And Pilate said unto them, "Behold the man!" (Joh 19:2-5)

There would be no point putting an Imperial purple cloak on a prince who merely wanted to become the king of Judaea. The symbology and meaning here is obvious - just like King Arthur, King Jesus-Izas also wanted to become the emperor of the entire Roman Empire.

Pelles and Pellehan

The accounts in *History* and *Quest* are therefore suggesting that the Jewish Revolt was a much wider conflict than Saul-Josephus makes out in *Jewish War*. While much of the military conflict took place in Judaea, the region ruled and controlled by the Edessan monarchy encompassed many of the lands to the east of the river Jordan. In which case, potential support for the uprising could have come from all the rich cities of the Syrio-Jordanian Decapolis, and so Rome was potentially faced with a major revolt in a vast swathe of its eastern territories, and Vespasian's re-conquest of Judaea was by no means a certainty. Had the Decapolis cities joined the Revolt, Vespasian would have had a major problem on his hands, and so much of Vespasian's military strategy depended on political negotiations with the Decapolis cities, and this is why the insufferable Saul-Josephus was so useful to Vespasian.

We have already seen Saul-Josephus' description of the Nazarene revolutionaries expecting assistance from their brethren who lived 'beyond the Euphrates', but there was also a great deal of sympathy for the revolution 'beyond the Jordan' too. One of the major cities of the Decapolis in the province of Perea, beyond the Jordan, was called Pella. There is not simply a nominative similarity between King Parian-Pellehan and Perea-Pella, for there is a close 1st century political link too. As we have just seen, the true era for these events is just after the Jewish Revolt. However, in his *Church History* Eusebius says that the 'Christians' had fled from Jerusalem just before the Jewish Revolt, and relocated to Pella:

> The people of the Church in Jerusalem were commanded by an oracle given by revelation before the war to those in the city who were worthy of it to depart and dwell in one of the cities of Perea which they called Pella. Those who believed on Christ traveled from Jerusalem to Pella, so that the holy men had altogether deserted the royal capital of the Jews and the whole land of Judaea... (Eusebius, Church History 3:5:3)

This account equates very well with the amnesty that was given by King Claudas, before the battle with the Arthurian army, when his nephew advised Claudas to let all those who would not be loyal to leave Gaunes. And the quote here is not a reference to Christians, of course, it is a reference to 'the Jerusalem Church' and 'those who believed in Christ'. As has been laboured many times in these books, Jesus was not a Christian and neither were his followers Christians. Jesus was a Fourth Sect Nazarene Jew, and so the 'followers of Jesus' who fled to Pella would have been Nazarene Ebionite Jews. Epiphanius in his *Refutation of Heresies* or *Panarion* confirms this when he says of this same migration:

Fig 13.1 The Decapolis, the ten great Roman cities in Syrio-Judaea, during the early centuries AD. Many are just ruins now, but Damascus and Philadelphia (Amman) are still large cities.

> For after all those who believed in Christ had generally come to live in Perea, in a city called Pella of the Decapolis of which it is written in the gospel that it is situated in the neighborhood of the region of Batanaea and Basanitis. As far as I know he (Ebion) first lived in a village called Kochaba ... also called Astaroth, in Basanitis ... the same place, if you please, as the Nazoreans. But I have already spoken at length ... about the locations of Kochaba and Arabia. (Epiphanius, Panarion 30:2:7)

> This heresy of the Nazoraeans exists in Beroea in the neighbourhood of Coele Syria and the Decapolis in the region of Pella and in Basanitis in the so-called Kochaba. From there it took its beginning after the exodus from Jerusalem when all the disciples went to live in Pella because Christ had told them to leave Jerusalem and to go away since it would undergo a siege. Because of this advice they lived in Perea after having moved to that place, as I said. (Epiphanius, Panarion 29:7:7-8)

Jesus-Izas and James were both Nazarenes (Math 2:23), as was Saul-Josephus before he went over to the Romans (Acts 24:5), and yet Epiphanius is now branding the people of Pella as believing in 'the heresy of the Nazoraeans'. Its is quite amazing how this history could have been be distorted, curved, folded, and bent back upon itself to such a degree, that by the time we reach the 4th century of Epiphanius, Jesus himself had become a Christian heretic! Christianity must be the only religious sect in history that despises and denigrates its own founding father.

Note also the standard chronological chasm. These quotes say that Jesus warned these Nazarene 'Christians' (the people who venerated the new christ or king) about the impending siege of Jerusalem in AD 70. But how could this have happened, if Jesus died in AD 30? Again this demonstrates that Jesus was actually an AD 60s prince and king who was closely involved in the tragic events of the Jewish Revolt. However, perhaps the most significant aspect of these quotes is that the Ebionites and Nazarenes who believed in King Jesus-Izas, and would not support the Romans, fled to Pella just before the Jewish Revolt. And this flight to Pella was made on the advice of either the biblical King Jesus or the Arthurian King Claudas.

The name for the Ebionite sect was derived from *ebyon* אביון meaning 'poor', and they were closely linked to the Essene community at Qumran. So the Ebionites were known as 'the poor'; the Essene were 'the poor'; the Nazarene Church of Jesus and James were 'the poor'; the Fourth Sect were 'the poor'; the Boethusians were 'the poor'; the Bethanyites were 'the poor'; and the Knights Templar were also 'the poor'. All of these sects ran a communist kibbutz-style social system, where new members gave up their wealth to the community and lived from the common purse - the very same *glossokomon* γλωσσοκομον or 'donations box' that Judas Iscariot kept for the Church of Jesus.*

And so many of the Fourth Sect Nazarene followers of Jesus-Izas and James fled to Pella in Batanaea, either before or after the Great Jewish Revolt. And yet Batanaea was the biblical Bethany, as has been amply proven in the previous books, and was also named after 'the poor'. And so the flight of these refugees was not to a completely new and unknown location, it was a flight back to the home of Simon the Leper (Simon Boethus) - the house in Bethany where Mary Magdalene had anointed Jesus-Izas with oil. Thus there had always been a strong Nazarene-Ebionite presence in Pella, to the east of the Jordan.

Interestingly, according to these quotes from *Refutation of Heresies*, this region around Pella had also been called Kochba כוכבא, and yet it was Simon bar Kochba כוכבא who started the third revolt against Rome, the Bar Kochba Revolt. And there is a definite link between these regions and events. King Jesus-Izas was the Star, the prince whose mother was identified with the Eastern Star (Venus-Isis) and whose birth was foretold and pinpointed by the Eastern Star (see Math 2:2). And a star in Hebrew-Aramaic is called a *kochab* כוכב. So the town or city of Kochba was actually the town or city of the Star - the city where the Eastern Star or one of his descendents had fled to. This is why the region was also known as Astaroth, which comes from the Greek *aster* αστηρ meaning 'star', and is the basis for the name of the goddess Astarte (Venus-Isis). So Kochba not only refers to the 'Star Family' it also refers to the 'Star City', and that city may well have been the Decapolis city of Pella.

It is also worth noting that these Decapolis cities to the east of the Jordan did not collapse into economic decay, following the Jewish and Bar Kochba revolts. Far from it. At Gedara, which lies just to the north of Pella they began the construction of a massive water system in the late first century, a project that lasted for perhaps a hundred years. Gadara overlooks the Jordan valley, in a very similar fashion to Pella. But to get a head of water for the city's water supply the intrepid Roman engineers went to modern Jillan in Syria, some 30 km to the northeast, which resides on one of the sources for the river Jordan itself.

* See John 13:29. Note that most Bibles call this a 'purse' or 'bag' to diminish its status and diminish the wealth of the Church of Jesus. But it was no such thing it was a 'donations box' or 'treasure chest', exactly as one might imagine being onboard a pirate ship. So while individual members of the Church were poor, the Church itself could be very rich. Especially in the case of the Boethus-Sadducee Church, whose members only used gold and silver cutlery and crockery.

But to get the water to Gedara, they had to penetrate the inhospitable badlands to the east of the Jordan valley, which consists of a myriad of ridges and valleys. The result was a winding aqueduct called the Qanat-Firaun, which runs for a total of 170 kilometers, including an underground section that is an incredible 94 kilometers long. And to ensure that the aqueduct did not lose its head of water, the gradient was restricted to an equally incredible 30 centimeters of fall per kilometer, which is an astonishingly shallow angle of descent.[2] This was the vibrant and dynamic culture that existed in Syria and the Roman East, before Islam conquered the region and turned it into a social and economic backwater.

So did King Pellehan live in and acquire his name from the city of Pella? Well, it is quite possible that this royal family controlled many of the lands to the east of the Jordan, which was also known as the Kingdom of Aurania. It has already been argued that the exiled Babylonian Jews were given all of the eastern borderlands between Judaeo-Syria and Parthia, with Edessa as its capital and Palmyra as its economic hub. The only difference with this new assessment is that the Kingdom of Edessa would have extended right down to the borders of Nabataea and as far west as the river Jordan itself, encompassing the major Decapolis cities of Pella, Gerasa and Gedara. And if this was so, then it was no wonder that Judaea and Rome would have felt threatened by this wealthy and ever-expanding principality right on its doorstep.

Remember also that the province of Perea was a central component in this Arthurio-Edessan story. The seventy emissaries of the Edessan monarchy who went to see Varus (Cestius Gallus) and were slaughtered, came from Ecbatana or ek-Batanaea meaning 'from Batanaea', in Perea. And in a similar fashion, two of the leaders of the Edessan army that subsequently attacked Cestius Gallus' Syrian legion, were Silas of Babylon and Niger of Perea. It has already been suggested that this Simon and Niger were one person: the Simon Niger mentioned in Acts 13:1, who must therefore have been an Edessan (Babylonian) from Perea.

There is also a possible link here between Simon Niger and Wolfram von Eschenbach's Feirefiz, the half-brother of Perceval. Feirefiz was piebald (black and white) as that is what his name means in the Norman French. But Simon Niger was also black, for that is what Niger means. (Although this blackness may refer more to Egypt rather than any skin pigmentation.) So Simon Niger, one of the leaders of the Babylonian Jewish Revolt, may be linked to Feirefiz of Zazamans, while Arthurian history records that Feirefiz commanded the largest army in Mesopotamia. Once more we can see here a huge circle of connections and interconnections, that link Arthurian history with Josephus' history of Syrio-Judaea and also with biblical history.

Thus it is entirely possible that King Parian-Pellehan was the king

Fig 13.2 The ancient city of Pella, one of the rich Decapolis cities of Judaeo-Syria. The city lies in the low hills to the east of the Jordan, and looks down upon the relatively lush Jordan valley.

Fig 13.3 The Qanat-Firaun aqueduct that supplied the city of Gedara. This tunnel runs for 94 kilometers.

or tetrarch of the province of Perea and the city of Pella, and so a branch of the Edessan family may well have been based in Pella. And while it is probably just coincidental, the name for Pella was derived from a capital city of Macedonia, just as Edessa was. Edessa was named after the first capital city of Macedonia, while Pella was named after the third.

Quest for the Grail

As we saw earlier, at the end of the account in *Quest* the Holy Grail had been given to Saul-Josephus (of Arimathaea). But we might reasonably presume that this Grail was merely the golden chalice. Saul-Joseph(us) had never been initiated into the mysteries of the Round Table and the Grail, and so he did not realise that the true Holy Grail was a sacred stone and a sacred bloodline, rather than a golden chalice. Saul-Joseph(us) would be like the unenlightened Feirefiz asking the Grail princess to stand to one side, so that he could see the Grail more clearly.

Having said this, perhaps the Romans did realise that they had not discovered the full truth about the Holy Grail, for *Quest* narrates that at just this very time a new foreign knight joined the quest for the Grail. And he managed to join the quest even though he was not a member of the Round Table, which caused some consternation within the ranks of the Arthurian knights. But the really strange thing about this new knight, is that he was Prince Claudin, the son of King Claudas, who we have already identified as being Titus and Emperor Vespasian respectively.

For some peculiar reason *Quest* seems to completely forget that Prince Claudin is the son of the most hated king in the world, who had just fought an epic battle with the Arthurian army, and so the Arthurian knights greet him like a brother. Does this not seem bizarre? Why would any author of a heroic Arthurian history write such nonsense? *Quest* does not even attempt to explain this peculiar state of affairs, and simply leaves the reader baffled. However, the answer is that within real Syrio-Judaean history the Arthurian knights would have been forced to do just this. In the real world, Claudin was Titus, the son of Emperor Vespasian, and as the indisputable victor of the Jewish Revolt he and his father now ruled this entire land. The surviving knights may have hated Prince Claudin-Titus' guts, but anyone who did not greet him warmly would have been placed in solitary confinement for ten years, and had their entire family taken to the slave markets in Rome.

Once again, the story being told in *Quest* only makes sense if we place Arthurian history into 1st century Judaea. And *Post Vulgate Quest* goes on to clarify the aims of Prince Claudin-Titus by saying:

> He had just recently left the kingdom of Gaunes (Judaea) and come to Logres (Edessa-Palmyra), because he had heard that the great quest for the Holy Grail had begun, and he wanted to join it like the knights of the Round Table. And know that he had already done many knightly deeds ... of which the tale does not speak because he was not of the Round Table. (Post Quest 108:363) (Author's brackets.)

The Jewish Revolt may have ended with Gaunes and Benoic (Judaea) in ruins and much of the southern and western parts of the Kingdom of Logres under Roman control. But the majority of Logres (the Osrhoene, Batanaea, Aurania and Perea) were untouched by the Revolt, and these vibrant and wealthy lands still harboured rebel forces and ancient mysteries. We have already seen in *Lancelot* how Claudin-Titus went to Logres and Camelot in disguise, in AD 68 or 69, to spy on King Arthur and the Grail. And here is Claudin-Titus in rebel lands once again. But this time he is not in disguise, he is bold and confident as the great victor of the Jewish Revolt, and yet still trying to understand the politics of the region and discover the secrets of the Holy Grail. Wealth and power are nothing without wisdom, and here we see Claudin-Titus as the complete outsider, almost begging for wisdom from the formerly defeated knights of the Round Table.

This also explains why King Arthur is largely absent from the narrative in *Quest*. In *Lancelot* we saw the events of the Jewish Revolt, from the first landing of the Romans in AD 66 all the way up to the departure of King Claudas-Vespasian to Rome in the spring of AD 70. At the end of the siege of Jerusalem in August of AD 70, King Jesus-Izas-Arthur was captured and crucified, according to the accounts in Saul-Josephus' *Life*. And according to the analysis in *King Jesus,* King Jesus-Izas was then sent into exile, firstly to Rome and then to Britain. And so the absence of King Arthur from the account in *Quest* is only to be expected. It is very difficult to make King Arthur the central character of a story, if he was in exile in Britain at the time.

However, this strange assertion that Prince Claudin-Titus was also on a quest for the Holy Grail may shed some more light on what this new quest was actually about. We have seen the previous quest for wisdom, but if the San Greal (the holy chalice) was also the Sang Real (the royal blood), then there may have been a quest during the early AD 70s to find and protect the princesses of the holy bloodline. And conversely, the Romans may have been on a parallel quest to find and imprison those same bloodline princesses. (The Judaic royal line passes through the female line.) And we see this pursuit and persecution of the surviving family of King Jesus Izas - the Desposyni - in the ecclesiastic history recorded by Sextus Aficanus and Hegesippus. Eusebius, quotes these two Church historians and says of the Desposyni:

> The relatives of our Lord according to the flesh ... have handed down the following account ... Among these are those already mentioned called Desposyni, on account of their connection with the family of the Saviour. Coming from Nazara and Cochaba, villages of Judea, into other parts of the world, they drew the aforesaid genealogy from memory and from the book of daily records as faithfully as possible. (Eusebius, History of the Church, 1:7:11, 13)

> There still survived of the kindred of the Lord the grandsons of Judas, who according to the flesh was called his brother. These were informed against, as belonging to the family of David, and Evocatus brought them before Domitian Caesar: for that emperor dreaded the advent of a christ, just as Herod had done. So he asked them whether they were of the family of David; and they confessed they were. Next he asked them what property they had, or how much money they possessed. They both replied that they had only 9000 denaria between them ... And then they held out their hands, exhibiting the roughness of their skin as proof of their manual labour.

> (Domitian) then asked concerning Jesus and his kingdom ... they said that it was not of this world, but belonging to the sphere of heaven and angels, and would make its appearance at the end of time. Thereupon Domitian passed no condemnation upon them, but treated them with contempt ... and let them go free. At the same time he issued a command, and put a stop to the persecution against the (Nazarene) Church ... When they were released they became leaders of the churches, as was natural in the case of those who were ... of the kindred of the Lord. (Eusebius, History of the Church, 3:20 :1-11) (Author's brackets).

In the first quote from Africanus we see that there were surviving family members of King Jesus-Izas, and they were based in Cochaba and Nazara. Cochaba (Kochba) is Pella, as we saw previously, the city of the Nazarene Ebionites. And no doubt Nazara is the city of the Nazarene, which may be a reference to Palmyra or Edessa. In the second quote from Hegesippus we see that the Flavian Emperors had been hunting down the surviving family members of King Jesus-Izas, and taking them to Rome in chains to be interviewed by Emperor Domitian. This would be the AD 80s, and so this is just the right sort of era for this (renewed) Grail quest in Logres (Syria).

In *Lancelot,* Sir Galahad was said to be just a boy when the Jewish Revolt ended (when King Claudas-Vespasian sailed for Rome). And in *Quest* and *Post-Quest* we see Sir Galahad being knighted as a young man. If Galahad was 16 years old when he was knighted, then the era of *Quest* is the late AD 70s and the early AD 80s - the very era when the Desposyni (the family of Jesus) were being hunted down all across Judaeo-Syria. As the quote says, Emperor Domitian feared the advent of a new Christ, a new King of the Jews, just as King Herod had in the gospel accounts.

The meaning of these quotes is clear. This was ten years after the Jewish Revolt. Judaea and parts of southern Syria had been turned into a wasteland by the Romans, but the heartlands of the Edessan monarchy were relatively untouched and a new generation of knights were agitating for revolt once more. This is what Domitian feared - the appearance of a new Christ, a new king of Edessa and Palmyra who would agitate for a renewed revolt against Rome. So the renewed persecution of the Edessan monarchy was a preventative measure, to nip this new revolution in the bud before it had even started.

That is why the descendents of Jesus-Izas who had been captured were being asked about their beliefs. The answers they gave to Domitian confirmed that they had (supposedly) been influenced by the Roman propaganda that had been crafted and broadcast by Saul-Joseph(us) (of Arimathaea) to the people of Sarras-Palmyra and those beyond the Euphrates (in Edessa). Domitian was satisfied that these grandsons or great nephews of Jesus-Izas had been suitably 'reeducated' into Saul-Josephus' new Rome-friendly Simple Judaism, and allowed them to go back to Judaea.

But Domitian was right to think that a new revolution was in the air, because the Bar Kochba Revolt broke out just 50 years later, in AD 132. And the name of this renewed revolt would suggest that these revolutionaries came from Kochba, the city of Pella where the Nazarene Ebionites had been based. Or should that be the city of King Pellehan?

So the renewed knightly quest that is narrated in *Quest* may have been a competitive venture between opposing forces. The Arthurian knights were trying preserve the bloodline of King Jesus-Izas, while the Romans were trying to eliminate it, because the Edessan monarchy were a direct threat to the Flavian emperors in Rome. So from the Roman perspective, the quest for the Holy Grail was a precautionary measure to prevent another uprising. And depending on how we understand the wording, *Quest* appears to say the very same thing:

> Gawain replied, "We should all serve him (Galahad) as the one sent by god to free our land from the great wonders and strange adventures that have been taking place here for so long." ... The king (Arthur) said (to Galahad). "Sir, we are in great need of your help to put to an end the extraordinary wonders of this land and bring to a close an adventure that no one among us has been able to accomplish ... This is why god has sent you among us: to do what others could never accomplish." (Quest 4:11)

But what were these great wonders and adventures, that Sir Galahad was about to end in the dual kingdoms of Logres and Gaunes? Well, firstly we have to ask: 'who is Galahad?' According to the analysis in this book, he is actually the younger son of Saul-Joseph(us) of Arimathaea, who was called Galahad. And according to the rather heretical account in *Merlin Grail,* Joseph(us) of Arimathaea was an enemy of Jesus-Izas who was working for the Romans (p16). (See the quote in Chapter VII.) But if Sir Galahad was also working for the Romans, and therefore an enemy of King Arthur, then this puts a rather different spin on the story. So let us change the wording of this quote from *Quest,* and see if it makes any more sense in this revised and Romanised context:

> Gawain replied, "We should all serve him (Galahad, the son of Saul-Josephus of Arimathaea) as the one sent by Emperor Vespasian to free our land from the many revolts that have been taking place here for so long." ... The king (Evalach?) said (to Galahad). "Sir, we are in great need of your help to put to an end the many uprisings in this land and bring to a close the revolution that no one among us has been able to succeed in ... This is why Emperor Vespasian has sent you among us: to do what others could never accomplish (and bring peace to the Roman east)." (Quest 4:11, revised.)

Indeed. So the renewed Roman quest for the Holy Grail would end these eastern bloodline claims to the Throne of Rome, and bring the Jewish Revolt to a final close, so that the Roman east would remain in peace. The people of Sarras-Palmyra and Edessa had been cornered in an uncompromising propaganda pincer, that had been ordered by Rome and executed by Saul-Josephus (of Arimathaea) and his sons, Josephus and Galahad. And so the next generation of Palmyrans and Edessans would have to genuflect before an image of a pacifist King Jesus-Izas in a white robe nailed to a cross, instead of a militant warrior King Jesus-Izas-Arthur in shining armour wielding his sword and shield.

Except that the establishment of this new creed did not immediately bring peace, and the seeds of the Bar Kochba Revolt were already being sown at this very same time. It is almost impossible to change the hopes, desires and aspirations of a single generation, especially if those hopes can be constantly reignited and reinvigorated by religious zeal, as the subsequent events in Judaeo-Syria proved. It took a full two to three generations and two major wars, before the religio-revolutionary designs of the Edessan monarchy were finally quashed.

And yet the tragic irony is that this new peaceful creed of Simple Judaism that Saul-Joseph(us) was peddling for Rome, in order to crush the revolutionary Nazarene creed of Edessa, led directly to the establishment of a controlling authority that was ten times worse than the Roman administration that the Edessans were in conflict with. Peaceful Simple Judaism eventually morphed into despotic Catholic Christianity, and the new Christian

Fig 13.5
An image of the real warrior King Izas-Jesus in shining armour (left).
An image of the Romanised pacifist King Izas-Jesus in priestly robes (right).
Note that the real King Jesus-Izas Manu wears the traditional Edessan Crown of Thorns.

establishment hated the Nazarene Church of Jesus and James even more than the Romans ever did, because it threatened the very core of their creed. The Edessans had fought with a lynx, only to see it replaced by a lion.

Rome had been a model of multinationalism and multitheism, with the only proviso being that everyone had to agree to conform to Roman culture and law. The Romans knew full-well that multiculturalism was a contradictory absurdity that had never worked in any society in the entire history of man, but they also understood that multinationalism and multitheism through syncretism were almost compatible and just about controllable. Under the socio-political umbrella of a single Roman culture and society, multinationalism and syncretic multitheism proved to be a winning formula that prospered and expanded for hundreds of years, while the multicultural cesspit that followed Rome resulted in the destitution and decay of the Dark Ages.

Death of Arthur

Quest ends with the death of Sir Galahad, the son of Lancelot-Arimathaea. But if Galahad died from nothing more than old age, as the text implies, then how does Lancelot become the central figure in *Mort Artu*? It would appear that much of the story in *Mort* is not only going back in time, it is relating slightly different events to the ones explored thus far. *Quest* was centered around kings Pelles and Pellehan and their knightly champions, Perceval and Galahad. But in *Mort* we have moved onto Camelot, King Arthur and the infamous deeds and amours of Sir Lancelot. So much of *Mort* is merely a different aspect of the story narrated in *Quest*.

The central theme of *Mort* is the love-triangle between Arthur, Gwenevere and Lancelot. A trap is set to catch Sir Lancelot and Queen Gwenevere together, but Lancelot escapes. The queen accidentally gives a knight a poisoned fruit and he dies, and so the queen is accused and convicted of murder by the court of King Arthur. Once again we can see the dire courtly conflict and fatal family feud that this illicit affair engendered, and how far this story strays from what is often considered to be classical Arthurian history.

Unlikely as it may seem, King Arthur and his court sentenced Queen Gwenevere to death. But as the queen stood upon her funerary pyre awaiting her doom, Lancelot and his men ride in to engage King Arthur's forces in battle and rescue her. King Arthur then declares war on Lancelot, who retreats to the Dolorous Castle. This is the scene that is engraved upon the door of Modena Cathedral, as was discussed in Chapter VIII. However, in this version of the story it is Lancelot who abducts or saves Queen Gwenevere, rather than Mordred-Mordrain. Whoever the saviour of Gwenevere really was, a truce is organised between the warring parties by the Pope, and Gwenevere is eventually returned to King Arthur. But Arthur declares war again on Lancelot, the very next year.

And if we continue with the theory that these events all belong in the 1st century, and that Lancelot was actually Saul-Joseph(us) of Arimathaea, then these events share a distinct similarity with the events in Judaea during the AD 60s. In his *Jewish War* and *Life*, Saul-Josephus Flavius narrates the many disputes and battles he had with his mortal enemies in Judaea. And the two main enemies of Saul-Josephus were (James) Justus of Tiberias and Jesus of Gamala. But as we have seen on many occasions, Jesus of Gamala was the biblical King Jesus-Izas of Edessa, while Justus was probably James the Just, the brother of Jesus. And if this seems a little complicated, then perhaps a short resume of the characters involved in this dispute is necessary:

Lancelot was Joseph(us) of Arimathaea.
We know this because both of these characters had a virginal son called Galahad, who became a king (a Galli high priest) of either Sarras or Britain. The reason for the name-change is that Joseph(us) was most definitely a 1st century character, while Lancelot was supposed to be a 6th century character, and so the two names were devised to separate them. But their life and deeds do appear remarkably similar. In addition, while the early Arthurian manuscripts mention Joseph(us) of Arimathaea on numerous occasions, they ***never*** mention Lancelot. Conversely, the manuscripts that mention Lancelot rarely mention Joseph(us) of Arimathaea.

Joseph(us) of Arimathaea was Saul-Josephus Flavius.
We know this because both of these characters took the leader of the Jewish Revolt down from the cross. And the leader of the Jewish revolt was called King Izas, while the leader of the biblical revolt was called King Jesus. In addition, both Joseph(us) of Arimathaea and Saul-Josephus Flavius were rescued from prison by Legatus Vespasian in about AD 68, and became close colleagues of the Emperor after the Jewish Revolt. There is also the comment in *Merlin Grail* that Joseph(us) of Arimathaea was plotting to arrest Jesus, just as was Saul-Josephus Flavius during his many battles with Jesus (of Gamala) in and around Galilee.

Jesus of Gamala was King Izas-Jesus.
We know this because both of these characters were Babylonian Jews who arrived in Judaea in the early 1st century. In addition: both became the high priest or king of Judaea; both led the Jewish Revolt against the Romans; and both carried the Gama-Kama title of the Edessan monarchy.

King Izas-Jesus of Adiabene was King Manu of Edessa.
We know this because: the mother of both of these princes was Queen Helena; the titles 'Izas' and 'Manu' were both Edessan royal titles; and both of these princes became king in the AD 60s.

King Izas Manu was the biblical King Jesus Em-Manuel.
We know this because: these kings share the same name; the same Nazarene religion; and a similar history - including both being kings who were crucified after a revolt in Judaea while wearing a Crown of Thorns.

King Izas Manu was King Arthur
This was proposed in *King Jesus*, because Jesus and Arthur were both kings who led twelve knights or disciples and sat them at a Round Last Supper Table. It was then noticed that: the King Arthur does not exist in the historical record; the standard chronology for King Arthur is impossible; the Arthurian manuscripts

often place their accounts in the 1st century; the author of the original Arthurian manuscript was probably Saul-Josephus Flavius; and the events he describes correspond very closely with events in 1st century Judaea. The correspondence between King Arthur and King Izas Manu is what this book has set out to prove, and hopefully it has achieved this.

Thus the two protagonists in this bitter battle in *Mort* were actually:

King Izas-Jesus-Manu-Arthur.
Izas-Arthur was the king of Edessa, Palmyra and all the lands to the east of the Jordan. And if his realm did indeed stretch from Edessa and Amida, all the way down to the Dead Sea, then this was quite an extensive, wealthy and influential realm. This realm may have been governed by vassal princes who included King Pellehan.

Prince Saul-Josephus-Lancelot of Arimathaea.
Saul-Josephus was a prince in his own right, who became a knight (a disciple) in the court of King Izas-Jesus. But he was rejected for some reason (after an affair with the queen, according to *Mort.*) The biblical and historical records indicate much the same story, with Saul-Josephus Flavius first allying himself with the Judaean administration and then with Vespasian and the Romans. And the principle enemy of Saul-Josephus in both cases was Jesus - in *Jewish War* his enemy was Jesus (of Gamala), while in the Gospels it was the biblical Jesus (Saul, Saul, why are you persecuting me? Acts 9:4). And if we now include Arthurian history in this equation, we now see a conflated Jesus-Arthur battling with a conflated Josephus-Lancelot.

We can now begin to see a number of similarities between the account of the battle between King Arthur and Lancelot in *Mort,* and the battle between King Izas-Jesus and Saul-Josephus in *Jewish War*. These include:

One combatant being a king and the other a knight.
Their being closely related.
That King Arthur (ie: King Jesus) was quite old at the time.
That Lancelot (ie: Saul-Josephus) was much younger.
The battle being fought in two lands separated by water (Jordan and Sea of Galilee).
The battles being fought in castles, or fortified towns.
Both combatants gaining the upper hand at some point.
Truces being organised by third parties.
72 emissaries being killed.
After the battle, the Romans arrive in the country.
The Romans want tribute (taxes) from Arthur.
Lancelot eventually becomes a priest.

Unfortunately it is not possible to prove that these many conflicts and battles between Arthur and Lancelot were the same as the conflicts and battles between King Jesus-Izas and Saul-Josephus, but the tone and tenor of these narratives are very similar. The one similarity that does stand out, is the killing of King Arthur's men in the first melee. Queen Gwenevere was condemned to die for the murder of a knight, but Lancelot and his men ride to the rescue and inflict heavy losses upon Arthur's knights. Lancelot then whisks Gwenevere away to his castle called the Dolorous Guard, which is a very similar story to the abduction of Gwenevere by Mordred, as we have seen previously. And when King Arthur accounts for those killed, he finds he has lost 72 men. Is this an oblique reference to the 70 Edessan ambassadors killed by Varus (Cestius Gallus)? *

When this event happened in the historical record, Saul-Josephus was still fighting against King Jesus-Izas of Gamala, and he was being accused of siding with the Romans. So it is entirely possible that Saul-Josephus acted alongside and in concert with Cestius Gallus (Varus). In fact, after the defeat of the Roman army by the rebels, it would appear that Saul-Josephus went straight to Cestius Gallus in Damascus. And it was agreed that he should then go to Greece to see Nero. But in *King Jesus* it was speculated that Saul-Josephus wanted to see Vespasian rather than Nero, because Vespasian was his spy-handler and he was also in Greece at this time:

> After this calamity had befallen Cestius, many of the most eminent of the Jews swam away from the city (of Jerusalem), as from a ship when it was going to sink (the flight to Pella). Therefore Costobarus and Saul, who were brethren, together with Philip, the son of Jacimus, who was the commander of king Agrippa's forces, ran away from the city, and went to Cestius (in Damascus) ... However, Cestius sent Saul and his friends, at their own desire to Achaea, to see Nero and inform him of the great distress they were in. And to lay the blame of the kindling the war upon (governor) Florus, hoping to alleviate his own danger by provoking (Nero's) indignation against Florus. (Jewish War 2:20:1) (Author's brackets.)

This is an interesting quote from *Jewish War*, because here we have someone called Saul doing exactly what Saul-Josephus Flavius would have done - going straight to the defeated Roman commander to apologise for the

* Twenty six different Bibles have been used in this research. Some of these relate that Jesus sent 70 new apostles on this mission, while others say that there were 72. The Syriac versions of the New Testament tend to favour 72 apostles. See Luke 10:1.

actions of the rebels and to distance himself from them. And then going to see Emperor Nero (or Vespasian) to apologise once more and to appraise the Romans on the situation and politics within Judaea. Once again we can be sure that Josephus was also called Saul, and so the biblical Saul was most definitely Josephus Flavius (Saul-Josephus).

It is fairly clear from this account that Saul-Josephus was already working for the Romans at the time of Cestius Gallus' defeat in September AD 66, long before he surrendered to Vespasian at the siege of Jotapata in the July of AD 67. During the intervening months commander (knight) Saul-

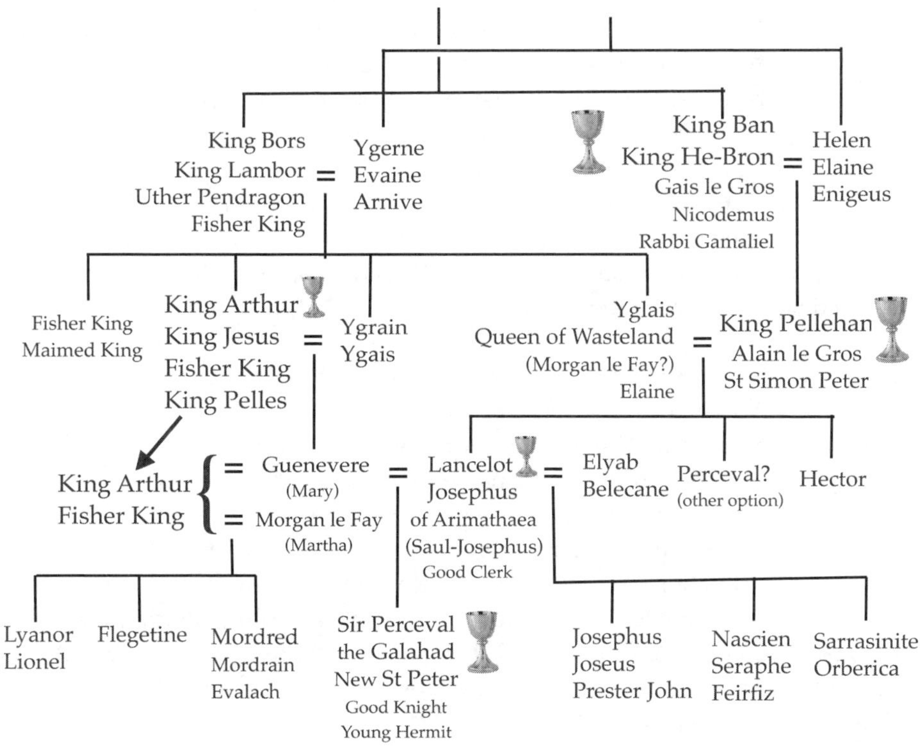

Fig 13.6 An idealised genealogy of the Arthurian monarchy that takes into account all the many permutations we have seen in the other genealogies. In order to get the generations correct, with King Arthur being older than Joseph(us) of Arimathaea, and yet Joseph(us)-Lancelot falling in love with Gwenevere, King Arthur is shown marrying his daughter. This is not so shocking as it may seem, because Queen Thea Muse Ourania of Parthia and Edessa did the very same thing, she married her son. And in a similar fashion, King Abgarus of Edessa married his sister, Queen Helena. Perceval-Galahad would have to be a late son of Queen Gwenevere, as he is supposed to be much younger than Mordrain and Nascien. There may be other permutations of this genealogy that achieve the same goals. The chalices indicate holders of the Grail.

Josephus was busy defending Galilee, but against whom is uncertain. He was defending Galilee against King Jesus-Izas (of Gamala) and supposedly defending Galilee from the Romans. But he was much keener on the former strategy than the latter, for obvious reasons, and was accused of siding with the Romans on numerous occasions. After all, this was a Judaean army commander (knight) who had already been on a secret mission to see Emperor Nero (and Vespasian) in the autumn of the previous year.

According to *Mort,* the war between Lancelot (Josephus) and King Arthur (Jesus) had degenerated into a stalemate, with neither gaining the upper hand. It was finally ended by Lancelot and Gawain, Arthur's nephew, engaging in single combat. It was a hard-fought fight but Lancelot, the younger of the two, wins the contest but spares the life of Gawain. But matters then went from bad to worse for King Arthur, because the Romans arrived in their country, destroying entire cities. And this time-line equates very well with the arrival of Vespasian and the Roman army in Judaea in April AD 67. A messenger came to the king and said:

> "Sir, I bring you bad news ... Sir, the Romans have entered your land; they have already burned and destroyed Burgundy and injured and killed the people and pillaged the land. Without doubt they will send an army against you this week ... and you have never seen such a large army." (*Mort* ch20 n205)

This is a contention that makes little or no sense for the 6th century Britain and Gaul in which these battles are supposed to have been fought. *Quest* places these events in the late 5th or early 6th century, with Galahad, Lancelot's son, sitting in the Perilous Seat 454 years after the crucifixion, or in the 480s according to the classical chronology. But there was no Rome in the late 5th century. The Western Roman Empire officially ended in 480, and so not only could there not have been a Roman invasion of the region, but there were no Romans left to invade, and so the chronology being presented here is completely wrong. In reality this is a story about 1st century Judaea, not late 5th century Britain, and Legatus Vespasian had just landed in Judaea with a huge Roman army.

Mordred

Mort ends with King Arthur finding out that his son, Mordred, had taken control of his realm while he had been away fighting the Romans, and Queen Gwenevere had fled to the 'Tower of London' for safety (or as his lover, according to some manuscripts). All of which appears to be a retelling of the saving of Queen Gwenevere by Lancelot, and their fleeing to the Dolorous

Tower or castle. But which of these stories is the original and which is the reproduction is difficult to tell.

A great battle ensues between Arthur and his son on 'Salisbury Plain', which ends up with the decimation of both armies and Mordred dead and Arthur mortally wounded. Arthur then asks a knight called Girflet to take him to the Ancient Black Chapel, and to throw Excalibur into a nearby lake, as per popular mythology. Arthur dies shortly afterwards and his sister, Morgan le Fay, takes his body by ship and sails away. Lancelot then declares war on the sons of Mordred and defeats the tattered remains of Mordred's army, before retiring to become a monk in a hermitage. Girflet eventually finds himself back at the Ancient Black Chapel and sees two new tombs, one for a knight called Lucan and the other for King Arthur. He asks the hermit if this is really Arthur's tomb and he is told it most assuredly is. However, in *Post Quest* the hermit gives a different answer, for he says:

> I think it is, for two ladies brought the body of a knight on a litter ... they told me it was King Arthur ... Then Girflet went to the tomb and saw nothing (inside) except for Arthur's helmet ... he showed the tomb to the hermit and said: "my lord isn't here, I want you to be my witness." said Girflet, "So I will go to find out how King Arthur died. Truly he is a mysterious king, whose death no man shall know." (Post Quest ch158 n471) (Author's brackets.)

The reason for this strange story of a battle between King Arthur and his son Mordred, remained a bit of a mystery for a long time during this research. It not only made for a poor fictional story, with the great hero having a traitorous son who turns on his own father and kills him, but there appeared to be no obvious parallel between this account and the history of King Izas-Jesus-Manu of Edessa. The only oblique evidence lay in the fact that King Izas-Jesus did not receive the support he expected from his brethren and followers who lived 'beyond the Euphrates' (ie: in Edessa and perhaps Palmyra). As Saul-Josephus says in the introduction to his *Jewish War*:

> Those Jews also who were for innovations, then rose up when the times were disturbed ... Some hoped for gain, and others were afraid of loss in such troubles; for the Jews hoped that all of their nation which were beyond Euphrates would have raised an insurrection together with them. (War, Preface 2)

So the hoped for support from Edessa and Palmyra never materialised, but the mystery remained. And then a breakthrough was made, which was the realisation that King Evalach-Mordrain of Sarras-Palmyra was named after the son of a Babylonian king who had destroyed Jerusalem and its Temple. But in late 1st century Judaea the (Babylonian) king who had just destroyed

Jerusalem and its Temple was actually King Jesus-Izas Manu of Edessa - the biblical Jesus. So if we draw a *pesher* parallel between these two stories, then King Evalach-Mordrain must have been the son of the biblical King Jesus-Izas. And if Arthur was a covert pseudonym for Jesus, then Prince Mordred and Prince Mordrain just have to be the same person - the son of King Arthur-Jesus.

Here is King Arthur-Jesus' son, King Evalach-Mordred-Mordrain, and he is covertly but clearly mentioned in *History* as being the king of Sarras-Palmyra in the post-Revolt era. And the first person that Saul-Joseph(us) (of Arimathaea) went to see after the Jewish Revolt, to negotiate the surrender of the Kingdom of Edessa to the Romans, was this very same king. Furthermore, we now have a good idea why this prince was said to

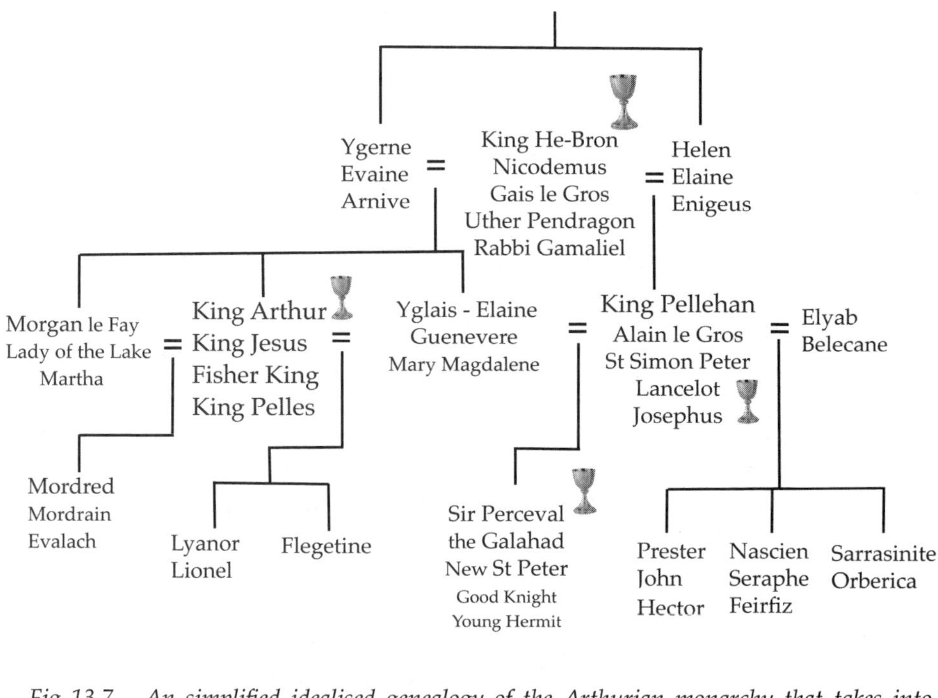

Fig 13.7 An simplified idealised genealogy of the Arthurian monarchy that takes into account Lancelot's infidelity. When Lancelot had an affair with Gwenevere he lost the Galahad title (the Wounded King and Guardian of the Grail), and so he only held it for one day. But the title of the Wounded Grail King also bypassed Alain li Gros, according to 'Merlin Grail'. It is therefore possible that the Lancelot-Josephus character was Alain li Gros, as depicted here. But Alain would have to be much younger than King Arthur-Jesus-Pelles, and Gwenevere might have to be a younger wife. Making King Arthur and Alain half brothers also sorts out a few of the other problems within this complex genealogy.

have rebelled. *Mort Artu* says of this:

> The queen's messenger came before the king (Arthur) ... he then related Mordred's actions: how he had been crowned king of Logres and how all the high-ranking barons who held the lands of King Arthur had paid homage to Mordred, so that if he (Arthur) came there he would not be received as their lord but as their enemy. Then he told him of how he had besieged the queen in the Tower (of London), and pressed the siege every day ... my lady implores you to come to her aid as soon as possible, because if you delay she will be surely captured. (*Mort* ch21 n210.) (Author's brackets)

It was not simply Prince Mordred-Mordrain who had rebelled, but the majority of the nobles in the land. Like Saul-Josephus, they too could see that a war with Rome was a futile exercise that would result in ruin, and so to preserve their lands and status, they had refused to send reinforcements to Judaea and had looked for a prominent figure to rally around. That leader turned out to be Prince Evalach-Mordred-Mordrain, the son of King Arthur-Jesus, and so the scene was set for a conflict between King Arthur-Jesus and his son.

The queen obviously did not agree with this strategy, according to this account of her 'abduction', and so she ended up being besieged in a tower. And since this conflict took place in Syria, rather than Britain, it is likely that Queen Gwenevere would have been held prisoner in one of the funerary Towers at Palmyra, rather than a tower in London (the present Tower of London is 11th century Norman). And these towers would indeed make a very good refuge or prison for a queen, as they are: solidly built like a fortress; only have one entrance; and normally only have one window for someone to escape from. So here was Queen Gwenevere imprisoned in a tower waiting for her hero-husband to return and save her, despite her reputed infidelity with one of King Arthur's knights.

In which case, we can probably take the arguments and comparisons made in earlier chapters, and advance them several steps further. Queen Gwenevere was most probably a priestess, and the priests of Edessa were called Mar, meaning 'bishop'. But since Queen Gwenevere was a lady, perhaps the title Mara מרה is more appropriate. But Mara Gwenevere had been locked in a tower, which is called a *magdal* מגדל, and so the queen was not only closely linked to the Magan star-tower of David, she was now incarcerated within a real tower, a real *magdal*. In the circumstances, perhaps it is not so surprising that she was thenceforth known as Mara Magdal(ah) מרה מגדלה or Mary Magdalene. And since it has also been demonstrated that King Arthur was King Jesus-Izas, the conflation of Queen Mary Magdalene and Queen Gwenevere seems to be almost guaranteed:

Husband king	**Queen wife**
Jesus-Izas	Mary Magdalene
Lord of the zodiac	Bishop of the Tower
Fought the Romans	Incarnation of Venus
Arthur-Uther	Gwenevere
Lord of the zodiac	Bishop of the Tower
Fought the Romans	Incarnation of Venus

Here was Gwenevere-Magdalene, locked in a tower just like Repunzel, awaiting the return of her prince charming who was fighting a desperate

Fig 13.8 The Palmyran funerary tower that Queen Gwenevere may have been imprisoned in. She was waiting for King Arthur-Jesus to return, so she could let her golden hair down from the solitary window.

battle against the Romans. Gwenevere-Magdalene had long golden or ginger hair, as just about every Renaissance painting of her demonstrates, and she was waiting to lower her fine golden tresses from that small window in the Palmyran tower, so her prince charming husband could save her. 'Gwenevere, Gwenevere, let down your golden hair....'

But in this particular case, prince charming never returned. And the reason for his absence was not because Prince Mordred-Mordrain had assumed control of the kingdom and declared war on King Arthur-Jesus, as Arthurian history suggests, but rather because he had assumed control of the kingdom and had refused to send reinforcements. And because the cavalry never appeared over the horizon to relieve the Alamo fortress (the city of Jerusalem), King Izas-Jesus-Arthur was defeated. Prince Evalach-Mordred-Mordrain may have been acting logically, and taking the best advice of all his ministers and barons, but his inaction still sealed the fate of his father.

The king was dead

XIV

Avalon

The king was dead

Or not quite dead. The book *King Jesus* made a compelling argument that King Jesus-Arthur was summarily crucified after the Jewish Revolt, but was reprieved by Saul-Josephus (of Arimathaea) and then taken in chains to Rome. And because Rome was too close to this conflict, with many Jewish factions in the city, King Jesus-Arthur was eventually taken to Fortress Dewa in Britain - a 1st century equivalent of Guantanamo Bay, constructed on the very fringes of the Empire in the AD 70s by Emperor Vespasian. And in a somewhat similar fashion, Geoffrey Monmouth says that King Arthur-Jesus was carried from the battlefield mortally wounded, but very much still alive. He was then placed upon a ship, and sent to Avallach or Avalon:

> He was bourne thence to the island of Avalon for the healing of his wounds, where he gave up the crown of Britain (Edessa) unto his kinsman. (History of Kings bkX1 ch2) (Author's brackets.)

And rather surprisingly for such a famous location within Arthurian history, the nine books of the *Vulgate Cycle* only mention Avalon once.* And even this solitary reference is not in the context that we might expect, for it speaks of Morgan le Fay, the sister of Arthur, and not King Arthur himself. It says that King Arthur invited his long-lost sister to come and live at the court of

* And mention the Lady of Avalon twice.

Camelot, to which Morgan replies:

> Dear Brother, don't ask me this, for I swear to you that I will never go to court. Instead, when I leave here, I will most certainly go to the Isle of Avalon, where the women live who know all the world's magic. (*Mort* ch5 n60)

And that is it. Out of the 3,500 odd pages that comprise the *Vulgate Cycle*, that is the only direct mention we have of Avalon. So if we want to find the location of this fabled burial site, the only clue we have from the *Vulgate* is that this land is famed for its female magicians. In the Roman world the primary land of the magicians was the exotic east: the Zoroastrian Magi from Parthia. But the Magi of the East tended to be male, rather than female. (Although Princess Flegetanis-Flegetine was certainly an exception.)

The other priesthood famed for its arcane wisdom and magic in this era were the Druids of Britain, who may well have had female priests. The name for the Druids probably comes from the Welsh *dryw* meaning 'seer', and so the Druids performed the same prophetic role as the augurs of Rome and the Israelite priests in Egypt. As *Lancelot* says:

> The damsel who carried Lancelot off into the Lake was a fairy. At that time the word 'fairy' was used for all women who used magic, and at that time there were more of them in Great Britain than in other lands. According to the British

Fig 14.1 The Last Sleep of Arthur in Avalon, Edward Burne-Jones.

> Chronicles, they knew the power of words, stones and herbs. (Lancelot ch6 n38)

But was the mention of Avalon really a reference to Britain, or was it another cryptic reference to Syrio-Judaea? The clue here is that the Lady of the Lake was also known as the Lady of Avalon, the sacred isle where the magical sword Caliburn (Excalibur) was forged. And the Lady of the Lake was called Ninanne or Viviane, the princess who took Lancelot away from her mother, when the lands of Gaunes and Benoic were invaded by King Claudas (Vespasian). The misspelling between Ninanne and Viviane may be due to the Greek 'v', which is the 'n' consonant, and this may suggest that a Greek text was involved at some point in time in these translations.

But who was this magical Lady of the Lake? The first piece of evidence that points to her identity, is that she was known as a fairy: a magician and sorceress. And the only other famous fairy in this tale is Morgan le Fay, the sister or half-sister of King Arthur. This link between the Lady of the Lake and Morgan le Fay is supported by Layamon in his *Chronicle of Britain*, who calls the Lady of the Lake 'Argante', which is no doubt a corruption of Morgan(t). This suggestion is also supported by Geoffrey of Monmouth's short poem *Life of Merlin*, which says that Morgan le Fay was the chief of the witches at Avalon:

> The Isle of Apples which men call 'The Fortunate Isle' (Avalon) gets its name from the fact that it produces all things of itself, as the fields there have no need of ploughs or tenant farmers ... There nine sisters rule by a pleasing set of laws those who come to them from our country. She who is first of them is more skilled in the healing art, and excels her sisters in the beauty of her person. Morgan is her name, and she has learned what useful properties all the herbs contain, so that she can cure sick bodies ...
>
> There after the battle of Camlann we took the wounded Arthur, guided by Barinthus to whom the waters and the stars of heaven were well known. With him steering the ship we arrived there with the prince, and Morgan received it with fitting honour, and in her chamber she placed the king on a golden bed and with her own hand she uncovered his honourable wound and gazed at it for a long time. At length she said that health could be restored to him if he stayed with her for a long time and made use of her healing art. (Life of Merlin)

Monmouth's *Life of Merlin* contains one of the first references to Avalon, and it closely links Morgan le Fay, Avalon, and the death of King Arthur. The Barinthus helmsman mentioned here is an equivalent of the Greek Charon, who ferried the dead across the river Styx to Hades, the land of the dead. This was the guy that you did not pay, until he got you to the other side. But remember that Charon was the helmsman of the underworld, and therefore an equivalent of the ferryman who guided the barque of the Sun-god Ra across the heavens.

In which case, the most obvious explanation for Avalon is that it is simply a Celto-Norman equivalent of the Greek Elysian Fields: a special land of the dead similar to Hades, but reserved for demigods and heroes. Like Avalon, the Elysian Fields were located across Okeanos, the sea that encircled the known world. Which is why the extremities of the circular Mappa Mundi in fig 14.9, that lie beyond the peripheral Okeanos sea, are marked with the letters M.O.R.S., the Latin for 'death'. In addition, the Elysian Fields were known as the Fortunate Isle, the same title that Monmouth gives to Avalon, and so we appear to have a direct correspondence here between Avalon and the Greek Elysian Fields. In his *Odes*, the 5th century BC Greek poet Pindar said of the Elysian Fields:

> The good receive a life free from toil, not scraping with the strength of their arms the earth, nor the water of the sea, for the sake of a poor sustenance. But in the presence of the honored gods, those who gladly kept their oaths enjoy a life without tears ... Those who have persevered ... follow Zeus' road to the tower of Cronus, where ocean breezes blow around the island of the blessed, and flowers of gold are blazing, some from splendid trees on land, while water nurtures others. (Odes 2.59–75.)

Yet this is more or less how Monmouth describes Avalon. In which case, it would appear that Avalon was nothing more than an Arthurian version of the Elysian Fields. But there may be more to Avalon than this, because the quote from Monmouth's *Life of Merlin* also cryptically links Avalon with the very secular and very historical tax revolts against Imperial Rome - because it says that the land of Avalon had no need for ploughs or tenant farmers *(colonis)*. So the Isle of Avalon may well be a temporal abode, as well as a spiritual paradise.

The British and Jewish revolts against Rome were primarily tax disputes, and the Judaean dispute was described in some detail in the gospel parable of the tenant farmer who refused to pay his rent (Math 21:33), as we saw in the last chapter. What Jesus-Izas was explaining in this parable, is that the Romans were living on Nazarene-Edessan lands in Syrio-Judaea, and so King Jesus was the landlord and the Romans were the tenant farmer. But a tenant farmer (the Romans) should pay rent to the landlord (King Jesus), and not the other way around. And this is why, according to the gospel parable, the evil tenant farmer (the Romans) deserved to be killed by the Landlord (King Jesus). Which is exactly what happened at the outbreak of the Jewish Revolt (the Nazarene Ebionite Revolt).

This simple explanation for this parable is supported by the Roman method of taxation, which was called 'tax farming'. Tax collectors like Vespasian, before he became a military commander and emperor, 'farmed' the land for taxes. A certain proportion of this 'farming income' was sent back to the treasury in Rome, while the rest was retained locally for regional expenditure and for the tax collector's own pocket. These were the sinful 'publicans' or tax collectors that Jesus consorted with in Matthew 9:10-11 and 11:19. However, these particular *publicani* tax collectors were not Roman, these were Jesus' own domestic *publicani* who gathered the income needed to maintain his own Kingdom of Osrhoene or Edessa.

And yet the term Monmouth has used for these 'tenant farmers', that Avalon apparently did not need, is quite revealing. This is a Latin text, but instead of calling these unwanted farmers in Avalon *agricolas* they are being called *colonis* meaning 'settlers' or 'colonists'. And yet this is what Rome called the cities it established in the outer regions of the Empire - *coloniae*. And so Monmouth's story is not simply alluding to Roman colonists and their Imperial taxation, it specifically mentions them and states that Avalon did not need them. The Isle of Avalon was indeed a Fortunate Land because it had no need of tenant farmers - it had no need of Roman colonists ploughing (tax farming) its lands.

Fig 14.2 Morgan le Fay, the sorceress of Avalon. Monmouth links Morgan with The Lady of the Lake, who raised Lancelot when he was a child. Painting by Frederick Sandy. Note that Sandy has depicted Morgan wearing the leopard skin of the Egyptian priesthood, the same 'animal skin' that John the Baptist wore.

Within the 1st century Roman Empire, there were two potential tax-free lands in which the temporal version of this semi-mythical island of Elysium-Avalon could have been located. Firstly, this may be a reference to Syrio-Judaea once more. Rome should not have been taxing most of Syrio-Judaea because the entire east of this region had been given to the Babylonian Edessans tax-

Fig 14.3 King Arthur and Morgan le Fay (the Lady of the Lake) sailing across the waters to Avalon. Note the anachronistic armour worn by King Arthur. Painting by Frank Topham (1838-1924).

free, by Emperor Octavian-Augustus. Secondly, this temporal Avalon may also be a reference to Britain. As we saw in Chapter II, Magnus Maximus and Constantine III had both led revolts against Rome, which were no doubt partly provoked by taxation. So in both of these regions we see a tax-dispute with Rome that ended in defeat for the local kings. And so the temporal 'Fortunate Isle' - Monmouth's tax-free Isle of Avalon - could either be a reference to Syrio-Judaea or to Britain.

And the British option is further enhanced through the compelling argument made in *King Jesus*, that King Izas-Jesus of Edessa had been captured after the Jewish Revolt and sent into exile in Fortress Dewa in Roman Britain, which had been purpose-built to hold these dangerous rebels. This was a remote location that had been deliberately chosen in order to distance King Jesus-Izas from his power-base in Syrio-Judaea; and in the mid AD 70s, the furthest one could possibly get from Judaea within the Roman Empire, was Fortress Dewa in Britain. And this is why the later 12th and 13th century Arthurian authors chose Britain as their alternate location for the history of King Jesus-Izas of Syrio-Judaea. King Jesus-Izas ***had*** lived in Britain, albeit as a prisoner of Rome, and so it was entirely appropriate that the history of his life was tagged onto the history of Britain in some manner. And by attaching the father of King Jesus-Arthur onto the royal-imperial family of Emperor Constantine III, this is exactly what these authors had achieved.

And while Morgan le Fay would certainly not have been in Britain before the Jewish Revolt, it is highly likely that she did go there afterwards. Jesus-Izas-Arthur's wounds had not been received in battle, they were the result of his summary crucifixion after the Jewish Revolt. And if Morgan le Fay was acting as Jesus-Izas' physician, then she too would have ended up in the British version of Avalon - in Fortress Dewa in Chester. And so it was Morgan le Fay who would become the mistress of Avalon, just as the *Vulgate* maintains. Please see *King Jesus* for a detailed discussion about this fortress, its unique Temple of the Zodiac, and the many reasons why the biblical Jesus-Izas of Edessa may have been exiled and incarcerated there.

Perceval and the Grail

It is only *Merlin Grail* that mentions the location for Avalon, and even then only in vague terms. At the beginning of this story, Jesus in spirit form* foretells the life of Alain li Gros and the Grail family. Alain is said to be the nephew of Joseph(us) of Arimathaea here, but this is merely the same old chronological

Fig 14.4
Phryne, an Athenian courtesan, enjoys the delights of the Elysian paradise. Painting by Henryk Siemiradzki, 1889.

dislocation we have seen many times before, and Alain is much more likely to have been one and the same as Saul-Joseph(us) (of Arimathaea). *Merlin Grail* then says that all of the main players in this saga will depart for new lands. Bron-Hebron is the Fisher King and Grail Guardian and so he takes the Holy Grail-stone and goes to the west. An unidentified Petrus or Peter follows Bron with a 'letter' or 'manual of secrets' for the Grail. Perceval follows Bron to the west at a later date. And then Alain is sent to 'strange lands', along with his brother-disciples. And since Alain has been identified as Joseph(us), the 'strange lands' he was sent to must surely be a reference to Joseph(us) of Arimathaea being sent to Sarras-Palmyra with 75 disciple knights by Emperor Vespasian.

And remember that when Arthurian history talks about the Holy Grail it is often referring to the Ark of the Covenant, because these sacred artifacts were two sides of the same coin. As we saw in Chapter X, Saul-Joseph(us) (of Arimathaea) was the previous Guardian of the Grail, but he deliberately likened himself to Uzziel or Izziel, the Torah's Guardian of the Ark. And as we saw in *Jesus, King of Edessa,* the Elagabal Grail-stone was depicted on Edessan coinage as being a rectangular box. Clearly, the Ark of the Covenant was simply the Bethel-box that contained the sacred Holy Grail-stones, just as it says in Deuteronomy 10:5.

But why was a separate 'Peter' carrying the 'manual of secrets' for the Grail, when either Bron, Alain or Perceval was the Guardian of the Grail-stone in the mid to late 1st century? The Peter or Kephas rock was a formal Nazarene title for the Guardian of the Holy Grail-stone, as we saw in Chapter VI, and so the Peter Kephas mentioned here must be a reference to either Bron, Alain or Perceval. And when Bron the Peter finally passed away, the next Peter in line was actually his grandson, Perceval the Peter. In the following quotes Robert Boron is actually using Petrus, the Latin form of Peter:

> Give the letter (manual of secrets) to Petrus (Peter) and bid him to go wherever he thinks best ... and he will tell you that he intends to go to the west, to the vales of Avalon ... You never saw a message more surely entrusted than this. I, Petrus

* This sounds more like Saul-Joseph(us) of Arimathaea talking, rather than the spirit of Jesus. Just like Muhummad, whose commands always conveniently came 'from god', so the Arthurian Joseph(us) often has a disembodied Jesus telling him what to tell people to do. This is rather like a little boy saying that he will get his big brother to beat up his enemies. Most people grow out of this phase by the time they are teenagers, but Joseph(us) and Muhummad never did - instead, they turned their imaginary 'big brother' into worldwide religions.

> (Peter), shall go to the Valley of Avalon, a lonely place in the west. (Merlin Grail p41) (Author's brackets.)
>
> When you have told Bron all this, commend the Holy Grail into his keeping, and all who hear tales of him will call him the Rich Fisher King, because of the fish he caught ... just as the world is and always will be moving towards night, so must Bron and his people move towards the setting Sun, into the west. As soon as the Fisher King has the Grail he must journey westwards wherever his heart leads him. And where he comes to rest there he must await the coming of his son's son. (Merlin Grail p42) (p62 says Alain also went to the west.)

In the second quote, Bron-Hebron is both the Fisher King of Pisces and the Guardian of the Holy Grail-stone. And so although *Merlin Grail* does not clearly identify the Peter, he just has to be Bron, the Guardian of the Grail-stone who was instructed to go to Avalon in the west. And since Bron Peter could hardly travel to the west from Britain, this has to be an account of Joseph(us) of Arimathaea in Judaea instructing Bron and Perceval (his son's son) to travel westwards from Judaea. Again we see that this has been a Syrio-Judaean story, right up until this point.

There are a number of contradictions in this account, because Bron-Hebron-Ban-Boni is likely to have been too old to travel to the west. In fact, he should have been dead by this time. So if we interpolate the confusing and conflicting assertions in this story, the true meaning is probably as follows (with all of these events happening in the late 60s and early 70s):

Fig 14.5
The Ark of the Covenant depicted in a small temple on a coin of King Wael of Edessa. This box is a Beth-El, a House of God that housed the sacred Holy Grail-stone(s). The Ark was located at Sogmatar near Edessa, in the 2nd century.

The Grail family are advised that they must go to the west.
Bron bequeathed the Grail to Perceval-Galahad in Judaea.
Bron (Ban) died shortly afterwards, much as *Lancelot* says.
Alain-Josephus is sent to 'strange lands' (Sarras-Palmyra).
Bron goes to the west. But this surely refers to his mortal remains.
Perceval Galahad the Peter also travels to the west.

And this agrees with the broad outline of the story narrated thus far. Monmouth did say that the father and uncle of King Arthur (Jesus) were buried at Stonehenge, so perhaps this explains how they got there. And the only real difference to the account in *History*, is that the (second) journey of Perceval-Galahad is now said to be towards the west rather than to Sarras Palmyra.

And the evidence confirming that this story is actually a hoary old history of events in Judaea, rather than a fantasy devised in 13th century Normandy, comes from the *Panarion* or *Against Heresies*, by the 4th century Epiphanius of Salamis. As we saw in Chapter VII the *Panarion* relates a story that is very similar to this Arthurian history; about a 4th century Count Josephus from the court of Constantine I, who was easily confused with Josephus Flavius. But this same text then goes on to say that this same 4th century Josephus received the Holy Grail and its manual of secrets:

> When Ellel (Gamaliel?) was dying he asked for the bishop who then lived near Tiberias ... For he had sent for him by Josephus, as though he were a doctor ... The bishop summoned the servants and ordered water prepared, as though intending to give the patriarch, who was very sick, some treatment for his illness ... And sending everyone out from pretended modesty, the patriarch **vouchsafed the chalice and the holy mysteries** (to Josephus and the bishop). (Panarion 4:30 Ebionites 5-7.) (Author's brackets.)

The *Panarion* is a 4th century text, from long before Norman Arthurian history was crafted. And while this text is a critique of perceived heretical beliefs, and may therefore suffer from distortion and embellishment, it is not intended as fiction. And the presence of a humble chalice cup at a deathbed scene is hardly something that a theologian is likely to get too animated about.

And yet this story of a Grail-chalice and a separate oral instruction or a letter of 'holy mysteries' being passed on to both Josephus and an unnamed bishop, is uncannily similar to the story in *Merlin Grail*. In *Panarion* we have an account of a patriarch called Ellel, who is supposedly descended from the family of the 1st century patriarch Gamaliel, passing on a Holy Grail-style chalice and its manual of secrets to his successor. And yet the 'Count Josephus' who oversaw this transfer was said to be easily confused with the 1st century's Saul-Josephus Flavius, as we saw in Chapter VII. In which case, this appears to be a 1st century story that has been deliberately and conveniently relocated into the 4th century, to distance it from the gospels, just as most of Arthurian history has been likewise displaced and relocated.

But if this is the same story that Arthurian history was narrating, then the source text that *Merlin Grail* and the *Vulgate* were using was obviously very old indeed. If Epiphanius of Salamis can tell a story in the 4th century, that has eventually been included in *Merlin Grail*, then the original source manuscript for both of these accounts must date from before this time. In addition, this particular chapter in *Panarion* is criticising Nazarene Ebionite teachings, and so this story must contain elements extracted from Nazarene Ebionite history and teachings - the history of the Church of Jesus and James. And this Nazarene Ebionite history appears to be closely related to Arthurian history, just as we might expect, including these Nazarene Ebionites possessing a secret and sacred Arthurian-style Holy Grail chalice.

Rather than being a 4th century story, this account in *Panarion* is much more likely to have been a 1st century history. And so this unknown elderly Ellel must surely be the venerable Gamaliel (Gamal-Ellel), who was a supporter and defender of the disciples in Acts 5:34 and the tutor of Saul-Josephus in Acts 22:3. But we have already seen that the Grail Guardian who was on his deathbed was actually Bron-Ban-Boni, the father of Alain li Gros. This would again imply that Bron-Ban and Gamaliel were the same person, which is what was tentatively suggested in Chapter X. And this can be further confirmed from another source. Acts of the Apostles identifies the tutor of Saul as being Gamaliel, as we have seen, and yet Josephus' *Life* identifies the tutor of Josephus Flavius as Banus. In which case, surely the conflated Saul-Josephus must have been tutored by a conflated Gamaliel-Ban-Banus-Bron-Boni - or perhaps Nicodemus for short.

Thus Saul-Josephus was at this touching deathbed-scene not simply because he was an acolyte, disciple and pupil of Gamaliel, but quite possibly because he was his son, just as the biblical Acts and Josephus' *Life* imply. And because the aged Gamal-Ellel was departing this life, Saul-Josephus has summoned the next Guardian of the Holy Grail, so that he can receive the Grail and its manual of secrets from the dying master. And this is the same touching deathbed scene that is recorded in *Merlin Grail* in the following quote:

> Then the aged Bron placed the vessel in Perceval's hands, and from it came a melody and a perfume so sweet they thought they were with the angels in Paradise. Bron, who was well advanced in years ... spread his arms wide to form a cross, and offered his thanks to the Lord. And with that he passed away. (Merlin Grail p155.)

And the vital information that *Panarion* had purposely omitted, is the fact that the wise old sage who was on his deathbed was called Bron-Hebron-Boni, the father of Alain li Gros (Saul-Josephus). As we have seen previously, *Merlin Grail* indicates that the Grail jumped a generation for some reason, and so the succession of Grail Guardians is likely to have been as follows:

Grail Guardian	Holder	Relationship
Gamaliel-Bron	yes	Father of Alain-Josephus
Alain-Josephus	no	Son of Bron-Ban-Boni
Perceval-Galahad	yes	Son of Alain-Josephus

And so the quote from Epiphanius' *Panarion* was actually a record of the Holy Grail being transferred from Bron to Perceval in the late 60s. And surprisingly, there is some evidence for this in the Gospels. In Acts 5:34 Gamaliel (Gamal-Ellel) stood up in the Judaean Sanhedrin parliament and addressed the high priest and his council, and defended the biblical disciples against charges of heresy. And the leader of the disciples at this time, who was speaking in this very meeting, was St Simon the Peter.

Jesus had already nominated Simon as the new Peter-Kephas, the new Guardian of the Grail-stone. But Simon could only become the new Peter after he had received the Grail from its former keeper. And so if Gamaliel was the old Peter, then Simon must have become the new Peter after this assembly at the Sanhedrin. And since Bron and Gamaliel have already been linked with one another, it is only fitting that we should go on to discover that the son of the biblical Gamaliel was similarly called Simon. And so both Gamaliel and Bron appear to have had sons or grandsons called Simon. And just like the biblical St Simon Peter, Simon ben Gamaliel was also a leader in the AD 60s Jewish Revolt:

> (Gamaliel) is also treated as the originator of many legal ordinances; as the father of a son, whom he called Simeon, after his father's name. (Catholic Encyclopaedia.)

> Beside his son, who inherited his father's distinction and position, and who was one of the leaders in the uprising against Rome, a daughter of Gamaliel is also, mentioned. (Jewish Encyclopaedia, Gamaliel)

Readers may have noticed that this analysis does give us some contradictions. These many similarities and connections sometimes indicate that the gospel St Simon Peter was one and the same as Saul-Josephus, because both have been identified with Alain li Gros on occasions. But this is simply not possible. Their characters are entirely separate within the New Testament accounts; they had widely opposing viewpoints; they argued with each other; and Saul-Josephus would never have become a Peter-Galli eunuch under any circumstance. Although Saul-Josephus could well have been a Lancelot-type character, who was only a Galli for one day and lost the title because of an amour with the queen (Quest 36:126).

However, many of the other similarities discussed in Chapter VI indicated that St Simon Peter was actually Perceval-Galahad, rather than his father. But that hardly seems possible, because Perceval-Galahad would have been far too young to have been involved in some of St Peter's gospel events: especially his appearance in the Epistle to the Galatians in the 50s.* And his promotion to Grail Guardian at such a young age seems optimistic too, because any potential son of Saul-Josephus-Alain could only have been a teenager at the time of the Jewish Revolt. However, since 'Peter' was a title that passed through the generations, there could have been several Peters in the gospel stories who have been blended into one. And remember that Bron and Alain held the same title, they were both surnamed 'Gros' meaning twelfth of the twelve (or perhaps first of the twelve). So the St Peter who makes a fleeting appearance in Galatians could have been Bron li Gros Peter, rather than Alain Peter or Perceval Galahad Peter.

In which case, the Grail succession given in *Merlin Grail* was probably correct. Robert de Boron claimed that the primary Grail Guardian or Peter during this era was Bron-Hebron, the father of Alain-Josephus-Lancelot. The Grail-chalice and the Peter title then skipped a generation past Alain-Josephus, because of his carnal thoughts and his affair with the queen, and onto Perceval the Galahad instead. So it was the younger Perceval Galahad who was the primary St Peter within the gospel stories, not Bron or Alain.

While this is not a comprehensive solution, it does explain most of the potential problems within these accounts. In this revised scenario, Saul-Josephus could easily have been arguing bitterly with a St Peter in the 50s, as he does in Galatians, because the Peter at this time was Bron, the father of Alain-Josephus. And so Alain-Josephus was arguing with his father, which is entirely reasonable and likely. And Perceval could well have been knighted as the new Peter and Galahad by Jesus-Izas, even though he was only a teenager at the time, because his father had forfeited the position and title. And this would have been the very same initiation ceremony that took place on the Mount of Olives, just before Jesus was arrested, as we saw in Chapter VI. (See Mark 14:51-52.)

* Interestingly, although Galatia is identified as being in Anatolia, the Thayer Greek Lexicon says that Galatia refers to the Galli. And although this is not specifically a reference to the Galli priesthood, this does remain an interesting possibility.

Zodiac Circle

So where in the west did the Holy Grail go to? Where was this lonely place in the far-off west called Avallach or Avalon, which became the last resting-place of King Arthur? The answer to this may be found in the Aramaic name for a circle which can be either *galiyl* גליל, the name for Galilee, or *khavalah* חוילה, the name for Havalah which is one of the lands that the first river of Eden circled around. But this Havalah circle can also be pronounced as Evalah or Avalah, just as the name for Khavah חוה, the wife of Adam, was eventually pronounced as 'Eve'.

So it is possible that Avallach or Avalon refers to a circle. But this would not be any old circle, this would be the great circle in the heavens above - the zodiac. And anyone wishing to journey to the west, to the land of the dead, would need a boat in the same manner that King Arthur travelled to the west; because the heavens above were one great celestial sea, upon which the Solar barque of Ra sailed every day. And at the very center of these celestial seas, lies the constellation of Ursa Major - the Great Bear symbol for King Arthur. So it is quite possible that Morgan le Fay sailed her small boat out into the heavens and across the celestial seas, and so King Arthur lies in a heavenly Avalon - the greatest of the northern constellations in the heavens above.

However, the old adage of the venerable sages was 'As Above, So Below', and so whatever lies in the heavens above can be mimicked on the Earth below. And one obvious candidate for the terrestrial equivalent of the heavenly zodiac lies on the shores of the Sea of Galilee. The Sea of Galilee is named after a *galiyl* גליל circle, and on the shores of the Sea of Galilee there lies the Hamat Teverya zodiac, a zodiac that was probably made in the 1st century by the Nazarene Galileans. What better location for a burial of a Syrio-Judaean monarch, than beside one of the greatest zodiacs in the Near East. If, of course, the Romans who controlled the region would allow this to happen.

Fortunate Isle

While this suggestion is possible, we have already seen that Joseph(us) told Bron-Peter and then Perceval-Peter to go to the west, to a lonely place as far away as the setting Sun. And that description does not suit the Sea of Galilee very well at all. Judaea lay at the very epicenter of the Medieval world, not the far west, as can be seen on the Mappa Mundi in fig 14.9. But if Alain and

Perceval went to the west, then where exactly did they go to? A possible answer may be found in the 7th century accounts of Isidore of Seville, who said that the Fortunate Isle (Avalon) was situated in the Atlantic to the left of Mauretania. The Roman Mauretania refers to Libya and Algeria, and it is not unreasonably presumed that 'to the left' means 'to the west':

> The name of the Fortunate Isle signifies that it bears all good things, as if happy and blessed in the abundance of their fruits ... Pagan error and the songs of the secular poets have held that these islands to be Paradise because of the fecundity of the soil. Situated in the Ocean to the left of Mauretania, very near the west, they are separated by the sea flowing between them. [1]

Isadore thinks that the fecundity of Avalon was not due to the favourable climate and soil, as the 'secular poets' maintained. But now we know why, because this 'abundance' was actually due to Avalon not being taxed by the Romans. Isadore then says that Avalon lay to the 'left' of Mauretania, which in his day would have referred to North Africa, and this would place Avalon somewhere out in the Atlantic. This strange claim persuaded some Medieval authors to link Avalon with the Canary Islands, which do indeed reside to the

Fig 14.6
The celestial seas of the cosmos, upon which the solar Barque of Ra sailed.

At the center of this cosmos, the very center of the circle of the zodiac, lies Ursa Major, the Great Bear of King Arthur.

west of North Africa. But Isadore did not say 'west' he said 'left'. But what did Isadore understand by 'left'? Where would Isadore have gone to, if he travelled to the 'left' of Mauretania in the 7th century?

In order to see how Dark Age authors viewed the world, we really need to use a Dark Age map, something like the Mappa Mundi from Hereford Cathedral shown in fig 14.9. And while this is a 13th century map we can be certain that it was not the nautical chart that the 13th century crusading navies were using to transport Templar knights to and from Judaea. If this had been the only map available in that era, the crusaders would never have found Judaea and the Crusades would never have begun. And so we can be fairly certain that the Mappa Mundi was based upon a much older ecclesiastic view of the world, something much closer to the map that Isadore might have been using. And where would we end up on this map if we travelled to the left of Mauretania?

The Mappa Mundi places Jerusalem at the very center of the world, as did all ecclesiastical maps, and the entire composition is orientated with east at the top instead of usual north. East was and still is the primary orientation of religious veneration, because the Sun rises in the east; which is why all Christian cathedrals and churches are aligned due east to greet the sunrise. But this east-facing tradition is much older than Christianity and actually goes back to the causeway at Stonehenge and the three causeways that run eastwards from the Giza pyramids. The Stonehenge causeway strides out to the north east and towards the summer solstice sunrise, as will be discussed later. In contrast, the Giza causeways face either due east to the equinox sunrise, or diagonally to the cross-quarter sunrises. See *Tempest & Exodus* for an illustration. And the reason for these orientations was so that the astronomer-priests of Egypt could track the annual cycle of the Sun, and also track the millennial precession of the equinox. To view the progress of precession, the priesthood would need an east-facing causeway to view the rising constellation at the vernal equinox sunrise, and that is what the Third Pyramid causeway provides. And this is why the Aramaic word *imon* or *timon* means both 'south' and 'right side'. The primary orientation for religious veneration was always to the east, and so the south lies on the right side.

Around the perimeter of the Mappa Mundi: east is marked as Oriens (the rising sun); the south is Meridiens (mid-day); the west is Occidens (the setting sun); while the north is Septentrio (the seven stars of the Great Bear). And since the left of this map is north, then the left is the land of Ursa Major, the Septentrio Great Bear, the land of King Arthur. Around the perimeter of the map there are four prominent letters spelling MORS, the Latin for 'death', and so the extremities of this map are being equated to the land of the dead, or the Greek Elysian Fields. So what we have here is a circular map surrounded by Okeanos, the river or sea that encircled the known world, which is being equated with the underworld, the Elysian lands of the dead. But since the heavens above were envisioned as a celestial sea, it is possible that the Mappa Mundi was viewed not just a map but also as a terrestrial equivalent of the zodiac. As Above, So Below.

While this terrestrial zodiac does portray the entire continent of Europe, locating the position of individual countries is not very easy. The best method is to look for the names of the capital cities. To the left of the central city of Jerusalem is Constantinople, and slightly below that is Athens and Greece. Further below Jerusalem is Rome and Italy, and further down towards the bottom of the map is Spain and the Straights of Gibraltar. And if we look to the extreme bottom left quarter of the map, there are some islands all squashed up together. This is England, Ireland and Scotland, with all the major rivers and cities marked upon it.

So if we were to travel to the 'left of North Africa' in order to find Avalon, just as Isadore claimed, then where would we end up? The arrow on this map marks a line that travels to the 'left' of Roman Mauretania or North Africa, and where does this take us? The surprising answer is that Isadore's travelogue takes us directly to Britain, and so Isadore's temporal version of Avalon may well have resided somewhere within the British Isles. Thus Isadore may have been correct.

Temple of resurrection

Although the Elysian Fields were a paradise in the heavens above, far across the celestial seas, the Temple of the Eleusinian Mysteries was a terrestrial temple complex located at Eleusis or Elysis, just to the west of Athens. It was here that the secrets of Persephone's autumn descent into the underworld to see Hades were taught. And since it was Persephone's absence from the world that caused the barren winter, and it was her return in the spring that brought fertility back to the land, this entire 'mystery' may appear to be a simple agrarian cult.

But the cycle of the seasons is intimately connected to the cycle of death and rebirth: the belief and creed of resurrection that became so central to Saul-Josephus' new Simple Judaic Christian creed. And the cycle of the seasons is also intimately connected with and dependent upon, the much greater cycles in the heavens above. Were it not for the rotation of the heavens, there would be no barren season during which Persephone could visit Hades. This is why the four seasons are depicted at the four corners of the Hamat Teverya zodiac, because the constellations and the seasons rotate together in the same heavenly circle and dance. And although we do not know what was taught at Eleusis, we do know that this was an initiatory cult that professed the teaching of lesser and greater mysteries. It would not be surprising to learn that those mysteries contained elements of astronomy concerned with the lesser movements of the zodiac during the solar year, and the greater movements of the zodiac during the precessional cycle.

Yet if the Elysian Fields can have a dedicated temple based at Eleusis,

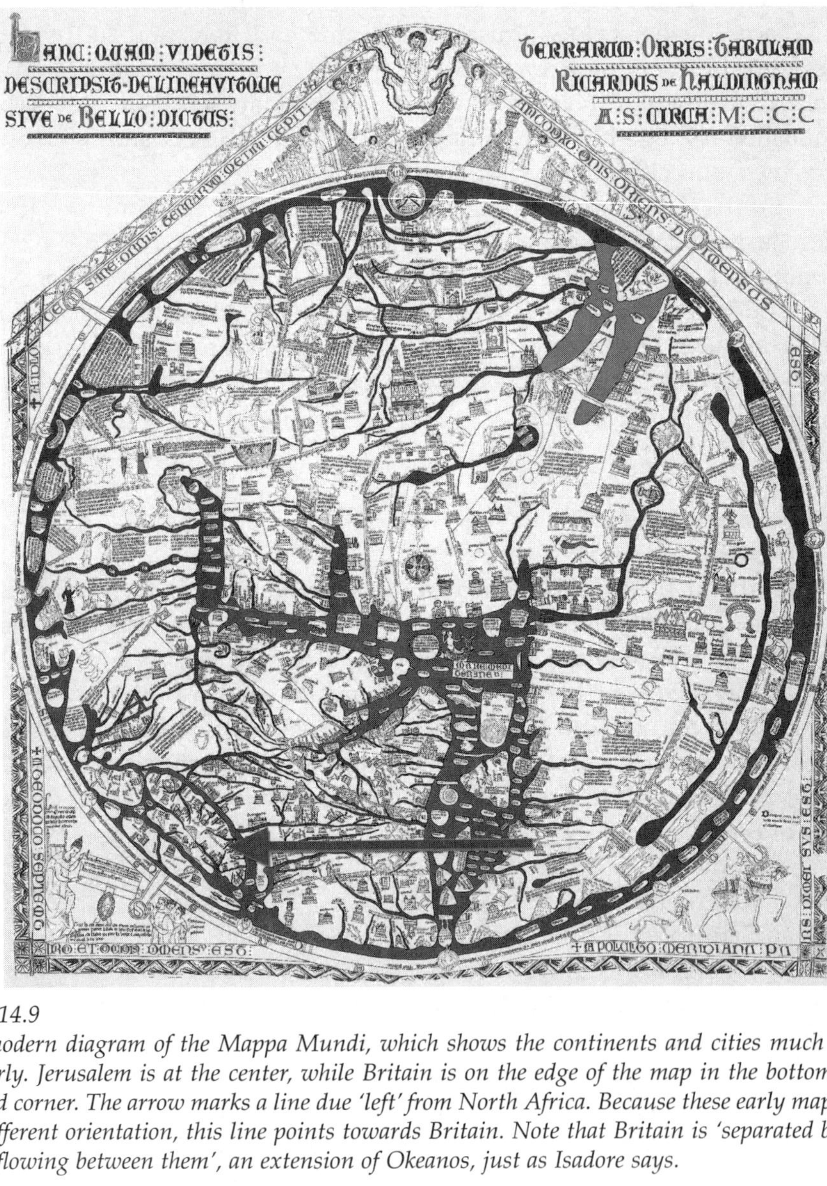

Fig 14.9
A modern diagram of the Mappa Mundi, which shows the continents and cities much more clearly. Jerusalem is at the center, while Britain is on the edge of the map in the bottom left-hand corner. The arrow marks a line due 'left' from North Africa. Because these early maps use a different orientation, this line points towards Britain. Note that Britain is 'separated by the sea flowing between them', an extension of Okeanos, just as Isadore says.

then perhaps the Avalonian Fields may also have had a dedicated temple. And since the Arthurian story has moved to the west, not simply to the land of the dead but also to Isadore's Avalonian Britain, then perhaps that temple may be found in Britain. But if King Arthur was taken to a sacred place in the west called Avalon, then what of his ancestors and descendants? As we saw back in Chapter II, Monmouth, Oxford and Boron, all say that the sepulchre or mausoleum for the Arthurian royal family was the great circle of stones at Stonehenge. King Aurelius Ambrosius, his brother King Uther ben Dragown, and King Constantine (IV), were all buried at Stonehenge.[2]

It is highly unlikely that this desecration of a sacred space would have been allowed when Stonehenge was a functioning Druidic temple of astronomy, because dead bodies were considered unclean within most religions. And although the Christian clergy saw the highly lucrative advantage of allowing the burial of rich patrons within churches, turning entire cathedrals into ritually unclean mausoleums, there are certainly no burials within the precincts of a Jewish synagogue, Islamic mosque, or Hindu Temple.*

Recent archaeology at Stonehenge appears to confirm that the original guardians of Stonehenge likewise did not allow burials within their sacred cathedral, for there are precious few burial remains to be found on this site. Most of the sparse human remains discovered thus far are cremations that had been deposited within the Aubrey holes, around the outer henge-ring, and all of these burials are more recent than the construction era for this site. Although it is possible that the Aubrey holes at Stonehenge were an exception to the sanctity rule, because they lie outside the sacred precinct. If we view the circular Stonehenge as a representation of the circular Earth, as the precessionary diagram in fig 14.12 suggests, then the outer ring of the henge is almost the equivalent of the outer ring on the Mappa Mundi. And the perimeter of the Mappa Mundi was marked with the letters MORS, which refer to the land of the dead. So it is possible that this outer ring of holes around the perimeter of Stonehenge was regarded as a Neolithic Elysian Field - a ring of 56 station points located in the heavenly abode of the dead,

* Except for the supposed shrine and tomb of John the Baptist, which lies in the middle of the Damascus mosque for some reason. But the Damascus mosque was previously a Byzantine cathedral and a Roman Temple of Jupiter before that, and so the shrine probably predates the mosque by a long margin.

The Roman Temple of Jupiter was pulled down to build the Byzantine cathedral in the 4th century, and this was in turn pulled down and rebuilt by the Muslim invaders in the 8th century. But the same Roman pillars were reused each time, and so the Mosque is still substantially Roman.

and depicted upon this huge terrestrial map of the cosmos.

However, it should be stressed that neither Aurelius nor Uther could have been buried at Stonehenge in the era when they died (if these earlier monarchs are indeed references to Edessan royalty, rather than being otherwise unknown British princes). Britain had only just been conquered by the Romans in the mid 1st century, so they could not have been buried in Britain. Besides, the Edessans already had a royal necropolis at Sogmatar, just east of Harran in Syria (now in Anatolia), so the initial burials of both of these kings would surely have been at Sogmatar.

And in addition to the necropolis at Sogmatar, the Edessan royalty had their very own stone-henge at Gobekli Tepe, a Neolithic and megalithic henge that is similar in many respects to the Stonehenge site and lies just 20 km east of Edessa. It is not entirely certain if Gobekli Tepe was a functioning temple during the early Roman era, because it was completely covered with soil at some point in time. But if it was open and venerated in any way by the Edessan monarchy, it is worth noting that many of the large standing-stones are carved as humanoid figures, as if they were representations of giants standing or dancing in a circle. Monmouth calls Stonehenge the Giants' Dance, so is Gobekli Tepe yet another Dance of the Giants?

So the Edessan monarchy appears to have been associated with two very similar megalithic monuments that were constructed thousands of kilometers apart during the Neolithic era, which is an interesting connection or coincidence in itself.* And while the earlier Edessan monarchy could not have been buried at Stonehenge when they died, their remains could easily have been interred there in a later era. By the mid AD 70s, Britain had been conquered; the last of the Druids had been defeated in Anglesey in AD 60; fortress Dewa had been constructed; and Stonehenge was no longer a functioning temple. So by the time that King Arthur-Jesus is likely to have been exiled to Britain in the mid 70s, it is highly likely that Stonehenge lay completely abandoned, and could have been used as a royal mausoleum - a British alternative to the Edessan Gobekli Tepe.

And if King Arthur-Jesus died in Britain in the late 90s, and the Romans would not allow his remains to return to Judaea for political reasons,

* Within classical archaeology, Gobekli Tepe is said to have been constructed in a much earlier than Stonehenge. However, we have to take these claims with a pinch of salt, because we cannot date stone. And if a site is kept clean of organic debris, then we cannot date the site either. However, the Gobekli site is dated to 8000 or 9000 BC, while the earliest carbon dates at Stonehenge are also from 8000 BC. It is entirely possible, therefore, that these two very similar sites share a common heritage.

then where is the most likely place for a secure but sacred burial in a foreign land? Since Arthur was the son of Uther ben Dragown, surely the royal son would be buried in the same royal mausoleum that his father and uncle were reputed to have been buried in - within the precincts of Stonehenge.

Celestial circle

In which case, the possibility exists that the temporal Avalon, the mausoleum for the mortal remains of the Arthurian monarchy, was closely connected with the abandoned temple of Stonehenge. And yet there may be a linguistic connection too, that links Avalon, Stonehenge, and the precessional zodiac.

The foundation for this interesting connection begins at the famous mountain in Hibernia-Ireland, where Stonehenge was said to have stood before Merlin brought it to Salisbury Plain. As we saw in Chapter II, the mountain was called Mount Killaraus or Killara, and it was suggested there that this name was derived from the Aramaic *kil* חיל meaning 'dance'. And so it may have been from 'Killara' that the Stonehenge circle was called the Giants' Dance. And while this link to Aramaic may have sounded unlikely

Fig 14.10
Stonehenge on Salisbury Plain, which was claimed to be the burial site of King Aurelius Ambrosius and his brother King Uther ben Dragown. Was King Arthur-Jesus buried here too? Was Stonehenge the site of the fabled Avalon?

back in Chapter II, we have now seen the great number of Celto-Welsh words and Arthurian names that have been derived from Latin and Aramaic.

And the Welsh scribes would have known all about the word *khil* חיל, because it was derived from Khaviylah or Havilah חוילה, which is the name of the land that the first river of Eden circled around. And every Welsh scribe worth his pot of ink would have known the names of the four rivers of Eden and the lands they ran through. However, Khaviylah חוילה also means 'circle', the encircled land, and this name was derived from *khiyl* חיל meaning 'whirl around' or 'dance'. And there is another closely related word in the Aramaic, which is *giyl* גיל meaning 'circle' and 'rejoice', from which we also derive Galiyl גליל meaning Galilee, the province in Judaea which also means 'circle'. And *giyl* גיל was obviously derived from *khil* חיל.

Readers may wonder where this explanation is going at this point, so let us go back to Stonehenge and see what we can find there. In *Brut Oxford,* Stonehenge is called the Cor y Cewri meaning the Choir of Giants, which was derived from the Welsh *cor* and the Old French *cuer* meaning 'choir', as in a church choir. But the Welsh *cor* may also be related to the Aramaic *khil,* via the standard 'l' to 'r' transliteration, and have a long history that includes

Fig 14.11
One of the megalithic circles at Gobekli Tepe, just 20 km from Edessa in Anatolia. Did the Edessan monarchy know of this sacred site in the 1st century AD? If so, who covered the entire site with soil, and when?

many linguistic connections. Perhaps the best way to illustrate the many connections and derivations of these two interconnected words, is via a long list. Starting with the Welsh and working backwards in time we have:

Language	word		meaning
Welsh	cor (kor)	*cor*	choir in a church
Old French	cuer	*cuer*	choir in a church
Irish	cor	*cor*	turn or twist
Latin	chorus	*chorus*	song and dance in a circle
Greek	khorus	χορος	group of dancers in a circle
Aramaic	khiyl (khiyr)	חיל	dance or whirl around
Irish	Mt Killara		dance mountain
Welsh	cylch (kyrch)	*cylch*	circle or district
Latin	gyrus	*gyrus*	circle or circuit
Greek	gyrus	γυρυς	round or circuit
Aramaic	giyl (giyr)	גיל	circle or district
Aramaic	Galiyl	גליל	Galilee - circle district
Aramaic	Galiylah	גלילה	Galilee - circle district
Aramaic	khavalah	חוילה	encircled
Aramaic	Havilah	חוילה	encircled land of Eden
Aramaic	Khavah	חוה	Havah or Eve (wife Adam)
Greek	Eua (Yewa)	Ευα	Eewah or Eve (wife Adam)

Again we can see that large sections of the Celtic languages have much older and more diverse origins than is commonly supposed. In this case, the progression takes us from the Welsh, through the Old French and Latin, via the Greek, and eventually back into the Aramaic. And it is interesting to see how the more informal Greek and Latin 'dance and song in a circle' has become a solemn Celtic 'choir in a church', no doubt with much merriment and enjoyment being lost along the way.

So *cor (kor), khil* and *cylch* were most probably all derived from the Aramaic *khiyl* חיל, via the standard 'l' to 'r' transliteration. And this gives us the surprising conclusion that Cor and Killara, the two names most closely linked to Stonehenge, were two variants of the same root word, with both meaning 'circle' and 'dance'. And so the Cor y Cewri stone henge and the Mt Killara mountain represent two sides of the same linguistic coin.

This is why many modern Welsh dictionaries translate Cor y Cewri as the Giants' Circle, while Geoffrey of Monmouth interpreted it as the Giants' Dance. This alternate translation is made clear in the Latin version of *History of Kings* which says of the original Stonehenge in Ireland:

> *Cui Merlinus: "Si perpetuo opere sepulturam virorum decorare volueris, mitte pro* ***Chorea Gigantum*** *quae est in Killarao mont Hiberniae."*
>
> Merlin said: "If you want to adorn the sepulchre of these men with a structure that will endure forever, place here the Dance of Giants that is in Mount Killarao in Ireland." (History of Kings, 8:10.)

Here we see that Geoffrey of Monmouth has chosen the Latin Chorea Gigantum (Dance of Giants), rather than the Latin Circus Gigantum (Circle of Giants). So both the mountain and the monument referred to a dance. But what does this 'dance' refer to, exactly? Were these stones merely seen as a ring of giants having a party, like the giant figures at Gobekli Tepe? Or was there a more esoteric and cosmic symbolism concealed within this fabled megalithic dance?

In the first degree of Elysian-Avalonian initiation, this circular dance is actually a reference to a great religions ceremony. The Israelites used to whirl around Mount Seir in a great procession or dance, just as the Torah says in Deuteronomy 2:1. And Muslims still perform this great circular dance around the Ka'ba in Mecca, to this very day. But what the Jews and Muslims will not admit, is that this great circular procession around a temple is actually a reenactment of the movement of the stars and constellations in the heavens above. The priesthood are simply getting their unthinking automaton followers to act out the daily rotation of the heavens and the zodiac. And if the Meccan priests prior to the advent of Islam had changed the symbology of each quadrant in their temple, as the centuries and millennia passed by, then they could reenact the precessional zodiac too.

This is why the temple at Mecca was originally adorned with 360 statues of the gods. No doubt they were all arranged around the perimeter of this circular temple precinct, and each statue represented a degree or day within the annual zodiac. And in a similar fashion, each statue would also represent 72 years within the precessional zodiac, because one degree or day of precession lasts roughly 72 years. But as we saw in Chapter XII, when Muhummad captured Mecca almost without a fight in 631, he ordered all of the 360 idolatrous icons to be destroyed, as it says in Bukhari 2.671, 3.658, 5.583-4, 6.244, and 6.442. But in destroying its own history and heritage, Islam was hollowing out its own heart and ensuring it would be relegated to the gutters of intellectual endeavor.

The closed and unthinking mind of orthodox Islam has completely destroyed the ancient esoteric symbolism upon which these ceremonies were based, and so Islam has withered into being no better than a Vanuatu cargo cult. Genuflecting to Allah in a mosque is no more spiritually or scientifically advanced than a Vanuatu tribesman building an aeroplane and radio out of bamboo sticks, and hoping that this will entice John Frum, the great American god, to return to their lands (with more cargo). All of the major religions have lost a great deal of their ancient esoteric knowledge, but none more so than the deranged and dangerous cult of Islam.

However, just as the temple at Mecca once contained a layout of the precessional zodiac, so too did the Giants' Circle at Stonehenge. But with the demise of the Druids and their esoteric knowledge, this information was also lost to the world. Yet the stones still survive and so we can still see this symbolism today, as was explained in the book *Thoth, Architect of the Universe.* And while the thirty stones of the Sarsen Ring at Stonehenge may look very different to the twelve segments of a zodiac, this merely means that the 30 Stonehenge stones are each separated by 12°, while the 12 zodiac segments are each separated by 30°. In which case, the ancient British year may well have contained thirty months of twelve days each, while the ancient British zodiac may well have contained thirty constellations. It is such a shame that the Druid liturgy has been lost, and we can no longer verify this suggestion.

And Stonehenge and the zodiac do appear to be closely linked within Arthurian history, because in *Merlin Grail* the construction of Stonehenge by Merlin is immediately followed by Merlin's construction of the Arthurian Round Table. It is as if the two projects were linked in some fashion (p92). And if Stonehenge was known to represent the zodiac and the precession of the equinox, just as the Hamat zodiac does, they were indeed intimately linked.

In fact, Stonehenge is a much more advanced precessional diagram than even Hamat Teverya, for it displays the true motion of the axis of the Earth during the precessional Great Year. The precessional motion of the Earth is depicted at Stonehenge by the smaller rings at the periphery of the ditch-and-bank ring, as can be seen in figs 14.10 and 14.12. The great Sarsen Ring represents the Earth itself, while the smaller rings on opposite sides of the henge represent the motion that the Earth's axis describes in the heavens above. The centers of those smaller rings are displaced by 22.5° from the axis of the henge, and this figure can be precisely calculated because of the presence of the 56 Aubrey holes around the perimeter. And in a very similar fashion, the center of the celestial circles described by the real Earth are displaced by 23.5° from the axis of the Earth. This 23.5° is the angle of inclination of the Earth, and it is just 1° different to the Stonehenge equivalent. However, this difference may not be a mistake, because the Earth's angle of inclination varies over the millennia by +/- 1.1°. And this angle was last at 22.5° some 22,000 years ago or even 63,000 years ago, as can be seen in fig 14.13, depending on how far back into the past we wish to go.

Dendera zodiac

There are two possibilities that would explain this 1.0° difference between the angle on the Stonehenge diagram and the Earth's present angle of inclination.

Firstly, the Stonehenge architect may have been studiously accurate with this design, and so the 22.5° ecliptic circles were a deliberate feature that precisely recorded the Earth's inclination when the henge was constructed. If so, then this precise angle can give us a precise date, as can be seen in fig 14.13, and the calculated angle-dates for 22.5° on this graph are 22,000 BC or 63,000 BC. Such early dates would mean that Stonehenge must be very old indeed, and however unlikely such early construction dates may seem, they are geologically and archaeologically possible. The ice-sheets of the Devensian glaciation terminated up in Shropshire, and so Wiltshire remained free of ice and Stonehenge would have survived the Ice Age. And because Stonehenge is a relatively clean site, with virtually no organic carbon-dateable artifacts, it is almost impossible to date this henge with carbon dating. Archaeologists cannot date stone or ditches, only the organic detritus associated with them,

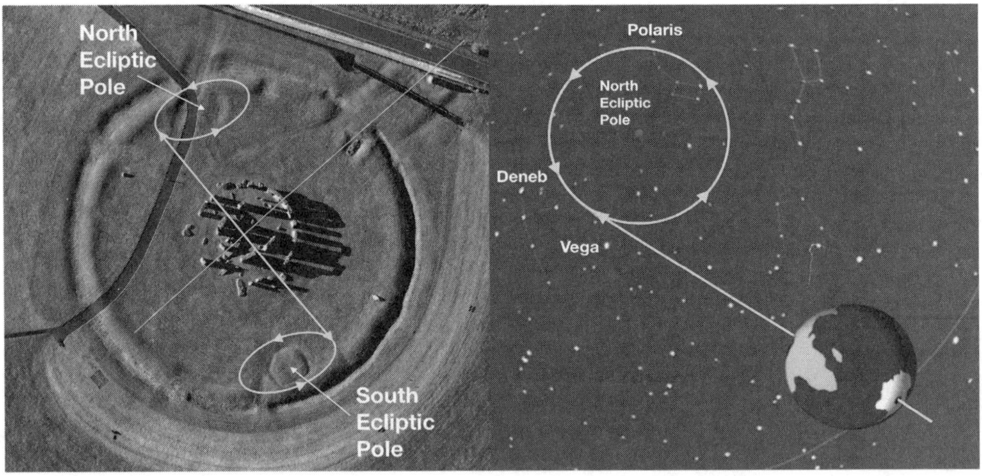

Fig 14.12
The layout of Stonehenge incorporates two smaller circles, which represent the circular motion of the celestial axis or pole of the Earth. These circles are the small inner circles depicted in fig 14.14. The Earth also describes a similar circle in the southern hemisphere, which is not shown on the planisphere animation. The Earth takes 25,680 years to draw these circles in the northern and southern heavens, and it is this same motion that drives the Great Months from Taurus, to Aries and to Pisces. Infrared image courtesy Cirrus Digital Systems, animation from Wiki.

but if a site is kept clean for a few thousand years it becomes impossible to properly date. And this appears to be what has happened at the Stonehenge site, which has no major deposition layers whatsoever.

The recent 2008 SPACES archaeological project at Stonehenge found a jumble of carbon dates from Neolithic all the way through to the 17th century, caused by later post-holes, diggings, pits, stone removals, and animal burrows, which have thoroughly churned up the site down to more than a meter below the current surface level. The majority of this disturbance was from after the site ceased to be a functioning temple, and so there is no stratigraphy to even remotely date the true origins of this henge. The only way we will ever obtain something approaching a secure date for Stonehenge, is by lifting a stone from the Sarsen Ring and hoping to discover datable material underneath it.

The second possible reason for this 1.0° angle difference, between Stonehenge and the present inclination of the Earth, is that the architect may have simply chosen 22.5° because it is precisely 1/4 of 90°. This convenient fraction would make the celestial and ecliptic planes or perimeter circles on a planisphere, be displaced from each other by exactly 1/8 of the diameter of those circles (180° divided by 22.5° equals 8). See fig 14.14 for an illustration of these astronomical circles and their 1/8 ratios of displacement. This

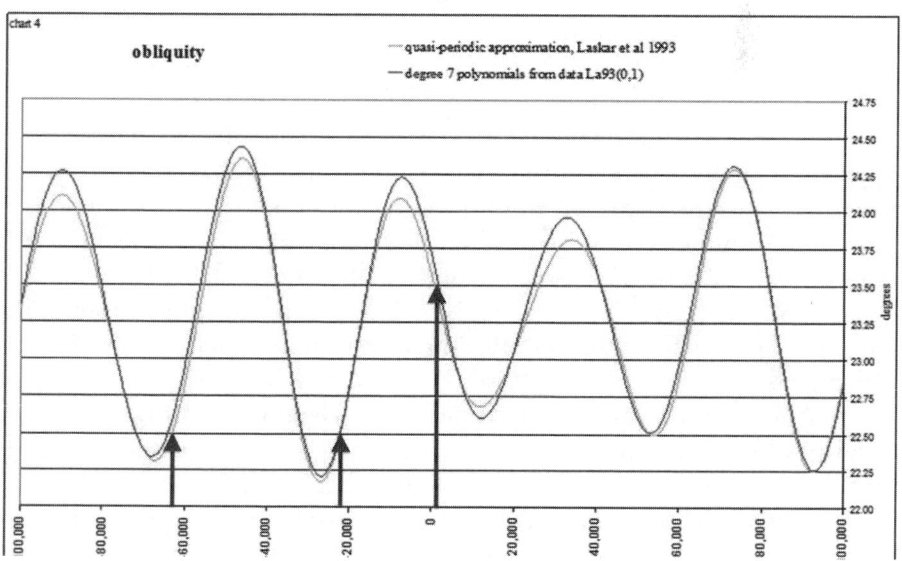

Fig 14.13
The angle of obliquity or inclination of Stonehenge is 22.5°. The Earth was last at that angle of obliquity in 22,000 BC or 63,000 BC. (Graph from Lasker et al. 1986 and 1999.)

conveniently exact ratio would impart this cosmic design with a great deal of harmony and symmetry, for those who subscribe to the role of a creator deity. Curiously, these displacement ratios are exactly half the proportions that have been used on the Dendera zodiac in fig 10.9, where the distance between the perimeters of these circles is exactly 1/4 their diameter. In which case, the Dendera zodiac is a very precise analogue of what we actually see in the heavens above, if we used the Stonehenge angle of inclination for the Earth of 22.5°. And this again demonstrates that the Dendera designer knew the angle of inclination for the Earth, as did the Stonehenge designer.

One presumes that a different displacement ratio for the Dendera zodiac - a 1/4 ratio instead of 1/8 - was chosen for artistic reasons rather than any errors of calculation. Had the true 1/8 diameter displacement ratio between these circles been used, there would have been no room to draw the constellations that lie outside the zodiac circle, and the difference between the ecliptic perimeter and the celestial perimeter would have been all but invisible to the viewer. Fig 14.14 illustrates how these circles would have looked when using the correct displacement ratio, and the very small space between the exteriors of these two circles. However, having made this change, the designer of the Dendera zodiac has cramped the central constellations that lie inside the arcuate or ellipse, resulting in some positional modifications. But devising a two dimensional map of a three dimensional world always involves compromises, even with today's cartographical expertise, and so the Dendera sculptor has actually made a very good job of this composition.

The arcuate (elliptical) outline created by these two circles is often called a Vesica Piscis, which is said to represent the symbol of Pisces. However, since the fundamental design of this symbol was derived from the rotation of the Earth and the precession of the axis of the Earth, which forms two pairs of circles in the northern and equatorial heavens, this is more of a Symbol of Precession than a Symbol of Pisces. The link with Pisces probably evolved because the outline does look like the Christian fish symbol, and the present precessional era is the Great Month of Pisces. But that link is specious, for this elliptical-arcuate outline is actually the Symbol of Precession.

And in a very similar fashion to the Dendera zodiac, the Temple of the Zodiac in Fortress Dewa in Chester has used the same kind of displacement ratios to form the same arcuate Symbol of Precession. And it is highly likely that this layout was deliberately designed to illustrate the same astronomical and precessional layout as on the Dendera zodiac. Fortress Dewa was a Roman prison fortress constructed in Britain in the AD 70s by Emperor Vespasian, where the surviving leaders of the Jewish Revolt may well have been incarcerated. This remote location on the edge of the Empire, was deliberately chosen to be as far from the power-base of these Syrio-Judaean leaders as it was humanly possible to get in this era. Two Temples of the Zodiac were eventually constructed in Fortress Dewa, on the same site in different eras, and although the external dimensions of these temples remained exactly the same, because the site available was restricted, the internal arcuates (ellipses) of these two temples used different displacement ratios, as can be seen in fig 14.15.

The first Temple of the Zodiac (top) used a very simple 1/4 displacement ratio, which is exactly the same as the ratio used on the Dendera zodiac. But as we have already seen, while this ratio may be a convenient fraction of the normal ratio, it results in a narrow arcuate (ellipse) and therefore a narrow and cramped temple. So when it came to building the second temple the new designer wanted to make the central arcuate (ellipse) broader, to make the temple interior larger. But since the external dimensions of the site were constricted to 60 Egyptian thoth or royal cubits, the options available were limited. The ratios that could have been used for this design are as follows (measurements in thoth or royal cubits):

Displacement ratio (circles) fraction	Arcuate width (tc)	Layout circle diam (tc)	Distance btwn circles (tc)
1/4	60	80	20
1/5	60	75	15
1/6	60	72	12
1/7	60	70	10
1/8	60	68.56	8.57

What the designer has done here, is to choose the smallest ratio and therefore the fattest arcuate (ellipse) for the interior of the temple, while still retaining whole numbers for the construction project. Using a true astronomical displacement ratio of 1/8 was possible, but metrologically messy, and so a 1/7 ratio was chosen instead. Despite this modification the designer has managed to retain a good approximation of the true layout of the ecliptic and celestial circles, and also included the division of twelve segments of the zodiac that lie within those circles. So this design is much more complex than a simple Temple of the Zodiac, like the Hamat Teverya zodiac, it is also a temple dedicated to the geometry and apparent movements of the Cosmos.

Interestingly, the dimensions used to create this Temple of the Cosmos were measured in Egyptian royal or thoth cubits. This is the same measurement system that was used by the Israelites, as it states in Ezekiel 43:13, but they were not a Roman unit of measure. So this is a temple that is utterly unique within the Roman world because it: celebrated precession;

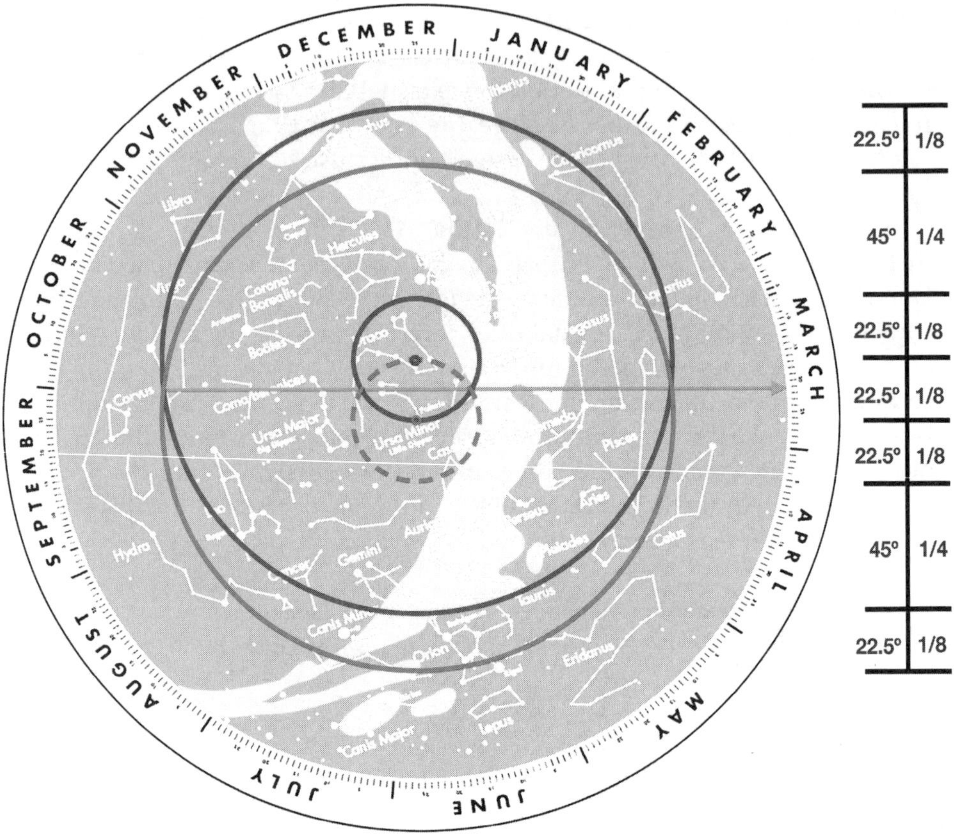

Fig 14.14
The intersection of the ecliptic perimeter (upper red) and the celestial perimeter (lower blue) form a broad arcuate (ellipse) in the heavens above. These are the same circles that are depicted on the Dendera zodiac in fig 10.9. Note that the Dendera circles are further apart, to facilitate the sculptor drawing all of the constellation symbols.

The diagram here is for the current era and so the intersections of the ecliptic and celestial circles almost point towards the conjunction of Pisces and Aquarius (at the vernal equinox on March 21st). This indicates a precessional date of about AD 2000 - the current era. The intersections on the Dendera zodiac point at the conjunction of Taurus and Aries, indicating a much earlier precessional date of 1,750 BC. This planisphere rotates in the usual 'looking up' fashion, like most planispheres do.

The Earth's axis is orientated with the center of the lower blue circle, located on the tail of Ursa Minor, the Pole Star. During precession, the Earth's axis - the center-point of the lower blue circle - rotates anticlockwise around the small upper red circle. It moves 30° every 2,140 years (a Great Month), and the full 360° in 25,680 years (a Great Year). The two inner circles are the same as the circles in fig 3.8, but in fig 3.8 the wheels have not been drawn large enough and so they do not intersect as much as they should.

understood the inclination angle of the Earth; mimicked the Egyptian Dendera zodiac; and was designed in Egypto-Israelite cubits. And yet this peculiar Egypto-Israelite temple was placed in a Roman fortress on the far western fringes of the Empire. But who within the Roman Empire would have been using Egypto-Judaic cubits to portray an Egypto-Judaic celestial map of the heavens? Perhaps readers can see some of the many reasons why it was previously suggested that this temple had been designed by fervent Egypto-Babylonian prisoners from the east of the Empire, rather than by disinterested Roman legionnaires stationed in a lonely outpost in the far west. See the book *King Jesus* for further details.

And since this Temple of the Zodiac at Dewa was constructed on the borders of Wales, it is interesting to see that the most accurate portrayal of the original 'Christian' cross symbol is to be found in the Celtic lands of Wales and Ireland. The Celtic cross is fundamentally an equal-armed cross

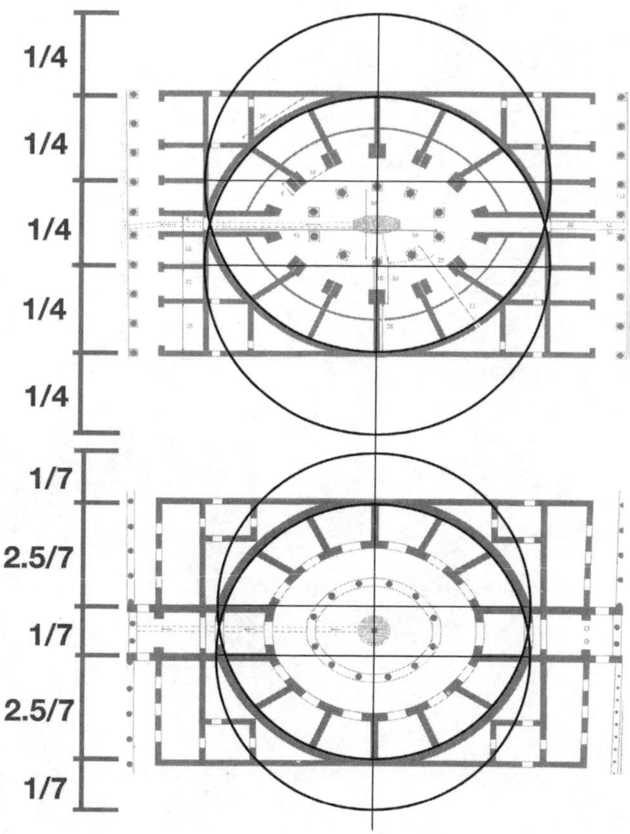

Fig 14.15
The designs of the two Temples of the Zodiac constructed at Fortress Dewa in Chester. The first temple (top) was destroyed, and then a second temple (bottom) was built on the foundations of the first. These designs purposefully use the same arcuate (elliptical) layout and symbolism that is created by the inclination of the Earth and the precession of its axis.

atop a pedestal, and so it is not a representation of a crucifixion cross at all. The circle on this cross represents the circle of the zodiac, while the four equal-length arms represent the four compass stations of the zodiac: the positions of the solstice and the equinox. And so these four quadrants also represent the four seasons of the annual cycle, just as they do on the Hamat Teverya zodiac, and are supposed to do on a circular 'four seasons' pizza.

The cross at Monasterboice in Ireland pictured here is known as Muiredach's High Cross. Interestingly, it depicts King Jesus-Arthur placed at its very center. The two dots either side of Jesus' waist are thought to be the Sun and Moon, while the bird under his feet is the Phoenix, the sacred avian of the precessional cycle. And so this is not a simple representation of

Fig 14.16
An artist's impression of the interior of the Temple of the Zodiac, constructed at Fortress Dewa in Chester. This temple was constructed when Roman rule in Britain was still in its infancy, and it was the finest building in the whole of the province up until that time. With thanks to Julian Baum, Take 27 Ltd. And to Dr David Mason and Peter Carrington of Chester Archaeology.

Jesus pinned to the crucifixion cross, it is King Jesus-Arthur standing at the center of the zodiac, just as either Ursa Major or the Helios-Sun is located at the center of a celestial zodiac. And so this particular Celtic cross could also be viewed as being a depiction of the Arthurian Round Table - with King Arthur again placed at the center of the table and surrounded by his twelve knightly disciple signs of the zodiac.

Giants' Circle - Giants' Dance

It is not simply the layout of Stonehenge that is of interest in this research, so too is its name. As we saw earlier, when Monmouth mentioned Stonehenge he translated the Welsh Cor y Cewri into the Latin 'Dance of the Giants'. He has taken the Welsh *cor* and 'incorrectly' translated it into the Latin *chorea* meaning 'dance'. No doubt this was due to existing traditions that had preserved the Aramaic meaning of this word, as they also appear to have been in the Gaelo-Irish. And yet the resulting dual designation that has been derived for Stonehenge - of Giants' Circle and Giants' Dance - is quite illuminating.

We can all understand how the name Giants' Circle was derived, because Stonehenge is obviously circular. But how did the various authors who have described this monument, know that Stonehenge also represented a Giants' Dance? What Monmouth appears to be describing here, is Stonehenge as an illustration of the precessionary movement of the Earth, as is shown in fig 14:12. As that diagram demonstrates, because of gyroscopic precession the axis of the Earth describes a great circle in the heavens above, and the equatorial constellations of the zodiac follow this motion and appear to waltz around the ecliptic perimeter circle. And if readers spin up a child's spinning top and watch it precess, just as the Earth precesses in its orbit, the seemingly erratic wobbling circular motion that the spinning top performs can best be described as a dance - just like the whirling dance of a Dervish. And so Monmouth was correct, Stonehenge is both a circle and a representation of a cosmic precessional dance.

In fact, without wishing to get diverted from the topic at hand, the Whirling Dervishes are from the Sufi sect, the mystical and esoteric branch of Islam. Dervish means 'The Poor', and so the Dervish appear to have the same prime doctrine as the Nazarene, the Ebionites, the Bethanites, the Boethusians, the Essene, the Kibbutznicks, and the Knights Templar, who were all named as 'The Poor'. In addition, the perfect Sufi is said to be the Qutb, who is considered to be the axis of the cosmos, and the whirling dance they perform represents the planets circling the Sun:

> As planets and stars circle the sun, the Dervishes turn counterclockwise, both around themselves and around the *halka* (circle). They turn first with crossed arms; then, taking flight, they open their arms, holding the right hand up and the left hand down, becoming transparent vessels for bringing divine blessings to earth. [3]

So each Dervish dancer represents the axis of a planet, spinning anticlockwise and circling the solar system in an anticlockwise fashion. Not only that, but the dancer also precesses like a spinning top, altering his angle of inclination just like the Earth does during the precessional Great Year. Readers can now perhaps appreciate how complex esoteric knowledge can be preserved in the most surprising of places: a child's bedtime story;

Fig 14.17
The 10th century Celtic cross at the Monasterboice monastery, just north of Dublin. The cross is effectively an equal-armed cross standing on a pedestal. So the circle represents the ring of the zodiac, while the cross represents the four stations or seasons on the annual zodiac.

The central figure on this Celtic zodiac is Jesus. So once again we see the King Jesus-Arthur figure sitting or standing in the center of the Round Table zodiac and representing (literally) the ring-master of the Cosmos.

an adventure story about knights in shining armour; a religious procession at Mecca; a circular megalithic monument; or even an entertaining dance for modern tourists.

And while the modern tourist will enjoy the exotic pageant and long history of the Dervish dance, do remember that Islam has a long history of persecuting and terminating all such forms of entertainment. The Turkish government, for instance, banned all Sufi sects and their Dervish dances back in 1925, and the custom only managed to survive in small, secretive village gatherings. So modern Islamic iconoclasm is not a simple prohibition against cartoons of Muhummad, as the servile Western media like to portray the problem. Just as night gives way to day, the Islamic prohibitions will inevitably expand into a comprehensive pogrom against all the liberal arts and sciences. The Taliban's destruction of cassette players and iPods; the traditional Islamic ban on bells; the ISIS destruction of statues and monuments; Muhummad's execution of poets; * the Sivas massacre of 37 poets and musicians in Turkey in 1993; and the Turkish ban on Dervish dances, are all manifestations of Islam's deep hatred of personal and cultural pleasures. Where is Islam's equivalent of the great Rio Carnival in Brazil, or the magnificent Patras Carnival in Greece? Western governments agreeing to outlaw cartoons of Muhummad will only be the first step on the long road to self-inflicted cultural suicide.

Yet through their long and perilous history of secrecy, obfuscation and periods of persecution, the Sufi Dervishes have still managed to preserve the motions of the planets and the Heliocentric model of the solar system. The planets do (mostly) rotate anticlockwise and precess on their axes, and rotate anticlockwise around the Sun, just like the whirling Dervish do. (When seen from the northern cultural perspective.) And if a Dervish dancer can preserve the knowledge of the precessional rotation of the Earth, then why cannot the design and outline of a monument like Stonehenge do likewise? If the knowledge of these celestial movements was known at the time these monuments were constructed, it is as simple to encode those celestial motions within the design of a henge as it is to encode them within an esoteric dance. And the evidence we see before us appears to demonstrate that this is exactly what has happened. And the employment of indestructible megaliths in the Stonehenge design, would suggest that this knowledge was intended to last for millennia.

Yet this is not the end of the many esoteric intrigues that have been hidden within these manuscripts. If Stonehenge was not simply an

* Muhummad himself ordered the murder of a number of poets, including Al Nadr bin al Harith, Uqbah bin Abu Muayt, Asma bint Marwan, and Kab bin al Ashraf.

illustration of the precessional dance of the Earth, but more of a tutor's technical drawing, then the layout of this great henge is actually instructional - it is preserving and imparting knowledge. And strangely enough this is more or less what *Brut Oxford* calls Stonehenge. The usual name for this monument is Cor y Cewri meaning 'Dance of the Giants', as we have seen, but when Uther ben Dragown is buried at Stonehenge it is actually called Ynghor y Cewri meaning 'Advice of the Giants', 'Instructions of the Giants' or perhaps even 'Tuition of the Giants'. But what sort of 'instructions' can a megalithic henge or mausoleum give to us? The answer, surely, is instructions about the motion of the Earth during its millennial dance and the equivalent precession of the zodiac during its millennial waltz. And so the many titles that we have for Stonehenge now include (celestial) 'circle', (celestial) 'dance', or even (celestial) 'tuition'.

Cor	Cewri
Chorea	Gigantum
Dance	of Giants

Fig 14.18
The Whirling Dervish Sufis of the East. Each dancer is representative of a spinning planet orbiting the center of the solar system.

Ynghor	Cewri
Tuition	of Giants

Did the full esoteric understanding of the design for Stonehenge endure the millennia? In other words, did Monmouth and Oxford know that Stonehenge was a technical drawing of the millennial pirouettes of the Earth? Or were the 'dance' and 'tuition' titles that they used simply ancient names and traditions that had been passed down, while their true meaning had been lost to the sands of time? And if Monmouth and Oxford did understand the celestial design of Stonehenge, then when was this knowledge lost to us?

Whichever is the case, if Monmouth had been taking some of his cues from the Aramaic then he would have known that a 'circle' can be either a *galiyl* גליל, the name for Galilee, or a *khavalah* חוילה, the name for Eden's Havalah. But this Havalah circle can also be pronounced as Evalah or perhaps Avalah, just as the name for Khavah חוה, the wife of Adam, is pronounced as Eve. And yet the Welsh spelling for the Isle of Avalon is actually the Ynys Avallach, as can be seen in fig 14.19. And the Welsh Avallach was amended into the English Avalon, just as Magdalah was changed to Magdalene. And so it is not beyond the realms of possibility that Stonehenge was also known as the Kepha Avallah כיפא חוילה, the Stone Circle, or even the Nephilim Avallah נפלים חוילה, the Giants' Dance.*

Kephas	Avalah	Stone Circle
Ynys	Avallach	Isle of Avalon
Nephilim	Avalah	Giants' Dance
Ynys	Avallach	Isle of Avalon

Garden of Eden

And it is entirely possible that Monmouth goes on to give us a cryptic clue, to confirm that this proposed link between Avalon, Avallach and Havalah-Avalah is correct. In *History of Kings* Monmouth calls this Elysian paradise, the Isle of Avalon, which is not very helpful for determining its location.

* And when viewed as an image of the Earth, as in fig 14.12, Stonehenge is also an island floating in the vast emptiness of space. Or, in Egyptian terms, an island floating in the cosmic sea of Nu, across which the Solar barque of Ra sailed each day. We would certainly need a boat to get to this celestial Stonehenge-Avalon.

But in his later *Life of Merlin* he translates the Isle of Avalon as the Island of Apples, which is classically presumed to be derived from the Welsh *afal* and the Breton *aval* meaning 'apple'.

However, this may not be entirely so. The English 'apple' was derived from the Anglo-Saxon *appel* and the Indo-European *abel*, which is a generic name for any fruit. It is presumed that the Welsh *afal* and the Breton *aval* meaning 'apple' were direct derivations of this Anglo-Saxon word. However, in 12th century Wales the poets were rhyming the *aval* apple with the biblical Eve, rather than with the Anglo-Saxon *appel* fruit.

> *Blas aual, blys Eua.*
> Taste the apple, that Eve desired.
>
> *Gomedwys Eua, aual diwed.*
> Led astray (was) Eve, the apple (her) downfall. [4]

Here we see the Welsh poets adopting the Greek Eua (Eyua) for Eve. And we also see an *aual* apple being forcibly rhymed with Eve's name, whether it likes it or not. The fruit of Eden was inextricably linked with Eua-Eve, and so the

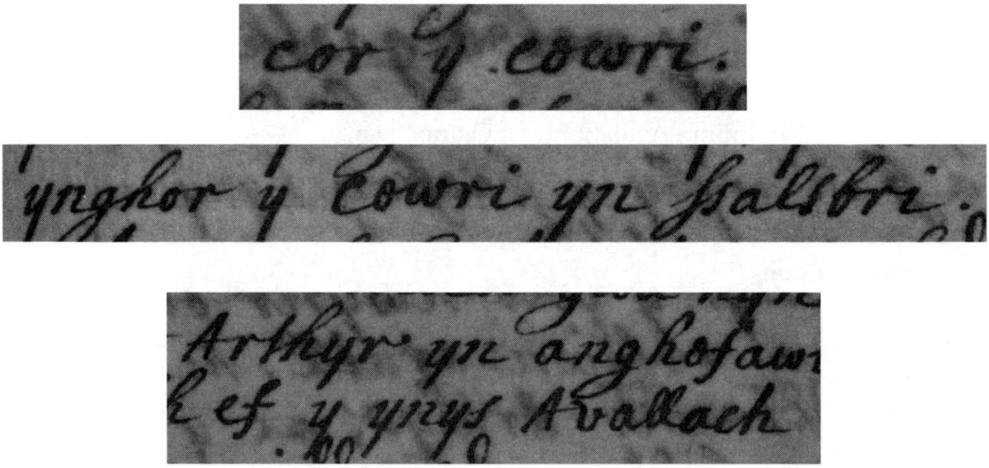

Fig 14.19
(top) The usual Welsh name for Stonehenge - Cor y Cewri - Circle of Giants.
(middle) The alternate Welsh name for Stonehenge - Ynghor y Cewri - Instructions of Giants.
(bottom) The Welsh spelling of Ynys Avallach, the Isle of Avalon.

Images from Jesus College Manuscript XXVIII at Oxford University, which is a 1695 copy of the original, made by Hugh Jones of the Ashmolean Museum.

fruit had to rhyme with her name - or else! But since the 'u' and 'v' were the same consonant in Latin, the Greek Eua eventually became the English Eve, and the *aual* apple likewise became the *aval* apple. So the Breton and Welsh *aval* may not be dependent on the Saxon *appel* at all, it may be more closely related to the biblical Eve and the famous fruit she picked in the Garden of Eden. (The modern Welsh spelling for Eve is Efa, which again invokes an *afal* apple.)

And if Monmouth was copying from the same 12th century Welsh sources as these poems, then the Arthurian Avallach-Avalon would not simply refer to the Isle of Apples but also to the Isle of Eden, or the Garden of Eden in which Eve's famous apple grew. And since the Garden of Eden was often viewed as a heavenly paradise, then it could also be seen as another Elysian Field, an Avalonian Isle of the dead. So in making this odd-sounding translation from Avalon to Apple, Monmouth is actually making a direct link to the Garden of Eden's encircled land of Havalah or Avallach. And it is only one short step from the circles of Avallach to the ecliptic and celestial circles of the zodiac, and thence to the ecliptic and celestial circles of Stonehenge.

Biblical	**Welsh**
Garden of Havalah	Garden of Avallach
Garden of Eve-apple	Garden of Apples
Garden of Eve	Garden of Aval
Garden of Efa	Garden of Afal
Garden of Eua	Garden of Aual
Evelon	Avalon

Exile

Despite Avallach-Avalon being the Norman equivalent of the Elysian Fields and a heavenly Garden of Eden, King Arthur was not quite dead when he was taken to Avalon. He was said to be mortally wounded, but Morgan le Fay claimed that she could still restore him to good health. But if all these events took place in Judaea, as the previous chapters have demonstrated, then why would a wounded King Arthur-Jesus be taken to Britain for treatment? Surely the healing waters at Hamat Teverya on the Sea of Galilee would be a better option, or perhaps even the renowned Asclepeion hospital on the island of Kos, where many Greco-Roman aristocrats went for medical assistance?

The answer to this is that King Arthur-Jesus was an enemy of Rome and his wounds had been received during his summary crucifixion, rather than in a desperate battle with his son, Mordred-Mordrain. And while Jesus-Izas may have been more useful to the Romans alive than dead, they still wanted to keep him as far from his rebel power-base in Syrio-Judaea as they possibly could. And the furthest that Rome could achieve from Judaea in the AD 70s, was Chester in Britain. And so it was in Chester, a 'lonely place in the west' over by the setting Sun, that Emperor Vespasian built Fortress Dewa, a prison fortress that was effectively a Roman version of Guantanamo Bay. And it was as a prisoner in Fortress Dewa that King Arthur-Jesus designed and built the Temple of the Zodiac.

King Arthur-Jesus would have remained incarcerated in this prison fortress at Chester until the late nineties, which is most probably when he died. But then the Romans would have had yet another problem on their hands - for what should they do with his mortal remains? In Jewish traditions the body was laid out in a special tomb and allowed to rot, so that the bones could be gathered up and placed in a small ossuary casket. The tombs at the Edessan necropolis at Sogmatar were designed for exactly this purpose, and had rolling stones to cover the entrance just as the gospels describe. The Palmyrans had traditions that were closer to the Egyptian than classical Judaic, for the spaces in the funerary towers at Palmyra were just about large enough to take a body, and the few remains that have been discovered indicate that the dead were mummified in the Egyptian tradition. And remember that Jesus-Izas was also being prepared for mummification in John 19:39, before it was discovered that he was still alive.

The point being made here is that cremation was not a standard Judaeo-Nazarene funerary custom, and so the Romans would have been left with the body or bones of a dangerous rebel to dispose of. They could not allow these remains to be taken back to Judaea for burial, as they may have become the focus for renewed dissent or even a new rebellion. And so they needed a burial site well away from King Arthur-Jesus' former power-base in Syria, that would nevertheless satisfy the demands of the Edessan monarchy for a dignified resting place. And if Stonehenge lay abandoned at this time, it would have satisfied all of those conflicting demands. Stonehenge would still have been considered a sacred site, to anyone who understood precessional astronomy; it would have been remarkably similar to the Edessan stone-henge at Gobekli Tepe; and it was sufficiently remote from Syrio-Judaea to prevent it becoming the focus for a renewed rebellion in Syrio-Judaea. Stonehenge would have been a fitting last resting place for the defeated Wise King.

And while there is little evidence for Roman constructions on Salisbury Plain, the results of the recent 2008 SPACES excavation within the stone circle of Stonehenge has revealed substantial Roman activity, including evidence of pits and stone removal during this period. The Romans were doing something at Stonehenge, but exactly what we do not know. And if Gobekli Tepe in Edessa was still a functioning site at this time, perhaps the

Romans deliberately buried this stone circle to prevent its veneration, just as they had closed down Stonehenge.

Unfortunately, it is not only the archaeology that runs out of steam at this point, so too does Arthurian history. And it does so just when these enigmatic texts get to the most significant and interesting part of the story - the final burial place of King Arthur-Jesus. After all the detailed knowledge that Arthurian history has displayed: of Pompey the Great, Mithras, Thera eruptions, Hippocrates, Mandylions, Charles Martel, City of Orange, Wheels of Fortune, Palmyra, Brennius and Belinus, Prester John, Julius Caesar, Vespasian, Floating islands, Galli priests, St Peter, Ophites, Hamat Teverya and even the Elagabal Holy Grail-stone that came from the heavens - the one thing that is really missing from these many stories is a detailed description of where the Wise King of Syrio-Judaea was laid to rest. So in the final analysis were are obliged to speculate that King Arthur-Jesus was interred at the Nephilim Avallah or Avalon נפלים חוילה - the precessional Dance of the Giants or Circle of the Giants that stands upon Salisbury Plain.

The Isle of Avallach-Avalon

Fig 14.20 Stonehenge photo: Max Alexander.

XV

Epilogue

We have come a long way in this analysis of Arthurian history - too far, some may say. And since it has been such a long and tortuous journey perhaps it is wise to summarise the most pertinent of the many points made, and bring this analysis to some sort of conclusion. In the author's opinion, the following represents the true sequence of events that gave rise to Arthurian history as we know it, and what it really meant to its authors and early readers.

Pre-Arthurian history

At the end of the Western Roman Empire there were several revolts organised by strong leaders who were based in or came from Britain. The first of these was Constantine I, the Great, who successfully fought his way onto the Throne of Rome in the early 4th century and became emperor. Then there was Magnus Maximus of the late 4th century, whose revolt and bid for Rome failed. And then there was Constantine III in the early 5th century, and again his bid for the throne of Rome failed.

Several venerable British historians recorded the events of these tumultuous times, including Gildas, Bede and Nennius. But none of these chroniclers said anything about the classical King Arthur, because he never existed in this era and in this region. The one or two references we have to a warrior Arthur were actually talking about a heroic semi-divine Hercules figure, who was supposed to come to the aid of an army in its time of need. In history there were two mighty guardians and ring-masters of the cosmos and zodiac, and they were Osiris-Hercules-Orion and Arthur-Ursa Major. This is why Nennius records that a warlord called Arthur was involved in twelve great battles, because these were hazy recollections of the twelve labours of Hercules and therefore symbolic of the precessional zodiac.

This threadbare Arthurian history, if one can call these few moth-eaten strands a history of Arthur, takes us all the way through to the beginning of the 12th century. And perhaps it is worth reinforcing this fact. Until we reach the 12th century there is absolutely no classical King Arthur whatsoever. According to the many chroniclers of this era, he simply did not exist.

Crusades

In 1096 the People's Crusade to the Holy Land began, as a popular revolt against the Muslim invasion and subjugation of the Judaeo-Christian Near East. The first wave of enthusiasts could hardly be described as an army, but this was swiftly followed by a second wave of more professional Crusaders led by Hugh I, the brother of King Philip I of France. Within this large force were Baldwin of Boulogne and Tancred of Norman Italy, who together besieged and took the city of Tarsus in southeastern Anatolia.

The army of Tancred then did the obvious thing and turned south towards Antioch-Orontes in Syria, while Count Baldwin kept marching east, capturing towns near modern Gaziantep. He then moved across the Euphrates and relieved the Christian city of Antioch-Edessa from Muslim oppression. The situation had been pretty grim in Edessa prior to Baldwin's arrival, and so he was invited in by Kouro Thoros as a liberating hero. But this Crusade had started out as a campaign to liberate Christian Syria and Judaeo-Christian Judaea from Muslim occupation and oppression, so why was Baldwin campaigning to the east of the Euphrates in Mesopotamia? Did he already know that Edessa had been a pivotal city during the tumultuous 1st century events that gave rise to the gospel stories?

Whatever the case, the literary realm of western Europe began to dramatically change from this time onwards, and the classical Arthurian genre was about to suddenly blossom. And it is worth taking a minute here to wonder why this event happened in Normandy at this very moment in time. Hand-written manuscripts of this magnitude were hugely expensive to manufacture, and the later *Vulgate Cycle* was about twice the size of the entire Bible. So why in the 1130s and 1140s did various aristocrats from Brittany and Normandy and eventually through to Holland, Germany, Italy and Spain, start producing these enormously expensive volumes about a history of a British king who never existed? And we know that the classical King Arthur of Britain never existed, because nobody had ever mentioned him up until this time. The answer lies in the history of the Knights Templar.

Count Baldwin of Boulogne and Edessa went on to become the king of Jerusalem in 1100, and successfully liberated many Christian cities in the Near East from Muslim control and oppression. The parasitical protection racket that Muhummad had created was at last being pushed back into the sands of Arabia where it belonged. King Baldwin I of Jerusalem was succeeded in 1118 by Baldwin II, the son of Hugh I. And then something strange happened. In 1119 Hugues de Payens and Godfrey de Bouillon approached Baldwin and requested permission to set up a monastic order for the protection of pilgrims in the Near East. This new martial monastic order was, of course, the Poor Soldiers of Christ and the Temple of Solomon - or the Knights Templar for short. And note that Hugues de Payens had chosen a name that reflected the 1st century Nazarene, Ebionites, Essene and Boethusians, in being called the 'Poor Knights', and so the Knights Templar were covertly declaring themselves to be the true heirs to the Nazarene-Ebionite sect of Jesus and James.*

The formation of the Knights Templar is central to this story. Not only did Wolfram von Eschenbach name the Templars as the Guardians of the Holy Grail-stone, but this was exactly the kind of secretive order that would have been required to carry out the dangerous literary mission that created the Arthurian genre. And the dates are suspiciously coincident too. It was immediately after the foundation of the Knights Templar in 1119 that novel manuscripts started turning up in Normandy, the very region and era that these European aristocrats originally came from. Baldwin of Boulogne was from eastern Normandy; Hugues Payens was from Troyes in northeastern France; while Godfrey Bouillon was from Ardennes and Lorraine which encompassed much of modern Belgium and Holland.

The novel texts that had been acquired in Judaeo-Syria, most probably from Edessa, were decidedly heretical - the sort of text that only a secretive and initiatory organisation like the Templars could possibly have handled. Norman aristocrats like Hugues and Godfrey were devout Christians, but obviously Christians with an open mind because what Count

* French Toast, which is battered and grilled on both sides, is often called a Poor Knight. It is claimed that this was a simple meal for poor knights, but the name was actually derived from the Knights Templar, who were called the Poor Knights of Christ. More specifically this name was derived from Jacques de Molay, the last Grand Master of the Knights Templar, who was slow-roasted to death by Catholic cardinals in Paris on 18 March 1314 - which is why a Poor Knight toast is battered and grilled on both sides.

Baldwin had discovered in Edessa represented a radically new perspective on classical Christian history. Here were texts that said that the biblical Jesus was a warrior king of Edessa, who had led the Jewish Revolt against Rome. The new story was much the same as the gospel story, but the import of this amendment - from pauper prince to warrior king - was incendiary to say the least. And yet the eastern bishops were adamant that this was the gospel truth: Jesus had been a king of Edessa.

Perhaps we can now see why the Knights Templar were set up as a monastic military order based upon a communal society. They were, in fact, copying the very same military, monastic, and communal order that King Jesus has founded back in 1st century Syrio-Judaea. In fact, many of the rules of the Knights Templar were drawn directly from the Community Rule of the Essene sect on the shores of the Dead Sea. And while this new Christian history recorded that King Jesus-Izas of Edessa had battled valiantly against the Roman occupation of these lands, the Knights Templar were similarly battling against the Muslim occupation and oppression of these very same lands. Essentially, the monastic military order of King Jesus had been resurrected in the early 12th century to perform exactly the same function - to claim the Near East in the name of Nazarene Judaism. Not in the name of Christianity of course, because Jesus was not a Christian in any shape or form, but in the name of Gnostic Nazarene Sabaean Ebionite Egypto-Judaism.

Subversive esoterica

But what could be done with texts that contained such a radical reevaluation of the gospel stories? The information these texts contained was decidedly heretical and incendiary, but it was the truth, and to a devoutly religious person this was god's truth. So these manuscripts were of such importance they could not be buried and forgotten, and yet this was not an era in which a count or even a king could challenge the established creed of the Catholic Church. In fact, the only way in which this information could be preserved for future generations, is if some courageous and creative authors crafted a fictional story about heroic knights that incorporated all of the many historical heresies contained within these Edessan manuscripts. What these Norman authors needed in order to achieve this, was a real history upon which this new semi-fictional history of Jesus could be hung, which could provide the new story with a degree of historical authenticity. These authors did not want to craft a fairy-story for children, they wanted a plausible history to intrigue an intellectual aristocrat. What they needed was a rebel prince or king who had been involved in a tax-dispute with the Roman Empire and had set out to become the next emperor, just as the biblical King

Jesus had likewise done in the 1st century.

This is why Wolfram von Eschenbach says that Master Kyot was sent out to search many other lands, including Ireland and Britain, in order to discover the rest of the story. But what Kyot was actually looking for was not 'the rest of the story', instead he wanted 'the ideal cover-story'. Kyot finally found what he was looking for in Anjou, in northwestern France, and what he discovered there was the history of the Bretton-British usurper emperors of Rome, Magnus Maximus and Constantine III. Here were two warrior monarchs of a small 'oppressed' land who could act as the perfect substitute and camouflage for the Edessan history of King Jesus. Both Maximus and Constantine had been kings of a small nation who had led a revolt against Rome, and just as importantly they had lived at the very start of the Dark Ages when much of the history of Europe had been lost to the sands of time.

It would have been difficult to have crafted a semi-fictional cover-story story about a well known emperor like Hadrian or Septimius Severus, as the deceit would easily be exposed. But who knew of Magnus Maximus or Constantine III? In fact, how many people know that these Bretton-British kings invaded Rome and became usurper emperors even today? So if these Arthurian authors added a couple of sons onto the line of these kings, who would ever notice the deception? In fact, there were so many ideal opportunities here that Monmouth and Oxford appear to have hedged their bets and alluded to both British usurper emperors for their cover-story, which has resulted in the confusing chronology that is Arthurian history.

The next thing that these intrepid authors required was a pseudonym for their hero, one that reflected Jesus' true status and position but would only be recognised by a few enlightened initiates. And since it was known that Jesus was often portrayed as the central Sun-god figure on a zodiac, as is depicted on the Beit Shean zodiac from Galilee in fig 12:15, the answer was obvious. All they needed to do was replace the central Helios Sun-king on this Christian zodiac, with the figure that was already displayed at the center of many of the more empirical zodiacs - the constellation of Ursa Major. Ursa Major was the central constellation around which the twelve signs of the zodiac rotated and it was therefore a perfect substitute for this king of the cosmos.

And the result of this academic subterfuge was a literary facade that would deflect Church suspicion for centuries. Ursa Major is surrounded by a circle of twelve subordinate signs of the zodiac; King Arthur-Ursa could now be encircled by the twelve knights of the Round Table; while king Jesus-Izas had always been surrounded by his twelve disciples of the Last Supper table. And since the Round Table was an allegoric circle of the zodiac, the symbolic synchronicity was now complete. And so in the newly crafted Arthurian gospels the biblical King Jesus-Izas was renamed as Uwth עות or Arth ערת, the Aramaic name for Ursa Major (Uther the Great), a name that eventually became pronounced as King Arthur.

In which case, the popular King Arthur of Britain from classical Arthurian history never existed, at least not in the manner which we expect. In reality, the history of the new King Arthur that had been crafted in the 12th century by the Knights Templar, represents the heretical gospel story that had been outlawed and destroyed by the Catholic Church - a version of Josephus Flavius' *Jewish War* that overtly called the 1st century Judaean rebel leader 'King Jesus of Edessa'. Such a gospel obviously existed at one time, but the 4th century Council of Nicaea had denounced the biblical King Jesus as a heretic of the very religion that bore his name. The newly created Catholic Christianity said that Jesus could not have been a created being - a son of greater god, as was advocated by the Arians - instead, he was an eternal god-figure co-substantial with god. At one stroke the Christian clergy had just outlawed the true history of their heroic figurehead, and turned the biblical Jesus-Izas into an apostate of Christianity.

This edict was reinforced at the 5th century Council of Chalcedon. But the revised creed issued there was not accepted by the Syriac, Armenian, Coptic or Ethiopian Churches, and this caused an irrevocable split within Christianity which effectively cut off the Syriac and Armenian Churches from Rome and Constantinople. The Syriac Church was centered on Edessa, the first city to convert to Nazarene 'Christianity' way back in the 2nd century. But Edessa and the Syriac Church had been cut off from mainstream Christianity by the Council of Chalcedon, and so the traditions and texts from Edessa were likewise cut off from Western theology and history.

This same doctrinal schism facilitated the Muslim conquest of Christian Mesopotamia and Christian Syria, because Constantinople was deliberately slow in coming to the aid of their heretical Christian cousins in Edessa. And so Christian Edessa and Christian Mesopotamia became cut off from the West behind the 5th century velvet curtain of the Chalcedon decree, and then imprisoned behind the 7th century iron curtain of Islam. And so the copious compositions of Aphrahat, Ephrem, Moses of Chorene, Yohannes Drasxanakertci, Dionysius of Tel Mahre and numerous others besides, were lost to Western theology and scholarship for hundreds of years - before East met West once again during the Crusades.

From the evidence outlined in this book, it is axiomatic that one of the forgotten manuscripts rediscovered in Edessa during the Crusades was the source for all of Arthurian history; and its rediscovery caused a muted sensation in the courts of northern France. There followed some consternation about how to handle these heretical texts, and then a great flurry of literary excitement and endeavour. The result was the creation of a pseudo-historical monarch called King Arthur, who valiantly attempted to free his people from Roman 'oppression'. But the unmentionable sub-text to this esoteric story, was that the semi-fictional King Arthur of Britain and Gaul was actually the historical King Jesus of Judaea and Edessa.

King Arthur was King Jesus

✠ ✠ ✠ End ✠ ✠ ✠

Appendix I

Arthur & Constantine

The analysis of early Arthurian history within chapters I & II demonstrated that there was a reasonable amount of real British history within the chronicles of Gildas, Bede, Nennius and the first part of Monmouth's account. But these accounts also exhibited some profound failings too, and so although the chronology developed in those chapters was satisfactory, it did not explain many aspects of this earlier British history. The main faults and fracture-lines within the previous chronology included:

> Four rebellions against Rome being orchestrated in Britain, which is possible but perhaps unlikely. (Constantine I, Magnus Maximus, Constantine III and King Arthur.)
>
> Aurelius Ambrosius being the son of an executed emperor, which means that King Arthur was probably the grandson of Constantine III. See point below.
>
> Because of this restriction, King Arthur has to be a mid to late 5th century monarch, or even an early 6th century monarch, who could not have invaded Rome. By the late 5th century, Rome would not have been demanding taxes; Britain was in no fit state to invade; and by the time we reach the late 5th century Western Rome no longer existed.
>
> King Arthur being a phantom monarch of the Dark Ages, who is never mentioned by Gildas, Bede or Nennius. And neither is there an equivalent monarch by any other name in any other historical record.

The many problems with this early Arthurian history have probably been created or at least facilitated by Bede's *Ecclesiastical History,* which has misidentified the recipient of the third British plea for Roman assistance, and therefore extended the chronology of these events into the mid 5th century. It is this late date that makes the possibility of a rich and influential King Arthur impossible, because such a powerful monarch, his extensive royal court, and his gallant expedition against Rome, could not have existed within the poverty-stricken mid to late 5th century AD.

This brief comparison between Gildas and Bede demonstrates Bede's extension of the chronology quite well.

Gildas	year	Bede
Maximus rebellion.	383	Maximus rebellion.
Maximus beheaded in Aquileia.	384	Emperor Gratian killed.
	388	Maximus executed in Aquileia.
No army left in Britain.	390	Gratian the British king killed.
First plea for Roman help, Legion sent. Turf wall.	394	
Second plea for Roman help, Legion sent.	398 400	
Honorius letter of no support.	404	
Third plea to Agitius-Arcadius.	406	
Saxon invasions	407	Constantine III and Constans.
	411	Constantine and Constans killed.
Ambrosius Aurelianus king.	411	No army left in Britain.
	?	First plea for Roman help, Legion sent. Turf wall.
	?	Second plea for Roman help, Legion sent. Stone wall.
	410?	Honorius letter of no support.
	446?	Third plea to Agitius-Aetius.
	450?	Saxon invasions
	450?	Ambrosius Aurelianus king.

Because Gildas did not mention the second British usurper emperor and his son, Constantine III and Constans, Bede has assumed that all the British pleas for assistance from Rome must have happened after these usurper emperors, rather than before. This has resulted in a misidentification of the recipient of the third plea for Roman assistance, who Bede identified as being Commander Aetius instead of Emperor Arcadius, and the result is a 40-year extension of the chronology.

And we can be reasonably sure that Gildas is the more correct here because there are some fairly secure chronological pegs to attach this time-line onto, which include the execution of the British usurper emperor Magnus Maximus in 388; the declaration of no assistance by Honorius in 404; the third plea to Arcadius in 406; and the actual Roman withdrawal from Britain in the early 5th century. Chapters I & II have dated this withdrawal to 404, shortly after Honorius' letter, but even classical Roman history will date this event to about 410. So there is absolutely no possibility that the Britons would have been making a plea for Roman assistance in 446, more than 36 years (or 42 years) after the Roman withdrawal from Britain. Rome was struggling with multiple invasions of its homeland at this time, and was in no position to provide Britain with military assistance.

And so the identification of the third plea for assistance, by Bede and all subsequent historians, is incorrect. In reality, because Western Emperor Honorius had already renounced all support for the province in about 404, a party of British ambassadors travelled all the way to Constantinople in 406 to see Eastern Emperor Arcadius. But they were again refused assistance, and despondently retraced their steps back to a vulnerable, raided, invaded and ravaged Britain.

The solution

If we are to blend an unknown King Arthur into this history of Britain, as Monmouth and Oxford have done, and end up with a chronology and genealogy that makes historical sense, then the British equivalent of Arthur must have lived some 50 or 60 years earlier than these authors assert. And so there is a solution to this chronological confusion, but only if we disregard Bede's error and bring the British Arthur back into the late 4th century or the very early 5th century. And although this solution changes much of the Arthurian side of this history, the historical chronology of Britain and Rome remains the same as before, and so the resulting narrative makes a great deal of sense. Furthermore, the basic premise for this solution is very simple:

The British King Arthur was Emperor Constantine III

And that is it. All we need to do now, is to shuffle all the other Arthurian characters around to match this suggestion. And the result of these amendments is quite logical, as we shall see. Effectively, this means that Emperor Maximus takes on the role previously given to Constantine III, while Constantine III takes on the role of the British version of King Arthur - so everyone has shuffled up the genealogy by two generations. More importantly, this places the British King Arthur into an era that could well have supported a wealthy monarch who invaded Rome. And we know this was possible in this era because Constantine III did exactly this - he invaded Gaul and Rome in about 408. Please see the revised genealogy in fig A1.2.

Do bear in mind that this is merely a reference to the British version of 'Arthur'. This is the earlier semi-mythological supposedly British king who had no name or history within the British chronicles until the 12th century. And he was not mentioned by Gildas, Bede or Nennius, because he simply did not exist. What Monmouth and Oxford have done here, is to hang the history of King Jesus-Izas of Judaea upon a convenient historical king and emperor from northern Europe. And the emperor who was chosen to be the grandfather of this semi-mythical King Arthur was either Constantine I, or

Fig A1.1
A gold solidus of Emperor Constantine III. If this alternate explanation for Monmouth's chronology is correct, then this is the British King Arthur. Or rather, this is the historical King Constantine-Arthur, upon which the cloak of King Jesus-Arthur was placed by the later Norman authors. Constantine III was merely a convenient backcloth, upon which the life of the historical King Jesus-Izas could be portrayed. And Constantine III was ideal for this task, for he was a usurper emperor who invaded Rome, just as Jesus-Izas was trying to do.

-- Constantine III may be the British King Arthur --

Magnus Maximus, or perhaps Constantine III - the accounts are uncertain and vary.

However, if Monmouth and Oxford had thought about this problem more rationally, then it would have been much more logical to make this new semi-mythical King Arthur the grandson of Emperor Magnus Maximus, rather than the grandson of Emperor Constantine III. And while this may seem like a radical and unwarranted suggestion, it does solve all the problems that were identified earlier within Monmouth's chronology. And these are:

> The four rebellions against Rome become just three. (Constantine I, Maximus, and Arthur-Constantine III.)
>
> Aurelius Ambrosius is still the son of an executed emperor. But in this case the emperor is Magnus Maximus, who lived in a much earlier and more realistic era.
>
> The semi-mythical King Arthur is not consigned to the impossible mid to late 5th century. Instead, he began his reign in 407, and this is definitely an era when an invasion of Rome could have occurred. See point below.
>
> The semi-mythical King Arthur becomes an early 5th century monarch, who we know invaded Rome - King Arthur-Constantine III.

As can be seen, although this new chronology has trampled all over the 'classical' Arthurian chronology, as given by Monmouth and Oxford, the order of the royal succession and the chronology of orthodox Romo-British history has remained the much same. In which case, the salient points in this new chronology are:

> When the Maximus rebellion ended, Britain was left without an army and without an arms manufacturing industry - because the remnants of Maximus' defeated army returned to Brittany instead of Britain. (388)
>
> The first usurper of the British throne was Maurice the son of Caradoc, who had wanted to take the throne when Maximus became king and emperor. This is the king called Marcus in the historical record, but he is deposed fairly quickly. (388)
>
> A new local king was crowned, who is called King Gratian in the historical record. Arthurian history may him King Pendragon or ben Dragown. (390)
>
> The Romans are no longer interested in Britain after the Maximus rebellion, and let the place fall apart. (392)
>
> Following the death of Pendragon his brother Uther takes the throne and

adopts his brother's title, becoming Uther ben Dragown. But his common hypocorism in the historical record was Aurelius Ambrosius. His new throne-name was derived from St Ambrose who had died that year, and because of this nickname he was commonly known as The Monk. (397)

The situation in Britain becomes so dire that King Uther requests assistance from Rome and receives a legion in return for a substantial tribute. (400)

Invasions continue, so Emperor Honorius writes to all the cities of Britain to say that Rome can no longer protect the province. (404)

In desperation, Uther writes to Emperor Arcadius in Constantinople for help, but none is forthcoming. Uther ben Dragown is killed in the battles with the invading Picts and Scots and is buried in Stonehenge. (406)

Uther's son, Constantine (III) takes the throne. Popular 12th century histories would rename Constantine as 'King Arthur', and link his life to the history of the biblical King Jesus in 1st century Judaea. (407)

Since the Romans have twice refused to help the beleaguered nation, Constantine-Arthur assembles a Bretton-British army and invades Gaul and thence Rome. (408)

King Constantine-Arthur's revolt against Rome fails, and he is killed in Arles, Gaul. (411)

Constantine-Arthur's (step) son reigned after him, and Monmouth calls this new king Constantine. This is Constans II, the son of Constantine III. (412)

This new chronology fits the known facts in Monmouth's account quite well. All the main players within Arthurian history have moved up by two generations, but everything else remains much the same as before. And Aurelius Ambrosius can still be the son of a murdered British Emperor of Rome, because he is now the son of Emperor Magnus Maximus instead of Emperor Constantine III. This is the story that Monmouth and Oxford should have written, because this is the chronology and history that would have made more historical sense. Rather than having their semi-mythical King Arthur living in the Dark Ages, they could have linked him to a king who was known to have invaded Rome.

Monmouth flirted with the idea of making King Arthur a grandson of Constantine I (the Great) but abandoned this effort, presumably because Constantine the Great was too famous and his family too well known. But he could have made Arthur the grandson of Magnus Maximus, and therefore made King Arthur one and the same as Constantine III. Why he did not do so is anyone's guess. Perhaps Constantine III was also too famous, and Monmouth's semi-mythical Judaeo-British king, Arthur-Jesus, needed burying in the depths of the Dark Ages. Or perhaps Monmouth and Oxford simply did not appreciate that the wealthy, powerful and expansionist King Arthur they were crafting from their 12th century Templar manuscripts, could not have existed in the Dark Age era.

Whatever the case, the many problems with this uncertain British chronology were easily solved by the later authors of Arthurian history by skipping over this entire episode. The entire *Vulgate Cycle*, for instance, has just one paragraph copied from Monmouth which mentions a Constantine. And the rest of British history is simply forgotten, as is all 4th and 5th century Roman history. There is no Constantine the Great, Maximus, Gratian, Marcus, Honorius, or Theodosius, and there are no appeals to Rome, assistance of legions or letters of withdrawal. Apart from a few mentions of place names in Britain, to keep the Church censors happy, there is absolutely nothing to suggest that these later Arthurian histories have anything to do with British history at all.

Just as Chapter XV explains, this earlier British history was merely a convenient backcloth, upon which the real life of King Jesus-Izas of Judaea

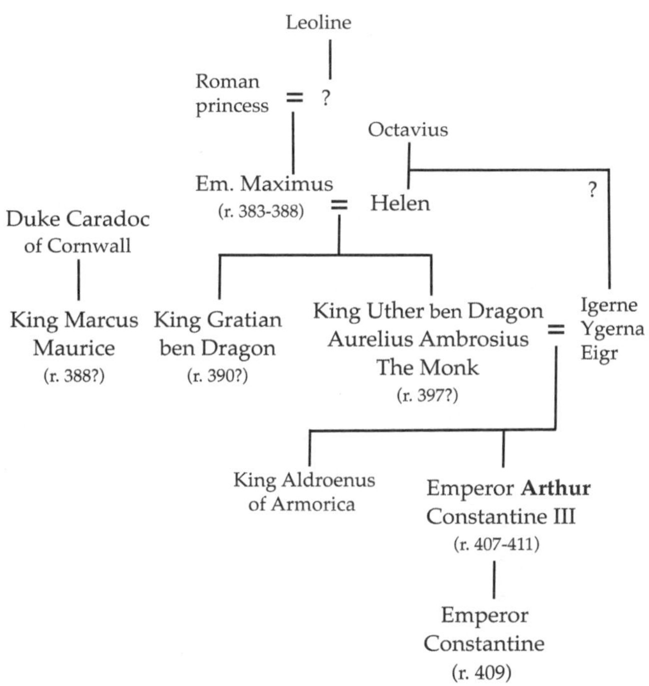

Fig A1.2
Genealogy of King Arthur, assuming that Arthur is one and the same as Constantine III. This shifts the life of King Arthur back to AD 407, and into an era when a British invasion of Rome was still possible.

could be overlaid and overtly displayed, while still remaining hidden. And the life of Constantine III would have been ideal for this, because it displayed many points of commonality with the life of Jesus-Izas. Constantine was a usurper emperor who may have had a tax dispute with Rome and who did embark on an invasion to conquer Rome, just as King Jesus had. However, Monmouth and Oxford chose to make King Arthur a grandson of Constantine III instead, and thus laid the foundations for a perennial chronological conundrum.

AII

Appendix II

Glossary

Locations:

Adiabene	= Supposed kingdom in Persia, around Arbela. More probably a reference to Edessa and Palmyra.
Armorica	= Brittany in NW Gaul.
Antioch	= City in northwestern Syria, now Antakya in Turkey.
Arthur	= Son of Pelles, husband of Gwenevere.
Aurania	= See Auranitis below.
Auranitis	= Region to the east of the Euphrates and Jordan. Probably the same as the Osrhoene.
Avalon	= Equivalent of the Elysian Fields.
Babylon	= Southern and eastern Iraq.
Badon	= Famous battle of Arthur, of uncertain location.
Berytus	= Beirut.
Bethanya	= Region to the east of the river Jordan.
Bithynia	= Northern Turkey.
Byblos	= Coastal city north of Beirut.
Caerleon	= City of the Legions. Either on River Usk, or is Chester.
Caesarea	= Coastal town in Israel, north of Joppa.
Camelot	= Arthur's capital, location unknown.
Carthage	= Roman city near Tunis in Tunisia.
Cilicia	= Southeastern Turkey.
Chaldaea	= Iraq, near the Persian Gulf.
Commagene	= Southeastern Turkey.
Corbenic	= City or castle of the Holy Grail.
Cyrenacia	= Northern Libya.
Dacia	= Western Black sea area.

Decapolis	=	The ten major Roman cities in Syria and Galilee.
Ecbatana	=	Capital of Assyria, but also referring to Bethanya.
Edessa	=	Modern Sanli Urfa in Turkey.
Egypt	=	Southern Egypt - Thebes.
Emesa	=	Modern Homs in Syria, known for its sacred stone.
Galatia	=	Region in central eastern Turkey.
Gallia	=	Southern France.
Gamala	=	Ancient city in Syria, NW of Amman: Umm el-Jimal.
Gamala	=	Also a small citadel on east-bank of Galilee.
Gaul	=	Supposedly France, but see Gaulanitis below.
Gaulanitis	=	Golan Heights northeast of the Sea of Galilee.
Israel	=	Region to the west of the Sea of Galilee.
Jabneh	=	University run by Josephus after Jewish War, located just south of Tel Aviv.
Judaea	=	Region around Jerusalem.
Lebanon	=	Coastal strip west of Syria.
Levant	=	Coastal strip of Judaea, Lebanon and Syria.
Logres	=	Land supposedly equivalent to modern England.
Lydia	=	Western Turkey, near the Maeander river.
Lycia	=	Southwestern Turkey.
Macedonia	=	Northern Greece.
Mauretania	=	Northern Morocco and Algeria, also Tunisia and Libya.
Nabataea	=	Arabian kingdom around southern Dead Sea.
Palmyra	=	Oasis city northeast of Damascus, a city founded by Thea Muse Ourania and Helena of Adiabene.
Pamphylia	=	Region in southern Turkey.
Pannonia	=	Hungry.
Parthia	=	Originally Bactria, but the empire spread to Iran,Iraq and eastern Turkey. Equivalent of earlier Persian Empire.
Petra	=	Rose-red city in Nabataea.
Phrygia	=	Region in central western Turkey.
Persia	=	An earlier empire occupying roughly the same region as Parthia.
Philippi	=	Town on the north coast of Greece, east of Thessalonica.
Osrhoene	=	The small kingdom governed by King Abgar V of Edessa. It encompassed Edessa, Amida, Harran and Palmyra.
Qumran	=	Settlement on northwest of Dead Sea.
Samaria	=	Region to the west of the river Jordan.
Sarras	=	City between Jerusalem and the Euphrates. Probably Palmyra.
Scythia	=	Ukraine. Sometimes called Bactria.
Sidon	=	Coastal city south of Beirut.
Syria	=	Modern Syria. Sometimes a term for all of the Levantine coast including Lebanon, Syria and SE Turkey.
Tiberias	=	City on west-bank of Sea of Galilee.
Thrace	=	North eastern Greece, southern Bulgaria, and north-bank Istanbul.
Troad	=	Region in northwestern Turkey.
Tyre	=	Coastal city south of Sidon and Beirut.

Characters and organisations:

Abgarus	=	Kings of Edessa. Abgarus V is the most important of these and he is identified as Jesus' father.
Addai	=	Apostle who visited King Abgarus in Edessa. Identified with Judas Thomas of the gospels.
Agabus	=	Pseudonym for Abgarus-Monobazus.
Agrippa I	=	King of Syria AD 37 - 44 and Judaea AD 41 - 44.
Agrippa II	=	King of Chalcis, Syria AD 48 - 53, Tetrarch of Bethnaya AD 53 - 100.
Alain li Gros	=	Father of Perceval, also called Pellehan. Was the 'Peter' (Guardian of the Grail) before Perceval. Son of Bron. May also be Lancelot and Josephus Flavius.
Albinus	=	Governor of Judaea, c. AD 62 - 64.
Alexander Severus	=	Severan Emperor of Rome AD 222 - 235.
Anfortas	=	The Wounded King. Also the Fisher King.
Antipas (Herod)	=	Tetrarch, or minor king of Galilee 4 BC - AD 39 and later of Judaea AD 7 - AD 39.
Archelaus (Herod)	=	Tetrarch, or minor king of Judaea 4 BC - AD 6.
Aurelius Ambrosius	=	Son of Constantine. Either Uther or Pendragon.
Ban	=	Father of Lancelot. Probably the same as Bron.
Barnabas	=	Comrade of Saul-Josephus on his travels - probably his brother, Matthias
Barsabas	=	See Barnabas.
Belacane	=	Wife of Gahmuret-Alain.
Berenice	=	Sister-wife of Agrippa II. Mistress of Emperor Titus.
Blaise	=	Merlin's secretary and scribe.
Boethus	=	Jewish aristocrat, (step) father of Mary Mag and Jesus.
Boni	=	Talmud's name for Nicodemus. Probably Bron and Ban.
Bors	=	Cousin of Lancelot.
Bretons	=	People from Brittany in NW Gaul.
Bron	=	Father of Alain li Gros. Full name is Hebron. Was the 'Peter' (Guardian of the Grail) before Alain. Same as Ban, Boni and therefore Nicodemus.
Brutas	=	Great-grandson of Trojan Aeneas.
Cabal	=	Arthur's dog.
Caliburn	=	The magical sword, Excalibur.
Caligula	=	Emperor of Rome AD 37 - 41.
Cephas	=	Another name for Peter.
Clarke, Adam	=	Composed a commentary on the Bible, 19th century.
Claudas	=	Roman enemy of Arthur and Lancelot.
Claudius	=	Emperor of Rome, AD 41 - 54.
Clemens (Titus Flavius)	=	Nephew of Emperor Vespasian. Husband of Domitilla, daughter of Vespasian. Known as Clement, the third 'Christian' pope.
Clement of Rome	=	See Clemens.
Cleopatra VII	=	Last Ptolemaic pharaoh of Egypt, 51 - 30 BC.
Constans	=	Son of Constantine III, also became emperor.

Constantine III	=	Usurper emperor of Rome 407-411.
Constantine	=	Father of Uther and Pendragon, same as Constantine III.
Cumanus	=	Governor of Judaea, c. AD 48- 52.
Dindrane	=	Sister of Perceval.
Domitian	=	Flavian Emperor of Rome AD 81 - 96.
Domna, Julia	=	Wife of Septimius Severus.
Drusilla	=	Wife of Felix.
Elagabalus	=	Priest of Elagabal. Emperor of Rome AD 218 - 222.
Elymas ben Jesus	=	A son of Jesus.
Essene	=	Ascetic Judaic revolutionary sect, based in Qumran on the Dead Sea. Peaceful, but composed the War Scroll.
Eusebius	=	Christian historian, bishop of Caesarea AD 313 - 339.
Evalach	=	King of Sarras in the AD 70s.
Fadus	=	Governor of Judaea, c. AD 44 - 46.
Feirefiz	=	Half-brother of Perceval.
Felix	=	Governor of Judaea, c. AD 52 - 58.
Festus	=	Governor of Judaea, c. AD 59 - 62.
Fisher King	=	Either Pelles or Pellehan, depending on the text.
Florus	=	Governor of Judaea, c. AD 64 - 66.
Gahmuret	=	Same as Alain-Pellehan.
Galahad	=	Son of Joseph of Arimathaea or Ban. Same as Perceval.
Galileans	=	The Nazarene Fourth Sect of Judaism. The same sect as the Church of Jesus and James.
Gawain	=	Son of Lot, nephew of Arthur.
Gill, John	=	Composed a commentary on the Bible, 19th century.
Gorlois	=	First husband of Ygerne, Uther's wife.
Gwenevere	=	Wife of Arthur. Mistress of Lancelot.
Hebron	=	See Bron.
Hector	=	Brother of Lancelot.
Hegesippus	=	Christianised Jew and historian, early 2nd century.
Helena, Queen	=	Queen of Adiabene in the AD 40s and 50s. Probable daughter of Queen Thea Muse Ourania. Probably Mary the Virgin, mother of Mary Magdalene and Jesus.
Herod (the Great)	=	King of Judaea, Galilee and Syria 37 BC to 4 BC.
Herod	=	See Archelaus, Antipas or Philip.
Herodias	=	Daughter of Aristobulus, asked for John's head.
Herzeloyde	=	Same as Yglais.
Ither	=	Same as Yder.
Ignatius	=	Bishop of Antioch.
Irenaeus	=	Bishop of Lyon, 2nd century.
Izas	=	Sons of Helena. Also called Izas-Monobazus I and II. Origin of the name 'Jesus'.
Izates	=	Same as Izas - see above.
Jesus Justus	=	Full name of Jesus, born AD 14.
James Justus	=	Brother of Jesus. Also called Stephen.
Jesus of Gamala	=	Son of Judas of Gamala, governor of Tiberias and Bethanya. Leader of Galileans c. AD 30s to AD 70s, Same as biblical Jesus, born approx AD 14. Also called Izas-Monobazus and Emmanuel.

Johanan b Zakkai	=	*De facto* high priest after the fall of Jerusalem. Established a university and Sanhedrin at Jabneh. Possible pseudonym for Saul-Josephus.
John the Baptist	=	Possible leader of the Essene, died about AD 33. Son of Zacharias and Elisabeth. Death incorrectly recorded as the death of Jesus.
Josephus Flavius	=	Judaean army commander turned traitor and author. The same person as Saul (St Paul). Confused with Joseph of Arimathaea and Lancelot.
Joseph Arimathaea	=	Aristocrat, member of the Sanhedrin Took Jesus down from the cross. Probably the same as Saul-Josephus.
Josephus	=	Son of Joseph Arimathaea. Confused with Josephus Flavius.
Joseus	=	Son of Pelles, confused with Josephus.
Joses	=	Brother of Jesus.
Julia Ourania	=	Daughter of Thea Muse Ourania. Probably Helena of Adiabene.
Judas of Gamala	=	Exiled Jew from Persia, governor of Bethanya. Leader of Fourth Sect. c. AD 4 to AD 30s.
Kay	=	Arthur's seneschal. Also Cai.
Kephas	=	Meaning 'stone'. The Kephas was the Grail Guardian. See Peter.
Lady of Lake	=	Fay or fairy foster mother of Lancelot. Morgan le Fay?
Lailoken	=	Also Myrddin. Probably origin of name for Merlin.
Lambor	=	Sometimes father of Pelles.
Lancelot	=	Knight of Arthur, lover of Arthur's wife. Son of Ban. Originally called Yder or Ither. May be Joseph of Arimathaea.
Lot	=	King of Lothian, father of Lancelot and Gawain. Sometimes he is brother-in-law of Arthur.
Luna	=	Partner of Simon Magus, also called Helena.
Macrinus	=	Emperor of Rome AD 217 - 218. Not a Severan.
Manu	=	Kings of Edessa. Manu V and VI. They are to be identified with James and Jesus.
Mary Magdalene	=	Daughter of Simon Boethus, sister-wife of Jesus, born c. AD 20. Name refers to a phallic tower.
Mary the Virgin	=	Mother of Jesus. Probably same as Julia Ourania and Queen Helena.
Matthias	=	Successor to Judas Iscariot. Saul-Josephus' brother.
Medraut	=	See Mordred.
Merlin	=	Wizard and advisor of King Arthur. His muse was probably Morgan le Fay, Arthur's sister.
Monobazus-Izas	=	Brother-husband of Queen Helena.
Morgan le Fey	=	Sister of Arthur, muse of Merlin.
Mordred	=	Son of Arthur, same as Mordrain.
Mordrain	=	King of Sarras, son of Arthur.
Morgan le Fay	=	Sorceress sister of Arthur. Lady of Avalon. Possible Lady of the Lake and guardian of Lancelot. Possible muse of Merlin.

Morgause	=	Half-sister of Arthur. Wife of Lot, mother of Lancelot and Gawain. Possibly another wife of Arthur, and mother of Mordred.
Myrddin	=	Early Welsh name for Merlin.
Nakdimon	=	Talmudic name for Nicodemus.
Nero	=	Caesarian Emperor of Rome AD 54 - 68.
Nicodemus	=	Rich man in gospels, (step) father of Mary and Martha. See Boethus. Talmud calls him Boni. Sometimes, father of Alain-Pellehan.
Niniane	=	Lady of the Lake. May be Morgan le Fay. Also Vivien.
Origen	=	Third century theologian.
Paul (St)	=	See Saul.
Pellehan	=	Father of Perceval, also called Alain li Gros. Grail Guardian. May be St Peter. Also called Pellinore.
Pelles	=	Often the father of Arthur, often the Fisher King.
Pendragon	=	Brother of Uther. May be Aurelius Ambrosius.
Perceval	=	Son of Alain-Pellehan. Same as Galahad. The Peter (Guardian of the Grail) after Alain-Pellehan. Was the new St Peter after Bron-Hebron.
Perilous Seat	=	Special and dangerous seat at the Round Table. Variously explained as the seat of Jesus or the seat of Judas.
Peter	=	St Simon Peter. Same as Bron and Perceval.
Peter	=	Formal title meaning 'rock' or 'stone'. The Peter was the Grail Guardian. See Kephas.
Petrus	=	See Bron or Hebron.
Philip (Herod)	=	Tetrarch, or minor king of Bethanya 4 BC to AD 34.
Phraataces	=	Son of King Phraates IV. King of Parthia 2 BC - 4 AD. Son-husband of Queen Thea Muse Ourania.
Phraates IV	=	King of Parthia (Persia) 38 - 2 BC. Husband of Queen Thea Muse Ourania.
Polycarp	=	2nd century Christian historian, bishop of Smyrna.
Pontius Pilate	=	Roman procurator of Judaea AD 26 - 36.
Poppaea	=	Errant wife of Emperor Nero.
Queen of Wasteland	=	Wife of Alain-Pellehan.
Red Knight	=	Was Alain-Pelehan, but became Perceval or Galahad.
Ron	=	Arthur's spear.
Round Table	=	Representation of a zodiac.
Sangrail	=	Holy Grail.
Septimius Severus	=	Severan Emperor of Rome AD 193 - 211.
Septuagint	=	Greek Tanakh, written by the 'seventy' scribes.
Saul	=	Later called St Paul. Author of many of the biblical Epistles, and possibly Luke and Acts. Same person as Josephus Flavius, the historian.
Sicarii	=	Title for Jewish revolutionaries allied to Jesus. Probably extreme wing of the Essene.
Simon	=	Another name for Peter Cephas.
Simon Boethus	=	Another name for Boethus.
Simon Magus	=	Gnostic pupil of John the Baptist. Possibly Jesus' (step)

		father, Simon Boethus. Partner of Helena-Luna, who may have been Queen Helena of Adiabene.
Stephen	=	Probably James Justus.
Talmud	=	Discussions on Judaic law and history.
Tanakh	=	Old Testament.
Tiberius	=	Emperor of Rome AD 14 - 37.
Titus	=	Roman commander in Judaea. Flavian Emperor of Rome AD 79 - 81.
Thea M. Ourania	=	Daughter of Cleopatra VII, wife of Phraates IV of Parthia. Probable mother of Queen Helena.
Theophilus	=	Possibly Clemens. Possibly Josephus' father.
Torah	=	First five books of the Old Testament.
Uther	=	Brother of Pendragon. May be Aurelius Ambrosius. Became Uther Pendragon after the death of his brother.
Vespasian	=	Roman commander in Britain and Judaea. Flavian Emperor of Rome AD 69 - 79.
Viviane	=	See Niniane.
Whiston, William	=	Translator of Saul-Josephus, 18th century.
Wounded King	=	Galli high priest. Either Pelles or Pellehan, depending on the text.
Yder	=	Appears to be a pseudonym for Lancelot.
Ygerne	=	Wife of Uther, mother of Arthur. Also Igerne.
Yglais	=	Wife of Alain-Pellehan. Also called Herzeloyde. Sometimes wife of Pelles.
Zacchaeus	=	Rich tax-collector. Son of Zacharias. May be identified with Saul-Josephus.
Zacharias	=	Father of John the Baptist and Zacchaeus, husband of Elisabeth. Possible father of Saul-Josephus.
Zakkai	=	See Zacharias and Johanan.
Zenobia	=	Queen of Palmyra AD 240s - 270s. The fleeting Queen of Egypt c. AD 270.

List of diagrams

Stonehenge images courtesy of:
Max Alexander, STFC,
WallpapersWA.com, and 123RF.

Notes & References

Bible: All references taken from the King James edition, although the text is often modernised for clarity.

Josephus: Ant = Antiquities, War = Jewish war, Life = Life.
Quotes and page references are to the William Whiston's translation, which was first published in 1736; some references are from the Penguin Classics edition by G. Williamson, first published 1959.

Acknowledgements

1. The charity with no shame. Founded to promote peace, the wealthy Rowntree trust now funds Muslim fanatics, former Irish terrorists and anti-Semitics. How can it justify its charitable status? Daily Mail 6th March 2015.
   http://www.dailymail.co.uk/news/article-2983488/Founded-promote-peace-wealthy-Rowntree-trust-funds-fanatics.html

Intro

1. The Arthurian Handbook, Norris Lacy, p10.
   Norris Lacy is one of the translators of the *Vulgate Cycle.*

Chapter 1

1. The Evolution of Arthurian Romance, James Bruce, Bk1 p3.
2. The names being used were Artusius (Arthur) and Galvanus (Gwain). See Gli eroi Brettoni onomastica Italiana, Pio Rajna. Romania, XVII, 161 355 (1888).

Chapter 2

1. Jesus College MS LXI, translated by Bill Cooper.
2. http://www.cngcoins.com/Coin.aspx?CoinID=240411
3. Merlin Grail p44, p47, History of Kings 8:24.

Chapter 3

1. Symbolism of Perlesvaus 1946, Prof Neale Carmen p42.
2. In Quest of the Holy Grail, An introduction to the legend, Sebastian Evans, 1898.
3. The Grail , Roger Loomis p97.
4. Glastonbury and the Holy Grail, William Nitze. Modern Philology. Vol. 1, No. 2 (Oct., 1903), pp. 247-257.
5. Ibid
6. In Quest of the Holy Grail, An introduction to the legend, Sebastian Evans, 1898.

Chapter 5

1. The Three Days' Tournament, A Study in Romance and Folk-Lore, By Jessie L. Weston. Project Gutenberg.
2. World Archaeological Congress (2006). Of the past, for the future: integrating archaeology and conservation. Proceedings of the conservation theme at the 5th World Archaeological Congress, 22-26 June 2003. Getty Conservation Institute. p. 266.
   http://www.getty.edu/conservation/publications_resources/pdf_publications/of_past_for_future.html
3. United Nations Development Programme.
   Arab Human Development Report 2002.
   Compiled by Arab scholars for the UNDP. See page 78.
   http://www.arab-hdr.org/publications/other/ahdr/ahdr2002e.pdf
   Also reported in The Economist, Jul 4th 2002.
   http://www.economist.com/node/1213392
   However, the figure of 100,000 Spanish translations a year in this report is incorrect. The figure is closer to 10,000, which invalidates the claim being made here. How these Muslim 'scholars' and the UN could not spot such a gross error, is a complete mystery.
4. Ctesiphon:
   History of the Islamic Civilization, Jurji Zaydan, 1905.
   Alexandria:
   Bar Hebraeus, Edward Pococke (1650).
   Included in: Specimen Historiae Arabvm (1806).
5. Islam and Science, Pervez Hoodbhoy p104.
   The Muguddimah, Ibn Khaldun.
6. The Closing of the Muslim Mind, Robert R. Reilly 2010.
   Robert R. Reilly is a fellow at the American Foreign Policy Council.
   See also Chapter VIII in *Mary Magdalene, Princess of Orange*.
   This chapters is summarised on the Academia.edu website:
   https://www.academia.edu/8749355/Islamic_Inventions_were_Roman_Greek_and_Persian
   This is a nice easy-read article on modern Islamic 'science':
   http://discovermagazine.com/2007/jul/science-and-islam
7. The Malay Mail, 4th Aug 2015.
   http://www.themalaymailonline.com/malaysia/article/avoid-intellect-logic-when-it-comes-to-islam-perak-mufti-tells-cabinet
8. List of universities in Dubai.
   http://www.dubaifaqs.com/universities-dubai.php
9. Jordanian pilot burned to death.
   http://www.dailymail.co.uk/news/article-2938299/One-sickening-acts-committed-film-Carefully-edited-highly-choreographed-footage-ISIS-knows-horrify-West-entice-jihadists-cause.html
10. The Story of Rome, Arthur Gilman, 1885. ch18 p289.
11. Halsall, Paul (1997). Otto of Freising: The Legend of Prester John. Internet Medieval Sourcebook. Retrieved June 20, 2005. Otto von Freising, Historia de Dua-

bus Civitatibus, 1146 Quoted from Friedrich Zarncke, Der Priester Johannes, Leipzig, Hirzel, 1879.

Chapter 6

1. White Gold, by Giles Milton.

Chapter 7

1. Zeitschrift für französische Sprache und Literatur, Bd 29, 1906, p82. L'Enserrement Merlin. Studien zur Merlinsage, Ernst Brugger. http://www.jstor.org/stable/40613834
2. Richard Carrier on his blog ... Thread 'Atwill's Cranked-up Jesus', comment 43.1, 56.1. Readers will note that anyone who argues with Prof Richard Carrier is instantly branded as being 'genuinely insane'. Since Carrier is not medically trained, these bald assertions say much more about Richard Carrier's state of mind, than the people he is arguing with and castigating.
3. Amplification as Gloss in Two Twelfth Century Texts, Joanne Rittey.

Chapter 8

1. Clement of Alexandria and a Secret Gospel of Mark. Harvard University Press, 1973.
2. Refutation of Heresies, V:6 n 139.
3. Ygern. Cambridge University Library manuscript EE426.

Chapter 9

2. Pseudo-Lucian, Erotes. See also Livy. xxix. 10, 14; xxxvi. 36; Juvinal. vi. 512; Ovid. Fast. iv. 237; Pliny. H. N. v. 32; xi. 49; xxxv. 13; Propert. ii. 18, l. 15; Herodian, 11. And, History of Phoenicia, G Rawlingson.
3. See Quest ch 20 sec 72, ch 23 sec 80, ch 25, sec 87, ch32 sec 110.
4. Hippolytus, Refutation of Heresies, V:7 or n 150.
5. Aufstieg Und Niedergang Der Roemischen Welt - Rise and Decline of the Roman World. Hildegard Temporini, pt II, Principat 9, 2, Volume 8, p.201).

Chapter 10

1. Otto von Freising, Historia de Duabus Civitatibus, 1146, in Friedrich Zarncke, Der Priester Johannes, Leipzig, Hirzel, 1879.
2. An online copy of Acton Griscome's translation of Oxford can be found here: http://www.maryjones.us/ctexts/tysillo.html
   And William Cooper's translation is here:
   http://www.annomundi.com/history/chronicle_of_the_early_britons.pdf
   Cooper only includes the 'Ben Dragown' as a footnote.
   The Jesus College Manuscript XXVIII can be viewed here:
   http://image.ox.ac.uk/show?collection=jesus&manuscript=ms28

Re-transcribed by Hugh Jones, Ashmolean Museum, in 1695.
3. NASA has a handy eclipse calculator, for major cities.
http://eclipse.gsfc.nasa.gov/JLEX/JLEX-index.html
http://eclipse.gsfc.nasa.gov/eclipse.html
4. Rousseau (trans. Angela Scholar), Jean-Jacques (2000). Confessions. New York: Oxford University Press. p. 262.
5. Critical Examination of the Life of St Paul, Boulanger, 1823. ch2, ch20.See also: A commentary on the Epistle to the Hebrews, Moses Stuart, 1834. p55. Dictionary of the Bible, 'Ebionites', 2001. p. 364.
6. George W Houston The Altar from Rome with Inscriptions to Sol and Malakbel. Syria Archaeology. 1990 vol 67-1 p189. The Pantheon of Palmyra, By Javier Teixidor, p47.
The Palmyrenes of Dura-Europos: A Study of Religious Interaction in Roman Syria. By Lucinda Dirven.

Chapter 12

1. Memoirs of the House of Medici, Nicholas Ten Hove, ch1 p3.

Chapter 13

2. http://www.spiegel.de/international/world/rome-s-tremendous-tunnel-the-ancient-world-s-longest-underground-aqueduct-a-612718.html

Chapter 14

1. Isidore of Seville's Etymologies XIV.6.8 tr Priscilla Throop.
2. Merlin Grail p44, p47, History of Kings 8:24.
3. Mevlevi Whirling Dervishes Order of America.
http://www.hayatidede.org

4. Gwaith Cynddelw Brydydd Mawr, Jones and Owen, ii-26.
Gwaith Meilyr Brydydd a'i Ddisgynyddion, Williams, 397.
From Geiriadur Prifysgol Cymru, the Dictionary of Welsh Language.

Additional bibliography:

1. A dictionary of Norman French.
https://archive.org/stream/dictionaryofnorm00kelhiala
https://archive.org/details/glossairecompara00mois
2. Brut y Brenhinedd, Dublin Institute for Advanced Studies, Brynley Roberts, 1971.
3. Neglected British History, by Flinders Petrie, November 7 1917.
http://en.wikisource.org/wiki/Neglected_British_History
4. Proceedings of the British Academy, Volume VIII, pp 251-278, 1917. The Chronicle of the Early Britons, MS LXI, William Cooper.
5. Center National de Ressources de Textualles et Lexicales.
http://www.cnrtl.fr

Index

Symbols

A

B

D

E

F

H

K

L

O

P

Q

R

S

T

U

V

W